Harmonizing language data

Digital Linguistics

Edited by
Andreas Witt

Volume 4

Harmonizing language data

Standards for linguistic resources

Edited by
Piotr Bański, Ulrich Heid and Laura Herzberg

DE GRUYTER

We gratefully acknowledge the support of the Volkswagen Foundation (the German VolkswagenStiftung), provided through the research project “Collection Replication for Enhanced Re-usability and Preservation Planning: A Case Study with the DOBES Archive” (grant number Az. 9A 966).

ISBN 978-3-11-914802-3
e-ISBN (PDF) 978-3-11-220821-2
e-ISBN (EPUB) 978-3-11-220953-0
ISSN 2751-1278
DOI https://doi.org/10.1515/9783112208212

Library of Congress Control Number: 2025943182

Bibliographic information published by the Deutsche Nationalbibliothek
The Deutsche Nationalbibliothek lists this publication in the Deutsche Nationalbibliografie; detailed bibliographic data are available on the Internet at http://dnb.dnb.de.

The book is published open access at www.degruyterbrill.com.
Cover image: piranka/E+/Getty Images
Typesetting: VTeX UAB, Lithuania
Printing and binding: CPI books GmbH, Leck

www.degruyterbrill.com
Questions about General Product Safety Regulation:
productsafety@degruyterbrill.com

Acknowledgments

The editors would like to express their gratitude to all those who contributed to the development and publication of this volume. We are particularly thankful to the chapter authors for their valuable and well-considered contributions, which form the foundation of this work.

We gratefully acknowledge the support of the Volkswagen Foundation (the German VolkswagenStiftung), provided through the research project "Collection Replication for Enhanced Re-usability and Preservation Planning: A Case Study with the DOBES Archive" (grant number Az. 9A 966). This funding made it possible to publish this volume as open access and thereby broaden its reach within the academic community.

We also wish to thank the editorial team at De Gruyter, past and present, for their competent and reliable support throughout the publication process. Our special thanks go to the series editor, Andreas Witt, whose continued engagement and guidance have been greatly appreciated.

The editors accept full responsibility for all mistakes and shortcomings in this volume.

https://doi.org/10.1515/9783112208212-202

Contents

Piotr Bański, Ulrich Heid, and Laura Herzberg

Towards an optimum degree of order in the field of language resources

Abstract: This chapter explores the role of standards and best practices in the creation, sharing, and sustainable use of language resources. As linguistic data becomes increasingly complex and varied, ranging from continuous corpora to multimodal annotations, the need for interoperability and long-term accessibility has grown. This chapter shows how encoding practices, metadata, and annotation frameworks contribute to the transparency, reproducibility, and reusability of language data. Emphasis is placed on the importance of consensus-driven standards, such as those developed by ISO (International Organization for Standardization), and the practical implementation of best practices within academic, archival, and computational contexts. By detailing the responsibilities and perspectives of data providers, analysts, and hosts, this chapter offers a comprehensive guide to achieving an optimum degree of order in the language resource ecosystem.

Keywords: language resources, data interoperability, standards and best practices, research data management, FAIR principles

1 Introduction

Standards can be seen as safeguards for the transmission of information: encoding information in a way advanced by a maintained standard based on the consensus in the given field ensures that the information is going to remain interpretable for the coming decades, that there will be a way to query that information in a uniform way, and that individual standardised information containers can be pooled together to form a larger coherent whole. This book provides readers with an overview of standards that are crucial in the task of ensuring sustainability of the data they produce and work with: from the selection of data-encoding formats, through methods of enriching data with annotations of various sorts – so that the result is transparent, easy to interpret and easy to query, to ways of ensuring that the resources are findable and accessible. These activities are central to the work of digital humanists,

Piotr Bański, **Laura Herzberg**, Digitale Sprachwissenschaft, Leibniz-Institut für Deutsche Sprache, R5 6-13, D-68161 Mannheim, Baden-Württemberg, Germany, e-mail: herzberg@ids-mannheim.de
Ulrich Heid, Institut für Informationswissenschaft und Sprachtechnologie, Universität Hildesheim, Universitätsplatz 1, 31141 Hildesheim, Germany

https://doi.org/10.1515/9783112208212-001

language documentalists, computational linguists working with spoken or textual data, and other researchers whose work involves the creation, maintenance, or simply use of language resources.

Digital humanists, language documentalists, etc., produce and use language data in various forms: contiguous text in numerous formats, item-based arrangements such as lexicons, thesauri, or encyclopaedias, as well as multiple kinds of parallel structures: aligned translations, manuscript witnesses, transcribed manuscript interpretations accompanied by their corresponding facsimiles, as well as audio or video recordings with corresponding transcriptions, etc.

In addition to data reflecting language behaviour (call that the *primary data*[1]), crucial roles are played by two types of derived or added data, typically referred to as *annotations* and *metadata*.

Annotations enrich the data component by classifying, describing, and relating data fragments to one another. They can be simple labels providing part-of-speech information to individual words, or complex feature structures expressing, e. g., morphosyntactic information, or additional arrangements that organize fragments of the primary data into, for example, syntactic structures or semantic dependencies.

"Metadata" is a broad notion encompassing various kinds of data used for identification and description – of entire resources, as well as of particular pieces of the primary data and of its annotations. Metadata may contain information about language resources themselves (i. e., cataloguing information on the entire corpora or collections), but also, for example, about the volume of primary data, its provenience, as well as about the particular properties of annotations and about tools and methods used to produce them.

The three mentioned types of data and their interrelationships are depicted in Figure 1, in a sort of an ideal setup; not all kinds of corpora contain all three of them: many data collections are un-annotated, just containing raw data and (some) metadata. Examples are the texts in the Gutenberg[2] collection or results of automatic crawls from the internet.

In this book, however, we take the 'ideal' situation as a starting point for our discussion.

1 The term "primary data" means different things in different contexts: for textual data (see e. g. Bański and Diewald 2025), the primary data is the stream of characters that make up documents of various sorts. For audiovisual resources (see e. g. Frick and Schmidt 2025), the primary data is the audio and/or video signal, with textual transcriptions being derived from the primary data in various ways, and potentially annotated.

2 Project Gutenberg is a collection of over 75,000 electronic books, cf. https://www.gutenberg.org/

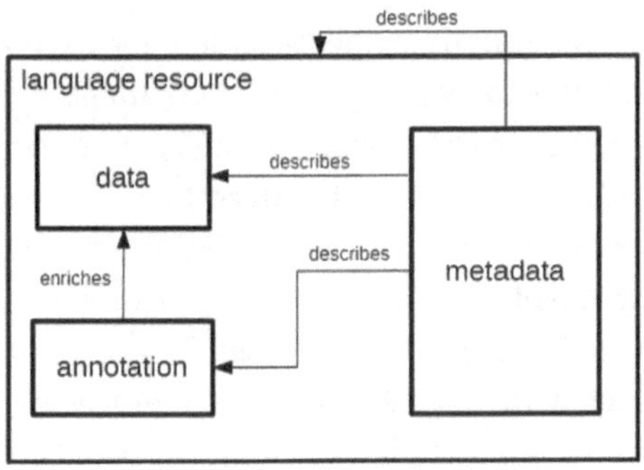

Figure 1: Data model of a language resource containing raw data, annotations and metadata.

All the abovementioned kinds of digital data come in a large variety of formats, depending on how they have been created or recorded, on their intended use, but also on the customs of the local academic, research or industrial communities. Some of those formats are well-defined, bearing a stamp of international standards organisations, and some are a matter of more-or-less local practice.

In the most recent natural language processing revolution instigated by the deployment of large computational models for the purpose of the analysis, transformation and generation of language, the variety of input formats is typically not a hurdle in the process of creating the resulting neural networks that are capable of connecting the disparate pieces of data in novel (and still largely unpredictable) ways. At the time of the publication of this book in 2025, the results are often stunning, enlightening, but not transparent, and – in many cases, unfortunately – hallucinatory. On the other hand, those linguists, language documentalists, digital humanists and others who encode manuscripts for the purpose of studying minute differences between witnesses, or who collect data in various modalities for the purpose of language documentation and preservation, have a restricted and precise set of goals. Apart from transparency and reproducibility of results, the primary goal in many projects is *sustainability* of the resulting data collections: making sure that both the primary language data and the information about that data is going to be interpretable in the future.

Sustainability entails at least some of the defining features of *interoperability*, i. e. the ability of data and tools to interact: if they interact in a predictable and reproducible way, data can be successfully queried, manipulated, aggregated and curated, and thus not only exploited, but also preserved, maintained, and used as a basis for further development and new research questions. Sustainability is not achievable without clear guidelines on how to prepare the data and on how the data can be processed, enriched, and aggregated. Guidelines of various kinds, known as best practices and technical standards, are ubiquitous in the field, and, for example, for a language documentalist concerned with preserving their observations in a transparent and sustainable form, it is not always easy to select the effective course of action. This book addresses this multitude of possibilities by suggesting, out of a variety of possible paths, a couple of routes that are coherent and well-documented by either international standards or firmly established best practices. This is not to say that other paths are not possible – given the richness of methods for gathering data and the spectrum of purposes for which data may be gathered and processed, no single set of guidelines can exhaust all possible paths from a raw datum to a structured query result (or a robust digital object in an archive). Nevertheless, we hope that the present volume – *a* guide to the diverse landscape of data representation, legal frameworks, and institutional expectations – is going to assist researchers in making informed decisions about their own workflows.

2 The scenario of interoperable resources

2.1 Guidelines, best practices and standards for harmonizing language resources

The topic of this book are best practice guidelines and standards that support the creation, archiving and exploration of resources that can be shared, exchanged and reused.

A simple taxonomy of language resources distinguishes between static and dynamic resources, as well as between text-based and item-based (particularised) ones (cf. Witt et al. 2009: 2); the authors count tools for the processing of language data among the dynamic resources, while corpora and lexicons are static resources. Text-based resources, according to their classification, consist of continuous, running text, whereas itemised resources include for example dictionaries, terminologies, or ontologies. As of 2025, pretrained (large or small) language models can equally be classified as static (numerical) item-based language resources. Within this two-by-two matrix, the present book focuses on static continuous-text resources, i. e. corpora of written and spoken language.

The definition of a standard, as provided by the ISO/IEC Guide 2:2004, def. 3.2, reads as follows: “standard – document established by consensus and approved by a recognised body that provides, for common and repeated use, rules, guidelines, or characteristics for activities and their results, aimed at the achievement of the optimum degree of order in a given context.”

This definition states that standards are based on consensus, which implies that they require a certain degree of maturity of a scientific field, such that researchers can come to a consensual description, guideline, or set of rules (this is pointed out in a note to the ISO/IEC definition). In this book, we thus focus on established practice and examples of the common understanding across the research community, at the time of writing.

The ISO/IEC definition also describes the objective of standardization: establishing the "optimum degree of order" in a given context. Establishing order in processes and in the artefacts handled in these processes is a prerequisite for cooperation and interoperability, i. e. – in the case of language resources – for data exchange that allows different tools (and their users) to combine data and functionalities.

Finally, the definition includes an element of officiality: standards are approved by a recognised body; ISO, the International Organization for Standardization, is one of the relevant international bodies that organize standardization processes. ISO work is organised, among other things, by "technical committees" (and subcommittees, see Preissner and Heid 2025); language resources are covered by one such committee whose national counterparts are expert groups organised by the respective national standardization bodies. Proposals for standards are then produced in a structured process to which experts from around the world can contribute.

In this book, numerous ISO standards are mentioned, but also best practice guidelines which are not (or not yet) official standards. Best practices equally come into existence through consensus. They may be proposed by individuals (e. g. in publications) or by organizers of shared tasks or benchmarks, and they may then be taken up by larger groups. An example of best practice guidelines that originate from a shared task in computational linguistics is the CoNLL-format for the representation of dependency structures.[3] It was suggested to the participants of the shared task (for the organizers to be able to compare individual results) and later taken up by many others.

A similar example, first proposed by a group of industrial companies and later taken up as an ISO standard, is TBX, TermBase eXchange (ISO 30042:2019), a widely used format for the exchange of terminological data from termbanks.

Creating "order in the field of language resources" by means of standards and best practice guidelines does not mean that all resources should be the same: the reasons and objectives behind the creation of a given resource obviously determine its contents and structure. However, adherence to standards or orientation taken from them support what is called "harmonization of language resources" in the title of this book. Harmonization here essentially means interoperability, the pos-

---

3 "CoNLL" stands for "Conference on Natural Language Learning"; see https://conll.org/

sibility for data providers and data users to combine resources, or resources and tools, or, even simpler, to just understand what information certain annotations or representational devices are meant to convey.

Examples of such harmonization effects include the combinability of certain corpus processing tools (e. g. part-of-speech taggers and syntactic analysis tools in a sequential setup) or the possibility for users to query several online textual resources through a common interface (relying on common encoding and representation formats, as well as annotations).

The order in the resource domain which standards and best practices allow to create more generally helps to ensure that resources follow the FAIR principles (Wilkinson et al. 2016), i. e. that they are Findable, Accessible, Interoperable and Reusable.

2.2 Actors in language data sharing

There are three main types of actors involved in the scenario of language data sharing that is discussed in this book:

- Data providers: researchers, projects, or institutions who produce language data and wish to share these data with other researchers, projects, or institutions, or simply with "the community" at large; or they wish to ensure that their data can be reused in the long term, which requires appropriate archiving.
- Data analysts: researchers, projects, or institutions interested in inspecting, using, and possibly further analyzing data that others have produced; in a sharing scenario, they are the "takers", while the data providers are the "givers".
- Data hosts: while two individual researchers intending to share a given single resource may not need any particular infrastructure, reuse of larger amounts of data, sharing between multiple parties or with parties not known a priori, as well as any form of non-synchronous reuse will typically rely on an intermediary who hosts the data and makes it available to interested parties.

Typical examples of both data providers and data analysts are researchers, research projects, or institutions that collect, structure or annotate language data. On either side, this includes not only collaborative research projects, but also, for example, PhD candidates who do empirical research.

Data hosts (also called "data stewards", see Kamocki 2025) are typically (members of) institutions that can guarantee some kind of medium- to long-term availability of the data they host. Examples of such institutions include universities or academies (and/or their computing centres), specialised public libraries or infrastructural institutions (such as, in Germany, the Leibniz-Institut für deutsche

Sprache[4] or the distributed “Zentrum für Digitale Lexikographie”[5]). Initiatives such as the German National Research Data Infrastructure,[6] NFDI, and the projects it is composed of (for text resources, in particular – the Text Plus project[7]), or the European CLARIN ERIC[8] intend, among other things, to create networks of such data hosting and data stewardship centres, and to make them accessible online to the research community.

The perspectives and needs of each of the three kinds of players in this scenario differ considerably.

Data providers may be planning to collect, to annotate or otherwise enrich data; or they may just be interested in making sure that their existing data are safely stored and can be reused also in five, ten or more years. This book provides them with the necessary knowledge to ensure that their data are in a shape that supports these goals: questions that are answered concern the choice of representation formats, of tools that can produce certain kinds of annotations or that can convert existing data from one format into another. These questions do not only play a role in the course, or at the end of, a project of any size, but also already in its planning phase. If long-term archiving is at stake, data providers should also be aware of the functions of data host institutions, of the processes that make a given data collection “ingestible” for an archive, of the attached expectations and requirements of the data hosts, but also of the support and services that can be expected from data stewards.

Data analysts are mainly interested in finding data that is useful for answering their research questions and also in accessing and possibly themselves enhancing such data as a result of their research. In a way, this involves a double perspective: on the one hand, data analysts need to know how to query data or how to get data from a data host, e. g. from an archive, a repository, or a shared online infrastructure; on the other hand, knowledge about the principles of representation, annotation and metadata-based description of spoken or written data is helpful for data analysts to ensure that they can make proper use of what they get access to.

Data host institutions typically follow principles that are shared worldwide, e. g. on the basis of agreements within the Open Archival Information System (OAIS);[9]

---

4 https://www.ids-mannheim.de/en/entrance-into-the-ids/

5 https://www.zdl.org/

6 https://www.nfdi.de/?lang=en

7 https://text-plus.org/en/

8 https://www.clarin.eu/

9 http://www.oais.info/

in addition, they need to know about the input formats and the peculiarities of different kinds of language data (e. g. spoken vs. written, entities linked to external knowledge sources, etc.).

2.3 Resource interoperability and the data lifecycle

The three parties are involved in a data sharing and reuse scenario which has an input side (data provision) and an output (or: access) side (data analysts searching for data and working with what they find), both linked by the data host which acts as an intermediary.

This scenario is known from general principles of research data management (RDM): the well-known data lifecycle (cf. Figure 2) describes the objectives of the three parties, focusing however rather on the processes involved than on the parties responsible for these processes. It involves creating data, processing and analysing data (i. e. for annotation, as a part of data provision), preserving data and giving access to data (i. e. the task of the data host), and finally re-using shared data.

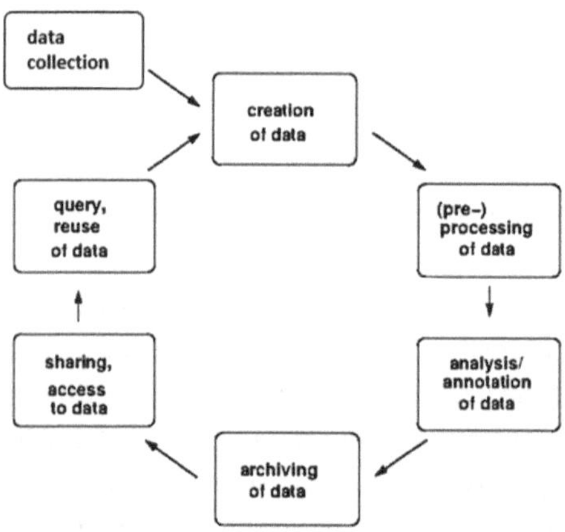

Figure 2: Data Lifecycle.

In many projects in (computational) linguistics, language documentation, or digital humanities, the elements of the data lifecycle are to some extent sequentially ordered; in Figure 3, we thus reproduce the phases of the data lifecycle in the form of a pipeline-like workflow, and we indicate the main actors involved.

The cooperation of the different actors requires, as any sharing and exchange does, a common understanding of formats, of properties that the resources should

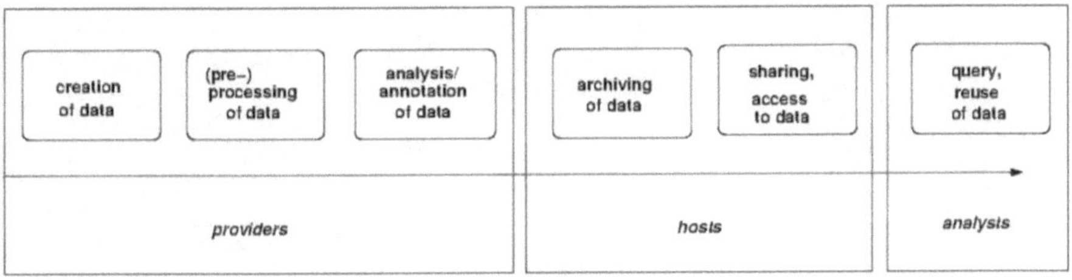

Figure 3: Data Lifecycle as a pipeline, with types of actors.

have, and of ways and means used to organize and realize the exchange. The standards, best practices and recommendations discussed in this volume are intended to contribute to this common understanding.

3 Overview of the book

The chapters in this volume are systematically structured around the key stages of the data lifecycle, as illustrated in Figure 2 above. The present Section 3 demonstrates how each chapter corresponds to a specific part of the lifecycle, showing the ways in which the contributions are thematically and conceptually interconnected. Before exploring the individual chapters, we give a brief overview of the volume's overall scope, followed by an explanation of these connections. The section concludes with concise summaries of each chapter's content.

This volume focuses on standards related to corpora, both of written and of transcribed spoken language. It does not discuss standards for dictionaries or for (Large) Language Models. As dictionaries involve a broad and highly complex range of data types and quite diverse structural models, depending on the dictionary functions and target user groups, they differ considerably from corpus data and thus should be considered as a field of study of their own. Similarly, this volume does not address standards for Large Language Models (LLMs) and for Machine Learning resources used in Natural Language Processing. These fields are dynamically evolving, and as of 2025, efforts are still underway to develop a comprehensive understanding of the artefacts and processes that should be taken into account in the development of best practices and standards in this area of research.

As illustrated in Figure 4, the lifecycle begins with the *input* stage, where data, whether textual, spoken, or audiovisual, is initially provided and prepared for further processing. In this stage, a variety of activities are undertaken to convert the raw data and to add annotations. These activities may include character encoding (see Wartena 2025), the classification and annotation of texts with codes for lan-

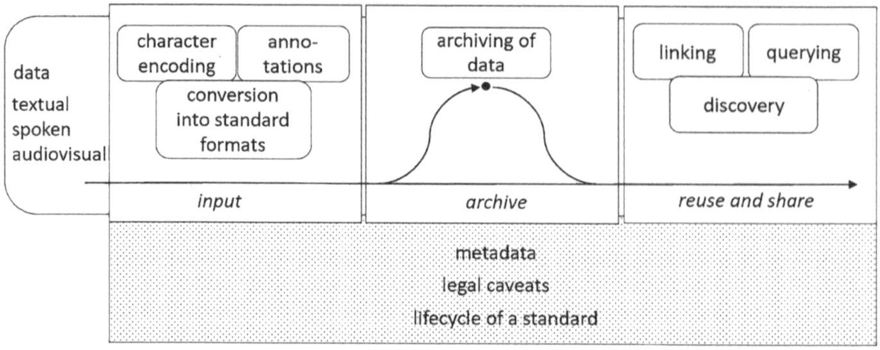

Figure 4: Contributions of the volume representing the data lifecycle.

guages and their varieties (see Romary 2025), part-of-speech tagging (see Ljubešić and Erjavec 2025), the identification and annotation of Named Entities (see Schwarz 2025), the conversion of data into standardised formats, ensuring consistency and interoperability across different platforms and applications (see Ferreira et al. 2025, Werthmann 2025) as well as managing multiple layers of annotation in linguistic corpora (see Bański and Diewald 2025).

The next stage in the lifecycle focuses on the potential *archiving* of data at host institutions (see Pisetta and Trippel 2025, Lüngen and Pisetta 2025). This phase is central for ensuring the long-term preservation and accessibility of data. Therefore, the chapters show how archiving encompasses a range of practices aimed at safeguarding data against loss. This stage also involves organizing and categorizing data in such a way that it remains discoverable and usable for future research, analysis, and reference.

Following archiving, the contributions turn to the *reuse and sharing* stage of data lifecycle. They emphasize the importance of making data accessible and available to a broader community. Tools that support data linking (see Khan 2025) and querying (see Evert et al. 2025, Frick and Schmidt 2025) play a significant role in this phase, enabling users to search and connect related datasets across various sources. Additionally, the Federated Content Search (FCS) system (see Körner and Eckart 2025) is introduced as a tool that allows users to perform searches across distributed data repositories; Federated Content Search provides a unified interface for accessing diverse data sources hosted in different places.

From an infrastructure perspective, certain core elements play a role throughout every stage of data processing. These include metadata (see Trippel 2025) legal and ethical aspects (see Kamocki 2025), and the development and application of standards (see Preissner and Heid 2025). The chapters in this volume demonstrate how these elements are closely connected to each phase of the data lifecycle. They are key to managing, maintaining, and using data responsibly and effectively from start to finish.

In the chapter "Character Encoding and its Importance for Text Resources" by Christian Wartena, the author lays the groundwork for understanding character encoding, i. e. the process of representing textual characters as binary data for computer storage and processing. Wartena begins by establishing the connection between human-readable characters and their underlying binary representations within computer systems. His discussion then explores the core principles and characteristics of character encodings specifically designed for Western European languages. Finally, Wartena offers guidance on best practices for corpus construction, showing the importance of proper encoding handling.

The chapter "International standards for the identification and the description of languages and their varieties" by Laurent Romary addresses the challenges and importance of standardizing how languages are identified and described, particularly within digital resources and data collections for language documentation and linguistic research. Romary presents two primary ISO standards: ISO 639, which deals with language codes, and ISO 21636, which focuses on characterizing language varieties. These frameworks support navigating linguistic diversity in a structured manner. Additionally, Romary suggests ways of refining existing coding proposals within the framework set by the Text Encoding Initiative (TEI) to capture the complexity of language documentation. The author points out that the overarching goal is to promote more adaptable, inclusive, and well-structured digital language resources.

Nikola Ljubešić and Tomaž Erjavec define in their chapter "Part-of-Speech Tagging and Related Annotation" part-of-speech (POS) tagging as a step in text annotation that involves assigning grammatical categories and morphosyntactic features to words in a body of text. POS tagging supports corpus searches based on grammatical properties and at the same time serves as the foundation for further linguistic analysis. Ljubešić and Erjavec provide an overview of POS tagging, covering its development, commonly used tagsets, tagging methods and tools, standard data formats, and related annotation levels such as those of tokenization, lemmatization, and syntactic analysis.

The chapter "Named Entity Recognition and Entity Linking" by Pia Schwarz presents Named Entity Recognition (NER) and Entity Linking (EL) as Natural Language Processing (NLP) techniques for extracting meaning from text. Schwarz introduces NER and EL, outlining their respective tasks, common methodologies, relevant data formats, and diverse applications, while also providing advice on applying these techniques to raw datasets. Schwarz shows how modern NER and EL systems leverage both statistical methods and advanced neural network architectures, particularly transformer models, to accurately recognize, disambiguate, and link entities.

Vera Ferreira, Hanna Hedeland and Kelsey Neely provide in their chapter "Annotated audiovisual language data: data quality and data maturity" a summary of data quality and data maturity considerations for annotated audiovisual collections. Based on recent research, the authors offer best practice recommendations for both audiovisual and derived data formats. Moving beyond format specifics, the chapter presents a broader discussion including criteria such as overall data quality and the principles of FAIRness. In the initial sections, the authors introduce relevant concepts and terminology, providing the background and a context to facilitate a deeper understanding of the rationale behind the presented recommendations. The authors aim at creating a reference guide for ensuring high-quality, mature, and FAIR annotated audiovisual data for research across linguistics and related disciplines.

In the article "From Spoken Language Data to TEI-based ISO Standard", Antonina Werthmann presents formats used for transcribing and annotating spoken language data across diverse linguistic domains. Her focus is placed on their conversion to the TEI-based international standard ISO 24624, "Language Resource Management – Transcription of Spoken Language." Following an introduction on the significance of standardised formats, Werthmann examines various widely adopted transcription and annotation formats, explaining their key characteristics and applications within different linguistic subfields. The author then describes the TEI-based ISO standard in detail. Furthermore, Werthmann presents practical use cases that demonstrate the standard's utility and applicability in linguistic research scenarios.

The chapter "Dealing with multiple annotations" by Piotr Bański and Nils Diewald focuses on corpora that feature multiple layers of annotation and looks at the phenomenon from an application-based perspective, couched in the real-life context of DeReKo (the largest linguistically motivated collection of contemporary written German) and of the analysis engine KorAP that makes it possible to analyse texts in complex queries across several query languages. The authors review the basic concepts needed for talking about multiple annotations, present the most notorious obstacles in dealing with them in an XML-based format, show the basic ways of tackling it that have been suggested in the literature, and conclude with a presentation of KorAP-XML, an internal format designed for the purpose of easy enrichment of DeReKo texts with many diverse annotation layers.

The chapter "Standards and practices for long-term digital archiving" by Ines Pisetta and Thorsten Trippel, illustrates principles and practices in digital long-term archiving within the language sciences. The authors begin by outlining different levels of preservation; binary, logical, and semantic, which are necessary for ensuring the medium- to long-term integrity of digital content. Pisetta and Trippel introduce the OAIS framework (Open Archival Information System), explaining the roles of Submission, Archive, and Dissemination Information Packages (SIP, AIP, and DIP) in structuring the archiving process. Their discussion extends to the importance of repository systems and persistent identifiers in maintaining data accessibility over time.

In the contribution "Conversion into the archival format I5" by Harald Lüngen and Ines Pisetta, the authors present the repository approach used at the Leibniz Institute for the German Language (IDS) for the long-term preservation of linguistic resources. They place emphasis on the archival format I5: I5 is a customised version of TEI, specifically adapted to the structure and needs of the IDS corpus collections, which have been developed since 1964. The format features a three-part macrostructure and includes modifications to TEI elements for better alignment with IDS data. Following a brief overview of I5, the authors illustrate how data from various formats are converted into I5 using examples from the archive. Additionally, two case studies are discussed: one involving the KED corpus of simplified German, and another one using Wikipedia corpora.

In the chapter "Metadata for Research Data" by Thorsten Trippel, the author examines the function of metadata in the management and accessibility of language data within research infrastructures. Trippel starts by outlining metadata elements, such as title, creator, identifier, and format, which are important for organizing and describing research data. The author then discusses metadata generated during the data deposition process, including technical details and file integrity information. The importance of established metadata standards like DataCite, DCAT, and Dublin Core is explored, along with the role of schema.org in promoting interoperability. Additionally, Trippel addresses the use of rich, discipline-specific metadata standards, focusing on ISO 24622-1 and ISO 24622-2 (CMDI: Component Metadata Infrastructure).

In "Linguistic Linked (Open) Data", Anas Fahad Khan introduces the principles of linked open data and the Semantic Web, stating their impact for the publication, access, and reuse of data, particularly in the linguistic domain. Aimed at linguists and others interested in sharing linguistic data as linked open data, Khan's chapter is designed for readers who may be new to these concepts. The author begins by explaining the foundational ideas behind linked open data and the Semantic Web, and then turns to the Linguistic Linked Open Data (LLOD) cloud. Key Semantic Web vocabularies relevant to linguistic datasets are also presented which offer practical tools for structuring and linking data within this framework.

In the chapter "Data exploitation: Corpus queries", the authors Stephanie Evert, Timm Weber, Steffen Bothe, Philipp Heinrich, and Alexander Piperski explore the landscape of corpus query languages (CQLs) and their close ties to underlying data models. The authors trace the fragmented development of CQLs and examine key technical concepts, alongside efforts to create a unified querying standard, the corpus query lingua franca (CQLF). Additionally, the authors discuss two paradigms: finite-state queries for tabular data, illustrated by the IMS Open Corpus Workbench (CWB), and anchored queries for graph-based models, exemplified by ANNIS (Annotation of Information Structure). The authors also examine recent initiatives to separate query design from specific systems using intermediate representations like KorAP/KoralQuery and to enhance accessibility through simplified languages and visual query construction tools.

In "Querying spoken language data", Elena Frick and Thomas Schmidt explore query methods for spoken language corpora, focusing on their use in fields like interactional linguistics and language documentation. The authors highlight the unique features of spoken data, such as spontaneity and interaction that set it apart from written language and require specialised query approaches. The authors review current tools and standardization efforts for querying annotated transcriptions. The chapter concludes with practical examples using the FOLK[10] corpus (Forschungs- und Lehrkorpus Gesprochenes Deutsch) on the ZuMult[11] platform (created in the project Zugang zu multimodalen Korpora gesprochene Sprache).

The chapter "Accessing Linguistic Content in Distributed Research Environments" by Erik Körner and Thomas Eckart presents the CLARIN Federated Content Search (FCS) as a decentralised framework designed to make linguistic resources easily accessible and searchable within a distributed research infrastructure. Emphasizing data ownership and flexibility, the authors describe how FCS 2.0 has matured into a robust and extensible *de facto* standard, building on established protocols and formats. They illustrate how the system is widely adopted across Europe and how it continuously evolves through user feedback by addressing challenges like authentication integration, content-specific displays, and the growing role of linked data.

Paweł Kamocki addresses in his chapter "Taxonomy of Legal and Ethical Metadata for Language Resources" the role of legal and ethical issues in the creation and reuse of language resources. The author introduces a structured metadata taxonomy aimed at improving transparency, compliance, and reusability in line with FAIR principles. Designed for researchers with limited legal expertise, Kamocki provides a guide to navigating lawful data use, covering topics such as copyright, data protection, ethical concerns, and the responsibilities of Data Stewards. The guide is

10 https://agd.ids-mannheim.de/folk.shtml

11 https://zumult.org/

intended as a helpful tool to ensure documentation and responsible data handling, while also acknowledging ongoing challenges in the field.

In "the life of an ISO standard" by Annette Preissner and Ulrich Heid, the authors highlight the importance of standards and best practices in promoting the longevity, transparency, and interoperability of language data particularly in the field of digital humanities. The authors explore the role of the International Organization for Standardization (ISO) in shaping these conventions. Focusing on the work of ISO/TC 37/SC 4, the subcommittee dedicated to language resource management, Preissner and Heid offer insight into how digital language resources are modeled, specified, and encoded to ensure consistency and reuse. They also explain the collaborative, consensus-driven ISO standardization process and outline possibilities for active participation.

Bibliography

Bański, Piotr & Nils Diewald. 2025. Dealing with multiple annotations. In Piotr Bański, Ulrich Heid & Laura Herzberg (eds.), *Harmonising language data: Standards for linguistic resources*. Berlin/Boston: De Gruyter.

Evert, Stephanie, Timm Weber, Steffen Bothe, Philipp Heinrich & Alexander Piperski. 2025. Data exploitation: Corpus queries. In Piotr Bański, Ulrich Heid & Laura Herzberg (eds.), *Harmonising language data: Standards for linguistic resources*. Berlin/Boston: De Gruyter.

Ferreira, Vera, Hanna Hedeland & Kelsey Neely. 2025. Annotated audiovisual language data: Data quality and data maturity. In Piotr Bański, Ulrich Heid & Laura Herzberg (eds.), *Harmonising language data: Standards for linguistic resources*. Berlin/Boston: De Gruyter.

Frick, Elena & Thomas Schmidt. 2025. Querying spoken language data. In Piotr Bański, Ulrich Heid & Laura Herzberg (eds.), *Harmonising language data: Standards for linguistic resources*. Berlin/Boston: De Gruyter.

ISO 30042:2019. *Management of terminology resources – TermBase eXchange (TBX)*.

ISO/IEC Guide 2:2004. *Standardization and related activities – General vocabulary (Multilingual)*. https://www.iso.org/resources/publicly-available-resources.html (accessed 30 January 2025).

Kamocki, Paweł. 2025. Taxonomy of legal and ethical metadata for language resources. In Piotr Bański, Ulrich Heid & Laura Herzberg (eds.), *Harmonising language data: Standards for linguistic resources*. Berlin/Boston: De Gruyter.

Khan, Anas Fahad. 2025. Linguistic linked (open) data. In Piotr Bański, Ulrich Heid & Laura Herzberg (eds.), *Harmonising language data: Standards for linguistic resources*. Berlin/Boston: De Gruyter.

Körner, Erik & Thomas Eckart. 2025. Accessing linguistic content in distributed research environments. In Piotr Bański, Ulrich Heid & Laura Herzberg (eds.), *Harmonising language data: Standards for linguistic resources*. Berlin/Boston: De Gruyter.

Ljubešić, Nikola & Tomaž Erjavec. 2025. Part-of-speech tagging and related annotation. In Piotr Bański, Ulrich Heid & Laura Herzberg (eds.), *Harmonising language data: Standards for linguistic resources*. Berlin/Boston: De Gruyter.

Lüngen, Harald & Ines Pisetta. 2025. Conversion into the archival format I5. In Piotr Bański, Ulrich Heid & Laura Herzberg (eds.), *Harmonising language data: Standards for linguistic resources*. Berlin/Boston: De Gruyter.

Pisetta, Ines & Thorsten Trippel. 2025. Standards and practices for long-term digital archiving. In Piotr Bański, Ulrich Heid & Laura Herzberg (eds.), *Harmonising language data: Standards for linguistic resources*. Berlin/Boston: De Gruyter.

Preissner, Annette & Ulrich Heid. 2025. The life of an ISO standard. In Piotr Bański, Ulrich Heid & Laura Herzberg (eds.), *Harmonising language data: Standards for linguistic resources*. Berlin/Boston: De Gruyter.

Romary, Laurent. 2025. International standards for the identification and the description of languages and their varieties. In Piotr Bański, Ulrich Heid & Laura Herzberg (eds.), *Harmonising language data: Standards for linguistic resources*. Berlin/Boston: De Gruyter.

Schwarz, Pia. 2025. Named entity recognition and entity linking. In Piotr Bański, Ulrich Heid & Laura Herzberg (eds.), *Harmonising language data: Standards for linguistic resources*. Berlin/Boston: De Gruyter.

Trippel, Thorsten. 2025. Metadata for research data. In Piotr Bański, Ulrich Heid & Laura Herzberg (eds.), *Harmonising language data: Standards for linguistic resources*. Berlin/Boston: De Gruyter.

Wartena, Christian. 2025. Character encoding and its importance for text resources. In Piotr Bański, Ulrich Heid & Laura Herzberg (eds.), *Harmonising language data: Standards for linguistic resources*. Berlin/Boston: De Gruyter.

Werthmann, Antonina. 2025. From spoken language data to TEI-based ISO standard. In Piotr Bański, Ulrich Heid & Laura Herzberg (eds.), *Harmonising language data: Standards for linguistic resources*. Berlin/Boston: De Gruyter.

Wilkinson, Mark D., Michel Dumontier & IJsbrand Jan Aalbersberg, et al.. 2016. The FAIR Guiding Principles for scientific data management and stewardship. *Scientific Data* 3. 160018. https://doi.org/10.1038/sdata.2016.18.

Witt, Andreas, Ulrich Heid, Felix Sasaki & Gilles Sérasset. 2009. Multilingual language resources and interoperability. *Language Resources and Evaluation* 43(1). 1–14. https://doi.org/10.1007/s10579-009-9088-x.

Christian Wartena

Character encoding and its importance for text resources

Abstract: This chapter provides an introduction to character encoding, exploring the fundamental relationship between characters and binary data. It discusses how computers store information and how characters are represented in binary form. The principles and characteristics of the most common encodings for Western European languages are examined. The chapter concludes with recommendations for corpus construction and finally explains some typical problems that can arise from improper handling of character encodings.

Keywords: character encoding, Unicode, character

1 Introduction

Character encoding is a fundamental aspect of digital text processing, and a basic understanding of character encoding is useful when dealing with texts encoded in different ways. Though programming at the bit level is never needed, a good understanding of what text editors and other programs do is helpful to avoid and repair errors that would cause mojibake and inconsistent texts.

A character encoding consists of three parts: 1) a definition of what a character is and the selection of characters that are part of the encoding: 2) a mapping from characters to numbers, called code points, and 3) a mapping of code points to actual bit patterns that can be saved in a computer memory.

In Section 2 we begin with a brief look at two fundamental problems: how information is stored in a computer's memory, and what exactly are characters. We see that for most early character encodings, the selection of characters, the first step mentioned above, was mainly determined by hardware limitations on the number of possible characters. These legacy encodings, discussed in Section 3, are important in the first place because some of them are still widely found. Secondly many aspects of modern encodings can only been understood on the basis of the historical development of character encodings. The ISO 2022 standard (cf. ISO/IEC 2022:1994, originally defined in 1971) and the Universal Character Set (cf. ISO/IEC 10646:2020, first draft published in 1990) sought ways to overcome the limitation of the number

Christian Wartena, Data | H Institute for Applied Data Science Hannover, Hochschule Hannover, Expo Plaza 12, 30539 Hannover, Germany, e-mail: christian.wartena@hs-hannover.de

https://doi.org/10.1515/9783112208212-002

of characters imposed by software and hardware. The approach of the Universal Character Set was the first one to introduce the third step mentioned above and make a systematic distinction between code points and their encoding. This distinction was adopted by Unicode and is described in Section 4. Finally, in Section 5 we look at practical implications and at typical errors and how to avoid them.

2 The relationship between characters and bits

Before we start with an overview of the most common character encodings for the Latin script, we need to look at two fundamental issues: how is information stored in a computer, and what are characters.

2.1 Storing information in bits and bytes

At the lowest level modern computers can only save two different symbols, usually referred to as 0 and 1. Natural numbers can be converted easily to a binary representation using only 0 and 1, as already described by Gottfried Wilhelm Leibniz (Leibniz 1703).

However, Leibniz' mathematical system is not sufficient to store numbers on a computer: a computer memory is not a long tape where we can write and read arbitrary 0's and 1's separated by spaces or line breaks, as a mathematician would do on paper. We only have two states, not a third state to separate two numbers. Also, not every location in memory is addressable. The smallest addressable unit is called a *byte* (Wikipedia 2025a). A byte nowadays usually consists of 8 *bits*, where a bit can be seen as a position that can be in the state 0 or 1. All the bits in a byte must be written and read at the same time. So when we store a number, we must always use at least one byte, or 8 bits, even if the number is shorter. The positions that are not needed are usually filled with 0's. If we need more than 8 bits (for numbers greater than 255), we need 2 or more bytes to store the information. The processor needs to know in advance how many bytes to read at once to read the next number. There are two ways of distributing the bits that represent a number over two bytes: Some processors put the bits that represent the largest numbers into the first byte, while others put the bits that represent the smallest numbers into the first byte. The first system is called big-endian (because it starts at the high end of the number), the others are called little-endian. The order within the byte is irrelevant because we cannot address the individual bits. Thus, if we read larger units than bytes from memory, we need to know how they were written. We will see that some character encodings also require more than one byte and have the same problem. Initially, however, all encodings always used one byte to store a character, as longer encodings were considered too inefficient or unnecessary.

2.2 Characters and glyphs

Before we get to the question of how to encode a character in a binary system, we need to answer the question of what a character is. A character such as the lowercase letter *a* can have several quite different shapes (see Figure 1 for an example). We call these different shapes *glyphs* and the abstraction of the particular shape a character. Linguists have drawn the parallel to sounds and phonemes and have come up with the notion of *grapheme* as the smallest unit in a script that causes a semantic difference (Dürscheid 2016: 130ff, Meletis 2019, André 2002). Thus, graphemes can be found using minimal pairs in the same way as with phonemes. According to this criterion, for example uppercase and lowercase variants of the same letter are different graphemes: at least in some cases, case helps to distinguish between proper names and nouns in English, or between nouns and otherwise identically spelled words with a different part of speech in German. In the following, we will equate graphemes with (printable) characters to keep things simple.

Figure 1: Different glyphs for the lower-case Latin letter *a*.

Glyphs can also be smaller than a character and can be combined to form a character: Usually diacritics are also considered glyphs, while a letter with a diacritic is considered a character. Different glyphs representing the same character are called *allographs*, parallel to allophones in phonology (Dürscheid 2016: 133). Like for phonemes we find free allographs and complementary allographs such as final or non-final sigma in Greek (ς or σ) or initial, middle and final variants of Arabic letters (Meletis 2020).

Homography is the situation where two different characters can be represented by the same glyph. For example, the uppercase I and lowercase *l* can be identical in sans-serif fonts. Homography also exists between letters from different scripts. For example, many capitals in Greek, Roman and Cyrillic scripts are homographs. In spam messages character homography is used to deliberately deceive readers (Holgers et al. 2006).

Although the basic principle of distinguishing between glyphs and graphemes or characters is simple and intuitive, it is not easy to apply the principle in all cases and, moreover, there are many different graphematic theories. Most character encodings appear to be based on characters rather than glyphs. A notable exception are encoding systems that have encodings for diacritics that can be combined with basic characters to form composite characters, such as ANSEL (American National Standard for Extended Latin Alphabet Coded Character Set for Bibliographic Use) or ITU T.61.[1] However, this decision is usually not made explicit, and in many legacy encodings it seems that the selection of characters and glyphs to be included in an encoding is more ad hoc than guided by any graphematic theory.

Of course, the use of a different glyph or shape can be important in a text, for example, it might be important that a word in a German text is set in bold. Since there is no pair of two German words that differ only in whether one letter is bold or not, bold letters are different glyphs (i. e. allographs) but not different characters. Since character encodings deal with characters (graphemes), not glyphs, the information that the words are bold must be included in the text markup, and one should not try to use different characters for this. The same applies to many other typographical details, such as special forms of letters, ligatures, abbreviations, etc.

2.3 Encoding characters

In most older encodings, the number of characters was limited by the number of bits available to represent a character, usually 7 or 8. If each character is encoded at a maximum of 8 bits, we can use one byte to store each character, which makes storing and processing text very efficient. As we will see below, the maximum of 256 characters that can be encoded using 8 bits is not enough to encode all the scripts used in the world, or even in Europe. This leads to a very confusing situation where different mappings have to be used for different scripts, and the same number is used to encode different characters in different scripts.

Unlike natural numbers, there is no system for converting characters into bit sequences. So each character we want to encode must be assigned to a bit sequence. This assignment is completely arbitrary and can be done in many different ways. Unfortunately, not only is it possible to assign a character to different bit sequences, but this has also been done many times over the past century, resulting in many different character encodings.

When a character, for example *a*, is assigned to a bit sequence, say 0110 0001, that bit sequence also represents a decimal number, in this case 97. So, instead of

1 Both encodings were created in the 1980s and withdrawn around 2013 (National Information Standards Organization 1993, International Telecommunication Union 2008).

specifying the bit sequence, we can just specify the number to which the character is assigned. Most tables that define character encodings give hexadecimal numbers. In the hexadecimal system we have 16 different symbols instead of 10 (the numbers 0 to 9 and the letters A to F). The advantage of hexadecimal numbers is that they are easier to convert to binary numbers and vice versa. The hexadecimal representation of binary 0110 0001 (or decimal 97) is 61 ($6 \cdot 16^1 + 1 \cdot 16^0$). This is easily found since hexadecimal 6 corresponds to 0110 and hexadecimal 1 to 0001. Normally, hexadecimal numbers are preceded by 0x to indicate that the following number is hexadecimal. So we could write 0x61 or 97 for the number used to encode the letter *a*.

Finally, a character needs to be printed or displayed on the screen. To do this, we need an image of a glyph that represents that character. A collection of such graphical representations is called a font. Obviously, not every font has glyphs for all characters of all existing encodings. If a character has to be displayed that is not present in the font used, it depends on the software used what is done. Some programs will instead display a glyph for the character from a default font, if available, while others will display a character to indicate that no glyph was available. This is usually an empty square or a square with a cross, question mark or the hexadecimal code of the missing character, or the so-called *replacement character* (see Figure 2) (Constable et al. 2022, Unicode Consortium 2024: 106,253).

Figure 2: Some glyphs commonly used to display characters missing in the font currently used. The last glyph is the so-called replacement character, defined in Unicode (Unicode Consortium 2024: 1070), that is especially used to display invalid bytes in Unicode based encodings.

3 From ASCII to Latin1

In 1870, Émile Baudot invented a 5-bit binary code, which was patented in 1874 and used worldwide for telegraphy, replacing the Morse code used previously (Haralambous 2007, Kurmis 2015: 128). With 5 bits, only 32 characters could be encoded. To overcome this problem, the code allows switching between two modes, thus allowing a maximum of 62 characters (two codes are needed to switch the mode). In the late 19th and early 20th centuries, various variants and standardisations of this code were used for telegraphy. In the 1950s, various non-standardised 6-bit codes were used in the first computers. In 1960 a 7-bit code, FIELDATA, became a standard for the US military (Haralambous 2007: 29).

3.1 ASCII

In 1961, Bob Bemer, a computer programmer at IBM, submitted a proposal for a 7-bit character encoding to the ASA (American Standards Association), which led to the first definition of the ASCII code (American Standard Code for Information Interchange) in 1963. The third version was published in 1967 and, with very minor changes, is ASCII as we know it today. In 1968 ASCII became the official standard for all US government agencies (Haralambous 2007: 31, McEnery and Xiao 2005).

Seven bits allow 128 characters to be encoded, which is obviously not enough to encode all the characters used around the world. Eight bits (256 possible characters) is still not enough but would at least allow a much wider range of characters to be encoded. However, in 1961 the size of a byte was not yet standardised, and some computers using 8 bits for a byte needed one bit as a check bit. ASCII has a number of further peculiarities from this early computer era. At that time, only one stream of data could be sent to a printer. So, the control statements had to be included in the character set as control characters, which still make up a large part of the ASCII character set. For example, at the end of the line a line feed (LF) and a carriage return (CR) command were needed. This is why Windows computers still use two control characters to mark the end of a line. The encoding for the upper and lower variants always differs by exactly 1 bit, making it easy to change case. The control character for *delete* is assigned to code 127, which is 1111111 in binary. This was useful for typing punch cards: if you make an error, you can invalidate or delete the character by punching all 7 positions.

3.2 Extensions of ASCII

In the original ASCII definition, the use of diacritics was foreseen. After typing a base letter, a backspace followed by a diacritic that would then be placed over or under the previous character should be entered. Thus, characters composed of a base letter and a diacritic were not encoded but could be handled perfectly as long as printers that worked like typewriters were the main computer interface (Haralambous 2007, Aivosto n. d.).

As computer screens became more prevalent and manufacturers began selling computers in non-English speaking countries, the ASCII standard was no longer sufficient, leading to the design of new character sets. From today's perspective, at least two significant mistakes were made during that time, which caused considerable issues with character encoding for several decades. First, character sets were often viewed as components of specific computers or operating systems. This approach works well as long as we consider computers as advanced standalone typewriters, but it leads to problems when exchanging data between different systems. Second, both vendors and standardization organizations focused on markets, countries, and nations when developing character sets, rather than on languages or scripts. For instance, character sets were created specifically for Germany, Switzerland, and France instead of for the German and French languages.

Initially, ASCII was adapted for use in non-English speaking countries by replacing some characters with those necessary for the local languages. The ISO 646 standard (cf. ISO/IEC 646:1991), first released in 1967, specifies which characters can be replaced for national use. The International Reference Version, defined in the 1973 release of this standard, is identical to ASCII except for the dollar sign. The characters @ [ ] { } \ | can be substituted for other characters in national versions (Aivosto n. d.). This led to the unsatisfactory situation where the same code can represent different characters in different countries, and two countries might use different codes for the same character. For example, é is encoded in ISO 646 for France and Canada as 0x7B while the Swiss version uses 0x5B (cf. ISO/IEC 646:1991). Clearly, seven (or in some cases, slightly more) positions are insufficient to encode all the characters needed for most languages. Additionally, the replaced characters may also be necessary, for example for writing program code.

Personal computers have always used 8-bit encodings. Manufacturers and developers of operating systems, such as Microsoft, IBM, and Apple, have created their own encodings, typically as extensions of ASCII. As computers began to be sold outside the USA, national variants, called code pages with Microsoft, were introduced. The ISO 2022 standard, defined in 1971, is an attempt to create some systematicity in all upcoming encodings (Haralambous 2007: 33ff). It provides a general framework for 8-bit encodings and mechanisms to switch between encodings within a single text. For 8-bit encodings it specifies that the first 32 positions (0x00 to 0x1F) and the first 32 positions of the second half of the table (0x80 to 0x8f) are reserved for control characters, and there are 94 and 96 positions in the first and second halves of the table, respectively, for printable characters. With the exception of Japan, the standard was not widely adopted, however, many subsequent standards have followed the general structure of ISO 2022 for the utilisation of the positions in the table.

3.3 ISO 8859 and its variants

The most important 8-bit character encoding standard is the ISO 8859 norm, defined from 1987 on. This encoding is primarily based on the Multinational Character Set (1983) from the computer manufacturer DEC (now Hewlett-Packard) and is compatible with ISO 2022 (André 2002: 43). The first 128 characters are still identical to ASCII. Currently ISO 8859 consists of 15 parts, each defining an encoding for alphabetic languages (Latin, Cyrillic, Greek, Arabic, Hebrew and Thai). For the Latin script it defines encodings for languages in various regions in Europe, such as Latin 1 (ISO/IEC 8859-1:1998) for western European languages and Latin 2 (ISO/IEC 8859-2:1999) for central and eastern European languages written with Latin script. The ISO 8859 standard represents a significant enhancement over ISO 646 but still has the same fundamental problems. For example, all characters required for German are identical in both Latin 1 and Latin 2. Consequently, from the perspective of a German user, both encodings appear indistinguishable. If a German user opens a text encoded with Latin 1 and decodes it as Latin 2, it may appear correct at first glance, but many characters that are used only for foreign words are encoded differently. For example, 0xE6 is used in Latin 1 for æ and in Latin 2 for ć. In almost all cases, a glyph that is part of several character sets defined by ISO 8859 gets the same code point in each encoding. However, a few exceptions still exist: the letter æ is encoded as 0xE6 in Latin 1, 4, 6, 8, 9 and 10 and Latin/Thai, but as 0xBF in Latin 7 (Baltic languages). Furthermore, 96 additional characters for several languages is quite tight. Consequently, in some ISO 8859 encodings, characters essential for languages that should be covered are absent, most notably the ligatures œ and ij[2] are missing for French and Dutch, respectively. Finally, some special characters like the copyright sign (©) are present in some encodings while absent from others.

Microsoft's Windows operating system, released in 1985, already used the ISO 8859-1 encoding. To be more precise, it used a draft from the American National Standards Institute (ANSI) that later became the ISO 8859-1 standard. This encoding is called Windows code page 1252 or Windows Latin 1, but is often referred to as ANSI, though it never was an ANSI standard (Microsoft 2017). Starting from Windows 2.0, the encoding deviated from ISO 8859-1 by using the positions 0x80 to 0x8F, reserved for control characters, for characters missing in the ISO standard. Windows code page 1252 became one of the most widely used encodings in Western Europe and is still in use today. According to W3Techs (2025b) in February 2025 still more than 1.5 % of all websites use ISO-8859-1 or one of its MS Windows variants (code page 1251 or 1252). For Websites from the .de-domain this is about 2.5 % (W3Techs 2025a). For texts locally stored in text files and databases this fraction might be much higher; this may also concern scientific legacy data.

In addition to the encoding specified in this section, there are numerous other encodings that have been defined and utilised. The English Wikipedia comprises dedicated pages for approximately 400 character encodings, categorised under the

2 Whether the Dutch ligature ij should be considered as an autonomous grapheme is subject to debate (Nunn 1998: 12, Haralambous and Dürst 2019: 152).

'Character sets' category and various subcategories. It is beyond the scope of this chapter to mention all of them.

4 The Unicode standard

As early as 1984 ISO established the Joint Technical Committee 1 (JTC1) that got the task of developing a universal character encoding (Aliprand 2000). The character set developed by the JTC1 was called the Universal Character Set (UCS) and became standard ISO/IEC 10646:2020, referencing ISO 646. UCS makes a systematic distinction between code points and encodings. A code point is simply a number assigned to a character, while the encoding is the bit sequence that is actually stored on disk. When a character set has less than 256 code points, we can encode each code point directly in one byte, meaning that there is only a theoretical difference between the code point and its encoding. However, if there are more than 256 code points, we may need to use two, three, or even four bytes per character, which would require significantly more memory for storage and more bandwidth for transmission. Therefore, usually encodings are used that minimize the number of bytes per character. This can be achieved either by employing variable-length encodings, where common characters have shorter representations and infrequent characters have longer ones, or by defining specific encodings for different parts of the character set along with a mechanism to switch between the encodings. The early drafts of ISO 10646 included several complex encodings that also utilized the mechanisms set out in the ISO 2022 standard.

In 1988 Joseph Becker from Xerox and Lee Collins and Mark Davis from Apple started to work on a simpler fixed length universal encoding, called Unicode and based on "Alternative B" from Peter Fenwick who was involved in the JTC1 (Bettels and Avery Bishop 1993, Unicode Consortium 1991: 5). In 1991 the Unicode consortium was established as a non-profit organization involving various important members from software industry. The goal of Unicode was to develop a 16-bit encoding that could represent all characters used in languages around the world. With 16 bits, there are 65.536 possible code points. To accommodate all characters within this limit, it was decided that characters from traditional Chinese, simplified Chinese, and Japanese that are based on the same abstract shape would share the same code point (Unicode Consortium 1991: 15). Whether a character is displayed in its Japanese, simplified or traditional Chinese form is then a matter of font selection. Note that this approach differs from the treatment of alphabetic languages, where e. g. the A from the Greek, Latin and Cyrillic alphabet get different code points.

As many companies feared the emergence of two competing standards, the JTC1 and the Unicode design group met in 1991 and decided to align their efforts (Bettels and Avery Bishop 1993). Since 1992 (Unicode Consortium 2000: 5) UCS and Unicode have defined the same code points.

Unicode started as a pure 16-bit encoding. However, already in version 2.0 (1996) a mechanism from UCS was adopted to allow for some 32-bit character encodings as well, although this mechanism was not yet in use (Unicode Consortium 1996: 6-118). Unicode version 4.0, released in 2003, began defining characters requiring more than 32 bits. Together with the possibility to define more characters also the concept of using different encodings for the same code points was introduced into Unicode.

4.1 Structure

As mentioned above, Unicode started as a 16-bit encoding, allowing for (at most) $2^{16} = 65.536$ characters. This part is now called the *Basic Multilingual Plane* (BMP). Two ranges of 1024 code points cannot be used directly for encoding characters. The excluded code points, called high and low surrogates, can be used only in combination to encode characters with 4 bytes. The 16-bit Unicode Transformation Format (UTF16), originating from UCS enables the combination of a high and a low surrogate to encode characters using 32 bits (see Table 3 for an example). Thus, $1024^2 = 1.048.576$ additional characters can be encoded. This results in a theoretical upper bound of $65.536 - 2.048 + 1.048.576 = 1.112.064$ Unicode characters. The additional 1.048.576 code points are organized in 16 additional planes of each 65.536 characters. Unicode version 16.0, however, only defines 154.998 characters from 168 scripts.

Plane 0, the Basic Multilingual Plane (BMP), contains the most important characters of almost all currently used scripts, including the (unified) Chinese and Japanese characters. The first 256 code points are identical to ISO 8859-1. Thus, the first 128 positions are identical to ASCII, including all weird control characters. The remaining code points are divided into blocks. Each block is used for one script, but most scripts are divided over several, often non-contiguous, blocks. Unicode code points are usually denoted by U+ followed by the hexadecimal representation of the number of the code point. For example, the small Latin letter a has the code point U+0061 (97 in decimal notation).

Plane 1, the Supplementary Multilingual Plane, is used for historical scripts, music notation, and special symbols, like mathematical symbols. The next plane, Supplementary Ideographic Plane, is used for rare or newly invented Chinese, Japanese and Korean (CJK) ideographs not included in the BMP. The Tertiary Ideographic

Plane, plane 4, is used for historical Chinese scripts. Planes 5 to 16 are currently not used to encode characters.

In the BMP, a block of 6,400 characters (from U+E000 to U+F8FF) is reserved for private use. It is recommended that end users use the lower regions of this so-called primary Private Use Area (PUA), while software companies should start defining characters at U+F8FF and extend downwards in values. If more characters need to be defined, almost the entire fifteenth and sixteenth planes are available as supplementary Private Use Areas (Unicode Consortium 2024: 1058ff). Companies may use the PUA for internal technical purposes or to encode a company logo for example (Unicode Consortium 2024: 1060). Similarly, the PUA is often used to encode icons (Microsoft 2024). Other uses include scripts that are not (yet) included in the Unicode standard (such as the Klingon scripts from the Star Trek movies; Wikipedia 2025b) and character sets that contain many different glyphs (remember that Unicode aims to define characters, not glyphs).

A character set using the PUA that might be of interest for corpus construction is the one defined by the Medieval Unicode Font Initiative (MUFI), which includes many ligatures, scribal abbreviations, and special character forms that are considered essential for the accurate representation of medieval texts (Haugen 2013, MUFI Board n. d.). It should however be noted that the PUA is outside the Unicode standardization and that most software and most fonts will not be able to render these characters. Moreover, various users can use the same code points for different purposes which could lead to similar confusion as arose with all 8-bit character sets extending ASCII. Therefore, the goal of MUFI is to make proposals for the official Unicode standard and to use the PUA mainly as an intermediate solution (MUFI Board n. d.).

4.2 Principles

Unicode is based on a number of design principles (Unicode Consortium 2024: 49ff), some of which are of interest in the context of the construction of corpora. One such principle is stability, which guarantees that a code point once used for one character will not be used for another character in any future version of Unicode. Consequently, when employing Unicode to encode a text, its proper decoding in any future version of Unicode is guaranteed. Another important principle is that Unicode is designed to be compatible with existing character encoding standards. Notably, any (plain) text can be transformed to Unicode without information loss and can be translated back again (round tripping). Therefore, when aiming to use a single encoding for an entire corpus, while source texts are encoded in various formats,

Unicode is the only encoding that guarantees this can be achieved without errors or loss of information.

The downside of the compatibility principle is that it can lead to conflicts with other principles. Unicode addresses characters rather than glyphs, meaning it does not assign different code points for different representations of the same character. However, if there is a widely accepted standard that defines multiple glyphs for the same character, Unicode must incorporate all of them. For this reason, Unicode, for instance, defines three positional alternates for each Arabic letter.

4.3 Normal forms

Unicode also allows for the composition of characters. This feature enables the definition of characters that are not commonly used but are easily imaginable, such as an *x* with a diaeresis added to it ($\ddot{x}$). This character could be defined as an *x* followed by the diaeresis (U+0078 U+0308). For commonly used composed characters now always two possible encodings exist: the pre-combined one and the dynamically defined version. Note that the two encodings define exactly the same character. A program that renders the character has to display them identically and it is up to the rendering program whether it stores composed characters as one picture or whether it combines two or more pictures to render a composed character.

Unicode defines a number of properties for each character including information about canonical and compatibility equivalence with other characters or character sequences. Canonical equivalence means that two character sequences define exactly the same character. For example, U+006F U+0308 and U+00F6 both define the letter ö and therefore are canonically equivalent. Compatibility equivalence is broader and also defines equivalence between different glyphs for one character, that are included in Unicode for compatibility reasons or because for example in mathematical texts a different font shape of a symbol might have a different meaning. Table 1 gives some examples of equivalent sequences.

Table 1: Example of compatibility equivalence of Unicode code point sequences.

Character (official name)	Code point	Equivalent character	Code point
ﬀ (Latin small ligature ff)	U+FB00	ff	U+0066 U+0066
² (Superscript two)	U+00B2	2 (Digit Two)	U+0032
ε (Mathematical italic small epsilon)	U+1D700	ϵ (Greek small letter epsilon)	U+03B5

Table 2: Schematic overview of Unicode normal froms.

	composed	*decomposed*
canonical	NFC	NFD
compatability	NFKC	NFKD

Not every program might treat equivalent sequences as being identical. This could cause problems for search or string comparison in general. Therefore, Unicode defines four normal forms: NFC, NFD, NFKC and NFKD. NFD and NFKD will replace all characters by decomposed sequences (when possible) while NFC and NFCD will do the reverse and use pre-composed characters if available. The forms NFC and NFD use only canonical equivalence, whereas NFKC and NFKD also use compatibility equivalence (see Table 2 for a schematic overview).

It is recommended to always use NFC to obtain a maximally normalized text (Korpela 2006: 240, Haralambous 2007: 133, Moran and Cysouw 2018: 18). Note that one should be careful with using the NFKC normalization, since it may change the meaning of the text, e. g. 4^2 might become 42. NFKC is e. g. useful to implement search applications, but usually not for archiving texts.

4.4 Encodings of Unicode

Unicode defines three encodings: UTF32, UTF16 and UTF8. Many other unofficial and obsolete encodings exist but are not found frequently.

UTF32 is simply the 32-bit binary representation of each code point. Since at most 21 bits are needed, the 11 most significant bits will always be zero. This makes UTF32 a very inefficient format for storing texts. Since most processors can handle sequences of 32 bits very efficiently, UTF32 is mainly used as a program internal representation.

UTF16 uses 16 bits or two bytes (in computer terminology a *word*) for all characters from the Basic Multilingual Plane. For all other characters two surrogates are used. An example is shown in Table 3. The surrogates start with one of two patterns of six bits. All possible surrogates (2048) do not represent a code point in the BMP. UTF16 always deals with words (pairs of two bytes), but words can be stored in two ways on a computer: in little-endian (LE) or big-endian (BE) format. Consequently, there are two versions of UTF16: UTF16-BE and UTF16-LE. In order to tell a program which version of UTF16 was used to encode a text, a UTF16 text starts with a byte order marker (BOM), the character U+FEFF. The BOM is encoded with two bytes that only can be interpreted in one order (since U+FFFE is not a valid code point). Thus,

Table 3: UTF16 encoding of the German letter sharp s, the (Chinese) Kangxi radical dog and the violin clef. Bits printed in red are the meaningful bits that represent the code point, gray bits are leading zeros to fill up a byte and the blue bits mark the high and low surrogate. The first bit of the last example is not encoded explicitly in the high and low surrogate, because 0x10000 is subtracted from the code point before the bits are distributed over the two surrogates.

Char.	Code point	Code point (binary)	UTF16 encoding
ß	U+00DF	11011111	00000000 11011111
⽝	U+2F5D	101111 01011101	00101111 01011101
𝄞	U+1D11E	1 11010001 00011110	11011000 00110100 11011101 00011110

Table 4: UTF8 byte sequences. The 0's and 1's at the beginning of each byte are used to identify the byte type. The positions marked with an x are used to store the bits belonging to the code point.

standalone byte				0xxxxxxx
initial and 1 following byte			110xxxxx	10xxxxxx
initial and 2 following bytes		1110xxxx	10xxxxxx	10xxxxxx
initial and 3 following bytes	11110xxx	10xxxxxx	10xxxxxx	10xxxxxx

this (invisible, zero width) character can be used to figure out the endianness of the encoding.

The most popular encoding for alphabetic languages is UTF8. UTF8 is a very clever encoding invented by Robert Pike and Ken Thompson in 1992 (Kurmis 2015) that encodes each code point in one to four bytes. The length of the encoding depends on the numerical value of the code point. The lower this number is, the shorter the encoding. Since frequently used characters (from an American/Western-European point of view) are positioned at low code points and rare characters at the end of the BMP or in higher planes, texts using the Latin script can be stored very efficiently.

In UTF8 there are three types of bytes: stand-alone bytes, bytes that mark the beginning of a multi-byte sequence and follow-up-bytes. The first type starts with a 0 and uses the remaining seven bits to encode the code point. A follow-up byte starts with 10 and has six positions left. A starting byte starts with two, three or four 1's followed by a 0. The number of 1's gives the length of the sequence. Table 4 gives an overview of the four possible patterns. We see here that all characters needing at most seven bits are encoded in one byte. Thus all ASCII characters are encoded exactly in the same way as in the original ASCII encoding and every pure ASCII text is a valid UTF8 encoded text as well! All characters that can be encoded with 11 bits (the first 2048 code points) are encoded with 16 bits. This includes among others most characters from the Greek, Hebrew, Arabic and Cyrillic alphabets. Using three bytes, exactly 16 bits are available for the encoding, which is exactly enough for all

Table 5: UTF8 encoding of an ASCII character, the German letter sharp s, the (Chinese) Kangxi radical dog and the violin clef. Bits printed in red are the meaningful bits that represent the code point, gray bits are leading zeros to fill up a byte and the blue bits mark the bits from the UTF8 patterns.

Char.	Code point	Code point (binary)	UTF8 encoding
A	U+0041	1000001	01000001
ß	U+00DF	11011111	11000011 10011111
⽝	U+2F5D	101111 01011101	11100010 10111101 10011101
𝄞	U+1D11E	1 11010001 00011110	11110000 10011101 10000100 10011110

characters from the BMP. Finally, we see that there are 21 bits available when using four bytes, which is exactly enough to encode all Unicode characters. Table 5 gives a few examples of characters encoded with UTF8. Since UTF8 deals with bytes, not words, endianness is not an issue. Nevertheless, a BOM is allowed but not recommended in UTF8 texts (Korpela 2006: 302).

5 Practical recommendations

In general, it is always a good idea to use Unicode, since it is a modern widely accepted standard, coding more characters than any other standard, and because texts in any other encoding can be recoded in Unicode without any loss of information. When texts are (mainly) written in Arabic, Hebrew or European scripts, UTF8 NFC is highly recommended (see also TEI Consortium 2025: LII, McEnery and Xiao 2005: 55, Schäfer and Bildhauer 2013: 42). When texts are collected from the Internet, also HTML-entities might be used to represent non-ASCII characters. These also should be replaced by Unicode characters.

Unfortunately, many texts are encoded with other encodings, and still many texts are produced using other encodings. To convert these texts into UTF8 (most modern text editors and corpus software offer functions to do so), we first need to know what encoding was used. If the text is part of an XML or HTML document the encoding is often specified in the header. However, there is no guarantee that this information is correct. Many people just copy a header and put text into it without knowing what they are doing. The second possibility is to use a tool that guesses the encoding. Since there are many encodings and many of them differ just for a few characters, this method is also not reliable.

If we open a text, assuming some encoding that is not correct this often results in a text with “strange” characters, called *mojibake*. Suppose e. g. that we have a German text encoded as ISO 8859-2 (Latin 2). If we open the text file assuming it is encoded with Windows-1252 (“ANSI”) we will hardly see any problem, since all characters that are needed to spell German words, have the same code in both encodings. However, if somewhere the Czech place name Děčín is used, it will be displayed as Dìèín: the characters ě, č and í are represented by the codes 0xEC, 0xE8 and 0xED in Latin 2, respectively.[3] In Windows 1252 these codes are then interpreted as ì, è and í. Longer sequences of strange characters often arise from reading UTF8 encoded texts as if they were encoded with some single byte encoding. In Unicode a character with diacritics can be represented by one or two (or even more) code points and most code points are encoded with more than one byte. If such a text is read assuming it is encoded as Latin 1, each byte will be interpreted as a character. For example the German word *Gefäß* (jar) is represented in UTF8 (using NFC) by the bytes 0x47, 0x65, 0x66, 0xC3, 0xA4, 0xC3, 0x9F (see also Table 5 for the encoding of the letter ß). In Latin 1 this sequence would be interpreted as `GefÃ¤ÃŸ`. The other way around will usually result in errors when reading the text. Many byte sequences are not valid UTF8 sequences and usually a text that was not encoded as UTF8 contains many such sequences.

However, strange characters in the text do not necessarily mean that there is an encoding error. It might just be the case that a character is missing in the font that is used to render the text. Ideally, in such cases the replacement character is rendered (see Figure 2).

Once a text is corrupted with mojibake, it is difficult to repair. This often occurs when a text is opened with the wrong encoding, and then new text is added using the new encoding. Now in fact various parts of the text use different encodings and any encoding that is used to read the text will misinterpret some parts of the text. It is important to realize that if we see something like `GefÃ¤ÃŸ` from the example above in our text, this is not a rendering problem but a fundamental misinterpretation of the encoding. Now if we would find `großes GefÃ¤ÃŸ` (large jar) in a Latin1 encoded document we have hardly any chance to repair the text except by manual correction: If we save the text in UTF8 Unicode representations for the “strange” characters will be used to represent them and there will be no magic backward conversion to the originally intended string. When composing a corpus, it is crucial to ensure at every stage that all texts are encoded and rendered correctly, as later attempts to fix earlier mistakes can be quite cumbersome.

While some parts of this chapter may seem technical and complicated, as users, we never have to deal with all these technical details. It is most important to be aware of potential problems and to work carefully with texts.

---

3 Just for fun: if one searches the Internet for Dìèín, one will find some pages referring to Děčín and misspelling this name.

Bibliography

Aivosto. n. d. *7-bit character sets*. Retrieved Febr. 2, 2025. https://www.aivosto.com/articles/charsets-7bit.html.

Aliprand, Joan M. 2000. The Unicode standard. *Library Resources & Technical Services* 44(3). 160–167.

André, Jacques. 2002. Caractères, codage et normalization. De Chappe à Unicode. *Document Numérique* 6(3). 13–49. https://stm.cairn.info/revue-document-numerique-2002-3-page-13.

Bettels, Jürgen & F. Avery Bishop. 1993. Unicode: A universal character code. *Digital Technical Journal* 5(3). 21–31. ISSN 0898-901X.

Constable, Peter, Ken Turetzky & Mike Jacobs. 2022. *Recommendations for OpenType fonts (OpenType 1.7)*. Retrieved Febr. 21, 2025. https://learn.microsoft.com/en-us/typography/opentype/otspec170/recom.

Dürscheid, Christa. 2016. *Einführung in die Schriftlinguistik*. 5., aktualisierte und korrigierte Auflage. utb. Göttingen: Vandenhoeck & Ruprecht.

Haralambous, Yannis. 2007. *Fonts & encodings*, 1st edn. Sebastopol, CA: O'Reilly.

Haralambous, Yannis & Martin Dürst. 2019. Unicode from a linguistic point of view. In Yannis Haralambous (ed.), *Graphemics in the 21st century*. Vol. 1 of Grapholinguistics and Its Applications, 127–166. Brest: Fluxus Editions. ISBN 978-2-9570549-0-9. https://doi.org/10.36824/2018-graf.

Haugen, Odd Einar. 2013. Dealing with glyphs and characters. Challenges in encoding medieval scripts. *Document Numérique* 16(3). 97–111.

Holgers, Tobias, David E. Watson & Steven D. Gribble. 2006. Cutting through the confusion: a measurement study of homograph attacks. In *Proceedings of the Annual Conference on USENIX '06 Annual Technical Conference. ATEC '06*. USA: USENIX Association.

International Telecommunication Union. 2008. *T.61: Character repertoire and coded character sets for the international teletex service*. Retrieved Febr. 22, 2025. https://www.itu.int/rec/T-REC-T.61.

ISO/IEC 10646:2020. 2020. *ISO/IEC 10646:2020 Information technology – Universal coded character set (UCS)*. Standard. Geneva, CH: International Organization for Standardization. https://www.iso.org/standard/76835.html.

ISO/IEC 2022:1994. 1994. *ISO/IEC 2022: Information technology – Character code structure and extension techniques*. Standard. Geneva, CH: International Organization for Standardization. https://www.iso.org/standard/22747.html.

ISO/IEC 646:1991. 1991. *ISO/IEC 646: Information technology – ISO 7-bit coded character set for information interchange*. Standard. Geneva, CH: International Organization for Standardization. https://www.iso.org/standard/4777.html.

ISO/IEC 8859-1:1998. 1998. *ISO/IEC 8859-1: Information technology – 8-bit single-byte coded graphic character sets. Part 1: Latin alphabet No. 1*. Standard. Geneva, CH: International Organization for Standardization. https://www.iso.org/standard/28245.html.

ISO/IEC 8859-2:1999. 1999. *ISO/IEC 8859-2: Information technology — 8-bit single-byte coded graphic character sets. Part 2: Latin alphabet No. 2*. Standard. Geneva, CH: International Organization for Standardization. https://www.iso.org/standard/28246.html.

Korpela, Jukka K. 2006. *Unicode explained*. Beijing et al.: O'Reilly. ISBN 0-596-10121-X.

Kurmis, Oliver. 2015. *Unicode. Geschichte und aktuelle Herausforderungen der digitalen Zeichenkodierung*. München: GRIN. https://www.grin.com/document/321725.

Leibniz, Gottfried Wilhelm. 1703. Explication de l'arithmétique binaire, qui se sert des seuls caractères O et I avec des remarques sur son utilité et sur ce qu'elle donne le sens des anciennes figures chinoises de Fohy. In *Mémoires de mathématique et de physique de l'Académie royale des sciences*. https://hal.science/ads-00104781/document.

McEnery, Anthony & Richard Xiao. 2005. Character encoding in corpus construction. In Martin Wynne (ed.), *Developing linguistic corpora: A guide to good practice*, 47–58. Oxford: AHDS Literature, Language and Linguistics.

Meletis, Dimitrios. 2019. The grapheme as a universal basic unit of writing. *Writing Systems Research* 11(1). 26–49. https://doi.org/10.1080/17586801.2019.1697412.

Meletis, Dimitrios. 2020. Types of allography. *Open Linguistics* 6(1). 249–266. https://doi.org/10.1515/opli-2020-0006.

Microsoft. 2017. *Glossary of terms used on this site*. Retrieved Febr. 21, 2025. https://web.archive.org/web/20181208141313/https://msdn.microsoft.com/en-us/goglobal/bb964658.aspx#a.

Microsoft. 2024. *Private use area (PUA) characters and End-user-defined characters (EUDCs)*. Retrieved March 2, 2025. https://learn.microsoft.com/en-us/globalization/encoding/pua.

Moran, Steven & Michael Cysouw. 2018. The Unicode cookbook for linguists Managing writing systems using orthography profiles. In *Translation and multilingual natural language processing*, Berlin: Language Science Press. ISBN 978-3-96110-090-3. http://langsci-press.org/catalog/book/176.

MUFI Board. n. d. *MUFI: The medieval Unicode font initiative*. Retrieved March 2, 2025. https://mufi.info/.

National Information Standards Organization. 1993. *Extended Latin alphabet coded character set for bibliographic use*. Bethseda, Maryland: NISO Press. ISBN 1-880124-02-5. https://web.archive.org/web/20140314191437/http://www.niso.org/apps/group_public/download.php/6451/Extended%20Latin%20Alphabet%20Coded%20Character%20Set%20for%20Bibliographic%20Use%20%28ANSEL%29.pdf.

Nunn, Anneke Marijke. 1998. *Dutch orthography: A systematic investigation of the spelling of Dutch words*. The Hague: Holland Academic Graphics.

Schäfer, Roland & Felix Bildhauer. 2013. *Web corpus construction*. Synthesis Lectures on Human Language Technologies. Morgan & Claypool Publishers. ISBN 978-3-031-02152-7. https://doi.org/10.1007/978-3-031-02152-7_2.

TEI Consortium. 2025. *EI P5: Guidelines for electronic text encoding and interchange*. https://tei-c.org/Vault/P5/4.9.0/doc/tei-p5-doc/en/Guidelines.pdf.

Unicode Consortium. 1991. *The Unicode standard worldwide character encoding, Version 1.0*. Reading, Mass.: Addison-Wesley. ISBN 0-201-56788-1. https://www.unicode.org/versions/Unicode1.0.0/.

Unicode Consortium. 1996. *The Unicode standard worldwide character encoding, Version 2.0*. Reading, Mass. Addison-Wesley. isbn: 0-201-48345-9. url. https://www.unicode.org/versions/Unicode2.0.0/.

Unicode Consortium. 2000. *The Unicode standard worldwide character encoding, Version 3.0*. Reading, Mass.: Addison-Wesley. ISBN 0-201-61633-5. https://www.unicode.org/versions/Unicode3.0.0/.

Unicode Consortium. 2024. *The Unicode standard worldwide character encoding, Version 16.0.0*. South San Francisco. ISBN 978-1-936213-34-4. https://www.unicode.org/versions/Unicode16.0.0/.

W3Techs. 2025a. *Distribution of character encodings among websites that use .de*. Retrieved Febr. 2, 2025. https://w3techs.com/technologies/segmentation/tld-de-/character_encoding.

W3Techs. 2025b. *Usage statistics of character encodings for websites*. Retrieved Febr. 2, 2025. https://w3techs.com/technologies/overview/character_encoding.

Wikipedia. 2025a. *Endianness*. Retrieved Febr. 21, 2025. https://en.wikipedia.org/wiki/Endianness.

Wikipedia. 2025b. *Klingon scripts*. Retrieved March 2, 2025. https://en.wikipedia.org/wiki/Klingon_scripts.

Laurent Romary

International standards for the identification and the description of languages and their varieties

Abstract: The present chapter explores the need for and methods of standardising, especially in digital and linguistic contexts. With thousands of languages and countless varieties spoken globally, the task of accurately identifying, coding, and representing them is complex but crucial for interoperability, information management, and linguistic research. The article presents two key ISO standards – for language codes and for describing – and discusses how these standards can help professionals across domains manage linguistic diversity. It also proposes enhancements to the framework to better accommodate the nuanced identification and documentation of languages and their varieties. Ultimately, the article advocates for more coherent, flexible, and comprehensive digital language resources, emphasizing the importance of community consensus, data modelling, and training in standardisation practices.

Keywords: standardisation, language description, language code, language varieties, TEI guidelines

1 Standardising languages, why and how?

1.1 Languages – what is there to be standardised?

The Ethnologue register[1] lists around 7,000 languages, while the Glottolog[2] database (Hammarström et al. 2024) identifies over 8,000 languoids (families, languages, dialects, see Forkel and Hammarström (2022). In reality, there is far greater variability

1 https://www.ethnologue.com
2 https://glottolog.org

Acknowledgement: The author acknowledges the use of Large Language Models (LLMs) as writing aids in phrasing this chapter, based on the authors' notes, ideas, and concepts. The author retains full responsibility for the content. My warmest thanks to all the colleagues and friends who have provided input or feedback on this text, in particular: Susanne Alt, Gaby Bodard, Veronika Engler, Charly Moerth, Daniel Schopper, Toma Tasovac and of course the editors of the present volume.

Laurent Romary, Direction de la Culture et de l'Information Scientifique, Inria, Domaine de Voluceau – Rocquencourt, B.P. 105, 78153 Le Chesnay, France, e-mail: laurent.romary@inria.fr

https://doi.org/10.1515/9783112208212-003

in how a language is spoken (Reppen et al. 2002) depending on geographical context, the circumstances of communication, and also on social or educational parameters.[3] When we look at the level of individuals, we find that each one of us embodies a whole spectrum of linguistic forms, shaped by our origins, our learning history, and the groups with which we have interacted. We learn to master different registers, we activate different vocabularies according to the situation, and all of this evolves over time.

This variety of linguistic forms that we can observe at both the level of an individual – and even more so among a group of individuals – can render the task of standardised language identification almost impossible in its entirety. Yet, we intuitively know how to recognise a language we are familiar with and we can communicate fluidly within groups sharing a given language. In the context of the widespread digital exchanges, we must be capable of exchanging oral or textual information within computer systems that rely on the accurate identification of the languages that are being used.

In this context, standardisation offers professionals in different fields – language specialists, archive and library curators or IT professionals exchanging language data – means to identify languages so that the information arrives where it should arrive, and is processed in the right way.

Behind this generic idea of why standardisation is important in the domain of languages, there is a deeper question of what is to be standardised. Should we try to catalogue languages so that they fit into a box associated with a code? Or should we standardise the method to identify languages so that professionals themselves have a word to say about, the level of granularity at which a language should be considered? The present chapter intends to offer a compromise between these two perspectives.

1.2 A whole range of possible applications

Language encoding is essential for digital applications as it enables systems to identify, process, and present content in the correct language, ensuring seamless communication across linguistic diversity and platforms. In library settings, properly encoded language metadata allow for accurate cataloguing, searchability, and retrieval of documents within a multilingual archive. On the web, it ensures that pages are correctly displayed and indexed, enhancing accessibility and user experience. Language encoding also supports spell-checking by enabling software to apply the

3 See for instance the work of Eugenio Coseriu (1970) on linguistic variation.

right linguistic rules, improving accuracy. In smartphones, it facilitates multilingual interfaces, predictive text, and voice recognition. Crucially, standardised language encoding promotes interoperability, allowing different systems and applications to exchange and interpret linguistic data consistently, supporting global communication and information management.

A strong framework for describing and identifying languages and their varieties is of course essential to academic purposes dealing in particular with language resources. This is the case for any corpus gathering activity. Exemplary applications range from dealing with specific heritage objects such as epigraphic research (Bodard 2010) to large-scale ambitions to harvest online content for training machine learning systems (Ortiz et al. 2019, 2020).[4] And of course, language identification is key to all dictionary projects where framing the intended language variety has a strong impact on the actual lexical coverage.

The ultimate application of language description and encoding is clearly that of field linguistics where a scholar has to determine the granularity at which he/she wants to observe linguistic data to define the dimensions (in the sense of ISO 21636, as we shall see below) to consider and the language families he/she wants to connect the observations to. A strong standardisation framework is essential to be able to compare observations across researchers and linguistic spheres. For instance, it is important when previous evidence such as recordings, lexicons or grammatical descriptions in order to compare observations over time. As demonstrated by the exemplary work carried out in the Wibarab[5] project, each observation should be characterised according to the actual variety it represents.

As we can see from the examples above, there might be a tension between constraints on the linguistic precision and the technical effectiveness of language identification. Still, it is not imaginable to provide a different technical solution for each application, with the risk that proprietary solutions lack a proper maintenance of schemas and associated tools. What we shall see in this chapter is that ISO has probably defined, over the course of more than 50 years of activity on the subject, a rather reasonable path with both a stable framework for the identification of languages and a flexible environment for the description of varieties.

1.3 The standardisation landscape

This chapter will focus on the two main standardisation efforts within the International Organisation for Standardisation (ISO): ISO 639, a standard defining a code

4 See also https://oscar-project.org/

5 "What Is Bedouin-type ARABic?", https://wibarab.acdh.oeaw.ac.at

for identifying languages, and ISO 21636, a standard for describing language varieties. Additionally, we will refer to other standards in the course of this chapter. It is thus useful to elicit some basic elements for those readers who are not necessarily accustomed to standardisation.

- Standards are documents that have no legal power but create a social contract between two parties having to exchange information, in our case, the exchange of digital information;
- Standards are being developed in different bodies, such as ISO, but also the W3C (World Wide Web Consortium) or the TEI (Text Encoding Initiative);
- Standards are usually the result of a consensus within a community. They rely on a design process involving experts working jointly on a document or, maintain an authority list of objects.

We need to keep in mind that a real-life application is always based on a whole range of standards, issued by potentially different standardisation bodies. Each contributes to the definition of specific aspects in the representation of a digital object or elicits the way standards can actually be composed. Figure 1 shows the various standardisation layers that allow the encoding of the language in which a text is expressed within the following element according to the TEI guidelines.

We can illustrate this with the following snippet:

```
<quote xml:lang="fr-FR" xmlns="http://www.tei-c.org/ns/1.0">Demain,
dès l'aube, à l'heure où blanchit la campagne…</quote>
```

Typically, language identification requires the provision of a localization code, a country code taken from ISO 3166, or a script from ISO 15924, when the language may be written in two different ways (e. g. for Serbian). The IETF standard BCP[6] 47, combined with the IANA language subtag registry,[7] elicits how such standards may be combined. In turn, the W3C recommendation for XML specifies how to incorporate a language identification tags within an XML element, ie. using the @xml:lang[8] attribute. Finally, the TEI guidelines, based on the XML recommendation, define a vocabulary of elements together with their possible combinations and the condition of integration of the @xml:lang attribute to them.

6 Best Current Practice, one of the ways standardisation documents are named in IETF.

7 https://www.iana.org/assignments/language-subtag-registry/language-subtag-registry

8 We use the notation @XXX to indicate the name of XML attributes in the flow of our text and <YYY> for XML elements.

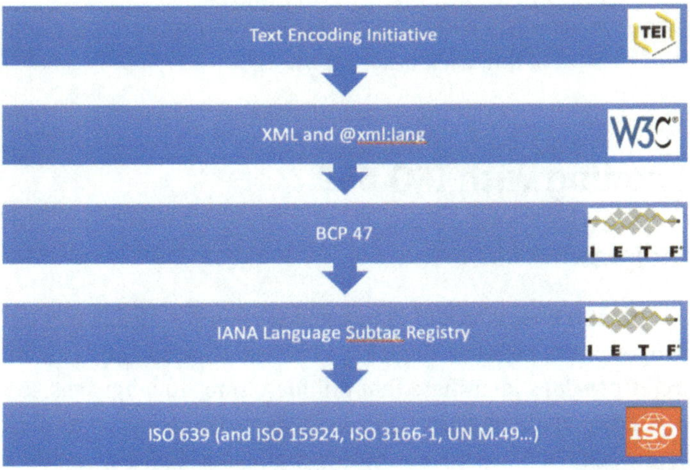

Figure 1: The multilayered standardisation landscape.

1.4 Identifying language as an object to be standardised

The central question when contemplating the standardisation of language codes is to define what a language actually is. There is a large literature on the subject and it is not the aim of the current chapter to dive into the details of the linguistic debates. Still, we want to provide here a glimpse into the complexity of the issue before we provide more details of ISO 639.

From a scholarly point of view, we can only speak of a language if we have observables. Observables can be primary sources such as written traces or recordings, or secondary sources, typically observations by field linguists, that a certain language exists and has certain linguistic properties. At this stage, we can already perceive two elements that contribute to the difficulty of identifying a language: a) the wide variety of evidence that we may have, from fragmented written traces to a whole body of observation and literature; b) such traces can never be about the language as a whole but are a compilation of elementary productions being part of the same "language". What we address here is indeed a central notion: whatever we do in the domain of linguistic documentation or description can only be conceived bottom up from the individual forms used by a given speaker, called his or her idiolect. On this basis, a language can be defined by a degree of commonness between idiolects, i. e. how much the way two speakers express themselves allows them to be understandable to one another. This is what we usually call mutual intelligibility.

A direct consequence is the difficulty to identify languages without actually describing them at least along the dimensions that are relevant for grouping or differentiating idiolects or groups thereof. The current chapter is thus an attempt to present the standardisation activities within ISO together with proposals as a contribution to the complex issues of linguistic description.

2 Language coding with ISO 639

2.1 ISO 639 principles

The main objective of the ISO 639 standard[9] is to provide a simple means to guarantee semantic interoperability between digital systems exchanging linguistic information. Therefore, it provides identifiers that uniquely refer to languages. ISO 639 defines a *language code*, made of elementary *language code elements* for each language covered by the standard, together with identifiers and names for each of the code elements.

In line with the vision provided in the introduction, the notion of language in ISO 639 is understood as the largest mutually intelligible set of idiolects.[10] The scope of ISO 639 is explicitly that of natural languages, as opposed for instance to computer languages. It covers spoken, written and signed languages, including extinct or historical languages. Under certain conditions, e. g. a living user community, it comprises constructed languages, such as Esperanto. In addition to individual languages, the standard covers macro-languages. For ISO 639 legacy reasons, this covers previously identified "languages" which actually are a superset of several distinct languages, for example Arabic or Chinese. It also applies to language groups when several languages share several linguistic or geographical properties, e. g. Caucasian languages.

In this framework, ISO 639 language code elements are associated with one to three identifiers:

- a mandatory three-letter identifier (give examples here);
- an optional second three-letter identifier, for some languages, corresponding to a, so-called "bibliographic use" or "terminological use";
- a two-letter identifier for a reduced number of "major, mostly national individual languages", also known as set 1 of ISO 639 (183 languages as of March 2025) – give examples here.

9 ISO 639:2023 Code for individual languages and language groups.

10 The definition of individual language precisely says "largest set of idiolects, used by different speakers, which are all interconnected through high mutual intelligibility, or through a chain of high mutual intelligibility, or which are socio-politically considered as a unit equivalent to such a largest set" (cf. https://www.iso.org/obp/ui/fr/#iso:std:iso:639:ed-2:v1:en:term:3.1.3)

For instance, the language with the reference name “French” has three identifiers, *fr*, *fra* (terminological use) and *fre* (bibliographical use).

In addition to these identifiers, ISO 639 provides them with language names. For each language code element, there is a single reference name. To achieve this, a differentiating element may be added to the name; for instance, “Leti (Cameroon)” vs. “Leti (Indonesia)”. Additional language names may be provided in English or French as part of the standard.[11] They correspond to names used in the literature or to forms used for indexing in archives or libraries. For example, the language with identifier *lrt* is associated with the reference name “Larantuka Malay” and an additional “inverted” name “Malay, Larantuka”.

The evolution of the ISO 639 language code is ensured by the ISO 639 maintenance agency which has been set up in 2023 and receives all online change requests addressed to it. Such change requests may both tackle the evolution of the language code at large, with proposals to create, merge, split or deprecate existing codes, as well as proposals of changes in naming existing language code elements. Typically, change requests related to the reference name of a code element are quite common in the work of the ISO 639 maintenance agency. They are often related to the observation that the reference name can be seen as derogatory for the corresponding speaker community or that another name has become a far more common designation for the language.

The maintenance of the ISO 639 language code is an activity that covers both linguistic but also political aspects since it can impact on the essence of certain communities or states. This is made all the more difficult because the existing language code is quite comprehensive and relies on a long-standing history (see below). The review mechanism for ISO 639 is essentially based on change requests issued by the community about which the maintenance agency should make an informed decision, possibly based on asking for further experts’ opinions. Still, in order to ensure some stability of the overall ISO 639 framework, there is little margin for creativity and the text of the ISO 639 standards clearly scopes conditions for such changes, in particular in terms of cross-intelligibility. Among the other constraints abiding to the evolution of the ISO 639 language code, we should also mention here that an identifier can never be re-used twice, even if it is part of a language code element that has been deprecated.

Another important observation at this stage is that the ISO 639 language code is the result of eight decades of standardisation activities and it is only recently that a single coherent framework for its maintenance has been set in place. As a result,

---

11 ISO 639 anticipates that its language code may be associated with other names by ISO member bodies.

some of the language code elements would not have necessarily been designed in the same way with the current rules, but are kept in place for legacy and thus backward compatibility reasons. This is in particular one of the reasons why macrolanguages exist in the ISO 639 framework. Still the new maintenance agency has put procedures in place whereby it documents – on a private github server – all decisions and action it takes, thus offering the possibility at each stage to fully justify its choices and also to create a corpus of case law for the years to come.

2.2 Looking back at history to understand the current stage of ISO 639

Even if the present chapter is intended to give the clues for a proper understanding and usage of the ISO 639 language code as it is now, we cannot avoid giving some historical elements as to how the standard was set up and evolved over time. This is all the more important that it impacts on both the structure of the ISO 639 language code and the current organisation of the maintenance agency.

The work on ISO 639 started as early as the 1960s with the publication in 1967 of a first recommendation (ISO/R 639) which had a scope beyond the sole encoding of languages (also covering countries and other identifiers), but which paved the way for the definition of an elaborate multi-part standard over the years.

The first part, published initially in 1988 as ISO 639 and in 2002 as ISO 639 part 1, addressed the encoding of languages using two-letter identifiers and thus could only address "major, mostly national individual languages". Still, it was somehow timely available for accompanying the development of web technologies such as HTML in particular.[12]

The limits of the 2-letter basis of ISO 639-1 for encoding a wide variety of languages was soon addressed by extending the ISO 639 framework with three letter identifiers and addressing, within ISO 639-2 (published in 1998), the encoding of a first larger group of languages. For this work, the Library of Congress took the lead in the definition and thereafter the maintenance of the standard and effected a strong library orientation in both the coverage and the choice of identifiers, so that it would actually match their own indexing practices. This explains for instance why a score of languages still has two three-letter identifiers.

The ISO 639-3 standard was published in 2007 to provide a more "comprehensive coverage of languages" by systematizing the allocation of codes to a portfolio

12 The first version of HTML was announced in 1991 (cf. Berners-Lee 1999), but the @lang attribute only appeared in HTML 4 (1999 – https://www.w3.org/TR/html4/), and defined according to RFC 1766 (1995 – https://www.ietf.org/rfc/rfc1766.txt).

that would not be limited to the mainstream languages as used in libraries or digital applications at that time. The work around this standard was strongly influenced by the existing Ethnologue registry maintained by SIL International, which as a consequence became the registration authority associated with the standard.

When ISO 639:2023 was published, it replaced the 5 existing ISO 639 parts so that, as described above a single language code was created encompassing the whole range of languages, language groups and macro-languages that were covered by them. Still, it was decided not to be completely disrupting, both from the point of view of the language maintenance organisation as of the language code structure:

- The three existing registration authorities associated to the former ISO 639 parts were integrated into the structure of the ISO 639 maintenance agencies as *language coding* agencies, so that their expertise would be kept in the work of the new agency;
- The scope of the four ISO 639 parts (1, 2, 3 and 5) were redesigned into the new language code as representing so called sets...

When looking at the organisation of the ISO 639 language code from a distance, we can see that the sets do not play a fundamental role. They are more a vestigial organ from the past than something that may impact on specific applications. All in all, language code elements are homogeneous units, whatever the number of identifiers that are associated with them and their belonging to some of these sets. We can anticipate that the notion of set may vanish in the years to come.

2.3 Which digital commons for ISO 639? A TEI-based proposal

At this stage, it is important to raise the issue of providing a comprehensive digital resource associated with the ISO 639 language code so that it could cover the whole spectrum of potential applications. As it stands currently, the availability of ISO 639 lies within a quite fragmented landscape. Because of the historical context of the creation of ISO 639, the three language coding agencies have their own websites where they provide access to the language code with more or less emphasis on the sets they are responsible for. Beyond these official sources, ISO 639 is available at various places, in particular Wikipedia, across various pages, and of course as part of the IANA Language Subtag Registry which maintains the reference implementation of BCP 47. Besides, those various sources are based on heterogeneous data models for representing ISO 639 content, in as much as we can call data models flat tables on a web page. Ideally, we should design both a precise data model and a resource that serves as a basis for all downstream consumers.

One issue with providing such a resource to all kinds of possible users is that it should be comprehensive enough not only for basic language identification mechanisms, like checking that two resources are similarly coded, but should allow extra consistency checks when needed. Typically, one should be able to identify that a legacy linguistic resource is coded using an identifier that is no longer in use. This implies that the ISO 639 resource should not only make active language code elements available, but also retired ones, such as Languedocien (lnc), which has been merged with Occitan (oci). This last example also shows that it may be useful to even provide the full change history associated with the language code at large.

At an early stage in our attempt to design a data model for describing languages and language varieties that would cover the various objectives and constraints that we have just delineated, it was clear that a central application domain could be linguistic resources and possibly digital humanities. This is why it occurred to us that a possible implementation of such a model should be compatible as much as possible with the general framework offered by the TEI guidelines, which are now the most widely adopted standards in these fields. Indeed, the TEI guidelines already contain a <language>[13] element, which, although its current scope is reduced to the tiny use case of registering the languages used within a TEI document, could be an interesting basis for a more elaborate descriptive component.

In the rest of this paper, we will thus place ourselves in the hypothesis of deeply revising this element to fulfil our purpose, while, in our view, not so much abusing the existing background of the TEI guidelines. We will try to show that this proposal could cover the basic identification needs related to ISO 639, but also more in-depth documentation associated with language varieties, as we shall see in the next section. Finally, we would like to see this new definition of the <language> element as a general tool that could be associated with a whole range of linguistic observations.

To deal with the basic needs of ISO 639, we propose to use the existing TEI attributes on <language> in the following manner:

- The @type attribute can indicate the type of language the description is about, individual language, macro-language or language group.[14] It is complemented by a @subtype attribute to indicate whether the language is considered as living, extinct, constructed, historical or special (for reserved ISO 639 codes);
- The @status attribute, which can take the values active or retired to mark the status of the language code element in the ISO 639 code and, as mentioned

13 https://tei-c.org/release/doc/tei-p5-doc/en/html/ref-language.html

14 As we shall see in the next section, these values will have to be complemented to deal with language varieties as well.

above, allow one to trace legacy code elements which may occur in long lasting document repositories for instance;
- The @ident attribute, in accordance with its current meaning in the TEI guidelines, would be kept to provide the identifier under which the language will be referenced in the rest of the encompassing TEI document. In general, it should be the identifier that BCP 47 would actually favour, e. g. two-letter identifiers for languages in set 1.

Identifiers are naturally provided with the <ident>[15] element associated with the following attributes:
- The @type attribute is used in strong alignment with the TEI guidelines practices to indicate the nature of the object being identified, and thus uniquely set to "languageIdentifier";
- The @subtype attribute is used to determine which of the ISO 639 is provided and can take one of the following values: "ISO639-2" (for two letter identifiers), ISO639-3L (for three letter identifiers for bibliographic use), ISO639-3T (for three letter identifiers for terminological use);

The names associated to the language code element can be easily represented using the TEI element <name>[16] in combination with the following attributes:
- The @type attribute is used in strong alignment with the TEI guidelines practices to indicate the nature of the object being names, and thus uniquely set to "languageName";
- The @subtype attribute may be used in addition to @type when the components of the name are inverted (e. g. "Creole French, Réunion"), and thus uniquely set to "invertedName";
- @xml:lang is provided to indicate, in conformance to the XML recommendation, the language in which the name is provided. Its content should be conformant to BCP 47. By construction, it is always English (en) for language reference names.

As an example, we can see below the two forms for the creole French of La Réunion (rcf) with first the reference name and the additional name with an inverted (bibliographic like) name.

15 https://tei-c.org/release/doc/tei-p5-doc/en/html/ref-ident.html

16 https://tei-c.org/release/doc/tei-p5-doc/en/html/ref-name.html

```
<name type="languageName" role="languageReferenceName"
xml:lang="en">Réunion Creole French</name>
<name type="languageName" subtype="invertedName"xml:lang="en">Cre
ole French, Réunion</name>
```

We can note that with this model, we could easily add names in other languages when, for instance, a national standardisation body would like to take up the standard in its national catalogue.

With such a data model associated with the transformation of the <language> element, we see that we have all the building blocks to integrate the core components of ISO 639 features. For instance, the entry associated to French (fr) could be represented as follows:

```
<language status="active"
     ident="fr"
     type="individual"
     subtype="living">
     <ident
          type="languageIdentifier"
          subtype="ISO639-3B">fre</ident>
     <ident
          type="languageIdentifier"
          subtype="ISO639-3T">fra</ident>
     <ident
          type="languageIdentifier"
          subtype="ISO639-2">fr</ident>
     <name
          type="languageName"
          role="languageReferenceName" xml:lang="en">French</name>
     <name type="languageName" xml:lang="fr">Français</name>
</language>
```

In addition, we can record the evolutions undergone by a given language code element by adding the <event>[17] element to the possible descriptive children of <language>. Its @type attribute categorises the event and can take the values "change", "merge", "duplicate", or "split". Depending on the event type, a child element <desc>[18] provides a more precise description of the event either by point-

17 https://www.tei-c.org/release/doc/tei-p5-doc/en/html/ref-event.html

18 https://www.tei-c.org/release/doc/tei-p5-doc/en/html/ref-desc.html

ing to the language element it has been replaced with or, in the case of a split, the list of languages that has resulted from its deprecation.

```
<language status="retired" xml:id="auv" ident="auv">
     <name       type="languageName"      role="languageReferenceName"
xml:lang="en">Auvergnat</name>
     <event type="merge" when="2007-03-14">
           <desc>
                <ref target="#oci">oci</ref>
           </desc>
     </event>
</language>
```

3 Beyond languages – language varieties – the 21636 series

3.1 The principles behind ISO 21636

The objectives of the work carried out around the ISO 21636 series within ISO committee TC 37/SC 2 (see Preissner and Heid 2025 for general information on ISO committees) are clearly complementary to the work achieved with ISO 639 and its maintenance agency. In a way, it has taken the reverse direction of what was initially intended with the now withdrawn part 6[19] of ISO 639, which intended to provide 4 letter identifiers for language variants, with the general agreement that it would be vain to try to catalogue in a comprehensive manner language variants or, as specified in ISO 21636, language varieties.

The ISO 21636 series actually aims at providing a descriptive method within which a wide range of types of language varieties can be described in coherence with the underlying setting offered by ISO 639. As a matter of fact, it identifies a language variety as a subset of an individual language which not only fulfils some structural criterion in terms of linguistic properties, but also some external criteria related to the conditions related to where the variety is used, by whom and under which socio-cultural circumstances. As such it follows the same principles that we saw for ISO 639, inspired by Lieb (1993), that a language or a variety thereof corre-

19 Withdrawn: ISO 639-6:2009 Codes for the representation of names of languages Part 6: Alpha-4 code for comprehensive coverage of language variants.

sponds to a set of idiolects that share certain characteristics, with at its centre, the notion of intelligibility.

The description of a language variety can be made along what ISO 21636 calls dimensions which, either in isolation or by combining several of them, may allow one to elicit how the variety can be singled out within a given individual language. The possible dimensions provided by ISO 21636 are the following ones:

- The *space dimension* is one of the most prominent dimensions to identify a language variety. It lies at the basis of the definition of dialects, seen as the way a language is used, (usually spoken) in a certain area and is often central to field linguistic studies;
- The *time dimension* can be used to characterise the period over which a given variety was to be observed, either for historical purposes or simply to characterise a specific trend for instance;
- The *social group dimension* corresponds to social circumstances where a certain variety is used. It can be related to certain types of gatherings, social strata or professional exchanges;
- The *person dimension*, which characterises a language spoken by a single person, can be seen as a special case of the social group dimension, and although a personal variety is not necessarily homogeneous,[20] there are many cases where this dimension can be useful in concrete applications. On can think of identifying an author of a series of texts (or online contributions), collecting a dictionary of a famous author (The dictionary of Goethe[21]) and of course to document each observation made during a field linguistics campaign;
- The *medium dimension* allows one to characterise a variety according to the actual way it has been communicated, i. e. whether it is just spoken, written or by default multimodal. The standard anticipates other modalities such as signed, whistled, drummed or resulting from specific augmenting devices in cases of impairment;
- Although it is positioned as a specific dimension in ISO 21636, we could see the *proficiency dimension* simply as a property attached to either the social group or the person dimension;
- Finally, ISO 21636 introduces a *communicative functioning* dimension which allows one to express how much the variety is specific to a person or group of persons with enhanced, normal or constrained communicative capacities. This

20 It may vary according to the situation, the interlocutors etc., all in all along many of the dimensions contemplated in ISO 21636.

21 See http://gwb.uni-trier.de/de/

may allow one to qualify specific impairments, diseases or above the average eloquent capacities.

It should be noted that many of these dimensions may rely on other standards that may exist to characterise them, such as the provision of spatial or temporal information, but also specific terminologies related to socio-cultural contexts for instance.

As we have seen above and we will further explore when further formalizing language varieties in the context of the TEI, there may even be dimensions that can be grouped as part of the description of a speaker or a speaker community, rather than to be seen as an autonomous property of a language variety.

3.2 Providing even more descriptive capabilities to the TEI <language> element

The definition of a language variety provided by the ISO 21636 series together with the provision of a comprehensive set of dimensions along which such varieties can be characterised is a very good basis to get one step further into the TEI based language modelling work we have started in the previous section. It seems we can now deeply revamp the <language> element so that we design a real "linguographic" element aimed at offering a variety of language descriptive capabilities.

We thus extend here the proposal made earlier by considering that the <language> element could bear all dimensions provided by ISO 21636 and be used as a component within a TEI document header to identify and describe the varieties used in its content or, when used within the body of a document, to list language references made within a text, as would be the case for text texts related to linguistic theory or grammar.

The core usage of the <language> element would then be very similar to its current purpose in the TEI guidelines which declares the occurrence of a language together with its identifier expressed according to the BCP 47 framework.

In the rest of this section, we suggest integrating the implementation of the 21636 dimensions as further child elements to <language>, with a systematic reuse of existing TEI elements. As we shall see and depending upon the intended application, some of the dimensions may be either reorganised into specific structures or even positioned elsewhere in the TEI header when necessary.

First, we need to extend the definition of the attributes attached to the <language> element to deal with varieties:

- By adding the value "variety" to @type;

- By adding additional values on @status to qualify the condition under which the variety has been put together, e. g., “observed”, “inferred”.

The space dimension can be easily implemented by using the <settingDesc>[22] element as a child of <language>. It does not have to be typed unless the locations have an impact for the definition of varieties (e. g. urban vs. countryside). The locations concerned can be described by means of elements such as <place>[23] or <listPlace>.[24] The TEI further provides various sub elements to them to refine their description, such as <placeName>,[25] <location> (for geographical details or addresses), etc.

```
<settingDesc>
    <place type="">
        <placeName/>
        <location type="address|geopolitical"/>
        <idno/>
        <note/>
    </place>
</settingDesc>
```

By means of the <idno>[26] element, the description of the place associated with a language variety can also be limited to a reference to an online standard such as ISO 3166 codes or the M49 Standard Country or Area Codes for Statistical Use[27] with the possible reference to the respective identifiers as illustrated in the following example:

```
<language ident="fr-FR">
    <name type="languageVariety">French as used in France</name>
    <place type="country">
        <placeName xml:lang="fr">France</placeName>
        <idno type="UN-M49">250</idno>
        <idno type="ISO-alpha3">FRA</idno>
    </place>
</language>
```

22 https://tei-c.org/release/doc/tei-p5-doc/en/html/ref-settingDesc.html
23 https://www.tei-c.org/release/doc/tei-p5-doc/en/html/ref-place.html
24 https://www.tei-c.org/release/doc/tei-p5-doc/en/html/ref-listPlace.html
25 https://www.tei-c.org/release/doc/tei-p5-doc/en/html/ref-placeName.html
26 https://tei-c.org/release/doc/tei-p5-doc/en/html/ref-idno.html
27 https://unstats.un.org/unsd/methodology/m49/

The implementation of the time dimension can be easily made by means of the <date> element, which, together with the large palette of dating attributes (@when, @notBefore, @notAfter, @from, @to), but also by naming a given period by using <name> as a child, allows one to represent a whole variety of temporal spans.

```
<language>
     <date notBefore="1900" notAfter="1940">
          <name type="period">early 20th century</name>
     </date>
</language>
```

Here again, there is a strong standardisation background for the expression of temporal information with the two parts of ISO 8601. Since the TEI guidelines potentially offer a whole range of attributes associated to the <date> element, the main issue will be to provide precise guidelines concerning a subset of these and how to use them to make sure that different varieties could be easily compared along this temporal dimension.

Since the social group dimension corresponds to the characterisation of a given speaker community one or several characteristics, there is again a straightforward implementation in the TEI framework using here the <personGrp> element.

```
<personGrp>
     <age/>
     <gender/>
     <faith/>
     <education/>
     <nationality/>
     <residence/>
     <occupation/>
     <socecStatus/>
</personGrp>
```

For instance, a simple description of business English could be as follows:

```
<language>
     <name type="languageVariety">business English</name>
     <personGrp>
          <occupation>business</occupation>
     </personGrp>
</language>
```

And here, a more complex example of a person group encoding inspired from the SHAWI project[28] (cf. Mörth and Procházka 2017):

```
<personGrp>
     <age>Different ages</age>
     <gender>Male and female</gender>
     <faith>Muslim (Sunni)</faith>
     <education>No specific level of education. Any formal education
     received in Turkish, no formal education in Arabic</education>
     <nationality type="citisenship">Turkish</nationality>
     <nationality type="ethnicity">Arab</nationality>
     <residence>No specific residence</residence>
     <occupation>No specific occupation</occupation>
     <socecStatus>The speakers of this variety were formerly sheep
     and goat rearing nomads.</socecStatus>
     <note/>
     <langKnowledge>
          <langKnown tag="Turkish"/>
          <p>All of the informants speak Turkish and Shawi Arabic,
          although they received no formal education in Arabic and
          therefore have no knowledge of Modern Standard Arabic. Data
          of other language knowledge was not collected.</p>
     </langKnowledge>
</personGrp>
```

Just as we have <personGrp> to implement the social group dimension, the TEI <person> element is the ideal candidate to implement the person dimension. Depending on the context, this element may contain further elements to either name the speaker or writer of the language (like in the example of the Goethe-Wörterbuch mentioned above), or just provide characteristics useful for the specification of the linguistic sample that is being recorded, as would be the case in field linguistics or when studying for instance the specificities of non-native speakers of a language (cf. Falko corpus). These kinds of examples are typical reasons why we suggest implementing the proficiency dimension as a component of the person dimension. This is all the more natural in the TEI framework as both elements (<person> and <personGrp>) actually contain the <langKnowledge> element that is perfectly fit to the purpose.

28 https://www.oeaw.ac.at/acdh/research/linguistics/research/corpus-linguistics/shawi-the-shawi-type-arabic-dialects

```
<langKnowledge>
     <langKnown tag=""/>
</langKnowledge>
```

By doing so, we can describe the linguistic profile of a person, whose idiolect we would want to qualify:

```
<person sex="m" role="speaker collaborator">
<!-- other details omitted -->
     <langKnowledge>
          <langKnown tag="mix">Mixtepec-Mixtec</langKnown>
          <langKnown tag="en">English</langKnown>
          <langKnown tag="es">Spanish</langKnown>
     </langKnowledge>
</person>
```

Here below, we further illustrate the person with the following example where we characterise a young non-native female speaker:

```
<language ident="en-x-nnyw">
     <person>
          <gender value="W">woman</gender>
          <age>between 18 and 22</age>
          <langKnowledge>
               <langKnown tag="en" level="nonNative"/>
          </langKnowledge>
     </person>
</language>
```

This is typically the kind of information that you would attach to corpora dedicated to language acquisition such as the Falko corpus[29] (Reznicek et al. 2012), where they try to attach to each entry the necessary metadata related to the education history, the first language (L1) together with the age and gender.

The characterization of the medium dimension for a language variety can be implemented by means of the <channel> element where we would suggest making the @mode attribute mandatory and constrained with a semi-open list of explicit values.

29 https://www.linguistik.hu-berlin.de/de/institut/professuren/korpuslinguistik/forschung/falko

```
<channel mode="multimodal">face-to-face conversation</channel>
```

Contrary to what is currently suggested within the TEI guidelines, we would suggest to avoid using mixed values for the @mode attribute (e. g. sw for spoken to be written, when dictating for instance), and use the @type attribute to clearly differentiate between the primary mode (how the language content is being produced) and the secondary mode (the intended use). For instance, the English language used in drama could be described as:

```
<language ident="en-x-drama">
     <channel type="primary" mode="written"/>
     <channel type="secondary" mode="spoken"/>
</language>
```

The implementation of the communication functioning dimension can also be covered by adapting the existing <interaction> element in the TEI guidelines. The simplest way would be to provide appropriate values for @type such as "regular", "enhanced" and "constrained" and provide an additional description as the content of the element. For instance, if we were to characterise the variety associated to drunken speech, we could have:

```
<interaction type="constrained">drunken speech</interaction>
```

With such a model for language description purposes we could imagine that language resource projects could systematise the precise description of the languages they deal with and further share such descriptions so that a real catalogue of linguographic objects could be made available for any type of TEI application as a common resource.

In some cases, though, some of the descriptive elements may not be directly associated to the languages present in a given language resource, but rather associated to the description of the language resource itself. If we take for instance the description of the medium using the <channel> element presented above, a given project may either consider that it characterises a specific variant within a heterogeneous corpus of, say spoken, written etc. content, or, on the contrary, that it characterises the way the corpus has been gathered by using the <textDesc> element within the <profileDesc> of the corpus.

As an example of how this model could be used to share more precise information about the languages used within a given language resource, we can foresee that, as suggested just above, a <language> element such as the one we are aiming at could be associated to each BCP 47 tag in a project, in particular when variant or private use subtags are present, where the meaning of the actual subcomponents may not be straightforward just from looking at the coding.

As an application of this and being aware that it would require some in-depth work to provide a complete coverage, we show below how a simple entry in the IANA language subtag registry[30] (left) could fit into the proposed TEI encoding (right):

Type: language Subtag: fr Description: French Added: 2005-10-16 Suppress-Script: Latn	<language ident="fr" source="https://www.iana.org/assignments/ language-subtag-registry/language-subtag- registry"> <name type="IANA- Description">French</name> <date type="whenAdded" when="2005-10- 16"/> <ident type="Suppress- Script">Latn</ident> </language>

In a mid-term perspective, this would present the advantage of proving a way to compare and align descriptions across standardisation initiatives.

4 Putting things in practice

The claim we make in this chapter is that any project, initiative or environment which has to signal the use of languages within a given corpus of linguistic content should go beyond the sole provision of tags that would not completely elicit the intention behind them. We have tried to show how the TEI guidelines, in complement to the background and features of such standards as ISO 639 and ISO 21636 could actually fulfil this need and even ensure a continuum with authority lists such as the IANA language tag registry and very specific projects.

In the context of a concrete corpus project, the proposed framework should be seen as a tool by implementers to help them precisely identify their needs and in particular make clear the level of granularity at which languages have to be defined

30 https://www.iana.org/assignments/language-subtag-registry/language-subtag-registry

for the purpose of the project and try to stay coherent in the precision with which languages are identified and documented.

If we consider the first class of use cases mentioned in the introduction, i. e. the basic interoperability between generic computer systems (web pages, computer interfaces etc.), we can observe that they can only work when the sender and the receiver of the information rely on the same level of granularity in terms of language identification. This implies that designers are more or less forced to ground their developments on the most common languages as covered by set 1 of ISO 639, possibly extending to set 2 with locale information for large linguistic regions (e. g. fr-CA), typically to facilitate the work of spell checkers.

In the case of large-scale corpus projects like the OSCAR project that we mentioned in the introduction, the situation is quite similar since the information available from scrapped online material is shallow. The corpus is actually sorted per language on the basis of a language classifier trained with corresponding language samples. New languages can only be identified if there is a training corpus at hand, meaning that, for instance, identifying a certain variety will require that it has enough available online presence, but also that it can be tagged with enough precision, so that it can be distinguished from other samples.

A project such as Wibarab could be seen as situated on the opposite side of the language granularity spectrum since it aims at identifying the language varieties of Bedouin communities down to each observation, more less boiling down to idiolects. Still the actual characterisation of these varieties closely depends on the linguists that will associate both intrinsic (e. g. phonetic or lexical) or extrinsic features (locational, situational, composition of the observed group) as relevant for the underlying research agenda. In a way, as is the case when studying the introduction of a new language in the ISO 639 language code, the experts will have to define precise criteria as to why two observations belong to the same variety or should be distinguished.

Finally, we could even think of using the framework as a way to provide metadata for elementary observations or recording as available on online platforms such as wiktionary. If we take for instance the entry for the esperanto word *scribis* in the French wiktionary,[31] we can see it contains an audio recording qualified for both the location and the language level of the speaker. A proposal encoding in this respect (within an <entry> element for the corresponding word) could be:

31 https://fr.wiktionary.org/wiki/skribis

```
<cit type="recording">
     <media
          url="https://fr.wiktionary.org/wiki/Fichier:LL-
     Q143_(epo)-Wierzbowski-skribis.wav"
          mimeType="audio/wav"/>
     <language ident="eo-Wierzbowski">
          <date type="recording" when="2023-04-13"/>
          <person>
               <persName>Wierzbowski</persName>
               <langKnowledge>
                    <langKnown tag="eo" level="good"/>
               </langKnowledge>
          </person>
          <settingDesc>
               <place>
                    <settlement>Białystok</settlement>
                    <country>Pologne</country>
               </place>
          </settingDesc>
     </language>
</cit>
```

It should be noted that one should not necessarily rely on the technical framework used for a given application to control the descriptive granularity that has to be employed. For instance, let us take a project that uses, and rightly so, the TEI guidelines for representing its language resources. As we have seen, the TEI relies on the generic @xml:lang attribute, whose content is based on IETF BCP 47, which allows a whole range of possibilities from the provision of a simple 2 letter code for usual languages down to precisely localised varieties. As a result, the encoder must have a clear strategy of which type of language information he/she will be using, for which type of object in his or her TEI representation. Just to make this point more concrete, in the case of the encoding of a lexical resource, there may be simple language codes for the working language (the one used for documenting the content) and more precise codes for the object languages (the ones being described in the lexical resource), taking into account the high level of precision that the lexicographer may need in identifying a specific variety.

5 Conclusion

In this chapter, we have tried to explore methods for standardising language identification and description, especially in digital and linguistic contexts. With thousands of languages and countless varieties spoken globally, the task of accurately identifying, coding, and representing them is complex but crucial for interoperability, information management, and linguistic research. The article presents two key ISO standards – ISO 639 for language encoding and ISO 21636 for describing language varieties – and discusses how these standards help professionals across domains manage linguistic diversity. It also proposes enhancements to the TEI (Text Encoding Initiative) framework to better accommodate the nuanced identification and documentation of languages and their varieties.

We hope this chapter has contributed to a better understanding of the tenets of the ISO standards related to language identification and language variety description and offered some perspectives for future designers of digital components, whether in applicative or research projects. Part of the methodology we have tried to put forward is that there must be a conceptual continuum from idiolects to large coverage language families, which can be coupled with a coherent data model applicable to any kind of granularity level in between. To this purpose, we have suggested a possible implementation using a revamped version of the TEI <language> element, but the same model could potentially be instantiated in other frameworks. All in all, the questions that are to be answered before the beginning of any kind of such projects is knowing what you want to describe for a given project, what approximations are allowed, what constraints are to be applied, and at the end of the day what you really want to differentiate as a language or language variety.

Finally, we want to insist that the proper use of existing standards is strongly based upon the wide dissemination of standardisation information not only within developers' communities, but also practitioners of language descriptions and content providers in the language industry at large. This requires a solid training strategy both in universities but also from international infrastructures such as CLARIN[32] and DARIAH[33] so that a large compendium of online or in-presential training resources are offered on a regular basis. Even if language identification and description standards seem to be very technical objects from a certain distance, they are so essential in providing interoperable digital systems that they should be taken very seriously within a wide range of academic and industrial contexts.

32 https://www.clarin.eu/

33 https://www.dariah.eu/

Bibliography

Berners-Lee, Tim. 1999. *Weaving the web: The original design and ultimate destiny of the World Wide Web by its inventor*. San Francisco: Harper San Francisco. https://dl.acm.org/doi/abs/10.5555/580812 (accessed 10 June 2025).

Bodard, Gabriel. 2010. EpiDoc: Epigraphic documents in XML for publication and interchange. In *Latin on stone: Epigraphic research and electronic archives*, 101–118.

Coseriu, Eugenio. 1970. *Einführung in die strukturelle Betrachtung des Wortschatzes*. Tübingen: Narr.

Forkel, Robert & Harald Hammarström. 2022. Glottocodes: Identifiers linking families, languages and dialects to comprehensive reference information. *Semantic Web* 13(6). 917–924. https://doi.org/10.3233/SW-212843.

Hammarström, Harald, et al. 2024. *Glottolog 5.1*. https://doi.org/10.5281/zenodo.14006617.

Lieb, Hans-Heinrich. 1993. *Linguistic variables: Towards a unified theory of linguistic variation*. Amsterdam & Philadelphia: John Benjamins Publishing Company.

Mörth, Karlheinz & Stephan Procházka. 2017. The Vienna Corpus of Arabic Varieties: Building a digital research environment for Arabic dialects. In *Lisan Al-Arab: Studies in contemporary Arabic dialects. Proceedings of the 10th international conference of AIDA, Qatar University, 2013*, 209–218. Berlin: LIT Verlag.

Ortiz, Suárez, Pedro Javier, Benoît Sagot & Laurent Romary. 2019. Asynchronous pipeline for processing huge corpora on medium to low resource infrastructures. In *Proceedings of the 7th workshop on the challenges in the management of large corpora (CMLC-7)*. Mannheim: Leibniz-Institut für Deutsche Sprache.

Ortiz, Suárez, Pedro Javier, Laurent Romary & Benoît Sagot. 2020. A monolingual approach to contextualised word embeddings for mid-resource languages. In *Proceedings of the 58th annual meeting of the Association for Computational Linguistics (ACL 2020), Seattle/Virtual, United States*. https://doi.org/10.18653/v1/2020.acl-main.156. https://hal.science/hal-02863875v2 (accessed 10 June 2025).

Preissner, Annette & Ulrich Heid. 2025. The life of an ISO standard. In Piotr Bański, Ulrich Heid & Laura Herzberg (eds.), *Harmonising language data: Standards for linguistic resources*. Berlin & Boston: De Gruyter.

Reppen, Randi, Douglas Biber & Susan Fitzmaurice. 2002. *Using corpora to explore linguistic variation*. Amsterdam: John Benjamins Publishing Company. http://digital.casalini.it/9789027296160 (accessed 10 June 2025).

Reznicek, Marc, Anke Lüdeling, Christiane Krummes, Florian Schwantuschke, Martina Walter, Katrin Schmidt, Helene Hirschmann & Andreas Torsten. 2012. *Das Falko-Handbuch. Korpusaufbau und Annotationen. Version 2.01*.

Cited standards

BCP: 47 *Tags for Identifying Languages, IETF*, September 2009.

ISO/R 639:1967 *Symbols for languages, countries and authorities*.

ISO 639-3:2007 *Codes for the representation of names of languages – Part 3: Alpha-3 code for comprehensive coverage of languages*.

ISO 639:2023 *Code for individual languages and language groups*.

ISO 3166-1:2020 *Codes pour la représentation des noms de pays et de leurs subdivisions – Partie 1: Codes de pays*.

ISO 8601-1:2019 *Date and time Representations for information interchange – Part 1: Basic rules*.
ISO 8601-2:2019 *Date and time Representations for information interchange – Part 2: Extensions*.
ISO 15924:2022 *Information and documentation – Codes for the representation of names of scripts*.
UN M49, *Standard country or area codes for statistical use (Series M, No. 49)*, United Nations, https://unstats.un.org/unsd/methodology/m49/.

Nikola Ljubešić and Tomaž Erjavec

Part-of-speech tagging and related annotation

Abstract: Part-of-speech tagging is a basic but crucial step in the automatic annotation of texts and consists of assigning part-of-speech and related morphosyntactic information to words in running text. As it adds grammatical properties to words, it is useful both for searching words or phrases in corpora according to these properties or as a basis for further annotation. This chapter describes PoS tagging, including its history, the part-of-speech tagsets commonly used, the methods and tools to perform it, and the data formats commonly used. It also gives an introduction of related linguistic annotation levels, in particular tokenisation, lemmatisation and syntactic analysis.

Keywords: part-of-speech tagging, PoS tagging, linguistic annotation, text processing, computer corpora, lemmatisation, tokenisation

1 Introduction

Part-of-Speech (PoS) tagging refers to the (usually) automatic process of assigning grammatical tags (e. g. word class labels) to words in running text. PoS tagging has, for a long time, been a very useful step in text processing. On the one hand, it allows for filtering of corpus queries depending on their grammatical category, e. g. it enables a linguist to search for phrases consisting of an adjective followed by a noun. On the other hand PoS tagging facilitates further linguistic and other processing of the text, such as lemmatisation, syntactic parsing, named entity recognition (NER, see Schwarz 2025), term extraction, etc.

Unlike automatic morphological analysis and especially syntactic parsing, which had a long tradition of rule-based methods (since the 1960s) but were mostly developed to test structuralist linguistic theories (especially the work by Noam Chomsky), automatic PoS tagging was the first large-scale natural language processing method to use machine learning, with initial methods appearing in the early 1990's, in a sense heralding the era of data driven methods in language processing. The main use case was PoS tagging of large corpora used for lexicography

Nikola Ljubešić, Tomaž Erjavec, Dept. of Knowledge Technologies, Jožef Stefan Institute, Jamova cesta 39, SI-1000 Ljubljana, Slovenia, e-mails: nikola.ljubesic@ijs.si, tomaz.erjavec@ijs.si

https://doi.org/10.1515/9783112208212-004

and for other corpus-linguistic research, with the most prominent such corpus being the British National Corpus[1] from the early 1990s.

Since then hundreds of papers have been published about it, implementing improvements to the machine learning methods or reporting on compilation of corpora that enable their training for particular languages, language varieties, and PoS tagsets.[2]

Figure 1 gives a short sentence along with its PoS tags from the Penn Treebank tagset (Marcus et al. 1993). It illustrates a number of points about PoS tags and tagging:

- PoS tagging is not the initial step in text processing, rather, text must be first split into tokens, i. e. words and punctuation symbols;
- a PoS tagset (i. e. the inventory of tags used in the annotation process) needs accompanying documentation to explicate the meaning of the tags, e. g. that VV means the base form of a verb or NNS a plural noun;
- PoS tags typically encode more than just the actual part-of-speech (noun, conjunction etc.) but also include other grammatical features of a word, such as the form of a verb or number for nouns;
- words can typically have more than one tag (e. g. *flags* can be a noun but also a verb) and it is the context in which a word appears that determines the actual PoS tag (in the given example, the preceding *the* would suffice to select NNS as the correct tag);
- not all words will be known to the tagger (i. e. the automatic tagging tool), and it might well happen that *Fallujah* is not in the tagger's lexicon, so a PoS tagger must also be able to tag unknown words;
- not only words, but all tokens are PoS tagged, which means that e. g. punctuation marks also receive their "part-of-speech" tag;

A PoS tagger thus takes as its input tokenised and preferably sentence segmented text (i. e. text, where word and sentence boundaries are marked), and attempts to predict the correct context-dependent PoS tag for each of its tokens.

The rest of this chapter is structured as follows: Section 2 introduces PoS tagsets, introduces their various types and mentions some better known ones; Section 3 discusses other annotation types related to PoS tagging, in particular tokenisation and sentence segmentation, lemmatisation, and syntactic parsing; Section 4 describes historical and especially current methods used for automatic PoS tagging, as well

---

1 http://www.natcorp.ox.ac.uk/ (accessed April 1st, 2025).

2 For an overview see https://www.clarin.eu/resource-families/tools-part-speech-tagging-and-lemmatisation (accessed April 1st, 2025).

1	Compare	VV
2	the	DT
3	flags	NNS
4	to	IN
5	the	DT
6	Fallujah	NNP
7	one	NN
8	.	.

Figure 1: Part-of-Speech tags of an example sentence.

as listing the better known PoS taggers; Section 5 introduces standards and best practices in the encoding of PoS-tagged text; and Section 6 attempts to contextualise the usefulness of PoS tagging in the age of large language models.

2 PoS tagsets

A part-of-speech tagset is a collection of labels denoting grammatical classes of word forms or, in general, tokens. As already mentioned, such tagsets typically do not only encode the part-of-speech of a word, but also its various lexical and inflectional features. For this reason, a more correct term is morphosyntactic tagsets (or tagging) i. e. using tags that, for the most part, encode features on the intersection of the morphological and syntactic layers, such as the type of verb (auxiliary vs. main) or the case of the noun (nominative, accusative, etc.) but not purely morphological (such as the conjugation or declension paradigm of a verb or noun) or syntactic features (such as verb transitivity). As tagsets must cover all the tokens of any free text, they also distinguish tags that have little to do with parts-of-speech or morphosyntactic features, such as tags for punctuation, mathematical and other symbols, abbreviations or foreign words.

The design of a good PoS tagset is a complicated and typically iterative process. It starts, as most other linguistic annotation tasks, with writing the annotation guidelines and manually annotating the first corpus. Often tagsets also take into account limitations of current PoS taggers, by not introducing distinctions when they could not be resolved automatically, for example because a given tool technology cannot take enough context into account. Nevertheless, the size and hence granularity of a PoS tagset will very much depend on its designers, with large differences in the number of tags.

PoS tagsets are also heavily dependent on the language, with typical tagsets for English having between 50 and 150 tags. On the other hand, heavily inflecting languages, such as some Slavic ones, typically have over 1,000 different tags, while for agglutinative languages, such as Hungarian, the very concept of a word-level set of PoS tags is a questionable one, as they would need tagsets with over 10,000 tags.

2.1 Synthetic tagsets

The first PoS tagsets developed were for English (Johansson 2008), starting with the tagset used in the 1 million word Brown University Standard Corpus of Present-Day American English, better known as the Brown corpus, with its development beginning in the mid-1960s. The Brown corpus tagset consisted of 86 PoS tags, and the corpus was first tagged automatically with a rule-based system, and afterwards manually checked, a very labour intensive process which took until the late 1970s to complete. The second well known "first generation" corpus was the Lancaster-Oslo/Bergen (LOB) corpus, which was similar to the Brown corpus, also in terms of its tagset, but covered British English and was compiled in the 1970s. The LOB tagset was then revised and used, e. g. for tagging the already mentioned British National Corpus, which was performed by the CLAWS tagger.[3] For this reason the tagset, which went through several revisions, is also called the CLAWS tagset, and is still used for tagging (British) English corpora. The latest version of the tagset, CLAWS8[4] from 2001, contains 175 PoS tags.

On the other hand, the most widely used tagset for American English is the one initially developed in the Penn Treebank Project (Santorini 1990). It is based on the Brown and LOB Corpus tagsets, although much smaller, with only 36 tags.

For the other languages of Europe, and often in the context of developing national reference corpora, further language-particular tagsets were developed, mostly in the 1990s. An example is the Stuttgart-Tübingen TagSet[5] (STTS) (Schiller et al. 1995), with the first version containing 54 tags, which became a de-facto standard for PoS tagging of German texts.

For the most part, these first tagsets were synthetic ones, i. e. a PoS tag was not directly decomposable into its grammatical features (such as number or case), and the meaning of a tag was specified only in textual form in the annotation guide-

3 https://ucrel.lancs.ac.uk/claws/ (accessed April 1st, 2025).

4 https://ucrel.lancs.ac.uk/claws8tags.pdf (accessed April 1st, 2025).

5 https://www.ims.uni-stuttgart.de/forschung/ressourcen/lexika/germantagsets/ (accessed April 1st, 2025).

lines. While this approach is not very problematic for small tagsets, it is much more difficult to use for large ones.

A breakthrough in PoS tagset development came with the proposal for a universal (i. e. applicable to any language) tagset with only 12 tags (Petrov et al. 2011), which largely only encode the traditional parts-of-speech. While this tagset does not give other morphosyntactic features, most applications make use only of the part-of-speech, hence it still had significant practical utility. Its authors also showed that PoS tagging with their Universal tagset gives competitive or better results if compared to tagging with standard tagsets that are then reduced to part-of-speech only.

2.2 Analytical tagsets

Starting with the EAGLES Guidelines (Leech and Wilson 1996) and continuing with the EU MULTEXT and especially MULTEXT-East projects[6] (Erjavec 2012), so called analytical (or logical) tagsets started to be developed in a multilingual setting.

Analytical tagsets are simply shorthands for feature structures, i. e. sets of attribute-value pairs. For example, the MULTEXT-East tag (or, in the terminology of the project, the morphosyntactic description) `Ncmsan` corresponds to the feature structure `Category = Noun, Type = common, Gender = masculine, Number = singular, Case = accusative, Animate = no`, with each feature (i. e. attribute-value pair) associated with one position in the tag string. Simple mapping tables then suffice to convert from tags to features or vice-versa.

This approach lends itself well to multilingual specifications: The MULTEXT morphosyntactic specifications covered Western European languages, while MULTEXT-East ones cover Central and Eastern European ones, with many of the MULTEXT and especially MULTEXT-East specifications adopted as de-facto standards for PoS tagging of particular languages.

The MULTEXT-East specifications define the set of attributes and their legal values, and, for each language covered, which attributes and which of their values are relevant to it. Because many feature combinations are invalid (e. g. assigning case to a verb) the language-particular specifications also give co-occurrence restrictions between the features, as well as the complete tagset for the language.

Finally, Interset (Zeman 2008) should also be mentioned, as it is a precursor of the Universal morphosyntactic features, as detailed in the following section. Interset started as a tool for conversion between morphosyntactic tagsets of multiple languages and was later employed as the morphological layer in HamleDT (Zeman

6 https://github.com/clarinsi/mte-msd (accessed April 1st, 2025).

et al. 2014), a project that brought treebanks (cf. Section 3.3) of many languages under a common annotation scheme.

2.3 Universal PoS and morphological features

The Universal Dependencies (UD) initiative (de Marneffe et al. 2021),[7] which started in 2013, has the goal of producing a general framework for morphosyntactic and syntactic annotation of language. The general philosophy of the initiative was to provide a universal inventory of categories and guidelines to facilitate consistent annotation of similar constructions across languages, while allowing language-specific extensions when necessary.

Many teams from many countries had by the 2010's already produced treebanks for their languages, i. e. corpora with manual word-level morphosyntactic as well as sentence-level syntactic annotations. However, they used a number of different linguistic formalisms with Universal Dependencies offering the possibility to contribute to a truly global undertaking. The success of the project is also due to the ease of development by using a well-maintained GitHub repository.

Each treebank that is part of the project needs a specification section, detailing the annotations (features) used, with which it is then also possible to automatically validate a treebank. The first treebanks contributed to the project were typically made on the basis of existing ones, by a combination of automatic and manual conversion methods. Later more and more languages previously without treebanks started their work directly in UD. At the time of writing, the latest published version of UD treebanks is 2.15 (Zeman et al. 2024) and contains treebanks for 165 languages, although of varying sizes and included text types.

It is therefore not surprising that the project has had a profound influence on linguistic annotation of a large number of languages. In particular, many pipelines for linguistic annotation have been trained on these treebanks and hence cover a multitude of languages, with the result that the UD annotation framework has in the last 10 years become a de-facto standard for morphosyntactic, as well as syntactic annotation.

On the morphosyntactic level, Universal Dependencies distinguishes part-of-speech labels from morphological features. Their Universal part-of-speech tagset[8] is based on the previously mentioned Universal PoS tagset, and distinguishes 17 labels. Some of these indeed correspond to the traditional parts-of-speech, with others

7 https://universaldependencies.org/ (accessed April 1st, 2025).

8 https://universaldependencies.org/u/pos/ (accessed April 1st, 2025).

either referring to their subtypes or are tags needed to process unrestricted text. Given the importance of UD in contemporary linguistic annotation, we list them here in full:

- Open class words: NOUN (Common noun), PROPN (Proper noun), VERB (Verb) ADJ (Adjective), ADV (Adverb), INTJ (Interjection);
- Closed class words: AUX (Auxiliary verb), PRON (Pronoun) NUM (Numeral), PART (Particle), DET (Determiner), CCONJ (Coordinating conjunction), SCONJ (Subordinating conjunction) ADP (Adposition, i. e. preposition or postposition);
- Other: PUNCT (Punctuation), SYM (Symbol, i. e. currency symbols, mathematical operators, emoticons and emoji), X (Other, i. e. unintelligible material, word fragments and unanalysed foreign words).

UD then specifies Universal morphosyntactic (or, in UD terminology, morphological) features,[9] which are based on the previously mentioned Interset / HamleDT ones. These Universal morphological features distinguish additional lexical and grammatical properties of words, not covered by the PoS tags, for example `Mood = Imp`, `VerbForm = Fin` for the imperative mood of a finite verb form.

It should be noted that UD does not propose a morphosyntactic tagset of the sort that has been discussed so far but stops at the part-of-speech labels and their morphosyntactic features. Thus the process that started with analytical tagsets has here been taken to its logical conclusion, i. e. atomic morphosyntactic tags are no longer used, rather, the morphosyntactic features are specified directly for each token. Given that the purpose of the traditional morphosyntactic tagsets was to have compact labels with which to annotate tokens, and this is, with vastly increased computer storage, no longer such an issue, the UD morphosyntactic markup was well placed to supplant previous tagsets.

Finally, UD treebanks use the so called CoNLL-U format for their annotations, which is detailed in Section 5.3.

3 Annotations related to PoS tagging

As already mentioned, PoS tagging is neither the first, nor the last step in linguistic annotation of text, and this chapter would not be complete without at least briefly mentioning the other three steps of the standard linguistic annotation pipeline, all the more so as the underlying contemporary methods, i. e. the use of a large lan-

9 https://universaldependencies.org/u/feat/ (accessed April 1st, 2025).

guage model, are now often employed together to perform most if not all of these tasks.

We here deal with the steps preceding PoS tagging (tokenisation and sentence segmentation), and those that typically follow and rely on it, or are performed simultaneously: lemmatisation and syntactic annotation. There are a number of other more or less standard annotation tasks which we will not treat here, such as terminology extraction, anaphora resolution and Named Entity Recognition, the last one the topic of a separate chapter.

3.1 Tokenisation and sentence segmentation

The first two steps in text processing split the text (i. e. a sequence of characters including spacing ones) into a sequence of tokens and sentences. Tokenisation and sentence segmentation are typically performed together, as they are interrelated, e. g. the period signals the end of a sentence, but can also be the last character of an abbreviation.

Compared to other linguistic markup, tokenisation and sentence segmentation is fairly simple and has traditionally been performed in a rule-based manner, by using regular expressions and small lexicons, typically of abbreviations. It should be noted that this simplicity is confined to languages that separate the written words by spaces. Tokenisation is much more complex for those that don't, e. g. Chinese or Japanese, where extensive lexicons were typically used.

Nevertheless, even for European and other alphabetic languages word and sentence segmentation has a number of pitfalls, esp. when tokenising free text with its mistakes and inconsistencies, or specialised texts containing many abbreviations. Further problems are caused by character encoding issues, as well as the complexities of Unicode with its many types of characters, some fairly common ones breaking many tokenisers, for example the soft hyphen character. Mistakes in tokenisation, as well as sentence segmentation are also very costly, as all further processing is affected, with errors likely to propagate to surrounding tokens.

There are several international standards that deal with tokenisation. The ISO standard on Word segmentation of written texts is composed of two parts: *Part 1: Basic concepts and general principles* (ISO 24614-1 2010) provides language-independent guidelines to enable written texts to be segmented, in a reliable and reproducible manner, into tokens, while *Part 2: Word segmentation for Chinese, Japanese and Korean* (ISO 24614-2 2011) concentrates on these specific languages, which are very difficult to tokenise. Furthermore, the Unicode consortium also published their recommendations for text segmentation (The Unicode Consortium 2024).

3.2 Lemmatisation

Lemmatisation, i. e. determining the base form of a word from an inflected one (e. g. *wolves* has the lemma *wolf*) enables, for example, corpus linguists to search for words regardless of their inflected form, and facilitates linking word tokens to dictionary headwords. This annotation step is fairly simple for English with its few word-forms but much more challenging for highly inflecting languages, such as Slavic ones.

For inflectionally poor languages rule-based methods were typically used to compute the lemma given the word form, while the more complex ones also need PoS information and soon adopted machine learning methods, for example LemmaGen (Juršič et al. 2010), which was trained to efficiently lemmatise 14 European languages.

3.3 Syntactic annotation

Syntactic parsing, i. e. determining the syntactic structure of sentences, was for a long time the holy grail of computational linguistics. Work on syntactic parsing started with Chomskyan formal grammar, and a large number of formal grammatical theories and their computational frameworks were developed in from the 1970's to the 2000's, with one of the better known being Head-driven phrase structure grammar (HPSG) (Pollard and Sag 1994). However, the implementations were mostly proof-of-concept, i. e. they worked for example sentences, but not on unrestricted text.

While this family of grammars was constituent-based, meaning that words in a sentence were taken to group into (e. g. noun or verb) phrases, another family of theories gained popularity in the context of computational linguistics in the 2000's and later, with the main formulation developed by Czech linguists (Sgall et al. 1986). This line of dependency-based syntactic annotation proved much more computationally tractable, with corpora being manually annotated for syntactic dependency annotations, and, of course, also including word-level morphosyntactic annotations. One of the earliest large and better known examples is the Prague Dependency Treebank (PDT) (Hajič et al. 2017), which started to be developed in the 1990's and is still actively maintained (Hajič et al. 2024).

In a dependency grammar, each word (except the top level word, typically the main content verb) is taken to be syntactically dependent on another word in the sentence, with all the words thus being nodes in a directed acyclic graph, and the connections in the graph being syntactic relations, as illustrated in Figure 2.

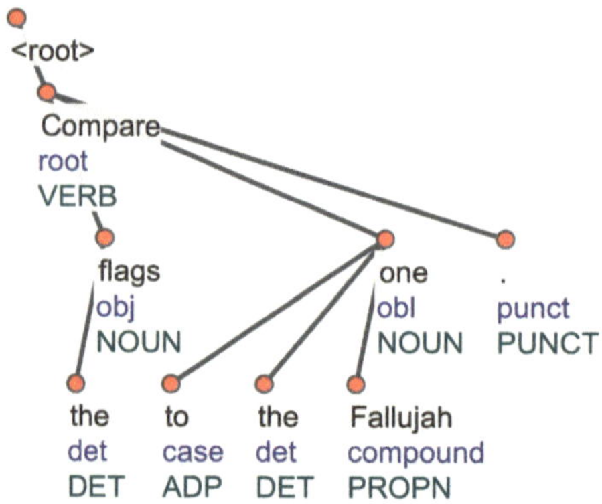

Figure 2: Example of a dependency syntax graph. Lower nodes are dependents of upper nodes.

As with constituent grammars, various dependency theories and implementations were proposed, but by far the most successful is the already introduced Universal Dependencies one.

4 Tagging methods and tools

This section gives an overview of various algorithms used for automating the PoS tagging task. It also gives a general understanding of the improvements in machine learning over sequential language data through time. The section ends with suggestions on tools to be used for PoS tagging.

4.1 Tagging as a sequence classification task

As already mentioned in this section, automating the task of PoS tagging is regularly performed via machine learning methods. Supervised machine learning is typically used, which means that the learning algorithm is supervised via (i. e. trained on) annotations of a corpus where each token had its PoS tag determined by a human annotator. The algorithm learns the regularities of the task, such as (1) *compare* is a verb, (2) determiners are most often followed by adjectives or nouns. Once trained, this algorithm is capable of performing the same task on new, previously unseen data.

In the world of machine learning, PoS tagging is considered a "sequence classification task", where each sequence is a sentence, the elements of that sequence are tokens, and each of these is classified into one of the categories defined in the

PoS tagset, as discussed in Section 2. This process of sequence classification results in outputs as already presented in this chapter in Figure 1.

Given the sequential nature of text, and of language in general, it is not surprising that natural language processing often applies sequence classification tasks. This is also the case with the related tasks described in (Schwarz 2025), as well as Sections 3.2 and 3.3 on lemmatisation and syntactic annotation. However, the last two related tasks come with their own challenges.

In the case of lemmatisation, the number of classes is much larger than those of a PoS tagset, as it comprises the whole lexicon of a language, which results in hundreds of thousands of categories i. e. lemmas. However, the number of these categories can be limited by taking as a class the transformation needed to generate the lemma from the word form. In case of the word form *flags* and its corresponding lemma *flag*, the corresponding transformation rule has to state that the final *-s* of the word is to be removed in order to compute the lemma. The same rule, or category, would be needed for transforming most English plural nouns into their singular forms. With such an approach, the number of categories in this sequence classification task drops from hundreds of thousands to just a few hundred categories (Gesmundo and Samardžić 2012).

Syntactic annotation also presents its own challenges. In case of dependency parsing, as discussed in Section 3.3, each word is to be classified by two criteria, the dependency relation in which this word takes part, and the (position of) the word on which this word depends. An example of the output of a dependency parse is given in Figure 2. The word *flags* depends on the predicate *Compare* by being its object, therefore having `obj` assigned as its dependency relation.

4.2 Traditional methods

In this subsection, we will discuss the two traditional supervised machine learning approaches that have been used extensively for PoS tagging. The common denominator of both methods is that they rely on surface words to assign PoS tags to each word. Different to that, in the following subsections neural approaches will be discussed, where technological progress allowed for numerical abstractions from the surface words in text to be used.

Hidden Markov Models (HMMs), (Baum and Petrie 1966) are the oldest supervised learning algorithm that has been massively applied to PoS tagging. There are two types of parameters the HMM model consists of. The first is emission probabilities, i. e., the probability of a specific word being assigned a specific tag. If we go back to our example, *Compare the flags to the Fallujah one*, and more specifically the polysemous word *flags*, from a manually tagged and large enough training dataset it is not hard to estimate that the two most probable tags for *flags* are verb and noun. The other type of parameters are transition probabilities, i. e., the probability of a tag being preceded by another tag. Our *flags* example benefits from this type of parameter greatly, since nouns are much more likely to follow determiners than are verbs. By combining the knowledge available from both emission and transition probabilities, the word *flags* obtains the correct tag, i. e. NOUN.

There are significant limitations to the HMM algorithm, the most severe one being that each word's tag is dependent only on the preceding word's tag. With that, it would be hard to predict that the word *flags* has an object function rather than a subject function, a feature that is indirectly included in many tagsets of languages with more complex morphology, such as the distinction between the nominative and accusative case of nouns. The method that allows the inclusion of a larger number of parameters per word, beyond transition and emission probabilities only, are conditional random fields (CRFs), (Lafferty et al. 2001). Most taggers based on the CRF algorithm represent each word also through the words that occur in a window of three positions before and after the word that is being classified. With this, in our example, the tagger would know that a verb (*compare*) was used two positions to the left of the word *flags*, which makes that word much more likely to have an object than a subject function due to the fact that English is an SVO (subject-verb-object) language. Taggers based on CRFs also popularised the inclusion of capitalisation information for each word. While tagging the word *Fallujah*, which is quite likely unseen in the training dataset, the fact that the word is title-cased would make the category of proper nouns most probable.

4.3 Embedding-based methods

The two most popular traditional methods for PoS tagging discussed above exploited features that can be extracted from the text's surface, like the word form and its capitalisation information. With the advent of neural methods, which revolutionised natural language processing, the opportunity emerged to use numerical representations of words, containing much more information on the word apart from its surface form. These numerical representations of words are called word embeddings.

The famous method that popularised word embeddings is called word2vec (Mikolov et al. 2013). The idea behind the method was to represent each word through a fixed number of numerical values that model the meaning and function of the word. These numerical values are actually parameters of a neural network that has the task of predicting a word from its context. With this, words of similar

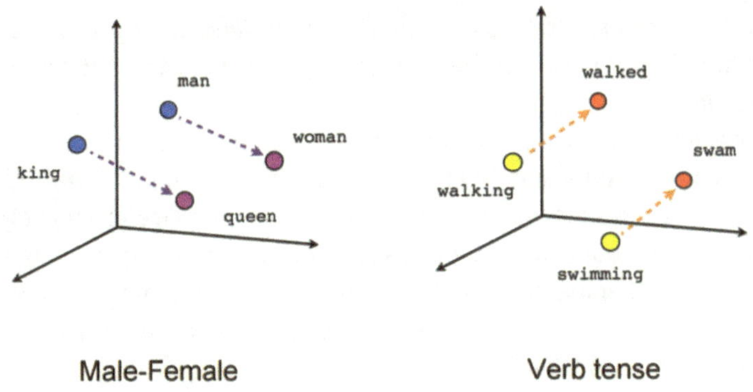

Figure 3: Example of word2vec numerical representations of words that allow for generalisation over the meaning and the function of words.

function and meaning, i. e., words occurring in similar contexts, would obtain similar numerical representations. Even more, words that are similar in some latent feature, such as animacy, would be similar in specific parts of their representation of a few hundred numerical values. The word embeddings are regularly learned on very large collections of texts, and the knowledge encoded in word embeddings comes from the regularities in word co-occurrences in this large body of texts.

Figure 3[10] shows the two most famous examples of word embeddings, based on associations between word embeddings. These word embeddings encode the meaning and function of each word so well that they allow for arithmetic operations over them. If we take the embedding of *king*, subtract the embedding of *man* from it, and add the embedding of *woman*, the word with the most similar representation would be *queen*. Similar arithmetic works also for the morphosyntactic function of words: if we take the word *walking*, subtract *walked* from it and add *swimming*, the most similar embedding would be the (irregular) form *swam*.

To showcase these capacities of word embedding numerical representations on the central example of this chapter, the word quite likely unseen by a tagger in its training data, *Fallujah*, represented through a word2vec word embedding, would have a very similar representation as *Anbar*, *Baghdad* and *Homs*, and would in general have encoded that this is a name of a city in Iraq. What is even more, if we investigated the semantic analogy "king is to queen what man is to woman" from Figure 3 on that word, moving *Fallujah* not between genders, but between countries, from Iraq to England, the closest matches would be *Notthingham*, *Norwich*, *Gloucester*, etc.

10 https://tinyurl.com/427kkrfj (accessed April 1st, 2025).

If we applied this analogy exercise to our other example, *flags*, taking the noun *car* as a reference, the closest match of the relationship between *cars* and *car* to *flags* is, as expected, *flag*.[11]

From the above examples, it is clear that the word embedding for each word has quite a significant amount of information encoded about both word meaning and function, which empowers PoS tagging, but also many other language processing tasks. While our discussion above touches on cases from our simple example, the knowledge encoded in word embeddings becomes even more prominent for low-frequency phenomena often occurring in domain-specific or nonstandard texts, such as those encountered on social media.

Word embeddings not only provide a significant knowledge boost for PoS tagging, but they are also the perfect input data format for neural networks trained to perform PoS tagging. That is, neural networks accept only numerical inputs of fixed size.

Analogously to HMMs and CRFs discussed previously, the first widely adopted neural sequence classification technique were recurrent neural networks (RNNs), (Rumelhart et al. 1986) and their subtype long-short term memory (LSTMs), (Hochreiter and Schmidhuber 1997). Word embeddings do hold quite a lot of knowledge about a specific word, which can be followed back to the large collection of text from which they were built, and RNNs use that knowledge to specifically learn regularities regarding PoS tags from manually annotated training data. Given that somewhere in the training data some city names will occur annotated as proper nouns, once the tagger arrives at our example sentence, it will label *Fallujah*, as well as other city names that might be less known, but still present in large collections of text, as a proper noun with ease.

Such a tagger will also successfully cover much more difficult cases. One important example for PoS tagging are long-range dependencies, e. g., differentiating between the already mentioned morphosyntactic categories of objects and subjects in very long sentences in languages with free word order, such as Slavic languages. Going back to our traditional algorithms, HMMs were capable of modelling dependencies between neighbouring words, while CRFs were able to take into account longer contexts, but were in practice useful only for immediate contexts of around three words to the left and three to the right. The reason for this limited context of CRFs is that they take into account every word that occurs in the seven-word context and cannot disregard words that are not important for a specific case and this specific task. Unlike that, neural networks learn numerical representations of problems, PoS

11 All the examples above have been tested through the word embedding interface available via https://embeddings.sketchengine.eu (accessed April 1st, 2025).

tagging being just one of them. With this neural networks learn which information to keep in their internal numerical representations, and which to skip, thereby being drastically better than traditional algorithms at isolating the relevant from the irrelevant signal for a specific task. To give an example on Slovenian and Croatian, two South Slavic languages with complex morphology, discriminating whether a masculine noun is in the nominative or accusative case used to be one of the most frequent errors in PoS tagging due to the very frequent syncretism (same surface form) of these two morphosyntactic categories. The solution to the problem lies in discriminating whether a noun is used as object (which would result in the morphosyntactic category of accusative case) or subject (nominative case) on the level of the whole sentence, which requires long-range-dependence modelling due to the free word order in Slavic languages. Once CRFs and RNNs are compared in how they deal with this problem, RNNs eliminate around 70 % of such error that CRFs generate in both languages (Ljubešić and Dobrovoljc 2019). This drastic improvement of performance occurs thanks to RNN's ability to isolate the signal of potential nominative and accusative nouns throughout the whole sentence to be highly relevant for the task of PoS tagging.

4.4 Contextualising word representations

In the previous subsection, we showed how capable neural word representations are, esp. if coupled with neural sequence classification algorithms. However, there is still a significant limitation to these word-level neural representations: they are not context-sensitive, meaning that the word *flags* will be represented by a single word embedding, and that this particular word embedding will have to represent both the noun and the verb meaning of this specific word. The leap forward from word embeddings, often also referred to as static embeddings, are dynamic embeddings that take into account the context inside which a specific word occurred during the process of constructing its numerical representation. With that, in our example, *flags* in that specific context will have a representation encoding that the word denotes a piece of cloth used as a sign, in its plural form. If the word *flags* occurred in a different context, e. g., *He flags these files for later use*, the representation of *flags* would encode the verbal function and the semantics that something was marked.

The dynamic embeddings are the result of much larger neural networks than those used to build static word embeddings. These neural networks are also often trained on much larger quantities of raw text than what is used for static word embeddings. However, the task both these neural networks are trained on is very similar – predicting a specific word given its context. Today, dynamic word embeddings are constructed with the help of Transformer models (Vaswani et al. 2017), the models that are the basis of the recent revolution of large language models. More details on how these models work and are built can be found in (Schwarz 2025).

To touch again on our example, the word *flags* in the context *Compare the flags to the Fallujah one* would be numerically represented inside a transformer model in such a way that it is very obvious that *flags* is a plural noun, making the final prediction from that representation very simple.

One could ask at this point whether these dynamic, contextualised word representations are really necessary for a task such as PoS tagging. We knew that *flags* is a noun in this specific context already with HMM models, given that the word is preceded by a determiner. For languages with more complex morphology and more free word order, such as the already mentioned Slovenian and Croatian languages, if the amount of training data was limited, as often is the case, dynamic word embeddings deliver a significant improvement in PoS tagging accuracy. To give an example, the Trankit tool (Nguyen et al. 2021) based on a Transformer model, that will be described in more detail in Section 4.6, achieves accuracies on these two languages of 98 % and 97 %. On the other hand, Stanza (described in Section 4.6), which is based on static word embeddings, when trained on the exact same training data, delivers accuracies of 90 % and 87 %. This represents a five-fold increase in error when moving from dynamic to static word embeddings.

4.5 Decoder-based models

In the previous subsection we introduced the Transformer model which enables learning dynamic word representations. There are two main types of Transformer models, (1) encoder models that encode each word's meaning and function into an embedding, and (2) decoder models, that generate only the representation of the word that is to follow some input text.

The use cases in the previous subsection have covered encoder models, and such models are by far the most frequently used Transformer models for sequence classification tasks. However, Transformer models have gained extreme visibility not through encoder, but through decoder models, the most famous being the Generative Pre-trained Transformer – GPT (Radford et al. 2018). Decoder models excel at text generation by producing the numerical representation of a word that should follow a specific piece of text.

While decoder models, which can be considered simply text generators, do not sound like a good choice for sequence classification, they have an important feature that can come in handy for PoS tagging as well. Namely, decoder models store the knowledge from pre-training data much better than encoder models. If the text to be PoS-tagged is written in a dialectal or historical language from which there is no training data available, the best option to PoS-tag such a text, but also process it in any other way, is through large decoder models.

There have been experiments on using GPT models to annotate 16th Century Latin (Stüssi and Ströbel 2024), showing best results when a GPT model is applied, but these models have, to date, still not been investigated enough on such tasks. To showcase here their capability on cases of nonstandard language, we have run dialectal texts written in the Slovenian Cerkno and the Croatian Chakavian dialect from the DIALECT-COPA dataset (Ljubešić et al. 2024) through a series of state-of-the-art PoS taggers for Croatian and Slovenian, but have also requested these sentences to be PoS tagged by the currently most popular GPT-4o model. State-of-the-art taggers, to be presented in the following section, do manage to provide reasonable annotations on around half of the sentences from the DIALECT-COPA dataset, however, they fail quite drastically at those that deviate more from the standard varieties. The state-of-the-art models, even if trained on a combination of standard and nonstandard Internet texts, still have a very limited experience with dialectal text. On the other hand, GPT-4o has been trained on trillions of words of text in various languages, which is also important for dialectal text understanding as dialects often feature influences from multiple languages, and its ability to "find its way around" even dialectal texts, not many of which exist online, is staggering.

To showcase the capabilities of the mentioned GPT-4o model, we present the processing of an exemplary Chakavian sentence in Figure 4. While the tags provided by the GPT model are all correct, the second-best model, trained on nonstandard and standard Croatian texts, has serious issues. These issues start already with the first word that, given that it is unknown to the tagger, but also badly represented in word embeddings (there are only 52 occurrences of this word in a two-billion-word web corpus of the Croatian language), is assumed to be a proper noun. Things deteriorate further in the second half of the sentence where the tagger starts producing the X (Residual) tags simply because most of the words are not present in the tagger's training data and are very badly represented by the word embeddings.

The reason why the GPT model excels at the task is simply because it has the capacity to assume the meaning of each word. While producing the correct tags, it also generates the explanation for its decisions: it assumed *šilica* to be a diminutive of *šila*, which the model assumes to mean *needle*, all of which is wrong, but close enough to generate the correct tag. Similarly, the GPT model correctly assumes that *iglo* is a dialectal form of the noun *igla* and that *va* is a dialectal form of the preposition *u*. Interestingly, the last two described deviations of the Chakavian dialect from the Croatian standard are rather close to the Slovenian standard, and large decoder models have knowledge of various languages at their disposal, compressed in their

Dialectal	Standard	English	GPT-4o	Best PoS tagger
Šilica	Krojačica	Seamstress	NOUN	PROPN
je	je	has	AUX	AUX
rinula	rinula / gurnula	pushed	VERB	VERB
iglo	iglu	needle	NOUN	VERB
s	s	with	ADP	ADP
koncien	koncem	thread	NOUN	X
va	u	into	ADP	X
robo	robu / tkaninu	fibre	NOUN	X

Figure 4: Comparison of the output of the GPT-4o model and the best-performing part-of-speech tagger on a hard case of the Chakavian dialect of Croatian.

model weights, which is a tremendous help with hard cases, such as dialectal or historical texts.

We can conclude that decoder models exhibit a large amount of stored knowledge, as well as linguistic reasoning, which can be very beneficial for hard cases of PoS tagging, such as dialectal texts that have no good online presence, and often no tagging training data available. Although GPT models are surely not needed for PoS tagging texts that are similar to those seen in large quantities online, or, even less, present in the tagger training data, for tagging texts that already require a significant amount of background knowledge and linguistic reasoning capacity, GPTs and similar decoder models are a very good solution.

4.6 Go-to tools for PoS tagging and related tasks

We wrap up this section with an overview of tools for PoS tagging and related tasks that we can suggest as strong solutions at the time of writing this article (2025). All the mentioned tools are quite mature, i. e. have been around for some time now and are actively maintained, and we expect them to be relevant in the foreseeable future as well.

Before going into specific tools, we have to stress again that the reason for the current good level of coverage of languages in all of the PoS taggers described below is the Universal Dependencies project, which ensured availability of training data for PoS tagging and related tasks across many languages. Given the availability of training data in many languages encoded in the same manner, it is extremely simple for a tagger developer to ensure that the tagger does not cover only one language, but all the languages that are present in the Universal Dependencies project. Of course, the quality of the tagger output for a specific language will depend on the amount of training data available, which varies significantly between languages.

The Universal Dependencies project is also the reason for all the tools discussed below to cover not only the PoS tagging, but other related tasks discussed in Section 3 as well, namely tokenisation, lemmatisation and syntactic parsing.

The first tagger to be mentioned is Stanza,[12] developed at Stanford University and available as a Python package. Using this tagger requires some basic coding skills, which are needed anyway if a larger amount of data is to be processed. Stanza is based on the RNN neural sequential classifier, using static word embeddings, as discussed in Section 4.3.

Another very popular tagger is UDPipe,[13] developed at the Charles University in Prague. It is written in C++ and therefore much faster than Stanza, which is written in Python. It is also not based on a neural model as Stanza, but uses a very specific non-neural implementation, primarily aimed at speed. Its implementation is the closest to the approaches described in Section 4.2. With this in mind, UDPipe would be preferred if speed of processing was the main concern. Another useful addition to UDPipe is its availability through a web interface.[14] The interface allows the user to try out the tool on exemplary sentences, which is very useful for testing, but also a great teaching method for students.

The final tool that we want to present is Trankit,[15] a tool based on Transformer models and dynamic word embeddings, discussed in Section 4.4. This tagger is based on a multilingual Transformer model and is therefore slower than Stanza.

The quality of the result of these three taggers reflects the technology that each tagger is based on. In Table 1, we represent some basic evaluation results of all the three taggers, performed on the language-specific tagsets of Arabic, Chinese and English. These evaluation numbers are taken from the Trankit documentation.[16] The lowest results of UDPipe are a consequence of the pre-neural technology it is using. However, if speed of processing is an issue, UDPipe is many times faster than the other two taggers. Stanza is expectedly positioned for each language in between the other two taggers. It features the addition of word embeddings, as well as the neural sequential modelling capacity. Finally, Trankit, with the Transformer technology representing each word depending on the context, and having significant knowledge encoded in the model beyond the task-specific fine-tuning, performs best for all three selected languages. The difference in performance between languages is also noticeable. While performance on Arabic and Chinese is comparable because

12 https://stanfordnlp.github.io/stanza/ (accessed April 1st, 2025).

13 https://lindat.mff.cuni.cz/services/udpipe/ (accessed April 1st, 2025).

14 https://lindat.mff.cuni.cz/services/udpipe/run.php (accessed April 1st, 2025).

15 https://trankit.readthedocs.io/en/latest/ (accessed April 1st, 2025).

16 https://trankit.readthedocs.io/en/latest/performance.html (accessed April 1st, 2025).

Table 1: Performance of the three taggers on the language-specific tagsets in three selected languages.

	Arabic	Chinese	English
UDPipe	84.00	84.04	92.75
Stanza	91.75	88.93	95.12
Trankit	94.08	94.02	95.71

of a comparable complexity of the PoS tagging problem, as expected, the problem on English is much simpler, therefore, the selection of the tagger is less crucial than in the case of the other two languages.

5 Data formats

This section introduces the data formats that are used for annotating tokens with PoS labels or morphosyntactic features, but also cater for the other related linguistic annotation levels introduced in Section 3.

The simplest format that can encode PoS tags is a tabular one, with each row for one token and the columns giving at least the token itself and the PoS tag, just as given in Figure 1. Of course, more columns can encode additional token-level annotations, such as the number of the token in the sentence or the lemma of the word token. As will be further detailed at the end of this section, the most common data format in natural language processing is indeed a tabular one, although with certain additional features.

There are, however, reasons to prefer more complex formats, the main one being that text can have many other annotations apart from token-level ones, and tabular formats soon run into trouble when attempting to model them.

5.1 TEI-XML

Historically, the Text Encoding Initiative Guidelines (TEI Consortium 2024) were the first attempt to model textual linguistic analyses in a comprehensive text annotation framework. TEI is a modular system based on XML, where different text and text analysis types can be combined, with the module for Simple Analytic Mechanisms containing the definitions for elements and attributes used for linguistic markup. One of the main goals of TEI is that any text or analysis type could be represented in it, with the down-side of this approach that many identical phenomena can be encoded in several different ways, with linguistic analyses being no exception.

Sentences and tokens are marked up with <s>, <w> (for words) and <pc> (for punctuation) tags, while a lemma is stored as the value of the lemma attribute on the token tags. The tags for tokens can also have the join attribute with possible values left, right and both, which encode the spacing between the tokens, e. g. join="right" means that there is no space following the token.

The encoding of PoS tags is more complicated, as TEI provides several attributes that can be used for this purpose:

- pos is meant to encode the part-of-speech assigned to a token, either a true part-of-speech (e. g. noun or adjective) or a PoS tag from a given tagset (e. g. CLAWS, STTS);
- msd encodes a morphosyntactic description of a token, such as the Universal Dependencies morphological features;
- function is an attribute that can be given to any linguistic segment and indicates its (linguistic) function, possibly a PoS tag;
- ana is a general pointing attribute that can also be used for analytical tagsets: the value of this attribute would point to the XML identifier of the definition of the PoS tag, i. e. its morphosyntactic attributes and values, which are typically encoded as a feature-structure elsewhere in the TEI document.

To illustrate one possible markup of a Universal Dependencies morphological analysis, Figure 5 gives the markup of an example sentence in TEI. Here the UD part-of-speech is encoded in the pos attribute, while the morphological features are given as the value of the msd attribute.

```
<s>
  <w lemma="compare" pos="VERB" msd="Mood=Imp VerbForm=Fin">Compare</w>
  <w lemma="the" pos="DET" msd="Definite=Def PronType=Art">the</w>
  <w lemma="flag" pos="NOUN" msd="Number=Plur">flags</w>
  <w lemma="to" pos="ADP">to</w>
  <w lemma="the" pos="DET" msd="Definite=Def PronType=Art">the</w>
  <w lemma="Fallujah" pos="PROPN" msd="Number=Sing">Fallujah</w>
  <w lemma="one" pos="NOUN" msd="Number=Sing" join="right">one</w>
  <pc lemma="." pos="PUNCT">.</pc>
</s>
```

Figure 5: An example sentence encoded in TEI.

TEI also supports the mark-up of syntactic analyses, either constituent or dependency based and offers a plethora of methods to do so. For in-line tree-based constituent analysis the module for Simple Analytic Mechanisms defines the <cl> (grammatical clause) and <phr> (grammatical phrase) tags. Other syntactic mark-up methods are all stand-off, i. e. the tokens are given XML identifiers and the syntactic analysis is encoded elsewhere in the TEI document where it refers to the tokens. Such analyses take advantage of elements defined in further modules of the TEI, such as Graphs, Networks, and Trees or Feature Structures.

As this section has briefly shown, TEI does offer mark-up constructs for all the annotation levels considered in this chapter, often with more than one encoding possibility. However, it should be noted that while TEI is heavily used in the field of digital humanities, in has not really gained traction among the natural language processing community, where it is seen as too complex and not prescriptive enough.

5.2 ISO standards

The development of standards in the scope of the International Standards Organisation (ISO) is performed by its Technical Committees (TC), which are subdivided into Subcommittees (SC). ISO/TC 37/SC 4 "Language and terminology / Language resource management" develops standards for the mark-up of various types of language resources, including, but not limited to computer corpora of written texts. In general, these standards concentrate on "meta-models" (i. e. abstract models) for the annotation of particular text and annotation types. However, they do have either informative annexes or associated standards for the concrete implementation of these meta-models, which is typically XML-based. Several of the developed standards simply took over the TEI recommendations for the particular text or annotation type, while others propose solutions that are more or less independent of TEI.

To date, ISO has released standards for the following aspects of annotation related to the linguistic levels discussed in this chapter:

- The Linguistic Annotation Framework (LAF) (ISO 24612 2012) provides general principles of linguistic annotation and a very general meta-model with its XML instantiation for arbitrary linguistic annotations.
- The Morpho-syntactic Annotation Framework (MAF) (ISO 24612 2012) gives a meta-model for morphosyntactic (i. e. PoS) annotations, also treating tokenisation and its mapping to word-forms. The standard gives two XML instantiations of the meta-model, one developed esp. for the standard, while the other is compliant with TEI, although much more specific and prescriptive in the kinds of elements and attributes to be used.
- The Syntactic annotation framework (SynAF) treats the annotation of both constituent and dependency based syntactic analyses and is composed of two parts: Part 1: Syntactic model (ISO 24615-1 2014) introduces the terminology and gives a meta-model for syntactic annotation, while Part 2: XML serialization (Tiger vocabulary) (ISO 24615-2 2018) gives a concrete instantiation of this model in

XML, following the TigerXML proposal, which gives syntactic analyses mostly in terms of graphs.

Similarly to TEI, it does not seem that the NLP community has made significant use of these ISO standards. The reasons for this are most likely, as with TEI, that they are viewed as too complex, and, furthermore, ISO sells its standards, i. e. they are not openly available.

5.3 The CoNLL-U format

As mentioned, the Universal Dependencies project has had a profound impact also on PoS tagging, so it is unsurprising that the format UD uses for its treebanks has also become a de-facto standard as one of the outputs of tool chains that perform annotation over the linguistic levels discussed in this chapter, such as Stanza or UDPipe.

The format, called CoNLL-U[17] is a tabular one, and is based on the CoNLL-X format developed for the Shared Task on Multilingual Dependency Parsing (Buchholz and Marsi 2006) that took place at the Conference on Computational Natural Language Learning (CoNLL).

Figure 6 gives an annotated sentence in CoNLL-U format. The complete specifications are available on the Universal Dependencies Web pages, and we here comment only on the main points:

- CoNLL-U files are plain text files using the Unicode UTF-8 encoding;
- comment lines start with hash (#) followed by the key and its value; some of these key (like the text of the annotated sentence) are prescribed by CoNLL-U, while others are user defined and can be used to store meta-data about the document, paragraph or sentence;
- blank lines mark sentence boundaries;
- the other lines contain the annotations of a token (word) in 10 columns separated by a single tab character
- the underscore is used for fields without values, while the pipe character is used to separate multiple features in a column;
- the first column (ID) gives the number of the token in the sentence, with CoNLL-U also being able to encode syntactic words, where one token corresponds to more than one such word;
- the next three columns give the token (FORM), its lemma (LEMMA) and the UD part-of-speech (UPOSTAG);

17 https://universaldependencies.org/format.html (accessed April 1st, 2025).

- the fifth column (XPOSTAG) gives the language-specific (legacy) part-of-speech tag, e. g. CLAWS for English;
- the sixth column (FEATS) lists the relevant morphological features from the UD feature inventory or from a defined language-specific extension;
- the seventh column (HEAD) gives the syntactic head of the current token, which is either its ID or zero (0) for the syntactic root of the sentence;
- the eight column (DEPREL) give the syntactic dependency relation of the token to its HEAD or to a defined language-specific subtype of one;
- the ninth column (DEPS) gives a list of so called secondary syntactic dependencies as HEAD-DEPREL pairs;
- the tenth column (MISC) gives any other token-level annotations, with `SpaceAfter=No` denoting that the token should not be followed by a space; this column can also be used for span-level annotations, such as NER using the IOB format, as further explained in (Schwarz 2025).

```
# sent_id = 1
# text = Compare the flags to the Fallujah one.
1  Compare   compare   VERB   VB   Mood = Imp|...      0  root      0:root      _
2  the       the       DET    DT   Definite = Def|...  3  det       3:det       _
3  flags     flag      NOUN   NNS  Number = Plur       1  obj       1:obj       _
4  to        to        ADP    IN   _                   7  case      7:case      _
5  the       the       DET    DT   Definite = Def|...  7  det       7:det       _
6  Fallujah  Fallujah  PROPN  NNP  Number = Sing       7  compound  7:compound  _
7  one       one       NOUN   NN   Number = Sing       1  obl       1:obl:to    SpaceAfter = No
8  .         .         PUNCT  .    _                   1  punct     1:punct     _

# sent_id = 2
...
```

Figure 6: An example sentence in CoNLL-U (Universal Dependencies) format.

As already mentioned in Section 5.3, Universal Dependencies also support validation, in particular CoNLL-U files can be checked whether they are correctly formatted, and use the correct features for a language.

6 Conclusion

We will start this section with a hard question that each computational linguist and natural language processing practitioner should ask himself these days. Namely, in the world where end-to-end, single-step computational language understanding has been achieved, with astonishing results of large language models, is the art and craft of PoS tagging, and their related disciplines, still necessary at all?

For many years, PoS tagging was assumed to be a crucial step in the layer-oriented approach to computational language understanding, where classifying each word by the function it has in a sentence was a preparatory step for the holy grail of language understanding for so many years – syntactic analysis. Once syntactic analysis was achieved, the assumption was that semantic and then pragmatic analysis would be within our reach and result in the understanding of a piece of text.

However, the deep learning revolution in the second decade of the 21st century, continued by the transformer large language model revolution in the current, third decade of this century, proved for the layer-wise approach not to be needed for highly capable computational language understanding and generation. Large language models answer questions in an end-to-end manner, receiving questions at their input and generating answers at their output. Image, video, and speech can also be embedded, making this interaction tool multimodal both in its input and in its output. Linguistically analysing any part of a text on any required level is also possible by simply providing the text, or audio, and the linguistic task at the input, the output being even structured if requested in input instructions.

Our claim that we will deliberate here is that PoS tagging and its related disciplines are still needed, however, not to achieve computational language understanding, but rather as a language analysis tool, in effect going back to the original task PoS tagging was developed for, i. e. corpus annotation.

Linguists still need large corpora to analyse language. There is work on investigating the capacity of large language models to deliver results that corpus linguists traditionally required corpora for.[18] However, the results are still very mixed, with quite many downsides of large language models, the biggest ones being the lack of scientific rigour regarding factuality and reproducibility of large language models. For that reason, corpora for linguistic research are still relevant, and they require PoS tagging and related processing on a scale for which the PoS taggers presented in Section 4.6 are still very much preferred to large language models.

Another strong use case for PoS tagging is the analysis of language input, but even more of language output of large language models. Large language models are huge black boxes that we simply do not understand. The most standard way of dealing with black boxes is to investigate their input and corresponding output. One of the techniques that will be useful for this analysis of input and output are PoS tagging, lemmatisation etc. There is already work showing that large language models are drastically changing the language of scientific communication (Kobak et al. 2025). And this is just the tip of the iceberg, both related to analysing the current

18 One example is https://www.english-corpora.org/ai-llms/ (accessed April 1st, 2025).

impact of large language models on language and communication, and the future impact given the expansion of the use of this and related technologies.

Such controlled linguistic analyses based on enriching text with PoS and related categories tremendously benefit from the recently improved availability and usability of PoS taggers for various languages. This improvement is to be followed to the availability of training data that is encoded with comparable tagsets and data formats in many languages, as discussed in Sections 2 and 5. Having such datasets at hand ensures two things: (1) a simplified development of taggers for a large number of languages and varieties, as discussed in Section 4.6, but also (2) much simpler use of the results of the tools regardless of the languages processed due to the uniform (a) data format and (b) linguistic formalism.

Bibliography

Baum, Leonard E. & Ted Petrie. 1966. Statistical inference for probabilistic functions of finite state markov chains. *The Annals of Mathematical Statistics* 37(6). 1554–1563.

Buchholz, Sabine & Erwin Marsi. 2006. CoNLL-X shared task on multilingual dependency parsing. In Lluís Màrquez & Dan Klein (eds.), *Proceedings of the tenth conference on computational natural language learning (CoNLL-x)*, 149–164. New York City: Association for Computational Linguistics. https://aclanthology.org/W06-2920/.

Erjavec, Tomaž. 2012. MULTEXT-East: Morphosyntactic resources for Central and Eastern European languages. *Language Resources and Evaluation* 46(1). 131–142.

Gesmundo, Andrea & Tanja Samardžić. 2012. Lemmatisation as a tagging task. In Haizhou Li, Chin-Yew Lin, Miles Osborne, Gary Geunbae Lee & Jong C. Park (eds.), *Proceedings of the 50th annual meeting of the Association for Computational Linguistics (Volume 2: Short papers)*, 368–372. Jeju Island, Korea: Association for Computational Linguistics.

Hajič, Jan, Eva Hajičová, Marie Mikulová & Jiří Mírovský. 2017. Prague dependency treebank. In Nancy Ide & James Pustejovsky (eds.), *Handbook of linguistic annotation*, 555–594. Dordrecht: Springer Netherlands.

Hajič, Jan, Eduard Bejček, Alevtina Bémová, Eva Buráňová, Eva Fučíková, Eva Hajičová, Jiří Havelka, et al. 2024. *Prague Dependency Treebank – Consolidated 2.0 (PDT-C 2.0)*.

Hochreiter, Sepp & Jürgen Schmidhuber. 1997. Long short-term memory. *Neural Computation* 9(8). 1735–1780.

ISO 24612. 2012. *Language resource management – Linguistic annotation framework (LAF)*.

ISO 24614-1. 2010. *Language resource management – Word segmentation of written texts – Part 1: Basic concepts and general principles*.

ISO 24614-2. 2011. *Language resource management – Word segmentation of written texts – Part 2: Word segmentation for Chinese, Japanese and Korean*.

ISO 24615-1. 2014. *Language resource management – Syntactic annotation framework (SynAF) – Part 1: Syntactic model*.

ISO 24615-2. 2018. *Language resource management – Syntactic annotation framework (SynAF) – Part 2: XML serialization (Tiger vocabulary)*.

Johansson, Stig. 2008. Some aspects of the development of corpus linguistics in the 1970s and 1980s. In Anke Lüdeling & Merja Kytö (eds.), *Corpus linguistics. An international handbook*, 33–53. Berlin: Mouton de Gruyter.

Juršič, Matjaž, Igor Mozetič, Tomaž Erjavec & Nada Lavrač. 2010. LemmaGen: Multilingual lemmatisation with induced Ripple-Down rules. *Journal of Universal Computer Science* 16(9). 1190–1214.

Kobak, Dmitry, Rita González-Márquez, Emőke Ágnes Horvát & Jan Lause. 2025. Delving into ChatGPT usage in academic writing through excess vocabulary. https://arxiv.org/abs/2406.07016.

Lafferty, John, Andrew McCallum, Fernando Pereira, et al.. 2001. Conditional random fields: Probabilistic models for segmenting and labeling sequence data. In *ICML*, Vol. 1. Williamstown, MA.

Leech, Geoffrey & Andrew Wilson. 1996. EAGLES recommendations for the morphosyntactic annotation of corpora. Technical Report, ILC, Pisa. https://www.ilc.cnr.it/EAGLES96/annotate/annotate.html.

Ljubešić, Nikola, Nada Galant, Sonja Benčina, Jaka Čibej, Stefan Milosavljević, Peter Rupnik & Taja Kuzman. 2024. DIALECT-COPA: Extending the standard translations of the COPA causal commonsense reasoning dataset to South Slavic dialects. In Yves Scherrer, Tommi Jauhiainen, Nikola Ljubešić, Marcos Zampieri, Preslav Nakov & Jörg Tiedemann (eds.), *Proceedings of the eleventh workshop on NLP for similar languages, varieties, and dialects (vardial 2024)*, 89–98. Mexico City, Mexico: Association for Computational Linguistics.

Ljubešić, Nikola & Kaja Dobrovoljc. 2019. What does neural bring? Analysing improvements in morphosyntactic annotation and lemmatisation of Slovenian, Croatian and Serbian. In Tomaž Erjavec, Michał Marcińczuk, Preslav Nakov, Jakub Piskorski, Lidia Pivovarova, Jan Šnajder, Josef Steinberger & Roman Yangarber (eds.), *Proceedings of the 7th workshop on Balto-Slavic natural language processing*, 29–34. Florence, Italy: Association for Computational Linguistics.

Marcus, Mitchell P., Mary Ann Marcinkiewicz & Beatrice Santorini. 1993. Building a large annotated corpus of English: The Penn treebank. *Computational Linguistics* 19(2). 313–330.

de Marneffe, Marie-Catherine, Christopher D. Manning, Joakim Nivre & Daniel Zeman. 2021. Universal Dependencies. *Computational Linguistics* 47(2). 255–308.

Mikolov, Tomas, Kai Chen, Greg Corrado & Jeffrey Dean. 2013. Efficient estimation of word representations in vector space. https://doi.org/10.48550/arXiv.1301.3781.

Nguyen, Minh Van, Viet Lai, Amir Pouran Ben Veyseh & Thien Huu Nguyen. 2021. Trankit: A light-weight transformer-based toolkit for multilingual natural language processing. In *Proceedings of the 16th conference of the european chapter of the Association for Computational Linguistics: System demonstrations*.

Petrov, Slav, Dipanjan Das & Ryan T. McDonald. 2011. A universal part-of-speech tagset. *CoRR*. arXiv: abs/1104.2086.

Pollard, Carl J. & Ivan A. Sag. 1994. *Head-driven phrase structure grammar*. Chicago: University of Chicago Press.

Radford, Alec, Karthik Narasimhan, Tim Salimans & Ilya Sutskever. 2018. Improving language understanding by generative pre-training.

Rumelhart, David E., Geoffrey E. Hinton & Ronald J. Williams. 1986. Learning representations by back-propagating errors. *Nature* 323(6088). 533–536.

Santorini, Beatrice. 1990. Part-of-Speech tagging guidelines for the Penn Treebank Project. Technical report, 3rd revision, 2nd printing, University of Pennsylvania.

Schiller, Anne, Simone Teufel & Christine Thielen. 1995. Guidelines für das Tagging deutscher Textcorpora, Technical report, University of Stuttgart and University of Tübingen.

Schwarz, Pia. 2025. Named entity recognition and entity linking. In Piotr Bański, Ulrich Heid & Laura Herzberg (eds.), *Harmonising language data: Standards for linguistic resources*. Berlin & Boston: De Gruyter.

Sgall, Petr, Eva Hajičová, Jarmila Panevova & Jacob Mey. 1986. *The meaning of the sentence in its semantic and pragmatic aspects*. Dordrecht: Springer.

Stüssi, Elina & Phillip Ströbel. 2024. Part-of-Speech tagging of 16th-century Latin with GPT. In Yuri Bizzoni, Stefania Degaetano-Ortlieb, Anna Kazantseva & Stan Szpakowicz (eds.), *Proceedings of the 8th joint SIGHUM workshop on computational linguistics for cultural heritage, social sciences, humanities and literature (LaTeCH-CLfL 2024)*, 196–206. St. Julians, Malta: Association for Computational Linguistics.

TEI Consortium (eds.). 2024. Guidelines for electronic text encoding and interchange. http://www.tei-c.org/P5/.

The Unicode Consortium. 2024. Unicode text segmentation (Unicode®Standard Annex #29). http://unicode.org/reports/tr29/.

Vaswani, Ashish, Noam Shazeer, Niki Parmar, Jakob Uszkoreit, Llion Jones, Aidan N. Gomez, Łukasz Kaiser & Illia Polosukhin. 2017. Attention is all you need. In *Advances in neural information processing systems*, Vol. 30.

Zeman, Daniel. 2008. Reusable tagset conversion using tagset drivers. In Nicoletta Calzolari, Khalid Choukri, Bente Maegaard, Joseph Mariani, Jan Odijk, Stelios Piperidis & Daniel Tapias (eds.), *Proceedings of the sixth international conference on language resources and evaluation (LREC '08)*. Marrakech, Morocco: European Language Resources Association (ELRA).

Zeman, Daniel, Ondřej Dušek, David Mareček, Martin Popel, Loganathan Ramasamy, Jan Štěpánek, Zdeněk Žabokrtský & Jan Hajič. 2014. HamleDT: Harmonized multi-language dependency treebank. *Language Resources and Evaluation* 48. 601–637.

Zeman, Daniel, Joakim Nivre, Mitchell Abrams, Elia Ackermann, Noëmi Aepli, Hamid Aghaei, Željko Agić, et al. 2024. Universal Dependencies 2.15. LINDAT/CLARIAH-CZ digital library at the Institute of Formal and Applied Linguistics (ÚFAL), Faculty of Mathematics and Physics, Charles University.

Pia Schwarz

Named entity recognition and entity linking

Abstract: Named Entity Recognition (NER) and Entity Linking (EL) are crucial tasks in Natural Language Processing (NLP) that enable the extraction and disambiguation of named entities in text data. NER involves identifying and labelling named entities, such as persons, locations, and organizations, while EL links these entities to external knowledge bases, providing additional context and information. NER and EL systems employ a range of techniques, including statistical and state-of-the-art neural approaches like transformer-based architectures, to recognize, disambiguate, and link entities to knowledge bases. The application of NER and EL has numerous use cases for automatic text analysis and information retrieval, and is generally useful to engage with text data in the area of digital humanities. This chapter provides an overview of NER and EL, including their tasks, techniques, relevant data formats, and applications, as well as some guidance on how to apply these technologies to raw data sets.

Keywords: named entity recognition, entity linking, knowledge base, data formats, language models

1 Introduction

There are many possible ways to process textual data in order to analyse its content or language. Linguistic annotations like tokenization or part-of-speech tags provide a lot of useful structural information (see Ljubešić and Erjavec 2025). In addition, text analysis can benefit a lot when it is enriched with semantic information. This way, humans as well as computers can make more sense of the data. One of the most common annotations in this respect are *named entities*: Persons, locations, and organizations are three types of entities that are very frequently labelled by *Named Entity Recognition* (NER) systems. The task of *Entity Linking* (EL) is a way to provide deeper understanding of these named entities. Links from a named entity pointing to further resources like an external knowledge base help to uniquely identify

Acknowledgement: This chapter is based on work within Text+, funded by the Deutsche Forschungsgemeinschaft (DFG, project number 460033370) as part of the German National Research Data Infrastructure (NFDI e. V.).

Pia Schwarz, Digitale Sprachwissenschaft, Leibniz-Institut für Deutsche Sprache, R5 6-13, D-68161 Mannheim, Baden-Württemberg, Germany, e-mail: schwarz@ids-mannheim.de

https://doi.org/10.1515/9783112208212-005

and disambiguate the entity and in the best case to even provide extra information about it, e.g. a person's birth date, their profession, affiliations to organizations or relations to other persons (see Khan 2025). If we think about a Wikipedia article opened in a browser tab: To quickly gain a better understanding of a less familiar topic it is extremely useful to have relevant entities in the text underlined and additionally be provided with more context information about the entity by hovering the mouse over it. Wikipedia is an application used very broadly, but there are many more specialised use cases where the techniques of NER and EL come into play. One example from the area of digital humanities are Vincent van Gogh's letters (Jansen et al. 2009). The electronically published version allows to browse through the letters in which named entities of type person were annotated manually. More context information about the entities is displayed using mouse-over (see Figure 1).

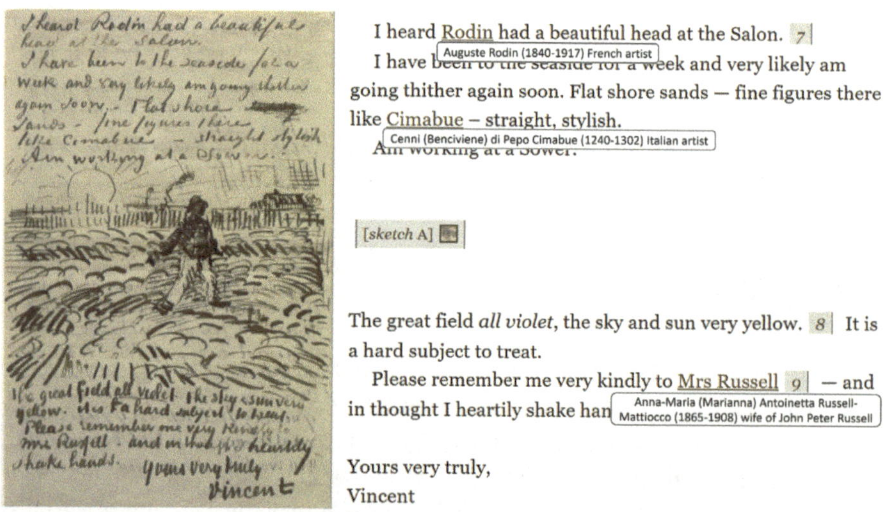
I heard Rodin had a beautiful head at the Salon. 7
Auguste Rodin (1840-1917) French artist
I have been to the seaside for a week and very likely am going thither again soon. Flat shore sands — fine figures there like Cimabue – straight, stylish.
Cenni (Benciviene) di Pepo Cimabue (1240-1302) Italian artist
Am working at a Sower.

[sketch A]

The great field *all violet*, the sky and sun very yellow. 8 It is a hard subject to treat.
Please remember me very kindly to Mrs Russell 9 — and in thought I heartily shake han[ds.]
Anna-Maria (Marianna) Antoinetta Russell-Mattiocco (1865-1908) wife of John Peter Russell

Yours very truly,
Vincent

Figure 1: Facsimile and translation of the transcription of the last two paragraphs of letter no. 627 from Vincent van Gogh sent to John Peter Russell on June, 17th 1888[1].

Another example use case are the person and location extraction services of the European Holocaust Research Infrastructure project (EHRI)[2] which aims at providing and improving the accessibility to documents and resources related to the Holocaust. Entities in the documents are tagged with a customised NER pipeline and in

1 https://vangoghletters.org/vg/letters/let627/letter.html (accessed 10 January 2025).
2 https://www.ehri-project.eu/ (accessed 9 January 2025).

part linked to their counterparts in knowledge bases like GeoNames[3] or Wikidata[4] (de Leeuw et al. 2018: 62). The result of this semantic enrichment can be seen in the EHRI portal[5] which is searchable for entities like persons and locations (i. e. concentration camps and ghettos). When searching for "Leon Blum" the first match[6] is an entry of type Person that shows some bibliographical properties as well as a list of related items. This list contains the links to items related to Léon Blum: terms (e. g. "Politicians and Statespersons"), locations (e. g. "Buchenwald concentration camp", where Léon Blum was an inmate) or documents (e. g. "Oral history interview with Arnold Weiss" in which Léon Blum's name is mentioned). Following the link to the location[7] on the EHRI portal, we are provided with a map with the geographic coordinates and a link to the camp's counterpart in Wikidata. To sum up, Named Entity Recognition and Entity Linking are two very common subtasks of information extraction leading to the discovery of new information. They reveal connections within data sets and make it possible to generate links pointing to other relevant (re-)sources. The additional value of NER and EL is twofold: Entity annotated data enables easier reusability of the data on the one hand, and an improved searchability in the data on the other.

2 Named entity recognition

NER as one of the most crucial downstream tasks in Natural Language Processing with the goal of identifying and labelling named entities is the first step in the pipeline for entity linking. In the context of part-of-speech tags, named entities fall into the grammatical word category of proper nouns, and just like part-of-speech tagging, NER falls in the category of so called sequence labelling tasks (see Ljubešić and Erjavec 2025). The input to a NER system is a text or a sentence, in other words, a sequence of words or tokens, and the output is a sequence of labels for every word in the sequence. Sometimes (especially in older literature) NER is also referred to as NERC, which stands for Named Entity Recognition and Classification. Example (1)

3 https://www.geonames.org/ (accessed 9 January 2025).

4 https://www.wikidata.org/ (accessed 9 January 2025).

5 https://portal.ehri-project.eu/ (accessed 9 January 2025).

6 https://portal.ehri-project.eu/authorities/ehri_pers-000046 (accessed 9 January 2025).

7 https://portal.ehri-project.eu/keywords/ehri_camps-43 (accessed 9 January 2025).

shows a very simplified representation of a sequence with a class[8] assigned to each token, in this case PER, ORG, LOC or no-NE for tokens that aren't named entities:

(1) **Input**: Chancellor Angela Merkel gave a speech to the United Nations General Assembly in New York.
Output: $[\text{Chancellor}]_{\text{no-NE}}$ $[\text{Angela Merkel}]_{\text{PER}}$ $[\text{gave}]_{\text{no-NE}}$ $[\text{a}]_{\text{no-NE}}$ $[\text{speech}]_{\text{no-NE}}$ $[\text{to}]_{\text{no-NE}}$ $[\text{the}]_{\text{no-NE}}$ $[\text{United Nations General Assembly}]_{\text{ORG}}$ $[\text{in}]_{\text{no-NE}}$ $[\text{New York}]_{\text{LOC}}$.

2.1 Entity classes

Three of the most common entity classes are PER (person), ORG (organization), and LOC (location). However, a comprehensive standardised list of entity classes does not exist, as a named entity can be any object denoted by a proper name (Jurafsky and Martin 2025: 6). For instance, we could decide to define a class EVENT to identify events like the Black Death, the German Federal Elections 2025 or the Olympic Games 2024. In addition to location, the class GPE which stands for geo-political entity, is often part of NER systems and denotes states or countries. This is a more fine-grained classification than only using the location class. An example for the opposite of fine-grained NER was established in the CoNLL-2003 Shared Task about language-independent NER where the goal was to recognize the three most common entity classes as well as the class MISC (miscellaneous) which can be any named entity not covered by the other three classes (Tjong Kim Sang and De Meulder 2003). Of course it always depends on the use case and the domain in which a named entity recognizer is applied. In a biomedical domain it might be rather useful to have entity classes for chemicals and proteins whereas if the domain is very broad and comprises social media posts or newspaper articles it is certainly more useful to have classes as offered by the some of the available fine-grained NER models of the natural language analysis package Stanza (Qi et al. 2020) from the Stanford NLP Group, listed in Table 1.

However, not all of these entity types are proper nouns, sometimes temporal expressions like weekdays or dates, or numerical expressions are included as entity classes. Tokens that should not be classified as named entities are pronouns referring to named entities, for example *he* in the sentence: *Barack Obama was 47 years old when he became president*. Although some linguists like Aufrant and Chasseur

8 Unlike in the introduction we use the term entity *class* or *label* instead of entity *types*. All three are often used interchangeably in the literature as well as in this chapter. However, the term *class* best fits the naming conventions of state-of-the-art machine learning algorithms used in NLP.

Table 1: Class labels for named entities of the Stanza NER package.

PERSON	person	LAW	law
NORP	nationalities, religious, or political group	LANGUAGE	language
FAC	facility	DATE	date
ORG	organization	TIME	time
GPE	geopolitical entity	PERCENT	percentage
LOC	location	MONEY	value in a currency
PRODUCT	product	QUANTITY	quantity
EVENT	event	ORDINAL	ordinal number
WORK_OF_ART	work of art	CARDINAL	cardinal number

(2024) propose to do so, we argue that this is rather part of coreference resolution. When labelling a data set to be used for training or evaluating a named entity recognizer it is extremely useful to provide clear definitions and examples of the desired entity classes. Such an annotation guideline would also need to clarify cases where there is more than one possible way to tag an entity, as shown in example (2), a short Wikipedia text[9] annotated with five different entity classes: person, location, organization, geo-political entity, and scientific discipline (SCD). For the entity *Friedrich August III, King of Saxony* the decision was made to tag it as a single entity of class person. We could have also decided to tag two separate entities instead, i. e. *Friedrich August III* and *King of Saxony*.

(2) *The main building of the [German National Library]$_{ORG}$ in [Leipzig]$_{LOC}$ was built 1914–1916 after plans of the architect [Oskar Pusch]$_{PER}$. The facade is 160 m long and faces the "[Deutscher Platz]$_{LOC}$" (German Plaza). The building was opened on 19 October 1916. The site of the library (near to today's [Alte Messe]$_{LOC}$) had been donated by the [city of Leipzig]$_{GPE}$, while [Friedrich August III, King of Saxony]$_{PER}$ provided the funds for the building. On the facade, the portraits of [Otto von Bismarck]$_{PER}$, [Johann Wolfgang von Goethe]$_{PER}$ and [Johannes Gutenberg]$_{PER}$ are displayed. Statues represent [Technology]$_{SCD}$, [Justice]$_{SCD}$, [Philosophy]$_{SCD}$, [Medicine]$_{SCD}$ etc.*

Another ambiguity arises regarding the entity *city of Leipzig*. In example (2) it was tagged as a geopolitical entity, but we could also argue that the actors behind the mentioned donation was not Leipzig as a place but rather the city council or the mayor of Leipzig. We could therefore decide as well to tag it as an organization.

9 https://en.wikipedia.org/wiki/German_National_Library#Building_in_Leipzig (accessed 13 January 2025).

However, we should not forget what such a decision would mean for similar cases that do not occur in the text but might appear in a larger corpus: Do we want to tag for example the mention of a university or the police as an organization or a location? Does it depend on the context or do we want to always decide for one of the classes? We can see that it is necessary to deal with several different ways to tag entities and that these ambiguities are probably not an exception, as they already occur in a relatively short text like example (2). This shows the importance of carefully designed guidelines to ensure a consistent annotation and illustrates that their development is certainly not a trivial task.

2.2 State-of-the-art NER systems

The research to automate the task of NER dates back to the early nineties. The first systems were rule-based, e. g. Rau (1991) designed an algorithm that follows a set of handcrafted rules and exception lists to extract company names in financial news texts. Other early studies deal with supervised machine learning where a model is designed to go through annotated text and learns to come up with discriminative features for disambiguation. Model architectures like Hidden Markov Models, Support Vector Machines or Conditional Random Fields were used for this (Nadeau and Sekine 2007). Around 2010, with computer hardware becoming more powerful, more approaches of tackling NER using neural networks started to emerge. This development was accelerated with research about the attention mechanism (Bahdanau et al. 2014) in combination with the invention of the neural network architecture of transformers (Vaswani et al. 2017). These encode-decoder models soon became state-of-the-art for many NLP tasks. The model type that is typically applied on sequence labelling tasks like NER is called BERT, short for Bidirectional Encoder Representations from Transformers (Devlin et al. 2019). In contrast to generative pre-trained transformers (GPT) which makes use of the decoder, BERT uses only the encoder. A crucial difference is BERT's ability to work bidirectionally: It can take the left context as well as the right context of an input sequence into account, unlike a GPT model which can only look at the previous, i. e. a sequence's left context. The self-attention mechanism of BERT has the effect that for each token the model determines how relevant every other token in the sequence is. In a first step, a BERT model is pre-trained on large amounts of data to be then fine-tuned on a specific task like NER in a second step (see Figure 2). Pre-training is done with the two learning objectives of Next Sentence Prediction (NSP) and Masked Language Modeling (MLM). The input are two sequences (i. e. sentences) separated by a special token ([SEP]) where some of the tokens are masked, much like a cloze text. The task of NSP requires to predict whether the second of the two sentences follows the first one or

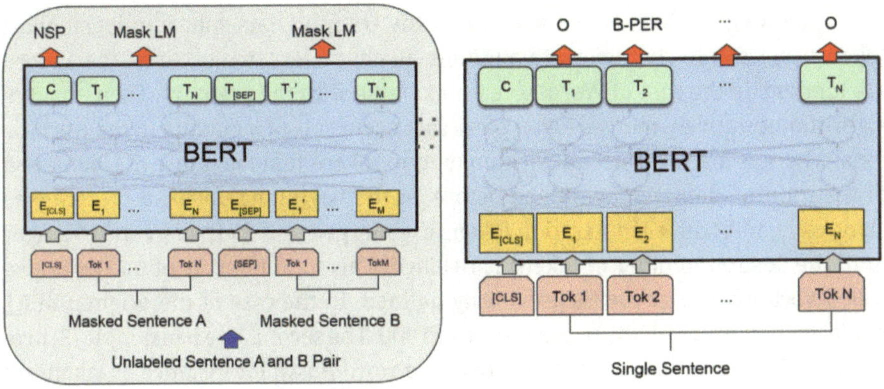

Figure 2: BERT model pre-training with Next Sentence Prediction (NSP) and Masked Language Modeling (MLM or Mask LM), and fine-tuning on NER. Tok stands for Token, E represents their embedding vectors and T their last hidden representation in the neural network. Red arrows indicate the classification tasks. Adapted from Devlin et al. (2019).

if it is unrelated.[10] For the MLM task the requirement is to predict the masked words. Both objectives have the advantage that they can be done using unlabelled training data and the model learns the basics of how human language works with regard to morphology, syntax and semantics and gains an understanding of long range dependencies between sentences. Going through more and more data, the model improves its predictions and adjusts its weights accordingly, until it converges after enough passes through the training data. Many such pre-trained models exist, some trained on only one language but also many trained on multilingual data.

There are many other popular BERT-like models with modifications for example in their pre-training methods or parameters, e. g. RoBERTa (Liu et al. 2019) or DistilBERT (Sanh et al. 2019) but they all have the powerful attention mechanism and some sort of pre-training in common. For the step of fine-tuning on NER the pre-trained encoder is extended by a classifier that predicts a label for each token of the sequence, either one of the class labels (e. g. PER, ORG, LOC) or a label designating tokens outside of named entities.

Like all transformer models, BERT works with tokenised input. Using algorithms like Byte Pair Encoding (BPE) or its variant WordPiece, sequences are split into tokens which do not necessarily correspond to words. Learning how to efficiently splitting text into subword tokens requires the training of a tokenizer with text data. During training the BPE and the WordPiece algorithm both start with a

10 This is the reason why the other special token [CLS] is needed. CLS is short for classification and holds the value that classifies whether the two sentences are either related or unrelated.

set comprising all distinct characters and the training data split into its smallest token size, i. e. into characters. In addition, all characters that occur inside a word are marked, in the case of WordPiece for example with the prefix ##. Then, the BPE algorithm iteratively merges token pairs that occur most frequently in the training data, whereas the WordPiece algorithm merges tokens that maximise the likelihood of the training data. As mentioned before, at the beginning tokens correspond to characters, but with each iteration tokens are merged and their size can get longer until the desired number of tokens is reached. This total number of tokens is also called vocabulary size and is previously defined. In the case of the original BERT model by Devlin et al. (2019) it amounts to 30,000. The second line in example (3) provides a tokenised sentence snippet where the word *Pusch* for instance, is tokenised into the three tokens *P*, *##us* and *##ch*. The advantage of the described tokenization algorithms is that they produce a vocabulary that can be used to encode previously unseen words by combining the appropriate subword tokens.

(3) ... in Leipzig was ... architect Oskar Pusch .

`...` `in` `Leipzig` `was` `...` `architect` `O` `##skar` `P` `##us` `##ch` `.`

2.3 Relevant data formats

The short Wikipedia text of example (2) illustrates what the output of a named entity recognizer looks like. However, if we want to use text data to train or evaluate a NER system, we need a different format. One challenge in NER is to determine where a named entity begins and ends, i. e. which tokens are part of the entity, as white space does not always correspond to the token boundary. If we take a phrase like *“Deutscher Platz”* or *Otto von Bismarck’s portrait* we would need a tokenizer that tokenizes the quotation marks of *“Deutscher Platz”* into separate tokens, and splits *Bismarck’s* into *Bismarck* and *’s*. It is also convenient to work with text that is segmented into sentences, as most NER systems require input in the shape of sentences or at least short paragraphs of text. A format that can handle both is the IOB/BIO tagging scheme. If no IOB annotated data set is available for training a NER system it is necessary to go one step back: If text data needs to be annotated first with a software, it is very probable that the annotation tool provides data export in JSON format only. Therefore, it is useful to take a closer look at both of these two formats. Finally, we will also cover TEI-XML, as it is especially useful for storing annotated data and preserving the annotations in a format well recognised in the fields of literature and linguistics.

2.3.1 IOB/BIO

IOB tags, also referred to as BIO tags, were originally proposed by Ramshaw and Marcus (1995: 87). The acronym IOB stands for inside-outside-beginning. IOB-annotated text is usually stored in text files, sometimes as TSV (tab-separated values) files. Figure 3 shows a text snippet with IOB tags.[11] The first column contains the tokenised text segmented into sentences by blank lines (lines 20 and 33). The second column lists the named entities: O, for outside, means that the token is not part of a named entity; if the tag starts with B, for beginning, it designates the first token belonging to a named entity consisting of more than one token. All following tokens

```
 1 # document_id = Wikipedia_German-National-Library_001
 2 # language = en
 3 The            O
 4 main           O
 5 building       O
 6 of             O
 7 the            O
 8 German         B-ORG
 9 National       I-ORG
10 Library        I-ORG
11 in             O
12 Leipzig        B-LOC
13 was            O
14 ...            ...
15 the            O
16 architect      O
17 Oskar          B-PER
18 Pusch          I-PER
19 .              O
20
21 The            O
22 facade         O
23 ...            ...
24 faces          O
25 the            O
26 "              O
27 Deutscher      B-LOC
28 Platz          I-LOC
29 "              O
30 (              O
31 ...            ...
32 .              O
33
34 The            O
35 ...            ...
```

Figure 3: IOB-tagged, tokenised and sentence segmented text. The line numbering on the left only serves as orientation and is not part of the format.

11 Another nice example of IOB-tagged data is EHRI-NER which was published by the EHRI project presented in the introduction: https://github.com/EHRI/EHRI-NER (accessed 17 January 2025).

of such a multi-token entity are tagged with I, for inside. Additionally, the tags B and I also provide information about the entity class as they are completed with a dash and the class label, e. g. in lines 8–10 in Figure 3. In case of more than one annotation more columns next to the named entity column can be present in the file (e. g. to accommodate POS tags). Columns can be tab-separated or white space-separated. If necessary, it is also possible to add metadata such as an identifier, a description etc. on top of each sentence or on top of a block of sentences (lines 1 and 2). A good convention for comments is to start them with a hash symbol at the beginning of each line to follow the CoNNL format,[12] originally developed for the shared tasks of the Conference on Natural Language Learning (Tjong Kim Sang and De Meulder 2003), and now widely adapted for many NLP tasks. Although for NER the IOB tagging scheme became almost the standard way of tagging, other variants of IOB exist, for example the IOE scheme that indicates the ending of a multi-token entity instead of its beginning as in IOB, or the IOBES scheme that marks the beginning and ending of a multi-token entity as well as entities consisting of only a single token with the S-tag. For a more detailed overview and description of IOB tagging scheme variants refer to Alshammari and Alanazi (2021: 295–296).

During the fine-tuning of a BERT model on the task of NER the input is a sequence tokenised into subwords and, for the task of NER, the output is a sequence of class labels. The third line of example (4) shows the class labels according to the IOB tagging scheme.

(4)	...	in	Leipzig	was	...	architect	Oskar		Pusch			.
	...	in	Leipzig	was	...	architect	O	##skar	P	##us	##ch	.
	...	O	B-LOC	O	...	O	B-PER	I-PER	I-PER	I-PER	I-PER	O

2.3.2 JSON

JSON (short for JavaScript Object Notation) is a standardised file format (ISO/IEC 21778 2017) developed in the early 2000s and is still very important for data interchange, especially the context of web development. It also plays a role for many software applications when it comes to storing or exporting data. Open source text annotation tools like doccano[13] or the NER Annotator[14] for example use JSON as an export format of annotated data sets. The JSON file contains the text alongside a list

12 https://www.clips.uantwerpen.be/conll2003/ner/ (accessed 17 January 2025).

13 https://github.com/doccano/doccano (accessed 20 January 2025).

14 https://github.com/tecoholic/ner-annotator (accessed 20 January 2025).

```
1  {
2      "annotations": [
3          [
4              "The main building of the German National Library in Leipzig was built 1914 after plans of the architect Oskar Pusch.",
5              {
6                  "entities": [
7                      [
8                          25,
9                          48,
10                         "ORG"
11                     ],
12                     [
13                         52,
14                         59,
15                         "LOC"
16                     ],
17                     [
18                         104,
19                         114,
20                         "PER"
21                     ]
22                 ]
23             }
24         ],
25         [
26             "The facade is 160 m long and faces the \"Deutscher Platz\" (German Plaza).",
27             {
28                 "entities": [
29                     [
30                         40,
31                         55,
32                         "LOC"
33                     ]
34                 ]
35             }
36         ]
37     ]
38 }
```

Figure 4: Two sentences tagged with named entities after data export as a JSON file using the tool NER Annotator. The line numbering on the left only serves as orientation and is not part of the format.

of entities that includes the entity class as well as the character counts (e. g. Figure 4, lines 8–9) indicating the start and end position of the entity.

2.3.3 TEI-XML

The Text Encoding Initiative Consortium created guidelines on how to represent textual data in a digital form (TEI Consortium 2024) using the markup language XML. The TEI encoding scheme allows to encode many different aspects of written language; this section focuses on how TEI-XML allows to represent named entities. If the entity classes comprise only person, organization, and place, it is possible to use

```
1  <?xml version="1.0" encoding="UTF-8"?>
2  <TEI xmlns="http://www.tei-c.org/ns/1.0"
3       xml:base="https://example.org" xml:id="example_v1">
4    <teiHeader/>
5  <standOff>
6      <listOrg>
7        <org xml:id="GY001">
8          <orgName>German National Library</orgName>
9        </org>
10     </listOrg>
11     <listPlace>
12       <place xml:id="LG001">
13         <placeName>Leipzig</placeName>
14       </place>
15       <place xml:id="DZ001">
16         <placeName>Deutscher Platz</placeName>
17       </place>
18     </listPlace>
19     <listPerson>
20       <person xml:id="OH001">
21         <persName>Oskar Pusch</persName>
22       </person>
23     </listPerson>
24 </standOff>
25 <text>
26     <body>
27       <p xml:id="para001">
28 The main building of the <orgName ref="#GY001">German National
29 Library</orgName> in <placeName ref="#LG001">Leipzig</placeName> was
30 built 1914-1916 after plans of the architect <persName
31 ref="#OH001">Oskar Pusch</persName>. The facade is 160 m long and
32 faces the "<placeName ref="#DZ001">Deutscher Platz</placeName> …
33       </p>
34     </body>
35   </text>
36 </TEI>
```

Figure 5: TEI-encoded text snippet with in-text references and a stand-off list of the annotated entities. The line numbering on the left only serves as orientation and is not part of the format.

<person>, <persName>, <org>, <orgName>, <place>, and <placeName>, respectively, as shown in Figure 5. The same elements can then be used to list persons, organizations, and places inside the element <standOff> (lines 5–24). Unique identifiers (e. g. line 7) connect the entities in the list to the corresponding in-text references (e. g. line 28).

The additional listing in <standOff> above the text is not mandatory but allows to add more information about each entity, for example, between lines 8 and 9 another an additional tag could be inserted holding the name of the entity in another language, as showed in example (5):

(5) `<orgName xml:lang="de">Deutsche Nationalbibliothek</orgName>`

Ideally, the tag holding the English name is then analogously expanded by `xml:lang="en"`. If more entity classes need to be represented, it advisable to choose a more general element like <name> that should contain a proper noun or noun phrase, or, even more general, the referencing string element <rs>. For the in-text references with <name> and <rs> a type attribute should be present to mark the entity type. The following examples (6) and (7) illustrate possible ways to do that:[15]

(6) ...(near to today's <name type="LOC">**Alte Messe**</name>) had been donated by the <name type="GPE">**city of Leipzig**</name>, while <name type="PER">**Friedrich August III, King of Saxony**</name> provided...

(7) ...(near to today's <rs type="NE_LOC">**Alte Messe**</rs>) had been donated by the <rs type="NE_GPE">**city of Leipzig**</rs>, while <rs type="NE_PER">**Friedrich August III, King of Saxony**</rs> provided...

3 Entity linking

If we read a text, for example about art and it mentions the Mona Lisa, many of us almost immediately have an image in front of our inner eye. Our world knowledge helps us to connect the name Mona Lisa to something we know from the real world: Leonardo da Vinci's painting exhibited in the Louvre Museum in Paris. This process can also be done by a machine; the task is called Entity Linking. But while humans can usually do this linking within an instant, it is not that obvious for computers. Admittedly, Mona Lisa is a rather straightforward example, but imagine a sentence like (8):

(8) Armstrong died in the early seventies...

Who do you think of when hearing the name Armstrong? A person, certainly, and from the context it is possible to know that this person has died already, but unless you have special knowledge about famous people named Armstrong, there are many options. Only the English Wikipedia page about this surname lists over a 140 famous persons with that family name.[16] We can already exclude the astronaut Neil Armstrong who lived until 2012. Louis Armstrong, the US-American trumpeter might be the one referred to in example (8), but this is only an assumption so far. Let's see how the sentence continues:

---

15 For more details, refer to Chapter "14 Names, Dates, People, and Places" of the *TEI P5: Guidelines for Electronic Text Encoding and Interchange*. Version 4.8.1. 2024. TEI Consortium. https://www.tei-c.org/release/doc/tei-p5-doc/en/html/ND.html (accessed 20 January 2025).

16 https://en.wikipedia.org/wiki/Armstrong_(surname) (accessed 23 January 2025).

(9) Armstrong died in the early seventies, the jazz musician was married to Louis Armstrong in her twenties.

Now it is obvious that the person in the text refers to the jazz musician Lillian Hardin Armstrong. With enough background information we were able to disambiguate between the various options.

In the context of NLP, Entity Linking is also known as Named Entity Disambiguation (NED), Named Entity Normalization (NEN) or Named Entity Recognition and Disambiguation (NERD). The latter refers to the whole pipeline including the task of recognizing the entity in the first place. In the context of EL, this first step is sometimes also called mention detection in the literature (Kolitsas et al. 2018, Kawata and Kikui 2019). In addition to context, humans use world knowledge for the disambiguation, machines acquire this knowledge through knowledge graphs. Among the popular knowledge bases for broad domain knowledge are the DBpedia,[17] Wiki-

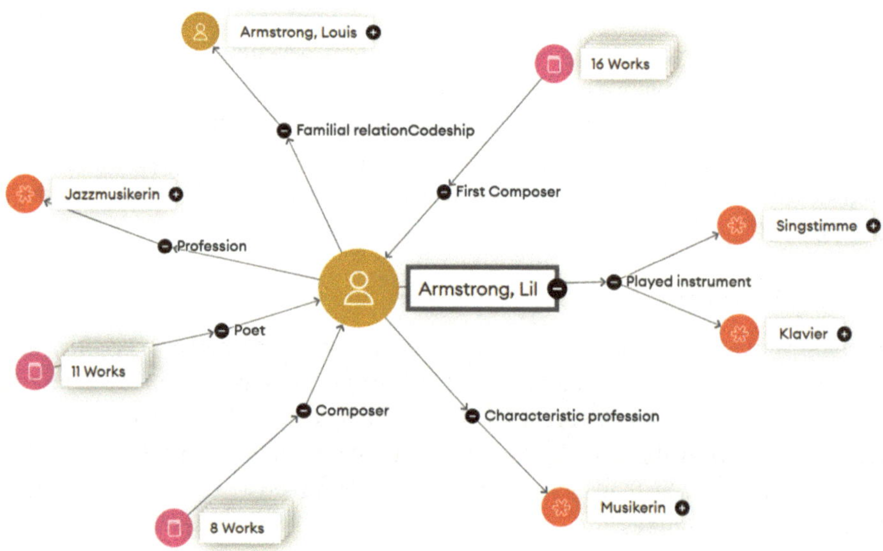

Figure 6: Part of the GND knowledge graph of Lil Armstrong[18]. The round + and – symbols allow to expand or collapse non-terminal nodes and relations to uncover further connections. Arrows indicate the direction in which the relation applies.

17 https://www.dbpedia.org/ (accessed 24 January 2025).

18 https://explore.gnd.network/en/gnd/13459004X/relations (accessed 24 January 2025).

data,[19] and GND[20] knowledge graphs (see Khan 2025). As illustrated in Figure 6 the nodes of a knowledge graph correspond to real world entities that are connected via named edges representing the relation between entities. For example, the central node for *Lil Armstrong* connected with the relation *Profession* to the node *Jazzmusikerin* is read as: Lil Armstrong has as a profession jazz musician. The relation between *Lil Armstrong* and *8 Works* via the *Composer* relation is directed towards Lil Armstrong, and is therefore read as: 8 works have as a composer Lil Armstrong, etc. Figure 6 shows the entities' labels (e. g. Armstrong, Lil), but in a knowledge base all entities also have a unique identifier. Wikidata for example calls these identifiers Q-identifiers and in the GND knowledge graph they are called GND IDs.

3.1 State-of-the-art EL systems

Systems that tackle the task of Named Entity Linking break down the problem into several subtasks. At first, NER is used to detect named entities, followed by the generation of candidate entities in a knowledge base, often in the shape of a knowledge graph. Finally, the subtask of candidate disambiguation is responsible for selecting the correct entity out of the list of candidates.

One of the major challenges of Entity Linking is to figure out when an entity mention does not have a corresponding entry in a knowledge base.[21] These unlinkable mentions are marked with the label NIL (not in lexicon). This is related to another difficulty that lies in the variation of names for an entity (Shen et al. 2015). The number of different surface forms for a single entity can be high, e. g. for Lil Armstrong (shown in Figure 6) aliases like Lilian Armstrong, L. H. Armstrong, only the first name, only the last name, etc. might be used in a text. Furthermore, mentions like the denomination *jazz musician* or *she* can also refer to the entity, and it depends on whether the NER system tags these kind of coreferences as named entities (refer to Section 2.1: Entity classes). Purely statistical approaches like the entity linker TAGME (Ferragina and Scaiella 2011) and other similar systems date fifteen to twenty years back, but just like NER, later entity linking systems are now often based

19 https://www.wikidata.org/ (accessed 24 January 2025).

20 GND (Gemeinsame Normadatei) are the authority files provided by the German National Library, the knowledge graph is browsable via https://explore.gnd.network/en/ (accessed 24 January 2025).

21 When we talk about entity linking in this chapter, we explicitly refer to the linking to external knowledge bases and want to clearly distinguish from entity coreference resolution where entity mentions *within* a text are linked with each other.

on neural approaches. The models encode the entities, the selected candidates, and the context of the mention and they work with vectorised representations, for example with a BERT encoder (refer to Section 2.2: State-of-the-art NER systems). The most successful type are entity linkers that keep the process of mention detection separate from entity disambiguation (Sevgili et al. 2022, see Figure 7).

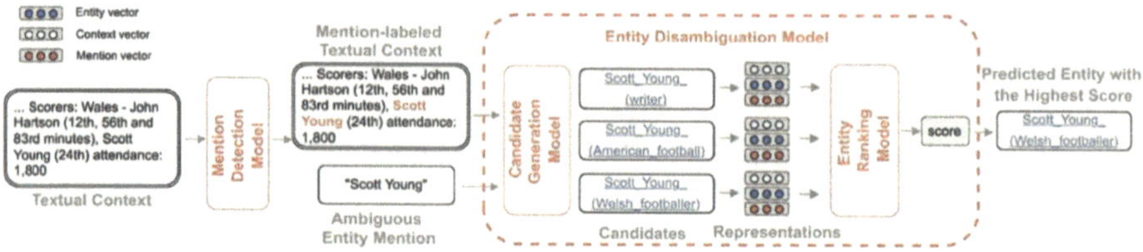

Figure 7: General architecture of neural entity linking systems, adapted from Sevgili et al. (2022).

For the generation of candidate entities many architectures use methods like the prior probability of a term, surface form matching, i. e. string matches between the entity as it is mentioned in the text and in the knowledge base, and expansions of a mention by using aliases of a mention found in a knowledge base or in a constructed dictionary of synonyms. The ranking of the candidates is then usually computed by a similarity measure like the dot product of the vector representations of the mention and the candidates. A probability distribution over the selected candidates then determines the final ranking. Sometimes the prior probabilities obtained during the candidate generation are additionally taken into account during the ranking process (Sevgili et al. 2022). Among the most well performing systems is such a neural architecture by Mulang' et al. (2020) who encode not only the entity mention and its context but also the textual information from triples retrieved from Wikidata (see Khan 2025). Another state-of-the-art entity linking system is DeepType (Raiman and Raiman 2018), as well as a neural approach that incorporates the entity type, e. g. person or place, retrieved from the nodes and edges of a knowledge graph, into the training data. This eliminates many candidates for ambiguous terms. For a mention like Washington, if the model can grasp that the entity type is person, then places like Washington D. C. etc. can be removed from the candidate list.

3.2 Incorporating entity links into the relevant data formats

3.2.1 IOB/BIO

The easiest way to incorporate entity links in a data set is to expand the IOB format. This can simply be done by adding an extra column that holds the links or the

```
# document_id = Wikipedia_German-National-Library_001
# language = en
...         ...       ...       ...
the         O         -         -
German      B-ORG     Q27302    10140798-1
National    I-ORG     Q27302    10140798-1
Library     I-ORG     Q27302    10140798-1
in          O         -         -
Leipzig     B-LOC     Q2079     4035206-7
...         ...       ...       ...
```

Figure 8: Excerpt of an IOB annotated data set including Wikidata Q-identifiers and GND IDs.

corresponding identifiers. Figure 8 illustrates an extension of parts of the data of Figure 3. The last two columns contain the Wikidata Q-identifiers and the GND IDs pointing to the respective entities. For the German National Library the Wikidata link resolves to the URL https://www.wikidata.org/wiki/Q27302, and the link to the GND has the following URL: https://d-nb.info/gnd/10140798-1. For a more extensive insight into an entity link annotated data set refer to the shared task HIPE (Identifying Historical People, Places and other Entities) in 2020 (Ehrmann et al. 2020) and 2022 (Ehrmann et al. 2022). They released a data set[22] of historical newspaper texts in English, German, and French annotated with Wikidata Q-identifiers for the subtask of entity linking.

3.2.2 TEI-XML

In addition to write down named entities, TEI also provides a way to encode entity links. The lists inside the element <standOff> containing persons, organizations and places can also hold entity links. Example (10) shows a <person> element as it was already present in Figure 5, but it now also has the attribute *sameAs*. The value of this attribute is a space-separated string with the links to the items in the respective knowledge bases.

(10)

```
<listPerson>
 <person xml:id="OH001" sameAs="https://d-nb.info/gnd/116313722
     https://www.wikidata.org/wiki/Q2033923">
  <persName>Oskar Pusch</persName>
 </person>
</listPerson>
```

22 https://github.com/hipe-eval/HIPE-2022-data/blob/main/README.md (accessed 27 January 2025).

```
...
<persName ref="#OH001" sameAs="https://d-nb.info/gnd/116313722
 https://www.wikidata.org/wiki/Q2033923">Oskar Pusch</persName>
```

If we would like to encode the entity links following the examples (6) and (7) we can use the additional attribute sameAs just like in (10) within the tags <name> or <rs> as illustrated in the following two examples:

(11)
```
<name type="LOC"
 sameAs="https://www.wikidata.org/wiki/Q99737336">Alte Messe</name>
```

(12)
```
<rs type="NE_LOC"
 sameAs="https://www.wikidata.org/wiki/Q99737336">Alte Messe</rs>
```

The advantage of encoding entity annotations within TEI is that one file contains all the information. However, if the textual data in the TEI-XML file underlies any copyright restrictions and cannot be shared easily, it might be worth to consider putting entity links together with the catalogue metadata, i. e. in a usually separate metadata file containing for example information about the author, data provenance, data size, access rights, etc. Although the exact reference to where the entity is found inside a text will be lost, the benefit of linking text resources to publicly available knowledge bases outweighs this drawback. Ways of enriching a corpus with such a stand-off annotation are thoroughly discussed in Ecker et al. (2024).

4 Applying NER and EL

This section wants to provide some guidance on how to start with NER and/or EL when having a raw data set at hand. Text data should be available in a digitised form, at best in a text file format such as TXT, TSV (tab-separated values), CSV (comma-separated values), etc. If the goal is to do entity linking it is still useful to read through the NER part, too, as Entity Linkers often do not include NER but rely on separate named entity recognizers or data where named entities are already tagged.

4.1 NER

The first questions to ask before using a NER system are: What kind of data do I have and what kind of named entities do I want to tag in my data? The following factors may play a role when selecting an adequate NER system:

i. *Language*: What language does the text have? Is it mono- or multilingual?
ii. *Domain*: Does the data rather belong to a broad domain such as newspaper articles, or is it a specific domain such as law or medical texts?
iii. *Register*: Is the language rather formal like in scientific reports or political speeches, does it have a more colloquial character as in social media comments, or is it maybe a historical text, e. g. literature of a certain literary period?
iv. *Entity types* to be tagged (and linked)?

When all these points are clarified the next step is to find out whether a corresponding NER model is readily available to do NER or whether it will be necessary to train a custom named entity recognizer specifically for one's own use case. Especially for academic use, there are many NER models out there:
- The *CLARIN website* hosts a list of available NER systems for many languages,[23] together with a short description.
- Another useful tool resource is *WebLicht*[24] offering models for mostly German data, but also English, Dutch, and Spanish.
- Also the commercially oriented initiative *Huggingface*[25] provides open source models that can be uploaded to the platform by anyone. Therefore, the list of models is long and a careful selection is necessary, but it is definitely worth to filter the website's model section for the NLP task of Token Classification and check the properties of eligible models.

Other very useful NLP platforms, tool sets or frameworks are:
- NLTK (Bird et al. 2009);
- Apache OpenNLP;[26]
- GATE (Cunningham et al. 2013);
- SpaCy (Honnibal et al. 2020);
- flair (Akbik et al. 2019);
- Software from the Stanford NLP group.[27]

23 https://www.clarin.eu/resource-families/tools-named-entity-recognition (accessed 30 January 2025).

24 https://weblicht.sfs.uni-tuebingen.de/weblichtwiki/Tools_in_Detail.html#named-entity-recognition (accessed 30 January 2025).

25 https://huggingface.co/models?pipeline_tag=token-classification (accessed 30 January 2025).

26 https://opennlp.apache.org/ (accessed 30 January 2025).

27 https://nlp.stanford.edu/software/ (accessed 30 January 2025).

It is also always useful to check on the model's architecture: the Stanford NLP group for example, offers rule based NER models[28] as well as others based on classical machine learning architectures,[29] and neural models with their Stanza (Qi et al. 2020)[30] framework. For a detailed overview refer to the survey papers of Jehangir et al. (2023) and Keraghel et al. (2024).

Depending on the use case, there are mainly two paths that allow you to apply NER to your data (see Table 2).

Table 2: Steps to consider on the way to applying NER.

	Use existing NER model	**Train custom NER model**[a]
Model selection	Make sure that the model properties fit your data (i. e. the data which the model was trained on should be similar to the data in the use case), and that the model is able to tag the types of entities the use case requires.	Select the model trained on data closest to your use case in order to fine-tune it.
Data preparation	If several models are on the short-list, create a gold-standard annotated test sample from the data and compare the results (refer to Section 4.4: Evaluation).	A model architecture like any type of BERT model uses supervised training which means that labelled training data is required. See if you can find an existing data set suitable to the use case. If not, it will be necessary to label your own data set[b] and split it into a training, development and test set.
Model usage / Model training	Select the appropriate way for you to make use of the model: Some models are embedded into a (web) user interface, others need to be called via API or downloaded and installed as a package in Python, etc.	Select an appropriate toolkit or framework that allows you to train or fine-tune the model. Evaluate it against the held out test set and apply it to further not yet annotated parts of your data.

[a]While other rule-based or older neural approaches might be interesting as well, we concentrate on models of the encoder architectures described in Section 2.2: State-of-the-art NER systems.
[b]Refer to Section 2.3: Relevant data formats.

28 https://nlp.stanford.edu/software/regexner.html (accessed 30 January 2025).
29 https://nlp.stanford.edu/software/CRF-NER.html (accessed 30 January 2025).
30 https://stanfordnlp.github.io/stanza/ner.html (accessed 30 January 2025).

4.2 EL

While for EL the range of possibilities is not as abundant as for NER, there are still many options to choose from. Guellil et al. (2024) list and compare many tools and frameworks as well as models for entity linking. They distinguish in their survey paper between disambiguation models only vs. models capable of joint entity recognition and linking. However, it is much more challenging to find a pre-trained entity linker than a readily available NER model due to the many properties that need to be predefined: the knowledge base to link to, the type of entities that it should resolve to, and finally the training data on which a model should be trained. Many broad domain entity linking systems tend to use Wikipedia or Wikidata (e. g. OpenTapioca[31] (Delpeuch 2019), or the multilingual end-to-end entity linker mGENRE[32] (De Cao et al. 2022)) but if the use case at hand requires to link to a custom data base it will obviously be necessary to train a model yourself, for example with the SpaCy framework.[33] When searching for entity link annotated data for model training the availability of existing data sets is similarly sparse as it is for EL models. Among the bigger data sets are Linked WikiText-2 (Logan et al. 2019) containing English text from Wikipedia with named entities linked to Wikidata Q-IDs, the AIDA CoNLL-YAGO data set (Hoffart et al. 2011) of newswire articles with links to the YAGO 2 knowledge base (Hoffart et al. 2013) or the DBpedia Abstract corpus (Brümmer et al. 2016) linking to DBpedia. While some of them are multilingual, most of the data is in English; this is as well reflected by the survey of Guellil et al. (2024). Another multilingual data set not mentioned there, is the data from the shared task HIPE[34] providing historical newspaper texts annotated with Wikidata Q-IDs in German, French, and English (Ehrmann et al. 2022). Just as for NER, for EL it might be useful to make a small comparison between available EL systems before selecting one, these data sets can be useful if no sample from one's own data is to be annotated. However, if it becomes necessary to annotate data it is worth to follow clear annotation guidelines[35] and take a look at annotation tools like brat[36] or tagtog.[37]

---

31 https://github.com/opentapioca/opentapioca (accessed 31 January 2025).

32 https://github.com/facebookresearch/GENRE (accessed 31 January 2025).

33 https://spacy.io/usage/linguistic-features#entity-linking (accessed 31 January 2025).

34 https://zenodo.org/records/6375600 (accessed 31 January 2025).

35 Possibly inspired by https://github.com/ad-freiburg/entity-linking-annotation-guidelines (accessed 31 January 2025).

36 https://github.com/nlplab/brat or https://brat.nlplab.org/normalization.html (accessed 31 January 2025).

37 https://github.com/tagtog or https://docs.tagtog.com/ (accessed 31 January 2025).

4.3 Using large language models for annotation

Since the emergence of large language models like GPT (Generative Pre-trained Transformers), they are applied to all kinds of tasks in NLP, of course also to NER and EL. To annotate named entities in data, the most straightforward way to use LLMs is to provide a system prompt which gives the LLM the instructions to solve a task, and some examples in the shape of annotated sequences of text. The number of examples depends on the approach using zero-, one- or few-shot prompting. In their survey on recent advances in NER, Keraghel et al. (2024) give an overview of several LLM-based approaches. When doing entity linking with a generative LLM, in addition to prompting it is necessary to make the database to be linked somehow available to the model. The technique to enhance a model's knowledge is called retrieval augmented generation (RAG) and is used for EL for example by Shlyk et al. (2024). In contrast, Liu et al. (2024) introduce an approach where LLMs only come into play for entity disambiguation which is *after* the step of candidate selection from a knowledge base. While LLM-based EL requires prompting a model several times during disambiguation, and prompt engineering can be time consuming, the advantage of working with LLMs is that there is no need for an annotated data set.

4.4 Evaluation

The usual way of evaluating NER systems is to compute precision, recall, and their harmonic mean, the F1-score. To count true positives, false positives, and false negatives when comparing the model predictions to the gold-standard annotation, three scenarios can occur: the string of the entity mention and the entity class matches the gold-standard, the model hypothesises an entity where there is none, or it misses to tag an entity. While this is enough to compute the above mentioned scores, some scenarios are ignored: the NER model could as well recognize the entity but assign the wrong class, it could predict the wrong entity boundaries (e. g. only detecting *Oskar* as a person instead of *Oskar Pusch* in example (4)) or the wrong prediction of both, entity class and entity boundaries.[38] While the evaluation of the CoNLL-2003 Shared Task for NER follows the simpler evaluation scheme, the metrics used for the Fifth Message Understanding Conference (Chinchor and Sundheim 1993) and the International Workshop on Semantic Evaluation, SemEval 2013 (Segura-Bedmar et al. 2013) follow a more fine-grained evaluation. For NER systems, an evaluation is often done per class type. Micro- or macro-averaged F1-scores then help to obtain a

---

38 This blog post nicely explains the scenarios in further detail including examples: https://www.davidsbatista.net/blog/2018/05/09/Named_Entity_Evaluation/ (accessed 31 January 2025).

score over all class types. The macro-averaged F1-score first computes the individual per-class F1 score and then takes averages which is why it is not recommended for an imbalanced class scenario as it assumes an equal contribution of each class. For imbalanced class distribution it is better to make use of the micro-average that computes a single F1-score by aggregating all true positives, false positives, and false negatives. The evaluation using the F1-score for entity disambiguation models is simpler as the step of NER is not part of the evaluation and therefore the problem of recognizing the entity boundaries becomes irrelevant. A framework used for the evaluation of EL systems is the general linked data benchmarking system GERBIL (Röder et al. 2018) with the GERBIL platform.[39]

5 Conclusion

Named Entity Recognition and Entity Linking are essential tasks in Natural Language Processing that enable the extraction and disambiguation of named entities in text data. This chapter provides an overview of NER and EL, including their tasks, techniques, relevant data formats, and applications. State-of-the-art NER systems, such as those based on transformer architectures like BERT, have achieved high performance in identifying and labelling named entities. Entity Linking systems aim to link these entities to external knowledge bases, providing additional context and information. The chapter also discusses the incorporation of named entities and entity links into relevant data formats, such as JSON, IOB/BIO, and TEI-XML, provides guidance on selecting suitable models, preparing data, evaluating system performance, and touches on the use of large language models for entity annotation and linking. Although both, NER and especially Entity Linking are nontrivial tasks, the effective application of NER and EL can lead to improved text analysis and information retrieval, with numerous use cases in areas such as digital humanities, enabling researchers and practitioners to extract valuable insights from text data.

Bibliography

Akbik, Alan, Tanja Bergmann, Duncan Blythe, Kashif Rasul, Stefan Schweter & Roland Vollgraf. 2019. FLAIR: An easy-to-use framework for state-of-the-art NLP. In *Proceedings of the 2019 Conference of the North American Chapter of the Association for Computational Linguistics (Demonstrations)*, 54–59. Minneapolis, Minnesota: Association for Computational Linguistics.

39 https://gerbil.aksw.org/gerbil/ (accessed 31 January 2025).

Alshammari, Nasser & Saad Alanazi. 2021. The impact of using different annotation schemes on named entity recognition. *Egyptian Informatics Journal* 22(3). 295–302.

Aufrant, Lauriane & Lucie Chasseur. 2024. UkraiNER: A new corpus and annotation scheme towards comprehensive entity recognition. In *Proceedings of the 2024 Joint International Conference on Computational Linguistics, Language Resources and Evaluation (LREC-COLING 2024)*. 16941–16952. Torino, Italia: ELRA and ICCL.

Bahdanau, Dzmitry, Kyunghyun Cho & Yoshua Bengio. 2014. Neural machine translation by jointly learning to align and translate. arXiv preprint arXiv:1409.0473 (accessed 03 February 2025).

Bird, Steven, Edward Loper & Ewan Klein. 2009. *Natural language processing with python: Analyzing text with the natural language toolkit*. O'Reilly Media Inc (Place is missing).

Brümmer, Martin, Milan Dojchinovski & Sebastian Hellmann. 2016. DBpedia abstracts: A large-scale, open, multilingual NLP training corpus. In *Proceedings of the Tenth International Conference on Language Resources and Evaluation (LREC'16)*, 3339–3343. Portorož, Slovenia: European Language Resources Association (ELRA).

Chinchor, Nancy & Beth Sundheim. 1993. MUC-5 evaluation metrics. In *Fifth message understanding conference (MUC-5)*, Baltimore, Maryland, August, 25–27.

Cunningham, Hamish, Valentin Tablan, Angus Roberts & Kalina Bontcheva. 2013. Getting more out of biomedical documents with GATE's full lifecycle open source text analytics. *PLOS Computational Biology* 9(2):e1002854.

De Cao, Nicola, Ledell Wu, Kashyap Popat, Mikel Artetxe, Naman Goyal, Mikhail Plekhanov, Luke Zettlemoyer, Nicola Cancedda, Sebastian Riedel & Fabio Petroni. 2022. Multilingual autoregressive entity linking. *Transactions of the Association for Computational Linguistics* 10. 274–290.

de Leeuw, Daan, Mike Bryant, Michal Frankl, Ivelina Nikolova & Vladimir Alexiev. 2018. Digital methods in Holocaust studies: The European Holocaust research infrastructure. In *2018 IEEE 14th international conference on e-science (e-science)*, 58–66.

Delpeuch, Antonin. 2019. Opentapioca: Lightweight entity linking for Wikidata. arXiv preprint arXiv: 1904.09131 (accessed 03 February 2025).

Devlin, Jacob, Ming-Wei Chang, Kenton Lee & Kristina Toutanova. 2019. BERT: Pre-training of deep bidirectional transformers for language understanding. In *Proceedings of the 2019 conference of the North American Chapter of the Association for Computational Linguistics: Human language technologies*, Vol. 1, 4171–4186. Minneapolis, Minnesota: Association for Computational Linguistics.

Ecker, Jennifer, Stefan Fischer, Pia Schwarz, Thorsten Trippel, Antonina Werthmann & Rebecca Wilm. 2024. Unlocking the corpus: Enriching metadata with state-of-the-art NLP methodology and linked data. In *CLARIN annual conference proceedings 2024*, 15–17 October, Barcelona, Spain, 181–184. Utrecht: CLARIN.

Ehrmann, Maud, Matteo Romanello, Alex Flückiger & Simon Clematide. 2020. Extended overview of CLEF HIPE 2020: Named entity processing on historical newspapers. In *Working notes of CLEF 2020 – Conference and labs of the evaluation forum*, Thessaloniki, Greece, 22–25 September. CEUR-WS.

Ehrmann, Maud, Matteo Romanello, Sven Najem-Meyer, Antoine Doucet & Simon Clematide. 2022. Overview of HIPE-2022: Named entity recognition and linking in multilingual historical documents. In *Experimental IR meets multilinguality, multimodality, and interaction: Proceedings of the 13th international conference of the CLEF Association, CLEF 2022*, Bologna, Italy, 5–8 September, 423–446. Berlin, Heidelberg: Springer-Verlag.

Guellil, Imane, Antonio Garcia-Dominguez, Peter R. Lewis, Shakeel Hussain & Geoffrey Smith. 2024. Entity linking for English and other languages: A survey. *Knowledge and Information Systems* 66. 3773–3824.

Hoffart, Johannes, Fabian M. Suchanek, Klaus Berberich & Gerhard Weikum. 2013. YAGO2: A spatially and temporally enhanced knowledge base from Wikipedia journal article. *Artificial Intelligence Journal* 194(C). 28–61.

Hoffart, Johannes, Mohamed Amir Yosef, Ilaria Bordino, Hagen Fürstenau, Manfred Pinkal, Marc Spaniol, Bilyana Taneva, Stefan Thater & Gerhard Weikum. 2011. Robust disambiguation of named entities in text. In *Proceedings of the 2011 conference on empirical methods in natural language processing*, 782–792. Edinburgh, Scotland, UK: Association for Computational Linguistics.

Honnibal, Matthew, Ines Montani, Sofie Van Landeghem & Adriane Boyd. 2020. SpaCy: Industrial-strength natural language processing in Python. Zenodo (online). https://doi.org/10.5281/zenodo.1212303 (accessed 03 February 2025).

ISO/IEC 21778. 2017. *Information technology – The JSON data interchange syntax*. International Standard, International Organization for Standardization (ISO), Geneva.

Jansen, Leo, Hans Luijten & Nienke Bakker (eds.). 2009. *Vincent van Gogh – The letters*. Amsterdam & The Hague: Van Gogh Museum & Huygens ING. https://vangoghletters.org (accessed 10 January 2025).

Jehangir, Basra, Saravanan Radhakrishnan & Rahul Agarwal. 2023. A survey on named entity recognition – Datasets, tools, and methodologies. *Natural Language Processing Journal* 3:100017.

Jurafsky, Daniel & James H. Martin. 2025. Sequence labeling for parts of speech and named entities. In *Speech and language processing: An introduction to natural language processing, computational linguistics, and speech recognition with language models*, 3rd edn. Online manuscript released January 12, 2025. https://web.stanford.edu/~jurafsky/slp3 (accessed 13 January 2025).

Kawata, Naotaka & Genichiro Kikui. 2019. Mention detection method for entity linking. In *IEEE international conference on big data, cloud computing, data science & engineering (BCD)*, Honolulu, HI, USA, 41–45.

Keraghel, Imed, Stanislas Morbieu & Mohamed Nadif. 2024. A survey on recent advances in named entity recognition. arXiv preprint arXiv:2401.10825 (accessed 03 February 2025).

Khan, Anas Fahad. 2025. Linguistic linked (open) data. In Piotr Bański, Ulrich Heid & Laura Herzberg (eds.), *Harmonising language data: Standards for linguistic resources*. Berlin: De Gruyter.

Kolitsas, Nikolaos, Octavian-Eugen Ganea & Thomas Hofmann. 2018. End-to-end neural entity linking. In *Proceedings of the 22nd conference on computational natural language learning*, 519–529. Brussels, Belgium: Association for Computational Linguistics.

Liu, Xukai, Ye Liu, Kai Zhang, Kehang Wang, Qi Liu & Enhong Chen. 2024. OneNet: A fine-tuning free framework for few-shot entity linking via large language model prompting. In *Proceedings of the 2024 conference on empirical methods in natural language processing*, 13634–13651. Miami, Florida, USA: Association for Computational Linguistics.

Liu, Yinhan, Myle Ott, Naman Goyal, Jingfei Du, Mandar Joshi, Danqi Chen, Omer Levy, Mike Lewis, Luke Zettlemoyer & Veselin Stoyanov. 2019. RoBERTa: A robustly optimised BERT pretraining approach. arXiv preprint arXiv:1907.11692 (accessed 03 February 2025).

Ljubešić, Nikola & Tomaž Erjavec. 2025. Part-of-speech tagging and related annotation. In Piotr Bański, Ulrich Heid & Laura Herzberg (eds.), *Harmonising language data: Standards for linguistic resources*. Berlin: De Gruyter.

Logan, Robert, Nelson F. Liu, Matthew E. Peters, Matt Gardner & Sameer Singh. 2019. Barack's wife Hillary: Using knowledge graphs for fact-aware language modeling. In *Proceedings of the 57th annual meeting of the Association for Computational Linguistics*, 5962–5971. Florence, Italy: Association for Computational Linguistics.

Mulang', Isaiah Onando, Kuldeep Singh, Chaitali Prabhu, Abhishek Nadgeri, Johannes Hoffart & Jens Lehmann. 2020. Evaluating the impact of knowledge graph context on entity disambiguation models. In *Proceedings of the 29th ACM international conference on information & knowledge management, CIKM'20*, 2157–2160. New York, NY, USA: Association for Computing Machinery.

Nadeau, David & Satoshi Sekine. 2007. A survey of named entity recognition and classification. *Lingvisticae Investigationes* 30. 3–26.

Qi, Peng, Yuhao Zhang, Yuhui Zhang, Jason Bolton & Christopher D. Manning. 2020. Stanza: A Python natural language processing toolkit for many human languages. In *Proceedings of the 58th annual meeting of the Association for Computational Linguistics: System demonstrations*, 101–108. Association for Computational Linguistics.

Raiman, Jonathan & Olivier Raiman. 2018. Deeptype: multilingual entity linking by neural type system evolution. In *Proceedings of the AAAI conference on artificial intelligence*, Vol. 32, 5406–5413.

Ramshaw, Lance & Mitch Marcus. 1995. Text chunking using transformation-based learning. In *Third workshop on very large corpora*, 82–94. Association for Computational Linguistics.

Rau, L. F. 1991. Extracting company names from text. In *The seventh ieee conference on artificial intelligence application*, 29–32. Beach, FL, USA: Miami.

Röder, Michael, Ricardo Usbeck & Axel-Cyrille Ngonga Ngomo. 2018. Gerbil – Benchmarking named entity recognition and linking consistently. *Semantic Web* 9(5). 605–625.

Sanh, Victor, Lysandre Debut, Julien Chaumond & Thomas Wolf. 2019. DistilBERT, a distilled version of BERT: Smaller, faster, cheaper and lighter. arXiv preprint arXiv:1910.01108 (accessed 04 February 2025).

Segura-Bedmar, Isabel, Paloma Martínez & María Herrero-Zazo. 2013. SemEval-2013 Task 9: Extraction of drug-drug interactions from biomedical texts (DDIExtraction 2013). In *Second joint conference on lexical and computational semantics (*SEM), volume 2: Proceedings of the seventh international workshop on semantic evaluation (SemEval 2013)*, 341–350. Association for Computational Linguistics.

Sevgili, Özgea, Artem Shelmanov, Mikhaile Arkhipov, Alexander Panchenko & Chris Biemann. 2022. Neural entity linking: A survey of models based on deep learning. *Semantic Web* 13(3). 527–570.

Shen, Wie, Jianyong Wang & Jiawei Han. 2015. Entity linking with a knowledge base: Issues, techniques, and solutions. *IEEE Transactions on Knowledge and Data Engineering* 27(2). 443–460.

Shlyk, Darya, Tudor Groza, Marco Mesiti, Stefano Montanelli & Emanuele Cavalleri. 2024. REAL: A retrieval-qugmented entity linking approach for biomedical concept recognition. In *Proceedings of the 23rd workshop on biomedical natural language processing*, 380–389. Bangkok, Thailand: Association for Computational Linguistics.

TEI Consortium. 2024. iv. About these guidelines. *TEI P5: Guidelines for electronic text encoding and interchange*. Version 4.8.1. 2024. TEI Consortium. https://tei-c.org/release/doc/tei-p5-doc/en/html/AB.html (accessed 20 January 2025).

Tjong Kim Sang Erik F. & Fien De Meulder. 2003. Introduction to the CoNLL-2003 shared task: Language-independent named entity recognition. In *Proceedings of the seventh conference on natural language learning at HLT-NAACL*, 142–147.

Vaswani, Ashish, Noam Shazeer, Niki Parmar, Jakob Uszkoreit, Llion Jones, Aidan N. Gomez, Łukasz Kaiser & Illia Polosukhin. 2017. Attention is all you need. In *Advances in neural information processing systems*, Vol. 30.

Vera Ferreira, Hanna Hedeland, and Kelsey Neely

Annotated audiovisual language data: data quality and data maturity

Abstract: This chapter gives an overview of different aspects of data quality and data maturity for annotated audiovisual data. It provides updated recommendations for audiovisual and derived formats and a more general discussion about quality and other relevant criteria, such as FAIRness, for annotated audiovisual language data and qualitative data in general. The recommendations provide guidance on source data, annotations, lexical resources, and metadata. Particular attention is given to the topic of audio and video specifications and the use of human- and machine-readable formats for annotations, metadata and other written resources. The recommendations are accompanied by concise explanations of relevant terms and concepts with the goal of empowering the reader to make informed decisions about which formats and tools are most appropriate to their research goals and project context.

Keywords: audiovisual collections, data formats, best practices, annotation, FAIR

1 Background

Annotated audiovisual data is the empirical basis for various types of research in linguistics, related fields, and non-related fields that rely on content and knowledge captured in this form. While the main aim of this chapter is to provide current best practice recommendations for file formats, configurations and conventions in a format suitable as a reference guide, we also want to provide background and context knowledge – on the one hand to make it easier to understand the reasoning behind these recommendations and on the other hand to allow for the assessment of future or less well-known formats, conventions and tools on the basis of more general principles. To begin with, we introduce some relevant concepts and terminology.

Vera Ferreira, Hanna Hedeland, Kelsey Neely, Berlin-Brandenburg Academy of Sciences and Humanities, Jägerstraße 22/23, 10117 Berlin, Germany, e-mails: vera.ferreira@bbaw.de, hanna.hedeland@bbaw.de, kelsey.neely@bbaw.de

https://doi.org/10.1515/9783112208212-006

1.1 Annotated audiovisual language data

This chapter has a rather narrow scope in that it only considers compiled and enriched sets of materials based on audiovisual recordings. Still, this is a very heterogeneous group of resources due to differences in content, research methods and specific research questions. These differences influence both the overall design of the resources and specific choices regarding file formats and annotation systems and conventions. These choices, in turn, determine to what extent the resources lend themselves to automatic/quantitative approaches. This is an important aspect of the aforementioned heterogeneity, as not all resources are in structured formats with different kinds of information explicitly encoded, and annotation is not necessarily applied systematically across the whole resource.

Resources belonging to this group are often referred to as "collections" or "corpora", but since there are no universal definitions or a widely accepted taxonomy of the resource group, it is not clear what to expect from a "learner corpus" or a "language documentation collection" beyond the content-related aspects (language acquisition vs. endangered languages). There is also little consensus on whether the use of terms such as "collection" or "corpus" implies specific types of resources, or resources with specific characteristics, and it seems that the preference for one term or the usage and contrasting of both sometimes mainly depends on the geographical location, or on the research tradition or community. As an example, while a distinction between "collections" and "corpora", as suggested by Jane Simpson and reported by Thieberger (2018), is often used within the field of language documentation (e. g., Sullivant 2020) for resources that have been prepared or curated to different extent, the best practice recommendations for language corpora of the German Research Foundation (DFG 104 2019) use another terminology. Here, the wide definition of "oral corpora" includes the entire spectrum from consistent, interlinked, aligned and fully transcribed datasets to sets of recordings in which only a few have accompanying (partial) transcripts (DFG 104 2019: 4). While we acknowledge that a distinction between collections and corpora is often made, which could maybe be simplified as browsable vs. queryable language resources, we will refrain from any existing or novel definitions in this chapter and instead refer to the various types of resources as "annotated audiovisual language data" as we begin with a description of their main characteristics.

Annotated audiovisual language data is a complex language resource type that comprises different data types and various types of relations between these. Figure 1 shows a typical resource with primary data (recordings, transcription/annotation files, other relevant materials), abstract objects such as (recording) sessions, participants and the resource itself, and metadata describing the various parts. Whether and how all of the contained information is available for analysis depends on the

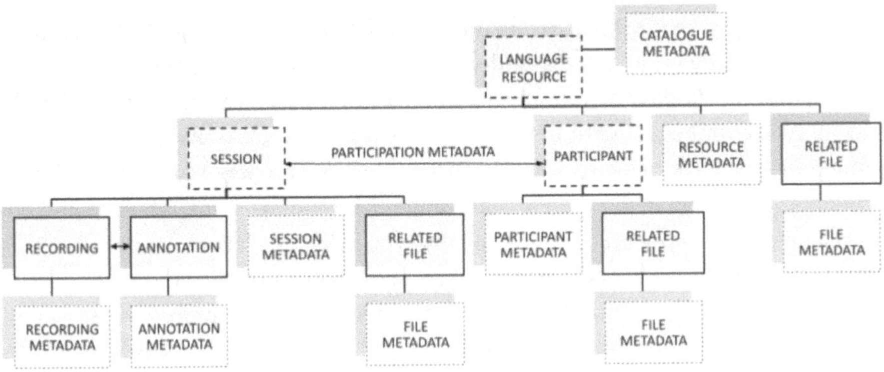

Figure 1: Annotated audiovisual language data.

choices described above, ranging from recording techniques and file formats to theoretical frameworks implemented as annotation schemas.

The description of the contents of the resource using metadata is also an important dimension along which resources differ. Depending on the metadata conventions, for example, there are differences regarding whether participants are treated as independent entities or as part of the description of a recording. Resources also differ regarding on which basis the original recorded materials are grouped into the next level units below the main resource, such as (recording) sessions, (file) bundles or (speech or communicative) events. While metadata formats usually provide this hierarchical structure, the semantics of these units are however usually not defined by the metadata conventions (cf. Hedeland 2021). A crucial aspect for the querying of annotated audiovisual language data has been left out in this figure – the potential linking of metadata on the (recording) session and participants to the actual language data inside recording and annotation files.

1.2 Data quality and data maturity

Today, researchers have access to digital infrastructures for archiving, distribution and reuse of research data. Funders increasingly not only expect researchers to make use of these possibilities to archive research data, but also to do it according to best practices in terms of data quality and other relevant requirements (RfII 2020, BMBF 2018). The FAIR principles (Wilkinson et al. 2016) have become widely accepted as requirements for research data and are now part of the code of conduct "Guidelines for Safeguarding Good Research Practice" of the German Research Foundation (DFG 2019: 17). The FAIR principles are related to different dimensions of data quality, most of which are not intrinsic (cf. Wang and Strong 1996). For example, the findability (F) and accessibility (A) principles are rather related to how the data is made available, which is something the individual researcher can only partly and indirectly influence with the choice of a suitable archive or repository. At the same time, the FAIR principles are generic in nature and how to implement these principles to comply with funders' requirements has not been fully defined and operationalised for many areas, including the type of research data described in this paper. As a consequence, the use of the FAIR principles as requirements relevant to researchers applying for funding without the necessary definitions or assessment methods in place in the disciplines have received criticism (Wilkinson et al. 2023).

As an example of their generic nature, the FAIR principles remain vague and refer to "domain-relevant community standards" (Principle R1.3, Wilkinson et al. 2016). This means that the principles cannot be applied without further specification of suitable formats and conventions that will make resources reusable (R). Since the principles are generic, the existing operationalization and assessment basis of the FAIR principles, the FAIR Data Maturity Indicators, also remain generic and refer to community standards (RDA FAIR Data Maturity Model Working Group 2020). What these community standards are and how they relate to the generic maturity indicators is still an open question. As pointed out by the authors (RDA FAIR Data Maturity Model Working Group 2020: 10), the idea of machine-understandable data and well-defined semantic models as required by the FAIR principles and maturity indicators is very different from community standards traditionally used in the Humanities. Even if some of the data formats are indeed machine-readable, the tradition of qualitative approaches and human interpretation possibly renders this aspect of the FAIR principles less relevant as a quality criterion for this community. A set of widely accepted community standards and an implementation of corresponding FAIR data maturity indicators are needed if the FAIR principles are to be used as a requirement on research data and for them to be assessable for funders.

Any kind of quality assessment also needs to consider the heterogeneity in the group of resources described in this chapter. The experiences with quality control in a data centre for spoken multilingual data (Hedeland and Ferger 2020), resulted in a tentative distinction between deposits, collections and corpora, for which different sets of requirements should be applied (Hedeland 2021). The aim was to avoid the use of requirements that were neither realistic nor relevant to the researchers, e. g., a research project that analyses conversational data by reading single transcripts while listening to the recording will not have the kind of structured and systematically annotated data that allows for reliable querying and automatic analysis. Instead of not succeeding in fulfilling these ideal requirements for "corpora", the resource can succeed in fulfilling other requirements for "collections" so that it is clear how the materials can be used. While maintaining this idea, to not cause confusion or conflict, the use of existing terminology was abandoned and the different resource subtypes were subsequently described as data maturity levels. Regardless of the terminology, the distinction aligns well with Jane Simpson's distinction between assemblage, collection and corpus, which implicitly describes how data matures within a language documentation project and results in different types of resources. Some tentative definitions of data maturity levels for annotated audiovisual language data are available in the final report of a German joint project on data quality and curation (QUEST, Wamprechtshammer et al. 2022: 11–12), but comprehensive tests across various archives and data centres would still be necessary for these definitions to evolve into data maturity indicators suitable for assessment scenarios. While FAIR assessment is desirable for funders, and a certain level of structure and consistency is necessary to ensure that a resource can be actively preserved and automatically migrated to future data formats, standardised data maturity levels would truly benefit those trying to reuse data. For each level, it would be possible to understand what to expect from a language resource and how it can be reliably reused.

The more intrinsic dimensions of data quality for this type of resource are related to what has been described as the inherently selective and interpretative nature of the data (Ochs 1979). This type of data cannot be objective, and the written (standard) language bias (Linell 2005) and other partly unconscious assumptions are brought into all processes of description, transcription and annotation. As Ayaß (2015) points out, even in video-based language resources, existing transcription systems, which were originally created for audio recordings, are still used, and as a consequence, non-verbal and other dimensions of communication are treated as subordinate to the spoken words. Figure 2 shows different aspects of data quality for recordings and annotation (adapted from Hedeland 2021). As data is created by the researcher, the degree of reduction and interpretation increases with the distance to the original communicative event. Standardised descriptions further define the result and possible ways of interacting with the data. One category is somewhat different: Basic oral annotation, so-called "careful speech" (cf. Section 2.2.1), translation and explications of cultural knowledge used as an additional basis for further description and analysis in language documentation, is provided by experts who are usually not linguists. The type of interpretation in these processes will probably thus also be different.

Traditionally, there are two essentially different ways to manage quality in this type of non-objective data. One is to formalise decisions and use special calculations to compare how well different annotators, or the same annotator over time, is able to describe the same data in the same way – this is called inter-annotator

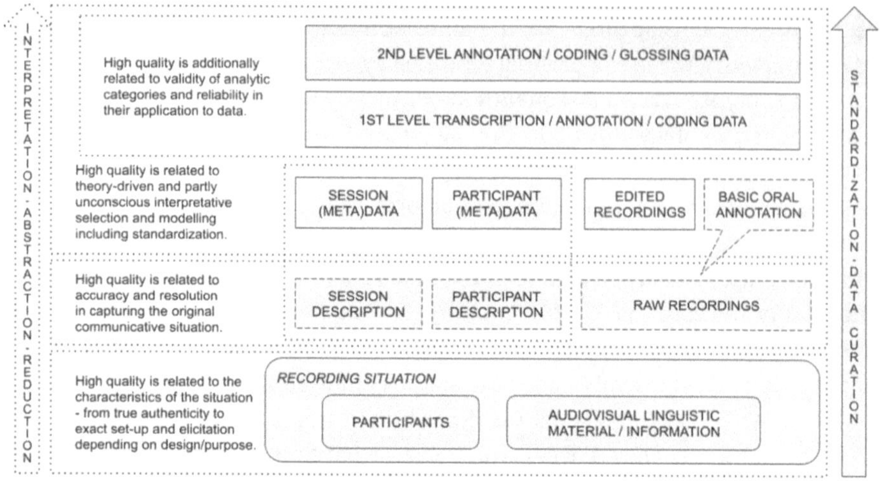

Figure 2: Aspects of data quality in annotated audiovisual language data.

and intra-annotator agreement, respectively. There are such coefficients for segmentation and labelling (annotation) tasks (cf. Reiter and Konle 2022, for a current overview), but these, or any kind of systematic comparison that can be reported in numbers, are very rarely used. The other option is to rely on the alternative quality criteria for qualitative research (cf. Steinke 2000, Strübing et al. 2018) and to focus on documentation of the processes, the context and the assumptions relevant for the resource creation. For reuse of this type of resource to be possible, it has to be possible to assess the quality of transcription and annotation. Without standardised processes for quality assurance, this can only be done if there is enough information available about the provenance of the resource. All the choices made regarding transcription, annotation and in other dimensions of the resource creation process, have to become understandable – this requires information on the qualifications and background of everyone involved in the project. Rich metadata and comprehensive documentation are crucial.

Following this discussion, it becomes clear that, on the one hand, no exact recommendations, let alone standardisation, are possible for transcription and annotation or any other areas where differences are motivated by different theoretical decisions. As Schmidt (2011) points out, any standard needs to retain these differences. On the other hand, there are often unnecessary differences in the use of formats and conventions between resources, which make resources incompatible although they contain the same information. In the following section we provide recommendations based on this distinction between required and unnecessary differences.

Existing conventions should be assessed and used where possible, if necessary, with documented adaptations, and they should be applied consistently.

Computational methods for controlling quality are in place in most archives and research data centres, e. g., the Endangered Languages Archive at the Berlin-Brandenburg Academy of Sciences and Humanities, assesses XML metadata automatically (and does a comprehensive manual quality control) before materials are uploaded, and then utilises further automatic checks to assess the uploaded files. Such checks are however usually only done on a generic level, not considering project or resource specific conventions. Applying automatic quality control methods continuously throughout the creation and curation of the data set will improve consistency and accuracy in the use of all sorts of conventions and reduce the amount of work needed when preparing the materials for archiving. While a detailed account is beyond the scope of this chapter, cf. Riaposov and Lazarenko (2024) for a description of quality control measures in a long-term project creating multi-level annotated corpora of lesser-resourced languages and Ferger et al. (forthcoming) for a report on the use of continuous quality control for multimodal corpora.

2 Recommendations

This section provides recommendations for data quality and data maturity relevant to annotated audiovisual language data. These recommendations are provided with the caveat that individual archives or repositories have different requirements, practices, and workflows. Our first and most important recommendation is for project teams to communicate early in the project planning phase with their archive or repository where the annotated audiovisual language data will be deposited. In some cases, it will be prudent or necessary that the requirements or recommendations of the repository override the recommendations given here.

The recommendations focus on source data (i. e., audiovisual recordings), transcriptions, translations, second-level annotations (e. g., interlinear glossing), lexical resources, metadata, and collection documentation. Individual projects may or may not make use of all of these data types, and it is certainly possible that other types of data can also be included (for example, photographs, scans, documents, or specialised types of data resulting from phonetic, psycholinguistic, or other experiments).

The recommendations presented here draw on and bring up to date other recommendations including Schmidt et al. (2010a,b), Seyfeddinipur and Rau (2020), Wamprechtshammer et al. (2022), and DFG (2019).

2.1 Source data

This section focuses on audiovisual data and includes explanations of how audiovisual formats work and how to choose the right formats and parameters to create long-term and flexibly reusable resources. Other types of data, such as images or original documents relevant to the communicative context, are briefly discussed.

Annotated audiovisual language data should include both high-quality audio in an uncompressed format and high-definition video. While the value of video data for sign language data is undisputed, video is also integral to the study of spoken language and should not be neglected (see Ashmore 2008, Seyfeddinipur and Rau 2020, interalia). Audio and video should be recorded with appropriate microphones, cameras, and/or audio recording equipment. The selection of recording equipment, its positioning relative to the participants in the recording, and the optimal audio or video settings for a given recording scenario are important considerations which are outside the scope of the recommendations presented here. Guidelines and recommendations on these aspects of audiovisual data collection are provided in Seyfeddinipur and Rau (2020), Ashmore (2008), Margetts and Margetts (2012), and Seyfeddinipur (2012).

In understanding audio and video, it is important to distinguish between codecs and file formats. Codecs encode electrical signals (such as that coming from a microphone) as a digital stream that can be played back (for example as sound over speakers). Codecs can also compress data to reduce the file size. A file format, on the other hand, is a standardised way of encoding information in a file. For example, WAV and MP3 are two common formats used for audio, and MP4 and MOV are two common formats used for video. These are also referred to as container formats because a file of a given format may contain video and/or audio streams encoded with compatible codecs. For example, a video file may contain a video stream encoded with one codec and an audio stream encoded with another codec.

2.1.1 Audio data

Audio codecs can be categorised into two main types, compressed and uncompressed. Audio for data concerning spoken language, whether collected as standalone audio or as part of a video recording, should be uncompressed. Uncompressed audio has not been altered by an algorithm to reduce the size or bitrate of the audio stream. The most common uncompressed codec type is LPCM (linear pulse-code modulation, sometimes referred to simply as PCM). LPCM codecs are the best choice for annotated audiovisual language data, as they will allow for the audio to later be used for spectral analysis and other purposes.[1] For audio files, the most common container format for LPCM audio is WAV. WAV files with LPCM audio are widely accepted by archives and repositories and are compatible with most software used for annotation and analysis of language data (e. g., ELAN, Praat, EXMARaLDA Partitur-Editor).

Compressed audio, on the other hand, has been altered to reduce the size. Broadly speaking, there are two types of compression: lossless and lossy. Lossless compression produces a smaller file that can still be decoded to restore the information in the uncompressed original stream. Some common lossless codecs are FLAC and ALAC. Lossy compression produces much smaller files, but some of the data is lost during compression and cannot be restored later. Some of the most well-known lossy codecs are MP3 and AAC. As storage media has grown in capacity and become more affordable, it is unlikely that most projects will need to compress audio for storage, so we do not recommend these types of codecs, even the lossless ones, as many software programs for language annotation and analysis are designed to work best with LPCM WAV audio.

Some projects may have limited resources and options for selecting recording equipment. If the video camera available to the project only has the option to use a compressed format like AAC, we recommend using the highest quality audio settings available on the camera to compensate. If phonetic quality audio is required, we recommend making a parallel recording using an audio recorder that records LPCM WAV audio.

Most audio and video file formats allow for the specification of multiple channels of audio to be included in the file. Some of the most common terms used to talk about the number of channels are mono, stereo, and surround sound.

Mono is composed of a single audio channel. A mono microphone has only one microphone component which will record sound for only a single channel. Mono sound is appropriate for recordings made of a single speaker.

Stereo is composed of two audio channels, with most stereo audio formats specifying which channel is the left side and which is the right side. A stereo microphone is actually composed of two microphones which are angled away from each other, often at a 90 or 120 degree angle. Stereo is ideal for recording situations where there are multiple speakers interacting, as it provides a more immersive experi-

1 Note that there are a number of different codecs of the LPCM type. One of the most common is pcm_s16le, which encodes 16 bit audio. Another option is pcm_s24le which encodes 24 bit audio. The codec(s) used different models of audio recorder or camera will differ, so it is important to consider the available codecs when selecting recording equipment.

ence where the listener can hear speakers on the left side more loudly on the left and speakers on the right side more loudly on the right.

Surround sound is composed of higher numbers of audio channels. One common type is the 5.1 specification which has 6 channels: front left, front centre, front right, back left, back right, and a low frequency effects channel. Surround sound is generally not used in annotated audiovisual language data collections, but some video cameras may have it as an option, so it is important to be aware of how it is different from mono or stereo.

Many recorders and cameras are configured to record stereo audio by default. If one records using a single mono microphone, this will usually result in having a second, empty audio channel. With uncompressed audio, this empty channel will take up as much space as the channel with audio, and when the recording is played back on headphones or stereo speakers, the audio can be heard only on one side. To remedy this, we recommend panning the audio from stereo to mono to eliminate the empty channel so that the same audio will play on both the left and right. This can be done using any of a number of audio editing software programs such as Audacity or FFmpeg.

Another important concept for audio data is the sample rate. The sample rate of an audio stream is the number of samples of audio that are recorded per second. In the real world, sound is produced as a continuous wave, but to capture this is digital format, the sound is measured and recorded at many discrete points in time. The higher the sample rate, the more faithfully the original sound wave can be represented in the audio stream. The most commonly encountered rates on modern recording devices are 44.1 kHz (used for compact discs, but still commonly encountered as a sample rate setting), 48 kHz (used for most modern digital applications), and 96 kHz. For annotated audiovisual language data, 44.1 kHz or 48 kHz are typically recommended as they capture the frequencies relevant to human spoken language. Higher rates like 96 kHz dramatically increase audio file sizes and are not generally used for linguistics, including most phonetic research.

The bit depth of audio is the amount of information recorded for a single sample. Audio bit depth can be thought of like the resolution in video – the higher the bit depth, the more fine-grained the information about the sample can be. Higher bit rates allow for recording audio with a higher amplitude (volume range). Recording devices commonly offer 16 bit or 24 bit options. As with the sample rate, the higher the bit depth setting is, the larger the resulting file size will be. Either 16 bit or 24 bit is appropriate for most annotated audiovisual language data. Higher rates such as 32 bit are generally not necessary.

Taken together, the sample rate multiplied by bit depth and the number of audio channels yields the bit rate of an audio file. For example, mono audio recorded at a sample rate of 48 kHz and a bit depth of 24 bits has a bit rate of 1152 kbps. Just because a given file's bit rate is high does not mean that it has appropriate quality for research purposes; rather, the sample rate, bit depth, and number of channels should each be considered.

The recommendations for audio data are summarised below:

- For both audio and video recordings, record using an (L)PCM audio codec if possible.
  - For standalone audio, use the WAV container format.
- Use stereo for recordings of multiple speakers interacting. Use mono in situations where there is only one audio channel (e. g., a phonetic elicitation session where the speaker is wearing a headset or lapel microphone).
- Record using a sample rate of 44.1 kHz or 48 kHz and a bit depth of 16 bit or 24 bit.

2.1.2 Video data

2.1.2.1 Formats and compression

In its simplest, raw form, video is simply a series of still images. Each digital image is composed of a large number of points referred to as pixels. Each pixel is a sample representing part of the image being recorded. Whereas a single data point in an audio stream consists of just the amplitude of that point in the sound wave, a single frame of raw video data records the hue (colour), saturation (intensity), and value (brightness) for each of the pixels recorded. For example, in raw 1080p video there are 2,073,600 pixels. This is more complex information than for audio due to the amount of data recorded, and raw and/or uncompressed video is generally hard to store and work with because of the extremely large file sizes. In fact, a raw video cannot even be viewed as a video stream until post-processing has taken place to interpret the file. Because of this, raw and uncompressed video are not recommended for annotated audiovisual language data.

Compressed video has already been interpreted and encoded so that it is ready to use when copied off the SD card. As with audio, compression can be lossless or lossy, but most of the types of video cameras used for audiovisual language research purposes record video with lossy compression. As of the time of this writing, it is not common that consumer video cameras offer lossless encoding. Some examples of lossy video codecs include H.264/AVC, H.265/HVEC, and AV1. Most video cameras use H.264/AVC, though 4K cameras often have H.265/HEVC which is better for this higher resolution video. As long as the video has an appropriate resolution, bit depth, and frame rate, it's okay for most audiovisual language data purposes if it is compressed, even with a lossy codec.

Common video container formats include MP4, MOV, AVI, MKV, and MTS. Most archives and repositories accept MP4 containing a video stream encoded with H.264/AVC or H.265/HVEC, and these are widely recommended (for example, see Seyfeddinipur and Rau 2020 and Schmidt et al. 2010a,b). MP4 video is also widely supported by software for the annotation of audiovisual language data.

In addition to the video stream, a video file typically contains one or more audio streams that provide the sound to go along with the images. Formats such as AVI, MKV, MOV, and MTS can contain LPCM audio. However, for MP4 video, the audio should be encoded in AAC. As discussed in Section 2.1.1, audio should be recorded in LPCM, meaning that the video container format must be AVI, MKV, MOV, or MTS for original recordings. The LPCM audio should be extracted from a video file as a WAV file before converting the video to MP4, in order to preserve the uncompressed audio. The extracted audio in WAV format should be archived alongside the video data.

2.1.2.2 Resolution

As mentioned in the previous section, the resolution of the image is expressed in terms of the number of pixels, or elements, in the image. In video, resolution is often expressed in terms of the number of pixels on the vertical axis (e. g., 1080 for 1080 pixels on the vertical axis). Designations with the letters p or i refer to how the rows of pixels in the video stream are displayed: p for progressive scanning and i for interlaced scan. Progressive scan is generally preferred and is widely available on most consumer video cameras currently available on the market. Table 1 lists some common resolutions by their most commonly used names.

Table 1: Some common video resolutions and their most commonly used names.

Name	Resolution (horizontal × vertical)
480p / Standard Definition	640 × 480
720p / High Definition	1280 × 720
1080p / Full HD	1920 × 1080
4K / Ultra HD	3840 × 2160 (UHD) or 4096 × 2160 (true 4K)

For audiovisual language data, we recommend at least 1080p / Full HD. It is not generally necessary to use 4K or UHD, and these higher resolution videos can sometimes be difficult to work with or convert depending on the specifications of one's computer. On the other hand, if one's research is concerned with tracking very fine gestural movements or gase, 4K or UHD may be beneficial to the project goals.

Researchers should check with the archive or repository where the video data will be deposited for their specific recommendations for video resolution and important information about file size limits, etc.

If the camera is able to record 4K/UHD, we recommend testing it first before committing to using it for the project. One way of testing is to make recordings that are at least 10 or 20 minutes long, allowing one to evaluate whether the computer(s) available to the project can process this video, if it will work when opened in software to be used in the research workflow, and how much hard drive space it will consume.

2.1.2.3 Bit depth, frame rate, and bit rate

The bit depth of video, sometimes referred to as the colour depth, is the number of bits used to represent the colour of a pixel in an image. Colour in digital video is represented by RGB (red, green, and blue) values. Most consumer video cameras record in 8 bit, meaning there are 256 (2^8) values for each of the colours red, green, and blue. This means there are 16,777,216 colours that can be represented in a single pixel. For audiovisual language data, recording in 8 bit is enough. Along with information about the bit depth, many cameras also indicate the chroma subsampling used to record different colours. This is an advanced colour topic which we do not discuss in detail, but most currently available consumer cameras use 4:4:0 or 4:4:2 and either of these is appropriate for language documentation applications.

The frame rate is the number of frames, or images, recorded per second. Frame rates are provided as a number followed by fps (frames per second), for example 24 fps for 24 frames per second. Over the history of video, from silent films until the present, a variety of frame rates have been adopted for different purposes in different parts of the world. Some of the most common frame rates and their applications are provided in Table 2.

Table 2: Examples of common frame rates and their applications.

Frame rate	Use
24 fps	Cinema video standard
25 fps	PAL analogue TV standard (Most of Europe, Oceania, parts of Asia and Africa) and SECAM analogue TV standard (France, Russia, parts of west Africa and Central Asia)
30 fps	online, digital video standard and NTSC analogue TV standard (Most of North America, western South America, Japan and the Philippines)
Higher rates	Higher rates like 48 fps, 50 fps, or 60 fps are sometimes used for both online and cinema video when there is fast action.

Recommendations for frame rate are highly variable in the literature, and often reflect the regional differences outlined above. For example, most (European) CLARIN centres recommend frame rates of 25 and accept 50 fps,[2] while the US Library of Congress prefers 30 or 24 fps.[3] The Language Archive Cologne recommends 30 fps, but also accepts 24 and 25 fps.[4] Much digital video online now uses 30 fps, which displays well on digital displays which often have refresh rates of 60 or 120 Hz.

Some video cameras can record at higher rates such as 60 or 120 fps. Higher rates significantly increase the file size and are not necessary for general documentation purposes. If the project focus is signed language or otherwise concerned with the details of gesture and/or gaze, it may be beneficial to record using a higher frame rate so that video can be slowed down for fine-tuned analysis of hand shape and/or gaze.

Ultimately, the choice of frame rate is dependent largely on how (and where) the video data is expected to be used, as well as the options available on consumer cameras in the region where recording equipment will be purchased. Many online streaming platforms, such as YouTube and Vimeo, support a plurality of frame rates. What is key is that a given project should endeavour to use a consistent frame rate for all video recordings in the collection, or use only combinations of rates which can easily be converted either by duplicating frames or dropping alternate frames (as is the case for 30 fps and 60 fps). Converting between other frame rates (such as 25 fps and 30 fps) will likely result in judder, a visual effect where the motion in the video is perceived by viewers as choppy or faltering. Note that judder can also occur when viewing video of a given frame rate on a display device that has an incompatible refresh rate.

As with audio, the bit rate of video is simply the product of the resolution, bit depth, and frame rate. With video, however, bit rates are often variable due to the compression of the video. The rate may be lower in some parts and higher in others. When viewing the file properties of a video in the file explorer on a computer, the bit rate listed is typically an average that combines both the rate of the video stream along with the rate(s) of the audio stream(s). For data quality, the resulting bit rate is not as important as the resolution, frame rate, and bit depth, which should be the primary considerations. However, it is important to consider the resulting bit rate when choosing appropriate storage media (i. e., SD cards) to be used with the

2 https://standards.clarin.eu/sis/views/view-format.xq?id=fMPEG-4-AVC

3 https://www.loc.gov/preservation/digital/formats/content/video_source.shtml

4 https://dch.phil-fak.uni-koeln.de/bestaende/language-archive-cologne/user-guides/submission-guidelines

camera, as different cards have different write speeds. This is particularly relevant to projects which will record in 4K and/or using high frame rates.

2.1.2.4 Summary of video recommendations

Video is still a rapidly evolving technology and there are many new and exciting developments with each passing year. Likewise, the standards for audiovisual data are constantly adapting to new technologies. Reputable archives and repositories are an indispensable scientific and cultural infrastructure, as they ensure that data is preserved and updated to new archival standard formats over time, preventing data loss due to format obsolescence. Because of their role in ensuring data permanence as well as due to technical limitations, some recent developments, such as 360° video may or may not be accepted by all repositories, or if they are accepted, the repository may not be able to guarantee long-term permanence. This underscores the importance of contacting the archive or repository early in the project planning process.

The recommendations for video data are summarised below:

- Record video as H.264/AVC (for HD/1080p) or H.265/HVEC (if recording in 4K).
- Record in a format that allows LPCM audio, if possible. Otherwise use AAC with the highest possible audio settings.
- Record in a resolution of at least 1080p.
- Record at a frame rate that corresponds with the requirements of the chosen archive/repository or with the anticipated uses of the audiovisual language data.

2.1.3 Images, scans, and documents

In this section, we turn to some other common types of language data: images, scans, and documents. Images, such as photographs, often constitute a type of primary data, while scans and documents may either represent primary data (such as written texts in the language(s) of study) or secondary data such as handwritten or typed field notes or annotations.

The standard for born-digital photographic images is JPEG (.jpg or .jpeg). Most consumer digital cameras, as well as smartphones, create JPEG images. Photographs from film cameras should be scanned with the highest quality possible and digitised in the TIFF format (.tif). Likewise, handwritten or printed documents should be scanned and digitised in the TIFF format. Both of these formats are widely accepted by language archives and other data repositories. Images such as figures or data visualizations which are created digitally may also be accepted by some repositories, most frequently in the PNG or SVG formats.

Born-digital documents created with word processing software and containing rich formatting should be saved in the PDF/A format. Note that not all .pdf files conform to the archival PDF/A standard, so care should be taken to save documents intended for archiving with the PDF/A option. Common word processing formats like .doc, .docx, or .rtf are not appropriate archival formats as the formatting may display incorrectly across different software or systems.

For textual data without rich formatting, plain text (.txt), HTML (.html), and XML (.xml) are also widely accepted by repositories as they are both human- and machine-readable. Textual data should follow the recommendations and guidelines provided by the Text Encoding Initiative (TEI) 2025) and by Bird and Simons (2003). Of key importance is the issue of character encoding: the TEI recommends UTF-8 encoding. Project teams should select widely-used fonts which map to the Unicode Standard (Unicode 2025). Non-Unicode fonts should be avoided. We strongly recommend selecting fonts which are freely available and widely used. If it is absolutely necessary to use a font which is not widely used, it should still map to the Unicode Standard and ideally be deposited alongside the text data. Some repositories accept fonts, often in TrueType (TTF) or OpenType (OTF) formats, but this should be discussed with the repository in advance.

2.2 Annotations

Audiovisual language data should ideally be accompanied by annotations of different types to make the data easier to understand for users who do not speak the language(s) used in the primary recordings and to improve searchability. This section provides recommendations for both primary annotations (i. e., transcriptions and translations), and for secondary annotations such as interlinear glossing and other forms of data coding or notes.

2.2.1 Transcription

Transcription is one of the most basic forms of audiovisual language data annotation. This section provides an overview of the different kinds of transcription systems and some approaches to transcription including careful speech recordings.

The most common form of transcriptions are written transcripts. These annotations seek to represent speech (or sign) in written format. The recommendations in this section pertain primarily to spoken language, although some points may be translatable to the annotation of sign language data. For an overview of sign language transcription systems, see Garcia and Sallandre (2013). Written transcriptions should be in a human- and machine-readable format, use UTF-8 encoding, and use only Unicode fonts (Bird and Simons 2003).

When working with audiovisual language data, transcriptions should ideally be time-aligned – that is, they should include timestamp data that allows each segment of the transcription to be linked to the time(s) where the speech represented can be heard in the primary recording. There are a number of software programs for annotation which make it easy to view and listen to audiovisual data and to create time-aligned transcriptions, translations, and other annotations. Two of the most widely used and recommended options are ELAN (2024) and EXMARaLDA's Partitur-Editor tool[5] (Schmidt and Wörner 2014). Both of these also allow for individual speakers on the recording to be transcribed on separate tiers, such that overlapping speech can be represented and the source speaker of each portion of speech can easily be identified. Transcriptions produced with either of these pieces of software are saved as XML and are accepted by most archives and repositories. Data in this format is easy to query and highly portable across different software and platforms. Both of these formats can also be converted into the TEI-based ISO standard for transcription of spoken language (ISO/TC 37/SC 4 2016), which allows for increased interoperability with textual data and additional use cases. These and other transcription formats are discussed and compared in more detail in Frick and Schmidt (2025).

The conventions used to create transcriptions should also be carefully considered. Some projects may make use only of an orthographic transcription which follows the conventions of a standardised orthography. Others may use a modified version of such an orthography. Projects may also use a phonetic transcription using the International Phonetic Alphabet, X-SAMPA, or another appropriate phonetic system. Phonetic transcriptions can be broad or narrow. It may be necessary to use more than one transcription type. For example, an orthographic transcription may be needed for some uses and a phonetic transcription for others. If using an orthography in a non-Latin script, it may be necessary to provide a transliteration to facilitate querying the data.

The choice of transcription convention(s) is left to research teams, but we strongly recommend that annotated audiovisual language data collections clearly identify the type(s) of transcription used (e. g., orthographic, narrow phonetic, transliteration) and document any relevant conventions (e. g., correspondences between a practical orthography and IPA, transliteration systems, etc.). Project teams should be careful to follow any conventions consistently and not to mix different

5 www.exmaralda.org

transcription types, as this makes the data much harder to query and use in a regular fashion. A distinct advantage of using annotation software such as ELAN or EXMARaLDA is that these allow for each of the transcription (or transliteration) types to be represented as separate data types (or tiers). Werthmann (2025) provides a detailed comparison of different transcription formats, their features, and their merits. By using machine-readable formats and conventions, including for pauses, interrupted or disfluent speech, and other "special tokens" as they are termed by Frick and Schmidt (2025), researchers can reliably query their data directly as well as convert it to other formats and, where a mapping exists, make it interoperable with transcription data encoded with other conventions.

In certain circumstances, it may be useful to collect oral "transcriptions" in the form of careful speech recordings to help facilitate the later production of written transcriptions. This is particularly useful if the researcher(s) do not speak the language, if the language does not have a widely-used orthography, and/or if the language is spoken by populations with limited literacy skills. The recording of oral annotations of this type form part of the Basic Oral Language Documentation workflow described by Reiman (2010). In this workflow, a fluent speaker of the subject language listens to an original recording and then records a careful speech repetition of each portion of speech. A transcriber can then listen to both the original recording and the careful speech recording to aid in creating a written transcription. These recordings could be made as a series of audio clips or using software such as SayMore.[6] This method is particularly useful when the language under study is highly endangered, and we return to it again in the following section on translation.

2.2.2 Translation

For audiovisual language data collections concerning endangered or minority languages, translations into a language of broader communication are indispensable data allowing a broader audience to understand the materials and for facilitating future research on the language(s) represented in the collection. As with transcriptions, translations should be time-aligned with reference to the original recording. The transcription software recommended in Section 2.2.1 (ELAN and EXMARaLDA) can be used to produce time-aligned translations at the same time as transcriptions and other annotations.

The choice of language, or languages, for translations depends on practical as well as socio-linguistic factors unique to each language, collection, and project. In

6 https://software.sil.org/saymore/

some cases, project teams may be working with a language community which is largely bilingual in a language of broader or global communication. In other cases, it may be the case that transcriptions must first be produced in a local contact language (which in some cases may be an endangered or minority language itself), after which these primary translations can be re-translated to a more widely-known language. Project teams may also opt to produce additional translations into a regional or national language to facilitate use of materials by users in the country or region where the data was collected.

Translations may be literal, free, or somewhere in between. Literal translations seek to represent the literal, word-by-word meaning of the original, as well as the original structure. Free translations take more liberty with the original structure and seek to represent the overall meaning of a particular segment of speech. Translations may also seek to strike a balance between literal meaning and free interpretation.

For highly endangered languages with only a few speakers or signers remaining, it is absolutely imperative to produce as many translations as possible. Should the language cease to be used, translations into a language which is not at risk will ensure that future generations can understand the content of recordings and creates possibilities for future revitalization, research, and other uses. Written translations, like written transcriptions, can be time-consuming to produce. Recording oral translations using a Basic Oral Language Documentation workflow (Reiman 2010) is one way to speed up this work and to allow non-literate or minimally literate project stakeholders to participate in the project. Oral translations into a primary contact language can later be used to produce written translations into the contact language or other translation languages used by the project.

Because translations are a key form of annotation for understanding audiovisual language data, researchers should thoroughly describe the translation workflow. The different translation languages used in a collection should be characterised in terms of how translations were produced into each language. For example, if translations were directly produced by native bilinguals from the language documented into a local contact language, and then the translations in the contact language were further translated into a language of broader/global communication, this should be noted explicitly. Likewise, project-internal conventions regarding free vs literal translations should also be made explicit in the metadata and collection description.

As with transcription, project teams should pay close attention to the use of special character sets, fonts, and encoding for translations. Translations should be provided in a human- and machine-readable format, use UTF-8 encoding, and use only Unicode fonts. If a project uses special fonts which are not widely available or used, the project team should consider including the font as a TrueType or OpenType font file as a supplementary file included in the archived collection.

2.2.3 Other second level annotation data

Audiovisual language data collections often include additional types of annotation in addition to transcription and translation. In this section, we provide some recommendations for different types of analytic annotation on various linguistic levels and discuss how data quality and maturity relate to the processes and formats of annotation. Often, these annotations include or encode linguistic or other analyses, and thus constitute a secondary level of annotation which draws on the primary levels of transcription and translation. One of the most widespread second level annotation types for language documentation data is interlinear glossing, to which we frequently refer as an example. For standardised languages like English or German, part of speech (POS) information, such as the spoken language variant of the STTS tagset for spoken German data (Westpfahl et al. 2017), is often added as a basic part of the resource creation process. Other types of annotation are more tightly related to linguistic theories and the research question at hand and vary across projects and contexts.

Second level annotations should conform to many of the same standards which we have already described for primary annotations: They should be human- and machine-readable, use UTF-8 encoding and a Unicode font, and link back to the original recording, ideally in a time-aligned format.

Care should be taken to produce consistent annotations and to document any coding schemes or other conventions used to produce second level annotations. To the greatest extent possible, project teams should strive to use standardised vocabularies and conventions which have already been widely adopted in their respective fields. For example, interlinear glossing should follow the conventions laid out by the Leipzig Glossing Rules. Where additional glosses, abbreviations, or conventions are needed to supplement these rules, these should be documented in detail and the result should be included in the archived collection. Other areas with existing annotation systems relevant in this context are the LISA guidelines for annotation of information structure (Dipper et al. 2007) and the GRAID system for grammatical relations and animacy (Haig and Schnell 2015).

There are several options for software which help maintain consistency in interlinear glossing, as well as other types of analytic annotations. ELAN has support for the creation and management of controlled vocabularies, and the most recent versions of this software now also offer an Interlinearization Mode for the creation of interlinear glosses. Transcriptions and translations from ELAN can also be exported to SIL's Fieldworks Language Explorer (commonly known as FLEx), software which facilitates interlinear glossing and the creation of lexical databases. These interlinear glosses can later be exported from FLEx back to ELAN so that they can be viewed and explored time-aligned to the original recordings. EXMARaLDA's transcription and annotation editor has integrated checks for adherence to the general data model, including checks to make sure that participants don't have several main transcription tiers, that second level annotations are used to annotate parts of the transcription for the same participants etc. There are also syntax checks for transcription conventions for several widely used transcription systems. The annotation panel allows for the definition of a hierarchical annotation system and the easy application of tags to avoid spelling mistakes etc. As an example, there are annotation panel configuration files available for German (spoken language) part of speech tagging.[7] The FOLKER transcription editor also provides syntax checks for the GAT transcription system.

Using software like ELAN or FLEx to manage interlinear glosses ensures that the data will be portable to other uses. For example, the Open Text Collections project is creating pipelines for interlinear glosses produced in ELAN or FLEx to be converted to TeX for publication as text collections (Nordhoff et al. 2024).

2.3 Lexical resources

This section discusses the formats used for lexical resources and in particular how to keep the important relations to the source data and transcription or other annotation files.

Lexical resources, like other text resources, should be human- and machine-readable and ideally stored in portable formats. Furthermore, data in lexical resources should be carefully organised and entered such that each field in the lexicon contains only one type of data in a single language. Data of different types, and even data of the same type that is provided in two or more languages, should be entered separately to maximise the machine-readability and portability of the resource. As always, the text should be encoded using UTF-8 and only fonts that map to the Unicode standard should be used.

To the greatest extent possible, lexical resources should link back to annotations and source recordings. This linking should ideally be as comprehensive as possible, such that the use(s) of particular tokens of a lexeme can easily be searched for and

7 https://exmaralda.org/en/utilities/

located within the source recordings. This is important to ensure transparent data provenance as well as to maximise the future possible uses of the lexical resource for purposes such as language revitalization or the creation of other products in the future.

Lexical resources can be created as comma-separated values (CSV) or as tab-separated values (TSV) files using spreadsheet software, or they can be created using specialised lexicon management software such as Fieldworks Language Explorer (FLEx), SooSL (for signed languages), or the lexicon tools in ELAN's *Interlinearization Mode*. These tools also allow the easy link between audiovisual materials and lexicon entries, which contributes to increase the transparency regarding data provenance regarding lexicon creation.

2.4 Metadata

Since there is a chapter in this book discussing metadata more in detail (see Trippel 2025), this section focuses on information that is particularly relevant as contextual information for annotated audiovisual data to make it understandable and reusable. We also point out relevant aspects when it comes to making the resource findable with public standardised/interoperable catalogue metadata. For more detailed recommendations on metadata, please also refer to Wamprechtshammer et al. (2022). As depicted in Figure 1, metadata is required to describe all parts of a resource. On the one hand, these are the original communicative event, represented by a "session", and its participants, on the other hand, it is important to describe the individual files and their provenance to document the digital resource and allow others to understand and reuse it. While a lot of the metadata needed for reusability is often highly specific and tailored to the characteristics of annotated audiovisual language data, standardised metadata plays a crucial role in making the resource findable in various contexts.

Annotated audiovisual language data collections are often organised into (recording) sessions or (thematic) bundles: groupings of files that share metadata such as the date, location, contributors, and content description. Descriptive metadata for a bundle should minimally include the following information about the original communicative event:

- The date the original audiovisual recording was created
- The location where it was created
- Information about the participants and other present people, including any relevant background information needed to fully understand the communicative event

- The language(s) used and in which constellation in case of multilingual conversations
- A rich description of the content of the recording, including any context needed to understand the communicative event documented in the recording
- A listing of the files included in the bundle and their key properties, e. g. formats, recording quality, content/provenance, the conventions and languages used for translation and analyses (e. g., "an .mp4 video file, a .wav audio file extracted from the video, and an .eaf ELAN file with time-aligned broad transcription in IPA with free translations in Spanish and English")
- Information on any and all contributors to the materials in the bundle, such as transcribers, language experts, annotators etc.

Depending on the archive or repository where the materials will be made available, there may be other types of descriptive metadata that are required. Some common types include descriptive titles and keywords.

Detailed information about contributors should be provided, whether they are a participant in the recording, a translator/annotator, or other member of the project team involved in the preparation, analysis, and depositing of the data. Ideally, key metadata including gender, age or birth year, and knowledge of other languages and other qualifications that lead to their involvement. As discussed in the introduction, without standardised methods for quality control of transcription and annotation, the only way of estimating their quality is by the qualifications of the involved contributors. Metadata about participants in the original audiovisual recordings can also be used to query data as described in Frick and Schmidt (2025).

Regarding the formats for metadata, these should follow our general recommendations and be machine-readable, open, well-documented file formats. Often, metadata is (initially) collected in a project-specific spreadsheet format, but there are also dedicated tools such as the EXMARaLDA Corpus Manager or the Lameta metadata editor that can assist in creating comprehensive and consistent metadata in the format required by the archive or research data centre that will host the materials, but also has other benefits: For example, the Lameta tool can export metadata files in different formats required at various DELAMAN archives. By using the EXMARaLDA Corpus Manager as a part of the EXMARaLDA software suite, it becomes possible to utilise metadata on sessions and individual participants in queries. An example would be to retrieve all occurrences of a particular word or gloss used by a female person of a certain dialect group – of course depending on the key-value pairs used in the metadata.

Apart from the formats used specifically for annotated audiovisual language data, there are several relevant formats for publication and exchange of metadata across different contexts. Some examples are the modular CMDI format (cf. Windhouwer and Goosen 2022), which is the ISO standard[8] used to describe language resources in all CLARIN centres, DataCite,[9] which is a generic format for research data and other research outputs, or Dublin Core,[10] which is a generic format used in many types of repositories and archives. Usually, standardised or generic formats are required by the archive or research data centre where materials will be deposited and can sometimes be automatically generated on the basis of existing resource metadata. One important aspect here is the availability of the different types of metadata. While metadata on the communicative event and the participants usually needs to be very detailed for the resource to be reusable by others, it is rarely possible to publish all of this metadata within an archive catalogue or similar contexts. What type of personal data can be made available to which type of audience, if any, will be determined by the informed consent given for recording and archiving. It is crucial to also handle metadata with different access levels separately to ensure that these distinctions can be reliably applied.

2.5 Documentation

All annotated audiovisual language data collections should be accompanied by thorough documentation that contextualises the collection as a whole and which provides details on organization and conventions which will allow users to comprehend and reliably use the materials. This type of documentation has been referred to as "meta-documentation" (see Austin 2013) and is also considered essential for reusability in non-linguistic fields working with qualitative data, such as the social sciences (cf. Heuer et al. 2020). This section provides recommendations on how to document the processes that resulted in the resource so that prospective users are able to evaluate the possibilities and limitations of the materials contained in it.

The documentation for an annotated audiovisual language data collection should describe the history and context of the project or projects that resulted in the collection. This should include any funding which the project(s) received, information about any legacy materials which may be included in the collection, and about any data processing, annotation, or analysis that took place outside of any funded periods. It should also describe the organization of the collection as a whole

8 cf. ISO/TC 37/SC 3 (2022a,b); ISO/TC 37/SC 4 (2015, 2019).

9 https://schema.datacite.org/

10 https://www.dublincore.org/specifications/dublin-core/

as well as the organization principles used for the sessions/bundles or any other sub-components of the collection.

This documentation should also include detailed descriptions of the core conventions used in the collection, such as file naming and annotation conventions. Where standardised conventions (e. g., the Leipzig Glossing Rules or the International Phonetic Alphabet) are used, these can simply be cited, but any workflows or conventions unique to the collection should be laid out in detail. For example, correspondences between the graphemes of a practical or non-standardised orthography and the IPA should be laid out in a table and any special abbreviations or transcription conventions used should likewise be listed so that future users can make sense of the collection contents. The file formats and fonts used in the collection should also be identified alongside any software that was used to produce annotations and analyses, or which may be needed to view and query the data.

Collection documentation can be further supplemented by collection guides which describe the context and content of the collection more richly (see, for example, the recommendations made by Sullivant 2020). Such guides can provide descriptive summaries of the collection contents (e. g., the genres of the communicative events or summaries of the ages or genders of the recording participants represented in the collection). Some good examples of such guides include Salffner (2015), Caballero (2017), Franjieh (2019), Skilton (2021) and the User documentation for the corpora of the project INEL[11] from the language documentation context, and the German learner corpus handbooks by Spiegel et al. (2020) and Muntschick et al. (2020).

Conclusion

Hopefully, this chapter has provided helpful recommendations and enough background for the reader to reflect on the processes relevant to the many dimensions of data quality and data maturity for annotated audiovisual language data and make informed choices in this area. While the recommendations are very concrete in some parts, such as specifications for audio quality, there are many open questions when it comes to linguistic annotation and how to ensure quality and related criteria such as interoperability and reusability in the narrow sense of the FAIR principles. We hope that this chapter can contribute to the discussion on how to define and assess relevant criteria of quality and FAIRness for different types of annotated

11 https://www.fdr.uni-hamburg.de/communities/inel

audiovisual language data in order to facilitate and enhance reusability of these valuable resources.

Bibliography

Ashmore, Louise. 2008. The role of digital video in language documentation. In Peter K. Austin (ed.), *Language documentation and description*, Vol. 5, 77–102. London: SOAS. http://www.elpublishing.org/PID/064 (accessed 10 June 2025).

Austin, Peter K. 2013. Language documentation and meta-documentation. In Mari Jones & Sarah Ogilvie (eds.), *Keeping languages alive: Documentation, pedagogy, and revitalisation*, 3–15. Cambridge: Cambridge University Press.

Ayaß, Ruth. 2015. Doing data: The status of transcripts in conversation analysis. *Discourse Studies* 17(5). 505–528. https://doi.org/10.1177/14614456155.

Bird, Steven & Gary Simons. 2003. Seven dimensions of portability for language documentation and description. *Language* 79(3). 557–582.

Bundesministerium für Bildung und Forschung. 2018. Bekanntmachung 1791. Richtlinie zur Förderung von Forschungsvorhaben zur Entwicklung und Erprobung von Kurationskriterien und Qualitätsstandards von Forschungsdaten im Zuge des digitalen Wandels im deutschen Wissenschaftssystem. https://www.bmbf.de/SharedDocs/Bekanntmachungen/DE/2018/06/1791_bekanntmachung.html (accessed 2 February 2025).

Caballero, Gabriela. 2017. Choguita Rarámuri (Tarahumara) language description and documentation: A guide to the deposited collection and associated materials. *Language Documentation & Conservation* 11. 224–255. http://hdl.handle.net/10125/24734.

DFG. 2022 [2019]. *Guidelines for safeguarding good research practice: Code of conduct*. Revised version 1.1. https://www.dfg.de/resource/blob/174052/1a235cb138c77e353789263b8730b1df/kodex-gwp-en-data.pdf (accessed 2 February 2025).

DFG-Fachkollegium 104 "Sprachwissenschaften". 2019. *Empfehlungen zu datentechnischen Standards und Tools bei der Erhebung von Sprachkorpora*. https://www.dfg.de/resource/blob/171632/383249f00d425a643bd8c120404bbff6/standards-sprachkorpora-data.pdf (accessed 29 January 2025).

Dipper, Stefanie, Michael Götze & Stavros Skopeteas (eds.). 2007. *Information structure in cross-linguistic corpora: Annotation guidelines for phonology, morphology, syntax, semantics, and information structure*. Vol. 7 of Interdisciplinary Studies on Information Structure (ISIS). Potsdam: Universitätsverlag Potsdam.

ELAN (Version 6.9) [Computer software]. 2024. Nijmegen: Max Planck Institute for Psycholinguistics, The Language Archive. https://archive.mpi.nl/tla/elan (accessed 10 June 2025).

Ferger, Anne, André Frank Krause & Karola Pitsch. Forthcoming. A workflow for creating, harmonizing and analyzing structured corpora of multimodal interaction.

Franjieh, Michael. 2019. The languages of northern Ambrym, Vanuatu: A guide to the deposited materials in ELAR. *Language Documentation & Conservation* 13. 83–111. http://hdl.handle.net/10125/24849.

Frick, Elena & Thomas Schmidt. 2025. Querying spoken language data. In Piotr Bański, Ulrich Heid & Laura Herzberg (eds.), *Harmonising language data: Standards for linguistic resources*. Berlin & Boston: De Gruyter.

Garcia, Brigitte & Marie-Anne Sallandre. 2013. Transcription systems for sign languages: A sketch of the different graphical representations of sign language and their characteristics. In Cornelia Müller, Alan Cienki, Ellen Fricke, Silva H. Ladewig, David McNeill & Sedinha Tessendorf (eds.), *Handbook body-language-communication*, 1125–1338. Berlin: Mouton De Gruyter. https://univ-paris8.hal.science/hal-01043755v1 (accessed 10 June 2025).

German Council for Scientific Information Infrastructures (RfII). 2020. *The data quality challenge: Recommendations for sustainable research in the digital turn*. Göttingen. http://www.rfii.de/?p=4203 (accessed 10 June 2025).

Haig, Geoffrey & Stefan Schnell. 2015. *Annotations using GRAID: (Grammatical relations and animacy in discourse): Manual Version 7.0*. Bamberg: opus. https://fis.uni-bamberg.de/handle/uniba/21446.

Hedeland, Hanna. 2021. Towards comprehensive definitions of data quality for audiovisual annotated language resources. In *Selected papers from the CLARIN Annual Conference 2020*, online, 5–7 October 2020, 93–103. https://doi.org/10.3384/ecp1801.

Hedeland, Hanna & Ferger Anne. 2020. Towards continuous quality control for spoken language corpora. *International Journal of Digital Curation* 15. https://doi.org/10.3384/ecp1801.

Heuer, Jan-Ocko, Susanne Kretser, Kati Mozygemba, Elisabeth Huber & Betina Hollstein. 2020. Kontextualisierung qualitativer Forschungsdaten für die Nachnutzung – eine Handreichung für Forschende zur Erstellung eines Studienreports. *Qualiservice Working Papers* 1-2020. Bremen. https://doi.org/10.26092/elib/166.

ISO/TC 37/SC 3. 2022a. *ISO 12620-1:2022 Management of terminology resources – Data categories. Part 1: Specifications*. https://www.iso.org/standard/79078.html (accessed 10 June 2025).

ISO/TC 37/SC 3. 2025b. *ISO 12620-2:2022 Management of terminology resources – Data categories. Part 2: Repositories*. https://www.iso.org/standard/79018.html (accessed 10 June 2025).

ISO/TC 37/SC 4. 2015. *ISO 24622-1:2015 Language resource management – Component metadata infrastructure (CMDI). Part 1: The Component Metadata Model*. https://www.iso.org/standard/37336.html (accessed 10 June 2025).

ISO/TC 37/SC 4. 2016. *ISO 24624:2016 Language resource management – Transcription of spoken language*. https://www.iso.org/standard/37338.html (accessed 10 June 2025).

ISO/TC 37/SC 4. 2019. *ISO 24622-2:2019 Language resource management – Component metadata infrastructure (CMDI). Part 2: Component metadata specification language*. https://www.iso.org/standard/64579.html (accessed 10 June 2025).

Linell, Per. 2005. *The written language bias in linguistics: Its nature, origins and transformations*. London & New York: Routledge.

Margetts, Anna & Andrew Margetts. 2012. Audio and video recording techniques for linguistic research. In Nicholas Thieberger (ed.), *The Oxford handbook of linguistic fieldwork*, 13–53. Oxford: Oxford University Press.

Muntschick, Eva, Adrian Portmann, Manuela Schwendemann & Klaus Wisniewski. 2020. *DISKO (Deutsch im Studium: Lernerkorpus): Handbuch*.

Nordhoff, Sebastian, Mandana Seyfeddinipur & Christian Döhler. 2024. Mobilizing archival collections: The Open Text Collections project. Paper presented at the Language Documentation and Archiving Conference, Berlin, Germany.

Ochs, Elinor. 1979. Transcription as theory. In Elinor Ochs & Bambi B. Schieffelin (eds.), *Developmental pragmatics*, 43–72. New York: Academic Press.

RDA FAIR Data Maturity Model Working Group. 2020. *FAIR data maturity model. Specification and guidelines (1.0)*. RDA technical report. https://doi.org/10.15497/rda00050 (accessed 10 June 2025).

Reiman, D. Will. 2010. Basic oral language documentation. *Language Documentation & Conservation* 4. 254–268. http://hdl.handle.net/10125/4479.

Reiter, Nils & Leonard Konle. 2022. Messverfahren zum Inter-annotator-agreement (IAA). *DARIAH-DE Working Papers* 44. Göttingen: DARIAH-DE. https://doi.org/10.47952/gro-publ-103.

Riaposov, Aleksandr & Elena Lazarenko. 2024. Corpus services: A framework to curate XML corpus data. In *Proceedings of the 2024 joint international conference on computational linguistics, language resources and evaluation (LREC-COLING 2024)*, 4030–4035. Torino, Italia: ELRA and ICCL.

Salffner, Sophie. 2015. A guide to the Ikaan language and culture documentation. *Language Documentation & Conservation* 9. 237–267. http://hdl.handle.net/10125/24639.

Schmidt, Thomas. 2011. A TEI-based approach to standardising spoken language transcription. *Journal of the Text Encoding Initiative* 1. 1–28. https://doi.org/10.4000/jtei.142.

Schmidt, Thomas, Kjell Elenius & Paul Trilsbeek. 2010a. Multimedia encoding and annotation. In Erhard Hinrichs & Iris Vogel (eds.), *Interoperability and standards: CLARIN-D5C-3*, 123–145. https://office.clarin.eu/pp/D5C-3.pdf (accessed 10 June 2025).

Schmidt, Thomas, Kjell Elenius & Paul Trilsbeek. 2010b. Multimedia corpora (media encoding and annotation): Draft submitted to CLARIN WG 5.7 as input to CLARIN deliverable D5.C3 “Interoperability and Standards”. https://ids-pub.bsz-bw.de/frontdoor/index/index/docId/2234 (accessed 10 June 2025).

Schmidt, Thomas & Kai Wörner. 2014. EXMARaLDA. In Jacqueline C. Evers & Martine Grice (eds.), *Handbook on corpus phonology*, 402–419. Oxford: Oxford University Press.

Seyfeddinipur, Mandana. 2012. Reasons for documenting gestures and suggestions for how to go about it. In Nicholas Thieberger (ed.), *The Oxford handbook of linguistic fieldwork*, 13–53. Oxford: Oxford University Press.

Seyfeddinipur, Mandana & Felix Rau. 2020. Keeping it real: Video data in language documentation and language archiving. *Language Documentation & Conservation* 14. 503–519. http://hdl.handle.net/10125/24965.

Skilton, Amalia. 2021. Ticuna (TCA) language documentation: A guide to materials in the California Language Archive. *Language Documentation & Conservation* 15. 153–189. http://hdl.handle.net/10125/24972.

Spiegel, Lena, Michelle Parker, Theresa Feldmüller, Lena Lenort & Klaus Wisniewski. 2020. *MIKO (Mitschreiben in Vorlesungen: Ein multimodales Lehr-Lernkorpus): Handbuch.*

Steinke, Ines. 2000. Gütekriterien qualitativer Forschung. In Uwe Flick, Ernst von Kardorff & Ines Steinke (eds.), *Qualitative Forschung. Ein Handbuch*, 319–331. Reinbek: Rowohlt-Taschenbuch-Verlag.

Strübing, Jörg, Stefan Hirschauer, Ruth Ayaß, Uwe Krähnke & Thomas Scheffer. 2018. Gütekriterien qualitativer Sozialforschung: Ein Diskussionsanstoß. *Zeitschrift für Soziologie* 47(2). 83–100. https://doi.org/10.1515/zfsoz-2018-1006.

Sullivant, Ryan. 2020. Archival description for language documentation collections. *Language Documentation & Conservation* 14. 520–578. http://hdl.handle.net/10125/24949.

Text Encoding Initiative (TEI). 2025. Languages and character sets. In *TEI: Guidelines for electronic text encoding and interchange. P5 Version 4.9.0*. https://tei-c.org/release/doc/tei-p5-doc/en/html/CH.html (accessed 2 February 2025).

Thieberger, Nick. 2018. Texts and more texts: Corpora in the CoEDL. Blog post. http://www.paradisec.org.au/blog/2018/02/texts-and-more-texts-corpora-in-the-coedl/ (accessed 2 February 2025).

Trippel, Thorsten. 2025. Metadata for research data. In Piotr Bański, Ulrich Heid & Laura Herzberg (eds.), *Harmonising language data: Standards for linguistic resources*. Berlin: De Gruyter.

Unicode, Inc. 2025. *About the Unicode Standard*. https://www.unicode.org/standard/standard.html (accessed 2 February 2025).

Wamprechtshammer, Anna, Jocelyn Aznar, Elena Arestau, Hanna Hedeland, Amy Isard, Ilya Khait, Herbert Lange, Nicole Majka & Felix Rau. 2022. QUEST: Guidelines and specifications for the assessment of audiovisual, annotated language data. *Working Papers in Corpus Linguistics and Digital Technologies: Analyses and Methodology* 8. 90 pages.

Wang, Richard Y. & Diane M. Strong. 1996. Beyond accuracy: What data quality means to data consumers. *Journal of Management Information Systems* 12(4). 5–33.

Werthmann, Antonina. 2025. From spoken language data to TEI-based ISO standard. In Piotr Bański, Ulrich Heid & Laura Herzberg (eds.), *Harmonising language data: Standards for linguistic resources*. Berlin: De Gruyter.

Westpfahl, Swantje, Thomas Schmidt, Jasmin Jonietz & Anton Borlinghaus. 2017. *STTS 2.0: Guidelines für die Annotation von POS-Tags für Transkripte gesprochener Sprache in Anlehnung an das Stuttgart Tübingen Tagset (STTS)*. Arbeitspapier. Mannheim: Institut für Deutsche Sprache.

Wilkinson, Mark D., Michel Dumontier, Jan Aalbersberg, Gabrielle Appleton, Myles Axton, Arie Baak, Niklas Blomberg, Jan-Willem Boiten, Luiz Bonino da Silva Santos, Philip E. Bourne, Jildau Bouwman, Anthony J. Brookes, Tim Clark, Mercè Crosas, Ingrid Dillo, Olivier Dumon, Scott Edmunds, Chris T. Evelo, Richard Finkers, Alejandra Gonzalez-Beltran, Alasdair J. G. Gray, Paul Groth, Carole Goble, Jeffrey S. Grethe, Jaap Heringa, Peter A. C. 't Hoen, Rob Hooft, Tobias Kuhn, Ruben Kok, Joost Kok, Scott J. Lusher, Maryann E. Martone, Albert Mons, Abel L. Packer, Bengt Persson, Philippe Rocca-Serra, Marco Roos, Rene van Schaik, Susanna-Assunta Sansone, Erik Schultes, Thierry Sengstag, Ted Slater, George Strawn, Morris A. Swertz, Mark Thompson, Johan van der Lei, Erik van Mulligen, Jan Velterop, Andra Waagmeester, Peter Wittenburg, Katherine Wolstencroft, Jun Zhao & Barend Mons. 2016. The FAIR guiding principles for scientific data management and stewardship. *Scientific Data* 3. 160018. https://doi.org/10.1038/sdata.2016.18.

Wilkinson, Mark D., Susanna-Assunta Sansone, Eva Méndez, Romain David, Richard Dennis, David Hecker, Mari Kleemola, Carlo Lacagnina, Anastasija Nikiforova & Leyla Jael Castro. 2023. Community-driven governance of FAIRness assessment: An open issue, an open discussion. *Open Research Europe* 2. 146. https://doi.org/10.12688/openreseurope.15364.2 (last updated 30 January 2024).

Windhouwer, Menzo & Twan Goosen. 2022. Component metadata infrastructure. In Darja Fišer & Andreas Witt (eds.), *CLARIN: The infrastructure for language resources*, 191–222. https://doi.org/10.1515/9783110767377-008.

Antonina Werthmann

From spoken language data to TEI-based ISO standard

Abstract: This chapter provides an overview of widely used formats for the transcription and annotation of spoken language data across various linguistic subfields, with a focus on their conversion to the TEI-based Standard ISO 24624, "Language Resource Management – Transcription of Spoken Language". After a brief introduction to the topic, the chapter examines prominent transcription and annotation formats, highlighting their core features and applications. It then introduces the TEI-based ISO standard and explores methods for converting diverse formats to align with its specifications. The last but one section presents practical use cases demonstrating the standard's applicability in linguistic research. The chapter concludes with a discussion of the challenges and benefits associated with format conversion, emphasizing the importance of interoperability and standardisation in spoken language data analysis.

Keywords: spoken language, transcription, annotation, formats, conversion, TEI, ISO 24624

1 Introduction

Spoken language data encompasses recordings, transcriptions, and annotations of human speech collected from diverse contexts. The variability of such data is high. This reflects the richness and diversity of human communication itself. It includes structured monologues, such as formal speeches and presentations, as well as elicited responses gathered through experimental or guided methodologies. At the other end of the spectrum are spontaneous dialogues, which capture unplanned

Acknowledgement: The author acknowledges the use of Large Language Models (LLMs) as a writing aid in phrasing this chapter, based on the author's own texts, ideas, and concepts. Full responsibility for the content remains with the author. This chapter is based on work within the project *Collection replication for enhanced re-usability and preservation planning. A case study with the DOBES Archive*, funded by the German VolkswagenStiftung (grant number Az. 9A 966), and *Text+*, funded by the Deutsche Forschungsgemeinschaft (DFG, project number 460033370) as part of the German National Research Data Infrastructure (NFDI e. V.).

Antonina Werthmann, Digitale Sprachwissenschaft, Leibniz-Institut für Deutsche Sprache, R5 6-13, 68161 Mannheim, Baden-Württemberg, Germany, e-mail: werthmann@ids-mannheim.de

https://doi.org/10.1515/9783112208212-007

conversational exchanges, and multilogue interactions involving dynamic communication among multiple participants. Additionally, spoken language data often features instances of code-switching, where speakers alternate between different languages or dialects within the same conversation.

The contexts in which spoken language data is collected add to its variability. Controlled, acoustically optimised environments, such as soundproof studios, produce recordings with minimal background noise, ensuring high quality audio. Field recordings in naturalistic or outdoor environments, on the other hand, often present challenges such as overlapping speech, background noise and other auditory artefacts. These environmental factors have an impact on both the quality of the recordings and the complexity of subsequent transcription and analysis processes.

The importance of spoken language data spans a wide range of academic and practical domains. For linguists, for example, they provide crucial insights into phonetic patterns, syntactic structures, semantic nuances and sociolinguistic phenomena. This is important for the documentation of endangered languages, where such data are essential for the preservation of linguistic diversity and cultural heritage. In the technological field, spoken language data, for example, are the foundation for advances in areas such as phonetic analysis, speech recognition or conversational artificial intelligence, and drive innovation in applications that interact with human speech.

To realise the potential of spoken language data, they must be systematically stored, shared, and analysed using established or standardised formats. Furthermore, standardisation is the only way to ensure that data from different sources can be seamlessly integrated, enabling large-scale studies and facilitating interdisciplinary collaboration. This necessity underscores the importance of data conversion – the transformation of annotations and metadata from one format to another – as a vital step in meeting research and development needs.

This chapter examines the different formats used for the transcription and annotation of spoken language, their applications, and the challenges associated with converting spoken language data between formats. It also introduces a range of tools designed to facilitate data conversion. By addressing these issues, this chapter aims to support a better understanding of different formats and of the conversion of spoken language data.

2 Formats for spoken language data

This section describes some considerations in choosing appropriate formats for transcribing and annotating spoken language data. It emphasises the complexity of spoken language and the different research objectives that influence format requirements. It also provides an overview of the most commonly used formats, their strengths and suitability for different linguistic research contexts.

2.1 Challenges and considerations in format selection

2.1.1 Challenges of working with spoken language data

Spoken language data presents complexities that set it apart from written text, which typically adheres to standardised grammatical conventions. Unlike written language, spoken interactions often feature hesitations, fillers, repetitions, overlapping speech, and paralinguistic elements such as tone, intonation, and pauses. While these features enrich spoken data with communicative detail, they also pose challenges for transcription and annotation, requiring careful planning and methodological precision. Given these complexities, several critical decisions must be made at the outset of working with spoken language data. These initial decisions – from the choice of transcription conventions, to the level of annotation granularity, and the inclusion of metadata – have long-lasting implications for the entire research workflow. Revisiting such decisions at later stages is often not easy, resource-intensive, and time-consuming, which highlights the importance of a deliberate and well-considered approach from the outset. Among these decisions, the choice of transcription and annotation format is central, as it is closely linked to the context of data collection, the theoretical framework of the study, and the specific research objectives.

2.1.2 Purpose of data collecting: language documentation vs. description

One of the key factors influencing the choice of formats for transcribing and annotating spoken language data is the purpose for which the data is being collected. In particular, the distinction between language documentation and language description is important. While both fields deal with linguistic data, their goals, audiences, and methodological requirements differ, and this is reflected in the choice of an appropriate format. Language documentation focuses primarily on the collection and preservation of the widest possible variety of natural spoken (and written) language data, collected in their appropriate social and cultural contexts, with the aim of creating comprehensive, high-quality resources – such as audio/video recordings, transcriptions and annotations – for long-term preservation and reuse. In contrast, language description emphasises the production of analytical outputs, including grammars, dictionaries, and linguistic analyses, which primarily serve linguists and support theoretical research (cf. Austin 2006, Austin and Grenoble 2007, Himmelmann, 1998, 2006).

These different goals influence the choice of transcription and annotation formats. Language documentation projects prioritise interdisciplinary accessibility, reusability, and comprehensiveness. Formats used in such projects must support multiple "entry points" such as transcription, translation, and metadata, to accommodate diverse audiences, including community members and researchers from different disciplines (cf. Austin and Grenoble 2007, Nathan and Austin 2004). On the other hand, language description formats are more closely aligned with linguistic conventions, emphasizing analytical precision and ease of integration into linguistic workflows. However, it should be noted that effective documentation often requires some degree of linguistic analysis to ensure data completeness and usability. For example, the identification of gaps in lexical or grammatical coverage during the documentation requires analytical tasks that overlap with description (cf. Austin and Grenoble 2007, Himmelmann 2012). The same is true the other way around: Detailed analyses benefit from comprehensive data representation, as required for language documentation. This shows that the boundary between documentation and description can be fluid, and we need formats that can do both.

2.1.3 Intended application and tool

When the different formats are examined in detail in the following subsection, it will become clear that each format offers distinct advantages and is often optimised for specific research domains, such as language acquisition, multimodal interaction analysis, or conversation studies. The suitability of a format depends strongly on its alignment with the intended application and the linguistic or paralinguistic phenomena being studied. In addition, the choice of tools used for transcription and annotation adds another layer of complexity. Many tools come with unique conventions, structures, and file formats that must be carefully evaluated in conjunction with the chosen format. Ensuring compatibility between the technological capabilities of these tools and the research goals is critical to achieving an efficient and cohesive workflow.

2.1.4 Long-term preservation and sustainability of the data

Another consideration when choosing a format for transcription and annotation is to ensure the long-term preservation and sustainability of the data. Beyond meeting immediate research needs, it is important to ensure the usability and accessibility of the data for future studies and potential interdisciplinary applications. To achieve this, researchers should prioritise formats that adhere to widely accepted standards and are supported by a variety of tools. Standardised formats not only facilitate data sharing and interoperability across research projects, but also reduce the risk of obsolescence as technological environments evolve.

In summary, the process of working with spoken language data requires navigating a complex interplay of theoretical, practical, and technological considerations. From dealing with the inherent complexities of spoken interactions to aligning format choices with the goals of language documentation or description, each decision has far-reaching implications. By adopting formats that balance interdisciplinary accessibility, analytical rigor, and long-term sustainability, researchers can maximise the value and usability of their data, ensuring its relevance for current and future research.

2.2 Overview of major annotation formats for spoken language data

This subsection provides an overview of the most commonly used and well-established formats for transcribing and annotating spoken language data. These formats have been widely adopted in linguistic research because of their functionality, adaptability, and ability to accommodate the complexities of spoken language. Each format reflects specific methodological priorities and research contexts, so it is necessary to understand its key features and applications.

2.2.1 CHAT format

The CHAT (Codes for the Human Analysis of Transcripts) is a plain-text file format widely used for the transcription and annotation of spoken language data, particularly in research on child language acquisition and development (cf. MacWhinney 2000). The format has gained prominence through its extensive use in TalkBank,[1] one of the largest repositories of spoken language data, which includes corpora on child language acquisition, second language learning, classroom interactions, and clinical studies of language disorders such as aphasia and stuttering. To facilitate the transcription, annotation, and analysis of data in the CHAT format, the CLAN[2] (Computerized Language ANalysis) software was specifically developed.

1 https://talkbank.org/ (accessed 09 April 2025).

2 https://dali.talkbank.org/clan/ (accessed 09 April 2025).

CHAT is designed to represent spoken language data by incorporating both structural and linguistic annotations, such as orthographic transcription, phonetic details, and morphological coding. To achieve this, the format uses a number of specialised conventions, including tabulators, colons, percentage signs, and control codes. These elements help define structural features such as speaker turns, tier types, utterance boundaries, and other linguistic or contextual details, which can then also be analysed. Each tier is clearly specified and linked to specific points or segments within the speech data. While CHAT is primarily optimised for linguistic transcription, it also allows the inclusion of quite detailed metadata, like speaker information (age, gender, language, etc.), contextual notes, and coding for specific research purposes, all of which can be stored in the header (see Figure 1). The transcription of speaker utterances is included in the main tier, indicated by a * symbol in front of a speaker ID. The annotations are listed in a dependent tier, indicated by a % symbol. Annotations of linguistic elements such as pauses (.), retracing [//] and other phenomena can be encoded within the conversation flow.

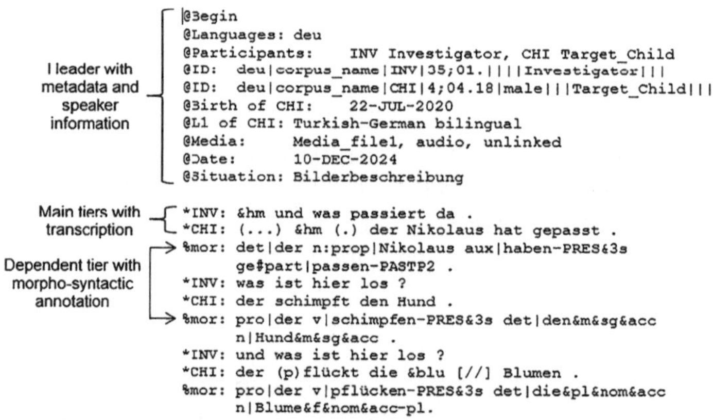

Figure 1: Excerpt of a CHAT transcription file.

CHAT is less suited for annotating multimodal material, such as gestures, gaze shifts, or body movements. Similarly, the format is less suitable for studies focusing on phonetics or prosody, where more specialised annotation systems may be required.

2.2.2 ELAN annotation format

The EAF (ELAN Annotation Format, also known as the EUDICO Annotation Format) is an XML-based data format based on the Abstract Corpus Model (cf. Brugman and

Russel 2004). It was developed by the Language Archive at the Max Planck Institute for Psycholinguistics in Nijmegen (cf. EAF Schema 2017) specifically for use with ELAN[3] (EUDICO Linguistic Annotator), one of the most widely used tools for the transcription and annotation of spoken language.

The EAF format is organised as a tiered structure, where a tier is a set of annotations that share common characteristics. There are two types of tiers: Independent tiers contain temporal annotations that refer directly to the timeline, e. g. used for orthographic transcriptions, while referential tiers contain annotations linked to annotations in another tier and therefore do not usually refer to the timeline itself, e. g. used for free translations or phonetic transcriptions. Annotations within a single tier cannot overlap, but annotations across tiers can. This structure allows users to represent hierarchical relationships in the dataset, where tiers can be linked as parent and child tiers.

As shown in the extract from an EAF transcription file below (see Figure 2), it includes a header section that stores metadata about the file, such as the au-

```
<?xml version="1.0" encoding="UTF-8"?>
<ANNOTATION_DOCUMENT AUTHOR="" DATE="2025-01-15T12:45:19+01:00" FORMAT="3.0" VERSION="3.0"
    xmlns:xsi="http://www.w3.org/2001/XMLSchema-instance"
    xsi:noNamespaceSchemaLocation="http://www.mpi.nl/tools/elan/EAFv3.0.xsd">
    <HEADER MEDIA_FILE="" TIME_UNITS="milliseconds">
        <MEDIA_DESCRIPTOR MEDIA_URL="../Media/EAF-example1.mpg" MIME_TYPE="video/mpg"
            RELATIVE_MEDIA_URL="../Media/EAF-example1.mpg"/>
        <!-- [...] -->
    </HEADER>
    <TIME_ORDER>
        <TIME_SLOT TIME_SLOT_ID="ts1" TIME_VALUE="0"/>
        <TIME_SLOT TIME_SLOT_ID="ts2" TIME_VALUE="2440"/>
        <TIME_SLOT TIME_SLOT_ID="ts3" TIME_VALUE="7520"/>
        <!-- [...] -->
        <TIME_SLOT TIME_SLOT_ID="ts12" TIME_VALUE="19240"/>
    </TIME_ORDER>
    <TIER LINGUISTIC_TYPE_REF="SPK01" TIER_ID="spk01">
        <ANNOTATION>
            <ALIGNABLE_ANNOTATION ANNOTATION_ID="a1" TIME_SLOT_REF1="ts1" TIME_SLOT_REF2="ts2">
                <ANNOTATION_VALUE>O.K., erzaehlst du mir das wieder?</ANNOTATION_VALUE>
            </ALIGNABLE_ANNOTATION>
        </ANNOTATION>
    </TIER>
    <TIER LINGUISTIC_TYPE_REF="SPK02" TIER_ID="spk02">
        <ANNOTATION>
            <ALIGNABLE_ANNOTATION ANNOTATION_ID="a2" TIME_SLOT_REF1="ts3" TIME_SLOT_REF2="ts4">
                <ANNOTATION_VALUE>ja</ANNOTATION_VALUE>
            </ALIGNABLE_ANNOTATION>
        </ANNOTATION>
        <ANNOTATION>
            <ALIGNABLE_ANNOTATION ANNOTATION_ID="a3" TIME_SLOT_REF1="ts5" TIME_SLOT_REF2="ts6">
                <ANNOTATION_VALUE>blue zuerst und dann die lilane,</ANNOTATION_VALUE>
            </ALIGNABLE_ANNOTATION>
        </ANNOTATION>
        <!-- [...] -->
    </TIER>
    <!-- [...] -->
</ANNOTATION_DOCUMENT>
```

Bracket labels (left of the listing, top to bottom): Header with metadata (HEADER); Timeline (TIME_ORDER); Tier for speaker SPK01 (first TIER); Tier for speaker SPK02 (second TIER).

Figure 2: Excerpt of an EAF transcription file.[4]

3 https://archive.mpi.nl/tla/elan (accessed 09 April 2025).

4 In this and all the following extracts, parts that are abbreviated for illustrating purposes are marked by [...].

thor, date, and media information. The timeline is defined in the <TIME_ORDER> section, where each <TIME_SLOT> assigns a timestamp (in milliseconds) to specific points in the media file. Speaker utterances and other annotations are organised into tiers defined by the <TIER> element. Each annotation is encoded within an <ALIGNABLE_ANNOTATION> element, which references the timeline via TIME_SLOT_REF1 and TIME_SLOT_REF2, linking the annotation to the start and end timestamps in the media file.

The EAF format's support for multimodal annotation makes it useful for researchers studying the interplay between language and nonverbal elements such as gestures, facial expressions, and body movements. It is widely used in linguistic and anthropological research, particularly in the documentation of endangered languages and the analysis of communicative behaviour.

2.2.3 EXMARaLDA transcription format

EXMARaLDA[5] (Extensible Markup Language for Discourse Annotation) is a system including data models, file formats, and free software tools designed for the creation, management, and analysis of spoken language corpora (cf. Schmidt 2004). Within the EXMARaLDA system, three main file formats are available: Basic-Transcriptions, Segmented-Transcriptions, and List-Transcriptions (cf. Cassidy and Schmidt 2017). Among these, the EXMARaLDA Basic-Transcriptions format, created and visualised in the Partitur-Editor,[6] plays an important role due to its interoperability. Therefore, when the term *EXMARaLDA format* is used in the following, it specifically refers to the EXMARaLDA Basic-Transcriptions format. Similar to ELAN's EAF format, the EXMARaLDA Basic-Transcriptions format is based on a STMT (Single Timeline, Multiple Tiers) data model, that organises annotation labels into tiers aligned with a fully ordered timeline (cf. Schmidt 2004). Each tier can be explicitly associated with a speaker and categorised into one of three types: transcription, description, or annotation.

As the extract from an EXMARaLDA Basic-Transcription below shows (see Figure 3), the general structure is similar to that of an EAF transcription. The header section stores metadata, including the project name, transcription name and media file reference. The timeline is defined in the <common-timeline> section, where each <tli> element assigns a timestamp to specific points in the media. Speaker

5 https://exmaralda.org/en/ (accessed 09 April 2025).

6 https://exmaralda.org/en/partitur-editor-en/ (accessed 09 April 2025).

```
<?xml version="1.0" encoding="UTF-8"?>
<!-- [...] -->
<basic-transcription>
    <head>
        <meta-information>
            <project-name>EXMARaLDA DemoKorpus</project-name>
            <transcription-name>Beckhams</transcription-name>
            <referenced-file url="BECKHAMS_MPEG-1.mpg"/>
            <!-- [...] -->
        </meta-information>
        <speakertable>
Header with     <speaker id="SPK0">
metadata and        <abbreviation>PAR</abbreviation>
speaker             <sex value="m"/>
information         <!-- [...] -->
              </speaker>
            <speaker id="SPK1">
                <abbreviation>VIC</abbreviation>
                <!-- [...] -->
            </speaker>
        </speakertable>
    </head>
    <basic-body>
        <common-timeline>
            <tli id="T15" time="0.0"/>
            <tli id="T0" time="0.21923076923076923"/>
Timeline    <tli id="T1" time="2.1866329681774834"/>
            <!-- [...] -->
            <tli id="T22" time="21.4"/>
            <tli id="T23" time="21.432"/>
        </common-timeline>
        <tier id="TIE0" speaker="SPK0" category="v" type="t"
            display-name="PAR [v]">
            <event start="T0" end="T1">And what comes through is
                your determination </event>
Tier for    <event start="T1" end="T2">at </event>
speaker SPK0 <event start="T2" end="T3">all </event>
            <event start="T3" end="T4">cost to actually </event>
            <event start="T4" end="T16">((0,35s)) </event>
            <event start="T16" end="T5">succeed. </event>
            <!-- [...] -->
        </tier>
        <tier id="TIE1" speaker="SPK1" category="v" type="t"
            display-name="VIC [v]">
            <event start="T2" end="T3">Yeah. </event>
Tier for    <!-- [...] -->
speaker SPK1 <event start="T18" end="T10">Yeah, I think that
                people don't realise that </event>
            <!-- [...] -->
        </tier>
    </basic-body>
</basic-transcription>
```

Figure 3: Excerpt of an EXMARaLDA Basic-Transcriptions file (from EXMARaLDA Media Test Battery[7]).

utterances and annotations are organised into `<tier>` elements, with each `<event>` specifying a start and an end time point on the timeline.

The EXMARaLDA format supports transcription and complex annotation tasks, including speaker turns, overlapping speech and detailed metadata integration, making it a format that can be used in different research contexts.

7 https://www.exmaralda.org/files/MEDIA-TEST-BATTERY.zip (accessed 09 April 2025).

2.2.4 FOLKER format

The FOLKER transcription format is an XML-based format used in FOLKER[8] (the FOLK EditoR) which was developed for the project "Forschungs- und Lehrkorpus Gesprochenes Deutsch (FOLK)"[9] (eng.: Research and Teaching Corpus Spoken German) at the Leibniz Institute for the German Language (cf. Schmidt and Schütte 2014). The FOLKER data format is a subset of the EXMARaLDA data model based on the STMT principle. This common foundation allows the two formats to share significant portions of their codebase, resulting in a commonality between them. Unlike the EXMARaLDA Basic-Transcription format, the data model of the FOLKER format does not support multi-level annotation tasks (cf. Schmidt and Schütte 2014). Instead, each tier is required to be assigned to a single speaker at the end time point on the timeline. This constraint simplifies the representation of speaker contributions, while allowing the temporal dynamics of turn-taking and overlapping speech to be captured. The format also supports annotations for linguistic elements such as words, pauses and other phenomena, following the GAT Transcription Conventions (cf. Selting et al. 1998).

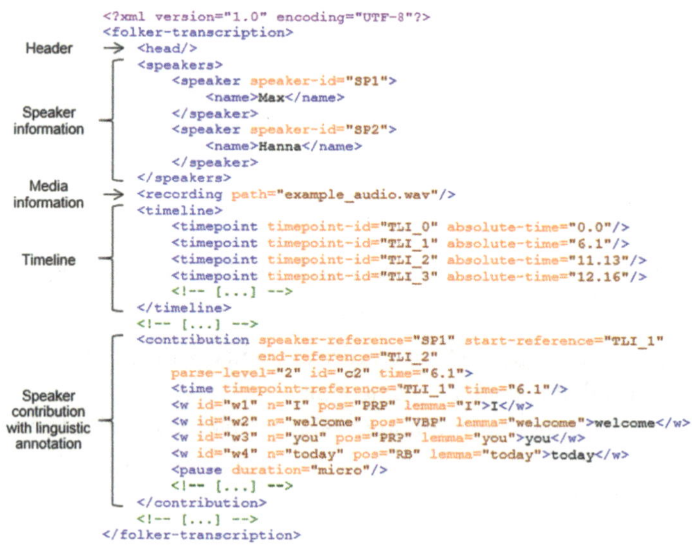

Figure 4: Excerpt of a FOLKER transcription file.

---

8 https://exmaralda.org/de/folker-de/ (accessed 09 April 2025).

9 https://agd.ids-mannheim.de/folk.shtml (accessed 09 April 2025).

As shown in Figure 4, the structure of the FOLKER format is flatter than the EXMARaLDA format. The speaker information, stored under the <speakers> element, and the media information, stored under the <recording> element, are not part of the header. Instead, they are structured as separate sections at the same hierarchical level as the header. The <timeline> section defines specific points in time in seconds using <timepoint> elements. Speaker contributions are encoded in <contribution> elements that reference the timeline to align utterances with time points on the timeline.

2.2.5 Transcriber format

The Transcriber file format (cf. Barras et al. 2001) is an XML-based file format designed specifically for use with the Transcriber tool,[10] which facilitates the segmentation, labelling and transcription of audio recordings. While it is primarily optimised for the transcription of audio files, the transcription of video files using the Transcriber tool depends on the operating system and specific configuration settings.

Header
Speaker information
Speech turn with start and end times for speaker spk1
Synchronization time point for aligning transcription with audio file

```
<?xml version="1.0" encoding="ISO-8859-1"?>
<!DOCTYPE Trans SYSTEM "trans-14.dtd">
<Trans scribe="myl" audio_filename="know" version="5" version_date="250322">
    <Speakers>
        <Speaker id="spk1" name="speaker#1" check="no" dialect="native"
            accent="" scope="local"/>
        <Speaker id="spk2" name="speaker#2" check="no" dialect="native"
            accent="" scope="local"/>
    </Speakers>
    <Episode>
        <Section type="report" startTime="0" endTime="23.962">
            <Turn speaker="spk1" mode="spontaneous" startTime="0"
                endTime="0.258">
                <Sync time="0"/> Excuse me, could you help me?
                How do I get to the nearest train station? </Turn>
            <Turn speaker="spk2" mode="spontaneous" startTime="0.258"
                endTime="2.41">
                <Sync time="0.258"/> Of course! Which train station
                are you looking for? </Turn>
            <Turn speaker="spk1" mode="spontaneous" startTime="2.41"
                endTime="4.77">
                <Sync time="2.41"/> I think it's called Central Station. </Turn>
            <Turn speaker="spk2" mode="spontaneous" startTime="4.77"
                endTime="9.202">
                <Sync time="4.77"/> Oh, Central Station is about a 10-minute
                walk from here. <!-- ... --> </Turn>
            <Turn speaker="spk1" mode="spontaneous" startTime="9.202"
                endTime="23.962">
                <Sync time="9.202"/> Thank you! Is it well signposted? </Turn>
        </Section>
    </Episode>
</Trans>
```

Figure 5: Excerpt of a Transcriber transcription file.

10 https://trans.sourceforge.net/en/Transcriber-LREC1998.php (accessed 09 April 2025).

Like the other formats described above, it can organise not only the orthographic transcription, but also information about turns, speakers, sections, acoustic state changes and other events. As shown in Figure 5, the speaker information is defined in the `<Speakers>` section, not in the header. The speaker contributions are recorded in `<Turn>` elements, which are linked to time points through `startTime` and `endTime` attributes.

The Transcriber format is well suited for creating simple, time-aligned transcriptions of spoken language data and is widely used in areas such as linguistic research, speech processing and corpus development.

2.2.6 TextGrid format

The TextGrid format is a specialised plain-text file format designed for use with Praat,[11] a widely used phonetic and acoustic analysis software. Similar to the tiered structures of the EAF and the EXMARaLDA format, the TextGrid format supports the creation of multiple annotation levels. However, unlike those two formats, TextGrid distinguishes between two types of tiers: interval tiers and point tiers. Interval tiers are used to annotate spans of time for events that have a defined start (`xmin` label for the starting time, see Figure 6) and end (`xmax` label for the end time), such as segments or words, while point tiers mark discrete moments within the timeline, such as minimum intensity points or maximum pitch. The tiers in TextGrid can operate independently or be organised hierarchically, allowing for versatile and detailed analyses of linguistic and acoustic phenomena. However, as Figure 6 illustrates, the hierarchy is not represented by the structure of the file format itself but rather indirectly through temporal overlap. For example, the `segments_text` tier covers the entire utterance from second 0.42 to 3.04, while the individual words in the `words_text` tier are arranged within this time span, creating an implicit hierarchical relationship between the segment and word levels. Furthermore, the excerpt from the TextGrid transcription file shows that there is no specific metadata about the speakers (such as name, gender, or age) or the media file. This information would have to be stored separately, for example, in a database or described in a CMDI[12] metadata file (cf. Zinn et al. 2016 or Trippel 2025).

---

11 https://www.fon.hum.uva.nl/praat/ (accessed 09 April 2025).

12 CMDI stands *for Component Metadata Infrastructure* and is a framework for modelling metadata to describe resources (https://www.clarin.eu/content/cmdi-component-metadata-infrastructure, accessed 09 April 2025).

```
File type = "ooTextFile"
Object class = "TextGrid"
```

Start and end time

```
xmin = 0.42
xmax = 3.04
tiers? <exists>
size = 2
item []:
```

Tier with transcription

```
    item [1]:
        class = "IntervalTier"
        name = "segments_text"
        xmin = 0.42
        xmax = 3.04
        intervals: size = 1
        intervals [1]:
            xmin = 0.42
            xmax = 3.04
            text = "Bonjour! Est-ce que vous allez bien?"
```

Tier with word segmention

```
    item [2]:
        class = "IntervalTier"
        name = "words_text"
        xmin = 0.42
        xmax = 3.04
        intervals: size = 7
        intervals [1]:
            xmin = 0.42
            xmax = 1.14
            text = "Bonjour!"
        intervals [2]:
            xmin = 1.14
            xmax = 1.92
            text = ""
        intervals [3]:
            xmin = 1.92
            xmax = 2.16
            text = "Est-ce"
        [...]
        intervals [7]:
            xmin = 2.58
            xmax = 3.04
            text = "bien?"
```

Figure 6: Excerpt of a TextGrid transcription file.

2.3 General comparison of formats

As outlined in the previous section, the different formats presented here use different strategies for structuring, presenting, and annotating data. While CHAT and TextGrid are plain-text file formats, the other formats described here are XML-based. Each storage format has its advantages. Plain-text file formats are characterised by simplicity, accessibility, and efficiency. Because they do not require complex parsing, they are lightweight and easy to process. Their human-readable nature enhances transparency, and they can be edited without the need for specialised tools. XML-based formats, on the other hand, offer advantages in terms of structure, flexibility, and interoperability. The XML-based data organisation can better support the representation of complex linguistic annotations, metadata, and relationships between different transcription layers. Furthermore, XML-based formats provide a well-defined schema that ensures validation and consistency, making them well suited for long-term preservation.

With respect to the structure of transcription formats, two primary types of data organisation and presentation can be distinguished: the list format and the partitur format. In the list format, speakers' utterances are organised vertically in chronological order, each entry typically beginning with the speaker's name, followed by their spoken production. This straightforward, top-to-bottom arrangement is used in Transcriber, CHAT and FOLKER, which are particularly suited for traditional orthographic transcription. These formats prioritise clarity and simplicity, offering a linear representation of spoken language data that is easy to read and interpret. As a result, they are well suited to projects that focus on textual transcription without the need for complex multimodal integration. In contrast, the partitur format is specifically designed to handle more complex data structures. Each speaker is allocated a horizontal tier that extends along the timeline from left to right. This format allows the inclusion of not only verbal data but also non-verbal elements, such as gestures, facial expressions, and gaze behaviour, as multiple tiers can be associated with a single speaker. Formats such as EAF, EXMARaLDA, and TextGrid are examples of this partitur-based structure. Their design provides flexibility and precision, making them well-suited for multimodal analyses and studies involving complex interactional data. This ability to seamlessly align disparate data streams is a key advantage for researchers working on projects that require a comprehensive and detailed examination of both verbal and nonverbal communication.

The formats can equally be categorised as single-level or multi-level, based on their ability to support annotation tiers (see Figure 7). Single-level formats, such as FOLKER (cf. Schmidt and Schütte 2014), are limited to one transcription level per speaker, but are suitable for simple dialogue transcription and basic linguistic tasks. Multi-level formats, such as CHAT, EAF, EXMARaLDA and TextGrid, allow any number of annotation levels for a given speaker. These formats support multiple, freely definable levels, enabling detailed and multi-dimensional annotation across categories such as orthography, International Phonetic Alphabet (IPA) transcription,

```
<contribution speaker-reference="SP1"
    start-reference="TLI_1"
    end-reference="TLI_2"
    <!-- [...] -->
    <w id="w1" n="I" pos="PRP" lemma="I">I</w>
    <w id="w2" n="welcome" pos="VBP"
       lemma="welcome">welcome</w>
    <w id="w3" n="you" pos="PRP" lemma="you">you</w>
    <w id="w4" n="today" pos="RB" lemma="today">today</w>
    <pause duration="micro"/>
    <!--  -->
</contribution>
```

```
<tier id="TIE0" speaker="SPK1" category="v" type="t"
    display-name="SPK1 [v]">
    <event start="T1" end="T2">I welcome
        you today</event>
</tier>
<tier id="TIE1" speaker="SPK1" category="lemma" type="a"
    display-name="SPK1 [lemma]">
    <event start="T1" end="T6">I</event>
    <event start="T6" end="T5">welcome</event>
    <event start="T5" end="T4">you</event>
    <event start="T4" end="T2">today</event>
</tier>
<tier id="TIE2" speaker="SPK1" category="pos" type="a"
    display-name="SPK1 [pos]">
    <event start="T1" end="T6">PRP</event>
    <event start="T6" end="T5">VBP</event>
    <event start="T5" end="T4">PRP</event>
    <event start="T4" end="T2">RB</event>
</tier>
```

Figure 7: Excerpt of an XML-based structure for single-level (left, FOLKER format) vs. multi-level (right, EXMARaLDA) annotation formats.

Part-of-Speech (POS), glosses and translations. The distinction between single-level and multi-level formats highlights the adaptability of the latter for complex linguistic and multimodal analyses, catering to different research needs.

Another difference is how timelines are represented within these formats (cf. Schmidt et al. 2009). For example, the EAF, EXMARaLDA and FOLKER formats use an explicit external timeline consisting of an ordered set of time anchors to which annotations refer (see Figure 8). This approach ensures precise temporal alignment and facilitates the analysis of multimodal data. On the other hand, formats such as CHAT and Transcriber use implicit timelines, where the order of timestamps in the transcription is directly linked to the media times in the recording. While this method is easier to manage, it may offer less flexibility in handling complex temporal relationships.

```xml
<Turn speaker="SPK-1" startTime="687.660"
endTime="688.900">
    <Sync time="687.660"/>A flower.</Turn>
<!-- [...]  -->
<Turn speaker="SPK-1" startTime="706.010"
    endTime="707.910">
    <Sync time="706.010"/>A cap and a flower.</Turn>
```

```xml
<TIME_ORDER>
    <!-- [...]  -->
    <TIME_SLOT TIME_SLOT_ID="ts126" TIME_VALUE="687660"/>
    <TIME_SLOT TIME_SLOT_ID="ts127" TIME_VALUE="688900"/>
    <!-- [...]  -->
    <TIME_SLOT TIME_SLOT_ID="ts130" TIME_VALUE="706010"/>
    <TIME_SLOT TIME_SLOT_ID="ts131" TIME_VALUE="707910"/>
    <!-- [...]  -->
</TIME_ORDER>

<ANNOTATION>
    <ALIGNABLE_ANNOTATION ANNOTATION_ID="a48"
        TIME_SLOT_REF1="ts126" TIME_SLOT_REF2="ts127">
        <ANNOTATION_VALUE>A flower.</ANNOTATION_VALUE>
    </ALIGNABLE_ANNOTATION>
</ANNOTATION>
<ANNOTATION>
    <ALIGNABLE_ANNOTATION ANNOTATION_ID="a49"
        TIME_SLOT_REF1="ts130" TIME_SLOT_REF2="ts131">
        <ANNOTATION_VALUE>A cap and
            a flower.</ANNOTATION_VALUE>
    </ALIGNABLE_ANNOTATION>
</ANNOTATION>
```

Figure 8: XML-based structure of an implicit (left, excerpt of a Transcriber transcription) vs. an explicit (right, excerpt of an EAF transcription) timeline.

The different strategies for structuring, presenting, and annotating data across formats become particularly relevant when data are converted between different formats. Inconsistencies in how data is organised and represented can lead to information loss or misalignment. For example, formats based on explicit timelines may have problems when converted to formats with implicit timelines, and vice versa. This includes calculating missing offsets when converting from explicit to implicit timelines, often through interpolation, and resolving conflicts between identical offsets when converting from implicit to explicit timelines (cf. Schmidt et al. 2009).

3 The TEI-based ISO standard "Transcription of Spoken Language"

The various formats and tools discussed in the previous section were designed to serve specific purposes effectively. However, their lack of interoperability posed challenges to data sharing and reuse across projects and disciplines. To address these limitations, the ISO 24624:2016 standard, entitled "Language Resource Management – Transcription of Spoken Language" (cf. ISO 24624 2016), was developed. This standard provides guidelines for encoding transcriptions and annotations of audio and video recorded spoken interactions in XML, following the widely recognised TEI Guidelines (cf. TEI Consortium 2025: Chapter 8 "Transcriptions of Speech"), which provide a framework for digital textual data encoding (more about standardising spoken language transcription: cf. Schmidt 2011).

The ISO 24624 is tailored to support transcription data in various fields, including sociolinguistics, conversation analysis, dialectology, corpus linguistics, lexicography, language technology, and qualitative social sciences. However, it explicitly excludes applications to other types of content, such as handwritten manuscripts. Its primary goal is to establish consistency by introducing standardised transcription conventions for spoken language, ensuring systematic and uniform annotation across datasets.

ISO 24624 conforms to the data models and encoding practices of transcription tools, like CLAN, ELAN, EXMARaLDA, FOLKER, and Transcriber. It is designed to be compatible with the formats of these tools and potentially others such as Praat, although additional conversion and annotation steps may be required to achieve full compatibility. The standard also takes into account transcription conventions such as CHAT (cf. MacWhinney 2000), DT (cf. Du Bois et al. 1983), GAT (cf. Selting et al. 1998), and HIAT (cf. Rehbein et al. 2014). However, achieving precise technical compatibility with these conventions is more complex due to their less formalised structure compared to software tool formats.

The modular design of the standard, based on the TEI framework, ensures adaptability to the diverse needs of transcription systems across disciplines while maintaining a unified encoding structure. It employs TEI elements to represent both the macrostructure and the microstructure of transcription data, as well as associated metadata. While the standard is primarily concerned with transcription encoding, metadata compatibility is addressed at a basic level through the TEI header, where the participants of the transcribed interaction are described in `<person>` elements inside the `<particDesc>` section of a `<profileDesc>`. The macrostructure organises the timeline (`<timeline>`) that defines points in the recording, speaker contributions (<u> elements) that contain the actual transcription text, as well as references to the timeline and to a participant, their temporal alignment (using attributes such as @start and @end attributes), and the overall structure of the interactions. Annotations can be represented using <spanGrp> and embedded <span> elements, with <annotationBlock> (see Figure 9) grouping speaker contributions with their related annotations to ensure coherence. The microstructure pertains to the fine-grained representation of spoken material, focusing on the linguistic and annotative granularity within the transcription. These include, for example elements such as tokens (<w> elements); pauses (<pause> elements), audible and visible non-speech events (<vocal>, <kinesic> and <incident> elements); punctuation (<pc> element); uncertainty, alternatives, incomprehensible and omitted passages (<unclear>, <choice>, <gap>). It also includes provisions for hierarchical divisions above and below the level of utterances (<u>).

```
<annotationBlock who="#SPK1" start="#T9" end="#T23" xml:id="ag10">
    <u xml:id="u10">
        <seg xml:id="seg30" type="utterance" subtype="declarative">
            <pause dur="PT0.4S"/>
            <w xml:id="w49">I</w>
            <w xml:id="w50">would</w>
            <w xml:id="w51">like</w>
            <w xml:id="w52">to</w>
            <w xml:id="w53">welcome</w>
            <w xml:id="w54">you</w>
            <w xml:id="w55">to</w>
            <w xml:id="w56">today's</w>
            <w xml:id="w57">meeting</w>
            <pc xml:id="pc2">,</pc>
            <pause dur="PT0.4S"/>
            <w xml:id="w58">and</w>
            <w xml:id="w59">thank</w>
            <w xml:id="w60">you</w>
            <!-- [...] -->
        </seg>
        <!-- [...] -->
    </u>
</annotationBlock>
```

Figure 9: Excerpt of a ISO 24624 transcription with an example for <annotationBlock> with tokens as <w> elements embedded in a <u> element (ISO 24624 2016: 26).

4 Tools for conversion of spoken language date to TEI-based ISO standard

Implementing ISO 24624 is not trivial. For researchers unfamiliar with XML-based encoding or with the Text Encoding Initiative, effective use of the standard may require specialised training. Another challenge is the perceived complexity of ISO 24624 for smaller-scale projects. The extensive and detailed coding requirements, while relevant for large-scale or multimodal studies, may seem overly burdensome for narrowly focused investigations or projects with limited resources.

Transcription tools such as FOLKER and EXMARaLDA have incorporated compatibility with the standard. These tools offer the ability to import and export annotated data directly in ISO 24624 format. For example, EXMARaLDA facilitates the annotation of multimodal interactions and supports the ISO 24624 format, enabling researchers to produce standardised datasets with minimal effort.

Converting a given transcription format to the ISO 24624 format is equally not a trivial task. As Schmidt et al. (2017) point out, the closer the structure of the original format is to the general TEI framework, the easier the conversion process will be. However, one advantage of the ISO 24624 format is that it can support more detailed and comprehensive information than any of the formats presented here, allowing lossless conversion. There are two main approaches to converting spoken language transcriptions and annotations from a given format to ISO 24624, or to another format. The first involves using tools designed for editing spoken language transcriptions, many of which include built-in format conversion utilities. The second approach relies on standalone conversion tools specifically designed to handle particular formats. These two approaches will be presented below.

4.1 Conversion using tools designed for editing spoken language transcriptions

The table below lists on tools related to the first approach, highlighting those that support the import and export of the formats introduced in Section 2.2. However, note that many of these tools also support additional formats beyond those discussed in this chapter. These additional formats are not included in this overview.

Table 1 illustrates the different capabilities of linguistic tools in managing specific data formats and in importing and exporting transcribed or annotated data. Among these tools, EXMARaLDA stands out for its support of multiple file formats, making it a versatile option for handling complex data workflows. Specifically, EXMARaLDA supports the import and export of all the formats discussed in Section 2.2. Moreover, it is the only tool observed here that provides full support for importing and exporting transcription and annotation data according to ISO 24624. In contrast, tools such as Praat and Transcriber appear to be more limited, either lacking export functionality or supporting a narrower range of import options. However, this limitation does not diminish their usefulness, but rather reflects their specialization in certain areas. For example, Praat is designed for phonetic analysis, while Transcriber is optimised for transcription-oriented tasks. CLAN is often used to analyse text corpora with language acquisition data. ELAN, on the other hand, is known for

Table 1: Tools for editing spoken language transcriptions and their supported formats.

Tool	Native file format	File extension	Supported import formats	Supported export format
CLAN	CHAT	*.cha	EAF, Textgrid	EAF, EXMARaLDA, TextGrid
ELAN	EAF	*.eaf	CHAT, TextGrid, Transcriber	CHAT, TextGrid
EXMARalDA	EXMARaLDA	*.exb	CHAT, EAF, FOLKER, TextGrid, Transcriber, ISO 24624	CHAT, EAF, FOLKER, TextGrid, Transcriber, ISO 24624
FOLKER	FOLKER	*.flk	EXMARaLDA, ISO 24624	EXMARaLDA, EAF, TextGrid, ISO 24624
Transcriber	Transcriber	*.trs	CHAT	
Praat	TextGrid	*.TextGrid		

its ability to handle multimodal data analysis. This comparison underscores the importance of selecting tools not only for their compatibility with specific formats, but also for their alignment with research goals.

It should be noted that the process of converting spoken language transcriptions and annotations from one format to another is inherently constrained by the capabilities and limitations of the tools used for conversion. As emphasised earlier, all of the tools and their formats mentioned here are typically designed to support specific features and structures, which means that the range of information they can accurately transfer is dependent on their implemented functionalities. A major challenge in this process is the potential loss or simplification of information, especially when certain data is supported differently in different formats. For example, in the CHAT format, essential metadata – such as age, gender, and native language of the participants – is stored in the header. When importing or exporting this data to another format, such as EAF or Transcriber, there is a risk that these critical details may not be retained, resulting in incomplete or inconsistent data sets. This highlights the importance of careful consideration when selecting data conversion tools and formats to minimise the risk of such losses.

4.2 Standalone conversion tools

Two other tools that must be included in this overview are standalone conversion tools whose primary function is not to edit spoken language data, but rather to convert data between different formats. Tools such as TEICORPO and TEIDrop automate data conversion, ensuring both consistency and accuracy while reducing the time required for such tasks.

4.2.1 TEICORPO

TEICORPO (cf. Parisse et al. 2020) is a conversion tool for spoken language transcriptions to the ISO 24624 standard. It is specifically designed to convert transcribed and annotated spoken language data from commonly used formats such as CHAT, EAF, Transcriber, and Praat files to ISO 24624. TEICORPO can also process other formats, but these are not the focus of this chapter. One of the main advantages of TEICORPO is its ability to perform bidirectional conversions. After converting the original transcription files to a target format, users can revert to their original format or convert them into other formats commonly used for spoken language transcription and editing.

TEICORPO is available both as a command-line interface, as a standalone operating system Java application, and as a Web service.[13] Beginners can use the web service for simple conversions, while advanced users and developers can integrate the command-line interface into more complex workflows. TEICORPO is open source (under the GPL-3.0 license) and available via the GitHub repository.[14]

4.2.2 TEI Drop

TEI Drop[15] is a Java-based application that is part of the EXMARaLDA toolset. Like TEICORPO, TEI Drop works according to ISO 24624 and supports file formats such as CHAT, EAF, EXMARaLDA, FOLKER and Transcriber. Reverse conversion from the TEI-based ISO standard to the abovementioned formats is not supported by the tool. TEI Drop allows the document to be parsed (i. e. analysed structurally) according to one of several transcription conventions specified in the Parse method drop-down menu. The HIAT (cf. Rehbein et al. 2014) and cGAT (cf. Schmidt et al. 2023) conventions are also supported. TEI Drop provides a user-friendly interface for batch processing, making it accessible to users with limited technical expertise.

In conclusion, the development of such standalone conversion tools facilitates the application of ISO 24624 across various research contexts. This is important for projects dealing with large or complex datasets, where manual conversion would otherwise be prohibitively labour-intensive.

13 https://ct3.ortolang.fr/teiconvert/index-en.html (accessed 09 April 2025).

14 Last version 1.41.16, from 7th December 2024, https://github.com/christopheparisse/teicorpo (accessed 09 April 2025).

15 https://exmaralda.org/en/tei-drop-en/ (accessed 09 April 2025).

5 Use of the TEI-based ISO standard for spoken language data

The research landscape focused on spoken language data shows that most researchers rely on well-established tools and formats that meet their specific research goals and methodological needs. These tools support the synchronization of audio and video recordings with transcriptions through graphical user interfaces, facilitating efficient data handling and analysis. However, the current observation suggests that the ISO 24624 format is rarely, if ever, used for the direct transcription or annotation of spoken language data.

As pointed out by Hedeland and Schmidt (2021), for a standard to be of real value to researchers and research infrastructure operators, it must be supported by sufficient use cases and software solutions that are compatible with existing tools and methodologies. Important steps have already been taken in this direction, as evidenced by the availability of several tools that not only support ISO 24624 import and export, such as EXMARaLDA, but also provide converters, such as TEICORPO and TEIDrop. Additionally, a set of XSLT stylesheets for ISO 24624 processing is available in the GitHub repository of EXMARaLDA.[16] Such resources and tools facilitate compatibility between different transcription and annotation frameworks and serve as a fundamental mechanism for enabling data exchange.

Another example of the use of data in ISO 24624 is ZuMult, an open source framework designed to provide flexible access to spoken language corpora distributed across different repositories (cf. Batinić et al. 2021). It uses an architecture that facilitates browsing and querying audiovisual corpora, while being adaptable to different technological infrastructures and user requirements (see Frick and Schmidt 2025).

ISO 24624 plays an important role in the long-term preservation of spoken language data. Its key characteristics – interoperability, flexibility, accuracy, and sustainability – ensure that data remain accessible and reusable over time. The high level of standardisation facilitates data integration across different tools, platforms, research projects, and infrastructures, thereby improving interoperability. This is important to ensure that archived data remains accessible and usable as tools and research methodologies evolve. Furthermore, ISO 24624 supports metadata, complex annotations and hierarchical structures. This adaptability enables archives to integrate and standardise data from multiple sources and formats without compromising specific research needs.

---

16 https://github.com/Exmaralda-Org/exmaralda/tree/master/src/org/exmaralda/tei/xml (accessed 09 April 2025).

6 Summary and conclusion

This chapter can be summarised as follows: spoken language data is inherently complex, characterised by features such as spontaneity, frequent overlap, prosodic elements (e. g. intonation, stress, pauses), non-linear structures, syntactic variability, and multimodal aspects such as gestures and facial expressions. To adequately capture this complexity, transcription and annotation must meet specific requirements, which has led to the development of specialised formats. Among the most established formats are CHAT, EAF, EXMARaLDA, FOLKER, Transcriber, and TextGrid. These formats differ in their approach to data structuring, organisation, and presentation, as well as in their methods of timeline representation. The choice of a particular format is typically determined by the theoretical framework, research goals, methodological priorities, and specific research context. Ultimately, the choice of transcription format should be guided by a careful balance between usability and the ability to meet specific needs.

Selecting an appropriate format in advance is crucial, as retrospective format changes or data conversion can be complex and time-consuming, often with the risk of losing, simplifying, or distorting the information embedded in the transcription and annotation. To mitigate this risk, efforts have been made to standardise spoken language transcription and annotation formats, leading to the development of ISO 24624. While ISO 24624 is not primarily designed for direct transcription and annotation of spoken language data, it offers advantages over established formats, including greater interoperability, long-term sustainability, and adaptability to evolving needs. ISO 24624 plays an important role in the archiving and long-term accessibility of linguistic data, ensuring that spoken language resources are preserved and remain available for future interdisciplinary research. Given its benefits, the expansion of ISO 24624-based resources and the development of tools to support them remain key priorities for advancing research in spoken language processing.

Bibliography

Austin, Peter K. 2006. Data and language documentation. In Jost Gippert, Nikolaus P. Himmelmann & Ulrike Mosel (eds.), *Essentials of language documentation*, 87–112. Berlin, New York: De Gruyter Mouton.

Austin, Peter K. & Lenore A. Grenoble. 2007. Current trends in language documentation. *Language Documentation and Description* 4. 12–25.

Barras, Claude, Edouard Geoffrois, Zhibiao Wu & Mark Liberman. 2001. Transcriber: Development and use of a tool for assisting speech corpora production. *Speech Communication (Speech Annotation and Corpus Tools)* 33. 5–22.

Batinić, Josip, Elena Frick & Thomas Schmidt. 2021. Accessing spoken language corpora: an overview of current approaches. *Corpora* 16(3). 417–445.

Brugman, Hennie & Albert Russel. 2004. Annotating multi-media/multi-modal resources with ELAN. In Maria Teresa Lino, Maria Francisca Xavier, Fátima Ferreira, Rute Costa & Raquel Silva (eds.), *Proceedings of the fourth international conference on language resources and evaluation (LREC'04)*. Lisbon, Portugal: European Language Resources Association (ELRA).

Cassidy, Steve & Thomas Schmidt. 2017. Tools for multimodal annotation. In *Handbook of linguistic annotation*, Vol. I, 209–227. Dordrecht: Springer.

Du Bois, John, Stephan Schuetze-Coburn, Susanna Cumming & Danae Paolino. 1983. Outline of discourse transcription. In Jane A. Edwards & Martin D. Lampert (eds.), *Transcription and coding in discourse research*, 45–89. Hillsdale, NJ: Erlbaum.

EAF Schema. ELAN Annotation Format. Schema version: 3.0 (Schema release date: January 2017). The Language Archive Max Planck Institute for Psycholinguistics. Nijmegen, The Netherlands. https://www.mpi.nl/tools/elan/EAF_Annotation_Format_3.0_and_ELAN.pdf (accessed 24 March 2025).

Frick, Elena & Thomas Schmidt. 2025. Querying spoken language data. In Piotr Bański, Ulrich Heid & Laura Herzberg (eds.), *Harmonising language data: Standards for linguistic resources*. Berlin: De Gruyter.

Hedeland, Hanna & Thomas Schmidt. 2021. The TEI-based ISO standard "Transcription of Spoken Language" as an exchange format within CLARIN and beyond, virtual edn. In *Proceedings of CLARIN Annual Conference 2021*, 27–29 September 2021, 100–104. CLARIN.

Himmelmann, Nikolaus P. 1998. Documentary and descriptive linguistics. *Linguistics* 36(1). 161–196.

Himmelmann, Nikolaus P. 2006. Language documentation: What is it and what is it good for. In Jost Gippert, Nikolaus P. Himmelmann & Ulrike Mosel (eds.), *Essentials of language documentation*, 1–30. Berlin, New York: De Gruyter Mouton.

Himmelmann, Nikolaus P. 2012. Linguistic data types and the interface between language documentation and description. In *Language documentation and conservation*, Vol. 6, 187–207. University of Hawai'i Press.

ISO 24624. 2016. *Language resource management – Transcription of spoken language*.

MacWhinney, Brian. 2000. *The CHILDES Project: Tools for analyzing talk*. Mahwah, NJ: Lawrence Erlbaum.

Nathan, David & Peter K. Austin. 2004. Reconceiving metadata: Language documentation through thick and thin. *Language Documentation and Description* 2. 179–188.

Parisse, Christophe, Carole Etienne & Loïc Liégeois. 2020. TEICORPO: A conversion tool for spoken language transcription with a pivot file in TEI. *Journal of the Text Encoding Initiative* (Issue 13).

Rehbein, Jochen, Thomas Schmidt, Bernd Meyer, Franziska Watzke & Annette Herkenrath. 2014. *Handbuch für das computergestützte Transkribieren nach HIAT*. Vol. Arbeiten zur Mehrsprachigkeit: Folge B, Sonderforschungsbereich 538 (56). Hamburg: Universität Hamburg.

Schmidt, Thomas. 2004. Transcribing and annotating spoken language with EXMARaLDA. In *Proceedings of the LREC – Workshop on XML based richly annotated corpora*, Lisbon 2004. European Language Resources Association (ELRA).

Schmidt, Thomas. 2011. A TEI-based approach to standardising spoken language transcription. *Journal of the Text Encoding Initiative* (Issue 1).

Schmidt, Thomas, Susan Duncan, Oliver Ehmer, Jeffrey Hoyt, Michael Kipp, Dan Loehr, Magnus Magnusson, Travis Rose & Han Sloetjes. 2009. An exchange format for multimodal annotations. In *Multimodal corpora. From models of natural interaction to systems and applications*, 207–221. Berlin: Springer.

Schmidt, Thomas, Hanna Hedeland & Daniel Jettka. 2017. Conversion and annotation web services for spoken language data in CLARIN. In *Linköping Electronic Conference Proceedings; Selected papers from the CLARIN Annual Conference 2016, Aix-en-Provence, 26–28 October 2016, CLARIN Common Language Resources and Technology Infrastructure*, Vol. 2017, 113–130. Linköping University Electronic Press.

Schmidt, Thomas & Wilfried Schütte. 2014. FOLKER: An annotation tool for efficient transcription of natural, multi-party interaction. In *Proceedings of the seventh international conference on language resources and evaluation (LREC 10), May 19–21, 2010, Valletta, Malta*, 2091–2096. European Language Resources Association (ELRA).

Schmidt, Thomas, Wilfried Schütte, Jenny Winterscheid, Mia Schürmann, Silke Reineke & Evi Schedl. 2023. *cGAT. Konventionen für das computergestützte Transkribieren in Anlehnung an das Gesprächsanalytische Transkriptionssystem 2 (GAT2).* Mannheim: Leibniz-Institut für Deutsche Sprache.

Selting, Margret, Peter Auer, Birgit Barden, Jörg Bergmann, Elizabeth Couper-Kuhlen, Susanne Günthner, Christoph Meier, Uta Quasthoff, Peter Schlobinski & Susanne Uhmann. 1998. Gesprächsanalytisches Transkriptionssystem (GAT). *Linguistische Berichte* 173. 91–122.

TEI Consortium (eds.). 2025. *Guidelines for Electronic Text Encoding and Interchange. P5 Version 4.9.0*. Last updated on 24th January 2025, revision f73186978. https://tei-c.org/release/doc/tei-p5-doc/en/html/index.html (accessed 24 March 2025).

Trippel, Thorsten. 2025. Metadata for Research Data. In Piotr Bański, Ulrich Heid & Laura Herzberg (eds.), *Harmonising language data: Standards for linguistic resources*. Berlin: De Gruyter.

Zinn, Claus, Thorsten Trippel, Steve Kaminski & Emanuel Dima. 2016. Crosswalking from CMDI to Dublin Core and MARC 21. In Nicoletta Calzolari, Khalid Choukri, Thierry Declerck, Sara Goggi, Marko Grobelnik, Bente Maegaard, Joseph Mariani, et al. (eds.), *Proceedings of the Tenth International Conference on Language Resources and Evaluation (LREC'16)*, 2489–2495. Portorož, Slovenia: European Language Resources Association (ELRA).

Piotr Bański and Nils Diewald
Dealing with multiple annotations

Abstract: The present chapter focuses on corpora that feature multiple layers of annotation and looks at the phenomenon from an application-based perspective, couched in the real-life context of DeReKo (the largest linguistically motivated collection of contemporary written German) and of the analysis engine KorAP that makes it possible to analyse texts with reference to multiple annotations. The authors review the basic concepts needed for talking about multiple annotations, present the most notorious obstacle in dealing with them in an XML-based format, show the basic ways of tackling it that have been suggested in the literature, and conclude with a presentation of KorAP-XML, an internal format designed for the purpose of easy enrichment of DeReKo texts with many diverse annotation layers.

Keywords: multiple annotations, overlapping annotations, KorAP, DeReKo, specialised format, parallel processing

1 Introduction

This chapter looks at a phenomenon that is nearly by definition present in multimodal language resources and by now also commonplace in all kinds of textual corpora – namely, the existence of multiple and oftentimes not fully complementary annotation components. We talk about some of the reasons for wanting or having to create multiple annotations and survey the means of accommodating them in language resources (mostly of the textual kind). We also talk about the roles that multiple annotations may play in various exploitation scenarios. Lastly, we present one possible way of handling multiple annotations in the complex real-life context of DeReKo and KorAP.

1.1 Basic assumptions

In approaching the topic, we make several assumptions. Some of them follow from the general nature of the present volume, while others are meant to heavily constrain the scope of the present study, in order to keep it chapter-sized and at the same time grounded in a well-defined use case.

Piotr Bański, Nils Diewald, Leibniz-Institut für Deutsche Sprache, R5 6-13, D-68161 Mannheim, Baden-Württemberg, Germany, e-mails: banski@ids-mannheim.de, diewald@ids-mannheim.de

https://doi.org/10.1515/9783112208212-008

The primary goal of this chapter is to address one of the putative actors of the book's scenario (see Bański et al. 2025): a researcher "with data on their hands" and with a willingness to "do something useful" with that data. The chapter provides an answer to the potential questions of why researchers should need to consider adding additional annotation layers to their data, and of what to pay attention to if they decide to do that in which cases.

What we therefore take as given is that – ideally, from the point of view of the standardisation scenarios espoused in this book – texts are encoded in Unicode (see Wartena 2025) and carry the appropriate language identification information (see Romary 2025). They may be enriched with part-of-speech and other annotations (see Ljubešić and Erjavec 2025 and Schwarz 2025). We also assume that the metadata follows the appropriate best practices (see Trippel 2025) and that, if the texts are transcriptions of speech, the relevant binaries are in the advocated standard formats (see Ferreira et al. 2025, while the transcription conventions and the internal structure of the resource follow the guidelines outlined in Frick and Schmidt 2025). At an abstract level, we view the information that is added, whether in the annotation or in the metadata component (see the discussion of Figure 1), as attribute-value structures, even if parts of those structures are only implied. When pressed for a technical implementation, we point at the ISO Feature Structure Representation (ISO 24610-1), available, among others, in the form of Chapter 19 of the TEI Guidelines.[1]

Before we move to present those of our assumptions that are strongly anchored in our everyday work, we also by necessity need to acknowledge the existence of less tangible circumstances that stem from the sociology of the field, and, ultimately, from the human nature: the existence of multiple schools of thought and various trends that govern their establishment and uptake, the existence of various corpus-oriented tools on the market – "seeing" different pieces of the original data and producing different output formats. Further, we acknowledge the existence of varying approaches to preparing the initial data set (by scanning, typing, transcribing, etc.), with ensuing varying approaches to tokenization (see e. g., Frick and Schmidt 2025, Section 3 for why there is no single way to tokenize; see Chiarcos et al. 2012, for another statement of the problem, with a suggested solution).

1.2 What we build on: DeReKo

The practical context in which we consider the topic at hand is the multi-layer, largely automated annotation of a very large corpus, DeReKo (Deutsches Referenz-

1 https://tei-c.org/release/doc/tei-p5-doc/en/html/FS.html

korpus, the German Reference Corpus), which poses specific additional and non-generalizable challenges. DeReKo (Kupietz and Keibel 2009, Kupietz et al. 2010, 2018) was developed and is maintained at the Leibniz Institute for the German Language in Mannheim, and presents the largest linguistically motivated corpus of written contemporary German. It is used in particular for basic linguistic research. With currently over 61 billion words, it consists of a wide range of texts of different genres, including news articles, legal texts, fiction, scientific texts or texts of computer-mediated communication. DeReKo is archived in a format referred to as I5 (Lüngen and Sperberg-McQueen 2012, see also Lüngen and Pisetta 2025), which is a customisation of TEI P5 (TEI Consortium 2025). For the purpose of further processing, DeReKo data are converted from I5 into KorAP-XML, which is enriched with multiple annotation layers and ingested into the corpus analysis platform KorAP (Bański et al. 2012, Diewald et al. 2016).

1.3 Our angle: the application perspective

When discussing the ways of handling multiple annotations, we do so mainly from the application perspective, and we categorize possible purposes for formats against the following use cases, whereby the formats generally allow all of them, but are more suitable for some of them than for others. We do not claim that the following list is exhaustive.

1. *Archiving*: The content and annotations are to be preserved in the format under consideration. In addition to the expected volume, the independence of special software for reading the data is decisive for this use case.
2. *Exchanging*: The content and annotations should be able to be exchanged between different processes. For this purpose, the format must be very generic in order to be convertible to and from a wide range of data.
3. *Post-processing*: The content and annotations should be easy to process. To this end, they must be easy to modify and enrich.
4. *Querying*: The content and annotations should be easily searchable and analysable in the format.

1.4 Overview of the chapter

Section 2 presents concepts and terms related to multiple annotations. Section 3 looks at the general challenges of representing and handling multiply annotated texts and presents established approaches to representing such texts in XML. Section 4 builds on this by presenting various formats and standards that have been established for linguistic corpora. Finally, Section 5 presents our approach for the representation of multiply annotated texts in a scenario for very large corpora and (extensively) automated annotation.

2 Multiple annotations: basic terminological distinctions

2.1 Corpus data models

The multitude of uses to which corpora are put nowadays necessitate a robust typology of corpus data models, i. e., abstract hierarchies of data containers as well as relations and constraints defined on them. Depending on what data containers the given model distinguishes (or licences), they can be effectively targeted by visualisation and query tools. Interoperability between data and tools can thus somewhat simplistically be defined as the ability to distinguish and target a shared inventory of data containers.

Figure 1 diagrams the data model of a typical textual corpus (see also Bański et al. 2025). Since, for the present chapter, it is relevant that the annotation component can come in multiples, the model diagram highlights that accordingly.

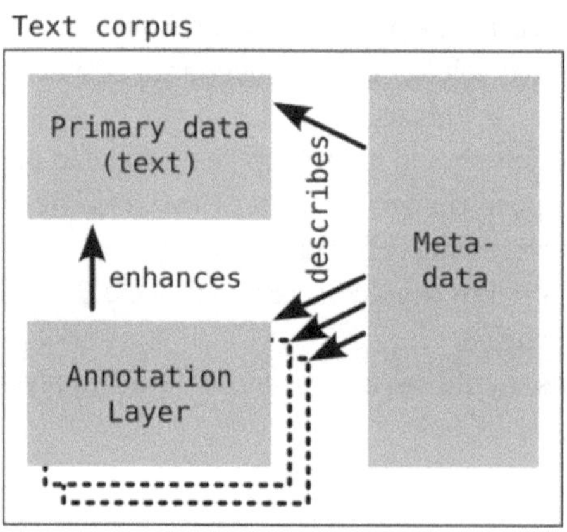

Figure 1: Diagram of the basic data model of an annotated text corpus with multiple annotation layers.

Textual corpus data essentially consists of three components: a) the primary textual data, which usually represents a textual unit such as a paragraph or a document, b) metadata describing this unit and optionally c) annotations that add additional information to the primary text, for example linguistic features.

2.2 Annotations and metadata

The diagram in Figure 1 contains distinctions based on certain compromises, typical for the modelling process, where only the relevant properties are highlighted while others are suppressed.

If the intuitive definitions of the terms *annotation* and *metadata* are considered, annotations are extra information attached to some fragments of data, whereas metadata is data about data. Both terms could be (and have been) used interchangeably, but, in general practice and for convenience, researchers tend to assign differing extensions to them. That practice is followed in this chapter, and an attempt at substantiating the difference in the usage of these two terms is made below.

In order to facilitate the exposition, the terminological distinctions in this section are introduced on the basis of a restricted data domain, namely textual resources with a single and uniform layer of tokenisation. Such a restriction makes it possible to (a) confine the discussion presented in this chapter to a well-defined, restricted range of cases, (b) offer a starting point for extending the potential taxonomy of kinds of multiple annotations, (c) base the present chapter upon the real use cases of DeReKo and KorAP.

In a typical monolingual electronic textual corpus, the stream of bytes interpreted as characters and divided into tokens provides a single continuous basis for the attachment of annotations.[2] This basis will in what follows be called an (*annotation*) *pivot*. A working distinction between the extensions of the terms "annotation" and "metadata" can be made on that basis: annotations are ontologically secondary data that are attached sequentially along the pivot, whereas metadata is ontologically secondary data that are attached elsewhere.[3] There is no restriction on the number of annotation pivots in a corpus. In particular, multi-layer annotation of a

2 In many cases, a distinction between word- and punctuation-tokens is invoked; the present exposition does not require that distinction.

3 Note that this opens the way to claims that ontologically tertiary data added to annotations, e. g. (references to) names of tools or annotators, or statements about the likelihood of the content of the given annotation to be a better fit than other, competing content, also deserve to be called metadata. We note this possibility but do not explore it any further.

text corpus may use the primary annotation pivot at the level of tokens, and a secondary pivot at the level of syntactic words, i. e., atoms of syntactic description, if the latter are not in a one-to-one relationship with the tokens (that is the case of, among others, the National Corpus of Polish, see Głowińska and Przepiórkowski 2010, and many other corpora that, e. g., tokenize texts into fragments smaller than those that correspond to broadly defined words).

Figure 2 shows the character data stream at the bottom, with tokens indicated as thick horizontal lines and forming the primary annotation pivot of the corpus. Upon that pivot, an annotation layer identifying parts of speech is built.[4]

Figure 2: The corpus data stream at the bottom, the tokenisation layer marked with thick horizontal lines (the primary annotation pivot of the corpus), with the POS annotation layer built upon it. The particular tags indicate, respectively from the left, a personal pronoun, the auxiliary *be*, the main verb in the progressive form, an adverb, and a punctuation mark.[5]

Figure 2 indicates that the annotation pivot should not be identified with the concept of the data stream.[6] Attested pivots for corpus representation include linear sequences of characters, linear sequences of tokens (as assumed here) or, for multimodal collections involving audio and/or video data streams, a pivot may be an abstract timeline of designated granularity (e. g. on the scale of seconds or milliseconds), which is either made more concrete by establishing a linear sequence of token-like events along it, or which is merely referenced in terms of time offsets (see Frick and Schmidt 2025, for discussion and illustrations).

4 In this case, the POS labels come from the CLAWS-5 tagset, and the text has been tokenised and tagged with the free tagger made available by the Lancaster University at https://ucrel-api.lancaster.ac.uk/claws/free.html

5 See https://ucrel.lancs.ac.uk/claws5tags.html for a more detailed explanation.

6 If the data stream is designated as the primary pivot, the tokenisation layer becomes the first annotation layer, and this is how conflicting tokenisations can be represented. In the real-life scenario outlined later in this chapter, the KorAP-XML format is agnostic with respect to whether it stores information about a single tokenisation layer or many. However, the specific fine-tuning of the KorAP analysis engine makes it necessary to only use a single tokenisation layer.

2.3 Kinds of multiple annotations

This section looks at the various kinds of what can be referred to as "multiple annotations" and sketches a basic taxonomy that is useful in the remainder of this chapter.[7]

Among annotations that are based on the same pivot, we distinguish the following major groups:

a. structurally complementary annotations
b. structurally stacked annotations (fully overlapping annotations)
c. structurally conflicting annotations (partially overlapping annotations)

These distinctions are exemplified in the diagrams in Figure 3.

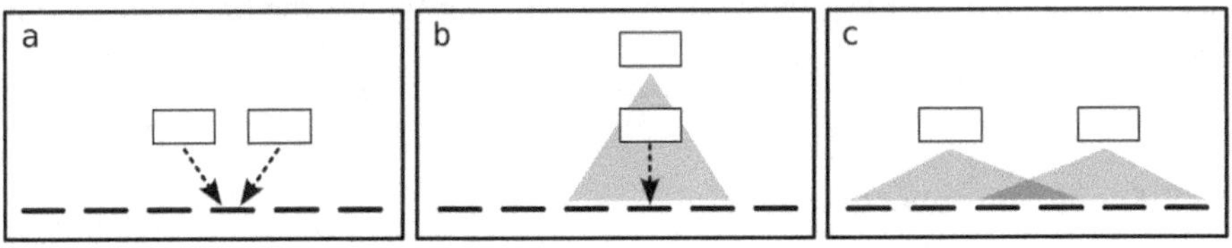

Figure 3: Diagrams showing various arrangements of multiple annotations based on the same pivot: complementary (a), stacked (b), and conflicting (c).

In the remainder of this section, we first look at these arrangements in more detail, and afterwards we briefly survey other ways of defining and referencing multiple annotations.

2.3.1 Complementary and stacked annotations

Structurally complementary and stacked annotations are illustrated in an extended version of Figure 2, shown in Figure 4.

In structural terms, the span dominated by the VP node in Figure 4 fully overlaps the annotations identifying the auxiliary, the main verb, and the adverb. The annotations for the NP node and the initial pronoun are structurally com-

---

7 The discussion in this section applies to the abstract, modelling level. For an important taxonomy of multiple, and specifically overlapping, annotations at the format (XML) level, see Durusau and O'Donnell (2001).

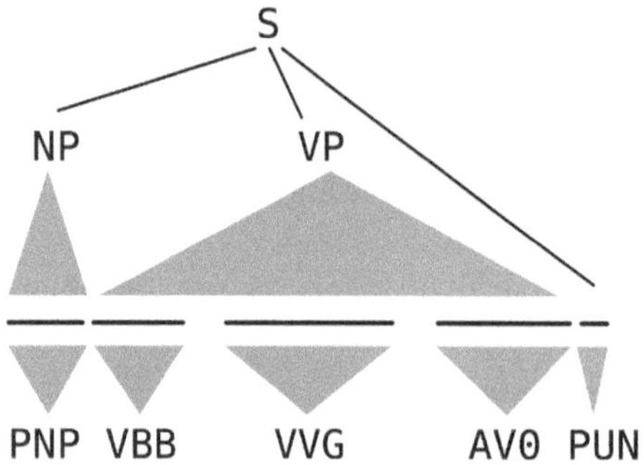

Figure 4: At the bottom is the POS-annotation familiar from Figure 2. The same annotation pivot is also used to create syntactic structure, with the labels “S”, “NP”, and “VP” standing for, respectively, a sentence node, a noun phrase node, and a verb phrase node.

plementary, and the same is the case for the token containing the final punctuation mark.[8]

2.3.2 Conflicting annotations

Annotations of structural linguistic ambiguity are an example of a conflict regarding competing tree representations. The sentence “The policeman saw the man with the telescope” (from Jurafsky and Martin 2000, p. 814) can be interpreted as indicated in Examples 1 and 2.

- [$_{S}$ [$_{NP}$ The policeman] [$_{VP}$ [$_{V}$ saw] [$_{NP}$ the man [$_{PP}$ with the telescope]]]]

Example 1: Labeled bracketing for the phrase “The policeman saw the man with the telescope”, interpreted with the prepositional phrase (PP) describing the noun *man*. Paraphrase: “The policeman saw the man who was holding the telescope”.

- [$_{S}$ [$_{NP}$ The policeman] [$_{VP}$ [$_{V}$ saw] [$_{NP}$ the man] [$_{PP}$ with the telescope]]]

Example 2: Labeled bracketing for the phrase “The policeman saw the man with the telescope”, interpreted with the prepositional phrase as a modifier of the verb *saw*. Paraphrase: “The policeman used the telescope to see the man”.

8 We stress that we use purely structural relationships. It might be argued that the POS annotation is ontologically primary, in the sense that the syntactic layer is built bottom-up, on the basis of the POS information. However, it is just as possible that, for languages with strict word order, the position of a token in a sentence serves as an indicator of its part-of-speech label. Restricting ourselves to structural distinctions allows us to avoid the above speculations.

Both readings are valid and could enrich the primary text as an annotation. However, their structural tree representations are not compatible with each other, i. e. they cannot be mapped without overlaps. Such conflicts (structurally conflicting annotations, illustrated in point (c) of Figure 3) can have their origin in ambiguities, but also in different interpretations by different annotators.

In addition to such conflicts within a single annotation layer, there may also be conflicts, i. e. overlaps, across the boundaries of individual linguistic layers, for example in structural annotations of poetry. Enjambment, for example, is a figure in poetry in which a sentence or its fragment stretches beyond a single verse line. In such cases, the syntactic annotation built over sentences has to conflict with the structural annotation (i. e. lines of verse). In the following poem from *The Winter's Tale* by William Shakespeare, the annotation trees of the two layers are incompatible:

```
<line><s>I am not prone to weeping, as our sex</line>
<line>Commonly are;</s> <s>the want of which vain dew</line>
<line>Perchance shall dry your pities;</s> <s>but I have</line>
<line>That honourable grief lodged here which burns</line>
<line>Worse than tears drown.</s></line>
```

Example 3: Incompatible annotation trees for lines of verse (marked with <line> tags in pseudo-XML) vs. sentence divisions (marked with <s> tags).

2.3.3 Competing annotations

Another distinction, not based on structural relationship but rather on the content of the labels, and thus orthogonal to the distinctions made above, is that of *competing annotations*. The metaphor invoked here is that of a competition for a single annotation "slot", and it may be illustrated by the arrangement well-known from Universal Dependencies,[9] where two sets of part-of-speech labels are typically used for annotating tokens, as shown in Example 4.

5 år år NOUN NN.NEU.PLU.IND.NOM Case=Nom | Definite=Ind | Gender=Neut | Number=Plur

Example 4: A line of the CoNLL-U format for the Swedish word *år* "year".[10]

The UD part-of-speech annotations ('NOUN' and 'NN.NEU.PLU.IND.NOM') compete to supply the content to the same information label, but they need not con-

9 https://universaldependencies.org/

10 See https://universaldependencies.org/format.html for more details.

flict – in most cases, the “universal” part-of-speech label is more general than the language-specific one, hence, in terms of content, the former subsumes the latter. For example, the “NOUN” label of the universal tagset is more general than the composite label of the Swedish tagset, which also indicates various morphosyntactic values (gender, number, definiteness, case). On the other hand, part-of-speech or named-entity labels may be supplied by different tools that make drastically different guesses – that kind of conflict is more obviously of a competing nature. The competing annotations in Example 4 are classified as structurally complementary. In what follows, we avoid using the term “competing” in favour of more neutral structural distinctions.

2.3.4 Annotations not based on shared pivots

Among annotations not based on shared pivots, two cases are worth highlighting for the sake of completeness: *aligned annotations* – which are built on separate pivots, based on separate data streams, and which are related only indirectly, by virtue of the fact that they annotate (for example) tokens in different languages, which are aligned, e. g. within aligned sentences. Note that such alignments need not be in a one-to-one relation.[11]

Another concept that needs to be mentioned is the concept of *data points*. It is relevant especially in the context of query systems, and encompasses not only annotations proper (however those are defined), but also metadata and primary data. Distinct data points need not (and in most cases, are not) built on the same pivot. An example query that illustrates the concept is “find sentences containing the lemma ‘knight’ and the surface form ‘ladies’ within a distance of 5 tokens, in plays by Shakespeare”. That query targets an element of the pivot, namely the token “ladies”, an annotation (lemma “knight”), and elements of metadata (genre: plays, author: Shakespeare). Data points are meant to be an all-encompassing concept, where more precise distinctions are not directly relevant.

2.4 Data models vs. their serialisations

An instance of a data model adheres to structures, relationships, and constraints defined by that model, while fixing the values of the particular data fields. Instances

11 Ide and Romary (2006), point out that the statements expressing the alignment between e. g. words of parallel corpora, are themselves a kind of impoverished annotations, which only consist of two or more targets.

of corpus data models are, very generally speaking, what query and visualisation tools operate with as their internal representations. In order for such an instance to be mapped onto the digital medium for the purpose of storage or exchange, the instance is serialised. *Serialisations* of corpora instances obey the corpus data model constraints on the one hand, and the constraints of the semantics and syntax of the particular serialisation format on the other. Thus, the principle is that the model provides the abstract scaffolding for the internal memory representation of an instance (with variable values set), and that instance is serialised into a format (or deserialised from a format).

A *format* is defined, by the Global Digital Format Registry (GDFR),[12] as "the set of syntactic and semantic rules for serializing an abstract information model, an expression of exchangeable knowledge. The format of a digital object must be known in order to interpret the information content of that object properly."

Matching a corpus data model against a particular serialisation format usually requires a trade-off of some kind: some aspects of the corpus data model may not readily be reflected in the serialisation format, and either need to be suppressed, or extra devices need to be introduced into the format.

In what follows, we concentrate on what is probably still the most popular corpus serialisation format in digital humanities, namely XML. XML itself provides only very basic constraints on its well-formedness, and delegates further syntactic validation to document grammars that impose additional constraints (often in various ways aligned with the constraints of corpus data models), while the various semantic constraints and interpretations are often a matter of written guidelines or user handbooks. That is the case of TEI XML (a robust toolkit for creating serialisation formats of a variety of corpus data models in digital humanities, cf. TEI Consortium 2025), and other more or less comprehensively described applications of XML, such as, a. o., PAULA, GrAF, or KorAP-XML, which we discuss in Sections 4 and 5.

XML offers the possibility of combining the various components of a corpus data model in a human- and machine-readable way and clearly assigning annotations to the text to be enriched. However, the so-called "inline" annotation markup of XML, in which information on parts of the primary text is represented as embedding elements, suffers from a drawback: it is not possible to represent concurrent hierarchies, i. e. overlapping annotations. Dealing with that restriction is one of the trade-offs mentioned above.[13]

---

12 https://www.loc.gov/preservation/digital/formats/intro/format_eval_rel.shtml

13 Another well-known trade-off case is tweaking the strictly tree-based nature of XML to represent graphs, by employing pointing mechanisms, which allow the creation of so-called secondary graph arcs in addition to those created between the mother and child nodes in the XML tree. Yet another

The present section began with a diagram of a corpus data model, identifying, among others, multiple *layers* of annotations. We follow Goecke et al. (2010) and assume the following distinctions between the terms "level" and "layer":

- annotation level – refers to the conceptual level of information represented in the digital resource; the term intentionally associates with the "levels of description", a term used often in theoretical linguistics to reference, among others, phonological, morphological, syntactic or semantic information, conceptualised as potentially distinct (even if related) sets of concepts. In the case of digital resources under consideration in the present chapter and volume, the nature of the given level is external to the particular modeling task, coming from the assumed architecture of language and linguistic theory.
- annotation layer – refers to the technical "packaging" of the relevant information in a digital form. In contrast to the concept of the level (of description), the nature of the layer is *not* external to the particular digital resource modelling task: it is rather one of the first fundamental decisions that the project needs to make already at the planning stage. It is a function of the data representation format and of the annotation system selected for the project, and of the expected complexity of the data exploitation systems (e. g. the query engines used). Here is where the issues of sustainability and interoperability come to the fore (see Bański et al. 2025).

Goecke et al. (2010) point out that it is often the mismatch between levels and layers that gives rise to overlapping annotations. In Section 5, we mention a particular (foundry-based) approach to this dichotomy that attempts to approximate a one-to-one ratio between levels and layers, within specified bounds.

3 Approaches to dealing with multiple annotations

SGML, the predecessor of XML, allows several parallel document type definitions (DTDs) with an optional concurrent document instance feature (CONCUR; Goldfarb

---

illustration involves the ease with which XML represents hierarchical information, e. g. simple cases of morpheme divisions inside words, compare <w><m>forget</m><m>ful</m><m>ness</m></w>, where "w" indicates a word, and "m" a morpheme, vs. the need to introduce extra devices and conventions into a CoNNL-U token stream, as is the case of, e. g., the Spanish sentence *Vámonos al mar* ("Let's go to the sea"), cf. https://universaldependencies.org/format.html, where both *Vámonos* and *al* are analysed as complex entities.

1990, p. 88f) in order to interpret the same content from different structural perspectives. This formalism allows overlapping annotations to be represented, albeit only to a limited extent. In contrast to that, XML relies on a strictly hierarchical, clearly nested tree structure. This reduction in functional complexity allowed for a simpler implementation of parsers and validators, which led to an increase in the interoperability of XML: "XML has been designed for ease of implementation", say Bray et al. (1998).[14] So while XML does not natively allow for the mapping of overlapping structures, which may seem limiting the use for linguistically annotated corpora, it offers a wider variety of tools for further processing compared to other formats. Established standard tools can be used for editing (e. g. Oxygen XML, XMLSpy), for validating instances (constrained with document grammars: DTD, XML Schema, Schematron, RelaxNG), for analysis (e. g. XPath, XQuery), for parsing and processing (e. g. XSLT, SAX, DOM) and for storage (XML databases like eXist-db, BaseX) – the plethora of tools and methods in most cases outweighs the limitations compared to SGML or more complex formats.[15] However, the lack of direct support for overlapping structures in the most common standardised format for document management led Jeni Tennison (2008) to conclude: "Overlap is arguably the main remaining problem area for markup technologists."

Numerous different formats have been developed for the representation of multiple annotations in texts based on XML (see Section 4). In addition, extensions for XML (or SGML) have been proposed to allow the representation of structures that exceed a simple tree (e. g. *TexMECS*, Huitfeldt and Sperberg-McQueen 2003, or *XCONCUR*, Schonefeld 2007). This variety is primarily due to the fact that the purpose or purposes of the formats determine how suitable a format is for the area of application; and different design decisions have different advantages and disadvantages with regard to different use cases.

3.1 Inline annotations in multiple documents

A simple way of mapping multiple, overlapping document trees is to duplicate the primary data to be annotated (cf. TEI Consortium 2025. 21.1). This approach enables very simple data handling with standard tools, provided that several annotation levels do not have to be taken into account at the same time. Example 5 is a realiza-

14 DeRose (2004, p. 3) mentions a rumor that there was only one SGML parser that supported the CONCUR feature, which considerably reduced the possibilities for its use.

15 OxygenXML: https://www.oxygenxml.com/; XMLSpy: https://www.altova.com/de/xmlspy-xml-editor; eXist-db: https://exist-db.org/; BaseX: https://basex.org/

tion of Example 3 using multiple document trees, where each instance uses inline markup.

```
<p n="1">
  <line>I am not prone to weeping, as our sex</line>
  <line>Commonly are; the want of which vain dew</line>
  <line>Perchance shall dry your pities; but I have</line>
  <line>That honourable grief lodged here which burns</line>
  <line>Worse than tears drown.</line>
</p>
<p n="1">
  <s>I am not prone to weeping, as our sex Commonly are;</s>
  <s>the want of which vain dew Perchance shall dry your pities;</s>
  <s>but I have That honourable grief lodged here which burns
    Worse than tears drown.</s>
</p>
```

Example 5: Overlapping annotations represented in multiple document trees.

One major disadvantage of this approach is the redundant data storage, which means that changes to the primary text have to be made in several places at the same time in order to keep the annotations synchronised.

This approach can be used as an exchange format, as all information in the format can be read using standard tools.

For archiving, the redundant data means a multiplication of the storage effort, which can be significant for large corpora, but negligible for smaller corpora. However, one advantage of archiving multiple documents with redundant annotation is their independence: each text document contains its information independently of other documents, which means that parts of an annotated document can still be intact if archiving is damaged.

However, this advantage can be a disadvantage in further processing, such as indexing for the use in a generic XML database or a dedicated corpus search engine, if data is deliberately not independent and has to be stored in a non-redundant and closely relational form for efficient querying.

If only one annotation level needs to be considered, querying the data is very easy with standard tools. But an analysis that involves several annotation levels simultaneously requires parallel synchronization of primary data in order to be able to relate the positions of the annotations in several documents.

3.2 Milestone annotations

The TEI P5 Guidelines propose so-called milestone elements to support annotations that combine several structural hierarchies (or are independent of hierarchies; TEI Consortium 2025, Ch. 3.11.3 and 21.2). Empty elements are used to mark the change in the reference system and thus to mark structural boundaries or content-related changes without hierarchical embedding. Example 6 is a realization of Example 3 with milestones (using "lb" for "line beginnings").

```
<p>
  <lb n="1"/><s>I am not prone to weeping, as our sex
  <lb n="2"/>Commonly are;</s><s>the want of which vain dew
  <lb n="3"/>Perchance shall dry your pities;</s><s>but I have
  <lb n="4"/>That honourable grief lodged here which burns
  <lb n="5"/>Worse than tears drown.</s>
</p>
```

Example 6: Overlapping annotation trees using milestones.

This approach can be applied to any annotation and thus allows overlapping annotations to be mapped without having to violate the tree structure of an XML document. However, it is primarily suitable for combining annotations of different levels, rather than representing different representations of a single level, as would be necessary for Example 2.

3.3 Fragment annotations

Fragments (TEI Consortium 2025, Ch. 21.3) are another way of allowing multiple annotations, whereby no empty elements are used but embedding elements, which are interrupted, i. e. closed, in the event of overlaps in the structure tree and then re-opened before the further insertion of primary data. Attributes in the fragments are used to mark their affiliation to a chain (so-called *virtual joints*) so that the original structure is fully described. Example 7 is a realization of Example 3 with fragments (using the "n"-Attribute to mark chain affiliations).

One problem that the TEI P5 guidelines directly address is that the number of fragment elements in the document does not provide any information about how often a feature occurs in a text. This can make quantitative analysis directly on XML documents more difficult.

```
<p>
  <l><s n="1">I am not prone to weeping, as our sex</s></l>
  <l><s n="1">Commonly are;</s> <s n="2">the want of which vain dew</s></l>
  <l><s n="2">Perchance shall dry your pities;</s> <s n="3">but I have</s></l>
  <l><s n="3">That honourable grief lodged here which burns</s></l>
  <l><s n="3">Worse than tears drown.</s></l>
</p>
```

Example 7: Overlapping annotation trees using fragments.

Another problem highlighted by the guidelines is the semantic inaccuracy. For example, a fragment only describes part of an element, but this only becomes apparent when the virtual joints are resolved.

For the same reasons as with milestones, fragments are primarily suitable for resolving conflicts between several different annotation levels and less suitable for resolving conflicts on one level, as illustrated in Example 2.

Fragments are usually mixed with inline annotations. It must be decided which annotation level is to be fragmented as "less important" (Dipper 2005, p. 46), which takes away the neutrality of the data modelling. However, unlike milestones, fragments preserve the hierarchical structure of the displayed trees. This means that searches for a nesting relationship and corresponding analyses can be carried out as long as the nestings are not mapped across fragment boundaries.

3.4 Standoff annotations

Standoff markup (TEI Consortium 2025, Ch. 17.9 and 21.4) separates the annotation from the primary text. Each annotation feature is stored apart in the XML document and refers to positions in the primary data by a reference, either pointing to text spans marked up using the ID/IDREF/XLink mechanisms or to offsets (usually token-, character- or byte-related). As the annotation trees are represented separately in this way, the elements cannot overlap. Example 8 is a realization of the first two lines of Example 3 with standoff annotations in two layers similar to Section 5.2.

One advantage over fragments and milestones is that the complexity of data management does not increase with additional annotation layers. This means that no further splitting is required, as is the case with fragments. In addition, annotations can also be stored in separate documents, which further increases their independence. With regard to the archiving use case, the simplified versioning of annotations should be emphasised in particular. This makes it possible to archive stable text versions of a document unchanged and to handle revisions of annotations separately.

```
<p>
    <seg xml:id="t1">I</seg>
    <seg xml:id="t2">am</seg>
    <seg xml:id="t3">not</seg>
    <seg xml:id="t4">prone</seg>
    <seg xml:id="t5">to</seg>
    <seg xml:id="t6">weeping</seg>
    <seg xml:id="t7">,</seg>
    <seg xml:id="t8">as</seg>
    <seg xml:id="t9">our</seg>
    <seg xml:id="t10">sex</seg>
    <seg xml:id="t11">Commonly</seg>
    <seg xml:id="t12">are</seg>
    <seg xml:id="t13">;</seg>
    <seg xml:id="t14">the</seg>
    <seg xml:id="t15">want</seg>
    <seg xml:id="t16">of</seg>
    <seg xml:id="t17">which</seg>
    <seg xml:id="t18">vain</seg>
    <seg xml:id="t19">dew</seg>
    ...
</p>

<layer>
  <spanList>
    <span target="#t1 #t10">
      <fs type="lex" xmlns="http://www.tei-c.org/ns/1.0">
        <f name="lex">
            <fs>
             <f name="structure">line</f>
            </fs>
        </f>
     </fs>
    </span>
      <span target="#t11 #t19">
       <fs type="lex" xmlns="http://www.tei-c.org/ns/1.0">
         <f name="lex">
```

Example 8: Overlapping annotation trees using standoff annotations similar to Section 5.2.

```
                <fs>
                 <f name="structure">line</f>
                </fs>
            </f>
         </fs>
      </span>
   </spanList>
</layer>
<layer>
   <spanList>
      <span target="#t1 #t13">
         <fs type="lex" xmlns="http://www.tei-c.org/ns/1.0">
            <f name="lex">
               <fs>
                <f name="structure">s</f>
               </fs>
            </f>
         </fs>
      </span>
      <span target="#t14 ...">
        <fs type="lex" xmlns="http://www.tei-c.org/ns/1.0">
         <f name="lex">
            <fs>
               <f name="structure">s</f>
            </fs>
         </f>
        </fs>
      </span>
   </spanList>
</layer>
```

Example 8: (continued)

One disadvantage, however, is that there is no inherent alignment between annotations and primary data in standoff annotations (cf. Dipper 2005, p. 40). Especially if the primary data reference is realised via offsets, this means that the annotations must be completely rebuilt if the primary text changes. Even when using the ID/IDREF/XLink mechanisms, it is possible for the reference targets to change and thus for the annotations to be effectively broken. Another disadvantage is the increased effort involved in searching in standoff annotations (Dipper et al. 2007,

p. 341), as many queries require the merging of distributed information, in particular annotations and primary data. The same is true for processing (Dipper 2005, p. 43).

4 Formats and standards

The need to model multiply annotated data in linguistics has driven the demand for specifications and formats. Different approaches to the representation and processing of annotated texts have spawned different formats, each addressing distinct needs in corpus analysis. In the following, we will briefly introduce a few formats to illustrate the range.

It should be noted that the list is by no means exhaustive or up-to-date, but rather reflects the state of research against which KorAP-XML was initially developed.

For instance, PAULA (Potsdamer AUstauschformat Linguistischer Annotationen, "Potsdam Exchange Format for Linguistic Annotations"; Dipper 2005) is a generic XML format for representing linguistically annotated textual and multimodal data based on a standoff architecture using the XLink mechanism with separated files. Corpus data is represented as arbitrarily labelled directed acyclic graphs (Zeldes et al. 2019). Inline serialization for partial data is also supported for processing steps.

<tiger2/> (Bosch et al. 2012) is a serialization format for the SynAF standard (ISO 24615 2014). This is a metamodel for representing syntactic structures that correspond to a general graph model, which can be mapped in <tiger2/> via standoff or inline annotations, even across file boundaries. <tiger2/> is also the successor format to *TigerXML* (Mengel and Lezius 2000), the corpus data format in which the TIGER corpus was created (Brants et al. 2004).

Instead of developing a format that covers all purposes (which, as shown, is not always sensible), the *SaltNPepper* framework (Zipser and Romary 2010) offers a different approach to keeping these formats intercompatible. As many formats refer to a similar metamodel, they can at least be conceptually mapped to each other – so they can often be converted into each other in order to be able to use the appropriate tools for the same database depending on the intended use. SaltNPepper, for example, allows the conversion of corpus data between TigerXML, <tiger2/>, PAULA, EXMaRALDA (Schmidt and Wörner 2009) and more. Salt is the internal general graph-based model and Pepper is the Salt-based conversion framework.

The *LAF/GRaF* model previously followed a similar approach, with LAF (Ide et al. 2003; ISO 24612 2012) as a general graph-based pivot model for linguistic annotations and GRaF (Ide and Suderman 2007) as an XML serialization of the model (cf. Section 2.4), but against the background of standardization and not against the background of a pragmatic compatibility solution.

Further formats for linguistically annotated text corpora have been developed over time, mostly in the context of specific corpus projects, some of which were based on the concepts presented here. For an overview of linguistically motivated annotation standards for textual corpora, especially with regard to multiple annotations, see Stührenberg (2012), who introduced the *XStandoff* format for similar purposes as KorAP-XML.

Another field in which overlapping annotations are occurring more frequently is the labelling of spoken language or multimodal data, since utterances and gestures, especially in situations with multiple actors (multi-party interaction), rarely have a clear linear sequence, as is the case in texts. Therefore, formats that are natively designed for these corpora must also support overlaps (see Frick and Schmidt 2025). One example here is EAF (The Language Archive 2025), the ELAN annotation format (Brugman and Russel 2004). Here, a standoff format is used which, instead of referring to character or token positions, refers to time slots that are defined separately. The situation is similar with EXMARaLDA (Extensible Markup Language for Discourse Annotation), which offers several tools for annotation, search and corpus management around the central model for storing multimodal annotation data. The format is based on the annotation graph model of Bird and Liberman (2001) and is conceptually compatible with EAF (Schmidt and Wörner 2009, p. 569). It should be noted that this format can also be converted using the SaltNPepper framework.

The KorAP-XML format presented in Section 5 has a purely practical background, which is why we take an application perspective when evaluating different approaches to representing multiple annotations in texts (see Section 1.3). A much more common perspective, however, focuses on the conflict to be dealt with, i. e., on which representation is best suited to represent an overlap. DeRose (2004) lists the following criteria (without claiming to be exhaustive) regarding the adequacy of a representation for an overlap: Human readability, Maintainability, Available implementations, XML compatibility, Ease of validation, Validation across hierarchies, Ease of formatting, Ease of extracting multiple views, Ease of extracting hierarchical subsets, and Continuity of text content. We follow the previously introduced application perspective and consider the following use case scenarios: Archiving, Exchanging, Post-Processing and Querying.

4.1 Archiving

None of the formats presented are primarily aimed at the application purpose of archiving, but all are based on XML (or are at least text-based) and encoded based on Unicode (see Wartena 2025), which can be seen as a necessary prerequisite for archiving data in these formats, as no additional tools need to be used to read the formats. Along with this, the character-based representation of revisions facilitates version control management systems such as Git[16] or Mercurial,[17] which is advantageous for archiving different states of corpus data. Some of the formats presented also allow metadata and annotations to be stored in separate files (compare with Section 5.2 below), which facilitates both the revision and the partial archiving of persistent parts of the corpus and thus serves the purpose of archiving very well.

4.2 Exchanging

Some formats that support multiple, overlapping annotations do not do so for a specific target use, but as a powerful intermediate format (pivot format) that can import any less expressive input data and export it to less expressive output formats. As the name suggests, PAULA was primarily designed as an exchange format. It is therefore very generic and thus suitable for mapping very different data relations. The use of a metamodel for <tiger2/> based on SynAF serves a similar purpose. The use of graphs as a data model in general enables the mapping of any relationships between text data, annotations and metadata, which is why formats based on them offer maximum compatibility for exchange.

4.3 Post-processing

Due to the extensive use of XLink, PAULA is less suitable for further processing, which is why it suggests an application-specific conversion into a reduced inline format for the purpose of further processing (Dipper 2005, Section 3). When converting conflicting annotations, the use of milestones (see Section 3.2) and fragments (see Section 3.3) in the converted documents is suggested to be more advantageous than standoff annotation for post-processing purposes. <tiger2/> proposes a similar approach and also specifies CoNLL as a possible non-XML-based format for post-processing (Bosch et al. 2012, p. 54).

16 https://git-scm.com/

17 https://www.mercurial-scm.org/

4.4 Querying

As already mentioned (see Section 3.4), standoff formats are not particularly suitable for direct searches. As for further processing, a conversion to a better integrated format that uses milestones and fragmentation or redundant documents can be advantageous in this case. The SaltNPepper framework is a helpful tool for converting corpus data for easy use in order to be able to use it efficiently with XPath, XQuery and represented in XML databases.

5 Dealing with multiple annotations in large-scale scenarios

5.1 The context of KorAP-XML

The KorAP-XML format (Bański et al. 2012) presented here was primarily developed as a representation and annotation format for DeReKo (Kupietz et al. 2010, 2018), the largest linguistically annotated corpus of written contemporary German, stored in the I5 format (a customisation of TEI P5; see Lüngen and Sperberg-McQueen 2012, Lüngen and Pisetta 2025). The aim was to develop a representation format based on the original text format with inline annotations, but capable of having any number and complexity of annotations added to the underlying primary text, ideally in parallel processing (i. e. the processing pipeline does not have to be sequential). These annotations should then be made accessible for research purposes via the newly developed corpus analysis platform KorAP (Bański et al. 2012, Diewald et al. 2016). Instead of a completely new design, components of the I5 format were adopted to guarantee little friction with regard to the continued use of the already existing tooling, and to the document structure adapted for parallel processing. KorAP-XML is an implementation of the KorAP data model (Bański et al. 2013).

The usage scenario outlined here is of crucial importance to many of the design decisions that were made for the KorAP-XML format. The format was never planned as a general-purpose format – it was optimised for the intended use.

5.2 Basic characteristics of the format

5.2.1 Physical storage

One of the main objectives of the KorAP data model is the physically separate storage of textual data and their interpretations (i. e. annotations). For this purpose, a

KorAP-XML document consists of several files containing primary data, metadata and annotations. Figure 5 shows the basic file structure of a corpus in KorAP-XML format, in which the primary data is stored in data.xml, metadata in header.xml and annotation layers in directories subordinate to the text, which represent the annotation sources, so-called “foundries” (Bański et al. 2013). The metadata can be stored not only for individual texts but also at the “document” and “corpus” levels in accordance with the “IDS text model” (Lüngen and Sperberg-McQueen 2012), whereby it is up to the corpus creator to decide how the corpus hierarchy is to be divided (for example, a corpus can correspond to a yearly edition of a newspaper, the documents to a month, etc.).

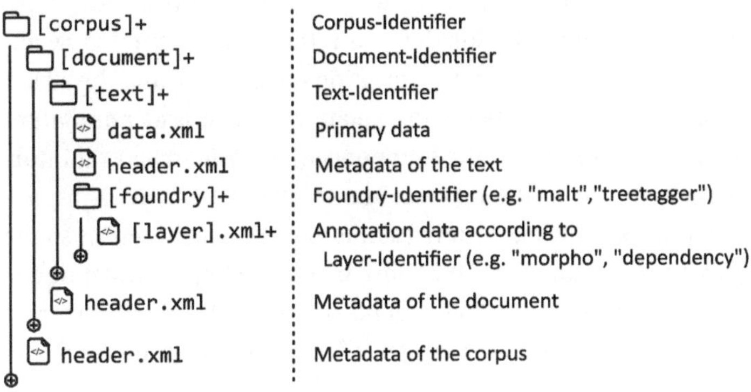

Figure 5: File structure of a KorAP-XML document.

Part of the inspiration for the directory design was the National Corpus of Polish[18] and subsequent related projects, where header documents for various levels of corpora were separated from the data and the full corpus documents could then be assembled as needed from the individual parts. That corresponds to solutions adopted in the PAULA format (see Section 4), in which, on the one hand, the easy addition, deletion and modification of individual annotations is emphasised as an advantage in this file layout, and on the other hand, the guaranteed immutability of the primary or raw data (Zeldes et al. 2019). The idea of leaving the primary data in a pristine state has been reiterated in a series of publications, mostly by Nancy Ide and Laurent Romary, concerning the use of stand-off markup for language resources (see, e. g., Ide and Romary 2006).

18 https://nlp.ipipan.waw.pl/TEI4NKJP/

One element of the KorAP-XML physical storage structure not mentioned yet is the header. The metadata in the header.xml files corresponds to the unchanged content of the original I5 documents. The underlying XML grammar of the header is accordingly a subset of the I5 grammar.

5.2.2 Foundry-based system

Adopting a foundry-based system in the KorAP data model allows, depending on one's information needs, to adopt a relatively theory-neutral stance or to maximise the recall in analysing linguistic phenomena. A foundry contains a specific view of the data, and the number of foundries for a single corpus text is theoretically unlimited. In particular, most foundries in KorAP contain information created by application of a specific analytic tool. A practical exception are the base and the struct foundries, the former containing tokenisation information (encoding an annotation pivot for the corpus, see Section 2.2), and the latter encoding basic structural information that allows to recreate the original textual hierarchy, e. g. text > paragraph > sentence. The *practical* nature of the exceptional status of these two foundries stems from the fact that, just like any other foundry, there may in theory be any number of base foundries, encoding various possible tokenisations for the given text, and the same is true of the struct foundry. A fragment of an example base foundry is provided in Example 9.

```
<layer docid="AAA_BBB_Sentence-1" ... >
  <spanList>
      <span id="t_0" from="0" to="2" />
      <span id="t_1" from="3" to="7" />
      <span id="t_2" from="8" to="9" />
      <span id="t_3" from="10" to="17" />
      ...
```

Example 9: A fragment of a KorAP-XML base foundry, containing tokenisation information, encoded as spans. The corresponding text (contained in data.xml, see Figure 5) is "To make a prairie (...)".

In terms introduced in Section 2.4, foundries are a way to approximate one-to-one correspondence between annotation levels and annotation layers – the former understood here broadly as views supplied by a single annotation tool (which is assumed to embody a certain kind of linguistic theory), and the latter as technical implementations of those views in a digital textual medium of choice. The researcher may choose to analyse the text through the lens of one theoretical approach (selecting the corresponding foundry), or they may maximise recall and use all available foundries, e. g. for the purpose of querying the given corpus.[19]

Figure 6 is a more articulated version of Figure 1, with explicitly named containers for groups of annotations (i. e., foundries), and with the internal structure of foundries sketched. Containers for the annotation layers are visible in the fragmentary listings in Examples 9 and 10.

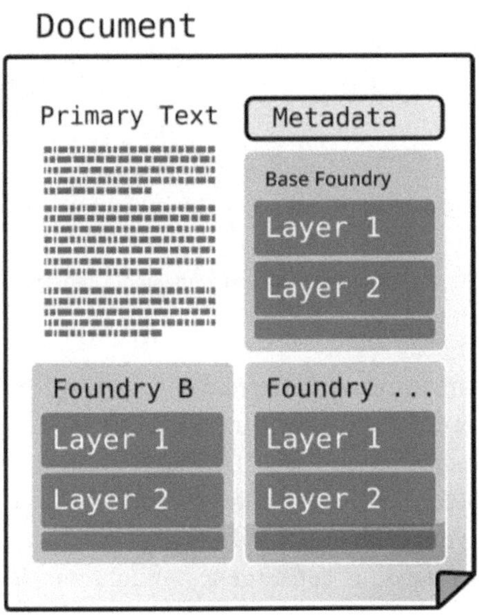

Figure 6: Model of a KorAP-XML document, with multiple annotation components grouped in foundries.

5.2.3 KorAP-XML annotations

We conclude the overview with an example of a KorAP-XML annotation.

Annotations are encoded as variants of the TEI-P5 typed feature structures (TEI Consortium 2025, Lee et al. 2004). The feature structures of the annotations reference character strings of the primary text, located within the <text/> element of the

19 In many ways, this is a similar approach to that which KorAP takes with regard to query languages (see Bingel and Diewald 2015), offering a selection of them, for the user to choose one suitable for the particular research need (or, sometimes, the one most familiar to the user).

data.xml. A single annotation containing the lemma of a token can have the structure shown in Example 10.

```
<layer ... >
 <spanList>
     <span from="0" to="3">
         <fs type="lex" xmlns="http://www.tei-c.org/ns/1.0">
             <f name="lex">
                 <fs>
                   <f name="lemma">zum</f>
                 </fs>
             </f>
         </fs>
     </span>
   ...
```

Example 10: A single KorAP-XML annotation enriching a span of the main text with lemma information.

The attributes “from” and “to” in the span structure refer to the beginning and end of the character span in the primary text, by addressing inter-character points (whereby the first such point is located at the very beginning of the targeted passage and indexed as “0”, and the next one is located after the first character of the passage and indexed as “1”, etc.). The structure can vary depending on the type of annotation (e. g. token-based for part-of-speech, span-based for constituency annotations, or relation-based for anaphoric relations).

5.3 Processing

The main advantage of standoff formats is the ability to add new annotations to existing corpus data without conflicting with the primary data or existing annotations (see Section 3.4; Dipper et al. 2007, p. 341). This flexibility can be increased by storing the annotations not only in separate areas of an XML document but in separate files (see Section 5.2). In this way, existing annotations and primary data do not have to be rewritten when new annotations are added, which makes it possible to add these annotations in parallel. This capability of standoff annotations is at the core of the KorAP-XML format and fundamental to the pertaining processing pipeline (Kupietz et al. 2023; see Figure 7).

However, the large number of files that are created when converting and annotating a single text into the KorAP-XML format also poses a challenge for large

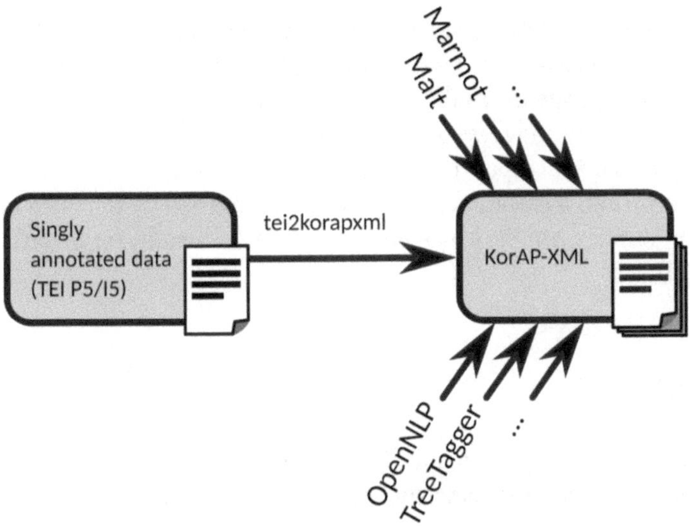

Figure 7: Preprocessing Pipeline for DeReKo. Various tools and sources (Marmot, Malt, OpenNLP, TreeTagger etc.) can annotate the data in parallel.

corpora. File systems can have problems with the large number of files, operating systems can have problems opening and closing these files (especially with highly parallelised processing) and, last but not least, the transfer of numerous individual files can lead to performance losses during processing.

The shorter the texts in a collection are, the greater these problems become, as the ratio of corpus size in tokens to the number of files increases significantly. An example here are corpora on computer-mediated communication, where single utterances are treated as texts that are only a few words long (an instance of this category is the NottDeuYTSch corpus, Cotgrove 2023, which was processed in this way). In order to be able to deal with this form of corpora while at the same time preserving the possibilities of parallel annotation, many corpora in the KorAP project were compressed in package formats such as Zip. This facilitates handling, e. g. transfer and storage in file systems,[20] but poses the additional problem that processing is sometimes significantly slower (as the data must first be decompressed for processing). However, Zip files are problematic with regard to the parallel addition of data, which is why the annotation pipeline creates separate Zip files for each annotation and only uses an immutable base Zip file (with the primary text and a tokenisation)

20 In particular, the storage of annotations in feature structures is very storage-intensive but can be compressed very efficiently due to the high data redundancy.

as input for the annotations. In addition to this difficulty, processing on the basis of Zip files also results in performance losses during compression and decompression and problems with interoperability, as libraries for handling Zip files in different programming languages do not always generate fully compatible files.

Tools for the conversion of corpus data to KorAP-XML (Diewald et al. 2024), for the enrichment with various annotation tools, and the preparation for indexing in KorAP (Diewald and Kupietz 2025) are available as open source software under a BSD-2 license on GitHub.[21]

6 Conclusion

The present chapter looks at large text corpora with multiple annotation components, mainly through the lens of specific application scenarios. We overview the major kinds of what can be understood under the term "multiple annotations" and the major ways of handling the most salient kind of multiple annotations, namely structurally overlapping annotations, in the context of XML. We also present some of the formats that have been around at the time when KorAP-XML was created, as an in-house format addressing specific application needs. The chapter concludes with a section on the context in which KorAP-XML was developed and the specific demands of the system in which it was deployed. We also mention the concept of annotation foundries as a way to introduce and maintain a measure of order in dealing with multiple annotations.

It has to be borne in mind that KorAP-XML is a format which has been optimised for a specific purpose, and which, in our application scenario, has some advantages over the formats presented in Section 4 (or did so at the time of development). Neither the enormous corpus size of DeReKo nor the need for parallel annotations are relevant in most of the application scenarios for which the formats presented in Section 4 are used, and therefore we do not present KorAP-XML as a panaceum for all corpus-related pain.

The advantages of KorAP-XML shine in particular in what, in Section 1.3, we call "post-processing", which can be thought of as a focal point for the use of this format and which is a weak point for the formats illustrated above (including the source format I5). The usage scenarios introduced in Section 4 show that different formats have advantages and disadvantages depending on the use case, and that the best tool should be selected depending on the purpose, or – as in the case of KorAP-XML – a specific format should be developed that uses established standards such

21 https://github.com/KorAP/

as the TEI-P5 metadata model and the TEI-P5 feature structures as a construction kit and thus supports the use of established tools for optimised formats.

Bibliography

Bański, Piotr, Ulrich Heid & Laura Herzberg. 2025. Towards an optimum degree of order in the field of language resources. In Piotr Bański, Ulrich Heid & Laura Herzberg (eds.), *Harmonising language data: Standards for linguistic resources*. Berlin & Boston: De Gruyter.

Bański, Piotr, Peter M. Fischer, Elena Frick, Erik Ketzan, Marc Kupietz, Carsten Schnober, Oliver Schonefeld & Andreas Witt. 2012. The new IDS corpus analysis platform: Challenges and prospects. In *Proceedings of the eighth international conference on language resources and evaluation (LREC'12)*, 2905–2911. Istanbul, Turkey: European Language Resources Association (ELRA). http://www.lrec-conf.org/proceedings/lrec2012/pdf/789_Paper.pdf (accessed 12 April 2022).

Bański, Piotr, Elena Frick, Michael Hanl, Marc Kupietz, Carsten Schnober & Andreas Witt. 2013. Robust corpus architecture: A new look at virtual collections and data access. In Andrew Hardie & Robbie Love (eds.), *Abstract book*, 23–25. Lancaster: UCREL.

Bingel, Joachim & Nils Diewald. 2015. KoralQuery – A general corpus query protocol. In *Proceedings of the workshop on innovative corpus query and visualization tools at NODALIDA 2015*, Vilnius, Lithuania, 1–5.

Bird, Steven & Mark Liberman. 2001. A formal framework for linguistic annotation. *Speech Communication* 33(1–2). 23–60. https://doi.org/10.1016/S0167-6393(00)00068-6.

Bosch, Sonja, S. Choi, Eric De la Clergerie, Alex Fang, Gertrud Faass, Kiyong Lee, Antonio Pareja-Lora, et al.. 2012. <tiger2/> as a standardized serialisation for ISO 24615 – SynAF. In *TLT11 – 11th international workshop on treebanks and linguistic theories*, Lisbon, Portugal, 37–60.

Brants, Sabine, Stefanie Dipper, Peter Eisenberg, Silvia Hansen-Schirra, Esther König, Wolfgang Lezius, Christian Rohrer, George Smith & Hans Uszkoreit. 2004. TIGER: Linguistic interpretation of a German corpus. *Research on Language and Computation* 2(4). 597–620. https://doi.org/10.1007/s11168-004-7431-3.

Bray, Tim, Jean Paoli & C. M. Sperberg-McQueen. 1998. *Extensible Markup Language (XML) 1.0*. https://www.w3.org/TR/1998/REC-xml-19980210.html (accessed 29 January 2025).

Brugman, Hennie & Albert Russel. 2004. Annotating multi-media/multi-modal resources with ELAN. In Maria Teresa Lino, Maria Francisca Xavier, Fátima Ferreira, Rute Costa & Raquel Silva (eds.), *Proceedings of the fourth international conference on language resources and evaluation (LREC'04)*, Lisbon, Portugal: European Language Resources Association (ELRA). https://aclanthology.org/L04-1285/ (accessed 4 February 2025).

Chiarcos, Christian, Julia Ritz & Manfred Stede. 2012. By all these lovely tokens... Merging conflicting tokenisations. *Language Resources and Evaluation* 46(1). 53–74. https://doi.org/10.1007/s10579-011-9161-0.

Cotgrove, Louis. 2023. THE NOTTDEUYTSCH CORPUS: A corpus of German-language YouTube comments. *Korpora Deutsch als Fremdsprache* 3(2). 225–229. https://doi.org/10.48694/kordaf.3841.

DeRose, Steven. 2004. Markup overlap: A review and a horse. In *Proceedings of extreme markup languages*, Montréal, Quebec, Canada.

Diewald, Nils, Michael Hanl, Eliza Margaretha, Joachim Bingel, Marc Kupietz, Piotr Bański & Andreas Witt. 2016. KorAP architecture – Diving in the deep sea of corpus data. In *Proceedings of the tenth international conference on language resources and evaluation (LREC 2016)*, 3586–3591. Slovenia: Portorož.

Diewald, Nils & Marc Kupietz. 2025. KorAP/KorAP-XML-Krill: v0.59. Zenodo. https://doi.org/10.5281/zenodo.14644758.

Diewald, Nils, Marc Kupietz & Peter Harders. 2024. KorAP/KorAP-XML-TEI: v2.6.0. Zenodo. https://doi.org/10.5281/zenodo.14170197.

Dipper, Stefanie. 2005. XML-based stand-off representation and exploitation of multi-level linguistic annotation. In *Proceedings of Berliner XML Tage*, Berlin, Germany, 39–50.

Dipper, Stefanie, Michael Götze, Uwe Küssner & Manfred Stede. 2007. Representing and querying standoff XML. In Georg Rehm, Andreas Witt & Lothar Lemnitzer (eds.), *Data structures for linguistic resources and applications*, 337–346. Tübingen: Gunter Narr Verlag.

Durusau, Patrick & Matthew Brook O'Donnell. 2001. Concurrent markup for XML documents. In *Proceedings of extreme markup 2001*. https://www.academia.edu/21040530/Concurrent_Markup_for_XML_Documents.

Ferreira, Vera, Hanna Hedeland & Kelsey Neely. 2025. Annotated audiovisual language data: Data quality and data maturity. In Piotr Bański, Ulrich Heid & Laura Herzberg (eds.), *Harmonising language data: Standards for linguistic resources*. Berlin & Boston: De Gruyter.

Frick, Elena & Thomas Schmidt. 2025. Querying spoken language data. In Piotr Bański, Ulrich Heid & Laura Herzberg (eds.), *Harmonising language data: Standards for linguistic resources*. Berlin & Boston: De Gruyter.

Głowińska, Katarzyna & Adam Przepiórkowski. 2010. The design of syntactic annotation levels in the National Corpus of Polish. In Nicoletta Calzolari, Khalid Choukri Bente Maegaard, Joseph Mariani, Jan Odijk, Stelios Piperidis, Mike Rosner & Daniel Tapias (eds.), *Proceedings of the seventh international conference on language resources and evaluation (LREC'10)*. Valletta, Malta: European Language Resources Association (ELRA).

Goecke, Daniela, Harald Lüngen, Dieter Metzing, Stührenberg Maik & Andreas Witt. 2010. Different views on markup. In *Principles and practice of semantic web reasoning*, 1–21. https://doi.org/10.1007/978-90-481-3331-4_1.

Goldfarb, Charles F. 1990. *The SGML handbook*. Oxford: Oxford University Press.

Huitfeldt, Claus & C. M. Sperberg-McQueen. 2003. TexMECS: An experimental markup meta-language for complex documents. University of Bergen. https://web.archive.org/web/20070629215455/https://decentius.aksis.uib.no/mlcd/2003/Papers/texmecs.html (accessed 14 April 2025).

Ide, Nancy, Nicoletta Calzolari, Judith Eckle-Kohler, Dafydd Gibbon, Sebastian Hellmann, Kiyong Lee, Joakim Nivre & Laurent Romary. 2017. Community standards for linguistically-annotated resources. In Nancy Ide & James Pustejovsky (eds.), *Handbook of linguistic annotation*, 113–165. Dordrecht: Springer Netherlands. https://doi.org/10.1007/978-94-024-0881-2_4.

Ide, Nancy & Laurent Romary. 2006. Representing linguistic corpora and their annotations. In *Proceedings of the fifth international conference on language resources and evaluation (LREC 2006)*. http://www.lrec-conf.org/proceedings/lrec2006/.

Ide, Nancy, Laurent Romary & Eric de la Clergerie. 2003. International standard for a linguistic annotation framework. In *Proceedings of the HLT-NAACL 2003 workshop on Software engineering and architecture of language technology systems – Volume 8 (SEALTS '03)*, 25–30. USA: Association for Computational Linguistics. https://doi.org/10.3115/1119226.1119230.

Ide, Nancy & Keith Suderman. 2007. GrAF: A graph-based format for linguistic annotations. In Branimir Boguraev, Nancy Ide, Adam Meyers, Shigeko Nariyama, Manfred Stede, Janyce Wiebe & Graham Wilcock (eds.), *Proceedings of the linguistic annotation workshop*, 1–8. Prague, Czech Republic: Association for Computational Linguistics. https://aclanthology.org/W07-1501/ (accessed 6 February 2025).

ISO 24610-1. 2006. *Language resource management – Feature structures. Part 1: Feature structure representation.*

ISO 24612. 2012. *Language resource management – Linguistic annotation framework (LAF).*

ISO 24615-1. 2014. *Language resource management – Syntactic annotation framework (SynAF) – Part 1: Syntactic model.*

Jurafsky, Daniel & James H. Martin. 2000. *Speech and language processing: An introduction to natural language processing, computational linguistics, and speech recognition.* Upper Saddle River, NJ: Prentice Hall.

Kupietz, Marc, Cyril Belica, Holger Keibel & Andreas Witt. 2010. The German Reference Corpus DeReKo: A primordial sample for linguistic research. In Nicoletta Calzolari, Khalid Choukri Bente Maegaard, Joseph Mariani, Jan Odijk, Stelios Piperidis, Mike Rosner & Daniel Tapias (eds.), *Proceedings of the seventh international conference on language resources and evaluation (LREC'10)*, 1848–1854. Valletta, Malta: European Language Resources Association (ELRA). http://www.lrec-conf.org/proceedings/lrec2010/pdf/414_Paper.pdf.

Kupietz, Marc & Holger Keibel. 2009. The Mannheim German Reference Corpus (DeReKo) as a basis for empirical linguistic research. In Makoto Minegishi & Yuji Kawaguchi (eds.), *Working papers in corpus-based linguistics and language education*, Vol. 3, 53–59. Tokyo: Tokyo University of Foreign Studies. https://citeseerx.ist.psu.edu/viewdoc/download?doi=10.1.1.475.9714&rep=rep1&type=pdf (accessed 8 April 2022).

Kupietz, Marc, Harald Lüngen & Nils Diewald. 2023. Das Gesamtkonzept des Deutschen Referenzkorpus DeReKo. Vom Design bis zur Verwendung und darüber hinaus. In Arnulf Deppermann, Christian Fandrych, Marc Kupietz & Thomas Schmidt (eds.), *Korpora in der germanistischen Sprachwissenschaft (Jahrbuch Des Instituts Für Deutsche Sprache 2023)*, 1–28. Berlin & Boston: De Gruyter.

Kupietz, Marc, Harald Lüngen, Paweł Kamocki & Andreas Witt. 2018. The German Reference Corpus DeReKo: New developments – New opportunities. In *Proceedings of the eleventh international conference on language resources and evaluation (LREC 2018)*. Miyazaki, Japan: European Language Resources Association (ELRA). https://aclanthology.org/L18-1689/ (accessed 23 January 2022).

Lee, Kiyong, Lou Burnard, Laurent Romary, Eric de la Clergerie, Thierry Declerck, Syd Bauman, Harry Bunt, et al.. 2004. Towards an international standard on feature structure representation. In *Proceedings of the fourth international conference on language resources and evaluation*, Lisbon, Portugal.

Ljubešić, Nikola & Tomaž Erjavec. 2025. Part-of-speech tagging and related annotation. In Piotr Bański, Ulrich Heid & Laura Herzberg (eds.), *Harmonising language data: Standards for linguistic resources*. Berlin & Boston: De Gruyter.

Lüngen, Harald & C. Michael Sperberg-McQueen. 2012. A TEI P5 document grammar for the IDS text model. *Journal of the Text Encoding Initiative* 3. https://journals.openedition.org/jtei/pdf/508.

Lüngen, Harald & Ines Pisetta. 2025. Conversion into the archival format I5. In Piotr Bański, Ulrich Heid & Laura Herzberg (eds.), *Harmonising language data: Standards for linguistic resources*, Berlin & Boston: De Gruyter.

Mengel, Andreas & Wolfgang Lezius. 2000. An XML-based representation format for syntactically annotated corpora. In *Proceedings of the second international conference on language resources and evaluation (LREC 2000)*, Athens, Greece.

Romary, Laurent. 2025. International standards for the identification and the description of languages and their varieties. In Piotr Bański, Ulrich Heid & Laura Herzberg (eds.), *Harmonising language data: Standards for linguistic resources*. Berlin & Boston: De Gruyter.

Schmidt, Thomas & Kai Wörner. 2009. EXMARaLDA – Creating, analysing and sharing spoken language corpora for pragmatic research. *Pragmatics* 19(4). 565–582.

Schonefeld, Oliver. 2007. XCONCUR and XCONCUR-CL: A constraint-based approach for the validation of concurrent markup. In Georg Rehm, Andreas Witt & Lothar Lemnitzer (eds.), *Datenstrukturen für linguistische Ressourcen und ihre Anwendungen / Data structures for linguistic resources and applications*, 347–356. Tübingen: Gunter Narr Verlag.

Stührenberg, Maik. 2012. *Auszeichnungssprachen für linguistische Korpora: Theoretische Grundlagen, De-facto-Standards, Normen*. Bielefeld: Universität Bielefeld. https://pub.uni-bielefeld.de/record/2492772 (accessed 29 October 2024).

Schwarz, Pia. 2025. Named entity recognition and entity linking. In Piotr Bański, Ulrich Heid & Laura Herzberg (eds.), *Harmonising language data: Standards for linguistic resources*. Berlin & Boston: De Gruyter.

TEI Consortium. 2025. *TEI P5: Guidelines for electronic text encoding and interchange*. http://www.tei-c.org/P5/.

Tennison, Jeni. 2008. Overlap, containment and dominance. https://www.jenitennison.com/2008/12/06/overlap-containment-and-dominance.html (accessed 31 January 2025).

The Language Archive. 2017. *ELAN annotation format EAF*. Schema version: 3.0. Nijmegen, The Netherlands: Max Planck Institute for Psycholinguistics. https://www.mpi.nl/tools/elan/EAF_Annotation_Format_3.0_and_ELAN.pdf (accessed 4 February 2025).

Trippel, Thorsten. 2025. Metadata for research data. In Piotr Bański, Ulrich Heid & Laura Herzberg (eds.), *Harmonising language data: Standards for linguistic resources*, Berlin & Boston: De Gruyter.

Zeldes, Amir, Florian Zipser, Arne Neumann & Thomas Krause. 2019. *PAULA v1.1. Documentation*. Potsdam: University of Potsdam and Humboldt-Universität zu Berlin. https://korpling.github.io/paula-xml/unpublished/PAULA%20XML%20Documentation.pdf.

Zipser, Florian & Laurent Romary. 2010. A model-oriented approach to the mapping of annotation formats using standards. https://inria.hal.science/inria-00527799 (accessed 5 February 2025).

Wartena, Christian. 2025. Character encoding and its importance for text resources. In Piotr Bański, Ulrich Heid & Laura Herzberg (eds.), *Harmonising language data: Standards for linguistic resources*. Berlin & Boston: De Gruyter.

Ines Pisetta and Thorsten Trippel

Standards and practices for long-term digital archiving

Abstract: This chapter delves into the critical aspects of digital long-term archiving, focusing on standards and practices in the language domain, based on the experiences gained in various projects and infrastructure activities. It begins by discussing various preservation levels – binary, logical and semantic – highlighting their importance in maintaining digital integrity over time. The chapter then explores the OAIS model, detailing the roles of Submission Information Packages (SIP), Archival Information Packages (AIP) and Dissemination Information Packages (DIP) in the archival process. It contrasts dark archives with open archives, explaining their respective purposes and benefits. The function of repository systems and the use of persistent identifiers are examined to underscore their roles in ensuring long-term accessibility. The chapter also defines digital objects and outlines the responsibilities of data stewards in managing these resources. Finally, it emphasizes the significance of certification in establishing trustworthy archives, discussing relevant standards and their benefits. This comprehensive overview provides essential insights into effective long-term digital preservation.

Keywords: digital preservation, OAIS model, repository systems, persistent identifiers (PIDs), data stewardship, certification standards, granularity

1 Introduction

Long-term digital archiving is the process of preserving digital data securely, ensuring its long-term accessibility and usability.

Acknowledgement: This chapter is based on work within Text+, funded by the Deutsche Forschungsgemeinschaft (DFG, project number 460033370) as part of the German National Research Data Infrastructure (NFDI e. V.). The authors acknowledge the use of Large Language Models (LLMs) as writing aids in phrasing this chapter, based on the authors' notes, ideas and concepts. The authors retain full responsibility for the content.

Ines Pisetta, Digitale Sprachwissenschaft, Leibniz-Institut für Deutsche Sprache, R5 6-13, D-68161 Mannheim, Baden-Württemberg, Germany, e-mail: pisetta@ids-mannheim.de
Thorsten Trippel, Digitale Sprachwissenschaft, Leibniz-Institut für Deutsche Sprache, R5 6-13, D-68161 Mannheim, Baden-Württemberg, Germany; and Seminar für Sprachwissenschaft, Eberhard Karls Universität Tübingen, Keplerstr. 2, 72074 Tübingen, Germany, e-mail: trippel@ids-mannheim.de

https://doi.org/10.1515/9783112208212-009

This includes data collected or generated in research. In the humanities, research data is the foundation of empirical inquiry, spanning fields from cultural heritage preservation to AI applications based on (large) language models. By archiving these data, research becomes more reproducible, reusable and easier to assess, thereby improving overall quality. Long-term digital archiving must address the following three key roles:

- the data provider
- the data user
- archive maintainer or data steward.

Researchers who contribute and deposit their data in a long-term archive play a crucial role as data providers. From their perspective, it is essential to ensure their data is securely stored to maintain good scientific practice. They also seek visibility and citability for their data, enabling them to reference the original dataset in publications and academic CVs. The process of depositing data should be straightforward to avoid becoming an additional burden. Many funding bodies require a Research Data Management Plan (RDMP), which outlines the collection, organisation and metadata creation processes (see Trippel 2025). Depending on the required level of preservation, the data is provided to an archive operating under the OAIS model (Section 3) as a Submission Information Packages (SIP).

The data user is a researcher who reuses data created by others and relies on the FAIR principles (Wilkinson et al. 2016) to locate, access and utilise data effectively. This includes evaluating and reviewing research results based on specific datasets, reproducing findings in academic teaching and applying existing data to new research questions. For data users, it is crucial to find relevant data, assess its quality and gain access to an authentic copy of the data. Moreover, data must be available in formats that are well-documented and reusable. Archives operating an appropriate repository system under the OAIS model provide data in the form of a Dissemination Information Package (DIP).

The archive maintainers or data stewards act as intermediaries between data providers and users and are responsible for quality assurance and long-term preservation. They ensure the integrity of the data from deposit to reuse, playing a vital but often unseen role. In long-term digital archiving, their function is critical, as they guarantee that deposited data meets the needs of researchers and the data is maintained in a trustworthy repository system. The responsibilities of data stewards are further discussed in Section 8.

This chapter explores the multifaceted domain of digital long-term archiving, with a particular focus on standards and practices within the language domain. Drawing on insights from various projects and infrastructures, it provides a comprehensive overview of the principles, models and tools that underpin successful digital preservation efforts.

1.1 Purpose of long-term archiving

The primary purpose of long-term archiving is to safeguard digital objects – ranging from text corpora and linguistic datasets to multimedia resources – against the inevitable threats of technological obsolescence, data degradation and loss of context. The integrity and accessibility of digital objects depend on the continuous availability of compatible software, hardware and expertise. Long-term archiving addresses these challenges by implementing strategies that ensure digital objects remain intact, functional and meaningful over extended periods, often spanning decades.

Long-term archiving is particularly vital in the language domain, where digital resources such as annotated text corpora, speech recordings and lexical databases are essential for linguistic research, language preservation and cultural heritage. The creation, collection and preparation of this data is both time consuming and resource intensive, hence expensive. These resources not only support current research but also serve as a foundation for future studies, enabling longitudinal analyses and cross-generational comparisons. Without robust archiving practices, the risk of losing these invaluable resources to technological change or neglect is significant.

1.2 Scope of the chapter

This chapter offers a comprehensive exploration of the key concepts, models and practices central to long-term digital archiving. It begins by examining the three levels of preservation – binary, logical and semantic – which are essential for maintaining the integrity, functionality and meaning of digital objects over time. The chapter then introduces the Open Archival Information System (OAIS) reference model, a foundational framework for digital archiving and contrasts dark archives with open archives, highlighting their distinct purposes and benefits.

The chapter also delves into the role of repository systems in managing and preserving digital objects, emphasizing features like version control, access management and metadata organization. It discusses the importance of persistent identifiers (PIDs) in ensuring long-term access to digital resources and defines digital objects as entities comprising content, metadata and structure, with models like the Oxford Common File Layout (OCFL) providing standardized approaches to their preservation. Additionally, the chapter explores the responsibilities of data stewards and the significance of certification standards, such as DIN 31644 (2012) (for example by nestor Section 9.1) and CoreTrustSeal, in establishing trustworthy archives.

It concludes with a summary of key points and a discussion of future directions in digital preservation. By providing a detailed yet accessible overview, this chapter aims to equip readers with the knowledge needed to navigate the complexities of long-term digital archiving and ensure the preservation of valuable digital resources for future generations.

2 Preservation levels

In the realm of digital preservation, ensuring the longevity and accessibility of digital objects requires a multi-layered approach. Different levels of preservation address various aspects of digital content, from its raw binary form to its logical structure and semantic meaning. These levels – *binary preservation*, *logical preservation* and *semantic preservation* – work together to safeguard digital objects against the inevitable challenges posed by technological obsolescence, data corruption and changes in user needs. Understanding these levels is crucial for designing effective preservation strategies that can adapt to the evolving digital landscape.

2.1 Binary preservation

At the most fundamental level, binary preservation, also referred to as bitstream preservation, focuses on maintaining the exact binary representation of digital objects. This involves ensuring that the sequence of bits – the zeros and ones that constitute digital files – remains unchanged over time. Binary preservation is the most basic of all digital preservation efforts, as even the slightest alteration to the binary data can render a file unreadable or corrupt its content.

To achieve binary preservation, archives employ techniques such as checksum verification, which involves generating a unique hash value for a file and periodically recalculating it to detect any changes. Examples for such checksum algorithms in use are the Message-Digest Algorithm 5 (MD5, Rivest 1992) or Secure Hash Algorithm with 256 bits, (SHA-256, National Institute of Standards and Technology (NIST) 2015). While binary preservation ensures the physical integrity of digital objects, it does not address higher-level concerns such as file format obsolescence or the ability to interpret the data. These challenges are addressed by the next level of preservation: logical preservation.

2.2 Logical preservation

Logical preservation goes beyond the binary level to ensure that the logical structure and functionality of digital objects are maintained. This involves preserving the file formats, software dependencies and data structures that allow digital objects to be rendered and used as intended. For example, a word processing document must not only retain its binary integrity but also remain readable by software that can interpret its format.

To ensure logical preservation proactive measures, such as format migration or emulation, may be required. Format migration involves converting files to newer, more sustainable formats, while emulation involves recreating the original software environment in which the files were created (Rothenberg 1999, Lorie 2001). Both strategies aim to ensure that digital objects remain accessible as technology evolves. However, logical preservation does not guarantee that the meaning or context of the digital objects will be preserved over time. This is where semantic preservation comes into play.

2.3 Semantic preservation

The most complex and nuanced level of preservation, semantic preservation, focuses on maintaining the meaning and context of digital objects. This involves ensuring that the information conveyed by the digital objects – whether text, images, audio, or video – remains understandable and interpretable by future users. Semantic preservation is particularly challenging because it requires not only technical solutions but also a deep understanding of the content and its intended audience.

To achieve semantic preservation, archives must document the context in which digital objects were created, including their provenance (history and origin), intended use and relationships to other objects. Metadata plays a crucial role in this process, as it provides the necessary context for interpreting the content. Additionally, archives may need to collaborate with domain experts to ensure that specialized knowledge is preserved alongside the digital objects (Hedstrom 1997). Semantic preservation ensures that the intellectual value of digital content is not lost, even as the technology used to access it changes.

2.4 Developing a strategy for preservation

While binary, logical and semantic preservation address different aspects of digital content, they are interconnected and must be integrated into a cohesive preservation strategy. The Open Archival Information System (OAIS) reference model provides a framework for achieving this integration (see ISO 14721 2012). By defining the roles and responsibilities of an archive and outlining the key packages of information – SIP, AIP and DIP– the OAIS model ensures that digital content can be preserved and accessed at all levels, from its binary representation to its semantic meaning. The next section will explore the OAIS model in detail.

3 The OAIS model

The Open Archival Information System (OAIS) reference model, developed by the Consultative Committee for Space Data Systems (CCSDS) and later adopted as ISO 14721 standard (ISO 14721 2012), provides a comprehensive framework for addressing the need for robust systems to manage, preserve and provide access to data. The OAIS model is not a prescriptive set of rules but rather a conceptual framework that guides the design and implementation of digital archives. It defines the roles, responsibilities and functional components necessary for the long-term preservation of digital information, ensuring that data remains accessible and usable over time.

"Open" refers to the fact that this model is developed in open forums. It does not mean that the archive can be accessed without restrictions.

3.1 Overview of OAIS

The OAIS reference model defines an archive as an organization that intends to preserve information long-term for a specific group of users, known as the "designated community" (ISO 14721 2012). This community could include researchers, historians, or any group with a vested interest in accessing the preserved information. The OAIS model emphasizes the importance of understanding the needs of this community, as it informs the archive's policies and procedures for preservation and access.

At its core, the OAIS model is structured around three key packages of information: the *Submission Information Package (SIP)*, the *Archival InformationPackage (AIP)* and the *Dissemination Information Package (DIP)*.

These packages represent different stages in the lifecycle of digital information within an archive, from its initial submission to its long-term preservation and eventual dissemination to users. Each package plays a critical role in ensuring the integrity, authenticity and accessibility of the archived information.

A common feature of each of these packages is that it contains the archival data (i. e. the object data) plus additional information required at the various stages of archiving, for example metadata required when submitting data to an archive, metadata required for processing within an archive, or metadata distributed together with the data by an archive when data is provided for reuse. It does not mean that these packages needs to differ from each other, but depending on the implemented processes they may.

3.2 Submission Information Package (SIP)

The Submission Information Package (SIP) is the first step in the archiving process. It represents the digital object(s), i. e. the object data and the associated additional information that is submitted to the archive by a producer, such as a researcher, institution, or organization. The SIP contains the digital content to be preserved, along with associated metadata that provides context and descriptive information about the content. This metadata is essential for understanding the provenance, structure and significance of the digital objects within the SIP.

The role of the SIP is to serve as a bridge between the producer and the archive. It ensures that the information is packaged in a way that aligns with the archive's requirements and standards. Upon receipt of the SIP, the archive performs a series of checks to validate the integrity and completeness of the submitted information. This may include verifying file formats, checking for viruses and ensuring that all required metadata is present. Once the SIP has been validated, it is transformed into the Archival Information Package (AIP) for long-term storage and preservation.

3.3 Archival Information Package (AIP)

The Archival Information Package (AIP) is the cornerstone of the OAIS model. It represents the information that is stored and preserved within the archive over the long term. The AIP contains the digital content from the SIP, along with additional preservation metadata that ensures that the content can be understood and used by future generations. This metadata may include technical details about file formats, information about the content's provenance and any actions taken to preserve the content, such as format migration or checksum verification.

The AIP is designed to be a stable and self-contained package that can withstand the test of time. It is stored in a secure and controlled environment, with regular monitoring and maintenance to ensure its continued integrity. The archive may also implement preservation strategies, such as format migration or emulation (Section 2.2), to address the challenges of technological obsolescence. By maintaining the AIP in a consistent and well-documented state, the archive ensures that the information remains accessible and usable for its designated community.

3.4 Dissemination Information Package (DIP)

The Dissemination Information Package (DIP) is the final stage in the OAIS model, representing the information that is delivered to users upon request. The DIP is derived from the AIP and is tailored to meet the specific needs of the user. It may include subsets of the original content, transformed formats, or additional contextual information to aid in interpretation. The DIP ensures that users can access and understand the archived information, even if they are not familiar with the technical details of its preservation.

The process of creating a DIP involves extracting the relevant information from the AIP and packaging it in a way that is suitable for dissemination. This may involve converting files into more accessible formats, adding user-friendly metadata or providing tools for searching and navigating the content. The DIP is designed to be flexible and adaptable, allowing the archive to meet the diverse needs of its users while maintaining the integrity of the original information.

3.5 Significance of OAIS

The OAIS model provides a robust and flexible framework for the long-term preservation of digital information. By defining the roles and responsibilities of an archive and outlining the key packages of information – SIP, AIP and DIP – the model ensures that digital content can be preserved and accessed over time. The OAIS model has been widely adopted by organizations around the world, from libraries and museums to government agencies and research institutions, as a best practice for digital preservation. As the volume and complexity of digital information continue to grow, the principles and practices outlined in the OAIS model will remain essential for safeguarding our digital heritage for future generations.

4 Dark archives vs. open archives

In research data archiving, two major types of repositories are commonly discussed: *dark archives* and *open archives*, sometimes referred to as *light archives*.[1] These

1 Erickson (2013) provides a list of definitions for dark and light archives.

archives serve distinct purposes, primarily differing in accessibility, security and integration with external systems. The distinction between these different types of archives is not related to the discussion of *open access* or *open research*, as these address questions of availability of data, not of the underlying archiving procedure. This section addresses these procedures.

4.1 Characteristics of dark archives

Dark archives are repositories that are not accessible to external users and are strictly limited to authorized archivists or data stewards. These systems are typically protected by strong firewalls and are neither available on the World Wide Web nor accessible through local networks. Their primary function is to ensure the long-term preservation and integrity of data without direct user interaction.

One of the key advantages of dark archives is their high level of security. Due to their restricted access, they require fewer security measures compared to systems with broader access. For example, they do not necessitate single sign-on integration, as access can be managed through functional accounts for a small number of users.

Dark archives are often integrated with front-end systems in a way that allows stored content to be exported for external access. A common example in language data archiving is storing a corpus in a dark archive, assigning it a persistent identifier (Section 6) and making it available via a long-term archival system. The dark archive remains invisible to end users, acting as a secure "black box," while external systems facilitate access to copies of the data. The persistent identifier serves as a reference for which data set was used.

The separation between ingestion (archival process) and data access enhances security: even if front-end systems experience security breaches, the original data within the dark archive remains unaffected. However, a major drawback is that external services, such as analysis tools, require separate access mechanisms. The front-end system and dark archive must establish a trust relationship, ensuring that privileged users can retrieve and process specific data. At each step in the research data life cycle the integrity of the data can be checked by comparing the data to the data in the dark archive as a reference. This is also true for the ingestion pipeline that needs to have a trusted gateway to store the data into the dark archive, which needs to be sufficiently secured.

4.2 Characteristics of open archives

In contrast, open archives are designed for public or institutional accessibility, enabling users to search, analyze and access data directly within the archival system.

Unlike dark archives, open archives do not rely on separate front-end systems to provide access to stored content.

The main advantage of open archives is their efficiency in facilitating research and data utilization. Since users can work directly with the archived data, there is often no need to create redundant copies for analysis. This reduces storage costs and simplifies data management; it is not necessary to assess the identity of the analyzed and the stored data, as there is no distinction.

However, open archives require a robust access control framework to balance long-term preservation with usability. Security measures must accommodate multiple users while ensuring that sensitive or restricted data is only accessible to authorized individuals. Additionally, maintaining an open archive requires more frequent updates to hardware, software and security protocols to support both preservation and active use.

4.3 Key differences and considerations

The fundamental distinction between dark and open archives lies in their architectural design and in security considerations:

- *Security:* Dark archives offer enhanced security through isolation and firewall protection, while open archives require more comprehensive access management strategies.
- *Data Access:* Open archives provide immediate and direct access to users, whereas dark archives necessitate front-end systems to process and retrieve data copies.
- *System Maintenance:* Open archives require ongoing system optimization to balance preservation and accessibility, whereas dark archives focus primarily on long-term data integrity. Hence questions of performance are less relevant.
- *Integration:* Dark archives function as long-term storage units that interact with other systems for data retrieval, while open archives integrate accessibility and preservation within a single system.

The choice between dark and open archives depends on specific use cases, priorities in long-term preservation and the need for active data access. In some cases, hybrid models may be implemented to combine the strengths of both approaches, optimizing security, usability and sustainability.

5 Function of repository systems

Repository systems play a pivotal role in the digital archiving ecosystem, serving as the backbone for the storage, management and preservation of digital objects. These systems are designed to ensure that digital content remains accessible, usable and interpretable over time, even as technologies evolve and formats become obsolete. By providing a structured environment for managing digital assets, repository systems enable archives to fulfill their mission of long-term preservation while supporting the needs of researchers, institutions and the broader public.

5.1 Role and importance of repository systems

Repository systems are essential for the effective management of digital archives. They act as centralized platforms where digital objects – ranging from text documents and images to audio recordings and other datasets – are stored, organized and made accessible to users. The primary role of a repository system is to ensure the integrity, authenticity and longevity of digital content, which is critical for preserving cultural heritage, scientific data and institutional records.

One of the key functions of repository systems is to provide a secure and reliable storage infrastructure. This involves not only safeguarding digital objects from physical threats such as hardware failures or natural disasters but also protecting them from digital threats like data corruption, unauthorized access and cyberattacks. Repository systems achieve this through redundancy, backup mechanisms and robust access control policies (Rosenthal et al. 2005).

Beyond storage, repository systems also play a crucial role in metadata management. Metadata – descriptive information about digital objects (see Trippel 2025) – is essential for ensuring that content remains discoverable and interpretable over time. Repository systems facilitate the creation, storage and retrieval of metadata, enabling users to search for and access digital objects efficiently. This is particularly important in large archives, where the volume of data can make manual management impractical (ISO 14721 2012).

Another important function of repository systems is to support the ingest and dissemination of digital objects. The ingest process involves receiving digital content from depositors, validating its integrity and packaging it for long-term storage. Repository systems often follow the Open Archival Information System (OAIS) model (Section 3), which defines standardized workflows for ingesting Submission Information Packages (SIPs, see Section 3.2) and transforming them into Archival Information Packages (AIPs, see Section 3.3) for preservation. On the dissemination side, repository systems provide tools for users to access and retrieve digital objects, often in the form of Dissemination Information Packages (DIPs, see Section 3.4).

5.2 Features and capabilities of repository systems

To fulfill their role in digital archiving, repository systems are equipped with a range of features and capabilities that support long-term preservation. These functionalities are designed to address the challenges of technological obsolescence, data degradation and changing user needs.

- *Version Control and Audit Trails:* Repository systems often include version control mechanisms that track changes to digital objects over time. This ensures that the history of an object is preserved, allowing users to access previous versions if needed. Audit trails provide a record of all actions performed on a digital object, including ingest, modification and access, which is critical for maintaining accountability and authenticity, and part of the provenance documentation.
- *Format Migration and Emulation:* To address the issue of file format obsolescence, repository systems may support format migration, which involves converting files to newer, more sustainable formats. Alternatively, some systems employ emulation techniques, which recreate the original software environment in which a file was created. Both strategies aim to ensure that digital objects remain accessible as technology evolves (Rothenberg 1999, Lorie 2001).
- *Metadata Management:* Repository systems provide robust tools for managing metadata, including the ability to create, edit and search metadata records. Many systems support standardized metadata schemas. A detailed discussion of metadata is found in Trippel (2025). Metadata management is essential for ensuring that digital objects remain discoverable and interpretable over time (see OAIS, ISO 14721 2012).
- *Access Control and Authentication:* To protect sensitive or restricted content, repository systems implement access control mechanisms that regulate who can view, download, or modify digital objects. Authentication protocols, such as Shibboleth (Cantor and Scavo 2005) or OAuth (Hardt 2012), ensure that only authorized users can access the repository. These features are particularly important for archives that contain confidential or proprietary information.
- *Scalability and Performance:* As the volume of digital content grows, repository systems must be able to scale to accommodate increasing storage and processing demands. Many systems are designed to support distributed storage architectures, such as cloud-based solutions, which provide flexibility and scalability. Performance optimization features, such as caching and load balancing, en-

sure that users can access digital objects quickly and efficiently (Cardellini et al. 1999).

- *Preservation Planning and Monitoring:* Repository systems often include tools for preservation planning, which involve assessing the risks to digital objects and developing strategies to mitigate them. Monitoring tools track the health of digital objects, alerting administrators to potential issues such as data corruption or format obsolescence. These features are critical for ensuring the long-term viability of digital content (Hedstrom 1997).
- *Interoperability and Standards Compliance:* To facilitate collaboration and data exchange between different archives, repository systems are designed to comply with international standards, such as the OAIS reference model (ISO 14721 2012) and the PREMIS (Preservation Metadata: Implementation Strategies)[2] data dictionary. Interoperability features enable repository systems to integrate with other tools and platforms, such as digital libraries, content management systems and research data repositories.

Repository systems are indispensable tools for digital archiving, providing the infrastructure and functionalities needed to preserve and manage digital content over the long term. By addressing challenges such as data integrity, format obsolescence and metadata management, these systems ensure that digital objects remain accessible and meaningful for future generations. As the volume and complexity of digital content continue to grow, the role of repository systems in supporting long-term preservation will only become more critical. The next section will explore the use of persistent identifiers, another key component of digital archiving that complements the functions of repository systems.

6 Use of persistent identification

In the digital age, the proliferation of scientific data, publications and other research outputs has necessitated the development of robust systems to ensure their long-term accessibility and citability. Persistent Identifiers (PIDs) have emerged as a cornerstone of digital preservation and scholarly communication. PIDs are unique, long-lasting references to digital objects, such as articles, datasets, software and other research outputs. Unlike URLs, which can break when content is moved or deleted, PIDs are designed to remain stable over time, ensuring that digital resources can be reliably accessed and cited for years to come.

---

2 See https://www.loc.gov/standards/premis/

The importance of PIDs lies in their ability to provide persistent, unambiguous and interoperable references to digital objects. This is particularly critical in scientific research, where the ability to access and verify prior work is fundamental to the advancement of knowledge. For example, Digital Object Identifiers (DOIs) are widely used in academic publishing to uniquely identify journal articles, books and datasets. When a DOI is assigned to a publication, it ensures that the resource can be accessed even if the underlying URL changes, as the DOI always resolves to the current location of the object through a centralized resolution service. This permanence is essential for maintaining the integrity of the scholarly record and enabling reproducible research.

PIDs also play a crucial role in enhancing the discoverability and interoperability of research outputs. By providing a standardized way to reference digital objects, PIDs facilitate linking between related resources, such as a journal article and its underlying dataset. This interconnectedness supports the growing emphasis on open science and data sharing, enabling researchers to build on existing work more effectively. Furthermore, PIDs are increasingly being used to track the impact and reuse of research outputs, providing valuable metrics for assessing the reach and influence of scientific work.

The central role of persistent identifiers is underlined by an International Standard. ISO 24619 (2011) defines properties and requirements. It describes the purpose of PIDs, with a scope on language resources. It specifies requirements for the creation and maintenance of PID systems in this field, ensuring their reliability and interoperability and outlines guidelines for using PIDs to reference and cite language resources in various contexts, such as publications, research data and online repositories. The standard defines criteria for PID systems and PID Usage. ISO 24619:2011 provides a crucial framework for ensuring the persistent identification and sustainable access of language resources.

6.1 Sources of PIDs

The implementation of PIDs involves a combination of technical infrastructure, governance frameworks and community adoption. Several organizations and initiatives provide PID services, each with its own focus and scope. Below are some of the most widely used sources of PIDs in the scientific community:

– *Digital Object Identifiers (DOIs):* DOIs are perhaps the most well-known type of PID, managed by the International DOI Foundation (IDF).[3] The DOI system is

3 See https://www.doi.org/ visited February 6th, 2025.

implemented through a network of registration agencies, such as Crossref[4] and DataCite,[5] which assign DOIs to scholarly content. Crossref primarily focuses on publications, while DataCite specializes in datasets and other research outputs. DOIs are widely adopted in academic publishing and are increasingly being used for datasets, software and other digital objects.

- *Handles:* The Handle System,[6] developed by the Corporation for National Research Initiatives (CNRI), is another widely used PID system. Handles are similar to DOIs in that they provide persistent references to digital objects, but they are not limited to scholarly content. The Handle System is the underlying technology for DOIs and it is also used independently in various contexts, such as digital libraries and institutional repositories.
- *Uniform Resource Names (URNs):* URNs are a type of PID defined by the Internet Engineering Task Force (IETF). Unlike DOIs and Handles, which rely on centralized resolution services, URNs are designed to be resolved through a distributed system. URNs are less commonly used in scientific research but have applications in specific domains, such as legal and governmental documentation.
- *Archival Resource Keys (ARKs):* ARKs are PIDs designed for long-term access to digital objects, particularly in archives and libraries. They are supported by the ARK Alliance[7] and are used by institutions such as the National Library of France and the University of California. ARKs are notable for their flexibility and ability to include metadata via inflections (adding question marks at the end of the identifier).

6.2 Challenges and the future of PIDs

Despite their many benefits, the implementation of PIDs is not without challenges. One major issue is the cost and complexity of maintaining PID systems, particularly for smaller institutions and research communities. Additionally, the proliferation of different PID systems can lead to fragmentation, making it difficult for researchers to know which system to use for a given purpose.

Looking ahead, the use of PIDs is expected to expand as the scientific community continues to embrace open science and data sharing. Emerging technologies, such as blockchain, may offer new ways to enhance the security and transparency

4 See https://www.crossref.org/ visited March 4th, 2025.

5 See https://datacite.org/ visited March 4th, 2025.

6 See https://handle.net/ visited March 4th, 2025.

7 See https://arks.org/ visited February 6th, 2025.

of PID systems. Furthermore, the integration of PIDs with artificial intelligence and machine learning tools could enable more sophisticated tracking and analysis of research outputs, opening up new possibilities for understanding the impact and evolution of scientific knowledge.

In conclusion, persistent identifiers are indispensable tools for ensuring the long-term accessibility, discoverability and interoperability of digital research outputs. By providing stable and unambiguous references to digital objects, PIDs support the integrity of the scholarly record and facilitate the advancement of science. As the scientific landscape continues to evolve, the development and adoption of robust PID systems will remain a key priority for researchers, institutions and policymakers alike.

7 Digital objects in archiving language data

Digital objects are central to the long-term archiving of electronic data. A digital object refers to the item being archived, along with the necessary metadata to describe it. These metadata can be technical or descriptive to facilitate discoverability. For more details, see Trippel (2025).

7.1 Content of a digital object

The content of a digital object includes the following:
- *Metadata:* Descriptive information to facilitate discoverability.
- *Technical Information* needed by an archival system, such as cryptographic checksums to ensure data integrity.
- *Access Control Lists (ACLs):* Data which defines who can access the data and what actions they can perform.
- *Object Data:* The actual data being archived, such as audio or video files and their annotations.

The internal structure of a digital object involves a defined directory structure, including required files and file names. This structure ensures that metadata, content data and technical information are organized systematically, facilitating efficient storage, retrieval and management. The following are two examples of such structures.

7.1.1 BagIt standard

The BagIt standard (Kunze et al. 2018) is a hierarchical file packaging format designed to support the transfer and storage of digital content. A BagIt package, or "bag," consists of a "payload" directory containing the object data and a set of "tag" files that provide metadata and checksums. The main components of a BagIt package include the following:

- *Payload Directory:* Contains the actual object data to be archived.
- *Manifest Files:* List the payload files along with their checksums to ensure data integrity.
- *Tag Files:* Provide metadata about the bag, such as the bag's creation date, contact information and other descriptive information.
- *BagIt.txt:* A required file that identifies the package as a BagIt bag and specifies the version of the BagIt standard used.

7.1.2 Oxford Commons File Layout (OCFL)

The Oxford Commons File Layout (OCFL, Jefferies et al. 2022) is a specification for organizing digital content in a consistent and transparent manner. It aims to ensure the long-term preservation of digital objects by providing a clear and understandable directory structure. Key features of the OCFL include the following:

- *Object Root:* The top-level directory for each digital object, containing all related files and metadata.
- *Version Directories:* Subdirectories within the object root that store different versions of the digital object. Each version directory contains the content files and metadata for that specific version.
- *Inventory File:* A JSON file located in the object root that lists all versions of the digital object, along with their associated files and metadata. The inventory file also includes checksums for data integrity.
- *Sidecar Files:* Optional files that provide additional metadata or checksums for the content files.

7.1.3 Organizing metadata and technical information

Both the BagIt standard and the OCFL emphasize the importance of organizing metadata and technical information separately from the content data. This separation allows for easier management and retrieval of metadata, which is crucial for the discoverability and integrity of digital objects.

7.2 Granularity and the archival units

With granularity, the level division of the archival data into digital objects is addressed. For illustrations a corpus will be used and the consequences will be discussed in this section.

7.2.1 Example: corpus with different granularities

Consider a national corpus consisting of multiple newspapers. This corpus can be structured in various ways:
- *Unstructured Dataset:* The entire corpus is provided as one unstructured dataset.
- *Substructured by Newspapers:* The dataset is divided by individual newspapers.
- *Substructured by Year:* Each newspaper is further divided by year.
- *Substructured by Issue:* Each year's data is divided by individual issues.
- *Substructured by Article:* Each issue is divided into individual articles.
- *Substructured by words:* Each article is divided into individual words.

The issue of granularity addresses the question with of these divisions should be used as the division of the digital object. Each level of granularity has implications for the creation of PIDs and metadata, as well as for search and analysis capabilities. Fine granularity (e. g., individual articles) allows for detailed analysis and precise referencing but increases costs and complexity. Broader granularity (e. g., entire newspapers or years) reduces costs and complexity but may limit detailed analysis.

7.2.2 Consequences of granularity selection: costs

Selecting the unit of a digital object involves considering the following aspects:
- *Persistent Identifiers (PIDs):* Fine granularity requires more PIDs, increasing costs and effort for minting the PIDs. Though one PID may be cheap – costing only a couple of cents – changing the granularity from national corpus level of detail to the level, where every newspaper article in the corpus receives a persistent identifier or even every word changes the number of needed PIDs significantly.
- *Metadata Creation:* Smaller units increase the costs for metadata creation. As each digital object contains some metadata, the increase of the number of objects also increases the costs – even if the creation by automatic processes may be cheap, the sum may become significant as well. And with manual creation of metadata by subject matter experts the costs will be too high as well.

To illustrate the difference, it is possible to look at the German Reference Corpus DeReKo (see for example Kupietz and Keibel 2009, Kupietz et al. 2010, 2018). It is possible to assign one PID on the corpus level, or on the word level, DeReKo as of January 2025,[8] has 61.5 billion words. For example, for 2025 the TIB consortium charges 500 EUR for up to 1999 DOIs to be assinged per year as part of a membership model, hence a granularity on the corpus level would be covered with the 500 EUR plan. For 61.5 billion words, each receiving its own PID, the largest package of this PID agency for 26 000 PIDs per year would have to be bought more than 6000 times, resulting in costs of almost 160 million EUR by this price model. Though a different price model would have to be negotiated, it is obvious that a decision for this kind of granularity has immense consequences.[9] The increase would be comparable also for the creation of the metadata files. Hence the selection has to balance the costs and the benefits.

7.2.3 Consequences of granularity: implications for addressing in research contexts

With specific metadata on the various levels of detail, it becomes possible to use the metadata also for searching without looking into the object data. In some research contexts, for example, it may appear natural to refer to an article of a specific newspaper issue, i. e. a specific date, with the title of the article. Taking the division of the newspapers into articles would allow for a search for a specific article and addressing it by its unique persistent identifier.

However, for distant reading purposes or statistics of word usages, for co-occurrences of words, such a fine granularity would not be necessary. In such scenarios, it would only result in additional structures to be ignored or removed during analysis, in the worst case leading to additional errors or processing requirements, or, in the best case, not causing any additional issues.

7.2.4 Consequences of granularity selection: technical implementation

The selection of granularity has significant implications for the technical implementation of archival systems. The granularity of digital objects directly affects the num-

8 See https://www.ids-mannheim.de/digspra/kl/projekte/korpora/ visited January 30th, 2025.

9 See the pricing at https://projects.tib.eu/pid-service/en/tib-doi-konsortium/become-a-member/ visited January 30th, 2025.

ber of files that need to be processed by an archival system. Finer granularity results in a larger number of smaller files, while broader granularity results in fewer, larger files. A large number of files can cause technical limitations in the underlying file systems. Although modern systems can handle thousands of files in a single directory, there are still limitations. These limitations may not only stem from the file system itself but also from operating system tools used for basic file operations, such as listing, copying and backing up files. Managing a vast number of files can lead to performance issues and increased complexity in file handling.

Conversely, combining multiple files into a single large file is not always a viable solution, as large files also present technical challenges. While file systems can process very large files, there are still limitations. For example, large files can be cumbersome to transfer, backup and restore. They may also require more robust hardware and software resources to manage effectively.

7.2.5 Finding the right granularity level

Finding the right balance in granularity selection is crucial for the reasons outlined above. Archivists must consider the trade-offs between having too many small details and too broad partitions.

ISO 24619 (2011), which provides a standard on PIDs for language resources, provides recommendations for selecting the granularity that will receive a persistent identifier. These can be used as a guideline also for the granularity of a digital object.

- If there is an existing identifier scheme for a type of resources, it is a good indication that this would be a suitable level of granularity. For example books having ISBNs are also often appropriate levels for digital objects in a corpus.
- If a resource is associated with the complete content of a digital file, it often makes sense to use this level of granularity. For example, if a publisher provides a single file containing the full year of a newspaper with all issues, then this is usually a good level of granularity for a digital object.
- If the resource is autonomous and exists outside a larger context, it could also serve as a digital object. For example a corpus being distributed as one unit, can also be combined into one digital object, even if it contains multiple files.
- If a resource should be citable without citing a containing resource, it should be a digital object of its own. For example if the articles of a newspaper should be citable, they should be individual digital objects.

A recommendation for archives is to maintain the level of granularity selected by the data provider whenever possible. If someone submits a dataset to an archive, the partitioning of this dataset should not be altered unless there are compelling reasons from the archive's perspective.

In selecting the right level of granularity for the digital object, the goal is to optimize the granularity to ensure efficient processing, storage and retrieval while minimizing technical limitations and costs. This balance involves evaluating the capabilities of the archival system, the nature of the digital objects and the intended use of the archived data. There is usually no obvious optimal selection, but there are trade-offs as indicated here.

7.2.6 Virtual digital objects

One solution to the granularity problem is to define Virtual Digital Objects (VDOs). A VDO initially appears to have the same structure as any other digital object, including metadata, checksums, etc. However, the key difference is that the object data within a VDO does not consist of the actual object data itself. Instead, it primarily comprises references to other digital objects, thereby pointing to the object data contained within those objects.

For example, consider the example of the national corpus above consisting of newspapers, annual volumes of a newspaper, individual issues and individual words. When choosing a granularity level at the annual volume level, a hierarchy can be formed. This hierarchy could include a digital object at the level of the newspaper or even the entire national corpus, by pointing to the (virtual) digital objects for each year of the newspaper.

Technically, this is usually implemented by using the persistent identifiers for the digital objects at the lower levels as pointers on the higher hierarchical levels. The object data of a newspaper corpus that is represented as a digital object hence would consist of some representation of the list of persistent identifier of the digital objects containing each year of the newspaper. A national corpus could then be a digital object, where the object data consists of all the newspaper corpora collected for the national corpus, with each one serving as a virtual digital object for the individual years. In this way, a construct is created where digital objects can contain hierarchical structures, allowing for citation of the entire construct without needing to reference individual parts separately, while on the other hand also the smaller constituents of the structures can be cited. Such a structure is not necessarily unique as individual parts may be constituents of different VDOs at the same time.

8 Role of a data steward in long-term archiving

The *data steward* is the central role in long-term archiving. The responsibility of the data steward is multifaceted for ensuring the integrity, accessibility and usability of data over extended periods.

8.1 Functions of a data steward in long-term archiving

The following are central functions of a data steward.

- *Data Quality Management:* Data stewards are responsible for maintaining the accuracy, completeness and consistency of data. They ensure that data meets quality standards and is reliable for future use.
- *Metadata Management:* They manage and update metadata.
- *Policy Enforcement:* Data stewards implement and enforce data governance policies across the organization. This includes ensuring compliance with regulatory requirements and organizational standards.
- *Data Security and Compliance:* They ensure that data is stored, accessed and shared in compliance with regulations such as the EU's General Data Protection Regulation (GDPR), copyright, confidentiality requirements and security needs. This involves safeguarding data against unauthorized access and breaches.
- *Collaboration with Stakeholders:* data stewards work closely with data contributors, i. e. owners, data analysts, IT teams and other stakeholders to ensure that data meets the needs of the organization and of researchers.
- *Long-term Preservation:* data stewards play a critical role in ensuring that data remains accessible and usable over time. This involves planning for technological changes, such as new media and data formats and addressing the needs of a changing user community.
- *Hierarchical Structuring:* They may also be involved in creating hierarchical structures for digital objects, ensuring that data can be cited and referenced appropriately at different levels of granularity.
- *Continuous Improvement:* data stewards continuously evaluate and improve data management practices to adapt to new challenges and opportunities, including the adoption of emerging standards and technologies in data management.

8.2 Skills and expertise for data stewards in language-related research data management

A data steward working with language-related research data needs a combination of specialized skills and expertise to effectively manage, preserve and ensure the quality of the data. They must possess a solid understanding of linguistic concepts, including familiarity with linguistic theories, syntax, semantics, phonetics and other language-related concepts. Additionally, they should have experience with language resources such as corpora, lexicons, language models and other linguistic datasets.

Proficiency in data management is crucial, including skills in data profiling, cleansing, validation and enrichment to ensure data accuracy and consistency. The ability to create and manage metadata is essential.

Technical proficiency is also important for a data steward. Among the skills should be the management of databases that store language data, including both SQL and NoSQL databases. Experience with tools and technologies for integrating and transforming language data from various sources is valuable, as is proficiency in programming languages such as Python or R, which are commonly used for data manipulation and analysis.

Understanding data protection laws is necessary, especially as they pertain to personal and sensitive data. Data stewards must be able to implement and enforce data governance policies to ensure compliance and ethical data handling.

Analytical and problem-solving skills are essential for analyzing language data to extract meaningful insights and support research objectives. The ability to identify and resolve data quality issues and other challenges that arise in managing language data is also important. Data stewards work collaboratively with various stakeholders to ensure that data meets the needs of the research community.

Finally, a commitment to continuous learning is vital. Data stewards should stay informed about the latest developments in data stewardship, language technology and related fields. They should also be willing to learn and adapt to new tools and technologies that can enhance data management practices.

Though this list is not necessarily complete and comprehensive, it indicates the diverse requirements for data stewards working with language related research data.

9 Contribution of certification for trustworthy archives

As digital data becomes central to research, education and cultural heritage, the need for trustworthy archives has never been greater. These archives safeguard valuable digital assets but face challenges like technological obsolescence, data corruption and institutional instability.

Certification addresses these challenges by ensuring archives follow best practices in digital preservation, fostering trust and accountability. It validates an archive's ability to preserve digital materials long-term, assuring researchers their data remains accessible, and guiding funders and policymakers in assessing sustainability. Ultimately, certification elevates archives from storage spaces to trusted custodians of the digital record.

9.1 Certification standards

Several certification standards have been developed to guide and evaluate the trustworthiness of digital archives. These standards provide a comprehensive set of criteria for assessing the technical, organizational and procedural aspects of digital preservation. All of the following standards are aligned with the Open Archival Information System (OAIS) reference model (Section 3).

- *nestor Seal:* The nestor Seal,[10] developed by the German nestor network of expertise in long-term storage of digital resources, is based on the DIN 31644 (2012) standard and provides a detailed checklist for evaluating the trustworthiness of digital archives (Neuroth et al. 2010, 2012).
  - *DIN 31644 – Criteria for Trustworthy Digital Archives:* The DIN 31644 (2012) standard, developed by the German Institute for Standardization (Deutsches Institut für Normung, DIN), is a widely recognized framework for certifying digital archives. It outlines a set of 34 criteria for ensuring the long-term preservation of digital objects, including requirements for organizational infrastructure, preservation planning and technical implementation. The standard emphasizes the importance of transparency, accountability and continuous improvement in digital preservation practices. DIN 31644 has been adopted by numerous archives and cultural heritage institutions.

---

10 See https://www.langzeitarchivierung.de/Webs/nestor/DE/Home/home_node.html visited February 6th, 2025.

- *CoreTrustSeal:* The CoreTrustSeal[11] is an international certification standard for data repositories, developed by the CoreTrustSeal Board. It builds on the earlier Data Seal of Approval (DSA) and World Data System (WDS) certification frameworks and is widely used in the scientific community. The CoreTrustSeal focuses on 16 core requirements, including data integrity, accessibility and sustainability. It is particularly relevant for research data repositories and is recognized by funding agencies and publishers as a mark of quality and reliability.
- *ISO 16363 (2012) – Audit and Certification of Trustworthy Digital Repositories:* ISO 16363 (2012) is an international standard for certifying trustworthy digital repositories, developed by the International Organization for Standardization (ISO). It provides a comprehensive set of criteria for evaluating the organizational, technical and procedural aspects of digital preservation.

9.2 Benefits of certification

Certification offers numerous benefits for digital archives, their users and the broader community. These benefits can be categorized into three main areas: trust and credibility, operational improvement and stakeholder engagement.

- *Trust and Credibility:* Certification enhances the trustworthiness of digital archives by providing an independent assessment of their capabilities and practices. For users, such as researchers and educators, certification serves as a guarantee that the archive adheres to recognized standards and is committed to preserving digital materials for the long term. This assurance is particularly important in the context of open science and data sharing, where the reliability of digital repositories is critical for ensuring the reproducibility and integrity of research.
- *Operational Improvement:* The process of certification encourages digital archives to critically evaluate and improve their policies, processes and infrastructure. By adhering to certification standards, archives can identify gaps and weaknesses in their preservation practices and implement targeted improvements. This continuous improvement process not only enhances the quality of the archive but also increases its resilience to technological and organizational changes.
- *Stakeholder Engagement:* Certification fosters stronger relationships between digital archives and their stakeholders, including funding agencies, publishers

---

11 See https://www.coretrustseal.org/ visited February 6th, 2025.

and user communities. For funding agencies, certification provides a clear indicator of the archive's commitment to best practices and long-term sustainability. For publishers, certification ensures that the archive meets the requirements for hosting supplementary materials and datasets associated with scholarly publications. For users, certification provides confidence that their digital assets will be preserved and accessible over time.

While certification offers significant benefits, it is not without obstacles. The process of certification can be resource-intensive, requiring significant time, expertise and financial investment. Smaller institutions and specialized repositories may find it difficult to meet the stringent requirements of certification standards. Additionally, the rapid pace of technological change poses challenges for maintaining the relevance and applicability of certification criteria.

In conclusion, certification is a vital component of the digital preservation ecosystem, providing a framework for ensuring the trustworthiness, reliability and sustainability of digital archives. By adhering to the above mentioned recognized standards, archives can demonstrate their commitment to best practices and build trust with their stakeholders. As the digital landscape continues to evolve, certification will remain a key tool for safeguarding the digital record and supporting the advancement of science and culture.

10 Conclusion

In this chapter, we have explored the multifaceted domain of digital long-term archiving, with a particular focus on standards and practices within the language domain. We began by discussing the various levels of preservation – binary, logical and semantic – highlighting their importance in maintaining the integrity, functionality and meaning of digital objects over time. The Open Archival Information System (OAIS) model was introduced as a foundational framework and the roles of Submission Information Packages (SIP), Archival Information Packages (AIP) and Dissemination Information Packages (DIP) in the archival process were discussed in detail.

We contrasted dark archives with open archives, explaining their respective purposes and benefits and examined the critical role of repository systems in managing and preserving digital objects. The use of persistent identifiers (PIDs) was emphasized as essential for ensuring long-term access and citability of digital resources. Additionally, we defined digital objects and outlined the responsibilities of data stewards in managing these resources, underscoring the importance of their role in ensuring data quality, security and compliance.

Finally, we discussed the significance of certification in establishing trustworthy archives, highlighting relevant standards such as DIN 31644 and CoreTrustSeal. Certification not only enhances the credibility and reliability of digital archives but also fosters continuous improvement and stakeholder engagement.

In conclusion, effective long-term digital preservation requires a comprehensive and integrated approach, combining robust technical solutions with sound organizational practices. By adhering to established standards and best practices and by leveraging the expertise of data stewards, we can ensure that valuable digital resources remain accessible, usable and meaningful for future generations. The insights and strategies presented in this chapter provide a solid foundation for navigating the complexities of long-term digital archiving and safeguarding our digital heritage.

Bibliography

Cantor, Scott & Tom Scavo. 2005. Shibboleth architecture. *Protocols and Profiles* 10(16). 29. https://doi.org/10.16.

Cardellini, Valeria, Michele Colajanni & Philip S. Yu. 1999. Dynamic Load Balancing on Web-Server Systems. *IEEE Internet Computing* 3(3). 28–39.

DIN 31644. 2012. *Information und Dokumentation – Kriterien für vertrauenswürdige digitale Langzeitarchive*. National Standard. Berlin: Deutsches Institut für Normung (DIN).

Erickson, Chris. 2013. Light, dark and dim archives: what are they? Blog article. Accessed: 6 February 2025. http://preservationmatters.blogspot.com/2013/05/light-dark-and-dim-archives-what-are.html.

Hardt, Dick. 2012. The OAuth 2.0 authorization framework. Tech. rep.

Hedstrom, Margaret. 1997. Digital preservation: A time bomb for digital libraries. *Computers and the Humanities* 31(3). 189–202.

ISO 14721. 2012. *Space data and information transfer systems – Open archival information system (OAIS) – Reference model*. International Standard. Geneva: International Organization for Standardization (ISO). https://www.iso.org/standard/57284.html.

ISO 16363. 2012. *Space data and information transfer systems – Audit and certification of trustworthy digital repositories*. International Standard. Geneva: International Organization for Standardization (ISO).

ISO 24619. 2011. *Language resource management – Persistent identification and sustainable access (PISA)*. International Standard. Geneva: International Organization for Standardization (ISO).

Jefferies, Neil, Rosalyn Metz, Julian Morley, Simeon Warner & Andrew Woods. 2022. Oxford common file layout specification. Tech. rep. Version 1.1. Updated 7 November 2024. Accessed: September 9, 2025. OCFL initiative. https://ocfl.io/1.1/spec/.

Kunze, J., J. Littman, E. Madden, J. Scancella & C. Adams. 2018. RFC: 8493 – The BagIt File Packaging Format (V1.0). IETF Standard 8493. Accessed: September 9, 2025. Internet Engineerint Task Force (IETF). https://datatracker.ietf.org/doc/html/rfc8493.

Kupietz, Marc, Cyril Belica, Holger Keibel & Andreas Witt. 2010. The German Reference Corpus DeReKo: A primordial sample for linguistic research. In Nicoletta Calzolari, Khalid Choukri Bente Maegaard, Joseph Mariani, Jan Odjik, Stelios Piperidis, Mike Rosner & Daniel Tapias (eds.), *Proceedings of the seventh conference on international language resources and evaluation (LREC 2010)*, 1848–1854. European Language Resources Association (ELRA).

Kupietz, Marc & Holger Keibel. 2009. The Mannheim German Reference Corpus (DeReKo) as a basis for empirical linguistic research. In Makoto/Kawaguchi Minegishi (ed.), *Workings papers in corpus-based linguistics and language education*, Vol. 3, 53–59. Tokyo: Tokyo University of Foreign Studies.

Kupietz, Marc, Harald Lüngen, Pawel Kamocki & Andreas Witt. 2018. The German Reference Corpus DeReKo: New Developments – New Opportunities. In Nicoletta Calzolari, Khalid Choukri, Christopher Cieri, Thierry Declerck, Sara Goggi, Koiti Hasida, Hitoshi Isahara Bente Maegaard, Joseph Mariani, Hélène Mazo, Asuncion Moreno, Jan Odijk, Stelios Piperidis & Takenobu Tokunaga (eds.), *Proceedings of the eleventh international conference on language resources and evaluation (LREC 2018)*, 4353–4360. Miyazaki, Japan: European Language Resources Association (ELRA). ISBN 979-10-95546-00-9.

Lorie, Raymond A. 2001. Long term preservation of digital information. In *Proceedings of the 1st ACM/IEEE-CS joint conference on digital libraries*, 346–352.

National Institute of Standards and Technology (NIST). 2015. Secure Hash Standard (SHS). FIPS PUB 180-4. U. S. Department of Commerce. https://doi.org/10.6028/NIST.FIPS.180-4.

Neuroth, Heike, Achim Osswald, Regine Scheffel, Stefan Strathmann & Karsten Huth (eds.). 2010. *nestor-Handbuch: Eine kleine Enzyklopädie der digitalen Langzeitarchivierung*. 2.3. Creative Commons License (Namensnennung-Keine kommerzielle Nutzung-Weitergabe unter gleichen Bedingungen 3.0 Unported). Glückstadt, Germany: VWH Verlag Werner Hülsbusch. http://www.nestor.sub.uni-goettingen.de/handbuch/index.php.

Neuroth, Heike, Stefan Strathmann, Achim Osswald, Regine Scheffel, Jens Klump & Jens Ludwig (eds.). 2012. *NESTOR HANDBUCH Forschungsdaten: Langzeitarchivierung von Forschungsdaten. Eine Bestandsaufnahme*. 1.0. Creative Commons License (Namensnennung-Keine kommerzielle Nutzung-Weitergabe unter gleichen Bedingungen 3.0 Unported). Glückstadt, Germany: VWH Verlag Werner Hülsbusch. http://www.nestor.sub.uni-goettingen.de/bestandsaufnahme/index.php.

Rivest, Ronald. 1992. RFC1321: The MD5 message-digest algorithm.

Rosenthal, David S. H., Thomas S. Robertson, Tom Lipkis, Vicky Reich & Seth Morabito. 2005. Requirements for digital preservation systems: A bottom-up approach. arXiv preprint arXiv: cs/0509018.

Rothenberg, Jeff. 1999. Avoiding technological quicksand: Finding a viable technical foundation for digital preservation. A report to the Council on Library and Information Resources. ERIC.

Trippel, Thorsten. 2025. Metadata for research data. In Piotr Bański, Ulrich Heid & Laura Herzberg (eds.), *Harmonising language data: Standards for linguistic resources*. de Gruyter.

Wilkinson, Mark D., Michel Dumontier, Jan Aalbersberg, Gabrielle Appleton, Myles Axton, Arie Baak, Niklas Blomberg, Jan-Willem Boiten, Luiz Bonino da Silva Santos, Philip E. Bourne, Jildau Bouwman, Anthony J. Brookes, Tim Clark, Mercè Crosas, Ingrid Dillo, Olivier Dumon, Scott Edmunds, Chris T. Evelo, Richard Finkers, Alejandra Gonzalez-Beltran, Alasdair J. G. Gray, Paul Groth, Carole Goble, Jeffrey S. Grethe, Jaap Heringa, Peter A. C. 't Hoen, Rob Hooft, Tobias Kuhn, Ruben Kok, Joost Kok, Scott J. Lusher, Maryann E. Martone, Albert Mons, Abel L. Packer, Bengt Persson, Philippe Rocca-Serra, Marco Roos, Rene van Schaik, Susanna-Assunta Sansone, Erik Schultes, Thierry Sengstag, Ted Slater, George Strawn, Morris A. Swertz, Mark Thompson, Johan van der Lei, Erik van Mulligen, Jan Velterop, Andra Waagmeester, Peter Wittenburg, Katherine Wolstencroft, Jun Zhao & Barend Mons. 2016. The FAIR Guiding Principles for scientific data management and stewardship. *Scientific Data* 3. 160018. https://doi.org/10.1038/sdata.2016.18.

Harald Lüngen and Ines Pisetta

Conversion into the archival format I5

Abstract: The IDS repository aims at long-term archival of linguistic resources and tools in the field of German studies. This chapter introduces I5, the archival format for textual data in the repository. I5 is characterised as a TEI customisation, featuring a tripartite corpus macrostructure and some renamings and restructurings of TEI elements to fit the corpus holdings compiled since 1964 at the IDS. After a brief introduction to I5, the contribution shows how the conversion to I5 is achieved for various input formats by using the examples of features of concrete corpora in the archive. The two cases covered are instances of the KED corpus of simple German which came as a CWB-based XML called VRT, and Wikipedia corpora which came in Wiki markup, both of which were converted to I5 using different strategies. We further show how I5 data are ingested into the archive and what happens if someone wishes to extract such data from the archive for their own subsequent use. Finally we mention some alternative archival formats used in other archives such as TEI proper or DTA-Bf.

Keywords: TEI, I5, XML, verticalised text format (VRT), Component Metadata Infrastructure (CMDI), InvenioRDM, repository

1 Introduction: I5 as an archival format

The IDS Repository aims at long-term archival of linguistic resources and tools in the field of German studies. It archives a most of the corpus holdings of the Leibniz Institute for the German Language (IDS), but also other, IDS-external corpus resources that are relevant in the field of German linguistics, provided they are (re-)encoded in the archival format I5.

Acknowledgement: Section 4 of this chapter by author Ines Pisetta is based on work within Text+, funded by the Deutsche Forschungsgemeinschaft (DFG, project number 460033370) as part of the German National Research Data Infrastructure (NFDI e. V.). Furthermore the author Ines Pisetta acknowledges the use of Large Language Models (LLMs) as writing aids in phrasing Section 4, based on the author's notes, ideas and concepts. The author retains full responsibility for the content.

Harald Lüngen, Ines Pisetta, Digitale Sprachwissenschaft, Leibniz-Institut für Deutsche Sprache, R5 6-13, D-68161 Mannheim, Baden-Württemberg, Germany, e-mails: luengen@ids-mannheim.de, pisetta@ids-mannheim.de

https://doi.org/10.1515/9783112208212-010

I5 is short for IDS-TEI P5. It is defined as a TEI customisation (a formal derivation of the official TEI format) that features a tripartite corpus macrostructure and some renamings and restructurings of TEI elements to fit all written corpus holdings compiled since 1964 at the IDS. It is used for the more than 60 billion tokens of text of DEREKO, the German Reference Corpus (Kupietz et al. 2022), i. e. for the IDS corpora that can be analysed online using the IDS corpus research software COSMAS II (older system, Bodmer Mory 2014) or KorAP (new system, Kupietz et al. 2022), which are both based on I5 as well. As a consequence, I5 is also used as an archival format in the IDS long-term data repository. This chapter describes the main features of I5 and gives an idea of what it takes to convert an annotated corpus to I5. The terms repository and archive will be used interchangeably.

IDS has been building written corpora since 1964, and they have not always been marked up as I5. Before I5, IDS corpora were formatted according to the XCES (Ide et al. 2000) standard. In fact, a large part of the definition of I5 consisted in customising the definition of TEI elements so that they matched the definitions and names of elements in XCES. For example, XCES had `@id` as a global attribute while TEI P5 has `@xml:id` for the same purpose, i. e. to indicate an identifier. Consequently, I5 uses `@id`, i. e. the formal customisation of I5 contains a renaming of `@xml:id` to `@id`. Other changes concern the introduction of IDS-specific elements such as <korpusSigle>, <dokumentSigle>, and <textSigle> for specific kinds of IDs relating to the three parts that make up the macrostructure of a corpus in I5. These three parts are the corpus level (the corpus file as a whole, characterised by the root element <idsCorpus>), the document level (a certain grouping of texts, characterised by the element <idsDoc>, and the text level (<idsText>). Each corpus has these three levels, and one <idsCorpus> must consist of at least one <idsDoc>, and one <idsDoc> must in turn consist of at least one <idsText> as depicted in Listing 1.

```
<idsCorpus>
   <idsHeader>...</idsHeader>
   <idsDoc>
      <idsHeader>...</idsHeader>
      <idsText>
         <idsHeader>...</idsHeader>
           [...]
      </idsText>
      <idsText>...</idsText>
       [... more idsTexts]
   </idsDoc>
    [... more idsDocs]
</idsCorpus>
```

Listing 1: Corpus macrostructure in I5.

For the record, this means that <idsCorpus> corresponds to the element <teiCorpus> in TEI P5, and <idsText> corresponds to the element <TEI> in TEI P5. It also means that for each corpus that is to be converted to I5 it has to be decided how to map the original corpus structure onto the tripartite macrostructure of an I5 file. For example, in the case of the press corpora in DeReKo, it was decided that each year of a newspaper source corresponds to an <idsCorpus>, each month corresponds to an <idsDoc>, and each single newspaper article corresponds to an <idsText> (sic: one day i. e. a single edition of the paper has no corresponding element in the I5 macrostructure). In the case of a corpus of novels, each <idsDoc> contains exactly one <idsText> which is one novel (book) as a whole.

Each macrostructure level will also contain an <idsHeader> element containing metadata pertaining to the specific level (cf. Listing 1). For example the <idsHeader> under <idsCorpus> will contain metadata on the corpus level, such as the name of the corpus and of the project and/or people responsible for compiling the corpus, information about the source of the corpus data, such as its bibliographical specification or an URL, about licensing the corpus, and also some textual and linguistic characteristics that pertain to the whole corpus such as its language(s) or text genre(s). The <idsHeader> under the <idsDoc> element will specify information about the particular grouping that <idsDoc> stands for, sometimes only scarce when the grouping is fairly arbitrary or only formal (such as the <idsDoc> elements representing initial letters within the IDS Wikipedia corpora). And finally, the <idsHeader> under <idsText> will contain metadata about the particular text, for example in case of a newspaper article the issue and the date when it was published, the page number, the column heading, its topic domain, its language, and its title and authors if available.

The history and setup of I5 is laid out in an article by Lüngen and Sperberg-McQueen (2012). When I5 was introduced at the IDS in 2012, the actual DeReKo corpora and their markup were not changed. They were merely no longer validated against the XCES DTD but instead validated against the new I5 DTD. Since then, the I5 schema has sometimes been extended e. g. to include new CMC-specific elements such as <posting>. The I5 ODD (TEI customisation file) and the derived DTD and other documentation can be found online.[1]

1 https://www.ids-mannheim.de/en/digspra/corpus-linguistics/projects/corpus-development/ids-text-model/

2 Conversion of features of specific sources into the archival format

2.1 Conversion of annotated verticalised text

Many corpora that have been built in corpus linguistic projects come in a one-word-per-line format called verticalised text format (VRT). Each token appears in one line of text, and its token-based annotations are added as columns to the same line. Such a vertical format is for example required by the analysis tools Corpus Workbench (Evert and CWB Development Team 2022) and Sketch Engine (Kilgarriff et al. 2014). Structural XML markup such as `<text>`, `<paragraph>` (or `<p>`) and `<sentence>` (or `<s>`) elements can also be included in VRT when each such XML element tag is placed on a single line.

Listing 2 shows a VRT-like encoded sentence from the source encoding of the corpus KED (Korpus einfaches Deutsch, Jach and Dietz 2024). The first column of each line representing a token contains the orthographic form of the token as it occurred in the primary text. The second column contains its base form or lemma, i. e. the nominative singular form for nouns or the infinitive in case of verbs (see Ljubešić and Erjavec 2025). The third column contains a part-of-speech (POS) tag according to the STTS tagset (Schiller et al. 1999) which is a de-facto standard for German in terms of a tagset for POS tagging and used by most German language taggers.[2] In fact, the triple consisting of orthographic form, base (lemma) form and POS tag corresponds to the typical output of a POS tagger such as the one integrated in the spacy NLP library for python (Honnibal et al. 2020) which was used for KED.

When a tagging structure like Listing 2 is converted to I5 or TEI, each token form should be represented by a `<w>` element, where the original form of the token (VRT column 1) appears as its immediate text content, and its base form (VRT column 2) and POS information (VRT column 3) should go into the attributes `@lemma` and `@pos`.[3] Note that while in VRT the order of the columns is crucial, in I5 (and generally in XML) the order of attributes is irrelevant. Similarly, while the newline character is used as a token delimiter in VRT, in I5 is it any amount of whitespace. That way, the VRT code in Listing 2 will be converted to the I5 snippet in Listing 3.

2 The STTS tags shown and their meanings are: ADJA: attributive adjective, APPR: preposition, ART: defininite or indefinite article, CARD: cardinal number, NN: common noun, PIAT: attributing indefinite pronoun, PIS: substituting indefinite pronoun, PRELS: substituting relative pronoun, VAFIN: finite auxiliary verb, VVPP: present participle of main verb, VVFIN: finite main verb, $,: comma, $.: sentence terminating punctuation.

3 A prefixed '@' marks an attribute name in XML parlance.

```
<paragraph>
<sentence>
Neandertaler    Neandertaler    NN
nennt           nennen          VVFIN
man             man             PIS
eine            ein             ART
bestimmte       bestimmt        ADJA
Art             Art             NN
von             von             APPR
Menschen        Mensch          NN
,               --              $,
die             der             PRELS
vor             vor             APPR
vielen          vieler          PIAT
tausend         tausend         CARD
Jahren          Jahr            NN
gelebt          leben           VVPP
haben           haben           VAFIN
.               --              $.
</sentence>
 [...]
</paragraph>
```

Listing 2: Tagged sentence from the corpus KED (Korpus Einfaches Deutsch/Corpus Simple German, Jach and Dietz 2024) in a verticalised format (corpus text KED_#05999_klexikon.xml, retrieved from https://klexikon.zum.de/wiki/Neandertaler 2023-03-09). Translation: 'Neanderthals are a specific type of human that lived many thousands of years ago'. Klexikon is a German online lexicon for children. The POS tags are from the tagset Schiller et al. (1999).

Within VRT, even more token-related annotations may be represented in additional columns, or positional attributes. The corpora of the Finnish Kielipankki corpus archive,[4] for example, make extensive use of this. Consider the token-based annotations contained in the first eight columns of a sentence in the Suomi 24 corpus (Suomi24 2021) in Listing 4. Here, the output of the TurkuNLP parser-tagger[5] in the form of the CoNLL-U standard[6] has been integrated into VRT (in the original, there are even more columns representing further analyses). For the sentence "Nukuin todella hyvin ja tosi pitkään" (engl. "I slept really well and very long"), the VRT column 1 contains the original token, column 2 the running number of the token in the sentence, column 3: the lemma (base form), column 4: lemmacomp i. e. lemma with compound segmentation information (nothing segmented in the cur-

4 https://www.kielipankki.fi/

5 https://turkunlp.org/

6 http://universaldependencies.org/docs/format.html

```
<p>
<s>
<w lemma="Neandertaler" pos="NN">Neandertaler</w>
<w lemma="nennen" pos="VVFIN">nennt</w>
<w lemma="man" pos="PIS">man</w>
<w lemma="ein" pos="ART">eine</w>
<w lemma="bestimmt" pos="ADJA">bestimmte</w>
<w lemma="Art" pos="NN">Art</w>
<w lemma="von" pos="APPR">von</w>
<w lemma="Mensch" pos="NN">Menschen</w>
<w lemma="--" pos="$,">,</w>
<w lemma="der" pos="PRELS">die</w>
<w lemma="vor" pos="APPR">vor</w>
<w lemma="vieler" pos="PIAT">vielen</w>
<w lemma="tausend" pos="CARD">tausend</w>
<w lemma="Jahr" pos="NN">Jahren</w>
<w lemma="leben" pos="VVPP">gelebt</w>
<w lemma="haben" pos="VAFIN">haben</w>
<w lemma="--" pos="$.">.</w>
</s>
...
</p>
```

Listing 3: VRT of Listing 2 converted to I5.

rent example), column 5 the POS according to the Finnish Universal Dependencies (Pyysalo et al. 2015),[7] column 6: a morphosyntactic description of the form ('_' in the case of function words), column 7: a pointer to the index of the token to which the current one stands in a dependency relation, and column 8: the name of the dependency relation.

Listing 5 shows the same sentence and its annotations converted to I5. The @head and deprel attributes were specifically introduced in I5 to represent the CoNLL-U columns for dependency relations. The pointer in @head naturally points to a <w> with a corresponding running number in @n, and marks it as the head of the current token. Hence, *pitkään* ("long"), for example, is the head of *tosi* ("very"), which is an adverbial modifier (advmod) of *pitkään* as annotated in @deprel. Note that @head and @deprel are not (yet) part of the official TEI P5. The attribute @msd contains the morphosyntactic description. For converting further VRT columns in I5, the best way would be to customise additional attributes for <w>, including one for the "lemma-

7 The POS tags shown and their meanings are: Adv: adverb, C[SUBCAT=CC]: coordinating conjunction, Punct: punctuation.

```
<sentence id="34" lang="fin" polarity="pos">
Nukuin   1 nukkua   nukkua   V     PRS_Sg1|VOICE_Act|TENSE_Prt|MOOD_Ind|CASECHANGE_Up
↪  0 ROOT
todella  2 todella  todella  Adv   _          3 advmod
hyvin    3 hyvin    hyvin    Adv   _          1 advmod
ja       4 ja       ja       C     SUBCAT_CC  3 cc
tosi     5 tosi     tosi     Adv   _          6 advmod
pitkään  6 pitkään  pitkään  Adv   _          3 conj
.        7 .        .        Punct _          1 punct
</sentence>
```

Listing 4: A sentence from the corpus Suomi 24 in VRT (from text 15105561:92340676). The original contains several more columns with further annotations.

```
<s id="s35" xml:lang="fin">
  <w n="1" lemma="nukkua" pos="V"
  ↪  msd="PRS_Sg1|VOICE_Act|TENSE_Prt|MOOD_Ind|CASECHANGE_Up" head="0"
  ↪  deprel="ROOT">Nukuin</w>
  <w n="2" lemma="todella" pos="Adv" msd="_" head="3" deprel="advmod">todella</w>
  <w n="3" lemma="hyvin" pos="Adv" msd="_" head="1" deprel="advmod">hyvin</w>
  <w n="4" lemma="ja" pos="C" msd="SUBCAT_CC" head="3" deprel="cc">ja</w>
  <w n="5" lemma="tosi" pos="Adv" msd="_" head="6" deprel="advmod">tosi</w>
  <w n="6" lemma="pitkään" pos="Adv" msd="_" head="3" deprel="conj">pitkään</w>
  <w n="7" lemma="." pos="Punct" msd="_" head="1" deprel="punct">.</w>
</s>
```

Listing 5: Conversion in I5 of the sentence tokens and tags in Listing 4.

comp" information in VRT column 4, which so far is not contained in the I5 conversion.

2.2 Conversion of corpora of computer-mediated communication: Wikipedia talk pages

In the case of corpora based on the online encyclopedia Wikipedia, the source data come as wiki markup (also known as wikitext or wikiCode), contained in a Wikipedia archive, i. e. the content of a Wikipedia at one specific point in time, deployed as a database dump by the Wikimedia foundation.[8] Wiki markup is a specific kind of light markup used on wiki platforms that are driven by the MediaWiki technology, such as Wikipedia.

8 at https://dumps.wikimedia.org/

Besides the well-known encyclopedic articles, Wikipedia also contains 'talk pages', which are a space where the Wikipedia authors discuss the composition of articles in the collaborative writing process, for example when they make changes, add images, or put forward criticism of what somebody else has written in the article. In fact, there is a talk page associated with each article in Wikipedia that can be reached via the "talk" link ("Diskussion" in German) under the title of the article page. These talk pages form very large and linguistically interesting archives of Computer-mediated communication (CMC), i. e. dialogic communication "mediated by digital technologies (such as text on web pages, written exchanges in chats and forums, interactions with artificial intelligence systems, [or] the spoken conversations in internet video meetings)" (TEI Consortium 2025). The IDS has built several corpora of Wikipedia articles and talk pages of different languages and from different Wikipedia snapshots (version at a specific point in time). For composing a contribution to a talk page on Wikipedia, authors use the wiki markup just as they use it for articles, while the Wikipedia Guidelines[9] encourage them to use indentations to mark their contribution on the talk page. The Media Wiki software generates a web page that looks for example like the one depicted in Figure 1.

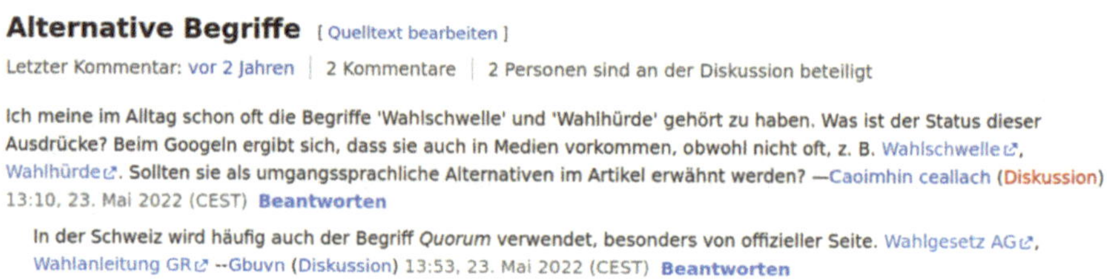
Alternative Begriffe [Quelltext bearbeiten]

Letzter Kommentar: vor 2 Jahren | 2 Kommentare | 2 Personen sind an der Diskussion beteiligt

Ich meine im Alltag schon oft die Begriffe 'Wahlschwelle' und 'Wahlhürde' gehört zu haben. Was ist der Status dieser Ausdrücke? Beim Googeln ergibt sich, dass sie auch in Medien vorkommen, obwohl nicht oft, z. B. Wahlschwelle, Wahlhürde. Sollten sie als umgangssprachliche Alternativen im Artikel erwähnt werden? —Caoimhin ceallach (Diskussion) 13:10, 23. Mai 2022 (CEST) **Beantworten**

In der Schweiz wird häufig auch der Begriff *Quorum* verwendet, besonders von offizieller Seite. Wahlgesetz AG, Wahlanleitung GR --Gbuvn (Diskussion) 13:53, 23. Mai 2022 (CEST) **Beantworten**

Figure 1: Part of the Wikipedia talk page for the article on Sperrklausel ("electoral threshold").

When comparing the wiki markup shown in Listing 6 with the screenshot of the talk page clip in Figure 1, we can see that in the wiki markup for example "==" is used to mark headings, single square brackets ('[ ]') are used to mark external links, double square brackets ('[[ ]]') are used to mark internal links ("Wikilinks"), ":" is used to mark indentations (marking user contributions), and "—" marks the insertion of a user signature and a timestamp, and the reply template ("Beantworten") which indicates the end of the contribution.

Listing 7 shows how the structure of this piece of dialogue in wiki markup is rendered in I5 using the elements `<div>`(ision), here used to mark a thread, and `<posting>`

9 https://en.wikipedia.org/wiki/Wikipedia:Indentation

```
== Alternative Begriffe ==
Ich meine im Alltag schon oft die Begriffe 'Wahlschwelle' und 'Wahlhürde' gehört
↪  zu haben. Was ist der Status dieser Ausdrücke? Beim Googeln ergibt sich, dass
↪  sie auch in Medien vorkommen, obwohl nicht oft, z. B.
↪  [https://www.tagblatt.ch/ostschweiz/
↪  rheintal/wir-liegen-offenbar-richtig-ld.217751 Wahlschwelle],
↪  [https://www.spiegel.de/politik/europaeische-union-eu-parlament-
↪  stimmt-fuer-sperrklausel-bei-europawahlen-a-c5de1b8a-f327-4bbe-
↪  9732-242acb392fe5 Wahlhürde]. Sollten sie als umgangssprachliche Alternativen
↪  im Artikel erwähnt werden? –[[Benutzer:Caoimhin ceallach|Caoimhin ceallach]]
↪  ([[Benutzer Diskussion:Caoimhin ceallach|Diskussion]]) 13:10, 23. Mai 2022
↪  (CEST)
:In der Schweiz wird häufig auch der Begriff ''Quorum'' verwendet, besonders von
↪  offizieller Seite.
↪  [https://gesetzessammlungen.ag.ch/app/de/texts_of_law/152.100/ versions/1270
↪  Wahlgesetz AG], [https://www.gr.ch/DE/publikationen/abstimmungenwahlen/
↪  Grossratswahlen-2022/faq/vier/Seiten/01_Doppelter_Pukelsheim.aspx
↪  Wahlanleitung GR] --[[Benutzer:Gbuvn|Gbuvn]] ([[Benutzer
↪  Diskussion:Gbuvn|Diskussion]]) 13:53, 23. Mai 2022 (CEST)
```

Listing 6: Wiki markup underlying the talk page clip in Figure 1.

which is used to mark a post in any CMC genre represented in I5. The original indentation is not reflected in the I5/XML structure but encoded in the `@indentLevel` attribute at `<posting>` (level "0" for the top level, "1" for the first indentation, and so forth). Links (internal and external) are encoded using the `<ref>` element, while `<signed>`, `<name>` and `<date>` are used to encode the signature, the user name, and the timestamp, respectively. There is also a list of users contained in the I5 header of the text, and the `@who` attribute at `<posting>` points to the respective `<listPerson>` element that represents information about the author of the post, such as their nickname and user page (not shown).

Wiki markup is difficult to parse which makes it a challenge to create corpora in I5 or TEI from the Wikipedia archives. The IDS approach based on the Sweble parser (Dohrn and Riehle 2011) and XSLT is described in Margaretha and Lüngen (2014).[10] An approach to convert wiki markup sources to the CMC-core TEI customisation is described in Ho-Dac (2024). Note that the official TEI Guidelines contain markup for CMC as of 2024 (TEI Consortium 2025). However, the I5 markup for CMC is based on the 2012 DeRiK proposal (Beißwenger et al. 2012) (with e. g. `<posting>` instead of `<post>`).

10 see also https://github.com/IDS-Mannheim/Wikipedia-Corpus-Builder

```
<div n="2" type="thread">
  <head> Alternative Begriffe </head>
  <posting id="i.1513683_1_1" indentLevel="0" who="WU00285477"
  ↪ when-iso="2022-05-23T13:10+02">
    <p>Ich meine im Alltag schon oft die Begriffe 'Wahlschwelle' und 'Wahlhürde'
    ↪ gehört zu haben. Was ist der Status dieser Ausdrücke? Beim Googeln ergibt
    ↪ sich, dass sie auch in Medien vorkommen, obwohl nicht oft, z. B. <ref
    ↪ target="https:// www.tagblatt.ch/ostschweiz/rheintal/wir-liegen-offenbar-
    ↪ richtig-ld.217751">Wahlschwelle</ref>, <ref target="https://
    ↪ www.spiegel.de/politik/europaeische-union-eu-parlament-
    ↪ stimmt-fuer-sperrklausel-bei-europawahlen-a-c5de1b8a-f327-
    ↪ 4bbe-9732-242acb392fe5">Wahlhürde</ref>. Sollten sie als
    ↪ umgangssprachliche Alternativen im Artikel erwähnt werden? &#x2014;<signed
    ↪ type="signed"><ref target="https://de.wiki-
    ↪ pedia.org/wiki/Benutzer:Caoimhin_ceallach"> <name>Caoimhin
    ↪ ceallach</name></ref><date>13:10, 23. Mai 2022 (CEST)</date> </signed>
    </p>
  </posting>
  <posting id="i.1513683_1_2" indentLevel="1" who="WU00075069"
  ↪ when-iso="2022-05-23T13:53+02">
    <p>In der Schweiz wird häufig auch der Begriff <hi rend="it"> Quorum</hi>
    ↪ verwendet, besonders von offizieller Seite. <ref
    ↪ target="https://gesetzessammlungen.ag.ch/app/de/texts_of_
    ↪ law/152.100/versions/1270">Wahlgesetz AG</ref>, <ref target=
    ↪ "https://www.gr.ch/DE/publikationen/abstimmungenwahlen/
    ↪ Grossratswahlen-2022/faq/vier/Seiten/01_Doppelter_Pukelsheim
    ↪ .aspx">Wahlanleitung GR</ref> --<signed type="signed"><ref
    ↪ target="https://de.wikipedia.org/wiki/Benutzer:Gbuvn">
    ↪ <name>Gbuvn</name></ref><date>13:53, 23. Mai 2022 (CEST) </date></signed>
    </p>
   </posting>
 </div>
```

Listing 7: Conversion to I5 of the thread shown in wiki markup in Listing 6.

3 Alternative formats

Why ist I5 a good format for archiving textual data? First of all, it is based on the established XML standard which has been published in 1998 and which is a non-proprietory, well-defined, well-understood data format, used and accepted widely in a variety of fields even outside text corpora, such as databases or web technologies. It comes with a wealth of tools and systems, even programming languages and programming libraries that are specifically designed to handle it. In short, the chances are quite high that XML will be used and understood for some time into the future. Even if it should get out of use, the semantics of data and data structures in XML can always be recovered to some degree by looking at the named elements and attributes and the document grammar (schema) that comes with valid XML files. This stands in contrast with e. g. tabular data formats like CoNLL-U or untyped formats like JSON, where the meaning of the lines and columns or hierarchy of the data structure must be encoded elsewhere, outside the structure itself, and can get lost or is sometimes never even recorded.

Applications of XML like the TEI that have the status of a community standard provide an even more elaborated level of semantics for data categories i. e. XML elements and attributes. The TEI Guidelines constitute a comprehensive semantics written in prose of the XML application that is TEI, which has been developed over the years by the international Digital Humanities community. This is of course also a plus for the sustainability of data and data categories. We think that all customisations derived from the TEI via the formal ODD mechanism are sustainable in the same way as any TEI. Such a customisation is I5, but also for example the DTA-Bf format developed for the German Text Archive (Haaf et al. 2014), which would consequently be a likewise suitable format for archiving textual data. In comparison with I5, DTA-Bf is more geared towards historical documents. One could argue that corpora marked up as VRT, which constitutes a kind of inofficial standard for corpus data as well, is already sufficient for long-term archiving and ingestion into a repository. But first of all, VRT, although it looks like XML, is not proper XML, hence it can frequently not be parsed using XML technology but needs to be manipulated by specific VRT corpus tools such as the CorpusWorkBench CWB. Second, there is no standard set of categories to be used in VRT and no established mechanism to encode the semantics of VRT structures, so that for example, the semantics of the positional attributes used for a corpus would be explained in a ReadMe file.

4 Ingestion into the archive: a detailed workflow for I5 data

After presenting the advantages of I5 as an archival format for textual corpus data and detailing how a conversion into I5 can be achieved, this section will show how such data is ingested into a long-term research data repository. The terms repository and archive will be used interchangeably. Furthermore, a pipeline graphic is provided as a supplementary material in the appendix (Figure A1) to guide the reader along the process in the most basic steps and is intended to serve as a general overview. The text will provide detailed information on the most important steps in the ingest process.

In the process of ingesting I5 data into the archive, several measures are employed to ensure the integrity, accessibility, and long-term preservation of the data. The steps range from the creation of the Submission Information Package (SIP) to the final publication of the data in the archive. The workflow adheres to the Open Archival Information System (OAIS) reference model, ensuring that the data is properly managed and preserved according to international standards. To achieve semantic preservation, descriptive metadata is included and the logical structure of the data is mirrored by arranging the digital objects in the archive in a strict hierarchy (see Pisetta and Trippel 2025).

4.1 Creating the metadata

The first step in the ingestion process is the generation of Component Metadata Infrastructure (CMDI) metadata for each I5 file. CMDI is a metadata standard within the Common Language Resources and Technology Infrastructure (CLARIN).[11] It is highly flexible through the use of components and profiles that can be recombined, reused or created from scratch and is usually specifically used for language data. For each I5 file, a TextCorpusProfile metadata file is created. This is done by parsing the `<idsHeader>` of the `<idsCorpus>` element of the I5 file (Section 1) and retrieving information about the content, structure, context, language, text type, and any annotations or markup that may be present. Subsequently this metadata information is then stored in the TextCorpusProfile CMDI file.

The TextCorpusProfile metadata uses the CMDI schema `clarin.eu:cr1:p_1696338267545`,[12] which is specifically designed for describing text corpora. This schema ensures that all relevant metadata is captured in a standardised format, making it easier for users to search and retrieve the data in the future.

In addition to the corpus-level metadata, CMDI metadata is also generated at the collection level. As an example, assume that all newspaper articles from a specific outlet from one year will form the corpus. Assembling all the corpora for each year will form the collection. The collection-level metadata provide an overview of the entire database and links to the different component corpora. These metadata files are created using the CMDI schema `clarin.eu:cr1:p_1659015263839`,[13] which is tailored for describing collections of linguistic resources.

11 https://www.clarin.eu/

12 TextCorpusProfile: clarin.eu:cr1:p_1696338267545

13 CollectionProfile: clarin.eu:cr1:p_1659015263839

4.2 Assembling a Submission Information Package (SIP)

After creating corpus- and collection-level metadata, the next step is to assemble the Submission Information Package (SIP), which is what is going to be ingested into the archive. A SIP can take multiple forms. As an example, we discuss a SIP that is realised as BagIt package (see Pisetta and Trippel 2025). A detailed overview can be found in Listing 8.

```
sip/
|-- data
|   |-- Metadata {1}
|        |-- CmdiCollection {1}
|        |        \-- Collection-CMDI-File {1,}
|   |    \-- I5 {1}
|        |        \-- TextCorpus-CMDI-File {1,}
|   \-- Content {1}
|   |    \-- I5 {1}
|        |        \-- I5 content file {1,}
|-- bagit.txt {1}
|-- manifest-sha512.txt {1}
|-- package-info.txt {1}
|-- recordmap.xml {1}
\-- tagmanifest-sha512.txt {1}
```

Listing 8: SIP example.

- *data/:* This directory contains the actual data and metadata that will be ingested into the archive. It is divided into two subdirectories: Metadata and Content.
  - *Metadata/:* This subdirectory contains the CMDI metadata files. It is further divided into CmdiCollection, which holds the collection-level metadata, and I5, which holds the corpus-level metadata for each I5 file.
  - *Content/:* This subdirectory contains the actual I5 content files. Each I5 file is stored in the I5 subdirectory, with a potential to also have other subdirectories besides I5.
- *bagit.txt:* This file contains basic information about the BagIt package, including the version of the BagIt specification used and the character encoding of the tag files.
- *manifest-sha512.txt:* This file contains a list of all the files in the `data/` directory, along with their SHA-512 checksums. This ensures the integrity of the data during transfer and storage.
- *package-info.txt:* This file contains information on the amount of files and total byte size in the `data/` directory.

- *recordmap.xml:* This file is a custom addition to the BagIt package and is required for the ingest process. It contains a mapping of the metadata and content files in the SIP to the corresponding records in the archive. This mapping is used during the ingest process to create the necessary records in the archive (Section 4.3.3).
- *tagmanifest-sha512.txt:* This file contains a list of all the aforementioned files, along with their SHA-512 checksums. This ensures the integrity of the entire package, including the metadata and manifest files.

4.3 From SIP to AIP

Following the OAIS model, the next step is to create the Archival Information Package (AIP) (see Pisetta and Trippel 2025), the form in which the data is stored within the archive. Converting the SIP into the AIP involves several procedures which will be laid out next.

4.3.1 Validation & upload

Before the SIP can be uploaded it needs to be validated first. The validation process checks that all the necessary files are present, that the checksums match and that the structure of the SIP is correct. In the subsequent upload process, the SIP is transferred to the archive's storage system. During this process, the archive system performs a series of checks to ensure that the data is complete and that there are no errors or inconsistencies.

4.3.2 InvenioRDM – a digital archive solution

To understand what happens next, it is important to go a little into detail about the archival system. There are several digital archive software solutions readily available, such as Dspace,[14] Fedora Commons[15] or Invenio.[16] As the goal is to store language data for research and preservation purposes, this chapter will focus specifically on InvenioRDM (Invenio Research Data Management). InvenioRDM organises

14 https://dspace.org/
15 https://fedorarepository.org/
16 https://invenio-software.org/

data in *records*. The most important parts of a record are the access restriction, the metadata and the actual data files. The access parameter decides whether the record is publicly visible or restricted to specific groups of users. It is also possible to only restrict file access and keep the metadata visible. InvenioRDM records have several metadata fields, most of which are optional. Beyond mandatory information like record title, creators, publication date and resource type, it is also possible to provide details about rights, subjects, languages, related work, alternate identifiers, size and many more. Apart from that it is even possible to create custom metadata fields.

4.3.3 Organizing records in a logical structure

The creation of records is guided by the `recordmap.xml` file, which defines the hierarchy, metadata and data of the records. An example recordmap for the DeReKo-2014-I corpus can be found in Listing 9.

The process begins with the creation of the root record, which represents the entire DeReKo release and is the top-level collection. Following that are lower-level collections like ZGE (the magazine *ZEIT Geschichte*). The necessary metadata information for an InvenioRDM record is extracted from the CMDI file and the CMDI metadata itself is stored in a custom CMDI metadata field. These collection-level records do not contain data in files and instead are "metadata-only" records. After creating all the records for the collections, the records for the I5 files will be set up next. These are created using the corpus-level CMDI metadata and are linked to the collection records they belong to via the InvenioRDM metadata field "related works" and "isPartOf"/"HasPart" relations. This ensures that the hierarchy and logical structure of the data is preserved. As with the collection-level records, the InvenioRDM metadata is retrieved from the CMDI file and the CMDI metadata itself is stored in the custom CMDI field. The I5 file is being uploaded and stored as a file with restricted access.

Deciding what should be a separate record requires knowledge about the data and its logical structure as well as careful consideration of granularity and cost (see Pisetta and Trippel 2025).

After the initial record creation, the records still remain in a draft state and are not yet published, since there are still some changes to be made.

4.3.4 Ensuring persistence & findability

A cornerstone of long-term digital archiving is to ensure that the data remains intact and findable over several years or even decades. To ensure lasting findability, the

```
<rootRecord title="DeReKo-2014-I">
  <metadata>
      data/Metadata/CmdiCollection/dereko-collection.cmdi
  </metadata>
  <records>
    <record title="zge-collection">
      <metadata>
          data/Metadata/CmdiCollection/zge-collection.cmdi
      </metadata>
      <records>
        <record title="zge12">
          <metadata>
              data/Metadata/I5/zge12.cmdi
          </metadata>
          <records/>
          <files>
            <file public="false">
                data/Content/I5/zge12.i5.xml
            </file>
          </files>
        </record>
        <record title="zge13">
          <metadata>
              data/Metadata/I5/zge13.cmdi
          </metadata>
          <records/>
          <files>
            <file public="false">
                data/Content/I5/zge13.i5.xml
            </file>
          </files>
        </record>
```

Listing 9: Example of a recordmap.

use of Persistent Identifiers (PIDs) (see Pisetta and Trippel 2025) is paramount. In this case, Digital Object Identifiers (DOIs)[17] will be created for each record. DOIs are persistent identifiers that provide a stable link to the records in the archive, ensuring that they can be easily cited and accessed over time.

The system connects to the DataCite API and generates a DOI for each record. This is called *minting*. As with the InvenioRDM records, any minted DOI will initially be in draft state. Draft DOIs are not yet registered in the global handle system and as such can still be deleted.

17 https://www.doi.org/

Once the DOIs have been minted, the next step is to edit the InvenioRDM records and CMDI metadata to include the minted DOIs that serve as persistent identifiers for these records.

With the information in the records now being complete, DOI and records are being published.

Once the records and DOIs have been published, the data is considered to be part of the repository's Archival Information Package (AIP). The AIP includes the Invenio record metadata, the CMDI metadata (as part of the Invenio metadata in the form of a custom metadata field) and the I5 content files (in the case of text corpora). The AIP is stored in the archive's long-term preservation system, where it will be managed and preserved according to the OAIS reference model.

4.3.5 Extracting data from the archive

Following the OAIS model it also needs to be possible to extract the data or information about it from the archive in the form of a Dissemination Information Package (DIP) (see Pisetta and Trippel 2025). With InvenioRDM there are several ways to extract information from the archive that can also be expanded upon and customised.

By default, InvenioRDM supports exporting records as JSON, DataCite,[18] Citation Style Language (CSL),[19] Dublin Core[20] and many more.[21] The uploaded files can only be accessed if they are set to public.

Beyond that, InvenioRDM also provides the option to harvest metadata via the Open Archives Initiative Protocol for Metadata Harvesting (OAI-PMH).[22] The standard formats here are `oai_dc` (Dublin Core), `oai_datacite` and `datacite` (not OAI-PMH v2 compliant). Again, because of the highly customisable nature, it is possible to deliver other metadata formats than the standard ones. After setting up a custom metadata field for CMDI metadata as explained previously, it is possible to adjust the OAI-PMH service so that it can also provide CMDI metadata by retrieving the information from that custom field. The CMDI metadata can then be harvested. These harvesting procedures are used, among other things, by services that provide infor-

18 https://datacite.org/

19 https://citationstyles.org/

20 https://www.dublincore.org/

21 https://inveniordm.docs.cern.ch/reference/export_formats/

22 https://inveniordm.docs.cern.ch/reference/oai_pmh/

mation about resources archived at different places, such as the Text+ Registry[23] or the Virtual Language Observatory (VLO).[24]

5 Conclusion

This chapter has provided a comprehensive overview of the I5 format, its role as an archival format for textual data within the German Reference Corpus (DeReKo), and the processes involved in converting various input formats into I5. The I5 format, as a TEI customisation, offers a structured and sustainable approach to archiving corpus data, ensuring long-term preservation and accessibility. By detailing the conversion of VRT tokens and their annotations, as well as Wiki markup from Wikipedia corpora, the chapter has demonstrated the flexibility and robustness of I5 in handling diverse data sources.

The ingestion process into the IDS long-term data repository, adhering to the OAIS reference model, further underscores the importance of metadata and persistent identifiers in maintaining the findability of archived data. The use of CMDI metadata ensures that the data is well-documented, while the integration with InvenioRDM facilitates efficient management, preservation and dissemination of the archived corpora.

In conclusion, the I5 format, with its strong foundation in XML and TEI standards, provides a reliable and future-proof solution for archiving textual data. The detailed workflows and examples presented in this chapter highlight the practical steps involved in converting, ingesting, and managing corpus data, ensuring that it remains accessible and usable for future research. As the field of corpus linguistics continues to evolve, the I5 format and the associated archival practices will play a crucial role in preserving and leveraging linguistic resources for years to come.

23 https://registry.text-plus.org

24 https://www.clarin.eu/content/virtual-language-observatory-vlo

Appendix

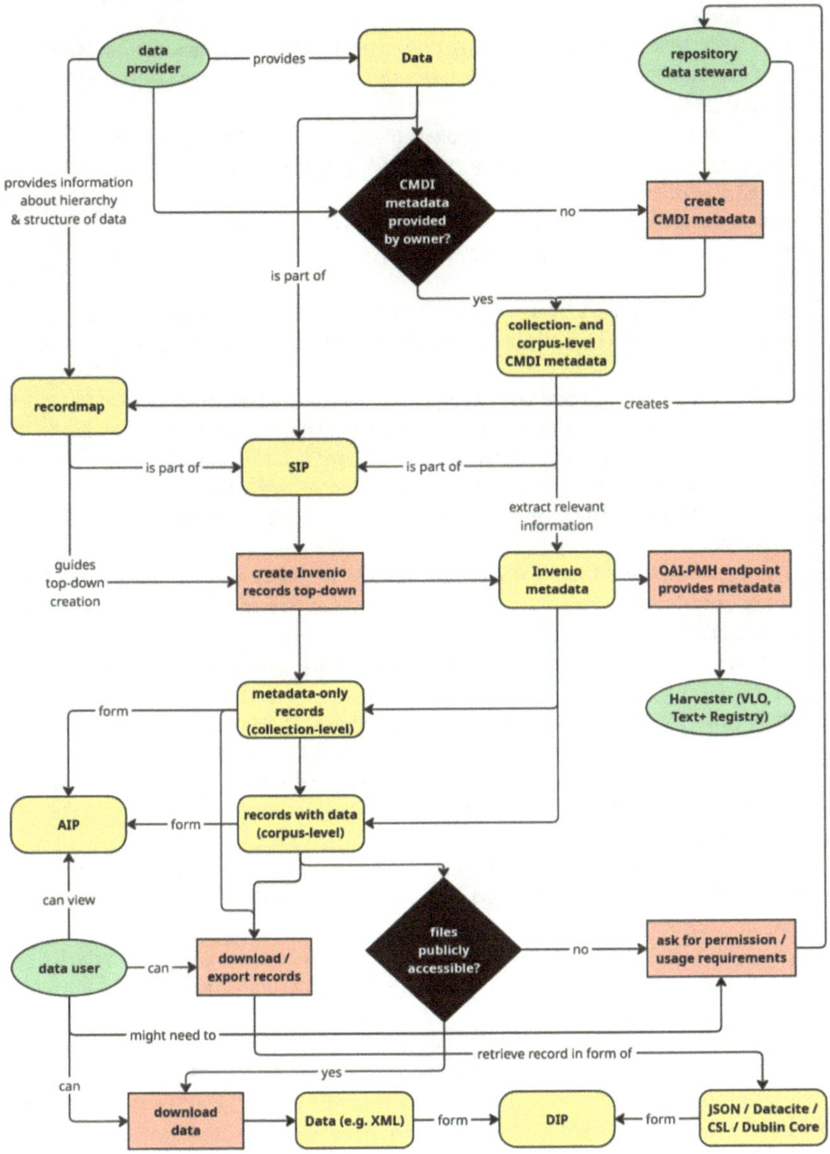

Figure A1: Simplified breakdown of ingest (SIP), preservation (AIP) and retrieval (DIP) of data in the repository. It also shows the involvement of key roles like the data provider, the data steward and the data user (see Pisetta and Trippel 2025).

Bibliography

Beißwenger, Michael, Maria Ermakova, Alexander Geyken, Lothar Lemnitzer & Angelika Storrer. 2012. A TEI schema for the representation of computer-mediated communication. *Journal of the Text Encoding Initiative* 3.

Bodmer Mory, Franck. 2014. Mit COSMAS II »in den Weiten der IDS-Korpora unterwegs«. In Melanie Steinle & Franz Josef Berens (eds.), *Ansichten und Einsichten. 50 Jahre Institut für Deutsche Sprache*, 376–385. Institut für Deutsche Sprache..

Dohrn, Hannes & Dirk Riehle. 2011. Design and implementation of the sweble wikitext parser: Unlocking the structured data of Wikipedia. In *Proceedings of the 7th international symposium on Wikis and open collaboration*, 72–81.

Evert, Stephanie & the CWB Development Team. 2022. The IMS Open Corpus Workbench (CWB). Corpus Encoding and Management Manual. CWB Version 3.5. https://cwb.sourceforge.io/files/CWB_Encoding_Tutorial.pdf.

Haaf, Susanne, Alexander Geyken & Frank Wiegand. 2014. The DTA "base format": A TEI subset for the compilation of a large reference corpus of printed text from multiple sources. *Journal of the Text Encoding Initiative* 8.

Ho-Dac, Lydia-Mai. 2024. Building a comparable corpus of online discussions on Wikipedia: The EFG WikiCorpus. In Céline Poudat, Harald Lüngen & Laura Herzberg (eds.), *Investigating Wikipedia*, 12–44. John Benjamins Publishing Company. https://doi.org/10.1075/scl.121.01hod.

Honnibal, Matthew, Ines Montani, Sofie Van Landeghem & Adriane Boyd. 2020. spaCy: Industrial-strength natural language processing in Python. *Zenodo*. https://doi.org/10.5281/zenodo.1212303.

Ide, Nancy, Patrice Bonhomme & Laurent Romary. 2000. XCES: An XML-based encoding standard for linguistic corpora. In *Proceedings of the second international conference on language resources and evaluation (LREC'00)*.

Jach, Daniel & Gunther Dietz. 2024. Korpus Einfaches Deutsch (KED). *Korpora Deutsch als Fremdsprache* 4(1). 123–130.

Kilgarriff, Adam, Vít Baisa, Jan Bušta, Miloš Jakubíček, Vojtěch Kovář, Jan Michelfeit, Pavel Rychlý & Vít Suchomel. 2014. The Sketch Engine: ten years on. *Lexicography* 1(1). 7–36.

Kupietz, Marc, Nils Diewald & Elisa Margaretha. 2022. Building paths to corpus data. In Darja Fišer & Andreas Witt (eds.), *CLARIN. The infrastructure for language resources*, Vol. 1, 163–189. Digital Linguistics. de Gruyter.

Ljubešić, Nikola & Tomaž Erjavec. 2025. Part-of-speech tagging and related annotation. In Piotr Bański, Ulrich Heid & Laura Herzberg (eds.), *Harmonising language data: Standards for linguistic resources*. de Gruyter.

Lüngen, Harald & Michael C. M. Sperberg-McQueen. 2012. A TEI P5 document grammar for the IDS text model. *Journal of the Text Encoding Iniative (jTEI)* 3. https://doi.org/10.4000/jtei.508. http://journals.openedition.org/jtei/508.

Margaretha, Eliza & Harald Lüngen. 2014. Building linguistic corpora from Wikipedia articles and discussions. *Journal for Language Technology and Computational Linguistics* 29(2). 59–82.

Pisetta, Ines & Thorsten Trippel. 2025. Standards and practices for long-term digital archiving. In Piotr Bański, Ulrich Heid & Laura Herzberg (eds.), *Harmonising language data: Standards for linguistic resources*. de Gruyter.

Pyysalo, Sampo, Jenna Kanerva, Anna Missilä, Veronika Laippala & Filip Ginter. 2015. Universal dependencies for Finnish. In *Proceedings of the 20th nordic conference of computational linguistics (NODALIDA 2015)*, 163–172.

Schiller, Anne, Simone Teufel, Christine Stöckert & Christine Thielen. 1999. *Guidelines für das Tagging deutsche Textkorpora mit STTS (Kleines und großes Tagset)*, Stuttgart: Universität Stuttgart.

Suomi24. 2021. The Suomi24 Corpus 2018-2020, VRT version. Accessed: 2025-02-10. http://urn.fi/urn:nbn:fi:lb-2021101524 (visited on 02/10/2025).

TEI Consortium (ed.). 2025. *TEI P5: Guidelines for electronic text encoding and interchange*. Last updated on 24th January 2025, Accessed: 2025-02-10. TEI Consortium. Chap. 9. Computer-mediated Communication. https://tei-c.org/release/doc/tei-p5-doc/en/html/CMC.html (visited on 02/10/2025).

Thorsten Trippel

Metadata for research data

Abstract: This chapter explores the critical role of metadata in language data and infrastructures, emphasizing its importance for data management and discoverability. It begins by defining basic metadata elements necessary for research data, such as title, creator, identifier, and format. The discussion then shifts to metadata derived during the deposition process, including technical specifications and file integrity checks. The chapter highlights the significance of metadata in adhering to the FAIR principles, particularly in enhancing data findability. It also examines the importance of utilizing established core metadata sets such as DataCite, DCAT, and Dublin Core, as well as the integration of schema.org for improved interoperability. Furthermore, the chapter delves into the use of discipline-specific rich metadata schemas, focusing on ISO 24622-1 and ISO 24622-2 (CMDI), and provides practical examples of their application. This comprehensive overview underscores the necessity of robust metadata standards in supporting effective research data infrastructures, including those for language-related research data.

Keywords: metadata, documentation, search, standards

1 Introduction

In the context of research data management, including the FAIR (Wilkinson et al. 2016) and CARE (Carroll et al. 2020) principles, the term *metadata* is ubiquitously used. As it is a central concept, this section will define metadata and discuss its importance. Competing abstract definitions of 'metadata' may initially cause confusion, even with authoritative sources such as international standards. For example, ISO/IEC 11179-1 (2023) defines metadata as 'data that define and describe other data',

Acknowledgement: This chapter is based on work within Text+, funded by the Deutsche Forschungsgemeinschaft (DFG, project number 460033370) as part of the German National Research Data Infrastructure (NFDI e. V.). The authors also sincerely thank their colleagues in the Metadata Section of NFDI for their invaluable contributions and insights. The authors acknowledge the use of Large Language Models (LLMs) as writing aids in phrasing this chapter, based on the authors' notes, ideas, and concepts. The authors retain full responsibility for the content.

Thorsten Trippel, Digitale Sprachwissenschaft, Leibniz-Institut für Deutsche Sprache, R5 6-13, D-68161 Mannheim, Baden-Württemberg, Germany; and Seminar für Sprachwissenschaft, Eberhard Karls Universität Tübingen, Keplerstr. 2, D-72074 Tübingen, Baden-Württemberg, Germany, e-mail: trippel@ids-mannheim.de

https://doi.org/10.1515/9783112208212-011

with 'data' being the 'reinterpretable representation of information in a formalised manner suitable for communication, interpretation, or processing'. Another international standard, ISO/IEC 19115-1 (2014), defines metadata as 'information about a resource'; ISO 17522 (2015) defines metadata as "'data about data'" (including the quotation marks), highlighting that the 'term is ambiguous, as it is used for two fundamentally different concepts'. The latter definition often appears in introductory texts, leaving novice readers with uncertainty about its precise meaning (for aspects on standardisation, see Preissner and Heid 2025). Despite these differences, all typical definitions agree that metadata provides descriptive information about *something*. Examples of such metadata include: a telephone connection described by phone numbers, time, duration, and date of the call; access to a webpage described by the time, IP address of the viewer, and the page address; a book identified by its title, author, publisher, and year of publication.

Metadata is an indispensable component of efficient research data management, particularly in language-related research. It provides essential descriptions and identifiers for language-related research data such as corpora, lexical resources, and digital literature. Metadata enhances discoverability and access, ensures interoperability and integration, supports preservation and archiving, and facilitates compliance with the FAIR principles. By providing detailed and standardised descriptions of data, metadata supports and documents quality criteria. Consequently, the quality, consistency, and usability of research data correlate with the presence of expressive and understandable metadata, promoting data sharing and collaboration among researchers. Thus, metadata is crucial for the cataloguing and archiving of research data.

This chapter outlines basic metadata found in collected data and metadata that is automatically derived during in the archival process. The role of metadata in the FAIR principles will be discussed. Regarding existing metadata schemas, some core metadata sets will be compared, and the semantic enrichment of data using schema.org will be discussed. As a use case, rich disciplinary metadata will be illustrated with a concrete example.

2 Basic metadata in collected data

Metadata provides a structured and detailed description of a data resource, which is essential for research data. The information entities, often called metadata fields, refer to fields of forms used for cataloguing and inventories. Common elements include the title, creator, date of creation, format, and language of the dataset. For language-related research, metadata might also include references to transcription and annotation conventions (for multiple annotations, see for example Bański and Diewald 2025), and descriptions tailored to disciplinary needs, such as dialect, phonetic transcription, or syntactic annotation, with additional keywords related to linguistic features, language families, or specific research methodologies. For example, a text corpus used in linguistic research could have metadata detailing the language, the period of the texts, the genre, and the source of the texts. This information helps researchers determine the suitability of the corpus for their specific research questions.

According to Schmidt (2004), the functions of metadata for research data are:

- Represent data in terms of the desired aspects as completely as possible.
- Provide contextual information and documentation of the data.
- Offer various routes of access to the data for a heterogeneous user group.
- Provide structural relationships between different datasets.

Metadata ensures that data can be found using different search strategies, which is a key objective (for metadata in search, see for example Frick and Schmidt 2025). Standardised metadata schemas ensure that users can rely on specific structures in their search processes. Metadata is used for searching for datasets based on its characteristics. For searching within datasets, see Frick and Schmidt (2025), Körner and Eckart (2025).

The aspect of documenting the data includes technical information about the file format, size, encoding (see Wartena 2025) and integrity checks (e. g., cryptographic checksums), which are necessary for maintaining the usability and authenticity of the dataset over time. Another crucial part of the documentation is provenance, which provides the detailed history and origin of the data, including how it was collected, processed, and transformed (for the transformation into an archival format see Pisetta and Trippel 2025). This helps ensure the dataset's authenticity, reliability, and reproducibility. It also documents its lifecycle from its creation to its current state. For language resources, this documentation ensures that the data can be used and preserved safely, for example, for endangered language corpora or historical linguistic records, making them accessible and usable for future generations of researchers.

Standardised descriptions and classifications in metadata help ensure that data is collected, documented, and stored consistently. This is particularly important in large-scale research projects where data is collected by multiple researchers or institutions. In language research, consistent metadata practices ensure that linguistic data from different sources can be compared and analysed together. The documentation of linguistic data by means of metadata is essential for promoting data sharing and collaboration among researchers, enabling them to replicate studies or use the data in new and innovative ways.

In language-related research, metadata provides detailed descriptions of linguistic resources, such as text corpora, tools, and experimental data. This information is crucial for researchers to understand the scope, methodology, and context of the data they are using. For instance, a metadata record for a phonetic database might include information about the recording conditions, the demographic characteristics of the speakers, and the annotation conventions used. This level of detail ensures that other researchers can accurately interpret and build upon the data.

2.1 Metadata types and the difference between rich and generic metadata schemas

Metadata is not only used in research data management but also in many other areas. The taxonomy in Figure 1 illustrates this.

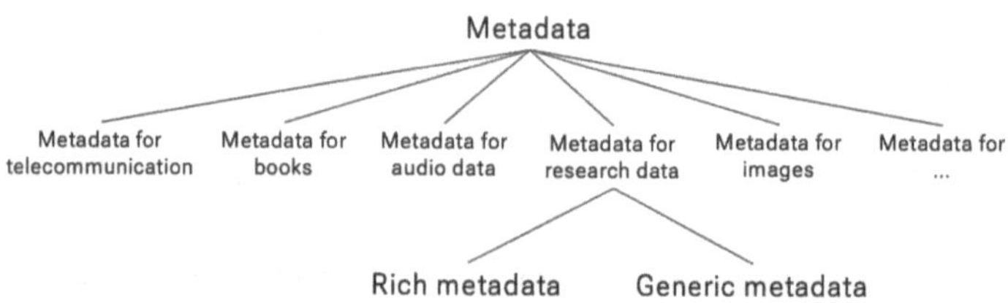

Figure 1: Simple taxonomy of metadata distinguishing between rich, disciplinary metadata and generic metadata.

This section focuses on the metadata used in research data management. Here, metadata can be subdivided into *rich metadata* and *generic metadata*.

2.1.1 The need for rich metadata schemas

Rich metadata aims to provide a comprehensive description of data, tailored to the specific needs of researchers, data analysts, and other domain experts. This necessitates a level of detail that goes beyond basic descriptive information. Rich metadata is often:

- Specific to the data type: The level and type of metadata vary significantly depending on the nature of the data (e. g., images, text, sensor data, simulations; for audiovisual language data, see Ferreira et al. 2025).
- Discipline-specific: Different research disciplines have unique metadata requirements. For instance, social scientists may prioritise metadata related to

sampling methods and ethical considerations, while biologists may focus on metadata describing experimental conditions and specimen information.
- Dependent on the research method: The metadata requirements can also vary depending on the research methods employed. For example, metadata for experimental data differ from those of observational studies or computational simulations.

The pursuit of a 'one-size-fits-all' approach to metadata in research data management is often unrealistic and counterproductive. Such an approach results in only generic mandatory descriptors, while the use of numerous optional elements to cover specific needs is difficult to enforce. This can lead to user confusion and pose quality assurance challenges, as the risk of misusing metadata elements increases.

Rich metadata aims to provide documentation for a dataset, offering a comprehensive description of the data for experts, allowing them to fully understand the data, its structure, purpose, and provenance. As it is intended to be understood and used by experts, it is highly discipline-specific and requires background knowledge and expertise regarding the individual datasets. For instance, metadata for a particle accelerator in physics or the metadata describing a medical study will differ completely from metadata generated for language research or the editorial process of old manuscripts. It is impossible to combine all metadata fields from all disciplines into one usable schema due to the overwhelming complexity such a schema would require.

2.1.2 Purpose of generic metadata schemas

In contrast to rich metadata, generic metadata aims to provide a basic, easily accessible overview of the data. It often has a limited set of core elements, making it more readily comparable across different datasets and disciplines. This approach does not provide full documentation for experts but offers an overview for non-experts in the discipline.

The concept of a 'one-size-fits-all' solution for generic metadata can be viewed as finding the 'lowest common denominator' among the rich metadata schemas across different domains. This involves identifying a core set of essential metadata elements that are universally applicable for all datasets. Beyond these mandatory fields, generic metadata can incorporate optional elements to allow for greater flexibility and accommodate specific needs when required.

The most commonly referenced core metadata set is the Dublin Core metadata schema (DCMI Metadata Terms 2020). Originating from a gathering of experts in Dublin, Ohio (USA) in 1995, it initially focused on describing bibliographic entities such as books and journal articles. The core set comprises fifteen essential elements: *Title*, *Creator*, *Subject*, *Description*, *Publisher*, *Contributor*, *Date*, *Type*, *Format*, *Identifier*, *Source*, *Language*, *Relation*, *Coverage*, and *Rights*.

These elements provide a standardised framework for capturing crucial information about a wide range of resources.

While initially developed for traditional publications, Dublin Core has proven remarkably adaptable. It has been extended and refined over time, including a significant modernisation for compatibility with the Resource Description Framework (RDF, see Tomaszuk and Haudebourg 2025, Hartig et al. 2025). This evolution has enabled its application in diverse contexts, including research data management. In this domain, Dublin Core often serves as a foundational layer, even when more specialised research-data-specific metadata schemas are employed. Hence, Dublin Core remains important for providing a common vocabulary for describing and understanding research outputs.

2.2 Principles for creating metadata

Discipline-agnostic core metadata schemas such as Dublin Core are not designed to comprehensively describe complex research data or to document the data, and hence are inadequate for this purpose. They may not capture the nuances of differen data types and research disciplines. To address this, disciplinary extensions and specialised metadata vocabularies have been developed. These extensions provide richer descriptions by incorporating domain-specific concepts and attributes relevant to specific research areas.

In addition, individual data centres and repositories often have unique metadata requirements. These requirements may include technical metadata that are essential for data management and preservation.

Figure 2 illustrates a shell model for metadata schemas, demonstrating that core schemas can be extended for specific disciplines and individual data storage facilities, also referred to as repositories, such as data centres.

Duval et al. (2002) have already outlined a number of principles for the creation of metadata schemas, recognising that there is considerable overlap between schemas developed for different purposes. According to their framework, four principles should be followed:

- *Modularity:* data elements should be combined into building blocks that can be used in different contexts. New metadata schemas can then build on top of existing ones, such as Dublin Core, while explicitly acknowledging overlap.

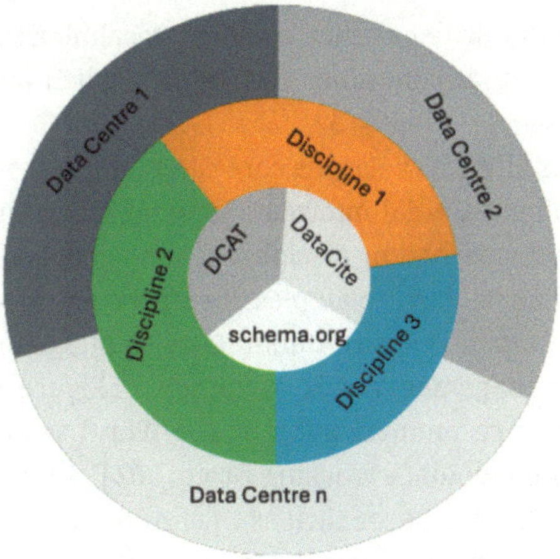

Figure 2: A shell model of metadata: At the core, generic metadata schemas are depicted, including DataCite (cf. Section 5.1), DCAT (cf. Section 5.2), and schema.org (cf. Section 6). These are extended for various disciplines and data centres.

- *Extensibility:* in practice, an existing metadata schema does not contain all the information required for a meaningful description. To ensure broader usability, a schema needs to be designed for extensibility.
- *Refinement:* although some metadata elements may be rather generic, they can often be further specified with minimal effort. For example, a date may be specified, but refining a date as a publication date, completion date, submission date, recording date, or archiving date provides additional detail without losing the general information that it is a date.
  Another approach to refinement is the use of controlled vocabularies and predefined entities, such as authority files (see Section 3 below), which increase semantic interpretability.
- *Multilingualism:* given the diverse linguistic landscape, metadata records often require multilingual capabilities. Addressing multilingualism not only improves accessibility, but also provides additional opportunities for semantic interpretability.

Duval et al. (2002) also offer suggestions, based on their experience, on the implementation of metadata schemas. For example, they define application profiles, which are structures used in an application and in which different metadata schemas can be combined with each other. These profiles also specify the cardinality of metadata elements, meaning that they are optional (appear zero or more times), mandatory (appear at least once), and how often they can appear (single or multiple occurrences). They also define value schemas such as closed vocabularies to be used for specific elements, or contextual conditions that specify when an element is required rather than optional.

Discipline-agnostic metadata schemas often serve as the core component, providing a common foundation for describing essential information about research data. This foundation is then extended and enriched by disciplinary metadata and the specific requirements of individual data centres. Examples of such extensions include DataCite and DCAT, which extend upon the core Dublin Core elements to meet the specific needs of research data management needs. At the core of Figure 2 are DCAT (Albertoni et al. 2024), which is a recommendation by the World Wide Web Consortium (W3C); DataCite (DataCite Metadata Working Group 2024) which is widely used for scientific metadata in infrastructures such as OpenAIRE and for registering DOIs. OpenAIRE[1] is a European infrastructure that supports Open Science by enabling the discovery, aggregation, and linking of research outputs across repositories, data centres, and other scholarly communication platforms. It plays a key role in promoting metadata interoperability, using standards such as DataCite for DOI registration and metadata management in scientific research. The third element in the centre of Figure 2 is schema.org (see Schema.org 2024), which is the result of an industry initiative to define and locate semantic properties within metadata.

Each of these metadata schemas serves as a basic structure and can be extended with disciplinary metadata tailored to specific data types or research areas, allowing for richer and more detailed metadata descriptions.

2.3 Classes of metadata serialisations

Metadata elements are primarily a concept for defining the units of information to be included in the metadata set. For practical purposes, these concepts do not appear outside of a concrete serialisation, such as the representation of a metadata document as a (database) table, or another format such as XML, RDF (Turtle, JSON-LD, or others).

Metadata for specific research data may either be embedded into the research data, as separate files that are part of the digital object that contains the object data (see Pisetta and Trippel 2025), or in a separate, independent format. An example of metadata embedded in research data in the text and language domains is the representation of metadata in XML files following the Text Encoding Initiative (TEI,

1 See https://www.openaire.eu/

see TEI P5: Guidelines for Electronic Text Encoding and Interchange 2025, see also Werthmann 2025). Here, the metadata elements are located in the TEI header, which is a specific, mandatory structure of each XML file following the TEI conventions. In the process of creating a TEI file, metadata must be included in the TEI header, either through a human-driven annotation process or via automatic generation, such as when converting data into a TEI file—for example, using the TEIWorLD application.[2] An example of the separation of object data can be seen in digital objects according to the OCFL format (see also Pisetta and Trippel 2025), where separate metadata files are part of the digital object. In this case, different metadata serialisations may also exist in parallel. The third option is complete separation, for example, by storing the metadata in a catalogue that points to the object, while the research data is stored elsewhere.

In practice, these representations appear in hybrid formats: for example, archives containing TEI files (with metadata in their headers) are contained in digital objects with separate metadata files, and data catalogues may list the digital objects. The challenge with this duplication is to maintain consistency and avoid duplication of effort. One way to achieve this is to use one of these as the authoritative version and generate the other formats from it.

For example, an archive that stores its data in TEI format can use the policy of authoritatively storing the metadata in the TEI header. In order to provide access to the metadata without having to verify compliance with access restrictions to the original data, the metadata may be extracted into a separate file. This separation allows the metadata to be handled independently of the object data. The metadata can even be automatically added to a catalogue, either in its entirety or as a selection. By using this approach, the benefits of each of these classes of serialisation – integrated, as part of the digital object, or completely separate on another system – can co-exist without inconsistency.

3 Metadata derived during deposition

Within the deposit process of language and text-related research data, understanding where metadata is created is crucial. Traditionally, metadata deposit has taken place within repository or archival systems, often using the Open Archival Information System (OAIS) (see also Pisetta and Trippel 2025) model and its associated Submission Information Package (SIP). The SIP typically contains the research data

2 See Ecker (2025) and https://teiwrld.github.io/TEIWorLD/

itself, along with additional structures. These structures may include specified directory structures with specific naming conventions and pre-existing metadata.

Traditionally, metadata for archives and libraries has primarily been manually created during the ingest process. Librarians, archivists or subject matter experts would meticulously catalogue each new book or publication, assigning Dublin Core or other metadata elements, including subject classifications, keywords, and other descriptive information.

For research data, the submission process typically involves user identification, often through a login process or a web-based form where users provide information about themselves and their research. This information, together with the data in specified structures and formats, is part of the SIP, which requires an editorial process maintained by a data steward on the archives' side.

The ingest workflow includes the initial populating of some core metadata elements, but also some technical information available in the system, such as the date and time of submission. Thise can be used to enrich the SIP. Available metadata include user credentials, especially when using single sign-on, which can be used to automatically pre-populate metadata fields related to the depositor's identity. Where appropriate linked databases exist, these can be queried for additional information to be included, such as the depositor's disciplines, institutions, authority file references, project context. While manual input is still essential for certain aspects of research data metadata, such as author names and dataset titles, information elements which are already part of the deposit process offer opportunities for automated metadata generation.

Data elements that can be extracted automatically by technical means, include:

- *File level information:* Filenames, cryptographic checksums (e. g., Message-Digest Algorithm 5 (MD5), Secure Hash Algorithm with 256 Bytes, SHA-256), and media types can be automatically determined. For textual data a tool such as Apache Tika (Apache Software Foundation 2025) can be used.
- *User information:* Single sign-on processes can automatically capture user names and possibly their positions, institutions, and project contexts. In some cases, disciplinary information can be inferred from the user's affiliation or project, also using authority file information such as that contained in the Integrated Authority File (*Gemeinsame Normdatei*, GND, hosted by the German National Library) or from the individual's ORCID record.
- *Data generation process information:* For research processes involving automated data generation, metadata may be automatically embedded within the data itself. This may include information about the tools and machines used, the date and time of data generation, and the specific parameters and settings used. Eckart (2018) (Section 1.2.4) describes *process metadata* recorded for automated processes. For example, the WebLICHT (Hinrichs et al. 2010a,b, Dima

et al. 2012),[3] which is a linguistic data annotation environment that automatically records information about the annotation tools, pipelines, and schemas used, which can be included in the cataloguing metadata.

- *NLP data extraction processes:* In addition, some tools can extract information directly from the data itself. Natural Language Processing (NLP) techniques can be used to identify named entities, topics, and keywords within text data (see also Wartena 2025, Romary 2025, Ljubešić and Erjavec 2025, Bański and Diewald 2025, Schwarz 2025). Although the robustness of these NLP techniques depends on the quality of the tools and the specific data, they can provide valuable assistance to human editors.

By automating the collection of these metadata elements during the deposit process, researchers and data managers can significantly improve the efficiency and accuracy of data discovery and reuse.

4 Metadata in FAIR research data management

It is no coincidence that the purpose of metadata is closely related to the FAIR Principles, which provide guidelines for ensuring that research data is properly managed and shared. Metadata is fundamental to compliance with these principles. It ensures that data is well documented and organised, making it easier to find, access, and reuse. This section considers the role of metadata in research data management as it implements the FAIR Principles.

4.1 The FAIR principles

The FAIR Principles (Wilkinson et al. 2016) provide a set of guidelines to ensure that research data is properly managed and shared. FAIR is an acronym for Findable, Accessible, Interoperable, Reusable. Since their publication, these principles have become ubiquitous in the field of research data management. Although the principles are concerned with research data as such, they have a direct impact on the metadata to be recorded and provide the background for the need for specific metadata elements. The principles are understood here in the following way, indicating the crucial role of metadata in supporting each of these principles: By providing

3 See https://weblicht.sfs.uni-tuebingen.de/

detailed and structured information about the data, metadata improves its discoverability, accessibility, interoperability, and reusability.

4.2 Findability metadata

Metadata enhances the discoverability of research data by including keywords, subject classifications, and persistent identifiers, which allow for efficient searching and retrieval within large repositories. Findability means that existing data can be found for use and analysis, and used data can be found for replication and evaluation of results, supporting the quality of research data. It is also important for researchers to document their work in creating or collecting data, thereby creating visibility for their contribution. Key metadata elements that contribute to findability of data include the following:

- *Persistent Identifiers (PIDs):* Unique and stable identifiers, such as Uniform Resource Names (URNs), Digital Object Identifiers (DOIs) and handle-system PIDs, ensure that data can be reliably located and cited over time, even if the location of the data itself changes (see Pisetta and Trippel 2025).
- *Keywords:* Well-chosen keywords describe the subject matter of the data, allowing researchers to easily discover relevant datasets through keyword searches in data repositories and search engines.
- *Indexing Information:* Metadata that provides information about the content of the data, such as controlled vocabulary terms, classifications, and subject headings, enables efficient indexing and retrieval of the data by search engines and discovery tools.
- *Descriptive Metadata:* Clear and concise descriptive metadata, including titles, abstracts, and author information, provides essential information about the data and its context, facilitating its discovery and initial evaluation by potential users.

By incorporating these elements, researchers can significantly improve the findability of their research data, making it more accessible to the wider research community.

4.3 Accessibility metadata

Accessibility metadata focuses on ensuring that authorised users can easily access and use the data. Key elements include the following:

- *Identifiers:* each dataset needs to be retrievable by using its persistent identifier.

- *Standardised Communication Protocols:* These protocols define technically specified methods for accessing data objects. For example, the Open Archives Initiative Protocol for Metadata Harvesting (OAI-PMH) is a publicly available protocol that enables libraries and archives to disseminate metadata and ingest it into catalogues. Standardised protocols facilitate seamless data access and transfer across different systems and platforms.
- *Descriptive Metadata in Catalogues:* Metadata serves as a descriptive layer on top of the data and is crucial for accessibility. A dataset's metadata record is independent of the dataset itself, allowing it to persist even if the original data is no longer available (e. g., due to loss or obsolescence). In such cases, the metadata acts as a *tombstone record*, preserving essential details such as the original location of the dataset, access rights, and relevant historical information.

4.4 Interoperability metadata

Interoperability ensures that research data can be easily integrated and reused with other datasets and software tools. To achieve this, the following information is often included in the metadata description:

- Data format and language: Data should be stored in open and widely supported formats and use common data exchange formats. Examples of such open formats in the domain of language data include XML, including for example the recommendations of the Text Encoding Initiative, but also various serialisations of structured data for example in JSON or RDF (see Khan 2025).
- Semantic definitions: The semantics of data components should be clearly defined and consistently applied. This can be achieved for example through the use of closed vocabularies and well-defined external vocabularies. Controlled vocabularies and ontologies provide a standardised set of terms and their definitions, ensuring consistent interpretation and comparison of data across different sources. They are often used as well-defined external vocabularies, that link data to established domain-specific knowledge bases.
- Data References to other data and authority file references. Metadata should include references to related datasets, publications, and other relevant resources, to facilitate the integration and contextualisation of the data within the broader research landscape. Using authority data references for named entities (e. g., using the GND,[4] the Open Researcher and Contributor ID (ORCID),[5] the Research

---

4 See https://www.dnb.de/EN/Professionell/Standardisierung/GND/gnd_node.html on the integrated authority file.

5 See https://www.orchid.org/

Organization Registry (ROR)[6] or Wikidata[7] for organisations and individuals) improves data quality and consistency by linking data to authoritative sources.

These elements increase the interoperability of research data, facilitating its integration and reuse within and across different research domains.

4.5 Reusability metadata

Ensuring the reusability of data requires the provision of clear and comprehensive information about data access, usage rights, and any necessary conditions for its reuse, including any restrictions or licensing terms, to ensure ethical and legal compliance (for legal issues see Kamocki 2025). This is particularly important to ensure that data is used ethically and in accordance with legal and institutional guidelines. For example, metadata might indicate that a dataset is available under a Creative Commons licence, allowing researchers to use and share the data freely while giving appropriate credit to the original creators.

Key metadata elements include the following:

- Access rights: Clearly defined access rights (e. g., open access, restricted access, embargoed access) and any associated conditions (e. g., data use agreements, terms of service) must be explicitly stated. For example, privacy-sensitive information, i. e. information covered by the European General Data Protection Regulation (GDPR)[8] legislation or similar information about individuals, or even classified data may require special rules for access to the data.
- Licensing information: Providing clear and concise licensing information (e. g., Creative Commons licences, open data licences) allows users to understand the permitted uses of the data and any restrictions that apply. This applies to language data which has copyright restrictions and hence may therefore require some form of contractual relationship between a data user and the owner of the original data.
- Authentication and authorisation procedures: If access to the data requires authentication or authorisation, the necessary procedures and any relevant contact information should be clearly documented, so that a potential data user understands which procedure to follow to gain access to the data.

6 See https://ror.org/

7 See https://wikidata.org/

8 See http://data.europa.eu/eli/reg/2016/679/

- Data usage notes: Providing guidance on the proper use and interpretation of the data, including any known limitations or caveats, is essential for its responsible reuse.
- Data Provenance, referring to the detailed history of a dataset, documenting its origins, transformations, and processing steps. This ensures transparency, reproducibility, and trust in data by allowing researchers to trace its lineage and assess its reliability, including information about data sources, applied modifications, versioning, and responsible entities, thereby supporting ethical and responsible reuse (see also Section 2).

The information on reusability is crucial for researchers to understand the conditions under which they can access and use the data, thus enabling its effective reuse within the research community.

4.6 The role of metadata in supporting FAIR data

Metadata is critical for achieving the goals of FAIR data management. As discussed, it improves data findability, accessibility, interoperability, and reusability. By providing structured, machine-readable descriptions, metadata enable researchers to implement sustainable research data management practices. These practices support the long-term reuse and archiving of research data, which often represents a significant investment of time and resources. While FAIR itself is not an end goal, its principles guide the process of enabling long-term access, visibility, reproducibility, and quality improvements in research by expanding data availability.

5 Core metadata sets

The previous section provided ample motivation for providing metadata for FAIR research data management. This section introduces some generic metadata schemas which are commonly used in research data management. Dublin Core (see Section 2.1.2 above) as a traditional bibliographic metadata standard has been mentioned before and will not be repeated here. It has been most influential for the development of newer metadata schemas that have been developed for artefacts that are not primarily for bibliographic data.

5.1 Datacite: a metadata schema for datasets

One prominent example is the DataCite Metadata Schema, developed by the non-profit organisation DataCite. While DataCite is best known for its DOI registration services, it has also created a robust metadata schema that is having significant impact on the research data landscape. Its adoption by major initiatives such as OpenAIRE[9] underlines its impact and importance.

The DataCite schema contains a comprehensive set of elements for effectively describing research data effectively. Key fields include the following:

- *Mandatory fields:*
  - *Identifier:* Unique identifier for the dataset (e. g., DOI).
  - *Creator:* Individual(s) or organisation(s) responsible for creating the dataset.
  - *Title:* Descriptive title of the dataset.
  - *Publisher:* Organisation responsible for making the dataset available.
  - *PublicationYear:* Year in which the dataset was published or made available to the public.
  - *ResourceType:* Type of resource being described (e. g., dataset, software, image).
- *Recommended fields:*
  - *Subject:* Keywords or controlled vocabulary terms that describe the subject matter of the dataset.
  - *Contributor:* Individuals or organisations that have contributed to the dataset but are not the creators.
  - *Date:* Dates associated with the dataset, such as creation date, update date, or availability date.
  - *RelatedIdentifier:* Identifiers of related resources, such as publications, software, or other datasets.
  - *Description:* Detailed description of the dataset, including its content, scope, and methods.
  - *GeoLocation:* Geographical locations relevant to the dataset.
- *Optional fields:*
  - *AlternateIdentifier:* Alternative identifiers for the dataset (e. g., URLs, local identifiers).
  - *Size:* Size of the dataset.
  - *Format:* File formats of the data files.
  - *Version:* Version number of the dataset.

9 See https://www.openaire.eu/

- *Rights:* Information on copyright, licensing, and access restrictions.
- *FundingReference:* Information about funding sources that supported the research.
- *RelatedItem:* Relationships to other resources, such as citations, references, or derived works.

The schema is supported by an XML Schema Definition (XSD), which allows automated validation and processing of metadata. Some fields, such as *contributor*, have substructures, but in most cases the content of each field is described in the specification but not formally restricted. It is therefore possible to include a controlled vocabulary with terms that have a formal definition of their semantics, but this is not enforced by the schema.

5.2 The Data Catalog Vocabulary (DCAT)

The Data Category Vocabulary (DCAT, Albertoni et al. 2024), published by the World Wide Web Consortium (W3C), provides a standardised schema for describing datasets. The aim is to facilitate the discovery, interoperability, and exchange of data. The European Union requires the use of DCAT for the description of public sector datasets, as described in a document on the DCAT application profile for data catalogues in Europe (Publications Office of the European Union 2025).

DCAT builds on the foundation of RDF (Resource Description Framework, Hartig et al. 2025); for thematic classification it can use the Simple Knowledge Organization System (SKOS, Miles and Bechhofer 2009) as an ontology. DCAT allows the description of different entities, such as *catalogs* and *datasets*, organised hierarchically so that for example *dataset* as a subclass of *resource* inherits the descriptive fields that are specified for the superclass. For datasets, this results in 40 fields, 32 of them are derived from a superordinate class. The specified fields include *identifier, creator, title, publisher, release date, type/genre, keyword/tag, description, spatial/geographic coverage, rights*. These are very similar if not identical, to those in the DataCite definition discussed in Section 5.1.

Note that some fields from DataCite are not available in DCAT, such as *contributor, related identifier, size, format, funding reference*. This indicates that DataCite has been defined for data that is created in a project context. Projects, such as research projects, typically have specific funders and additional contributors that need to be mentioned. In contrast to that, DCAT specifies other fields that are not available in DataCite, such as detailed options to indicate previous versions of a resource, a current version and other related resources.

5.3 Semantic overlap and transforming schemas into each other

While DataCite, Dublin Core, and DCAT can all be used to describe datasets, they address slightly different use cases and communities. However, there is significant semantic overlap between these core metadata sets. This overlap allows data annotated according to one schema to be mapped to another to some extent.

Semantic mismatches between the mappings can arise from different levels of granularity or the presence of fields specific to the domain of a particular schema. Transforming data from one schema to another may therefore involve some loss of information.

In specific cases, where one schema is more comprehensive than another one for a particular data element (e. g., DataCite's 'Creator' field compared to Dublin Core's 'Contributor' field), it may be possible to achieve a lossless transformation. In other cases, decisions may need to be made about how best to represent the data in the target schema.

A working group of the Research Data Alliance (RDA) provides a table with a mapping of the different data elements of these and other metadata schemas (see Research Data Alliance 2021). Datacite also provides a crosswalk to the RDA schema (Research Data Alliance 2024). Some of these mappings are obvious, others are only applicable in specific contexts, so that a concrete mapping requires a detailed analysis for specific domains and repositories, taking into account their practices and requirements.

Semantic markup can play a crucial role in facilitating more accurate schema transformations. By enriching data descriptions with semantic annotations, it becomes possible to identify the most appropriate corresponding fields across different schemas based on the meaning and content of the data. However, both DataCite and DCAT lack detailed semantic representation within their core elements.

For cultural institutions such as galleries, libraries, archives, and museums (GLAM), CIDOC-CRM (ISO 21127 2023) is proposed as a solution for semantic interoperability. It provides an ontology for concepts used in information catalogues maintained by GLAM institutions. CIDOC-CRM is often integrated with the Resource Description and Access framework (also abbreviated RDA, see Joint Steering Committee for Development of RDA 2013) for descriptive cataloguing. RDA provides comprehensive instructions and guidelines for formulating bibliographic data, ensuring consistency of metadata representation across various institutions. Designed for use by libraries, museums, and archives, RDA, together with CIDOC-CRM, enhances semantic interoperability, facilitating the structured exchange of cultural heritage and bibliographic information across different domains. Although there is an overlap with research data in general, and specifically with language and text data, additional methods for cataloguing and describing these types of research data need to be identified.

6 Integrating schema.org

Unlike previous schemas, schema.org provides a richer semantic framework for annotating data. By using schema.org's semantic markup capabilities, data providers can improve the interoperability of their data and enable more precise transformations between different descriptive schemas.

6.1 Introduction to schema.org

Schema.org is a collaborative effort between major commercial search engines, such as Google, Bing, and Yandex, and other organisations to create a standardised set of vocabularies for web page markup. The goal is to improve the way search engines understand the meaning and context of information on web pages. By embedding schema.org markup within web pages, website owners can provide structured data descriptions of their content, enabling search engines to return richer and more informative results.

Beyond its core function in search engine optimisation, schema.org's relevance extends to various data formats, including metadata for research data. This relevance is based on several key aspects. Schema.org provides a comprehensive set of semantic types and properties that can be used to describe a wide range of entities and concepts. This rich semantic representation goes beyond simple keywords or tags and allows for a more nuanced understanding of the meaning of the data. By adhering to schema.org's standardised vocabularies, data providers can ensure that their metadata is interpretable by a wider range of applications and platforms. In addition, schema.org markup can be embedded within web pages or catalogues of datasets created for data in repositories. The hierarchy of elements and their definitions are publicly available and maintained, ensuring their ongoing development and adaptation to new requirements.

6.2 Implementation

The integration of schema.org metadata into language data infrastructures involves several key concepts and methods. Many rich metadata sets can be partially mapped to schema.org, improving their interoperability and discoverability. When the serialisation of the metadata record is done in JSON-LD or some other RDF serialisation, the linked data can refer to schema.org vocabulary. This approach allows schema.org terms to be seamlessly integrated into the metadata, facilitating a structured and semantically rich representation of the data. Another method of incorporating schema.org metadata is to embed microdata enriched with schema.org information within HTML serialisations.

Schema.org contains a large number of possible metadata concepts. However, schema.org may not be comprehensive enough to cover all types of research data comprehensively. If the required information is not already included in schema.org, it may be difficult to accurately represent certain metadata elements. To address this limitation, schema.org provides an extension process. From the years 2011 to 2014, the extension process was based on schema.org's ontology, allowing users to extend the ontology by adding user-defined information to the hierarchically organised existing elements. The closest matching concept was used and an extension was appended by adding a slash character and the extension, i. e. / *EXTENSION*, where EXTENSION is a meaningful extension to schema.org. This method is no longer supported.

There are currently two main ways to extend schema.org. One way is to propose an extension to the editorial group. Users can propose new terms or modifications to the existing schema.org vocabulary by submitting their proposals to the schema.org editorial group. This process involves community discussion and review to ensure that the proposed changes are useful and widely applicable. However, as research data can be very specialised, and the editorial group is an external entity, this process may not always be successful. Another option is to host an extension to schema.org. Communities can define and host their own extensions to schema.org. These extensions can be tailored to specific needs and domains, and provide a way to include specialised metadata that may not be covered by the core schema.org vocabulary. Hosted extensions are maintained separately but can be linked to the main schema.org framework.[10]

6.3 Benefits

Including schema.org information into HTML serialisations of a metadata set or by providing JSON-LD offers several significant advantages. This technique is particularly beneficial because it allows major search engines to index the HTML pages and

10 An example of such an extension from the research data domain is https://bioschemas.org/ for biological and bioinformatics data.

access the embedded structured data. This can significantly improve the visibility and accessibility of the metadata in search engine results, making it easier for users to discover and access the data through standardised descriptions that allow search engines to better 'understand' the meaning and relationships of the data, resulting in richer and more informative search results. As a result, researchers and other users can find relevant data more efficiently, facilitating better data sharing and collaboration; this is particularly important for novice users not used to specialised search engines.

However, it is important to note that specialised search engines for research data are often limited to data sources registered with them, with the metadata accessible through standard and open APIs, as required by the FAIR principles (see Section 4.3 in this chapter). For example, a search engine such as the Virtual Language Observatory (VLO, Van Uytvanck et al. 2010) will harvest from enabled repositories using OAI-PMH and specific metadata schemas, rather than using a schema.org implementation. This approach ensures that the metadata is consistently accessible and interoperable across different platforms and systems.

Despite this limitation, the use of schema.org can still provide significant benefits for general web visibility and accessibility by broadening the audience through general web search engines. This dual approach can maximise the reach and impact of the metadata, making it more widely available and useful to a wide range of users.

7 Discipline and data type specific metadata schemas

The previous examples dealt with discipline agnostic metadata. However, rich documentation is much more subtle and includes discipline-specific aspects. For example the metadata specification Lightweight Information Describing Objects (LIDO, see LIDO v1.1 2021 2021) is a metadata schema designed for museum object documentation and cultural heritage data exchange. It is based on CIDOC-CRM and is widely used for publishing and sharing museum collections online.

This section presents a disciplinary approach specifically designed for language and text related research data.

7.1 The importance of discipline-specific metadata schemas

Discipline-specific metadata schemas provide detailed descriptions that reflect the unique characteristics of different types of research data. These schemas ensure accurate documentation for researchers and users. Community-accepted descriptive practices, developed and maintained by experts, play a critical role in the effectiveness of these schemas. They ensure that metadata is consistent, reliable, and interoperable within the research community.

Established repositories often use these schemas to store and share research data, preserving it for future use. Expert descriptions, written by subject matter experts, contribute to the overall quality and documentation of the data. By using these schemas, researchers ensure that their data is well documented, accessible, and interoperable, promoting better data sharing and collaboration.

7.2 Component Metadata Infrastructure (CMDI)

The Component Metadata Infrastructure (CMDI), formalised in the ISO standards ISO 24622-1 (2015) and ISO 24622-2 (2019), provides a flexible and modular framework for the definition and exchange of metadata. Unlike rigid, pre-defined schemas, CMDI allows for the creation of customised metadata models tailored to specific needs and domains. Following the principles of Duval et al. (2002) (see also Section 2.2 above), it is a modular approach that allows the recombination of building blocks consisting of metadata elements, defines their cardinality, allows for refinement and extensibility.

CMDI relies on different infrastructures for the definition of a metadata schema:

- *a Component Registry* which is a system in which the schema itself is defined and made available for the use in a metadata instance;
- *a Concept Registry* which is a system in which the semantics of the concepts used in the schema is defined.

Additional infrastructure components such as editors, metadata catalogues, evaluation systems are not required. As CMDI is serialised in XML, any editor that handles generic XML can be used, but also specialised tools can be used, either for manual editing or for automatic generation of metadata. As a modular approach with a high degree of flexibility, CMDI is particularly useful for its application in a federated research infrastructure (see Eckart 2016 and Körner and Eckart 2025, where metadata are used in a federated content search).

The genesis of this standard has been described in detail before (see for example Broeder et al. 2011, 2012a,b, Goosen et al. 2015).

7.3 Functionality of the component registry

At its core, CMDI is based on the concept of *components*. These are reusable building blocks that represent individual metadata elements or groups of related elements. These components can be combined and recombined to create 'profiles' that define the specific set of metadata elements required for a particular data type, domain, or data centre. This modular approach promotes flexibility and interoperability by allowing existing components to be reused and new profiles to be created as required.

CMDI's key features include modularity and reusability, flexibility, interoperability, and extensibility. The component-based approach allows for the creation of reusable metadata models, reducing redundancy and promoting consistency across different repositories and data types. CMDI enables the creation of customised metadata profiles tailored to specific needs and types of data, providing flexibility for different research domains and applications. By promoting the reuse of common components and adherence to standardised definitions, CMDI facilitates interoperability between different metadata schemas from different vendors. In addition, the framework allows for the continuous evolution and extension of metadata models as new requirements and use cases emerge; these extensions and can be built on top of existing schemas.

CMDI has been successfully applied in various domains, most notably within the language technology and digital humanities research communities (see for example Trippel et al. 2012) but also in fields as diverse as bioinformatics (see for example Brandt et al. 2021). By providing a flexible and modular framework for the definition and exchange of metadata, CMDI makes a significant contribution to the advancement of research data management and interoperability.

7.4 Registering the concepts used

Metadata schemas define metadata elements and their associated value schemas. To ensure that these elements and values can be properly interpreted, their semantics are provided in a registry. Registries provide a set of well-defined, persistent, and uniquely identifiable concepts for metadata descriptions. In the context of metadata schemas in CMDI, each element is assigned a persistent identifier that links to a concept and provides its definition. This identifier can point to a concept in the CLARIN Concept Registry,[11] or to any other persistently defined concept, such as a concept in schema.org.

The functions of such a registry are as follows:

11 https://vocabularies.clarin.eu/, last accessed on 4 February 2025.

- *Standardisation of metadata concepts:* a concept registry provides PIDs for metadata concepts, ensuring that metadata elements have stable, well-defined meanings across different datasets and institutions.
- *Interoperability between metadata schemas:* By linking metadata elements to common concepts in the registry, CMDI records become more machine-readable and interoperable. This enables the seamless integration of metadata from different sources.
- *Reuse of commonly defined concepts:* Rather than defining new concepts for each metadata schema, users can reuse existing concepts from the registry. This promotes consistency and reduces redundancy.
- *Improving search and discovery:* Metadata records that reference concepts in a registry can be indexed and searched more effectively because they are based on a common conceptual framework.
- *Support for linked data and semantic web:* As each concept in the registry is uniquely identifiable via a URI, CMDI metadata can be more easily integrated with Linked Open Data (LOD) and semantic web technologies (see Khan 2025).

7.5 Case studies and examples

The Component Metadata Infrastructure (CMDI) has been successfully deployed in various archives and research infrastructures, demonstrating its flexibility and effectiveness in managing metadata. Below are some practical examples of how CMDI is being used in different contexts, in particular within the CLARIN and Text+ initiatives. Practical examples show how these standards are applied in different archives, in CLARIN (see for example Hinrichs and Krauwer 2014a and Hinrichs and Krauwer 2014b) and Text+ (see for example Hinrichs and Trippel 2024).

The CLARIN infrastructure makes extensive use of CMDI to make language resources discoverable and interoperable. The Virtual Language Observatory (VLO, Van Uytvanck et al. 2010) within CLARIN uses CMDI to harvest metadata from different repositories, enabling researchers to efficiently search and access language resources.

In the Text+ initiative (Hinrichs and Trippel 2024),[12] CMDI is also used to manage metadata for text and language resources. Text+ supports the use of standards-based tools and practices to ensure the interoperability and accessibility of research data. The German Text Archive (DTA)[13] uses CMDI to provide a standardised format

12 See also https://text-plus.org

13 The website of the German Text Archive offers a download for all texts in various formats and metadata for example in CMDI, see https://www.deutschestextarchiv.de/

for metadata, ensuring high accuracy in data capture and annotation. This approach enables the reliable and consistent description of German-language texts from the 1600s to the 1900s, making them accessible for linguistic and historical research.

These case studies illustrate the practical application of CMDI in various research infrastructures, highlighting its benefits in terms of flexibility, interoperability, and effective metadata management. By using CMDI, archives and research initiatives can ensure that their metadata is well structured, accessible, and interoperable, supporting the advancement of research and collaboration across different domains. A detailed introduction to CMDI can be found in Windhouwer and Goosen (2022), Broeder et al. (2011) or on the CLARIN website.[14]

8 Conclusion

In this chapter, we have explored the critical role of metadata in research data management, particularly within the context of language data and infrastructures. We began by defining basic metadata elements and their importance for data management and discoverability. We then examined metadata derived during the deposit process and highlighted the importance of adhering to the FAIR principles to improve data findability, accessibility, interoperability, and reusability.

We also discussed the use of established core metadata sets such as Dublin Core, DataCite, and DCAT and the integration of schema.org for improved interoperability. We also looked at the application of discipline-specific rich metadata schemas, with a focus on ISO 24622-1 (2015) and ISO 24622-2 (2019) (CMDI), and provided practical examples of their implementation.

By adopting these metadata standards and practices, researchers can improve the quality, consistency, and usability of their data, ultimately contributing to the advancement of knowledge and the preservation of linguistic diversity.

Bibliography

Albertoni, Riccardo, David Browning, Simon J. D. Cox, Alejandra Gonzalez Beltran, Andrea Perego & Peter Winstanley. 2024. Data Catalog Vocabulary (DCAT) – Version 3. Tech. rep. Invited Experts: Riccardo Albertoni (CNR – Consiglio Nazionale delle Ricerche, Italy), David Browning (Previously at Refinitiv.com), Simon J. D. Cox (Previously at CSIRO), Alejandra Gonzalez Beltran (Scientific Computing Department, Science and Technology Facilities Council, UK; Previously at the

14 See https://www.clarin.eu/content/cmdi-component-metadata-infrastructure

University of Oxford), Andrea Perego, Peter Winstanley. World Wide Web Consortium. https://www.w3.org/TR/vocab-dcat-3/.

Apache Software Foundation. 2025. Apache Tika. Website. Apache Tika is a content analysis toolkit that detects and extracts metadata and text from over a thousand different file types. https://tika.apache.org/.

Bański, Piotr & Nils Diewald. 2025. Dealing with multiple annotations. In Piotr Bański, Ulrich Heid & Laura Herzberg (eds.), *Harmonising language data: Standards for linguistic resources*, de Gruyter.

Brandt, Olaf, Holger Gauza, Steve Kaminski, Mario Trojan, Thorsten Trippel & Johannes Werner. 2021. Extending the CMDI Universe: Metadata for bioinformatics data. In *Selected papers from the clarin annual conference 2020*. Linköping Electronic Conference Proceedings. https://doi.org/10.3384/ecp1806.

Broeder, Daan, Oliver Schonefeld, Thorsten Trippel, Dieter Van Uytvanck & Andreas Witt. 2011. A pragmatic approach to XML interoperability – the Component Metadata Infrastructure (CMDI). In *Proceedings of balisage: The markup conference*, Montréal, Canada. https://doi.org/10.4242/BalisageVol7.Broeder01.

Broeder, Daan, Dieter van Uytvanck, Maria Gavrilidou, Thorsten Trippel & Menzo Windhouwer. 2012a. Standardizing a component metadata infrastructure. In Nicoletta Calzolari (Conference Chair), Khalid Choukri, Thierry Declerck, Mehmet Uğur Doğan, Bente Maegaard, Joseph Mariani, Asuncion Moreno, Jan Odijk & Stelios Piperidis (eds.), *Proceedings of the eight international conference on language resources and evaluation (LREC'12)*. Istanbul, Turkey: European Language Resources Association (ELRA). ISBN 978-2-9517408-7-7.

Broeder, Daan, Menzo Windhouwer, Dieter van Uytvanck, Thorsten Trippel, Twan Goosen, Victoria Arranz, Daan Broeder, Bernhard Gaiffe, Maria Gavrilidou, Monica Monachini & Thorsten Trippel. 2012b. CMDI: A Component Metadata Infrastructure. In *Proceedings of the LREC 2012 workshop describing language resources with metadata: Towards flexibility and interoperability in the documentation of language resources*, Istanbul, Türkei.

Carroll, Stephanie Russo, Ibrahim Garba, Oscar L. Figueroa-Rodríguez, Jarita Holbrook, Raymond Lovett, Simeon Materechera, Mark Parsons, Kay Raseroka, Desi Rodriguez-Lonebear, Robyn Rowe, Rodrigo Sara, Jennifer D. Walker, Jane Anderson & Maui Hudson. 2020. The CARE principles for indigenous data governance. *Data Science Journal* 19(1). 1–12. https://doi.org/10.5334/DSJ-2020-043. Publisher: Committee on Data for Science and Technology. ISSN 1683-1470.

DataCite Metadata Working Group. 2024. DataCite metadata schema for the publication and citation of research data and other research outputs. Version 4.6. https://doi.org/10.14454/csba-e454.

DCMI Metadata Terms. 2020. https://www.dublincore.org/specifications/dublin-core/dcmi-terms/.

Dima, Emanuel, Erhard Hinrichs, Marie Hinrichs, Alexander Kislev, Thorsten Trippel & Thomas Zastrow. 2012. Integration of WebLicht into the CLARIN infrastructure. In *Service-oriented architectures (SOAs) for the humanities: Solutions and impacts joint CLARIN-D/DARIAH workshop at digital humanities conference 2012*, 17–23. http://clarin-d.de/images/workshops/proceedingssoasforthehumanities.pdf.

Duval, Erik, Wayne Hodgins, Stuart Sutton & Stuart L. Weibel. 2002. Metadata principles and practicalities. *D-Lib Magazine* 8(4). https://doi.org/10.1045/april2002-weibel. ISSN 1082-9873.

Eckart, Kerstin. 2018. *Task-based parser output combination: Workflow and infrastructure*. PhD thesis. Universität Stuttgart. https://dx.doi.org/10.18419/opus-9853.

Eckart, Thomas. 2016. *Einsatz und Bewertung komponentenbasierter Metadaten in einer föderierten Infrastruktur für Sprachressourcen am Beispiel der CMDI*. PhD thesis, Universität Leipzig.

Ecker, Jennifer. 2025. *Standardising language data through the conversion pipeline TEIWorLD*. IDSopen, Vol. 15. Mannheim: IDS-Verlag. https://doi.org/10.21248/idsopen.15.2025.54.

European Parliament & Council of the European Union. 2016. Regulation (EU) 2016/679 of the European Parliament and of the Council of 27 April 2016 on the protection of natural persons with regard to the processing of personal data and on the free movement of such data, and repealing Directive 95/46/EC (General Data Protection Regulation). https://eur-lex.europa.eu/eli/reg/2016/679/ (visited on 04/13/2023).

Ferreira, Vera, Hanna Hedeland & Kelsey Neely. 2025. Annotated audiovisual language data: Data quality and data maturity. In Piotr Bański, Ulrich Heid & Laura Herzberg (eds.), *Harmonising language data: Standards for linguistic resources*, de Gruyter.

Frick, Elena & Thomas Schmidt. 2025. Querying spoken language data. In Piotr Bański, Ulrich Heid & Laura Herzberg (eds.), *Harmonising language data: Standards for linguistic resources*, de Gruyter.

Goosen, Twan, M. Windhouwer, Oddrun Ohren, Axel Herold, Thomas Eckart. Matej Ďurčo & Oliver Schonefeld. 2015. CMDI 1.2: Improvements in the CLARIN component metadata infrastructure. In Jan Odijk (ed.), *Linköping Electronic Conference Proceedings* https://doi.org/10.3384/ecp116.

Hartig, Olaf, Pierre-Antoine Champin, Gregg Kellogg & Andy Seaborne. 2025. RDF 1.2 Concepts and abstract syntax. Working Draft. Latest version available at https://www.w3.org/TR/rdf12-concepts/. World Wide Web Consortium (W3C). https://www.w3.org/TR/2025/WD-rdf12-concepts-20250220/.

Hinrichs, Erhard, Marie Hinrichs & Thomas Zastrow. 2010. WebLicht: Web-based LRT services for German. In *Proceedings of the ACL 2010 system demonstrations. ACLDemos '10*, 25–29. Uppsala, Sweden: Association for Computational Linguistics.

Hinrichs, Erhard & Steven Krauwer. 2014a. CLARIN: Resources, tools, and services for digital humanities research. In *ADHO – 2014 "Digital Cultural Empowerment"*. Lausanne, Switzerland: ADHO. https://dh-abstracts.library.virginia.edu/works/1872.

Hinrichs, Erhard & Steven Krauwer. 2014b. The CLARIN research infrastructure: Resources and tools for eHumanities scholars. In Nicoletta Calzolari (Conference Chair), Conference Chair, Khalid Choukri, Thierry Declerck, Hrafn Loftsson, Bente Maegaard, Joseph Mariani, Asuncion Moreno, Jan Odijk & Stelios Piperidis (eds.), *Proceedings of the ninth international conference on language resources and evaluation (LREC'14)*, Reykjavik, Iceland.

Hinrichs, Erhard & Thorsten Trippel. 2024. Text+ – Concept and benefits for empirical researchers. *Cybernetics and Information Technologies* 24(4). 143–163. https://doi.org/10.2478/cait-2024-0040.

Hinrichs, Marie, Thomas Zastrow & Erhard Hinrichs. 2010. WebLicht: Web-based LRT services in a distributed eScience infrastructure. In Nicoletta Calzolari (Conference Chair), Khalid Choukri, Bente Maegaard, Joseph Mariani, Jan Odijk, Stelios Piperidis, Mike Rosner & Daniel Tapias (eds.), *Proceedings of the seventh international conference on language resources and evaluation (LREC'10)*. Valletta, Malta: European Language Resources Association (ELRA). ISBN 2-9517408-6-7.

ISO 17522. 2015. *Health informatics – Provisions for health applications on mobile/smart devices*. International Standard. Geneva: International Organization for Standardization (ISO).

ISO 21127. 2023. *Information and documentation – A reference ontology for the interchange of cultural heritage information*. International Standard. Geneva: International Organisation for Standardization (ISO).

ISO 24622-1 2015. *Language resource management – Component Metadata Infrastructure (CMDI) – Part 1: The Component Metadata Model*. International Standard. Geneva: International Organization for Standardization (ISO). https://www.iso.org/standard/37336.html.

ISO 24622-2 2019. *Language resource management – Component Metadata Infrastructure (CMDI) – Part 2: The Component Metadata Specification Language*. International Standard. Geneva: International Organization for Standardization (ISO).

ISO/IEC 11179-1. 2023. *Information technology – Metadata registries (MDR) – Part 1: Framework*. International Standard. Geneva: International Organization for Standardization (ISO).

ISO/IEC 19115-1. 2014. *Geographic information – Metadata – Part 1: Fundamentals*. International Standard. Geneva: International Organization for Standardization (ISO).

Joint Steering Committee for Development of RDA. 2013. Resource Description and Access (RDA). Last updated: 25 July 2013. http://www.rda-jsc.org/rda.html.

Kamocki, Paweł. 2025. Taxonomy of legal and ethical metadata for language resources. In Piotr Bański, Ulrich Heid & Laura Herzberg (eds.), *Harmonising language data: Standards for linguistic resources*, de Gruyter.

Khan, Anas Fahad. 2025. Linguistic linked (open) data. In Piotr Bański, Ulrich Heid & Laura Herzberg (eds.), *Harmonising language data: Standards for linguistic resources*, de Gruyter.

Körner, Erik & Thomas Eckart. 2025. Accessing linguistic content in distributed research environments. In Piotr Bański, Ulrich Heid & Laura Herzberg (eds.), *Harmonising language data: Standards for linguistic resources*, de Gruyter.

LIDO v1.1 2021. 2021. LIDO v1.1 – Lightweight Information Describing Objects. LIDO v1.1 XML Schema Definition (XSD). https://www.lido-schema.org/schema/v1.1/lido-v1.1.html. https://www.lido-schema.org/schema/v1.1/lido-v1.1.xsd.

Ljubešić, Nikola & Tomaž Erjavec. 2025. Part-of-speech tagging and related annotation. In Piotr Bański, Ulrich Heid & Laura Herzberg (eds.), *Harmonising language data: Standards for linguistic resources*, de Gruyter.

Miles, Alistair & Sean Bechhofer. 2009. SKOS: Simple knowledge organization system. Tech. rep. Accessed: 2025-02-24. World Wide Web Consortium. https://www.w3.org/TR/skos-reference/.

Pisetta, Ines & Thorsten Trippel. 2025. Standards and practices for long-term digital archiving. In Piotr Bański, Ulrich Heid & Laura Herzberg (eds.), *Harmonising language data: Standards for linguistic resources*, de Gruyter.

Preissner, Annette & Ulrich Heid. 2025. The Life of an ISO standard. In Piotr Bański, Ulrich Heid & Laura Herzberg (eds.), *Harmonising language data: Standards for linguistic resources*, de Gruyter.

Publications Office of the European Union. 2025. DCAT-AP: DCAT application profile for data portals in Europe. Accessed: 2025-02-24. https://op.europa.eu/en/web/eu-vocabularies/dcat-ap.

Research Data Alliance. 2021. RDA crosswalks from 15 metadata schemas to schema.org. PDF document. Version 1.0. This document provides a crosswalk between various schemas and schema.org, facilitating metadata interoperability. https://www.rd-alliance.org/wp-content/uploads/2021/12/RDA20Crosswalks20from20schemas20to20schema.org2028V1.02C202021-12-1629.pdf.

Research Data Alliance. 2024. A crosswalk of the DataCite schema to RDA metadata standard for DMPs. Website. This document provides a mapping between the DataCite schema and the RDA metadata standard for Data Management Plans (DMPs). https://support.datacite.org/docs/a-crosswalk-of-datacite-and-rda-mapping.

Romary, Laurent. 2025. International standards for the identification and the description of languages and their varieties. In Piotr Bański, Ulrich Heid & Laura Herzberg (eds.), *Harmonising language data: Standards for linguistic resources*, de Gruyter.

Schema.org. 2024. Schema.org. Website. Schema.org is a collaborative project that provides schemas for marking up web pages, email messages, and beyond with structured data. https://schema.org/.

Schmidt, Ingrid. 2004. Modellierung von Metadaten. In Henning Lobin & Lothar Lemnitzer (eds.), *Texttechnologie: Perspektiven und Anwendungen*. Handbücher. Tübingen, Germany: Stauffenburg.

Schwarz, Pia. 2025. Named entity recognition and entity linking. In Piotr Bański, Ulrich Heid & Laura Herzberg (eds.), *Harmonising language data: Standards for linguistic resources*, de Gruyter.

TEI P5: Guidelines for Electronic Text Encoding and Interchange. 2025. Tech. rep. Text Encoding Initiative. https://tei-c.org/release/doc/tei-p5-doc/en/html/index.html.

Tomaszuk, Dominik & Timothée Haudebourg. 2025. RDF 1.2 Schema. Working Draft. Latest version available at https://www.w3.org/TR/rdf12-schema/. World Wide Web Consortium (W3C). https://www.w3.org/TR/2025/WD-rdf12-schema-20250224/.

Trippel, Thorsten, Christina Hoppermann & Griet Depoorter. 2012. The Component Metadata Infrastructure (CMDI) in a project on sustainable linguistic resources. In *Proceedings of the Workshop Describing Language Resources with Metadata at LREC 2012*, Istanbul, Türkei. http://www.lrec-conf.org/proceedings/lrec2012/workshops/11.LREC2012%20Metadata%20Proceedings.pdf.

Van Uytvanck, Dieter, Claus Zinn, Daan Broeder, Peter Wittenburg & Mariano Gardelleni. 2010. Virtual language observatory: The portal to the language resources and technology universe. In *Proceedings of the seventh conference on international language resources and evaluation (LREC'10)*. 900–903. European Language Resources Association. http://www.lrec-conf.org/proceedings/lrec2010/pdf/273_Paper.pdf.

Wartena, Christian. 2025. Character encoding and its importance for text resources. In Piotr Bański, Ulrich Heid & Laura Herzberg (eds.), *Harmonising language data: Standards for linguistic resources*, de Gruyter.

Werthmann, Antonina. 2025. From spoken language data to TEI-based ISO standard. In Piotr Bański, Ulrich Heid & Laura Herzberg (eds.), *Harmonising language data: Standards for linguistic resources*, de Gruyter.

Wilkinson, Mark D., Michel Dumontier, Jan Aalbersberg, Gabrielle Appleton, Myles Axton, Arie Baak, Niklas Blomberg, Jan-Willem Boiten, Luiz Bonino da Silva Santos, Philip E. Bourne, Jildau Bouwman, Anthony J. Brookes, Tim Clark, Mercè Crosas, Ingrid Dillo, Olivier Dumon, Scott Edmunds, Chris T. Evelo, Richard Finkers, Alejandra Gonzalez-Beltran, Alasdair J. G. Gray, Paul Groth, Carole Goble, Jeffrey S. Grethe, Jaap Heringa, Peter A. C. 't Hoen, Rob Hooft, Tobias Kuhn, Ruben Kok, Joost Kok, Scott J. Lusher, Maryann E. Martone, Albert Mons, Abel L. Packer, Bengt Persson, Philippe Rocca-Serra, Marco Roos, Rene van Schaik, Susanna-Assunta Sansone, Erik Schultes, Thierry Sengstag, Ted Slater, George Strawn, Morris A. Swertz, Mark Thompson, Johan van der Lei, Erik van Mulligen, Jan Velterop, Andra Waagmeester, Peter Wittenburg, Katherine Wolstencroft, Jun Zhao & Barend Mons. 2016. The FAIR Guiding Principles for scientific data management and stewardship. *Scientific Data* 3(1). 160018. ISSN 2052-4463.

Windhouwer, Menzo & Twan Goosen. 2022. Component Metadata Infrastructure. In Darja Fišer & Andreas Witt (eds.), *CLARIN: The infrastructure for language resources*. Digital Linguistics, Vol. 1. Funded by CLARIN ERIC. De Gruyter.

Anas Fahad Khan

Linguistic linked (open) data

Abstract: In this chapter, we explore the concepts of linked open data and the Semantic Web, explaining their relevance and highlighting their role in the publication, access, and utilization of data. In particular, the chapter is aimed at readers who are linguists or who are interested in publishing linguistic data as linked (open) data but who may not have prior knowledge of the core concepts in the field. We begin with an introduction to the most relevant concepts for understanding linked open data and the Semantic Web in general. Following on from this we focus on the Linguistic Linked Open Data cloud and look at some of the main Semantic Web vocabularies, which are available for linguistic datasets.

Keywords: linked open data, RDF, semantic web, linguistic linked open data

1 Introduction

In 1999 Tim Berners-Lee, inventor of the World Wide Web, laid out his vision for a Semantic Web in the following words:

> I have a dream for the Web [in which computers] become capable of analyzing all the data on the Web – the content, links, and transactions between people and computers. A 'Semantic Web,' which makes this possible, has yet to emerge, but when it does, the day-to-day mechanisms of trade, bureaucracy, and our daily lives will be handled by machines talking to machines. The 'intelligent agents' people have touted for ages will finally materialize.
>
> (Berners-Lee and Fischetti 1999)

In short, Berners-Lee's vision was of an enhanced version of the then existing Web where computers would be able to analyse all content, links, and transactions with minimal necessity for human input (at least in what concerned more banal technical matters relating to trade and bureaucracy), resulting in seamless machine to machine interaction all along the line. Although the state of technology has moved on since 1999 – and often in quite drastic ways – this vision remains a compelling one, and is still far from being an everyday reality. From that time, the Semantic Web has been promoted by the World Wide Web Consortium (W3C)[1] and is being

1 https://www.w3.org/ (accessed: Feb 12, 2025).

Anas Fahad Khan, Consiglio Nazionale delle Ricerche – Istituto di Linguistica Computazionale, Via Moruzzi 1, 56124 Pisa, PI, Italy, e-mail: fahad.khan@ilc.cnr.it

https://doi.org/10.1515/9783112208212-012

implemented through the use of common, open standards for data and exchange protocols, together with the use of linked data for publishing datasets. The most important of these standards and technologies are often represented in terms of a stack, the so-called Semantic Web stack, with the standards in each layer dependent on the standards in the layer below.[2] The following are the principal elements of the stack:

1. Uniform Resource Identifiers (URIs) and the UNICODE character set form the foundation; see Wartena (2025).
2. XML: A common serialisation[3] format.
3. RDF (Resource Description Framework): A data interchange framework that specifies data organisation at an abstract level.
4. RDFS (RDF Schema): A language for creating taxonomies and simple ontologies.
5. OWL (Web Ontology Language) and SPARQL: Standards for defining complex relationships and querying linked data.

We will look at URIs, RDF, RDFS, and OWL later in this chapter (Sections 2.1 to 2.6 below), since they are key to understanding the Semantic Web. Before that however, we will look at the meaning of the term linked data.

2 What is linked data?

Linked data, to put it succinctly, is a method of publishing structured and interlinked data on the World Wide Web via standard web technologies such as HTTP, XML, and URIs. The data in question can potentially belong to any domain, however, in this chapter we will focus on language data. Linked data was originally devised as a means of enabling semantic querying – that is, the retrieval of data based on the *meaning* of that data – across datasets, including those hosted in servers at different locations. Along with this focus on semantic querying, is a related concern with promoting interoperability, machine accessibility and data interconnection. We will look at each of these briefly in turn.

Interoperability: Linked data relies heavily on shared standards, namely, those in the Semantic Web stack, in order to ensure a seamless integration of data from different sources. To this end the recommended best practice is to use common vocabularies whenever possible. In the case of language data, for instance, this entails

2 https://www.w3.org/2000/Talks/1206-xml2k-tbl/slide10-0.html (accessed: Feb 12, 2025).

3 The concept of serialisation is discussed below in Section 2.5.

the use of shared data categories and vocabularies for defining lexicons, corpora and annotations, as we will see below, Section 3.1.

Machine Accessibility: Linked data uses standard web technologies to publish and share datasets, as is indeed the case with traditional HTML pages. In particular, these datasets have HTTP addresses and are accessible via web browsers. However, the unique value of linked data datasets lies in their enhanced machine accessibility or readability. So that, unlike standard HTML pages, linked data datasets are designed to:

- Allow for complex data relationships.
- Support advanced queries across multiple datasets simultaneously.
- Facilitate automated data integration and analysis.

It bears repeating that this machine readability is underpinned by the use of shared standards and technologies, something which ensures that datasets can be effectively combined and integrated together regardless of their source.

Data Interconnection: Providers of linked data are encouraged to link their datasets to other linked data datasets with the idea of fostering a highly interconnected web of data. Indeed this aspect of linked data – that is, the 'linking' together of different datasets – is so important that it has lent its name to the concept itself. When it comes to language data, for instance, linked data facilitates the linking together of different kinds of linguistic resources such as lexicons, corpora and data category registers.

All three of these linked data desiderata are embodied and given a practical gloss in the four principles of linked data which were originally articulated by, once again, Tim Berners-Lee.[4] These are as follows:

1. Use Uniform Resource Identifiers (URIs) as names for things.
2. Use HTTP URIs so that these names can be looked up easily.
3. Provide Useful Information: When a URI is looked up, it should return meaningful data.
4. Include Links to Other URIs: This allows users to discover related information effectively.

These principles were later simplified into three key tenets:[5]

- Conceptual entities have HTTP-based names.
- Looking up these HTTP names returns data in a standard format.
- This data includes relationships, linking to other HTTP-named entities.

4 https://www.w3.org/DesignIssues/LinkedData (accessed: Feb 12, 2025).

5 https://web.archive.org/web/20110410204952/http://www.ted.com/talks/tim_berners_lee_on_the_next_web.html (accessed: Feb 12, 2025).

Linked Data (LD) is data that is published according to these principles. If this data is published with an open license then it becomes Linked Open Data.

Since its inception, linked data has gained significant traction within a number of different disciplines and subject areas, although up until now it has had most success in the sciences and especially the biomedical sciences. It has recently started to attract more attention as a means of publishing humanities datasets (Nurmikko-Fuller 2024), however, and in Section 3 of the current chapter, we will look at its application to linguistics and the domain of language resources and technologies.

One important reason for the popularity of linked data is that it helps to resolve the problem of data silos – isolated databases that make it difficult to access, integrate, or query data across multiple sources – and that it therefore facilitates data re-use. Most notably, linked data simplifies the process of integrating data from disparate sources, something that was often problematic in the past due to the proliferation of different formats and standards, many of which were discipline-specific. Ultimately, therefore, it encourages the reuse and enrichment of existing datasets, making it easier for users to build upon established resources rather than starting from scratch; as such it also fosters innovation by enabling new ways of combining and analysing information.

Since there is often confusion between the two closely related concepts of the *Semantic Web* and *linked data* it is worth distinguishing between them here.

1. Semantic Web: An expanded vision of the World Wide Web where documents are structured in order to allow them to be processed by computers based on their content.
2. Linked Data: A specific approach for implementing the Semantic Web by publishing interconnected datasets using open standards.

In essence then linked data should be considered a foundational technology for achieving the vision of the Semantic Web. By adopting linked data practices, data providers contribute to a more structured, interoperable, and machine-readable web, bringing us closer to Berners-Lee's initial motivating vision.

In the rest of this section we will look at four of the standards: URI, RDF(S) and SPARQL which we mentioned above.

2.1 Uniform Resource Identifiers (URI)

For the Semantic Web to be viable, we need a way of identifying the things which we wish to describe in our datasets and that can also be re-used in other datasets across the Web. Uniform Resource Identifiers (URIs) are a technological standard answering this need and that have been adopted as a means of uniquely identifying resources on the Semantic Web. Note that by resources here we don't just mean documents on the web, but anything that we intend to refer to or describe in a Semantic Web dataset, so for instance, Donald Trump, the SARS-CoV-2, Sudan, the number 2, or the class of Birds, can all be resources with their own URIs. Furthermore, resources can also be relationships: X located in Y, X bigger than Y, X has name Y.

So now that we know the role that URIs play, the obvious question arises as to what they actually are. In essence, they are strings that are structured according to a standard schema that can be represented as follows:

```
URI = scheme:[//authority]path[?query][#fragment]
```

where `scheme` can be for instance `http(s)` or `urn`.[6] The authority part contains elements such as user information, e. g., `user:password@` (this is optional), host information, e. g., `dbpedia.org` (this is mandatory), and port information, e. g., `:8080`, (this is optional). The `path` contains the location of the resource on a server. The `query` part includes additional parameters for the resource, and the `fragment` part narrows down a specific part of a given resource. We will not look in any detail at these latter two elements. As a very simple example (i. e., without the query and the fragment part), take the following URI:

```
https://dbpedia.org/resource/Pisa
```

In this case the scheme is `https`, the host is `dbpedia.org`, the path part of the URI is `/resource/Pisa`.

One important property of URIs is that they are (or should be) dereferenceable: that is, whenever we enter a URI in a browser or make a GET request, we should get back some relevant data. For instance on entering or clicking on a URI in a browser, a user should get back a relevant HTML document or the browser should automatically download an RDF file (this depends on the browser). In addition, URIs should ideally be stable (they should not be re-used for different things) and persistent (they should be around for the long term). Moreover, in order to help linked data function as it should, anyone publishing a dataset is encouraged to favour pre-existing URIs to refer to things (where they exist) and not just coin new ones ad hoc.

6 This stands for Uniform Resource Name. These are persistent identifiers that, unlike URIs, do not provide a means to access a resource but are location independent. We will not discuss these in any detail in what follows.

Finally, if URIs seem familiar to the non-technically minded reader it is likely because they are accustomed to Uniform Resource Locators (URLs), the latter being merely one kind of URI, the kind that identifies internet domain resources.[7]

2.2 Resource Description Framework (RDF)

Having established the use of URIs as universal IDs for identifying resources in the Semantic Web – where as the reader will recall, resources can be names for concrete things in the world, or abstract things including classes and events or even relationships between things – one might ask how we might go about employing these URIs to make statements about the world, to put together datasets? In fact, in order to do this we will need a language with a formal syntax and a semantics. In our case this is provided by the Resource Description Framework (RDF), a standard metamodel for data interchange, with its own clearly defined syntax and semantics, that utilises the linking structure of the World Wide Web via URIs to make statements about things.

In a few words, the RDF stipulates that data (of whatever kind) be structured in the form of (subject, predicate, object) triples where the subject and predicate must be resources with their own URI, and the object of the triple can be either a URI resource or a data value that is, a literal; such literals can be expressed using the ^^ syntax followed by the XSD datatype or @ and a language tag. We describe these RDF literals in more detail below, in Section 2.3. A set of these triples, associated together as part of a single RDF dataset, describes a directed, labelled graph. URIs that play the role of predicates are called properties, and the convention is to represent them as labelled arrows; they are the edges of the directed labelled graph.

To make this a little bit more concrete we represent a very simple RDF graph in Figure 1 where we make two statements about the city of Pisa: firstly that it is a city belonging to the nation of Italy and secondly that it has a population of 89,541 inhabitants.

Note that in this graph we have re-used already existing URIs for *Pisa*, *Italy* and the properties of city and population total (instead of, for instance, creating our own). In this case the URIs are taken from DBpedia, the linked data version of Wikipedia, see below for more details.

As well as being a metamodel, RDF is also a vocabulary which offers users a number of built-in resources which users can re-use in their own linked data

7 The reader might see reference to IRIs, Internationalized Resource Identifiers, these are an extension of URIs that permit the use of a range of characters, including non-ASCII characters.

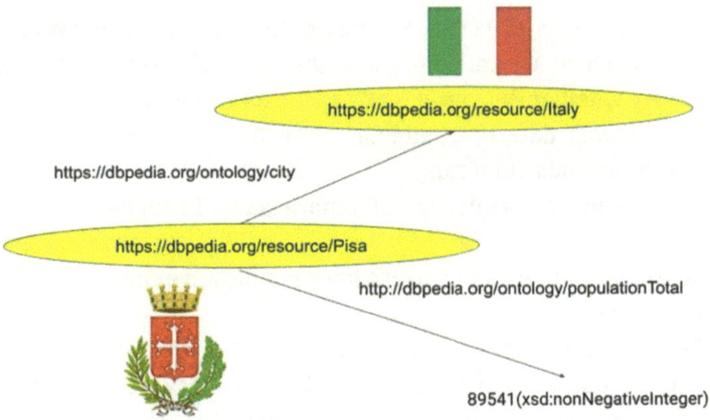

Figure 1: An Example RDF graph describing two aspects of the city of Pisa.

datasets; these are basic objects and properties which can be extremely useful in the creation of RDF datasets. The most important of these built-in resources is the *type* property with the URI https://www.w3.org/1999/02/22-rdf-syntax-ns#type; note that for readability we can abbreviate this as rdf:type where the 'rdf:' stands for 'https://www.w3.org/1999/02/22-rdf-syntax-ns#'. This property can be used to specify that a given resource is an instance of another resource, for instance, that *Piotr Banksi* is an instance of the class *Person*. An example of the use of rdf:type is given in Figure 2, to state that Italy is an instance of type Country (both of which are resources for which we've re-used URIs from dbpedia).

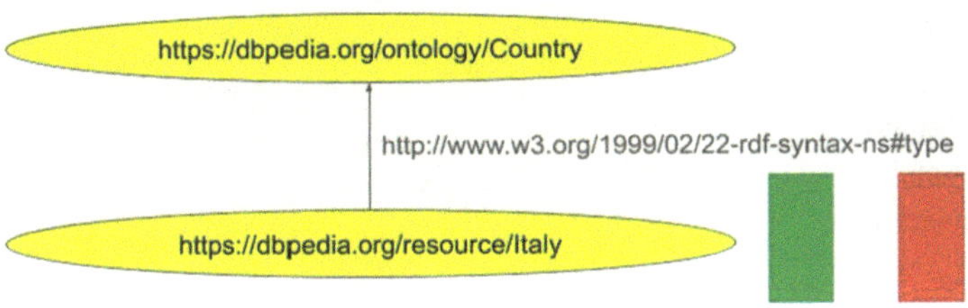

Figure 2: An Example of the Use of rdf:type.

2.3 RDF literals

We can add information to RDF literals, specifying the datatype of the literal in question or, in the case in which it is a string, the language to which it belongs. We will start with the former and look at XSD (XML Schema Definition) datatypes (Walmsley 2002). These are tags which are added to the end of any RDF literal following two '^' symbols to specify whether the literal is any of the following: string, integer, decimal, boolean, float, double, date, time, and dateTime. In what follows, we give an example of each of these kinds of literal:

- `xsd:string`: Represents a sequence of characters. Example: `"Hello World"^^xsd:string`
- `xsd:integer`: Represents an integer (can also have nonnegativeinteger). Example: `"42"^^xsd:integer`
- `xsd:decimal`: Represents a decimal number. Example: `"3.14"^^xsd:decimal`
- `xsd:boolean`: Represents a boolean value. Example: `"true"^^xsd:boolean`
- `xsd:float`: Represents a floating point number. Example: `"3.14"^^xsd:float`
- `xsd:double`: Represents a double precision floating point number. Example: `"2.71828"^^xsd:double`
- `xsd:date`: Represents a date (YYYY-MM-DD). Example: `"2024-06-21"^^xsd:date`
- `xsd:time`: Represents a time (HH:MM). Example: `"14:30:00"^^xsd:time`
- `xsd:dateTime`: Represents a date and time (YYYY-MM-DDTHH:MM). Example: `"2024-06-21T14:30:00"^^xsd:dateTime`

If, on the other hand, we wish to indicate the language of a given string literal, we can use language tags. In this case, the syntax consists of the string literal followed by @ and the language code (e. g., from ISO 639 (International Organization for Standardization 2023), see Romary 2025). We can also use more complex language tags to specify varieties and dialects of languages (see Khan et al. 2022).

Example:

- "Ciao"@it (Italian)
- "Olá"@pt (Portuguese)
- "Hello"@en (English)
- "Hola"@es (Spanish)
- "Hallo"@de (German)
- "你好"@zh (Chinese)

NB: RDF literals cannot have both an XSD datatype and a language tag simultaneously.

2.4 Resource Description Framework Schema (RDFS)

RDF, then, gives us a basic framework for constructing statements with the ultimate aim of modelling complex kinds of data in a standardised, interoperable way, on the basis of its meaning; but it is only really a first step towards realising this aim. One of the most important follow-up steps comes in the form of another standard vocabulary, the Resource Description Framework Schema (RDFS). RDFS builds on top of RDF, extending the latter in a way that allows users to begin adding more semantics to their data:

> [RDFS] provides mechanisms for describing groups of related resources and the relationships between these resources. ... These resources are used to determine characteristics of other resources, such as the domains and ranges of properties[8]

In particular, RDFS offers a number of built-in resources allowing us to explicitly categorise URI resources as classes (sets of things) and properties (relationships between individual things as we have already mentioned) as well as describing how they relate to other classes and properties in a standardised way.[9] Thus, RDFS allows us to build up hierarchies of resources and create taxonomies. These features of the RDFS vocabulary are at the basis of most Semantic Web technologies.

For instance, we can use the rdfs `Class` resource[10] to define a class, in addition to using the rdfs resource `Property`[11] to define a property (a relationship), see Figure 3. Moreover, we can use the properties `rdfs:subClassOf` and `rdfs:subPropertyOf` to define subclass and subproperty hierarchies.

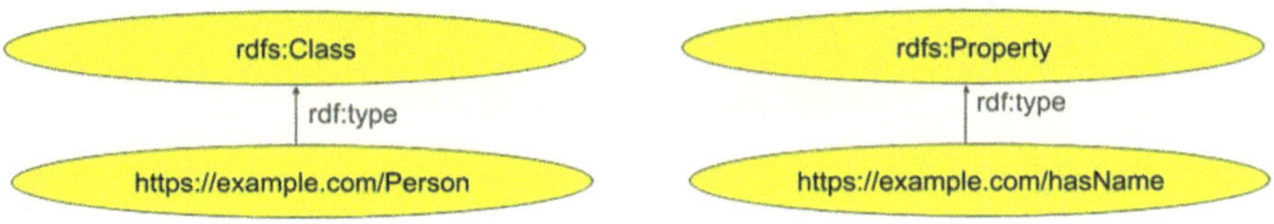

Figure 3: Example Use of rdfs:Class and rdfs:Property.

With these resources, we can create a simple RDF graph to describe the kind of thing that the President of Italy, Sergio Materella, is, in Figure 4, in terms of a simple hierarchy.

Two other important RDFS resources (available to re-use as part of the RDFS vocabulary) are the `Domain` and `Range` classes, together with their related properties. The `Domain` class helps to specify the set of things that a given property ap-

---

8 https://www.w3.org/TR/rdf-schema/ (accessed: Feb 12, 2025).

9 These classes and properties in question can be consulted at https://www.w3.org/TR/rdf-schema/

10 http://www.w3.org/2000/01/rdf-schema#Class or rdfs:Class for short.

11 http://www.w3.org/2000/01/rdf-schema#Property or rdfs:Property.

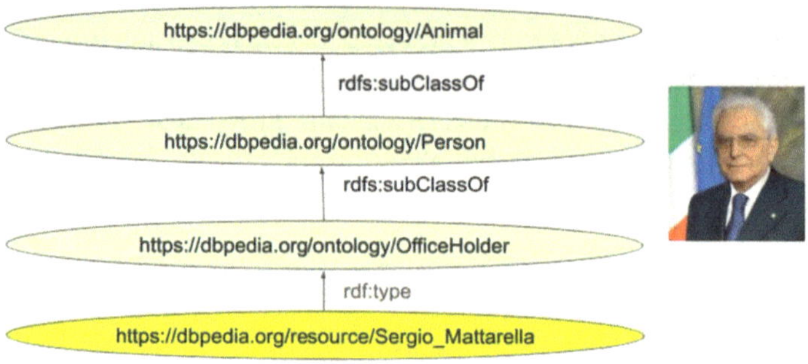

Figure 4: A Simple RDF Graph Describing the Current President of Italy.

plies to, e. g., the property X name of Y has as domain the class Person; it does this together with the RDFS property `domain`. The `Range` class, together with the `range` property, helps instead to define the class or datatype of the property value; e. g., the property X husband of Y has as (domain and) range Person `range`. In Figure 5 we have a simple graph specifying that `http://example.com/hasAge` is of type `rdf:Property`, that its domain is the class `http://example.com/Person` and that its range is `xsd:integer`. That is, X hasAge Y applies to persons and that it associates a person with an integer indicating their age.

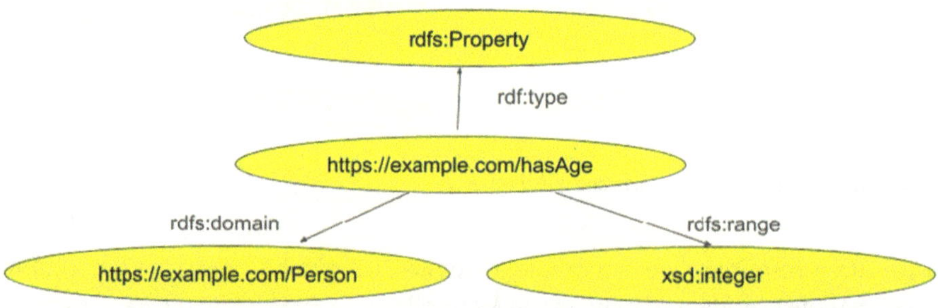

Figure 5: An Example Use of rdfs:domain and rdfs:range.

To summarise the last two subsections, then: RDF is a framework (as well as a meta-model, a language and a vocabulary) which imposes a basic structure on linked data datasets, that is, as a series of subject-predicate-object triples in which the subject and predicates are URIs, and the objects can be either URIs or data literals; since URIs are often shared among triples, RDF datasets can be visualised as networks or graph structures. These URIs represent arbitrary resources which we want to describe in our datasets. In addition RDF also provides a number of fundamental resources which are meant to be re-used in linked data datasets. RDFS, instead, is an extension of RDF which offers further resources allowing data modellers to distinguish a given resource as a class or a property and to define the domains and ranges of properties.

2.5 Serialisations

So far we have represented our RDF examples as diagrams of graphs. This was for purposes of exposition and is obviously not the most efficient means of sharing RDF graphs. Instead, when it comes to actually producing RDF files in a format that we can store, process, or query, then there are a number of different so-called serialisations (or serializations in American English) we can choose between in a given situation based on such desiderata as compatibility with other technologies, human readability, and/or efficiency of processing. All of these serialisations capture the same information so that we can pass between them (that is, convert from one serialisation to another) without losing any information (however, we might lose desirable properties such as efficiency and compatibility with certain kinds of software).

The most common of these serialisation formats are the following:
- RDF/XML
- N-TRIPLES
- TURTLE
- JSON-LD
- RDF-A

Note that the first of these, XML, has long been regarded as the 'default' serialisation for RDF. As XML is not the most readable or efficient of formats, the others are preferable from numerous different points of view. TURTLE, for instance, is the most readable of all these formats for human beings and is often used for didactic or illustrative purposes, but it is less efficient for purposes of machine processing than N-TRIPLES or JSON-LD, which are therefore preferable for most practical purposes. RDF-A, on the other hand, is a means of embedding RDF triples in HTML (and potentially any kind of XML), that is very popular among websites for search engine optimization.

Due to limitations of space we will not go into any detail on these different serialisation formats here or provide any examples, but the interested reader is referred to introductory texts such as (Sakr et al. 2018).

2.6 SPARQL

SPARQL (SPARQL Protocol and RDF Query Language)[12] is the standard Semantic Web query language used to retrieve and manipulate linked data via special online interfaces called SPARQL endpoints. SPARQL looks similar to the SQL standard used for querying relational databases (so the similarity in names isn't a coincidence), but it is designed specifically to query RDF triples via graph traversal, that is, by exploring the graph structure which is native to the RDF framework. By leveraging the interconnected nature of linked data, SPARQL allows users to retrieve information from multiple datasets as though they were a single, unified source. This possibility is vital for the smooth running of the Semantic Web, where data is distributed across thousands of different servers.

A basic SPARQL query consists of a SELECT statement for specifying the variables the user wants to retrieve; a WHERE clause to define the pattern of triples which the query should match; and optional modifiers like LIMIT or ORDER BY to modify the results of the previous clause.

For example, a simple query to find the names of all authors in a dataset might look like this:

```
SELECT ?authorName
WHERE {
  ?author <http://example.org/hasName> ?authorName.
}
```

Here, `?author` and `?authorName` are variables, and the triple pattern in the `WHERE` clause specifies that the query should match any resource (`?author`) with a hasName property, retrieving its corresponding value (`?authorName`). Note that SPARQL also supports advanced features such as `FILTER` for constraints, `UNION` for combining patterns, and `OPTIONAL` for retrieving data that may not always be present.[13]

One thing that should be emphasised in closing this section, is just how useful a language SPARQL is: in terms of allowing users to be able to work with RDF datasets and, more generally, allowing them to fully appreciate the utility and power of linked data as a means of publishing and accessing information. It is therefore important for beginners to gain a familiarity with it early on.

12 A recursive definition as is frequently encountered in such cultural contexts.

13 A full description of the language can be found at https://www.w3.org/TR/sparql11-query/ (accessed: Feb 12, 2025).

3 The Linguistic Open Data cloud

So far, around a couple of thousand datasets have been published as Linked Open Data and the number is growing constantly. Taken together, this collection can be understood as a large network of interlinked datasets (recall the importance of interlinking is part of the definition of linked data itself) that have high levels of interoperability amongst themselves (especially within subject areas and kinds of resource) and each of which is downloadable and reusable with an open license.[14] The Linguistic Open Data (LOD) cloud is a visualisation of this massive RDF knowledge graph, one that is periodically updated to reflect its growth;[15] it can be accessed at https://lod-cloud.net/.

The LOD cloud has been divided into several subject areas, each represented by nodes of a different colour:

- Cross-Domain: Datasets spanning multiple disciplines and contexts.
- Government: Data related to public administration, policies, and operations.
- Publications: Bibliographic data, citation networks, and publishing metadata.
- Life Sciences: Biological, medical, and healthcare data.
- Geography: Geographic and spatial information, including maps and geospatial datasets.
- Social Media: Data from platforms like blogs and social networks.
- User-Generated Content: Collaborative content like wikis, reviews, and comments.
- Media: Metadata about multimedia content, including audio, video, and images.
- Scholarly Data: Academic research data, such as experimental results and collaborations.
- Linguistics: Language-related resources, including lexicons, thesauri, corpora and annotations.

Two of the most well-connected nodes in the whole LOD cloud are DBPedia and Wikidata, the first of these datasets is directly based on the information contained in Wikipedia (Auer et al. 2007), and the second is inspired by Wikipedia (Vrandečić and Krötzsch 2014). In fact DBpedia is a result of the periodic extraction of structured data from Wikipedia, and more precisely the conversion into RDF triples of the information contained in Wikipedia info boxes. The end result is a vast linked

---

14 See Kamocki (2025) for more on open license models.

15 This visualisation only gives a rough estimate of the number of datasets available as linked open data since not all of the links in the graph are still live and a large number of linked open data datasets are not included in the visualisation.

data graph describing relationships between well-known entities such as people, places, and events. Wikidata, on the other hand, is a collaboratively curated knowledge graph and database maintained by the Wikimedia community. Unlike DBpedia, it is not extracted from Wikipedia but built from the ground up, with the aim of offering a multilingual, centralized repository of structured data. Each entity in Wikidata is assigned a unique identifier and enriched with detailed metadata, references, and links to other datasets. Together, DBpedia and Wikidata exemplify the potential of linked data to integrate and enhance human knowledge and to make it accessible on a global scale, both to machines and human beings.

3.1 The Linguistic Linked Open Data cloud

As mentioned above, the LOD cloud is divided into numerous discipline-specific subclouds, one of these, the Linguistic Linked Open Data (LLOD) cloud, focuses specifically on language resources. The LLOD cloud is itself further divided into categories based on the kind of dataset and/or kind of content concerned. These categories are as follows:

- Corpora and Linguistic Annotations
- Lexica and Dictionaries
- Terminologies, Thesauri, and Knowledge Bases
- Linguistic Resource Metadata
- Linguistic Data Categories
- Typological Databases

This list of categories was originally proposed by the Open Linguistics Working Group (OWLG) of the Open Knowledge Foundation (Chiarcos et al. 2012), and in the rest of what follows we give a brief overview of each of them. In particular, we will look at the different vocabularies that exist for encoding resources in each category, as well as some of the most well-known resources in that category. Note that the availability of shared vocabularies is crucial to the success and the smooth running of the linked data cloud insofar as it facilitates the interoperability and reusability of linked data datasets. Therefore, the existence of commonly used vocabularies in each of the categories listed below is a good indicator of the 'health' of that part of the linguistic linked open data cloud.[16]

16 The main indicator being, of course, the number of resources in that category; however the linguistic linked open data cloud diagram may only give a rough estimate of the number of existing linguistic linked open data datasets.

3.2 Corpora and linguistic annotations

The most well-known vocabularies for creating linked data corpora or publish annotations are the NLP Interchange Format (NIF) (Hellmann et al. 2013) and Web Annotation Data model.[17] The first of these, NIF, is a Semantic Web vocabulary for describing strings and their annotation and has a specific focus on NLP pipelines and web services. NIF is used in both academic and industrial applications, and is especially popular among the DBpedia community.

Key NIF vocabulary terms include:

- `Context`: Represents the context of a text fragment.
- `String`: Represents a string within the text.
- `beginIndex` and `endIndex`: Indicate the start and end positions of a text span.
- `annotation`: Links to annotations of the text span.

The Web Annotation Format, on the other hand, is a W3C recommendation that offers a framework for creating and sharing annotations of web resources.

Key terms from this latter vocabulary include the following:

- `Annotation`: Represents an annotation.
- `hasBody`: Links to the body of the annotation.
- `hasTarget`: Links to the target resource being annotated
- `Motivation`: Represents the purpose or intention of the annotation.

Other vocabularies in this category include POWLA (Chiarcos 2012) and CoNLL-RDF (Chiarcos and Fäth 2017). The former is an ontology for representing linguistic annotations, particularly those derived from previous XML-based formats like PAULA (Zeldes et al. 2013); the latter is a subset of NIF, which was designed to be interoperable with (pre-LOD) standards in NLP, especially CoNLL-based ones.

The publication of corpora, especially annotated corpora, as linked data, helps to make them highly interoperable (and permits the use of corpus queries in the powerful SPARQL language that take into consideration information from linked resources) as well as helping to overcome the expressive limitations associated with standards for text encoding such as TEI-XML. The downside is that resulting RDF datasets can be extremely verbose, and this can lead to a large storage overhead and query complexity. Corpora currently listed as being on the LLOD Cloud include:

17 https://www.w3.org/TR/annotation-model/ (accessed: Feb 12, 2025).

- News-100 NIF NER Corpus (100 German news articles from the online news platform news.de annotated for named entities[18]) and the Reuters-128 NIF NER Corpus (128 Reuters' articles annotated for at least one named entity[19]).
- DBPedia abstract corpus NIF: A corpus of manually disambiguated DBpedia abstracts.[20]
- A number of universal dependency treebanks.
- A number of Latin corpora made available by the Linking Latin (LiLa) project (Passarotti et al. 2020) including the Index Thomisticus Treebank,[21] St. Augustine's Confessions[22] and the Fibonacci Corpus.[23]

3.3 Lexicons and dictionaries

One of the most notable success stories in the whole field of linguistic linked data, the OntoLex-Lemon vocabulary was first published in a community report by the W3C Ontology-Lexicon group in 2016,[24] and was originally designed as a model for enriching ontologies with linguistic information; it has however evolved far beyond this initial motivation. Today, it is widely regarded as the *de facto* standard for creating and publishing lexicons on the Semantic Web (whether or not they are directly linked to ontologies). Its structured approach to representing lexical data has made it an essential tool for researchers and developers working with lexical resources in linked data environments.

The OntoLex-Lemon model has been widely adopted in numerous projects and has played a key role in the conversion of significant linguistic datasets. It has been used to publish resources such as the Princeton Wordnet (as well as many other wordnets[25]), Wiktionary (Sérasset 2015), and the Apertium series of dictionaries (Gracia et al. 2018). Moreover, the LiLa project has made a number of lexical resources available; these include an RDF version of the 19th century Lewis Short

18 https://aksw.org/Projects/N3NERNEDNIF.html (accessed: Feb 12, 2025).

19 https://raw.githubusercontent.com/AKSW/n3-collection/master/Reuters-128.ttl (accessed: Feb 12, 2025).

20 https://downloads.dbpedia.org/2015-04/ext/nlp/abstracts/https://downloads.dbpedia.org/2015-04/ext/nlp/abstracts/ (accessed: Feb 12, 2025).

21 https://lila-erc.eu/data/corpora/ITTB/id/corpus (accessed: Feb 12, 2025).

22 https://lila-erc.eu/data/corpora/CIRCSELatinLibrary/id/corpus/Confessiones (accessed: Feb 12, 2025).

23 https://lila-erc.eu/data/corpora/CorpusFibonacci/id/corpus (accessed: Feb 12, 2025).

24 https://www.w3.org/2016/05/ontolex/ (accessed: Feb 12, 2025).

25 https://globalwordnet.github.io/schemas/#rdf (accessed: Feb 12, 2025).

Latin-English dictionary,[26] the Latin wordnet,[27] and Latin Vallex 2.0, a Latin valency lexicon.[28] By providing a standardized framework for representing lexical data, it has facilitated interoperability and accessibility across diverse lexical resources, demonstrating the potential of linked open data as a means of making language resources available.

The popularity of OntoLex-Lemon can, at least in part, be attributed to how naturally the content of many kinds of lexicons lends itself to being represented in a graph-based format. Lexical data tends to be highly structured, with clear relationships between words, meanings, and related concepts, making it (relatively) easy to capture in a conceptual model; moreover, this structure tends to be quite regular, or highly conventionalised, which again makes the use of shared, standard vocabularies highly appropriate. OntoLex-Lemon provides an efficient and intuitive way to organize and publish lexical data, producing results that are typically concise rather than overly verbose. Another important factor in the OntoLex-Lemon's success is the active status of the W3C Ontology-Lexica group[29] which originally published the original OntoLex-Lemon model and which continues to maintain and to expand upon it. For instance, in 2019, the W3C group published its first extension to the original model, lexicog, dealing with lexicographic resources[30] and the group is currently developing two new extensions to the original, one of which is concerned with the encoding of detailed morphological information, and the other with frequency, corpus and attestation information. The group was and remains open to participation from anyone interested in contributing regardless of background. Regular meetings foster collaboration and reinforce the role of community-driven efforts in shaping linguistic linked data standards.

Some of the principal classes and properties in OntoLex-Lemon are:

- `Lexicon`: The object representing the lexicon as a whole.
- `Lexical Entry`: An entry in a lexicon is a container for one or several forms and one or several meanings of a lexeme.
- `Lexical Form`: An inflectional form of an entry. A given lexical form may have several representations in different orthographies.
- `Lexical Sense`: A sense links the lexical entry to the ontological reference used to describe its meaning.

---

26 https://lila-erc.eu/data/lexicalResources/LewisShort/Lexicon (accessed: Feb 12, 2025).

27 https://lila-erc.eu/data/lexicalResources/LatinWordNet/Lexicon (accessed: Feb 12, 2025).

28 https://lila-erc.eu/data/lexicalResources/LatinVallex/Lexicon (accessed: Feb 12, 2025).

29 https://www.w3.org/community/ontolex/ (accessed: Feb 12, 2025).

30 https://www.w3.org/2019/09/lexicog/ (accessed: Feb 12, 2025).

3.4 Terminologies. Thesauri, and knowledge bases

In terms of vocabularies/models for encoding knowledge organisation systems, that is structured vocabularies, taxonomies, thesauri, and basic classification schemes, as RDF, we can single out the SKOS (Simple Knowledge Organization System) (Miles and Pérez-Agüera 2007). SKOS allows for the description of concepts and their relationships (above all hierarchical relations) using a small number of core classes and properties. Everything is based around the core SKOS class `Concept`. Individuals of this class can be assigned to concept schemes and arranged in hierarchies using the SKOS properties `narrower` and `broader` (there also exist SKOS properties for specifying how closely two concepts match across concept schemes and for adding definitions and notes). In addition SKOS concepts can have labels in different languages, these labels can be either preferred labels (marked using the property `skos:prefLabel`) or alternative labels (marked using the property `skos:altLabel`). Take, for instance, the following listing, which shows the association of different labels with the same concept (that of butterfly)

```
ex:butterfly rdf:type skos:Concept;
     skos:prefLabel "butterfly"@en;
     skos:altLabel "rhopalocera"@en;
     skos:prefLabel "papillon"@fr;
     skos:prefLabel "farfalla"@it.
```

We illustrate the use of the narrower and broader labels to define a small hierarchy of three elements (insect >butterfly > painted lady) in the following listing:

```
ex:insect rdf:type skos:Concept;
     skos:prefLabel "insect"@en;
     skos:narrower ex:butterfly.
ex:butterfly rdf:type skos:Concept;
     skos:prefLabel "butterfly"@en;
     skos:broader ex:insect;
     skos:narrower ex:paintedlady.
ex:paintedlady rdf:type skos:Concept;
     skos:prefLabel "Painted Lady"@en;
     skos:broader ex:butterfly.
```

SKOS has become a popular way of publishing knowledge organisation systems, especially taxonomies and thesauri. This is thanks in no small part to the existence of numerous different free tools for working with SKOS resources. Here we can mention SKOSMOS, a well-known open source vocabulary browser for SKOS resources which has been adopted as an interface by a number of national/infrastructure specific vocabulary platforms, including Rossio,[31] a Portuguese national platform, Vocabs[32] the DARIAH vocabulary platform, and the CESSDA thesaurus service.[33] Another popular SKOS based tool is VocBench which is used for editing SKOS vocabularies (along with other kinds of resources) (Stellato et al. 2020).

Moving on to terminologies, a number of proposals have been made over the last few years for encoding terminological resources, and OntoLex-Lemon also has some provision for encoding terminological information, but so far there is no popular, widely used dedicated vocabulary for encoding terminologies in RDF and no general agreed upon approach to converting terminologies bases from TermBase Exchange (TBX) (International Organization for Standardization 2019) into RDF (something which would be a useful step towards encouraging terminologists to adopt linked data more widely). However, there are plans to update the core of OntoLex in order to facilitate interoperability with standards like TBX.

3.5 Linguistic resource metadata and linguistic data categories

Vocabularies for creating linguistic metadata (to be made use of in addition to more general vocabularies for metadata such as Dublin Core[34] and DCMI Metadata Terms[35]) are key for making linked data linguistic resources findable in the first place. Two key models in this respect are lime (Fiorelli et al. 2015), the metadata module of OntoLex-Lemon, which is inspired by the VoID vocabulary[36] and provides metadata categories for OntoLex-Lemon lexical resources, and the more broadly focused MetaShare ontology, which provides extensive coverage for language resources of all kinds (Gavrilidou et al. 2012, Khan et al. 2022).

Another important category of resources for ensuring interoperability across separate individual linguistic datasets, are Linguistic Data Category Registries, as they provide standardized descriptors for linguistic concepts and annotations. One of the most well-known of these within the context of linguistic linked data is Lex-

31 https://vocabs.rossio.fcsh.unl.pt/pub/en/ (accessed: Feb 12, 2025).
32 https://vocabs.dariah.eu/en/ (accessed: Feb 12, 2025).
33 https://thesauri.cessda.eu/en/ (accessed: Feb 12, 2025).
34 https://www.dublincore.org/ (accessed: Feb 12, 2025).
35 https://www.dublincore.org/specifications/dublin-core/dcmi-terms/ (accessed: Feb 12, 2025).
36 https://www.w3.org/TR/void/ (accessed: Feb 12, 2025).

Info[37] (Cimiano et al. 2011), which incorporates categories from the now-defunct ISOCat registry, and provides OntoLex-Lemon with standardized linguistic categories, helping to maintain consistency and clarity in linked data representations of language resources.

3.6 Typological databases

There are not any widely used vocabularies for the creation of typological databases in linked data (at the time of writing there are no resources of this category in the linguistic linked open data cloud either); however, see Khan et al. 2022 for a summary of the various different efforts which have been so far made towards defining vocabularies for the creation of typological databases. In fact, the latter article gives a reasonably in depth detailed overview of past and existing vocabularies for all of the categories listed above.

4 Conclusions

In this chapter, we have given a brief overview of linked open data, focusing on those aspects of the latter which are of most relevance when it comes to publishing linguistic data. In particular, in the latter half of the chapter, we have looked at the linguistic linked open data (LLOD) cloud, the sector of the linked open data cloud which deals specifically with linguistic datasets. At the time of writing (31-01-2025), the linguistic linked open data cloud consists of 1,350 datasets according to the site hosting the cloud; however, the actual number of linguistic linked open data datasets is likely to be much higher – for instance a lot of SKOS vocabularies aren't listed on the cloud but are available via numerous vocabulary platforms with an open license. In any case, as the popularity of linguistic linked data grows, thanks in large part to the success of projects such as Linking Latin (Passarotti et al. 2020), but also to the increasing uptake of linked data as a means of publishing data in a Findable Accessible Interoperable and Reusable (FAIR) way, we foresee a much more sustained augmentation in the linguistic linked open data cloud in the near future.

37 https://lexinfo.net/ (accessed: Feb 12, 2025).

Bibliography

Auer, Sören, Christian Bizer, Georgi Kobilarov, Jens Lehmann, Richard Cyganiak & Zachary Ives. 2007. DBpedia: A nucleus for a web of open data. In Karl Aberer, Key-Sun Choi, Natasha Noy, Dean Allemang, Kyung-Il Lee, Lyndon Nixon, Jennifer Golbeck, et al.. (eds.), *The semantic web*, Vol. 4825, 722–735. Berlin & Heidelberg: Springer. https://doi.org/10.1007/978-3-540-76298-0_52.

Berners-Lee, Tim & Mark Fischetti. 1999. *Weaving the web: The original design and ultimate destiny of the World Wide Web by its inventor*. San Francisco: Harper San Francisco.

Chiarcos, Christian. 2012. POWLA: Modeling linguistic corpora in OWL/DL. In Elena Simperl, Philipp Cimiano, Axel Polleres Oscar Corcho & Valentina Presutti (eds.), *The semantic web: Research and applications*, Vol. 7295, 225–239. Berlin & Heidelberg: Springer. https://doi.org/10.1007/978-3-642-30284-8_22.

Chiarcos, Christian & Christian Fäth. 2017. CoNLL-RDF: Linked corpora done in an NLP-friendly way. In Jorge Gracia, Francis Bond, John P. McCrae, Paul Buitelaar, Christian Chiarcos & Sebastian Hellmann (eds.), *Language, data, and knowledge*, Vol. 10318, 74–88. Cham: Springer. https://doi.org/10.1007/978-3-319-59888-8_6.

Chiarcos, Christian, Sebastian Hellmann & Sebastian Nordhoff. 2012. The Open Linguistics Working Group of the Open Knowledge Foundation. In Sebastian Hellmann, Christian Chiarcos & Sebastian Nordhoff (eds.), *Linked data in linguistics*, 153–160. Berlin & Heidelberg: Springer. https://doi.org/10.1007/978-3-642-28249-2_15.

Cimiano, Philipp, Paul Buitelaar, John McCrae & Michael Sintek. 2011. LexInfo: A declarative model for the lexicon-ontology interface. *Journal of Web Semantics* 9(1). 29–51. https://doi.org/10.1016/j.websem.2010.11.001.

Fiorelli, Manuel, Armando Stellato, John P. McCrae, Philipp Cimiano & Maria Teresa Pazienza. 2015. LIME: The metadata module for OntoLex. In Fabien Gandon, Marta Sabou, Harald Sack, Claudia d'Amato, Philippe Cudré-Mauroux & Antoine Zimmermann (eds.), *The semantic web. Latest advances and new domains*, Vol. 9088, 321–336. Cham: Springer. https://doi.org/10.1007/978-3-319-18818-8_20.

Gavrilidou, Maria, Penny Labropoulou, Eleni Desipri, Stelios Piperidis, Monica Monachini, Francesca Frontini, Thierry Declerck, Gil Francopoulo. Victoria Arranz & Valérie Mapelli. 2012. The META-SHARE metadata schema for the description of language resources.

Gracia, Jorge, Marta Villegas, Asunción Gómez-Pérez & Núria Bel. 2018. The Apertium bilingual dictionaries on the web of data. *Semantic Web* 9(2). 231–240. https://doi.org/10.3233/SW-170258.

Hellmann, Sebastian, Jens Lehmann, Sören Auer & Martin Brümmer. 2013. Integrating NLP using Linked Data. In Camille Salinesi, Moira C. Norrie & Óscar Pastor (eds.), *Advanced information systems engineering*, Vol. 7908, 98–113. Berlin & Heidelberg: Springer. https://doi.org/10.1007/978-3-642-41338-4_7.

International Organization for Standardization. 2019. *Management of terminology resources – TermBase eXchange (TBX) (ISO 30042:2019)*. https://www.iso.org/standard/62510.html.

International Organization for Standardization. 2023. *Code for individual languages and language groups (ISO 639:2023)*. https://www.iso.org/standard/74575.html.

Khan, Anas Fahad, Christian Chiarcos, Thierry Declerck, Daniela Gifu, Elena González-Blanco García, Jorge Gracia, Maxim Ionov, et al.. 2022. When linguistics meets web technologies: Recent advances in modelling linguistic linked data. *Semantic Web* 13(6). 987–1050. https://doi.org/10.3233/SW-222859.

Miles, Alistair & José R. Pérez-Agüera. 2007. SKOS: Simple knowledge organisation for the Web. *Cataloging & Classification Quarterly* 43(3–4). 69–83. https://doi.org/10.1300/J104v43n03_04.

Nurmikko-Fuller, Terhi. 2024. *Linked data for digital humanities*. London & New York: Routledge.
Passarotti, Marco, Francesco Mambrini, Greta Franzini, Flavio Massimiliano Cecchini, Eleonora Litta, Giovanni Moretti, Paolo Ruffolo & Rachele Sprugnoli. 2020. Interlinking through lemmas: The lexical collection of the LiLa Knowledge Base of Linguistic Resources for Latin. *Studi e Saggi Linguistici* 58(1). https://doi.org/10.4454/ssl.v58i1.277.
Romary, Laurent. 2025. International standards for the identification and the description of languages and their varieties. In Piotr Bański, Ulrich Heid & Laura Herzberg (eds.), *Harmonising language data: Standards for linguistic resources*, de Gruyter.
Sakr, Sherif, Marcin Wylot, Raghava Mutharaju, Danh Le Phuoc & Irini Fundulaki. 2018. *Linked data: Storing, querying, and reasoning*. Cham, Switzerland: Springer.
Sérasset, Gilles. 2015. DBnary: Wiktionary as a Lemon-based multilingual lexical resource in RDF. *Semantic Web* 6(4). 355–361. https://doi.org/10.3233/SW-140147.
Stellato, Armando, Manuel Fiorelli, Andrea Turbati, Tiziano Lorenzetti, Willem Van Gemert, Denis Dechandon, Christine Laaboudi-Spoiden, et al.. 2020. VocBench 3: A collaborative Semantic Web editor for ontologies, thesauri and lexicons. *Semantic Web* 11(5). 855–881. https://doi.org/10.3233/SW-200370.
Kamocki, Paweł. 2025. Taxonomy of legal and ethical metadata for language resources. In Piotr Bański, Ulrich Heid & Laura Herzberg (eds.), *Harmonising language data: Standards for linguistic resources*. Berlin & Boston: De Gruyter.
Vrandečić, Denny & Markus Krötzsch. 2014. Wikidata: A free collaborative knowledgebase. *Communications of the ACM* 57(10). 78–85. https://doi.org/10.1145/2629489.
Walmsley, Priscilla. 2002. *Definitive XML schema*. Upper Saddle River, NJ: Prentice Hall PTR.
Wartena, Christian. 2025. Character encoding and its importance for text resources. In Piotr Bański, Ulrich Heid & Laura Herzberg (eds.), *Harmonising language data: Standards for linguistic resources*. Berlin & Boston: De Gruyter.
Zeldes, Amir, Florian Zipser & Arne Neumann. 2013. *PAULA XML Documentation*, Technical report.

Stephanie Evert, Timm Weber, Steffen Bothe, Philipp Heinrich, and
Alexander Piperski

Data exploitation: corpus queries

Abstract: This chapter provides a systematic overview of corpus query languages (CQLs) and their close relation to the underlying corpus data models. Starting from an overview of the recent history of CQLs, which has led to a plethora of specialised and mutually incompatible corpus management systems, we explain key technical concepts and outline recent efforts towards standardisation of a corpus query lingua franca (CQLF). We then take a closer look at two major paradigms that have become widely-used de facto standards: finite-state queries for tabular data models, exemplified by the IMS Open Corpus Workbench (CWB), and anchored queries for graph-based data models, exemplified by the ANNIS platform. Recent developments aim to decouple query language design from specific implementations via an intermediate representation (most notably KorAP/KoralQuery) and to provide better support for end users through simplified query languages and visual query builders. The chapter aims to guide both developers and users in choosing or designing corpus query systems that meet their linguistic and technical requirements.

Keywords: corpus query language (CQL), corpus management system, data model, corpus query lingua franca (CQLF), CWB, CQP, ANNIS, KorAP

1 Introduction

Modern-day corpus research would not be possible without sophisticated computational tools for analysing corpora, i. e. databases of machine-readable text together with metadata and linguistic annotation of varying complexity. Besides corpus linguistics itself, many other fields also are concerned with analysing and interpreting natural language texts, including the digital humanities, computational lexicography, computational social science, discourse studies, and corpus-assisted language learning. Providing corpus management systems with user-friendly interfaces is essential for enabling broader adoption (McEnery and Hardie 2012), and the functionality of software solutions largely determines the practical toolbox of researchers (Anthony 2013: 141).

Stephanie Evert, Timm Weber, Steffen Bothe, Philipp Heinrich, Alexander Piperski, Computational Corpus Linguistics, Germanistik und Komparatistik, Friedrich-Alexander-Universität Erlangen-Nürnberg, Bismarckstr. 6, Erlangen, Germany, e-mails: stephanie.evert@fau.de, timm.weber@fau.de, steffen.bothe@fau.de, philipp.heinrich@fau.de, aleksandr.piperski@fau.de

https://doi.org/10.1515/9783112208212-013

Databases are only useful if they can be searched for specific information, which is called *querying*. For instance, researchers interested in lexico-grammatical patterns (e. g. constructions such as *the X-er the Y-er*) or specific grammatical structures (e. g. deeply nested noun phrases) need to choose a corpus management system that enables them to search for such structures with suitable corpus queries. They also have to make sure that the corpus includes the necessary linguistic annotation (e. g. part-of-speech tags or syntactic parse trees). Such choices are complicated by the fact that many corpus management systems and query languages have been developed over the years. They are often specialised for a particular application setting or corpus and have widely different capabilities and little interoperability. Moreover, precise documentation of the query language and underlying data model is often lacking. This chapter aims to help readers navigate the ecosystem of corpus query languages. We outline recent efforts towards standardisation and better interoperability and take a closer look at two major paradigms that have become de facto standards, with mature and widely-used software implementations.

1.1 A brief history of corpus management systems

Since the beginnings of corpus linguistics in the mid-20th century, developers of corpus management systems have faced a fundamental challenge: how to structure large amounts of linguistically annotated text in a way that allows for efficient retrieval and meaningful analysis. The solutions to this challenge evolved significantly over the years, as new technology became available and increasingly complex linguistic annotation had to be supported, leading to a plethora of data models and storage representations. While structured data (e. g. the tables of a relational database) are typically searched with standardised query languages such as SQL (Chamberlin and Boyce 1974), no comparable standard has been established for querying semi-structured corpus data.

When the first machine-readable corpora were compiled – such as the million-word Brown Corpus stored on 1,600 feet of magnetic tape – they had to be searched with bespoke computer programs running on mainframe computers such as the IBM 7070 Data Processing System at Brown University (Kučera and Francis 1967: xxiv–xxv). However, the need for user-friendly interfaces for querying corpora was soon recognised; writing a separate program for each corpus search and running it on a mainframe computer was not tenable in the longer term.

While early text processing tools such as TUSTEP go back as far as the 1960s and are still in active development (Schälkle and Ott 2023), we want to focus here on the history of the last 35 years, and especially on query languages. We are not concerned with additional quantitative functionality such as collocation analysis (Evert 2009) or keyword analysis (Culpeper and Demmen 2015) provided by corpus platforms such as BNCweb (Hoffmann et al. 2008) or CQPweb (Hardie 2012) without significant extensions of the underlying search logic.[1]

Corpus tools have developed rapidly since the early 1990s, with query systems evolving from simple text-based tools to sophisticated platforms handling billions of tokens across multiple languages and annotation layers. They have evolved alongside linguistic corpora. Early on, most corpora were monolingual and relatively small, but large-scale initiatives soon followed, such as the 100-million word British National Corpus (BNC, Aston and Burnard 1998) or the billion-word corpora of LDC's Gigaword project (Graff and Cieri 2003). Parallel and multilingual corpora like the 90-million-word corpus by Armstrong-Warwick et al. (1994) and later Europarl (Koehn 2005) further broadened the scope. The 2000s saw an explosion in the scale and diversity of corpora, with web-based resources like WaCKy (Baroni et al. 2009) and the COW family of corpora (Schäfer 2015) offering many billions of tokens of text in multiple languages, which created new challenges for storage and search (Gärtner and Jung 2020: 6308).

Meanwhile, as digital infrastructure matured, corpus representation transitioned to more standardised formats like Standard Generalized Markup Language (SGML) and, later, XML with UTF-8 encoding, enabling broader compatibility and web-based access (Gärtner and Jung 2020: 6307). Tools such as SARA (the SGML Aware Retrieval Application developed for the BNC) mirrored these changes, in this case with the development of the successor XAIRA adapted to XML-based corpora (Burnard and Dodd 2003: 142). More general corpus management systems followed the same trajectory: early tools like COSMAS (Bodmer 1996), IMS Corpus Workbench (CWB), and Linguistic DataBase (LDB, Halteren et al. 2002) offered some of the first powerful query languages. Perhaps the most influential system from this era was the CWB architecture (Christ 1994, Evert and Hardie 2011) with its corpus query processor (CQP) component, which was adopted widely and continues to serve as the back end for many corpus platforms today (Gärtner and Jung 2020: 6309), together with closely related implementations such as (No)Sketch Engine, Corpuscle (formerly Korpuskel, Meurer 2012), Poliqarp (Janus and Przepiórkowski 2007). Other systems based their implementation on a relational database, automatically translating corpus queries into SQL. Well-known examples are Mark Davies's web-based corpus platforms[2] (Davies 2005) and the LiRI Corpus Platform (LCP, Schaber

1 Of course, the list of corpus management systems mentioned in this section is by no means exhaustive.

2 https://www.english-corpora.org/, https://www.corpusdelespanol.org/

et al. 2023). Stand-alone tools such as WordSmith (Scott 2024) or AntConc (Anthony 2005) also offer their own search systems, often based on regular expressions.

The next generation introduced logic- and tree-based querying with tools such as TIGERSearch (Lezius 2002), TGrep2 (Rohde 2005), and ICE Corpus Utility Program (ICECUP, Nelson et al. 2002), supporting increasingly complex syntactic and semantic annotations and shifting over time from phrase structure to dependency trees and layered annotation models. This period also saw the emergence of commercial platforms, with the Sketch Engine (Kilgarriff et al. 2004) offering paid corpus management and exploration on a web-based platform. Systems like ANNIS (Dipper et al. 2004) started creating ecosystem approaches with metamodels such as Salt (Zipser 2012), converters, and search modules (Gärtner and Jung 2020: 6310). XPath and XQuery emerged as a query method for XML-based corpora, and specialised tools were developed for morphologically rich languages such as Poliqarp (Janus and Przepiórkowski 2007). As multimodal corpora began to emerge and annotation became increasingly complex, new query languages such as the NXT Query Language (NQL) emerged (Carletta et al. 2003). These supported multi-level segmentation, addressing the needs of richly annotated multimodal corpora (Gärtner and Jung 2020: 6310).

1.2 Chapter overview

Despite decades of progress, the field remains rather fragmented due to technological diversity, inconsistent data models and query languages, lack of widely accepted standards, and limited reuse of existing solutions, which hints at a lack of cooperation (Gärtner and Jung 2020: 6314). This is also highlighted by the overview of platforms for spoken-language corpora in Frick and Schmidt (2025). The present chapter aims to help readers navigate the ecosystem of corpus query languages. We begin with an overview of the most important technical concepts (Section 2) and look at recent standardisation efforts and progress towards a *corpus query lingua franca* (CQLF, Section 3). We then address the two most important de facto standards for corpus management systems, with a particular focus on their data models and query languages: Section 4 describes the tabular data model and finite-state queries implemented by CWB and its derivatives; Section 5 describes the graph-based data model and anchored queries underlying the different incarnations of ANNIS. Finally, Section 6 deals with current developments towards better interoperability (achieved in KorAP/KoralQuery via an intermediate representation layer between query language and implementation) and improved user-friendliness (e. g. in the form of visual query builders).

2 Basic concepts

We begin by defining some fundamental concepts and terminology. A corpus is understood to be a collection of machine-readable texts, the primary data, together with metadata (information about the texts such as author, date, genre, etc.) as well as structural markup (e. g. sections, headings, paragraphs, footnotes) and linguistic annotation (most typically part-of-speech (POS) tags and lemmatisation, but also more complex annotation such as dependency parsing). We refer to metadata, structural markup, and linguistic annotation jointly as annotation. Our focus in this chapter is on text corpora consisting of written language or transcripts of spoken language, while querying multimodal corpora of spoken language is addressed in Frick and Schmidt (2025). From a formal perspective, a text corpus contains semi-structured data: unstructured text as primary data (essentially a sequence of characters) combined with clearly structured annotation (usually represented via mathematical data structures and pre-defined tagsets). Note that we do not make any assumptions about the particular representation format and encoding of the corpus.

In order to work with corpora, i. e. to search for relevant information or carry out quantitative analyses, the primary data and annotation are usually accessed via specialised software tools that we refer to as corpus management systems. A corpus management system minimally combines functionality for indexing corpora, storing them either in an efficient custom file format or a database back end, and for querying the indexed corpora, i. e. searching for patterns of interest to users and returning matches with selected annotation (as illustrated in Figure 1).

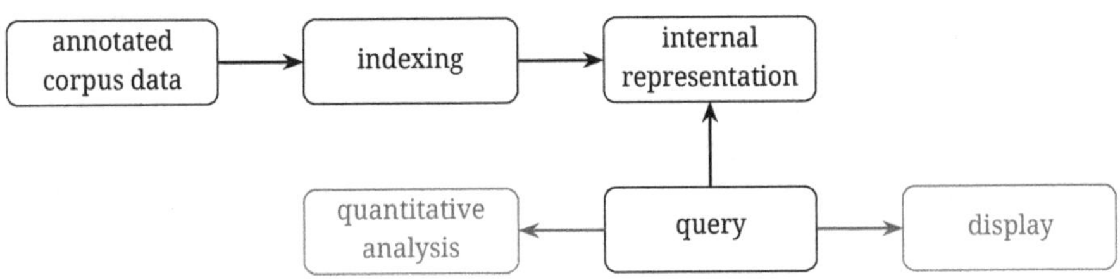

Figure 1: Basic architecture of a corpus management system. Additional components often included in a more comprehensive corpus platform are shown in blue.

Corpus management systems might also encompass additional components such as a graphical user interface or modules for quantitative analysis and visualisation (shown as blue boxes in Figure 1); well-known examples of such comprehensive corpus platforms are Corpus Explorer (Rüdiger and Oliver 2018), CQPweb (Hardie 2012), and Sketch Engine (Kilgarriff et al. 2014). Our focus here is entirely on indexing and querying, which are central components of any corpus platform. Different corpus query languages (CQLs) have been developed. CQLs are domain-specific languages (DSLs) tailored to the semi-structured combination of primary text and annotation in a text corpus.

The particular design of a CQL is usually deeply intertwined with the corpus data model (or simply "data model") of the corpus management system that implements the CQL. A corpus data model defines the logical representation of corpus data – primary texts, metadata, structural markup, and linguistic annotation – within the context of a corpus management system. It is "the set of concepts and data categories that underlies all [...] indexing and querying" (Evert and Hardie 2011: 5). The primary texts are almost always represented as a sequence of tokens, which are "non-empty contiguous sequence[s] of graphemes or phonemes in a document" (ISO 24623-1: 3.10) that roughly correspond to words and punctuation symbols. Whitespace between tokens is often omitted from the data model, though some data models preserve the primary data as a sequence of individual characters, with tokens linked to character spans. Annotation is usually encoded in the form of one or more annotation layers over the token sequence. Metadata, structural markup, and different kinds of linguistic annotation require annotation layers of many different types, including token-level annotation (e. g. POS tags, lemmata), text-level annotation (e. g. metadata), span-level annotation (e. g. structural markup, named entities), inter-corpus span alignment (e. g. sentence alignment), ordered trees (e. g. XML markup, phrase-structure parsing), and directed acyclic graphs (e. g. dependency graphs over tokens). The formal representation chosen for such layers crucially determines which patterns can efficiently be indexed and queried.

The purpose of a corpus query is to satisfy the search need of a user, which is an "information pattern that [the] user wants to locate in a corpus, based on the primary data stream and/or simplex or complex annotation" (ISO 24623-2: 3.6). Search needs range from (possibly case-insensitive) search for fixed words or phrases over flexible lexico-grammatical patterns (involving POS tags, lemmata, structural markup, and metadata) to complex syntactic patterns in parse trees or dependency graphs. The result set of a corpus query consists of all occurrences in the corpus that match the desired information pattern. In the simplest case, it can be represented as a list of token spans; occurrences of more complex patterns may be discontinuous and extend over multiple annotation layers. CQLs differ both in their expressiveness – which determines the complexity of patterns that can be searched for and the types of annotation layers that can be processed – and their query syntax – i. e. the specific notation used to express a corpus query. For example, the CQP query language has powerful capabilities for searching sequences of tokens, e. g. three or more adjectives immediately preceding the lemma *house*. In CQP query syntax, this search need can be expressed as shown in Listing 1.

```
[pos = "ADJ"]{3,} [lemma = "house"]
within s;
```

Listing 1: Example of a query in CQP syntax (with line numbers added in the left margin).

Each item in square brackets matches a single token with the specified properties, the quantifier `{3,}` requires at least three repetitions, and `within s` ensures that matches do not cross sentence boundaries. Note that it is a mistake to think of a CQL merely as a query syntax: the same search pattern could be expressed in an entirely different notation, or the same syntax might have different semantics in two CQLs. A CQL is best understood as the combination of a query syntax (i. e. the notation of a query) and corresponding semantics (i. e. the search need expressed by the query) with an underlying data model (which delimits the types of annotation accessible to queries).

In addition to the corpus data model, a corpus management system also has to define index data structures and file formats for storing corpus data in memory and on disk (possibly delegated to a database back end). This physical representation may impose additional limitations on the corpus data that can be stored (for example, the maximum size of a CWB-indexed corpus is slightly over two billion tokens); it also determines which access patterns can be implemented efficiently (within the boundaries set by the data model) and whether an indexed corpus can be modified or extended. Similarly, a CQL has to be implemented by a query engine in order to carry out the actual corpus search. The design and coding of this query engine (as well as the indexing library used for access to the corpus data) can have a profound impact on how efficiently different queries can be matched. A well-known example is that the CQP query engine is relatively slow for the query in listing 1. The same query is matched far more efficiently by other engines such as Corpuscle (Meurer 2012, 2020) and Sketch Engine (Rábara et al. 2017), but with the help of entirely different optimisation strategies. Finally, a corpus management system has to specify the input format(s) in which the primary data and annotation layers can be provided for indexing. Despite their importance for practical applications, input formats have no bearing on the data model and expressiveness of a CQL. Like physical storage models and the implementation details of query engines, they are thus beyond the scope of this chapter.

3 CQLF – a metamodel for corpus query languages

The standardisation of data models for structured data (e. g. relational databases, XML, RDF/OWL) quickly led to the development of standardised retrieval DSLs (SQL,

XQuery, SPARQL) with (more or less) precisely defined semantics. This provided enormous benefit both to users (who have a choice between different query engines using the same query language and API, so they can easily benefit from technological innovation) and to developers (who do not have to invent their own query language and can focus on a robust and efficient implementation). Unfortunately, a similar standardisation process has not taken place for corpus queries, resulting in a plethora of competing corpus management systems with diverging data models, query languages, physical storage models, and query execution strategies. Users have to settle on one of these systems with all its strengths, weaknesses, and limitations, their choice often dictated by a corpus platform or graphical user interface they want to use.

A likely explanation for this discrepancy is the fact that data models and query languages for structured data are usually based on a well-understood mathematical formalism such as relational calculus (Codd 1970). By contrast, the complexities of semi-structured corpus data were often addressed by specialised corpus management systems that targeted the specific requirements of a particular user group or the annotation of a particular corpus (cf. Section 1). The CQLs emerging from these efforts not only used their own query syntax but were also fundamentally different in their expressiveness and query semantics, often relying on mutually incompatible data models. As an additional problem, many of these corpus management systems lack thorough documentation. Typically, the focus is on explaining the query syntax, while the data model and query semantics are only sketched broadly or described in colloquial terms (e. g. CWB in Christ 1994). Quite often, the source code of a system is the only precise documentation (if it is available at all). A notable and relatively early exception is the NITE XML Toolkit (NXT, Carletta et al. 2003) with its NXT object model (NOM, Evert et al. 2003) and query language (NQL, Evert and Voormann 2003), both of which have precise mathematical definitions.

More recently, efforts have begun to work towards an international standard for a Corpus Query Lingua Franca (CQLF). Due to the reasons outlined above and the resulting lack of common ground, it was unrealistic for the community to agree quickly on a standardised data model and CQL.[3] Instead, two ISO standards now provide a metamodel for characterising CQLs as a first step. CQLF-1 (ISO 24623-1) broadly classifies CQLs into three levels according to their capabilities. Recognising the importance of the underlying data model for a query language, the levels are

3 While the LAF standard (ISO 24612) proposes a common data model in the form of annotation graphs, most existing corpus management systems prefer to rely on custom data models tailored to their indexing approach and query engine.

described primarily in terms of the types of annotation layers that can be queried. Each level is further subdivided into multiple modules (Bański et al. 2016: 2806):

- Level 1 (Linear): (a) plain-text, (b) segmentation, (c) simple annotation
- Level 2 (Complex): (a) hierarchical, (b) dependency, (c) span containment
- Level 3 (Concurrent): (a) paradigmatic, (b) overlapping

Level 1 CQLs typically focus on corpora as sequences of tokens (module 1a) with token-level annotation (1c) and simple structural markup (1b).[4] Section 4 discusses CWB as a typical example of such a data model and CQL in detail. Level 2 CQLs focus on more complex structural annotation, either in the form of hierarchically nested trees (2a) or directed acyclic dependency graphs (2b). A simplified form of structural annotation is containment between character or token spans, which provides an approximation of hierarchical structure in CWB (module 2c). CQLs need not support all three modules in order to be classified into level 2. Section 5 takes a closer look at ANNIS with a data model and CQL that support all level 2 modules. Level 3 CQLs support concurrent annotation including overlapping spans (module 3b); see Bański and Diewald (2025) for a more thorough account. In practice, it is often difficult to assign a given CQL to a unique level. The CQP query language of CWB is primarily a level 1 CQL, but also covers aspects of level 2 (span containment, 2c) and level 3 (overlapping spans, 3b).

CQLF-2 (ISO 24623-2) refines this coarse classification into a fine-grained taxonomy for describing the expressiveness of different CQLs and comparing their capabilities, called the CQLF Ontology (Evert et al. 2020: 3347).[5] It seems natural to think of CQL capabilities in terms of general functionalities such as Annotation (search based on linguistic annotation), Repetition (multiple occurrence of an object), ConstraintCombination (the ability to combine multiple constraints, often addressing different annotation layers, with logical operators), LinearRelation ("horizontal" sequences of objects), or TreeRelation ("vertical" dominance relations in hierarchical tree structures) (ISO 24623-2: 5.4). However, this characterisation is still too coarse because (i) functionalities can be implemented in different ways (e. g. PartialMatch as simple wildcard search vs. regular expressions) and (ii) the true expressive power of a CQL arises from the degree to which functionalities can

4 Technically, module 1a refers to plain-text search of texts represented as character sequences, with tokenisation understood as a form of segmentation (1b). This approach is rarely adopted by corpus management systems, presumably because token-level representations are much more efficient for large corpora.

5 To pick a nit, ISO 24623-2: 3.15 allows for multiple CQLF ontologies, which are required to adhere to the structure specified in the standard. We consider it unlikely that many competing ontologies will emerge and hence continue to refer to *the* CQLF Ontology.

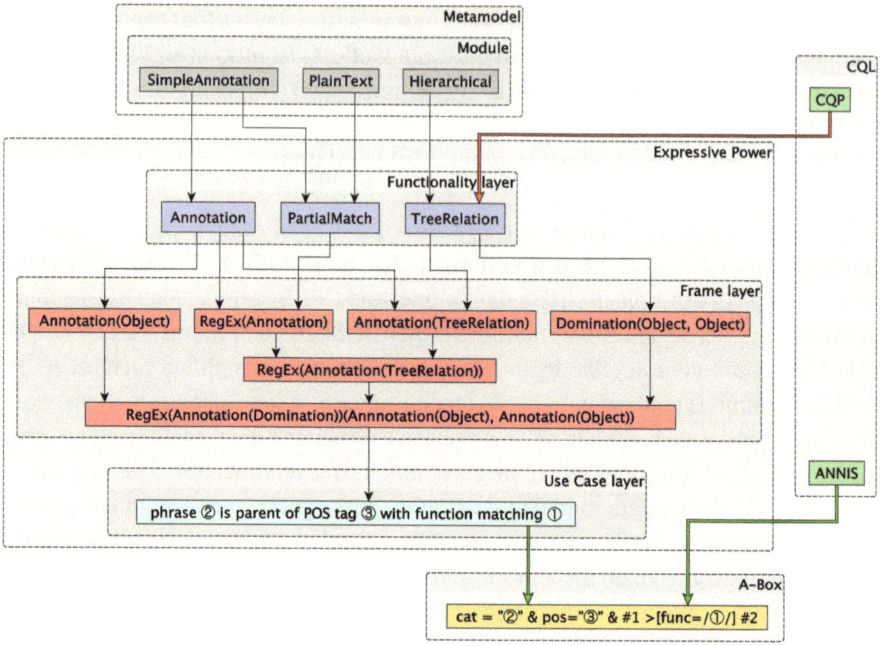

Figure 2: Illustrative visualisation of a fragment of the CQLF Ontology (Evert et al. 2020: 3350), showing examples of CQLF-1 modules (grey), functionalities (purple), frames (red), and use cases (turquoise). CQLs (green) are linked to use cases via positive conformance statements (yellow). ANNIS supports this use case (green arrows to conformance statement), whereas CQP cannot search for dominance relations in tree structures at all (red arrow).

flexibly be combined. As it is impossible to provide an exhaustive inventory of all potentially relevant combinations of functionalities, CQLF-2 introduces an open-ended ontology of frames and use cases based on common search needs identified by the community. Concrete use cases are linked to more general frames, which are in turn linked to functionalities and through them to CQLF-1 modules and layers. This hierarchical structure of the CQLF Ontology is illustrated in Figure 2. The capabilities of a given CQL are described by linking it to use cases via (positive) conformance statements, which must be supported by a (parameterised) query expression. Conformance statements thus also help to connect query syntax with the corresponding query semantics (in the form of the search need expressed by the use case). The conformance statement at the bottom of Figure 2 shows that the ANNIS query language is able to combine Annotation, PartialMatch, and TreeRelation functionalities because it can search for a specific POS tag (Annotation) dominated by a phrase node (TreeRelation) whose syntatic function is matched against a regular expression (PartialMatch). Negative conformance statements can be used to explicitly indicate that a CQL does not cover a particular functionality, frame, or use case. The red arrow in Figure 2 shows that the CQP query language is incapable of searching for dominance relations in tree structures (TreeRelation) and hence cannot possibly support the use case in the example.

4 Finite-state queries for tabular data models

For corpus management systems that are primarily designed for CQLF level 1, a tabular data model is a convenient and efficient choice. Inspired by the columnar representation format used by information retrieval systems (Witten et al. 1999), the tabular model represents the token sequence and all token-level annotations in the form of an annotation table.[6] Each row of the table corresponds to a single token, and the columns contain the token in its original form as well as token-level annotations (POS tag and lemma in the table shown in Figure 3). An equivalent data model, differing in implementation details only, is described in Körner and Eckart (2025). Tabular data models became popular in corpus and computational linguistics in the early 1990s. One of the first corpus management systems to adopt this approach was the IMS Corpus Workbench (CWB, Christ 1994), very closely following the recipe of Witten et al. (1999). Today, the popular CoNLL-U format of the Universal Dependencies Project[7] is also based on the tabular data model (with some extensions). Most corpus management systems that have adopted a tabular model provide only limited support for annotations beyond the token level, often with ad-hoc solutions for particular use cases. However, the Ziggurat corpus data model (Evert and Hardie 2015) has recently demonstrated how the concept of annotation tables can be extended to cover all three CQLF levels.

Tabular data models are usually combined with finite-state queries, which use regular expression notation (ISO/IEC/IEEE 9945) at two levels. Character-level regular expressions match word forms and token-level annotations, while regular expressions over token descriptions match sequential patterns of tokens in a highly

6 The tabular data model is quite similar to a table in a relational database. A crucial difference is that the rows of an annotation table are *ordered*, listing the tokens in their natural sequence. Relational tables, by contrast, are unordered sets and any ordering has to be imposed explicitly when querying the table. The tabular data model is thus particularly suited for searching sequential patterns of tokens efficiently.

7 https://universaldependencies.org/docs/format.html

flexible way.[8] An introduction to regular expression notation is beyond the scope of this chapter; see e. g. Friedl (2006) for an accessible treatment.

Still in active use today (now open-source and branded as the IMS *Open* Corpus Workbench), CWB has been very influential in corpus and computational linguistics. It has become a de facto standard, resulting in the development of several related tools that use (almost) the same data model and query language. These include the corpus management system Manatee (Rychlý 2007), which was designed as an open-source clone of CWB, and its commercial successor Sketch Engine (Kilgarriff et al. 2014), Poliqarp (Przepiórkowski et al. 2004), and Corpuscle (Meurer 2012). The remainder of this section focuses on the specific data model of CWB and its extension in Ziggurat (Section 4.1), as well as the finite-state CQP query language implemented by CWB (Section 4.2).

4.1 The CWB data model and Ziggurat

The data model of CWB was first described by Christ (1994) and is further explained in Evert and Hardie (2011). Aside from these high-level summaries, there is no precise formal definition of the abstract data model and its physical representation. As was often the case with such early tools, the program code itself is the documentation. A practical guide to indexing corpora in CWB and searching them with CQP queries can be found in the user manuals (Evert and The CWB Development Team 2022a,b).

The main component of the CWB data model is an annotation table that represents the primary data as a single sequence of tokens spanning the entire corpus. Rows of the annotation table are enumerated by their *corpus position* (cpos), starting at 0. The columns of the table represent different token-level annotations and are called *positional attributes* (or p-attributes). The first p-attribute is labelled *word* and plays a special role, as it contains the original surface forms of the tokens and must always be present. In order to keep the CWB data model and its implementation simple, all annotated values are represented as strings. While not strictly a property of the logical data model, a key feature of CWB is that once a corpus has been indexed, no further text can be added and the number of table rows n_{tokens} is fixed. However, further columns can always be added to the annotation table (facilitated by the columnar storage model of CWB), which is convenient for incremental

8 The term “finite-state queries” derives from the fact that such queries can be implemented as finite-state automata with token descriptions as edge labels (cf. Figure 6).

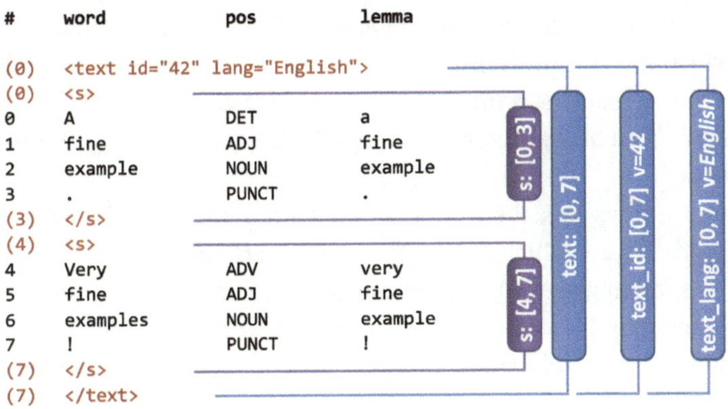

Figure 3: The tabular data model of CWB. Columns of the main annotation table correspond to p-attributes. Regions of s-attributes are linked to their start and end corpus positions.

annotation of corpora.[9] Figure 3 shows an example of an annotation table for a very small corpus ($n_{\text{tokens}} = 8$) with POS and lemma annotation. The initial column labelled # indicates corpus positions. The table row with cpos 6 contains all information available for the seventh token in the corpus: its surface form *examples*, its POS tag *NOUN*, and its lemma *example*.

CWB also supports a simple form of segmentation annotation in the form of *structural attributes* (s-attributes), completing its coverage of CQLF level 1. Each segmentation region corresponds to a token span represented as a pair of start and end cpos. Regions of the same type (e. g. sentences or texts) form an s-attribute. They must not be nested and must not overlap, but overlaps between different s-attributes are allowed. The s-attributes visualised in Figure 3 represent XML elements in the input data, but the hierarchical structure of the XML markup is broken up into independent s-attributes.[10] Regions may be annotated with a single string value, indicated by *v* = in the illustration. The XML elements enclosing texts in Figure 3 include multiple items of metadata in their start tags. These can only be indexed with a redundant work-around in the form of multiple parallel s-attributes (*text* for the regions themselves, *text_id* for their unique IDs, and *text_lang* for a language indication). Because of these limitations, CWB cannot be used for parse trees

9 In our own use of CWB, we often annotate German corpora with the POS tagger SoMeWeTa (Proisl 2018), index the tagged corpus in CWB, and then add lemmatisation as a new p-attribute with the morphological analyser SMOR (Schmid et al. 2004).

10 CWB does not allow elements of the same type to be nested, e. g. in a sequence such as <np> ... <np> ... </np> ... </np>. As a work-around, CWB can automatically rename nested elements in the indexing stage, creating multiple s-attributes *np*, *np1*, etc.

and other complex hierarchical structures mandated by CQLF level 2.[11] However, s-attributes are used extensively in CWB practice to encode metadata, structural markup, span annotations (such as named entities), and shallow syntactic structure. A CWB-indexed version of the richly annotated British National Corpus uses 124 distinct s-attributes.

As an extension of s-attributes, the CWB data model provides so-called *alignment attributes* (or a-attributes), which link a set of (non-overlapping) token spans in one corpus to corresponding spans in a different corpus. Their main purpose is to encode sentence alignment between parallel corpora. Interestingly, a-attributes belong to the class of multi-stream architectures that CQLF-1 leaves for future work (Bański et al. 2016: 2806).

Ziggurat (Evert and Hardie 2015) is the successor of the CWB data model and provides a comprehensive formal specification both of the logical data model and the physical storage format (Evert et al. 2023). Ziggurat generalises the notion of annotation tables beyond the primary layer of token-level annotations, referring to their columns as *variables*. Figure 4 shows how a segmentation layer (sentence regions) can be represented as a second annotation table, allowing an arbitrary number of annotations for each region. Rows of this annotation table are linked to token spans in the primary layer and are accessed via their layer position (starting from 0). In the CWB data model, three parallel s-attributes (*s*, *s_id*, *s_len*) would be needed

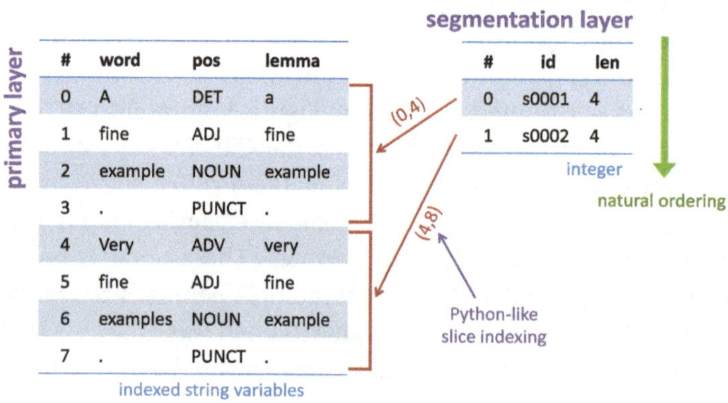

Figure 4: The Ziggurat data model represents segmentation layers as annotation tables similar to the primary layer. Each row corresponds to one segment, which is linked to a token span in the primary layer and can be annotated with multiple variables.

11 Which does not mean, of course, that it has never been used in this way (see e.g. Kermes and Evert 2002).

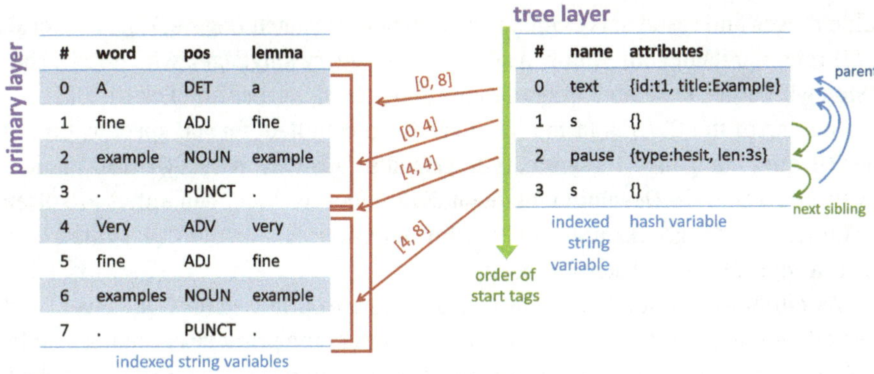

Figure 5: Even hierarchical tree layers are represented as annotation tables in Ziggurat, with each row corresponding to one node of the tree (here, an XML element in the input data). Special pointers encode dominance relations between nodes and precedence relations between siblings. As for segmentation layers, every node can be annotated with multiple variables in the annotation table. Nodes are linked to token spans in the primary layer, and even empty elements can be represented.

to represent the same information. As a second extension, Ziggurat allows for variables of different data types (e. g. integer numbers) to enable more efficient storage and retrieval.

Figure 5 shows that even hierarchical tree structures can be represented as annotation tables. The tree layer represents the hierarchical XML markup from Figure 3 extended with an empty <pause/> element between cpos 3 and 4. Each row of the table corresponds to one node of the tree, which is linked to a token span in the primary layer (with a zero-length span for the empty XML element between cpos 3 and 4). Rows are ordered in the sequence of the corresponding XML start tags. Additional pointers are required to represent dominance relations and the ordering of sibling nodes unambiguously and to allow efficient navigation of the tree.

4.2 Overview of the CQP query language

The CQP query language is a finite-state query language used by the corpus query processor (CQP) of CWB. Like the tabular data model, it has become a de facto standard in the field and has been implemented in several other corpus management systems. All implementations support the same core syntax, but with differences in details and sometimes with extensions. For example, Poliqarp offers extended support for tagsets in p-attributes, new disambiguated matching operators, and non-standard context markers (Przepiórkowski et al. 2004). Corpuscle features extended syntax for matching across structural boundaries and new operators for value ranges and result sets from parallel corpora.[12] Sketch Engine (Kilgarriff et al. 2014) refers to its flavour simply as CQL (*corpus query language*), which risks confusion with other, unrelated query languages (see e. g. Körner and Eckart 2025).

Similar to the CWB data model, there is no complete formal specification of the CQP query language. Its syntax is described extensively in the CQP user manual (Evert and The CWB Development Team 2022b), but its query semantics are often documented through examples only. A formal grammar for the CQP syntax only exists as part of the CQP source code.[13]

As a finite-state query language, CQP queries are optimised for CQLF level 1 and specialise on matching flexible sequences of rows in the primary annotation table. CQP syntax "employs regular expression patterns at two levels: at the level of character strings for word forms and annotation values, and also at the level of token sequences" (Evert and Hardie 2011: 8). CQP queries can thus be divided into two levels: individual tokens are matched by *token descriptions* enclosed in square brackets. Such token descriptions specify constraints on surface forms or token-level annotations in terms of literal values or regular expression patterns. Multiple constraints (usually involving different p-attributes) can be combined with logical operators such as *and* (`&`), *or* (`|`), and *not* (`!`). For example, the token description

```
[word = ".*icious" & pos = "JJ.*"]
```

matches any token that ends in *-icious* and is tagged as an adjective.[14] Regular expressions at the character level are used here to carry out prefix and suffix searches.

CQP syntax matches sequences of tokens by applying regular expression operators to complete token descriptions as basic units, in particular quantifiers `?` (optional), `*` (any number of repetitions), `+` (one or more), `{3,}` (three or more) and `|` to mark alternatives. In this way, the query

```
[lemma = "be"]? [word = "very"%c]+
[word = ".*icious" & pos = "JJ.*"];
```

finds an optional copula verb *be*, followed by any number of repetitions of the surface form *very* (case-insensitive due to the modifier `%c`) and an adjective ending in *-icious*. Its result set might contain the token span *was very VERY delicious*. Note that the query is split across multiple lines for better readability. Line breaks have no significance in CQP syntax, and the query must be terminated with a semicolon. As a convenience feature for interactive use, token descriptions that consist of a single

12 See https://clarino.uib.no/korpuskel/documentation/The_query_language

13 https://sourceforge.net/p/cwb/code/HEAD/tree/cwb/trunk/cqp/parser.y

14 Examples in this section assume the Penn Treebank tagset (Marcus et al. 1993).

constraint on the surface form can omit the square brackets and attribute. In this way, the second token description above could be shortened to "very"%c.

Listing 2 shows a more complex CQP query. Its first part (in parentheses) matches one of three alternatives: a noun phrase consisting of optional determiner and adjectives followed by a common noun (line 1), a name consisting of one or more proper nouns (line 2), or a single pronoun (line 3). This first part must be followed by an instance of the verb *say* (line 4). The result set is stored under the name SimonSays.[15]

```
1  SimonSays = ( [pos = "DT"]? [pos = "JJ.*"]* [pos = "NNS?"]
2              | [pos = "NPS?"]+
3              | [pos = "PP"] )
4              [lemma = "say" & pos = "V.*"];
```

Listing 2: Example of a complex CQP query, which matches a noun phrase (line 1), proper name (line 2), or pronoun (line 3) followed by the verb *say* (line 4). The result set of the query is named SimonSays.

Regular expressions can be translated into finite-state automata (FSA), which can then be matched efficiently against corpus data. CQP takes this approach and will translate the query from Listing 2 into the FSA shown in Figure 6. The FSA accepts any sequence of tokens that corresponds to a path from the start state q_0 to the final state q_4. Edges can only be traversed if the current token matches their token description. For example, the token span *the silly professor said* would be accepted with the path $q_0 \rightarrow q_1 \rightarrow q_1 \rightarrow q_2 \rightarrow q_4$.

CQP syntax also has limited facilities for accessing s-attributes in queries. XML-like tags can be inserted to match the start or end of an s-attribute region. For example, the query below finds a lowercase word at the start of a sentence.

```
<s> [word = "[a-z].*"];
```

Annotated values of regions can be matched in start tags, and if tags are used in matching pairs they mark a single region: <np> []* </np> matches any single noun phrase; note that the empty token description [] represents an arbitrary token. Label references give access to annotation values from anywhere within a region. The query

```
<np> []* a:[lemma = "dog"] []* </np>
:: a.text_author = ".*Dickens.*";
```

finds noun phrases containing the lemma *dog* within texts written by someone named *Dickens*. The marker :: introduces a "global" constraint that applies to the

15 Named after the children's game *Simon Says*, which is one of the matches of the query.

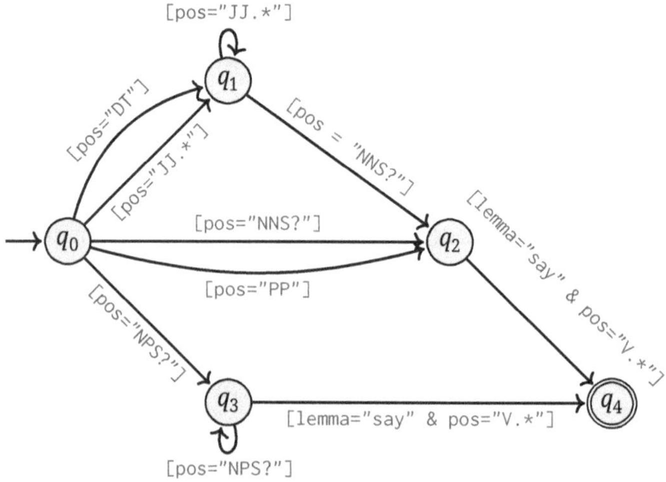

Figure 6: Representation of the query SimonSays (see Listing 2) as a finite-state automaton (Evert 2021: Figure 1.5).

entire query match and can involve multiple tokens (though it only refers to the token labelled a here).

CQP syntax offers many other features that are far beyond the scope of this chapter. For example, macros can be defined to make complex queries more manageable and readable; subqueries can be used to filter the result set of a query; result sets can be combined with set operations; and special TAB queries match fixed phrases (as well as skip-grams with optional gaps between the words) efficiently. See Evert and The CWB Development Team (2022b) for a user-friendly introduction to all features.

5 Anchored queries for graph-based data models

Corpora can also be represented in the form of more general graph-based data models, which are especially well-suited for CQLF level 2 (and to some extent level 3). They are needed in particular for rich annotation that involves general structural hierarchies (like trees), many cross-references between elements (like dependency graphs), or complex multi-level annotation schemes (Dipper 2005). Especially with the rise of treebanks and reliable automatic parsing, hierarchical annotation schemes became commonplace in corpus research. In contrast to the large corpora with mostly token-level annotation discussed in Section 4, treebanks and other types of corpora with many complex annotation layers tend to be smaller and often result from (partially) manual annotation processes.

Notable first efforts to develop specialised query tools for treebanks were tgrep/TGrep2 for the Penn Treebank (Rohde 2005) and TIGERSearch for the German TIGER treebank (Lezius 2002), both of which introduce bespoke query languages and rely on greedy search algorithms that require keeping the indexed annotation graph in main memory. The NXT query language (Evert and Voormann 2003) took a similar approach, but aimed to support annotation layers from all CQLF levels and modules, including concurrent annotation over a common timeline. Other developments have tried to make use of established technologies such as XQuery, either via off-the-shelf XML database systems like BaseX (Martens 2012) or via mapping schemes on top of relational database systems (Steiner and Kallmeyer 2002, Rosenfeld 2010).

Due to the very generic nature of graphs, further specifications are needed to determine how certain annotations and their properties are mapped to the elements of a graph (nodes, edges, and their attributes); such a specification is called a *metamodel*. There is a large body of work around formalising exchange formats for richly annotated multi-level corpora and around defining metamodels for the description and mapping of these annotations. Many exchange formats are based on XML, ensuring a natural representation of nested hierarchical structure as outlined by Carletta et al. (2003) and Chiarcos et al. (2008). The work of Ide and Romary (2004) and Ide and Romary (2006) has led to the creation of an international standard for a linguistic annotation framework (LAF, ISO 24612), which defines a metamodel for multi-level annotation. Later work like GrAF (Ide and Suderman 2007) directly applies this standard for mapping multi-level annotations to a representation as a directed acyclic graph (DAG). These exchange formats and metamodels have found application within the data models of some recent corpus management systems. Notably, the work surrounding GrAF and PAULA (Dipper 2005) is cited as a base for the later Salt metamodel (Zipser 2009, 2014), which is closely related to the ANNIS corpus management system described below and forms a superset of its data model.

Graph-based data models are usually combined with anchored queries, which select a tuple of graph nodes (matching certain annotation constraints) as anchors and then specify structural relations between the anchors via edges of multi-step paths. The ANNIS query language described in Section 5.2 is a typical example of this approach.

5.1 The ANNIS corpus data model

ANNIS is perhaps the most capable and widely used corpus management system for corpora and search needs beyond CQLF level 1. It is implemented on top of a fully graph-based data model and is capable of expressing all three levels of the CQLF metamodel. The first version of ANNIS was developed in a collaborative research centre (SFB 632) at the University of Potsdam and first published in Dipper et al. (2004). The system has since seen continued development, including multiple re-implementations of its underlying data model and indexing engine. The current version of ANNIS (Krause and Zeldes 2016) "is a query system that aims to support not only one type of annotation (like trees or spans), but integrates the different types of annotations into one query language and search tool" (Krause 2018: 16). Historically, ANNIS has stood in the tradition of TIGERSearch, taking inspiration from its query language and setting the explicit goal of supporting TIGER-style annotation (Dipper et al. 2004: 254). The internal representation of corpus data has varied significantly between different versions of ANNIS. While the initial release of ANNIS used a fully memory-based graph representation (Dipper et al. 2004), ANNIS2 and ANNIS3 (also known as relANNIS) switched to a mapping scheme on top of the relational database PostgreSQL (Zeldes et al. 2009, Krause and Zeldes 2016). An additional ongoing re-implementation of ANNIS returns to an in-memory graph model called graphANNIS (Krause et al. 2016, Krause 2018) and promises better query performance. Our description of the ANNIS data model uses the Salt metamodel as a proxy for the logical data model, since both have been developed concurrently. Any references to the physical representation are based on the concrete implementation in graphANNIS.

The ANNIS corpus data model is entirely based on a labelled directed acyclic graph (LDAG). Formally speaking, all aspects of a corpus are modelled as nodes and edges of the same LDAG, both data and metadata. Logically, different corpora form subgraphs that may not be interconnected. Corpora can be assigned labels (for metadata) and can be further hierarchically structured into subcorpora that eventually contain document nodes with associated raw text data. For each document there exists an annotation (sub)graph that defines all linguistically relevant elements. The data model makes a clear distinction between primary data and annotation, as the annotation graph is always defined over a layer of initial token nodes that are linked to character spans in the primary data.[16] This strict separation of primary and secondary data is known as stand-off annotation. This seamless graph-based model de-

16 Other forms of primary data, e. g. audio or video recordings, are also possible. In this case, character offsets are replaced with other appropriate anchor points such as timestamps.

scribed here is not realised in practice, though. All existing implementations of ANNIS model documents and annotation graphs separately, with different mappings for the different node types in both relANNIS and graphANNIS.

The model for the annotation graph in Salt is split into several layers of metamodels, with the generic model for an LDAG forming the bottom layer. In this metamodel, an LDAG is made up of a set of nodes, directed edges between the nodes, and labels that can be assigned to both nodes and edges. On the higher, more specialised layers, the metamodel specifies subclasses of these generic objects in order to capture the semantics of specific linguistic annotation types. It includes concepts such as tokens, annotations, metadata, and relations between objects (Zipser 2009: 49–66).

Figure 7 illustrates an incomplete fragment of the idealised annotation graph, omitting the document node as well as the raw text data to which the individual tokens are linked. Nodes of the token type are shown as rectangles. They link both to a character span (omitted) and to the next token in the sequence via an ordering relation (blue arrows). In contrast to the tabular data model, there is no inherent sequential ordering of the tokens. The surface form of each token is stored as annotation on the corresponding token node (redundantly to the linked character span), together with additional annotation for POS tags (corresponding to CWB's p-attributes). For the purpose of query evaluation, token nodes are treated as leaves of the annotation graph.

In addition to token annotations, the Salt meta model can represent arbitrary hierarchical and non-hierarchical structures. Trees (hierarchical structures) are represented via additional structure nodes (shown as ellipses) that connect to other structure nodes and/or to token nodes via a dominance relation (red arrows). Non-hierarchical segmentation works in a similar way, but uses nodes of span type (shown as rectangles with rounded corners). Span nodes have explicit coverage relations (green arrows) to all tokens contained in the span, so non-contiguous ranges can easily be modelled. An additional pointer relation (which does not imply text coverage) is used for dependency links between individual tokens, but does not appear in Figure 7. This very generic data model aims to fit many different kinds of corpora, allowing for unified search across diverse annotation schemes and layers.

The implementation of relANNIS has shown that it is difficult to map such a generic data model to a relational database and SQL queries. Corpus queries need to execute many join operations across tables when translated to SQL, leading to unsatisfactory performance. The number of joins can be reduced by materialising additional index tables in the database, but at the cost of considerable storage overhead (Krause et al. 2016). A further issue is inefficient query planning by the relational database system because of semantic mismatches between the relational model of the database and the ANNIS data model, leading to infelicitous cost estimations for

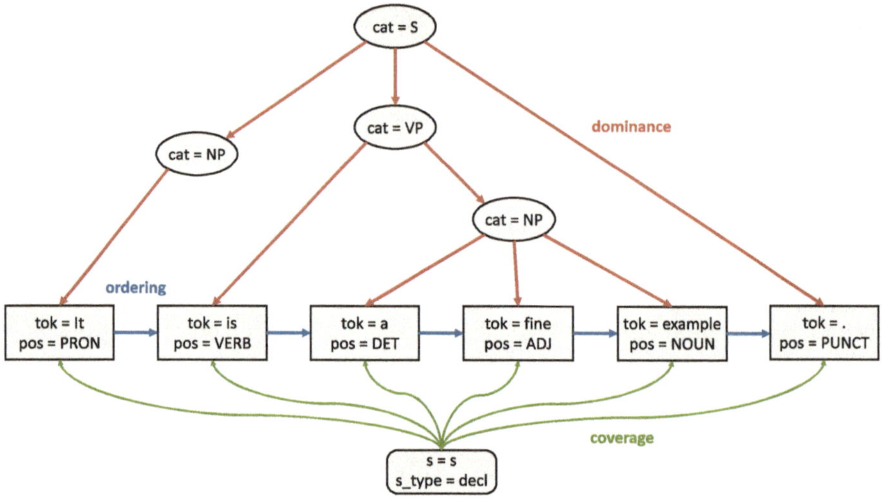

Figure 7: The ANNIS data model represents both primary data and annotation in the form of graph structures. Nodes are tokens and annotation elements, and all structural relations between nodes are encoded as directed edges. Even the sequence of tokens is encoded as an explicit ordering relation (blue arrows). Segmentation is indicated by a coverage relation (green arrows) between a segment and the tokens spanned by it, while tree structures are represented by a dominance relation (red arrows). Illustration adapted from Krause et al. (2016: 10).

query execution. For these reasons, graphANNIS no longer builds on top of a relational database system, but has returned to a custom in-memory representation (Krause 2018).

5.2 Overview of the ANNIS query language

ANNIS supports queries in the ANNIS query language, or AQL for short.[17] AQL needs a high degree of expressiveness to support the powerful ANNIS data model, which is achieved by allowing flexible combinations of a small number of basic elements and operators.[18] AQL is essentially a general graph query language, but takes into account semantics from the Salt metamodel in order to map different linguistic phenomena in a natural way. One design goal for AQL has been to use concepts and

17 AQL is no less problematic as an abbreviation than CQL. There are at least three other query languages called AQL, which are not related to corpus linguistics.

18 This is similar to regular expressions, which need only a handful of operators to search for complex sequential patterns.

terms that are familiar to linguists even if they might not always correspond directly to the underlying graph representation (Krause 2018). Since all corpora accessible through ANNIS are mapped to the Salt metamodel, AQL can be understood as a query language for the Salt data model – although not all Salt concepts are accessible through AQL. A complete overview of the AQL syntax can be found in the official user guide.[19] As is the case with many other corpus management systems, this user-oriented documentation does not provide a complete formal specification and fails to cover all corner cases.

The basic elements of an AQL query correspond to (token or annotation) nodes in the graph. Nodes can be selected based on their surface form (e. g. `"dog"`), based on the presence of a certain annotation (e. g. `pos` finds all nodes annotated with a POS tag), or based on a specific annotation value (`pos = "NN"`) or a regular expression (`pos = /VV.*/`). Annotation names can be qualified with a namespace, e. g. `stts:pos = "NN"` to distinguish multiple POS annotation layers.

A query usually consist of multiple terms combined with the operator `&`. All terms in a query are implicitly numbered (`#1`, `#2`, …) and the relationships between them have to be specified using additional predicates with structural operators.[20] For example, the phrase *cute cat* can be found with the AQL query

```
"cute" & "cat" & #1 . #2
```

where `.` is the operator for direct precedence according to the ordering relation between token nodes (but precedence is also defined for other nodes based on the token spans they cover). For conciseness and readability, it is also possible to put the operator directly between two elements and avoid the numeric references: `"cute" . "cat"`. This shorthand notation can be extended to three or more elements, which are chained together from left to right.

AQL offers almost 20 structural operators, including `>` for direct and `>*` for transitive dominance. The query `cat = "np"> lemma = "cat"` finds occurrences of the lemma *cat* and their containing noun phrases. The `->type` operator expresses a pointing relation of the given type and can optionally specify constraints on edge annotations in square brackets. All operators based on graph edges have direct and indirect versions (marked by `*`) and can be negated with `!`. Finally, a number of operators compare the token coverage of nodes. For example, `#1 _=_ #2` requires that `#1` and `#2` cover exactly the same tokens, while `#1 _i_ #2` specifies inclusion (`#2` must be contained in `#1`).

19 https://korpling.github.io/ANNIS/4.0/user-guide/aql/

20 Without specifying such relationships, the result set of the query would be the Cartesian product of the occurrences of the individual terms.

Unlike CQP syntax, AQL does not allow multiple constraints in the specification of a single element. To search for the lemma *light* not tagged as a noun, we have to specify two elements and make sure that they cover exactly the same token span:

```
lemma = "light" _=_ pos != /N.*/
```

With its syntax, AQL is thus able to express queries with almost arbitrarily complex structural relations. The result set of a query consists of tuples of nodes in the graph (instead of token spans or corpus positions), which are connected through structural operators specifying paths between the nodes. AQL is thus fundamentally different from the CQP query language: while CQP specifies flexible sequences of (complex) token descriptions along a single dimension (immediate precedence), AQL selects a tuple of nodes as anchors and then tests for structural relations between the anchors.

6 Perspectives

Recent developments in the realm of corpus queries and corpus management systems reflect three key trends (Gärtner and Jung 2020: 6311): (1) scalability, to handle massive corpora; (2) accessibility, with user-friendly interfaces and graphical query builders; and (3) standardisation, such as the CQLF initiative. With regard to corpus query languages, there have been efforts to generalise the implementation of corpus query capabilities: Query interoperability frameworks like KoralQuery (Diewald and Bingel 2017) implement multiple query languages on top of a common abstract query protocol to allow users to write queries in their preferred syntax, providing a clear accessibility advantage (Gärtner and Jung 2020: 6312). A third generation of query systems has also seen the development of example-based search systems like LSE (Resnik and Elkiss 2005) and GrETEL (Augustinus et al. 2012), which allow users to query by providing natural language examples instead of writing a query in any particular formal language. Scalable solutions for extremely large corpora emerged such as KorAP, Fangorn, and BlackLab using Apache Lucene in client-server setups, or initiatives like CLARIN Federated Content Search giving unified access to distributed resources (cf. Körner and Eckart 2025).

These developments can best be illustrated with the "next-generation corpus-analysis platform" KorAP developed at IDS Mannheim since 2011. KorAP was first introduced by Bański et al. (2012), followed by publications providing more details on its concrete implementation (Bański et al. 2014, Diewald et al. 2016). It is the main corpus platform for hosting the German reference corpus DeReKo (Kupietz et al. 2018), which currently comprises over 60 billion tokens of text data (as of January

2025). The self-proclaimed goal of the KorAP project is to develop a corpus management and query system that supports very large corpora featuring many annotations layers, implements several of the most common query languages, and can cope with the complex licensing and access-control scenarios surrounding DeReKo.

End users interact with KorAP in the form of a centrally hosted, server-based system. Unlike CWB and many other corpus management systems, KorAP has not been designed as a monolithic piece of software but instead is implemented as a collection of individual components in a microservice architecture. This helps achieve the project's scaling goals, as individual services can be deployed in parallel and even spun up on demand. Communication and control between the individual services is facilitated through a set of defined protocols and interfaces, which also enables relatively independent development of the individual components. KorAP features a three-level design, dividing its software stack into a user-facing frontend, middleware dealing with corpus query serialisation and user management, and corpus storage and retrieval back ends. This flexible approach to systems design uncouples the query engine from the data model and any specific corpus query language.

Currently, KorAP has only a single retrieval back end (Krill) based on Apache Lucene, although it would be possible to implement different back ends optimised for the retrieval of different types of annotations.[21] The data model employed by the platform is centered around individual documents, with separate storage of primary text data, document metadata, and linguistic annotations. All annotations are represented in stand-off format; potentially conflicting annotations are divided into individual "foundries". This document-based approach makes it easy to add new documents to the corpus, which is needed to support the constant growth of DeReKo as a monitor corpus by around 3 bilion tokens per year (Kupietz et al. 2018). The data model of the underlying Lucene index remains token-based and tabular – although it has been extended to allow for more complex structural information (CQLF level 2) and concurrent annotations (CQLF level 3). A more detailed description of the document data model and exchange format used by KorAP can be found in Bański and Diewald (2025).

6.1 First steps towards generic query representations

To enable the flexible combination of different query languages with its retrieval back ends, KorAP adopts a new approach: it translates corpus queries from the user-

21 According to earlier publications, a second back end based on the Neo4j graph database was planned but never realised.

facing syntax into a generic intermediary representation called KoralQuery. KoralQuery should be seen as a pivot language that is not intended to be directly written and read by human users, but rather as a standardised exchange format for corpus queries that can directly be processed by query engines. This effectively decouples the execution of corpus queries from any specific CQL syntax. In its current form, KoralQuery is an object schema expressed in JSON-LD syntax (Sporny et al. 2014) that was first proposed by Bański et al. (2014) to support the automatic rewriting of corpus queries for the purpose of access control and policy enforcement within KorAP. Its precise specification was subsequently developed by Bingel (2015) and published in Bingel and Diewald (2015). KoralQuery representations take the form of a set of standardised objects that are hierarchically nested in a tree structure to express arbitrary queries. One of the stated goals of KoralQuery was to be a candidate for the common serialisation format of a future CQLF.

The expressiveness provided by KoralQuery is similar to other current corpus query languages. Its capabilities closely follows the functionalities and frames specified in the CQLF Ontology (ISO 24623-2), which is descriptive in nature and in turn derived from typical query patterns in established CQLs. Koral, the software library implementing parsers for different CQLs and the KoralQuery serialisation format, supports a considerable range of input languages: Cosmas-II QL, ANNIS QL, two CQP dialects in the form of Poliqarp QL and CQP syntax, and query languages used by the CLARIN infrastructure (CQL and FCS-QL, see Körner and Eckart 2025). The expressiveness of KoralQuery should thus be a superset of all these languages, although it has to be noted that the KorAP platform cannot process corpus queries of arbitrary complexity yet. In practice, the scope of KoralQuery seems limited to the context of KorAP, so it cannot fulfil the vision of a universal query pivot format. For example, KorAP implements a version of ANNIS QL that is more limited in terms of capabilities than the version implemented by ANNIS itself, due to significant differences in the underlying data models. Similar limitations can be observed for the other CQLs supported by Koral, which often differ slightly in syntax and semantics from their implementation in the original corpus management systems.

Nevertheless, this approach of a generic query representation format has its merit. Intermediary representations have a long and successful history in the context of compiler construction, where they decouple high-level, user-friendly languages from the level of machine instructions, enabling better analysis and optimisation of the compiled programs. KoralQuery applies this principle to corpus query languages: the front-end CQL is translated into an intermediary representation, which then undergoes several passes of query rewriting to implement access control, user preferences, normalisation, and query planning optimisation (Diewald and Margaretha 2016: 78). Supporting additional CQLs is merely a matter of parsing and transformation into KoralQuery, while the rest of the query execution logic remains generic. Some other recent corpus management systems follow a similar strategy in the design of their query engine, such as the new LiRI Corpus Platform (Schaber et al. 2023) with its JSON-based intermediary query representation format (cf. Frick and Schmidt 2025).

6.2 Simplified query languages and visual query builders

Corpus query languages often use a very formal and complex syntax in order to ensure high expressiveness and precise interpretation. This can make them inconvenient for daily use and difficult to learn, especially for less experienced users. For this reason, corpus platforms often aim to make life easier for their users, either by offering a simplified query language with compact and user-friendly syntax (which is then translated into the original CQL) or by supporting the formulation of complex queries with a visual query-building tool.

Some CQLs already provide limited syntactic sugar, especially for simple word or phrase searches. These are implicitly applied to a selected default attribute, often the surface form itself. The CQP query `"good" "ideas";` is synactic sugar for `[word = "good"] [word = "ideas"];`. In Sketch Engine, the quotation marks can be omitted and the query will search for the term both as a lemma and as a case-insensitive surface form. The simple query `eye` is thus translated into `[lc="eye"| lemma="eye"]`. Simple queries may also help users with the details of tokenisation. For instance, searching the Polish National Corpus with the Poliqarp query `[orth = "przyszedłem"]` (`orth` denotes the orthographic form of a token) does not find any instances of the verb form *przyszedłem* 'I (masc.) came'. This is because such past-tense forms are analysed as two tokens in the corpus: the lexical verb *przyszedł* 'came' followed by the auxiliary suffix *-em* '1SG'. However, a simple query `przyszedłem` is automatically split into two tokens by Poliqarp and yields the expected result. Such facilities cannot be provided by more general corpus management systems such as CWB, which have to work with many different corpora as well as tokenisation and annotation schemes. In Sketch Engine, a double hyphen in a simple query matches single-word, multi-word, and hyphenated spellings: `multi--billion` finds *multi billion*, *multibillion*, and *multi-billion*. A corresponding query in CQP syntax is much longer and inconvenient:

```
[lc = "multi"] [lc = "billion"] | [lc = "multi-?billion"]
```

While most CQLs support regular expressions for matching surface forms and annotation values, this is often perceived as unfamiliar and too complex for inexperienced users. In simplified query languages, they are often replaced with simple wildcards such as `?` for a single character and `*` for any number of characters.

One of the most expressive simple query languages is CEQL (Hoffmann et al. 2008: ch. 6), which translates into CQP syntax. In addition to the usual wildcards, alternative spellings can be listed comma-separated options within square brackets, e. g. `neighbo[,u]r`. Case-insensitive or diacritic-insensitive search can be activated by appending `:c` or `:d` to a token. In contrast to most other simple query languages, CEQL also gives access to POS tags (separated by an underscore) and lemmata (in curly braces). The CEQL query `{light}_V*` finds instances of the lemma *light* tagged as a verb. CEQL uses regular expression notation for sequences of tokens. The CQP query in listing 2 can thus be written succinctly as

```
( (_DT)? (_JJ*)* _NN* | (_NP*)+ | _PP ) {say}_V*
```

Note that parentheses are required to help CEQL distinguish between character-level wildcards and token-level regular expression operators. CQPweb and other corpus platforms such as Kontext and Korp optionally show the generated CQP to users, which can assist them in learning the full-fledged query language (Hoffmann et al. 2008: 218–223).

When working with a full-fledged CQL, users need to know the annotation scheme of the corpus and have to be familiar with the relevant tagsets. As a minimal form of support, CQPweb displays a list of positional and structural attributes available in the selected corpus. To help users formulate queries even more easily, many corpus platforms offer visual query builders. Sketch Engine's query builder helps users to create a sequence of token descriptions, selecting attributes, POS tags, and comparison operators from drop-down menus. In Figure 8, it has been used to formulate a query for two or three adjectives starting with *r* followed by a noun, such as *rich red velvet*. The resulting CQP query is

```
[lemma = "r.*" & tag = "JJ"]{2,3} [tag = "N.*"]
```

Query builders become more complex when tags include rich morphological annotation. In the Russian National Corpus, tokens are annotated for multiple features. Selecting feminine adjectives in the dative or locative case in the superlative yields the logical expression `(A) & (dat | loc) & (supr) & (f)` generated from

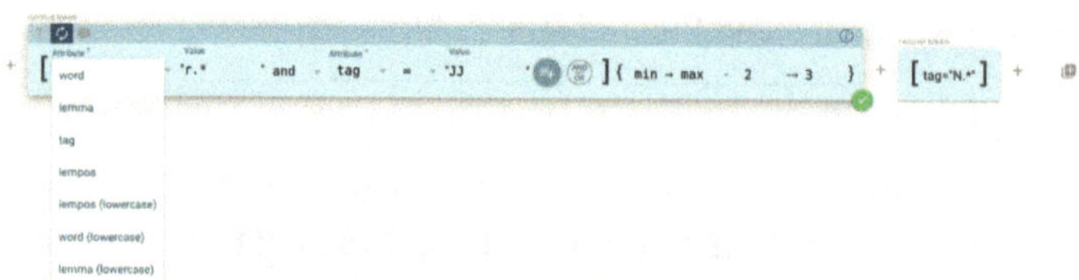

Figure 8: Sketch Engine's visual query builder for adjective–noun sequences.

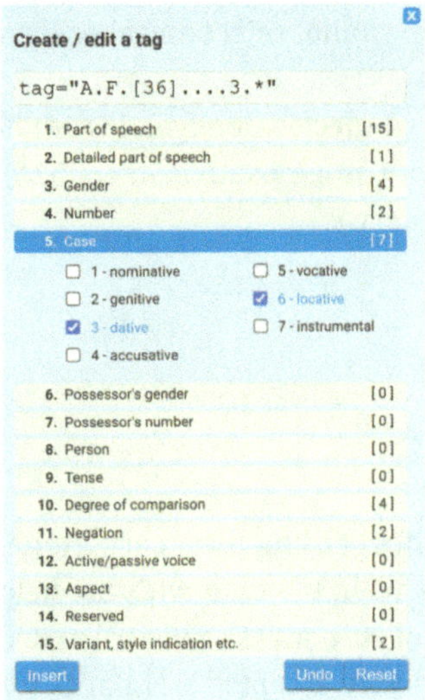

Figure 9: Czech National Corpus: visual query builder for positional tagset schemas.

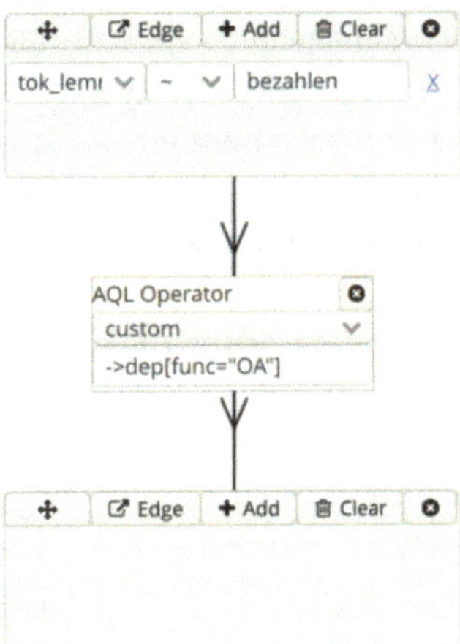

Figure 10: ANNIS query builder: creating a non-linear query.

the corresponding checkboxes. No feature names are needed since the tagset guarantees unique values even across features. In the most recent corpora within the Czech National Corpus, a POS tag is a 15-character string, each position encoding a morphological feature. The builder shown in Figure 9 converts checkbox selections to a regular expression; using the same example for Czech as previously for Russian, we get `[tag="A.F.[36]....3.*"]`, where `A` in position 1 stands for adjective, `F` in position 3 means feminine, `[36]` in position 5 are dative (3) and locative (6), and `3` in position 10 is superlative. This query builder also enforces well-formedness: adjectives, e. g., cannot have tense values, entailing that one cannot select any checkbox for position 9 once adjective has been selected.

The ANNIS query builder allows creation of nodes connected by edges. Figure 10 shows a search for the German verb *bezahlen* 'pay' with an accusative object (OA), irrespective of their linear order. The resulting AQL query is

```
tok_lemma = /bezahlen/ & node & #1 -> dep[func = "OA"] #2
```

7 Conclusion

As for other machine-readable databases, the usefulness of linguistic corpora depends crucially on being able to search flexible patterns in the data with the help of highly expressive corpus queries. The complexities of corpora as semi-structured data have been an obstacle to the development of broadly accepted standards for corpus query languages (CQLs) based on formal mathematical models, in contrast to standards such as SQL, XQuery or SPARQL for structured data. Most existing CQLs have been developed in the context of specific corpus management systems and are thus closely tied to the respective data models. As a result, corpus researchers must first decide on a corpus management system to use (based on their particular search needs and practical aspects such as scalability, ease of use, and software availability) and then learn the peculiarities of the system, most importantly its data model, input format, and query language. Over the years, two major paradigms have emerged as de facto standards in the field: (i) finite-state queries on the basis of a tabular data model (described in Section 4 with CWB as a prototypical example), and (ii) anchored queries in a graph-based data model (described in Section 5 with ANNIS as main representative). KorAP and some other recent systems aim to break up the tight connection between CQL, data model, and implementation by introducing an intermediary representation (KoralQuery) that decouples the query engine from a specific end-user CQL (Section 6).

Like many other fields, corpus research and the developers of corpus management systems would benefit greatly from better standardisation. First steps have been taken by recent work on a corpus query lingua franca (CQLF), which has so far resulted in the publication of two international standards: (i) a metamodel for the classification of CQLs based on their underlying data models (ISO 24623-1), and (ii) a community-driven taxonomy for the fine-grained description and comparison of the capabilities of individual CQLs (ISO 24623-2). What is still missing is a true CQLF that enables interoperability between different corpus management systems and query engines, i. e. the specification of a common data model and query language based on a formal mathematical model. We believe that such a future CQLF can only be successful if it meets several requirements: (i) it has to encompass existing de facto standards for which efficient and well-tested implementations exist, in particular supporting both tabular and graph-based data; (ii) it has to be normative, specifying precise query semantics rather than documenting the behaviour of existing CQLs; (iii) it has to provide a procedure for creating mappings to existing and new CQLs, even if they do not support all capabilities of CQLF;[22] (iv) it has to be modular and extensible so that it can be adapted to future search needs.

Bibliography

Anthony, Laurence. 2005. AntConc: Design and development of a freeware corpus analysis toolkit for the technical writing classroom. In *2005 IEEE International Professional Communication Conference Proceedings*, 729–737. https://doi.org/10.1109/IPCC.2005.1494244.

Anthony, Laurence. 2013. A critical look at software tools in corpus linguistics. *Linguistic Research* 30. 141–161.

Armstrong-Warwick, Susan, Henry S. Thompson, David McKelvie & Dominique Petitpierre. 1994. Data in your language: The ECI Multilingual Corpus 1. In *Proceedings of the International Workshop on Sharable Natural Language Resources*, Nara, Japan.

Aston, Guy & Lou Burnard. 1998. *The BNC handbook*. Edinburgh: Edinburgh University Press. http://www.natcorp.ox.ac.uk/.

Augustinus, Liesbeth, Vincent Vandeghinste & Frank Van Eynde. 2012. Example-based treebank querying. In Nicoletta Calzolari, Khalid Choukri, Thierry Declerck, Mehmet Uğur Doğan, Bente Maegaard, Joseph Mariani, Asuncion Moreno, Jan Odijk & Stelios Piperidis (eds.), *Proceedings of the Eighth International Conference on Language Resources and Evaluation (LREC'12)*, 3161–3167. Istanbul, Turkey: European Language Resources Association (ELRA). https://aclanthology.org/L12-1442/.

Baroni, Marco, Silvia Bernardini, Adriano Ferraresi & Eros Zanchetta. 2009. The wacky wide web: A collection of very large linguistically processed web-crawled corpora. *Language Resources and Evaluation* 43(3). 209–226. https://doi.org/10.1007/s10579-009-9081-z.

Bański, Piotr, Joachim Bingel, Nils Diewald, Elena Frick, Michael Hanl, Marc Kupietz, Piotr Pęzik, Carsten Schnober & Andreas Witt. 2014. KorAP: The new corpus analysis platform at IDS Mannheim. In Zygmunt Vetulani & Hans Uszkoreit (eds.), *Human Language Technology Challenges for Computer Science and Linguistics. 6th Language & Technology Conference*, December 7–9, 2013, Poznań, Poland, 586–587.

Bański, Piotr & Nils Diewald. 2025. Dealing with multiple annotations. In Piotr Bański, Ulrich Heid & Laura Herzberg (eds.), *Harmonising language data: Standards for linguistic resources*. de Gruyter.

Bański, Piotr, Nils Diewald, Michael Hanl, Marc Kupietz & Andreas Witt. 2014. Access control by query rewriting: The case of KorAP. In Nicoletta Calzolari, Khalid Choukri, Thierry Declerck, Hrafn Loftsson, Bente Maegaard, Joseph Mariani, Asuncion Moreno, Jan Odijk & Stelios Piperidis (eds.), *Proceedings of the Ninth International Conference on Language Resources and Evaluation (LREC'14)*, 3817–3822. Reykjavik, Iceland: European Language Resources Association (ELRA). https://aclanthology.org/L14-1582/.

22 The CQLF Ontology and its design (ISO 24623-2) might provide an excellent starting point for such mappings.

Bański, Piotr, Peter M. Fischer, Elena Frick, Erik Ketzan, Marc Kupietz, Carsten Schnober, Oliver Schonefeld & Andreas Witt. 2012. The new IDS corpus analysis platform: Challenges and prospects. In Nicoletta Calzolari, Khalid Choukri, Thierry Declerck, Mehmet Uğur Doğan, Bente Maegaard, Joseph Mariani, Asuncion Moreno, Jan Odijk & Stelios Piperidis (eds.), *Proceedings of the Eighth International Conference on Language Resources and Evaluation (LREC'12)*, 2905–2911. Istanbul, Turkey: European Language Resources Association (ELRA). https://aclanthology.org/L12-1467/.

Bański, Piotr, Elena Frick & Andreas Witt. 2016. Corpus Query Lingua Franca (CQLF). In Nicoletta Calzolari, Khalid Choukri, Thierry Declerck, Sara Goggi, Marko Grobelnik, Bente Maegaard, Joseph Mariani, Helene Mazo, Asuncion Moreno, Jan Odijk & Stelios Piperidis (eds.), *Proceedings of the Tenth International Conference on Language Resources and Evaluation (LREC'16)*, 2804–2809. Portorož, Slovenia: European Language Resources Association (ELRA). https://aclanthology.org/L16-1446/.

Bingel, Joachim. 2015. *Instantiation and implementation of a Corpus Query Lingua Franca*. Master's thesis, University of Heidelberg.

Bingel, Joachim & Nils Diewald. 2015. KoralQuery – A general corpus query protocol. In *Proceedings of the Workshop on Innovative Corpus Query and Visualization Tools at NODALIDA 2015*, May 11–13, 2015, Vilnius, Lithuania, Vol. 5. http://www.ep.liu.se/ecp_article/index.en.aspx?issue=111;article=001.

Bodmer, Franck. 1996. Aspekte der Abfragekomponente von COSMAS-II. In *LDV-INFO 1996. Informationsschrift der Arbeitsstelle Linguistische Datenverarbeitung (LDV-INFO 8)*, 112–122. Mannheim: IDS.

Burnard, Lou & Tony Dodd. 2003. Xara: An XML aware tool for corpus searching. In *Proceedings of the Corpus Linguistics 2003 conference*, 142–144.

Carletta, Jean, Stefan Evert, Ulrich Heid, Jonathan Kilgour, Judy Robertson & Holger Voormann. 2003. The NITE XML toolkit: Flexible annotation for multimodal language data. *Behavior Research Methods, Instruments, & Computers* 35(3). 353–363. https://doi.org/10.3758/BF03195511.

Chamberlin, Donald D. & Raymond F. Boyce. 1974. Sequel: A structured English query language. In *Proceedings of the 1974 ACM SIGFIDET (now SIGMOD) Workshop on Data Description, Access and Control*, 249–264. ACM. https://doi.org/10.1145/800296.811515.

Chiarcos, Christian, Stefanie Dipper, Michael Götze, Ulf Leser, Anke Lüdeling, Julia Ritz & Manfred Stede. 2008. A flexible framework for integrating annotations from different tools and tag sets. In Patrice Enjalbert, Kalina Bontcheva & Benoit Habert (eds.), *Traitement automatique des langues, volume 49, numéro 2 : Plate-formes pour le traitement automatique des langues [platforms for natural language processing]*, 217–246. ATALA (Association pour le Traitement Automatique des Langues). https://aclanthology.org/2008.tal-2.9/.

Christ, Oliver. 1994. A modular and flexible architecture for an integrated corpus query system. In *Papers in computational lexicography (COMPLEX '94)*, Budapest, Hungary, 22–32.

Codd, E. F. 1970. A relational model of data for large shared data banks. *Communications of the ACM* 13(6). 377–387. https://doi.org/10.1145/362384.362685.

Culpeper, Jonathan & J. Demmen. 2015. Keywords. In *The Cambridge handbook of English corpus linguistics*, 90–105. Cambridge: Cambridge University Press. https://doi.org/10.1007/9781139764377.006.

Davies, Mark. 2005. The advantage of using relational databases for large corpora: Speed, advanced queries, and unlimited annotation. *International Journal of Corpus Linguistics* 10(3). 301–328. https://doi.org/10.1075/ijcl.10.3.01dav.

Diewald, Nils & Joachim Bingel. 2017. KoralQuery 0.5. Edition: 0.3 2015-03-22. http://korap.github.io/Koral/.

Diewald, Nils, Michael Hanl, Eliza Margaretha, Joachim Bingel, Marc Kupietz, Piotr Bański & Andreas Witt. 2016. KorAP architecture – diving in the deep sea of corpus data. In Nicoletta Calzolari, Khalid Choukri, Thierry Declerck, Sara Goggi, Marko Grobelnik, Bente Maegaard, Joseph Mariani, Helene Mazo, Asuncion Moreno, Jan Odijk & Stelios Piperidis (eds.), *Proceedings of the Tenth International Conference on Language Resources and Evaluation (LREC'16)*, 3586–3591. Portorož, Slovenia: European Language Resources Association (ELRA). https://aclanthology.org/L16-1569.

Diewald, Nils & Eliza Margaretha. 2016. Krill: KorAP search and analysis engine. *Journal for Language Technology and Computational Linguistics* 31(1). 63–80. https://jlcl.org/article/view/202.

Dipper, Stefanie. 2005. XML-based stand-off representation and exploitation of multi-level linguistic annotation. In *Berliner XML Tage*. https://api.semanticscholar.org/CorpusID:6017695.

Dipper, Stefanie, Michael Götze, Manfred Stede & Tillmann Wegst. 2004. ANNIS: A linguistic database for exploring information structure. *Interdisciplinary studies on information structure: ISIS; working papers of the SFB632* 1. 245–279.

Evert, Stefan. 2009. Corpora and collocations. In Anke Lüdeling & Merja Kytö (eds.), *Corpus linguistics. An international handbook*, Vol. 2, 1212–1248. Berlin, New York: De Gruyter Mouton. https://doi.org/10.1515/9783110213881.2.1212.

Evert, Stefan. 2021. Finite state queries in CWB3. Tech. rep., Friedrich-Alexander-Universität Erlangen-Nürnberg. https://sourceforge.net/p/cwb/code/HEAD/tree/doc/technical/CWB3_finite_state_queries.pdf?format=raw.

Evert, Stefan, Jean Carletta, Timothy J. O'Donnell, Jonathan Kilgour, Andreas Vögele & Holger Voormann. 2003. The NXT object model. Tech. rep., Version 2.1. IMS, University of Stuttgart.

Evert, Stefan & Andrew Hardie. 2011. Twenty-first century corpus workbench: Updating a query architecture for the new millennium. In *Proceedings of the Corpus Linguistics 2011 conference*, 21–41.

Evert, Stefan & Andrew Hardie. 2015. Ziggurat: A new data model and indexing format for large annotated text corpora. In Piotr Bański, Hanno Biber, Evelyn Breiteneder, Marc Kupietz, Harald Lüngen & Andreas Witt (eds.), *Proceedings of the 3rd Workshop on Challenges in the Management of Large Corpora (CMLC-3)*, Lancaster, 20 July 2015, 21–27. Institut für Deutsche Sprache. https://nbn-resolving.org/urn:nbn:de:bsz:mh39-38335.

Evert, Stefan, Oleg Harlamov, Philipp Heinrich & Piotr Banski. 2020. Corpus Query Lingua Franca Part II: Ontology. In Nicoletta Calzolari *et al.* (eds.), *Proceedings of the Twelfth Language Resources and Evaluation Conference*, 3346–3352. European Language Resources Association. https://aclanthology.org/2020.lrec-1.410/.

Evert, Stefan & Holger Voormann. 2003. NQL – A query language for multi-modal language data. Tech. rep. IMS, University of Stuttgart. Version 2.1.

Evert, Stephanie, Andrew Hardie & Timm Weber. 2023. The Ziggurat data model and file format (draft 1.5). Tech. rep. Friedrich-Alexander-Universität Erlangen-Nürnberg. https://osf.io/n75es/.

Evert, Stephanie & The CWB Development Team. 2022a. Corpus encoding and management manual, CWB version 3.5. https://cwb.sourceforge.io/files/CWB_Encoding_Tutorial.pdf.

Evert, Stephanie & The CWB Development Team. 2022b. CQP interface and query language manual, CWB version 3.5. https://cwb.sourceforge.io/files/CQP_Manual.pdf.

Frick, Elena & Thomas Schmidt. 2025. Querying spoken language data. In Piotr Bański, Ulrich Heid & Laura Herzberg (eds.), *Harmonising language data: Standards for linguistic resources*. de Gruyter.

Friedl, Jeffrey. 2006. *Mastering regular expressions*, 3rd edn. Sebastopol, CA: O'Reilly Media.

Gärtner, Markus & Kerstin Jung. 2020. To boldly query what no one has annotated before? The frontiers of corpus querying. In Dan Jurafsky, Joyce Chai, Natalie Schluter & Joel Tetreault (eds.), *Proceedings of the 58th annual meeting of the association for computational linguistics*, 6307–6321. Online: Association for Computational Linguistics. https://aclanthology.org/2020.acl-main.562/.

Graff, David & Christopher Cieri. 2003. English Gigaword (LDC2003T05). Philadelphia: Linguistic Data Consortium. https://catalog.ldc.upenn.edu/LDC2003T05.

Halteren, Hans, Theo Heuvel & Ian Lancashire. 2002. Linguistic exploitation of syntactic databases: The use of the Nijmegen LDB program. *Language* 68. https://doi.org/10.2307/416875.

Hardie, Andrew. 2012. CQPweb — combining power, flexibility and usability in a corpus analysis tool. *International Journal of Corpus Linguistics* 17(3). 380–409. http://www.jbe-platform.com/content/journals/10.1075/ijcl.17.3.04har.

Hoffmann, Sebastian, Stefan Evert, Nicholas Smith, David Lee & Ylva Berglund Prytz. 2008. *Corpus linguistics with BNCweb – A practical guide*, Vol. 6. English Corpus Linguistics. Frankfurt am Main: Peter Lang.

Ide, Nancy & Laurent Romary. 2004. International standard for a linguistic annotation framework. *Natural Language Engineering* 10(3). 211–225. http://www.journals.cambridge.org/abstract_S135132490400350X.

Ide, Nancy & Laurent Romary. 2006. Representing linguistic corpora and their annotations. In Nicoletta Calzolari, Khalid Choukri, Aldo Gangemi, Bente Maegaard, Joseph Mariani, Jan Odijk & Daniel Tapias (eds.), *Proceedings of the Fifth International Conference on Language Resources and Evaluation (LREC'06)*, 225–228. Genoa, Italy: European Language Resources Association (ELRA). https://aclanthology.org/L06-1339/.

Ide, Nancy & Keith Suderman. 2007. GrAF: A graph-based format for linguistic annotations. In *Proceedings of the Linguistic Annotation Workshop – LAW '07*, 1–8. Association for Computational Linguistics. http://portal.acm.org/citation.cfm?doid=1642059.1642060.

ISO 24612. 2012. *Language resource management – Linguistic annotation framework (LAF)*. https://www.cs.vassar.edu/~ide/papers/ISO+24612-2012.pdf.

ISO 24623-1. 2018. *Language resource management – Corpus query lingua franca (CQLF) – Part 1: Metamodel.*

ISO 24623-2. 2021. *Language resource management – Corpus query lingua franca (CQLF) – Part 2: Ontology.*

ISO/IEC/IEEE 9945. 2009. Information technology – Portable Operating System Interface (POSIX®) Base Specifications, Issue 7. https://www.iso.org/standard/50516.html.

Janus, Daniel & Adam Przepiórkowski. 2007. Poliqarp: An open source corpus indexer and search engine with syntactic extensions. In *Proceedings of the 45th Annual Meeting of the Association for Computational Linguistics: Companion volume, Proceedings of the demo and poster sessions*, 85–88. Prague, Czech Republic: Association for Computational Linguistics. https://aclanthology.org/P07-2022.

Kermes, Hannah & Stefan Evert. 2002. YAC – A recursive chunker for unrestricted German text. In Manuel González Rodríguez & Carmen Paz Suarez Araujo (eds.), *Proceedings of the Third International Conference on Language Resources and Evaluation (LREC'02)*, 1805–1812. Las Palmas, Spain: European Language Resources Association (ELRA). https://aclanthology.org/L02-1202/.

Kilgarriff, Adam, Vít Baisa, Jan Bušta, Miloš Jakubíček, Vojtěch Kovář, Jan Michelfeit, Pavel Rychlý & Vít Suchomel. 2014. The Sketch Engine: Ten years on. *Lexicography* 1(1). 7–36. https://journal.equinoxpub.com/lexi/article/view/17961.

Kilgarriff, Adam, Pavel Rychlý, Pavel Smrz & David Tugwell. 2004. The Sketch Engine. In Geoffrey Williams & Sandra Vessier (eds.), *Proceedings of the 11th EURALEX international congress*, 105–115. Lorient, France: Université de Bretagne-Sud, Faculté des lettres et des sciences humaines.

Koehn, Philipp. 2005. Europarl: A parallel corpus for statistical machine translation. In *Proceedings of Machine Translation Summit X: Papers*, Phuket, Thailand, 79–86. https://aclanthology.org/2005.mtsummit-papers.11/.

Körner, Erik & Thomas Eckart. 2025. Accessing linguistic content in distributed research environments. In Piotr Bański, Ulrich Heid & Laura Herzberg (eds.), *Harmonising language data: Standards for linguistic resources*. de Gruyter.

Krause, Thomas. 2018. *ANNIS: A graph-based query system for deeply annotated text corpora.* Dissertation, Humboldt-Universität zu Berlin.

Krause, Thomas, Ulf Leser & Anke Lüdeling. 2016. graphANNIS: A fast query engine for deeply annotated linguistic corpora. *Journal for Language Technology and Computational Linguistics* 31(1). 1–25. https://doi.org/10.21248/jlcl.31.2016.199. https://jlcl.org/article/view/199.

Krause, Thomas & Amir Zeldes. 2016. ANNIS3: A new architecture for generic corpus query and visualization. *Literary and Linguistic Computing* 31. 118–139. https://doi.org/10.1093/llc/fqu057.

Kučera, Henry & W. Nelson Francis. 1967. *Computational analysis of present day American English.* Providence, RI: Brown University Press.

Kupietz, Marc, Harald Lüngen, Paweł Kamocki & Andreas Witt. 2018. The German Reference Corpus DeReKo: New developments – New opportunities. In Nicoletta Calzolari *et al.* (eds.), *Proceedings of the Eleventh International Conference on Language Resources and Evaluation (LREC 2018)*, 4353–4360. Miyazaki, Japan: European Language Resources Association (ELRA). https://aclanthology.org/L18-1689/.

Lezius, Wolfgang. 2002. TIGERSearch – ein Suchwerkzeug für Baumbanken. In Stephan Busemann (ed.), *Proceedings der 6. Konferenz zur Verarbeitung natürlicher Sprache (KONVENS 2002)*, 107–114.

Marcus, Mitchell P., Beatrice Santorini & Mary Ann Marcinkiewicz. 1993. Building a large annotated corpus of English: The Penn Treebank. *Computational Linguistics* 19(2). 313–330. https://aclanthology.org/J93-2004/.

Martens, Scott. 2012. TüNDRA: TIGERSearch-style treebank querying as an XQuery-based web service. In *Proceedings of the Joint CLARIN-d/DARIAH Workshop on Service-Oriented Architectures (SOAs) for the Humanities*. http://www.clarin-d.de/images/workshops/proceedingssoasforthehumanities.pdf.

McEnery, Tony & Andrew Hardie. 2012. *Corpus linguistics: Method, theory and practice.* Cambridge: Cambridge University Press.

Meurer, Paul. 2012. Corpuscle – A new corpus management platform for annotated corpora. In Gisle Andersen (ed.), *Studies in corpus linguistics*, Vol. 49, 31–50. John Benjamins Publishing Company. https://benjamins.com/catalog/scl.49.02meu.

Meurer, Paul. 2020. Designing efficient algorithms for querying large corpora. *Oslo Studies in Language* 11(2). 283–302. https://doi.org/10.5617/osla.8504. https://journals.uio.no/osla/article/view/8504.

Nelson, Gerald, Sean Wallis & Bas Aarts. 2002. *Exploring natural language: Working with the British component of the International Corpus of English.* John Benjamins. https://www.jbe-platform.com/content/books/9789027275356.

Proisl, Thomas. 2018. SoMeWeTa: A part-of-speech tagger for German social media and web texts. In Nicoletta Calzolari *et al.* (eds.), *Proceedings of the Eleventh International Conference on Language Resources and Evaluation (LREC 2018)*, 665–670. Miyazaki, Japan: European Language Resources Association (ELRA). https://aclanthology.org/L18-1106/.

Przepiórkowski, Adam, Zygmunt Krynicki, Łukasz Dębowski, Marcin Woliński, Daniel Janus & Piotr Bański. 2004. A search tool for corpora with positional tagsets and ambiguities. In Maria Teresa Lino, Maria Francisca Xavier, Fátima Ferreira, Rute Costa & Raquel Silva (eds.), *Proceedings of the Fourth International Conference on Language Resources and Evaluation (LREC'04)*, 1235–1238. Lisbon, Portugal: European Language Resources Association (ELRA). https://aclanthology.org/L04-1145/.

Rábara, Radoslav, Pavel Rychlý, Ondřej Herman & Miloš Jakubíček. 2017. Accelerating corpus search using multiple cores. In *Proceedings of the Workshop on Challenges in the Management of Large Corpora and Big Data and Natural Language Processing (CMLC-5 + BigNLP)*, Birmingham, UK, 30–34. http://nbn-resolving.de/urn:nbn:de:bsz:mh39-62629.

Resnik, Philip & Aaron Elkiss. 2005. The Linguist's Search Engine: An overview. In Masaaki Nagata & Ted Pedersen (eds.), *Proceedings of the ACL interactive poster and demonstration sessions*, 33–36. Ann Arbor, Michigan: Association for Computational Linguistics.

Rohde, Douglas L. T. 2005. TGrep2 user manual. https://www.cs.cmu.edu/afs/cs/project/cmt-55/lti/Courses/722/Spring-08/Penn-tbank/Tgrep2/tgrep2_manual.pdf.

Rosenfeld, Viktor. 2010. An implementation of the ANNIS 2 query language. Tech. rep. Humboldt-Universität zu Berlin.

Rüdiger, Jan Oliver. 2018. CorpusExplorer. Software package. http://corpusexplorer.de.

Rychlý, Pavel. 2007. Manatee/Bonito – A modular corpus manager. In *Proceedings of the 1st Workshop on Recent Advances in Slavonic Natural Language Processing*, 65–70. Brno: Masaryk University.

Schaber, Jonathan, Johannes Graën, Daniel McDonald, Igor Mustac, Nikolina Rajovic, Gerold Schneider & Noah Bubenhofer. 2023. The LiRI corpus platform. In Krister Linden, Jyrki Niemi & Thalassia Kontino (eds.), *CLARIN annual conference proceedings*, 145–149. CLARIN ERIC. https://doi.org/10.5167/uzh-257131.

Schäfer, Roland. 2015. Processing and querying large web corpora with the COW14 architecture. In Piotr Bański, Hanno Biber, Evelyn Breiteneder, Marc Kupietz, Harald Lüngen & Andreas Witt (eds.), *Proceedings of Challenges in the Management of Large Corpora 3 (CMLC-3)*, Lancaster, UK: UCREL. http://rolandschaefer.net/?p=749.

Schmid, Helmut, Arne Fitschen & Ulrich Heid. 2004. SMOR: A German computational morphology covering derivation, composition, and inflection. In Maria Teresa Lino, Maria Francisca Xavier, Fátima Ferreira, Rute Costa & Raquel Silva (eds.), *Proceedings of the Fourth International Conference on Language Resources and Evaluation (LREC'04)*, 1263–1266. Lisbon, Portugal: European Language Resources Association (ELRA). https://aclanthology.org/L04-1275/.

Schälkle, Kuno & Wilhelm Ott. 2023. TUSTEP: Tübinger System von Textverarbeitungs-Programmen. https://www.tustep.uni-tuebingen.de/.

Scott, Mike. 2024. WordSmith Tools version 9. Stroud: Lexical Analysis Software. https://www.lexically.net/wordsmith/.

Sporny, Manu, Dave Longley, Gregg Kellogg, Markus Lanthaler & Niklas Lindström. 2014. JSON-LD 1.0 – A JSON-based serialization for linked data. https://www.w3.org/TR/json-ld/.

Steiner, Ilona & Laura Kallmeyer. 2002. VIQTORYA – A visual query tool for syntactically annotated corpora. In Manuel González Rodríguez & Carmen Paz Suarez Araujo (eds.), *Proceedings of the Third International Conference on Language Resources and Evaluation (LREC'02)*, 1704–1711. Las Palmas, Spain: European Language Resources Association (ELRA). https://aclanthology.org/L02-1116/.

Witten, Ian H., Alistair Moffat & Timothy C. Bell. 1999. *Managing gigabytes: Compressing and indexing documents and images*, 2nd edn. Multimedia Information and Systems Series. Elsevier Science. https://books.google.de/books?id=2F74jyPI48EC.

Zeldes, Amir, Anke Lüdeling, Julia Ritz & Christian Chiarcos. 2009. ANNIS: A search tool for multi-layer annotated corpora. In *Proceedings of the Corpus Linguistics 2009 conference*. https://doi.org/10.18452/13437.

Zipser, Florian. 2009. *Entwicklung eines Konverterframeworks für linguistisch annotierte Daten auf Basis eines gemeinsamen (Meta-)modells*, MA thesis, Humboldt-Universität zu Berlin. https://hal.science/hal-00606102.

Zipser, Florian. 2012. Salt model guide. Tech. rep. Humboldt-Universität zu Berlin. https://raw.githubusercontent.com/korpling/salt/master/gh-site/doc/salt_modelGuide.pdf.

Zipser, Florian. 2014. SaltNPepper und das Formatpluriversum. Presentation at the LAUDATIO workshop. https://doi.org/10.5281/zenodo.17557.

Elena Frick and Thomas Schmidt

Querying spoken language data

Abstract: This chapter is about query mechanisms for spoken language corpora as used in different fields of linguistics. After discussing properties specific to this type of data and setting it apart from written language (see Evert et al. 2025), an overview of existing technology and approaches to standardisation for querying spoken language data is provided. The chapter concludes by illustrating some of the concepts in more detail using the FOLK corpus in the ZuMult platform as an example.

Keywords: corpus query platforms, querying transcriptions, spoken language, audiovisual data, interaction corpora

1 Introduction

Spoken language data, recorded on audio and/or video, is an object of study in different subdisciplines of linguistics, such as interactional linguistics, variational linguistics (dialectology), language documentation, or phonetics, and it also plays an important role in other academic disciplines, for instance in oral history studies or qualitative social sciences. Spoken language can have different degrees of interactivity, naturalness and spontaneity. At one end of the spectrum, there is highly natural, spontaneous interaction data, such as a casual face-to-face conversation; on the other end, there is monologic "speech" that is elicited in experimental settings or follows a written script. This chapter is focussing on the former type of data as it is typically used in interactional linguistics. As far as data structures are concerned, this is the most complex case, so solutions developed for this scenario can be expected to be fruitful also for the other types.

For spoken language data, corpus linguistic queries are just one approach to analysis besides many others (such as, e. g. acoustic analysis of the speech signal or qualitative micro-analysis of transcript sequences). Querying spoken language data

Acknowledgement: The authors acknowledge the use of Large Language Models (LLMs) as writing aids in phrasing this chapter, based on the authors' notes, ideas, and concepts. The authors retain full responsibility for the content.

Elena Frick, Pragmatik, Leibniz-Institut für Deutsche Sprache, R5 6-13, Mannheim, Germany, e-mail: frick@ids-mannheim.de
Thomas Schmidt, Institut für Kommunikationswissenschaft, University of Duisburg Essen, Universitätsstraße 2, 45141 Essen, Germany, e-mail: thomas@linguisticbits.de

https://doi.org/10.1515/9783112208212-014

means querying (annotated) *transcriptions* of audio or video recordings. The immediate target for the query is therefore not the primary data, but secondary data derived from it through a systematic, methodologically grounded process. Still, although transcriptions are a form of texts, they have specific properties that distinguish them from normal written text and that make adaptations to query technology necessary. These specific properties will be discussed in the following section.

The chapter is structured as follows: Section 2 provides an overview of the specific properties of spoken language data that set them apart from written language data. Section 3 briefly summarises the most important standards for this type of data. Section 4 gives an overview of existing systems for working with spoken language corpora, organised according to the solutions they choose for query. Section 5 illustrates different queries of spoken language data on the concrete example of the FOLK corpus in the ZuMult platform. Section 6 concludes the chapter with a summary and outlook.

There are many other aspects of spoken language data that are directly or indirectly related to the topic of querying. For more comprehensive accounts of the subject, the reader is referred to Edwards and Lampert (1992), Leech et al. (1995), Ruhi et al. (2014), Kirk and Andersen (2016), or Love (2024).

2 Specific properties of (working with) spoken language data

2.1 Primary and secondary data: recordings and transcripts

As a rule, querying spoken language data means querying written transcripts of audiovisual recordings. While many aspects can thus be understood in a recourse to written data, it is important to be aware of the fundamentally different epistemological status that transcripts have in comparison to a "born-written" text: a digital transcript is not a simple reproduction of the language recorded on audio or video, but a model of it (Schmidt 2005). It involves informed and systematic decisions on which phenomena to include, how to represent them, and which aspects of spoken language to leave out of the representation. Transcription is thus to a significant part guided by theory and research interests (Ochs 1979). For corpus query, this means, on the one hand, that a researcher can have a more precise expectation of what to look for, because transcription conventions may take active measures to reduce variation (e. g. by prescribing a certain spelling variant for a word). On the other hand, it limits the possibilities of what to find, because only those phenomena which are represented in the transcription can be addressed by a query (for instance, if transcription follows standard orthography, deviant dialectal pronunciation cannot be found via a query).

2.2 "Special" tokens

The "token" is a fundamental unit for queries. In most written language corpora, tokens are either words or punctuation characters. These units figure in spoken language transcripts, too, but spontaneous speech often contain further types of tokens. Most importantly, transcripts typically include pauses, i. e. silences between or within words, and audible non-speech items, such as laughing, coughing, sighing, etc. Transcription conventions will prescribe if and how such additional types of tokens find their way into the transcript, and they both expand and complicate possibilities for querying the data. For example, it may be interesting in some cases to do queries for specific words followed by a pause, while in other cases, an intervening pause may be a factor interfering with the calculation of token distances.

Furthermore, spoken language can contain special tokens that owe to the "performance" aspect of spontaneous speech: disfluencies can manifest themselves as incomplete or repeated words, and filled pauses (aka hesitation markers, such as "euh") can occur at any place in the speech stream. Again, such phenomena can be the target of some queries (see e. g. Wieling et al. 2016 for an advanced study of hesitations markers in Germanic languages), while they may constitute an undesired complication in others.

Last but not least, general features of colloquial speech as well as the regional or dialectal variation of spoken language, if they are taken into account during transcription, can lead to a greater diversity of lexical tokens. "Literary transcription" or "eye dialect" (see, for example, Bowdre 1964) may be used to represent one and the same lexical form in different ways if it occurs in a contraction (e. g. "dunno" for "do not know") or if it is pronounced in a non-standard or casual way (e. g. "lil" instead of "little"). In some corpora, an additional annotation layer for orthographic normalisation (Blevins 2023) is introduced in order to balance the precision of literary transcription against the better predictability of standard orthographic forms.

2.3 Parallel/simultaneous structures

At the heart of most query languages is the concept of language as a "stream of tokens", i. e. a linear, one-dimensional sequence of basic units of language. Query expressions operate with this concept, for example, in their definition of co-occurrences and token distances. In contrast to written language, spoken language does not unfold in a completely linear sequence. Most importantly, spoken interaction will contain instances of simultaneous speech when speakers are signalling their attention to what is being said ("backchannels") or when whole utterances partly or fully overlap. In these cases, there is no clear ordering of tokens, which constitutes another challenge for data modelling and querying.

While this simultaneity on the verbal level of interaction can still be viewed as an exception to the rule, parallel structures are ubiquitous when other modalities are taken into account. For video-recorded interactions, visible, "bodily" aspects of communication, such as gestures, facial expression, body posture, may also be transcribed or annotated. These constitute additional streams of annotation on the primary data which are structurally independent of (or at least: not trivially related to) the text of transcribed utterances. Specialised approaches to integrate this additional level of complexity into corpus queries exist (e. g. Rühlemann and Ptak 2023, Knight 2010, Parian-Scherb et al. 2024), but they will not be treated in depth in this chapter.

2.4 Speaker metadata

Metadata are a crucial component of queries, because they are used to relate linguistic phenomena to extra-linguistic properties (as in, for instance, "Find occurrences of the word 'Covid' in newspaper texts after 2023"). For written texts, metadata typically refer to the text as a whole (e. g. "text type=newspaper article" or "author gender=female"). The interactive nature of spoken language, by contrast, entails the necessity to assign individual parts of the "text" (i. e. the transcript) to a speaker, and metadata about that speaker will consequently only be applicable to parts of that text. Data models underlying the representation of transcripts with their metadata will have to take this additional complexity into account, and query languages must be able to formulate corresponding constraints (for instance: "find adjectives uttered by female speakers under 40 years of age").

2.5 (Re-)contextualisation of query results

Spoken interaction is "situated" communication: more than written language, it is embedded within and influenced by the specific context or environment in which it occurs. To understand and interpret a query result, researchers will need information about this context. The classical means in corpus linguistics to provide context is the KWIC (Key Word In Context) concordance, which displays a small amount of preceding and following tokens for a query result. While this is as efficient and effective for spoken language as it is for written language, it often turns out to be insufficient to fully understand and interpret a given occurrence of a spoken form. Corpus platforms dedicated to spoken language therefore need to provide additional means of accessing additional context of a query result. Most importantly, this includes access to a wider context in the transcript (to see what other speakers said or did previously), a recourse to the underlying recording (e. g. to get prosodic cues necessary to interpret an utterance) and the possibility to retrieve specific metadata (e. g. to get an idea of speakers' familiarity with each other). As an example, consider the KWIC in Figure 1 which shows query results for the form "why" in the Research and Teaching Corpus of Spoken German (FOLK, Schmidt 2016b) in the Database for Spoken German (DGD, Schmidt 2014). For the query result in line 8 of the KWIC, displaying the utterance in its transcript context reveals that the speaker is reading an error message from a computer system. Likewise, retrieving metadata about the "medial realisation" of the interaction shows that this utterance occurs in a video conference. Both facts would have been impossible to deduce from the KWIC representation alone.

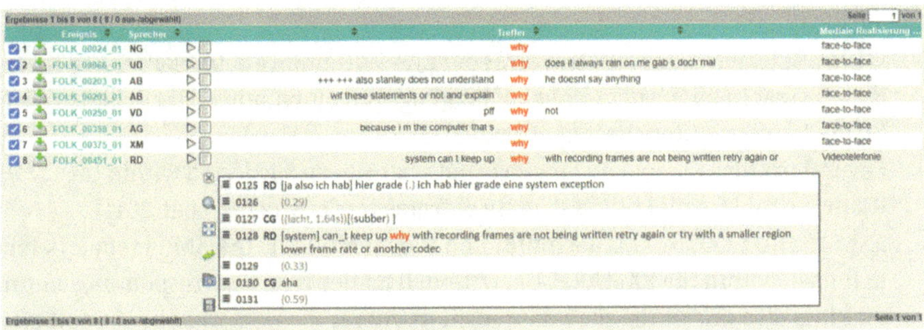

Figure 1: The result of a query in the Database for Spoken German (DGD) on the Research and Teaching Corpus of Spoken German (FOLK): All results are displayed as KWIC (Key Word In Context). An additional column on the right displays metadata ("medial realisation") about the interaction. For the last query result, additional context is provided via a folded-out transcript excerpt. The corresponding part of the underlying audio recording can be played back by double clicking on any position in the transcript excerpt.

3 Standards for data

All spoken language corpus queries rely on the corpus data adhering to established standards. Before turning to standards for querying proper in the following section, the most important standards for data are briefly recapitulated here.

3.1 Audio and video

Industry standards exist for digital audio and video recordings. While uncompressed PCM-WAV with sample rates of 44.1 kHz or 48 kHz is the most commonly used standard for encoding audio, MPEG-4 (as a codec and a container) is the most widely used standard for encoding video recordings. HD resolution (1080p) is desirable to be able to identify details of facial expression, body posture etc. (for more information see Ferreira et al. 2025).

3.2 Metadata

Metadata for spoken language corpora need to be able to record comprehensive and diverse information on communicative events and interlocutors. While XML or tabular formats (CSV, spreadsheets, etc.) can be regarded as a common ground for representing metadata in a structured manner, no single solution so far has managed to achieve the status of a real standard (cf. e. g. Lange 2022). The following solutions, however, are widely used and can be regarded as candidates for further standardisation:

- IMDI (ISLE Metadata Initiative, Broeder and Wittenburg 2006) serves as a metadata format in different archives of language documentation data. It is also used by the Lameta editor (Hatton et al. 2021)
- Several profiles for spoken language data have been suggested within the CMDI (Component Metadata Infrastructure) framework (Broeder et al. 2011)
- EXMARaLDA COMA XML (Schmidt and Wörner 2014) is the XML metadata format used within the EXMARaLDA system. It comes with a corresponding editor, and it is also one of the metadata formats currently supported by ZuMult (see Section 4.2.3.5 for the description of the ZuMult platform)

To integrate a spoken language corpus into a corpus platform, appropriate conversion of metadata into the format supported by the platform may be necessary. As long as one of the above solutions is used consistently, this is usually not a major problem.

3.3 Transcripts and annotations

As described in more detail in Werthmann (2025), a small number of (usually XML based) tool formats (ELAN, EXMARaLDA, etc.) can be viewed as de-facto-standards for representing spoken language transcription and annotation (see Schmidt et al. 2009). The TEI-based standard "ISO 24624:2016 – Language resource management –

Transcription of spoken language" is a published international standard, largely compatible with these tool formats. The ZuMult platform described in Section 4.2.3.5 operates with data in this standard.

3.3.1 Transcription conventions

An often-overlooked aspect of standardisation for spoken language corpora concerns the conventions used for transcription. The International Phonetic Alphabet (IPA) is a well- established standard for phonetic transcription and can nowadays be used in any solution with support for Unicode characters. For orthography-based transcription, the landscape is much more diverse and fragmented, with conventions often specific to a single language or a single corpus. Some proposals for orthographic transcription have at least become widespread for certain languages and research paradigms. For example, GAT (Selting et al. 2009) is widely used in German conversation analysis, and there are adaptations for other languages (English, Spanish, Portuguese), as well as a dedicated version cGAT (Schmidt et al. 2023) for computer-assisted transcription. For language acquisition data, CHAT (MacWhinney 2024) is a long-standing, international de-facto standard.

3.3.2 Annotation schemes

Last but not least, spoken corpus querying profits from annotations adhering to existing standards. Few solutions specifically dedicated to spoken language have achieved the status of a standard. Among the more widely established solutions is the STTS 2.0 Part-of-Speech tagset (Westpfahl et al. 2017) which builds on a widely used tagset for written language and has adaptations specific to spoken German in interaction.

4 Platforms and query languages

An increasing number of spoken language corpora are being made accessible online for research purposes. However, only a part of these corpora is available for transcript analysis through specialised tools, such as concordances, which enable efficient and systematic querying of linguistic patterns (see *Spoken Corpora Overview* in *CLARIN Resource Families*[1]). This limited availability may be attributed, on the

1 https://www.clarin.eu/resource-families/spoken-corpora (accessed 27 January 2025).

one hand, to the relatively small size of spoken language corpora (in comparison to text corpora) and the fact that access to primary data, such as audio or video, is traditionally considered more essential for the analysis of spoken language. On the other hand, it could be due to the fact that specialised software solutions capable of handling the complexity of spoken language (see Section 2) are still in earlier stages of development. Furthermore, a major challenge remains the lack of standardised query tools that can be easily used for different spoken language data formats.

Currently, the query options available for spoken language corpora are limited in the number of existing tools, but the technologies applied are diverse and range from simple transcript editors with basic search functions to more complex analysis platforms based on powerful search engines. In the following, some important tools will be listed, providing the reader with an overview of different approaches for querying spoken language transcriptions.

4.1 Desktop tools

Nowadays, specialised transcription editors are used to transcribe and annotate audio and video recordings. These tools usually work with tier-based data models and provide a visual representation of overlapping structures (e. g. simultaneous utterances by different speakers) in a musical score view (see Figure 2) synchronised with the underlying media stream (see Schmidt (2022) for more information). Some of the editors have extensive features that not only facilitate the creation and annotation of spoken language transcripts (e. g. by automating certain processes) but also enable in-depth data exploration through various query functions. Praat, Exmaralda, ELAN and SPPAS are some of the well-known and widely used editors that can be mentioned here as examples.

4.1.1 PRAAT

PRAAT (Boersma 2014) is a versatile tool for speech and acoustic analysis that uses the text-based TextGrid format to store linguistic annotations of audio files. It provides a simple “Find in Text” option that allows users to search through annotations and jump to the corresponding intervals. For more complex searches and statistical analysis, the Praat scripting language can be used to automate and customise queries across multiple TextGrid files.

4.1.2 EXMARaLDA

EXMARaLDA (Schmidt and Wörner 2014) is a suite of complementary tools designed for working with oral corpora. Among its components is a graphical query interface called EXAKT (EXMARaLDA Analysis and Concordance Tool, see Figure 2), which allows users to search for transcribed and annotated phenomena within a corpus by using keywords, regular expressions, and XPath expressions for complex structural queries. The search results display all occurrences within their context and can be filtered by metadata and annotations from other layers. The KWIC view can be saved and exported in various formats (e. g. HTML, XML), and customised using XSL stylesheets. While EXMARaLDA primarily works with its own (XML-based) EXB file format, it also supports import and export of many other formats, including PRAAT, ELAN, and ISO/TEI standard for transcriptions of spoken language (24624:2016).

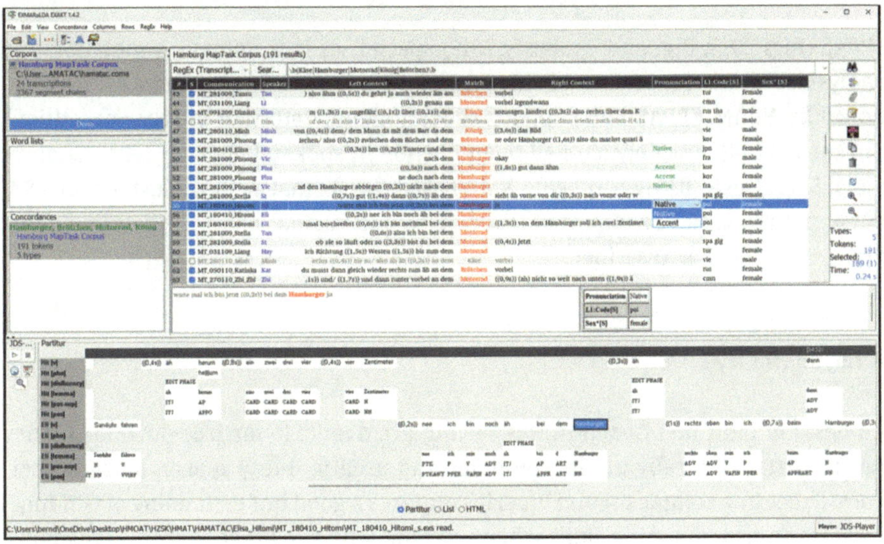

Figure 2: A query in EXMARaLDA EXAKT on the Hamburg Maptask Corpus (HaMaTaC, Hedeland and Schmidt 2012): The query is formulated as a regular expression (top), the result is shown as a KWIC with selected speaker metadata (sex and first languages of the speaker) displayed in additional columns. Another column ("pronunciation") is used to manually annotate individual query results. In the lower part of the screen, the full transcript context with all annotations is displayed in musical score format. The underlying audio can be played back from there.

4.1.3 ELAN

ELAN (Sloetjes 2014, Wilbur 2019), developed for working with video data, provides more advanced query options. It allows users to search across multiple transcript files and query specific annotation patterns based on their position (e. g. whether one annotation follows or precedes another), alignment (e. g. overlap or identical start points), and parent-child relationships in hierarchical tiers. Additionally, it is possible to use variables and search for annotations that meet specific duration criteria (e. g. longer than two seconds). ELAN primarily uses the (XML-based) EAF (ELAN Annotation Format) file format but also supports the import and export of TextGrid, CHAT, and other formats for exchanging annotation data.

4.1.4 SPPAS

SPPAS (Bigi 2015, Bigi and Saubesty 2015) specialises in automatic annotation and analysis solutions for audio and video data. In addition to the search functions mentioned by ELAN, SPPAS also supports the automatic detection of other-repetitions (Bigi et al. 2014), a widely studied phenomenon in spoken language. Like the other tools, SPPAS uses its own specific XML-based file format with the extension XRA, but annotations can be imported and exported in various other formats, including Praat, ELAN, and Transcriber.

4.1.5 Summary

All desktop tools mentioned in this section are available for free download. They can be installed locally on the computer and used to query spoken language corpora. Executing complex search queries requires a good understanding of GUI functions (even programming skills when working with the Praat scripting language), and some training may be needed. However, these editors are indispensable when working with one's own data. Each of them has its strengths in the presentation or evaluation of search results and can complement the others.

4.2 Online platforms

Researchers looking for alternatives to collecting their own datasets can turn to corpus resources available online through various corpus analysis platforms. Typically, users need to register to gain access. Once registered, they can utilise a wide range of linguistically annotated datasets and powerful tools designed for systematic search and in-depth analysis of these corpora.

Corpus analysis platforms that provide access to spoken language data vary widely in terms of search capabilities and the underlying query technologies. Starting with how users submit queries, these platforms can be categorised into two main groups: those without a dedicated query language, but with graphical query solutions that allow a visual and menu-based composition of queries, and those that support a dedicated corpus query language enabling users to formulate linguistically motivated search requests using specialised syntax. A further distinction can be made regarding the specific type of query language supported by these platforms (CQP, CQP-like or another query language).

4.2.1 Platforms without dedicated query language

What characterises platforms in this category is their focus on spoken language. These platforms were specifically developed for working with oral data and are well-equipped to handle audio and video recordings, with particular emphasis on ensuring the alignment between sound and transcription. Additionally, they provide access to full transcripts and include browsing features, such as detailed filters for speaker and event metadata and even interactive maps showing the locations where recordings were made. Notable examples of such platforms include:

4.2.1.1 DGD

DGD (Datenbank für Gesprochenes Deutsch, Schmidt 2014) is a database offering access to a vast audio and video collection of spoken German corpora from various regions of Germany and around the world. Built on an Oracle relational database, the platform supports token-based concordance searches, which can be combined with metadata and context filters. For selected corpora, a positional filter is available, allowing users to specify the position of searched tokens relative to parts of contributions, speaker changes, overlaps, pauses, and other non-verbal events.

The following example of a query in DGD exemplifies how queries can be built up step-for-step in a GUI.

1. The first query element (tab POSITION, see Figure 3) restricts searches to positions where the item to be found is in the second position of a pair of assimilated words (such as *has_te* – 'hast Du' in German or *y_all* – 'you all' in English).

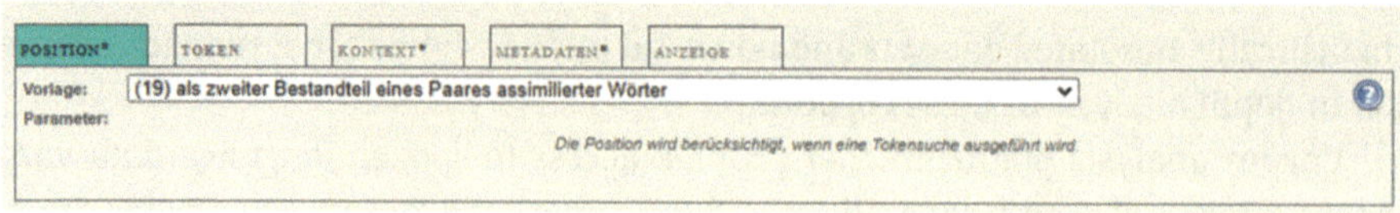

Figure 3: Specifying the position.

2. The second query element (tab TOKEN, see Figure 4) specifies the normalised form *Du* ('you') as the actual form to be searched.

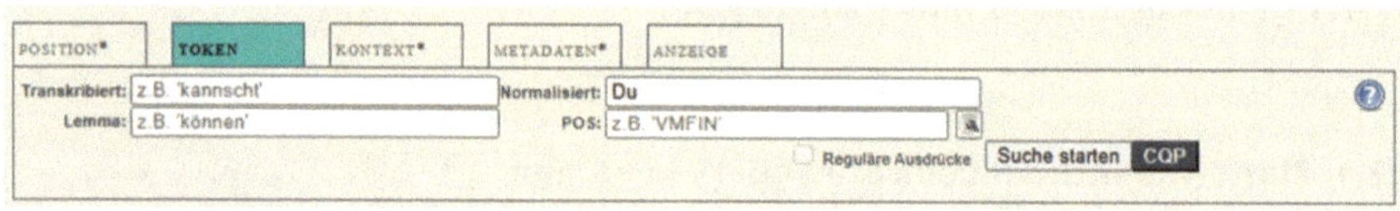

Figure 4: Specifying properties of the token.

3. The third query element (tab KONTEXT, see Figure 5) restricts results to those places where a modal verb (inflected or not: this is the regular expression (`VMFIN|VMINF`)) occurs in the left context of the token with a distance not greater than 5.

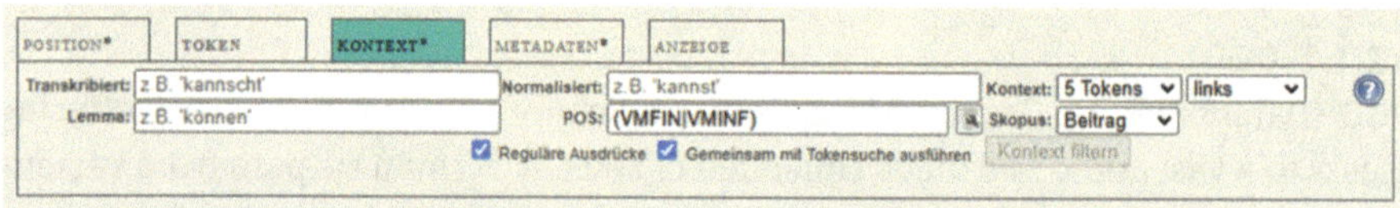

Figure 5: Specifying properties of tokens in the context.

4. The fourth query element (tab METADATEN, see Figure 6) restricts results to interactions recorded in the north of Germany (regular expression `nordost|nordwest`) and to speakers born between 1950 and 1980.

Figure 6: Specifying metadata.

The result is displayed as a KWIC (Figure 7) where each line can be expanded to provide additional transcript context (line 3). Double clicking inside such a transcript excerpt will playback the corresponding audio. Individual lines of the KWIC can be deselected and removed, for instance when they represent a false positive (line 13).

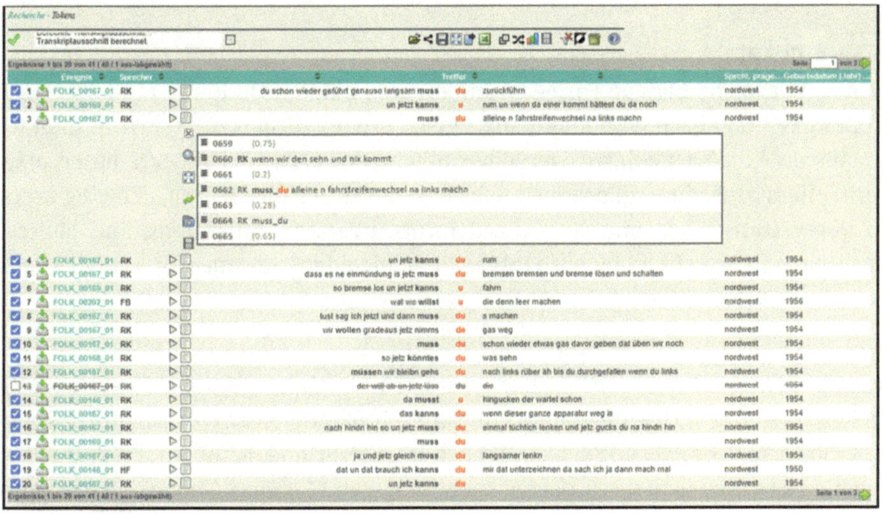

Figure 7: KWIC with one line expanded as a result of a query in the DGD.

4.2.1.2 GeWiss

GeWiss (Gesprochene Wissenschaftssprache, Slavcheva and Meißner 2014) is a platform of a comparable corpus of spoken academic language. It includes recorded and transcribed L1 and L2 speech from German, English, Polish, and Italian, focusing on oral exams and presentations by researchers and students. Users can browse the corpus and search for transcribed tokens and segment-based annotations, such as code-switching and discourse comments. Hits can be displayed and listened to within a broader context, with transcripts shown in the musical score view and synchronised with the playing audio. Extended search offers a comprehensive metadata filter. The platform uses a PHP/MySQL solution for storing and querying data.

4.2.1.3 ESLO

ESLO (Enquêtes Sociolinguistiques à Orléans, Baude and Dugua 2017) is a large corpus of audio-recorded interactions (mostly sociolinguistic interviews, but also free conversation, service interactions, etc.) documenting spoken French in Orléans in a micro-diachronic perspective. The first set of recordings were made in the 1970s, the second after 2000 until now. Search capabilities include a preselection of data according to properties of interviews or speakers (e. g. category of interaction, speakers' age) and a query on the transcribed text with some possibilities to formulate regular expression-like patterns as query terms. Search results are linked to the full transcriptions, which can run in parallel with the audio playback.[2]

4.2.1.4 CLAPI

CLAPI (Corpus de Langue Parlée en Interaction, Baldauf-Quilliatre et al. 2016) is a multimedia database with audio and video corpora of spoken French in interactional contexts, particularly everyday conversations. The PHP/MySQL-based platform offers browsing, collocation analysis and concordance search, allowing users to query transcribed and stem-based forms, overlaps, repetitions, and pauses. Searches can be refined by partial matching, metadata, distance, precedence, and sensitivity constraints.

4.2.1.5 OFROM

OFROM (Le corpus Oral de Français de Suisse Romande, Avanzi et al. 2016) is a corpus platform for analysing spoken French in Switzerland. It supports searches for tokens, character sequences, part-of-speech tags, and lemmas. The search functionalities include metadata options for speaker and social contexts, as well as a comprehensive filter that allows users to apply multiple conditions on the surrounding transcript context. This includes the ability to include and exclude specific tokens and define their distance, including within specified time intervals.

4.2.1.6 GOS

GOS (GOvorni korpus Slovenščine, Verdonik et al. 2013) is a corpus platform for spoken Slovenian, containing audio recordings of academic speech as well as public and private events such as descriptions or explanations, free dialogue conversations, workshops, round tables, interviews, parliamentary speeches. Its concordancer, built on OpenSearch and PostgreSQL, offers both simple searches (for words or phrases based on either standardised or pronunciation spelling) and advanced searches (by specifying grammatical and contextual features). The KWIC view includes playback functionality and a metadata filter to refine search results. Unlike other platforms listed above, GOS is open source, allowing users to set it up for their own corpora.

---

2 The ESLO platform is currently being remade. The corpus will eventually be available on a ZuMult platform with much extended query options.

4.2.1.7 Summary

The KWIC concordances of the platforms in this section use graphical search interfaces (= search forms) that vary depending on the specific phenomena annotated in the corpora (e. g. DGD allows to search for assimilated words, CLAPI for repetitions and GOS for pronunciation). The search forms typically consist of one or more input fields, each corresponding to the available annotation layers in the corpus (e. g. transcribed or normalised form, lemma, part-of-speech, etc.). Users can enter tokens or token sequences into these fields for search. Additionally, the search interface is enhanced with a variety of filtering options that allow users to refine their queries by specifying token contexts (e. g. preceded or followed by a certain token) and other search parameters (e. g. case sensitivity, consideration of accents/diacritics, inclusion of alternative spellings, etc.). Detailed filters for speaker and event metadata are available in each platform. Since these platforms are specifically designed to meet the needs of spoken language analysis, they also account for spoken language-specific phenomena, such as pauses, overlaps, repetitions, etc., and provide search functionality to explore these features.

While the platforms described so far do not offer a dedicated query language, they nevertheless allow users to perform sophisticated searches across transcriptions, annotations, and metadata, including speaker details and event metadata. Their search functionality is, however, often limited to a fixed set of annotation types. To incorporate corpora with new annotation types, the platforms themselves usually require modifications such as adapting the backend or expanding the user interface. In summary, platforms in this category are designed for a specific corpus or corpus type of spoken language and focus their search functionality on the specific annotations available in those corpora.

4.2.2 Platforms with CQP as a dedicated query language

A large group of online corpus analysis platforms is built on top of the IMS Corpus Workbench (CWB)[3] and the Corpus Query Processor (CQP) making it possible to query corpora using a formal language with a specialised syntax called CQP.[4] To illustrate the syntax of CQP, some example queries are provided below, emphasizing the distinctive features of the query language for different corpus search tasks:

(1) `[lemma="smile" & pos="V.*"]`
returns all verb forms of the lemma *smile*

3 https://cwb.sourceforge.io/ (accessed 27 January 2025).

4 https://cwb.sourceforge.io/files/CQP_Manual.pdf (accessed 27 January 2025).

(2) <u>[ ]
finds any token at the beginning of an utterance

(3) [word="some"] []{0,2} [pos="NN"] within u
searches *some* followed directly or indirectly (up to 2 tokens in between) by any noun within an utterance

CQPWeb, SpoCo, Glossa and TEITOK can be cited as representative examples of corpus platforms using CQP as a query language.

4.2.2.1 CQPWeb

CQPWeb (Hardie 2012) is a web-based graphical user interface for CWB. Experienced users can query and analyse texts using the CQP query language. For beginners, CQPWeb offers a simplified query language, CEQL, covering the most common CQP features. The following are examples selected from the CEQL manual:[5]

(4) super+_V*
searches verb forms starting with *super-*

(5) !on_{PREP} fire
searches *fire* not preceded by preposition *on*

(6) {waste/V} <<s>> (time <<3>> money)
searches the verb *waste* that must co-occur with *time* as well as *money* in the same sentence; but time and money must be closer together (within a 3-token window)

As an open source tool, CQPWeb is widely used across various corpus platforms (cf. the CQPWeb family, Xu 2015). The main instance of CQPWeb, hosted at Lancaster University,[6] provides access to an extensive collection of text corpora. In recent years, the collection has expanded to include several spoken language corpora, such as Spoken BNC2014 (Love et al. 2017), Longman Spoken American Corpus (Stern 1997), and ICNALE Spoken Dialogue (Ishikawa 2019), among others. CQP and CEQL can be used to query transcriptions of these corpora. Features for working with audio and video are either not yet available, as in the CQPWeb instance at Lancaster University (see Figure 8), or are limited to providing links for displaying media data in the browser, as for example in the CQPWeb instance hosted at the University of Erlangen.[7]

5 https://cqpweb.lancs.ac.uk/doc/cqpweb-simple-syntax-help.pdf (accessed 27 January 2025).

6 https://cqpweb.lancs.ac.uk/ (accessed 27 January 2025).

7 https://multimodalcorpora.org/web/ (accessed 27 January 2025).

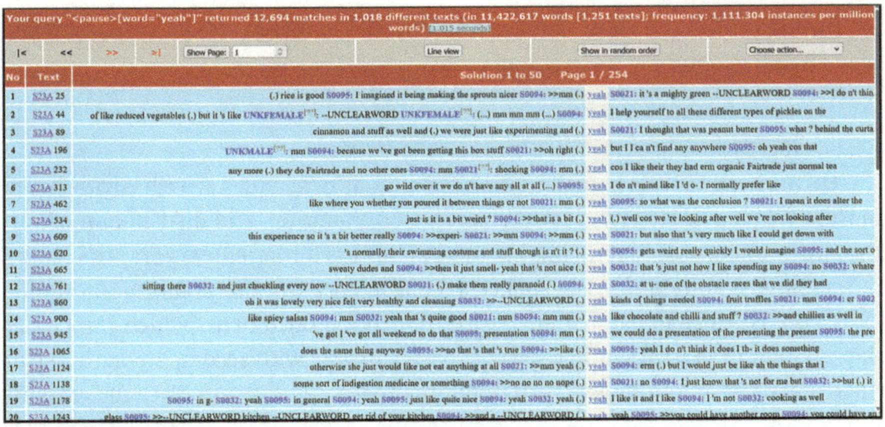

Figure 8: KWIC view in CQPWeb user interface: Query looking for the form *yeah* occurring after a pause, performed on Spoken BNC2014.

4.2.2.2 SpoCo

SpoCo (von Waldenfels and Woźniak 2016) is a web-based system designed for querying spoken language corpora with aligned audio files. Developed for dialect research, it is widely used in a network of Slavic dialect projects, cf. e.g. SpoCo instances for the Ustja River Basin Corpus[8] (von Waldenfels et al. 2014) and for the Corpus of Spoken Rusyn[9] (Rabus and Šymon 2015). For storing and querying corpus data, the platform utilises the CWB and the CQP query language. Each corpus hit in SpoCo is accompanied by audio playback and can also be downloaded for further analysis using PRAAT or other speech analysis software.

4.2.2.3 Glossa

Glossa (Kosek et al. 2015, Nøklestad et al. 2017, Priestley et al. 2024) is an open source corpus search system designed to process both multilingual (parallel) and multimodal corpora, including those with audio and video content. Built on the CWB, it features a web-based interface that aims to simplify the creation of complex CQP queries through the use of graphical elements and annotation filters. For spoken corpora, such as the Nordic Dialect Corpus[10] (Johannessen et al. 2009), search results

8 http://www.parasolcorpus.org/Pushkino/login.php (accessed 27 January 2025).

9 www.russinisch.uni-freiburg.de/corpus (accessed 27 January 2025).

10 https://tekstlab.uio.no/nota/scandiasyn/, GLOSSA instance under https://tekstlab.uio.no/glossa3/ (accessed 27 January 2025).

are linked to audio and video streams, and can be visualised through spectrographic analysis and geographic distribution maps.

4.2.2.4 TEITOK

TEITOK (Janssen 2016) is another online corpus platform with a search engine based on the CWB. It was designed for the creation, annotation, and distribution of various types of corpora, including historical manuscript-based corpora, treebanks, and audio-visual datasets. For spoken language corpora, the platform allows the KWIC context to be expanded into full transcription documents which can be displayed either in TEI/XML or in a speaker-based format, with accompanying audio or video playback. Additionally, TEITOK offers the Wavesurfer interface for working with audio files (see Figure 9). To facilitate the search process, the platform provides a graphical query builder, enabling users to easily construct CQP queries. As an open source platform, TEITOK is highly customizable, making it adaptable for a wide range of research projects, cf. e. g. TEITOK instances for MADISON[11] – A Sound Map for Portuguese Dialects and CoOrAJe[12] – The Annotated Oral Corpus of Judeo-Spanish.

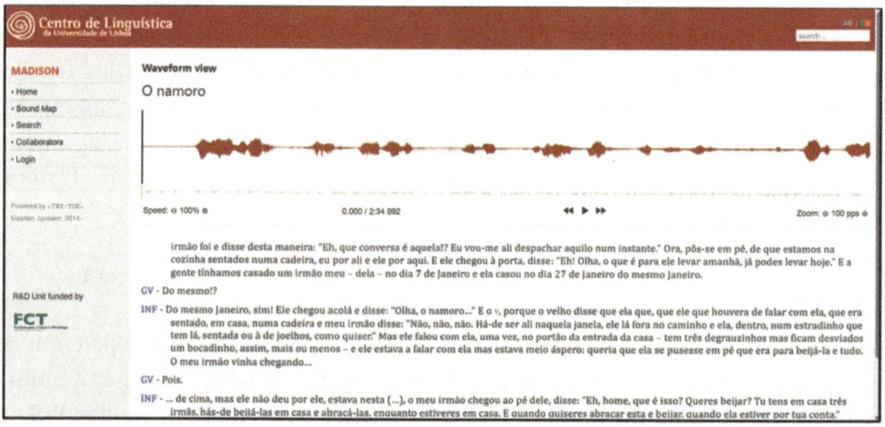

Figure 9: Wavesurfer interface of the TEITOK instance for the MADISON corpus.

11 http://teitok.clul.ul.pt/madison/en/ (accessed 27 January 2025).

12 https://recursos-glif.upf.edu/teitok/cooraje/ (accessed 27 January 2025).

4.2.2.5 Summary

Using a query language makes search options more flexible. However, the CWB and the CQP query language originally developed for querying written texts are used in the listed platforms for querying transcriptions of spoken language without being adopted to the specifics of spoken data (e. g. it is not possible to search for speaker overlaps).

4.2.3 Platforms with a CQP-like query language

This section lists platforms comprising search systems that support a CQP-like query language but are not based on CWB. Some important corpus platforms in this group are Sketch/No Sketch Engine, KonText, OpenSoNaR and ZuMult.

4.2.3.1 Sketch Engine

Sketch Engine (Kilgarriff et al. 2014) is a commercial online corpus management system that provides access to a vast collection of corpora in various languages and modalities, including, among others, Spoken BNC2014 (Love et al. 2017). The tool features its own query language, CQL (Corpus Query Language),[13] which extends the syntax of the CQP processor. For users who are not familiar with this query language, Sketch Engine offers a query builder, as well as simple search options that allow users to search for individual words, phrases, or grammatical categories. Initially developed for text data analysis, the platform does not yet support the display of full transcripts or audio playback.

4.2.3.2 NoSketch Engine

NoSketch Engine is an open source version of Sketch Engine. Despite some limitations, such as the absence of the Word Sketch and N-Gram tools, the concordancer in NoSketch offers the same functionality and is thus a powerful corpus search tool. It is used by numerous corpus platforms worldwide (see (No)Sketch Engine installations around the world[14]). The KIParla Corpus (Mauri et al. 2019) is one example with a NoSketch Engine installation.[15] After transcripts are searched, users can view hits in a broader context, and there is a link to the corresponding audio.

13 https://www.sketchengine.eu/documentation/corpus-querying/ (accessed 27 January 2025).

14 https://nlp.fi.muni.cz/trac/noske#no1 (accessed 27 January 2025).

15 https://search.corpuskiparla.it/corpus/crystal/#dashboard?corpname=KIPARLA (accessed 27 January 2025).

4.2.3.3 KonText

KonText (Machálek 2017) is a multimodal corpus analysis platform that offers access to an extensive collection of both written and spoken corpora from the Czech National Corpus (CNC, Křen 2015). The search tool is based on NoSketch Engine and utilises CQL as its query language. However, KonText implements its own user interface with advanced capabilities, such as an enhanced CQL editor with syntax highlighting and attribute recognition. Additionally, it provides support for spoken corpora, allowing text segments to be played back as audio, and displays hits within a broader context, with speaker turns easily distinguishable (see Figure 10). KonText is available as open source and is also used by other corpus providers, cf. e. g. LINDAT/CLARIAH-CZ instance[16] of KonText.

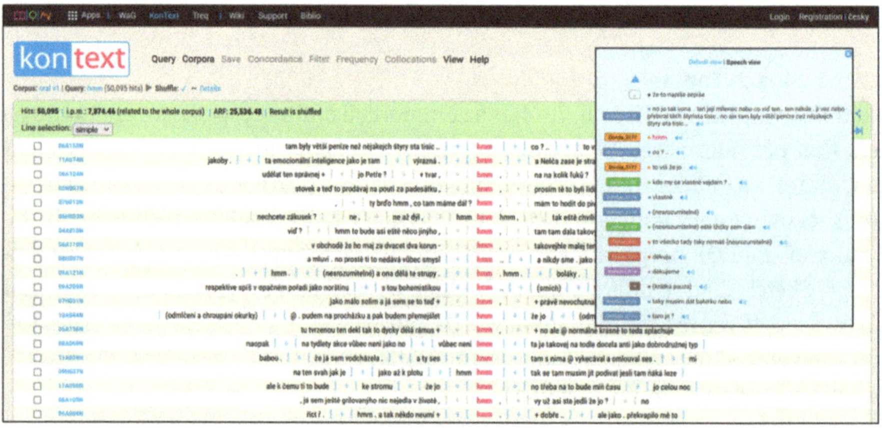

Figure 10: KWIC view in KonText user interface: Query for the form *hmm* was performed on the ORAL[17] corpus, first hit is opened in the speech view in a separate window.

4.2.3.4 OpenSoNaR

OpenSoNaR (van de Camp et al. 2017) is a web-based application designed for the search and exploration of large corpora. It provides online access to the Reference Corpus of Written Dutch (SoNaR-500) and the Spoken Dutch Corpus (Corpus Gesproken Nederlands, CGN). Built on the BlackLab search engine, it supports BlackLab's Corpus Query Language (BCQL), a dialect of the CQP query language. In addition

16 https://lindat.mff.cuni.cz/services/kontext/corpora/corplist (accessed 27 January 2025).

17 https://wiki.korpus.cz/doku.php/en:cnk:oral (accessed 27 January 2025).

to directly typing CQL queries, users can use various graphical search forms (simple, extended, advanced), or simply browse through the documents. For spoken language transcripts, the platform also offers audio playback functionality.

4.2.3.5 ZuMult

ZuMult (Fandrych et al. 2023) is an open source architecture for flexible access to spoken language corpora. As a framework, it provides base functionality for browsing and querying audiovisual corpora and can be adapted to different technological environments in the backend and various usage scenarios in the frontend. ZuMult has already been implemented for the Archive for Spoken German (AGD)[18] and for the Texas German Dialect Archive[19] (Boas et al. submitted). Further instances are currently being constructed for the French corpus ESLO (Schmidt in print), and for the multimodal corpora of the institute for communication science at the University of Duisburg-Essen (Ferger et al. 2023). The ZuMult architecture is designed to support various search engines, enabling even the use of multiple engines with different query languages in parallel. Currently, all ZuMult instances apply MTAS (Brouwer et al. 2016) to query corpora via a modified version of CQP.

4.2.3.6 Summary

The platforms listed in this section apply a modified version of the CQP query language. While the available search options differ across platforms, the syntax remains consistent. It consists of a sequence of token specifications, each composed of one or more attribute-value pairs, which are enclosed in square brackets. Although the syntax is straightforward and intuitive, it still requires some degree of familiarisation and practice. Moreover, users must be familiar with the elements present in the corpus as these may vary from corpus to corpus, even within a single platform.

4.2.4 Platforms with other query languages

The majority of corpus analysis platforms employing a corpus query language use CQP syntax. This section lists some platforms supporting a query language with a syntax distinct from CQP. These are Spokes, TalkBank, ANNIS and the LiRI Linguistic Corpus Platform (LCP).

18 https://agd.ids-mannheim.de, Zumult instance: https://zumult.ids-mannheim.de/ (accessed 27 January 2025).

19 https://tgdp.org/, Zumult instance: https://tgdp-zumult.la.utexas.edu/ (accessed 27 January 2025).

4.2.4.1 Spokes

Spokes (Pęzik 2015) is a web-based corpus query and visualisation tool originally developed for the PELCRA Conversational Corpus (PELCRA CC). It uses a query syntax called SlopeQ with a Solr-based backend for processing it (see (7)–(9) for some examples of the SlopeQ syntax from Pęzik 2015). The platform makes it possible to browse and search transcripts, which can also be played back. Additionally, it provides visualisations of pitch annotations for utterances and matched concordance spans. Spokes supports a metadata filter but also allows users to formulate and run metadata queries using the Solr Extended DisMax syntax.

(7) słuchaj <lemma=ja>
searches a sequence of surface tokens and lemmas

(8) (<lemma=jechać> tam)~2
finds a lemma and a surface token separated by up to 2 tokens, tokens may occur in any order

(9) <lemma=prosić>|!proszę
searches for any form of *prosić* except for *proszę*

4.2.4.2 TalkBank

TalkBank (MacWhinney 2007, 2017) is the world's largest online repository of spoken language data. It contains corpora of spoken communication in over 42 languages. All corpora are available in the CHAT transcription format and can be analysed and queried by using CLAN commands. Examples (10)–(12) illustrate the most basic CLAN commands: KWAL, FREQ and COMBO.[20]

(10) kwal +sgonna -w2 +w2 file.cha
searches for the keyword *gonna* and shows both the two sentences preceding it, and the two sentences following it in the file file.cha

(11) freq +t*CHI +s"*ed" *.cha
counts the frequencies of words ending with *-ed* in all the files at the child's tier (+t*CHI)

(12) combo +t*MOT +s"feel^free" file.cha
find instances where a speaker says "feel free" within a single utterance at the mother's tiers (+t*MOT) of the specified file file.cha

20 For more command examples see CLAN manual under https://talkbank.org/manuals/CLAN.html (accessed 27 January 2025) or MacWhinney and Wagner 2010.

The platform is well-equipped for working with audio and video data; it offers features such as playback with synchronised transcriptions, download options in common spoken language formats (e. g. ELAN, EXMARaLDA, Praat) and the ability to search for conversational features based on the CHAT conventions (e. g. pitch and voice annotations).

4.2.4.3 ANNIS

ANNIS (Krause and Zeldes 2016) is a web-based search and visualisation system designed for multi-layer linguistic corpora. Initially developed for text corpora, ANNIS has since been expanded to support a variety of corpus types (parallel, historical, learner corpora, etc.) with diverse annotation layers (syntax, semantics, morphology, prosody etc.). It also accommodates corpora with multiple and conflicting tokenisations, subtoken segmentations, and spoken corpora with overlapping speakers. Additionally, the system enables audio and video playback and offers a musical score view to visualise overlapping structures (see Figure 11). ANNIS provides its own graph-based query language, the ANNIS Query Language (AQL), which allows users to search desired elements (e. g. token- and span-based annotations) as nodes by defining relationships between them. These relationships can include distance, precedence, structural, hierarchical, dependency, and overlapping relations. Refer to (13)–(15) for some query examples selected from the ANNIS manual:[21]

(13) `lemma="give" & pos=/VV.+/ & #1 _=_ #2`
finds inflected forms of the verb *give*

(14) `pos=/VV.*/ & tok & #1 ->dep[func!=/.*obj.*/] #2`
searches all non-object dependants of lexical verbs

(15) `cat="PP" & cat="NP" & #1 > #2`
returns all NP being dominated by a PP

ANNIS is an open source platform, and numerous instances of ANNIS are currently in use across different research projects, cf. e. g. Berlin Map Task Corpus (BeMaTaC).[22]

---

21 https://korpling.german.hu-berlin.de/annis/VAADIN/help/aql/index.html (accessed 27 January 2025).

22 https://www.linguistik.hu-berlin.de/de/institut/professuren/korpuslinguistik/forschung/bematac, ANNIS instance under https://korpling.german.hu-berlin.de/annis/ (accessed 27 January 2025).

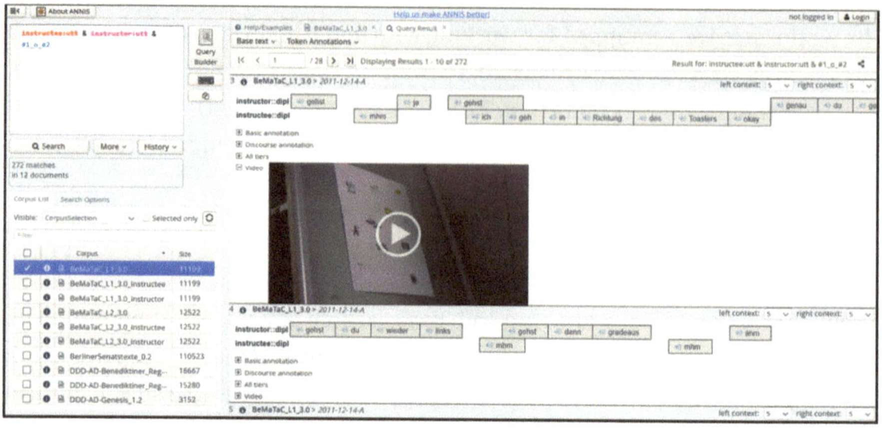

Figure 11: ANNIS user interface. Query search for overlapping utterances, performed on the BeMaTac_L1_3.0 corpus.

4.2.4.4 LiRI Linguistic Corpus Platform

The LiRI Linguistic Corpus Platform (LCP, Graën et al. 2024) is a relatively new platform designed for handling and querying very large corpora with complex annotation structures. It consists of three specialised tools, each tailored to work with a specific type of corpus: text, speech, multimodal. Users can not only query corpora available in the platform but also import their own corpora via a command-line interface, share them with selected users and use LCP tools to query and analyse these corpora directly in the browser. The open-source platform uses PostgreSQL and Redis for data storage and querying, and offers its own query language, DQD (Descriptive Query Definition), based on an Entity-Relationship (ER) modelling of corpora. DQD features two interchangeable representations: one in JSON and one in a textual format. Additionally, users can query corpora using CQP syntax, as the platform includes a converter from CQP to DQD. Figure 12 provides an example of a search query in DQD syntax (for further details, see the DQD manual[23]).

4.2.4.5 Summary

While the first two platforms described in this section were specifically developed for spoken language corpora, the latter two platforms are designed as multimodal, aiming to provide access to various types of data (text, audio, video) and to enable users to search across these modalities using the same query language and methodology.

23 https://lcp.linguistik.uzh.ch/manual/dqd.html (accessed 27 January 2025).

```
# Instantiate an entity labeled 'u' on the annotation layer 'Utterance'
Utterance u

# Instantiate an entity labeled 't' on the annotation layer 'Token'
# The character-containment operator @ requires t be part of u
Token@u t

# Look for token entities whose 'form'-attribute is "bien"
    form="bien"

# Constrain the position of t to the position of u
    position(t)=position(u)

# Return matching entities in the context in which they occur
res => plain

# Show in the context of u that contains t
    context
        u
# Show each t
    entities
        t

```

Figure 12: DQD query searching for the form *bien* at the beginning of an utterance.

4.2.5 Discussion

Overall, the overview of the current state of spoken language corpora and corpus platforms demonstrates significant collaboration and reuse in this field. While platforms build upon each other and strive to ensure interoperability through data formats and query language converters, corpus providers make their corpora accessible through multiple corpus platforms, which expands the usage and, in particular, the search options of these resources. For example, the GOS corpus is currently accessible not only through its own platform but also via the noSketch[24] and Kontext[25] services. Similarly, the OFROM-corpus, which has its own platform, is also integrated into the LiRi platform.[26] This approach addresses the needs of users with different research purposes and particularly those with varying levels of proficiency in different query languages.

Furthermore, it is also important that not only are corpora made available through different platforms, but that these platforms are designed for flexible deployment across various locations. This is particularly relevant when corpora cannot be shared due to data privacy concerns. Many of the corpus analysis platforms

24 https://www.clarin.si/ske/#open (accessed 27 January 2025).

25 https://www.clarin.si/kontext/corpora/corplist (accessed 27 January 2025).

26 Access to OFROM-corpus via LiRi platform: https://soundscript.linguistik.uzh.ch/query/40/OFROM (accessed 27 January 2025).

discussed here offer their code as open source, enabling users with expertise – especially in programming and software development – to deploy instances of these platforms on further servers and provide access to their own corpora. Moreover, when platforms are implemented in a modular way, individual components such as a search engine or a query language converter can be used independently of other elements such as the user interface. This modularity offers considerable flexibility and reusability, facilitating the development of new corpus search platforms tailored to spoken language corpora.

5 Practical illustration: FOLK in ZuMult

In what follows, typical use cases for querying spoken language corpora are illustrated through FOLK, the Research and Teaching Corpus of Spoken German (Forschungs- und Lehrkorpus Gesprochenes Deutsch, Schmidt 2016b). FOLK is a large (> 3 million tokens) and diverse corpus of spoken interactions in German, transcribed according to cGAT (Schmidt et al. 2023) and annotated with orthographic normalisation, lemmatisation and part-of-speech tagging. For several years, this corpus has been available for browsing and searching through the Database for Spoken German (DGD) along with other corpora from the Archive for Spoken German (AGD). Recently, the ZuMult architecture with MTAS-based search functionality has been implemented, to enable querying FOLK via CQP-based syntax.

FOLK transcripts are originally created in the XML format of the FOLKER tool (Schmidt 2012) according to the AGD's corpus data model and formats (see Schmidt 2016a). For ZuMult, those transcripts were converted to the ISO/TEI standard for transcriptions of spoken language (24624:2016). This conversion made it possible to add span- and time-based annotations and index FOLK for the MTAS search engine.

5.1 Base example

Since transcriptions of spoken language are written documents, basic text-based queries (such as searches for words, phrases, or word combinations) can be carried out on spoken language data in the same way they are applied to written language. For example, query (16) retrieves all occurrences of the transcribed forms of *sehr* ('very'), *voll* ('very'), and *ziemlich* ('quite') followed by an adjective (ADJA) and a noun (NN), enabling the analysis of the co-occurrence patterns of these semantically similar modifiers.

(16) `[norm="(sehr|voll|ziemlich)"] [pos="ADJA"] [pos="NN"]`

Figure 13 illustrates an excerpt of search results presented in the KWIC format:

FOLK_E_00253_SE_01_T_01	FN	hm ja genau ((kichert)) **voll nette menschen** eben weil ich ...
FOLK_E_00253_SE_01_T_02	FN	... ich hab ne **ziemlich kleine küche** bei mir da ...
FOLK_E_00253_SE_01_T_02	NJ	... für würzburg n **sehr guter preis** so definitiv °h was ...
FOLK_E_00253_SE_01_T_02	ML	sehr wohlhabend hm **sehr wohlhabende leute** da also da ...

Figure 13: Excerpt of the KWIC result of query (16).

However, when searching for phrases or grammatical patterns in spoken language transcriptions, special transcription elements (see Section 2.2. "Special tokens") should be taken into account. These elements (e. g. annotated pauses) can occur between word tokens, which could influence the search results. In the Zumult implementation for AGD corpora, these "special" tokens are indexed at their own token positions. This is made possible by MTAS, which provides a configurable file that can be easily modified without programming expertise, enabling users to parse corpus data according to custom specifications. As a result, the query above can be extended to accommodate the occurrence of short pauses or hesitation markers occurring between the modifier and the adjective-noun sequence. The modified query is as follows:

(17) [norm="(sehr|voll|ziemlich)"] (<pause/>|[pos="NGHES"])? [pos="ADJA"] [pos="NN"]
Looks for all transcribed forms of *sehr* ('very'), *voll* ('very'), and *ziemlich* ('quite'), followed by an adjective (ADJA) and a noun (NN), whereby a pause or a hesitation marker (NGHES) can occur between the modifier and the adjective-noun sequence.

This ensures that the search results also include sequences with minor interruptions, as demonstrated in Figure 14.

FOLK_E_00287_SE_01_T_03	AF	... der hat en **voll (0.21) kanonegeprelltn zeh** °h un geht zum ...
FOLK_E_00419_SE_01_T_01	PB	... s jetzt auch **voll (.) volle kanne** angehen und äh ...
FOLK_E_00450_SE_01_T_01	AB	... es gab n **sehr (0.24) gutes frühstück** also das war ...
FOLK_E_00429_SE_01_T_01	MF	... haaren und ähm (.) **ziemlich ähm schönen tattoos** °h (0.2) aber ähm

Figure 14: Excerpt of the KWIC result of query (17).

5.2 Example of searching with speaker metadata

Generally, there are two main approaches to metadata-based searches. Some platforms, e. g. DGD, provide metadata filters, which allow users to refine search results by metadata. An alternative approach, used e. g. by ANNIS, involves incorporating metadata constraints directly into the search query syntax. The ZuMult implementation for AGD corpora supports both methods: users can either integrate metadata constraints into the search query itself or sort the search results according to available metadata.

Integrating speaker metadata constraints directly into ZuMult queries is made possible by storing speaker metadata (see Section 2.4 for this particular type of metadata) alongside the speaker utterances in the search index. This data can then be treated similarly to annotation spans. For example, the following query searches for causal question words *warum* ('why') and *wieso* ('why') in teacher utterances, enabling the investigation of argumentative discourse in an educational context (cf. Volodina 2021):

(18)
```
[norm="(wieso|warum)"] within <ses_rolle_s="Lehrer/in"/>
```
looks for *wieso* ('why') and *warum* ('why') within teacher (German 'Lehrer/in') utterances, the metadata key "ses_rolle_s" stands for "speaker role in speech"

It is also possible to combine multiple metadata constraints, including both speaker and event metadata, in a single search query. The following example demonstrates how to search for question words used by female teachers during vocational school lessons:

(19)
```
([norm="(wieso|warum)"]
 within (<s_geschlecht="Weiblich"/>
 fullyalignedwith <ses_rolle_s="Lehrer/in"/>))
 within <e_se_art="Unterrichtsstunde in der Berufsschule"/>
```
looks for *wieso* ('why') and *warum* ('why') within female (German 'Weiblich') teacher (German 'Lehrer/in') utterances during vocational school lessons (German 'Unterrichtsstunde in der Berufsschule'), the metadata key "s_geschlecht" stands for "gender", "ses_rolle_s" for "speaker role in speech", "e_se_art" for "type of speech event".

5.3 Example of searching for time-based annotations

A part of the FOLK corpus has been manually annotated for action sequences – selected short excerpts of speaker interactions that illustrate various interaction situations, such as conversation openings and closings, requesting or giving advice, making proposals, etc. These interactions may involve two or more speakers and are annotated by reference to points in the timeline. MTAS allows to index such time-based annotations enabling users to search for complete action sequences as well as for specific tokens or token sequences within these annotations. The following queries provide examples of such searches:

(20) <as/>
looks for all annotated action sequences

(21) <as="Vorschlag/Angebot"/>
looks for all action sequence annotated with 'Vorschlag/Angebot' ('proposal/offering')

(22) <as="Er"offnung"/> containing [norm="jetzt"]
looks for all action sequence annotated with "Eröffnung" ('opening') and containing all transcribed forms of *jetzt* ('now')

5.4 Overlaps

Speaker overlaps are an important subject of study in conversation analysis, which aims to understand why one speaker interrupts another, how the interruption occurs, and how the original speaker reacts. The ability to systematically query overlaps within interaction corpora is a valuable and practical search function. To support this, AGD corpora are automatically annotated for speaker overlaps which are identified by comparing the start and end times of a contribution (represented by the <*annotationBlock*>-element in the ISO/TEI standard (24624:2016)) with those of other speakers' contributions in the transcript. Indexing these annotations of speaker overlaps (for more information see Frick et al. 2022) enables the following types of queries within the FOLK corpus:

(23) <speaker-overlap/>
looks for all spans annotated as speaker overlap

(24) <speaker-overlap/> containing [lemma="(Herr|Frau)"]
looks for all spans annotated as speaker overlap and containing any forms of *Herr* ('Mr.') or *Frau* ('Ms.')

(25) <speaker-overlap>[norm="also"]
looks for any transcribed form of also ('well') at the beginning of speaker overlaps

(26) `<speaker-overlap="SZ"/>`
looks for all token sequences overlapping with the contributions of the speaker “SZ”

Building on the discussion of conflicting tokenisations in spoken corpora presented in Sauer and Lüdeling (2016), two distinct search indices were created for the FOLK corpus: a transcript-based index, which indexes tokens based on their sequential position in the transcript document, and a speaker-based index, which goes through the tokens for each speaker separately, treating the tokenisations of other speakers as annotations of the current speaker. Consider the following query:

(27) `[lemma="ja"] precededby <pause/>`

This query will return all forms of “ja” preceded by a pause. However, if two speakers begin their utterances simultaneously and both say “ja”, only one occurrence will be returned, specifically that of the speaker whose utterance appears first in the transcript document after the pause element. Searching within the speaker-based index, however, will return both instances of “ja” from each speaker.

Additionally, searching by individual speakers allows for constraints related to speaker changes within queries. For example, the following query will find all instances of postponed “oder” as a tag question (‘or is it?’) occurring at the final position before a speaker change:

(28) `([lemma="oder"] !within <speaker-overlap/>) followedby <another-speaker/>`

5.5 Repetitions

For querying repetitions in the AGD corpora, an MTAS-based approach has been implemented. With this approach, users can submit a CQP search query for an element to be repeated and define the properties of the repetition through a graphical user interface. Users can specify various parameters, such as

- the maximum allowed distance to the repeated element
- whether the repetition should occur at least once or multiple times
- if the speaker repeats himself or is repeated (“echoed”) by another speaker
- if speaker changes may or not may occur between repetitions of the same speaker

etc.

The search process builds on the MTAS search indices. First, spans matching the CQP query and containing only word tokens from a single speaker are retrieved.

Next, word tokens within a user-defined distance following the match are fetched and compared with the match itself. If a repetition is found, additional user-defined conditions are checked. All processing is done within the search index, retrieving the necessary annotation values for specified token positions. The search is parallelised, with results written to a temporary document, sorted, and returned.

As an example, Figure 15 demonstrates how to search for specific German constructions *X* – *Was für X*? or *X* – *Was ist (denn ein) X*? (both 'X – What kind of X?') in the FOLK corpus.

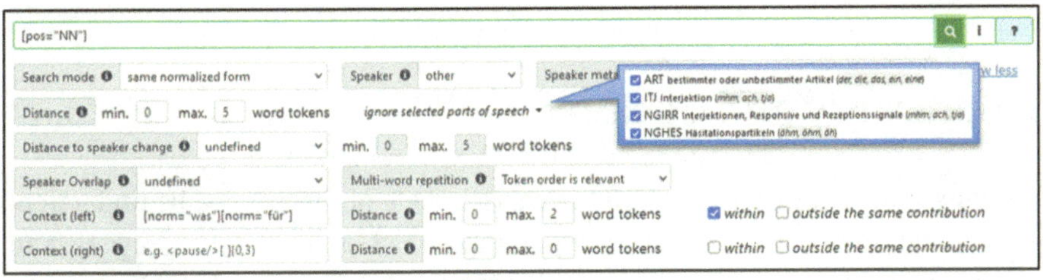

Figure 15: Search form for querying repetitions.

Since the focus is on the repetition of nouns, the CQP expression used is [pos="NN"] (see the green input field in Figure 15). The "Search mode" menu enables users to specify the method for identifying repetitions, including which token form (transcribed, normalised, or lemmatised) should be compared, and whether GermaNet[27] or custom synonym lists should be used to determine the repetition form. In this case, the repetitions will be searched by comparing normalised forms. Further settings determine that the repetitions should be realised by other speakers and within the maximum distance of 5 tokens, while ignoring articles (ART), interjections (ITJ), responsive/reception signals (NGIRR), hesitations (NGHES), abortions (AB) and other non-words (XY, e. g. stuttering) (this is specified in the drop-down menu under the "ignore selected parts of speech"). The field "Context (left)" contains the CQP pattern [norm="was"][norm="für"] and together with the distance and position settings determines that the repair initiator "was für" ('what kind of') may have different pronunciations and should occur in front of the repetition with the maximum distance of 2 tokens and within the same contribution. Figure 16 illustrates some hits returned by this search request:

27 GermaNet (Kunze and Lemnitzer 2009) is a lexical-semantic network for German verbs, nouns and adjectives: https://uni-tuebingen.de/fakultaeten/philosophische-fakultaet/fachbereiche/neuphilologie/seminar-fuer-sprachwissenschaft/arbeitsbereiche/allg-sprachwissenschaft-computerlinguistik/ressourcen/lexica/germanet-1/ (accessed 27 January 2025).

1	FOLK_E_00014_SE_01_T_01	CJ TJ	... für dis ein gehege (.) oh was für ein gehege denn °h ein holzgehege da freu ich mich °h und und (.) und einen (0.22) ein (.) ein rutschegehege oh ja ...
2	FOLK_E_00027_SE_01_T_01	AM PB	... um ne andere arbeit (0.82) ach so (1.65) um was für ne arbeit die arbeit die ich jetzt schreibe über mit diesen (0.55) wörtern °h hm hm die muss ...
3	FOLK_E_00027_SE_01_T_01	AM PB	... könn wir die haare rasieren theoretisch (.) was für haare sch (0.34) an den beinen damit du braun wirst nee hh° °h ja des mach ich dann nächste woch ...
4	FOLK_E_00049_SE_01_T_02	AM PH	sollen mer n film schauen (0.44) was für n film (0.34) na wenn dann eher was älteres (0.71) das ich schon lang nimmer gsehen hab (4.39) ja pass äh ...

Figure 16: Excerpt of the KWIC result for repetition search.

For more information on searching repetitions, see Frick et al. (2024).

6 Summary and outlook

Querying spoken language data, in the current state of the art, can be understood as a transfer and adaptation of techniques developed for written language to transcripts and annotations of audiovisual language data. This transfer takes into account the additional complexity arising from specific characteristics of spoken language and works out solutions, for instance, for handling parallel structures, for inclusion of non-word tokens, or for an extended contextualisation of search results.

Most of the platforms described in Section 4 went online in the last five to ten years, and quite a few of them are still in active development. This section is therefore a snapshot whose details may become outdated quickly as the existing platforms are further developed or new ones implemented. The recency of the developments may also partly explain why there is as yet little common ground between different solutions. As standardisation on the data level progresses, however, different approaches to querying may also converge. Presently, the CQP language seems to have the status of a de-facto standard for a query language.

For researchers working with spoken language data and aiming to make them queryable in solutions like the ones presented here, the most general and important recommendation is to follow existing standards as far as possible from the first stages of data creation onwards. If the primary data (audio and video), secondary data (transcripts and annotations) and metadata are generated with established tools and represented in established formats (WAV, MPEG-4, XML etc.) and according to widely used practices (e. g. TEI), the resulting structured corpus will be adaptable without major difficulties to the requirements of different query solutions. In the simplest case, researchers can remain in a single (desktop-based) “eco-system” which caters not only for the needs of data transcription, annotation and documentation, but also for query and analysis (see Section 4.1. “Desktop tools”). For more advanced (web-based) solutions, having standard conformant, structured data is likewise the single most important prerequisite. On that basis, most specialised centres (e. g. the Archive for Spoken German or CLARIN-B centres with a specialisation in spoken language data, such as BAS Munich, LiRI Zürich, etc.) will be able to archive the data and make it available for querying in the platform(s) they support.

Bibliography

Avanzi, Mathieu, Marie-José Béguelin & Federica Diémoz. 2016. Présentation du corpus OFROM – Corpus oral de français de Suisse romande. Université de Neuchâtel. https://ofrom.unine.ch/uploads/Documents/AM-MJB-FD_GC_LAJ_OFROM_23.pdf (accessed 27 January 2025).

Baldauf-Quilliatre, Heike, Isabel Colón de Carvajal, Carole Etienne, Emilie Jouin-Chardon, Sandra Teston-Bonnard & Véronique Traverso. 2016. CLAPI, une base de données multimodale pour la parole en interaction: apports et dilemmes. *Corpus [Online]* 15. http://journals.openedition.org/corpus/2991 (accessed 27 January 2025).

Baude, Olivier & Céline Dugua. 2017. Les ESLO, du portrait sonore au paysage digita'. *Corpus [Online]* 15. https://journals.openedition.org/corpus/2924 (accessed 27 January 2025).

Bigi, Brigitte. 2015. SPPAS – Multi-lingual approaches to the automatic annotation of speech. *The Phonetician* 111–112. 54–69.

Bigi, Brigitte, Roxane Bertrand & Mathilde Guardiola. 2014. Automatic detection of other-repetition occurrences: Application to French conversational speech. In *9th international conference on language resources and evaluation (LREC)*, Reykjavik, Iceland, 2648–2652.

Bigi, Brigitte & Jorane Saubesty. 2015. Searching and retrieving multi-levels annotated data, In *Proceedings of gesture and speech in interaction*, 4th edn., Nantes, France.

Boas, Hans, Margo Blevins & Thomas Schmidt. Submitted. TGDA 2.0 – A corpus platform for the Texas German Dialect Archive. *Language Resources and Evaluation.*

Evert, Stephanie, Timm Weber, Steffen Bothe, Philipp Heinrich & Alexander Piperski. 2025. Data exploitation: Corpus queries. In Piotr Bański, Ulrich Heid & Laura Herzberg (eds.), *Harmonising language data: Standards for linguistic resources*. Berlin/Boston: De Gruyter.

Bowdre, Paul. 1964. *A study of eye dialect*. Dissertation thesis, University of Florida. Republished 2011, Place: Nabu Press.

Blevins, Margaret. 2023. The language-tagging & orthographic normalisation of spoken mixed-language data, with a focus on Texas German. *UT Electronic Theses and Dissertations*. https://doi.org/10.26153/tsw/43598 (accessed 27 January 2025).

Broeder, Daan & Peter Wittenburg. 2006. The IMDI metadata framework, its current application and future direction. *International Journal of Metadata, Semantics and Ontologies* 1(2). 119–132. https://doi.org/10.1504/IJMSO.2006.011008 (accessed 27 January 2025).

Broeder, Daan, Oliver Schonefeld, Thorsten Trippel, Dieter Van Uytvanck & Andreas Witt. 2011. A pragmatic approach to XML interoperability – The Component Metadata Infrastructure (CMDI). In *Proceedings of Balisage: The Markup Conference 2011*, Vol. 7 of Balisage Series on Markup Technologies, Montréal, Canada, August 2–5, 2011.

Brouwer, Matthijs, Hennie Brugman & Marc Kemps-Snijders. 2016. MTAS: A Solr/Lucene based Multi-Tier Annotation Search solution. In *Selected papers from the CLARIN annual conference 2016*, Aix-en-Provence, 19–37. https://ep.liu.se/ecp/136/002/ecp17136002.pdf (accessed 27 January 2025).

Boersma, Paul. 2014. The use of Praat in corpus research. In Jacques Durand, Ulrike Gut & Gjert Kristoffersen (eds.), *The Oxford handbook of corpus phonology*, 342–360. Oxford: Oxford University Press.

van de Camp, Matje, Martin Reynaert & Nelleke Oostdijk. 2017. WhiteLab 2.0: a web interface for corpus exploitation. In Jan Odijk & Arjan van Hessen (eds.), *CLARIN in the low countries*, 231–243. London: Ubiquity Press.

Edwards, Jane & Martin Lampert (eds.). 1992. *Talking data – Transcription and coding in discourse research*. Hillsdale: Erlbaum.

Fandrych, Christian, Thomas Schmidt, Franziska Wallner & Kai Wörner (eds.). 2023. *Korpora Deutsch als Fremdsprache* 3(1). Themenschwerpunkt: Zugänge zu mündlichen Korpora für DaF und DaZ: Das ZuMult-Projekt Darmstadt: KorDaF, 2023. https://kordaf.tujournals.ulb.tu-darmstadt.de/issue/92/info/ (accessed 27 January 2025).

Ferger, Anne, André Krause & Karola Pitsch. 2023. A continuous integration (CI) workflow for quality assurance checks for corpora of multimodal interaction. In Krister Lindén, Jyrki Niemi & Thalassia Kontino (eds.), *CLARIN annual conference proceedings 2023*, Leuven, 106–110. https://office.clarin.eu/v/CE-2023-2328_CLARIN2023_ConferenceProceedings.pdf (accessed 27 January 2025).

Ferreira, Vera, Hanna Hedeland & Kelsey Neely. 2025. Annotated audiovisual language data: data quality and data maturity. In Piotr Bański, Ulrich Heid & Laura Herzberg (eds.), *Harmonising language data: Standards for linguistic resources*. Berlin/Boston: De Gruyter.

Frick, Elena, Thomas Schmidt & Henrike Helmer. 2022. Querying interaction structure: Approaches to overlap in spoken language corpora. In *Proceedings of the thirteenth language resources and evaluation conference*, 715–722. Marseille, France: European Language Resources Association.

Frick, Elena, Henrike Helmer & Dolores Lemmenmeier-Batinić. 2024. Querying repetitions in spoken language corpora. In *Proceedings of the 20th conference on natural language processing (KONVENS 2024)*, 309–316. Vienna, Austria: Association for Computational Linguistics.

Graën, Johannes, Jonathan Schaber, Daniel McDonald, Igor Mustač, Nikolina Rajović, Gerold Schneider, Teodora Vuković, Jeremy Zehr & Noah Bubenhofer. 2024. The LiRI corpus platform. In Krister Lindén, Jyrki Niemi & Thalassia Kontino (eds.), *CLARIN annual conference 2023*, Leuven, 62–75. https://office.clarin.eu/v/CE-2023-2328_CLARIN2023_ConferenceProceedings.pdf (accessed 27 January 2025).

Hardie, Andrew. 2012. CQPweb – Combining power, flexibility and usability in a corpus analysis tool. *International Journal of Corpus Linguistics* 17(3). 380–409.

Hatton, John, Gary Holton, Mandana Seyfeddinipur & Nick Thieberger. 2021. Lameta [software]. https://github.com/onset/laMETA/releases (accessed 27 January 2025).

Hedeland, Hanna & Thomas Schmidt. 2012. Technological and methodological challenges in creating, annotating and sharing a learner corpus of spoken German. In Thomas Schmidt & Kai Wörner (eds.), *Multilingual corpora and multilingual corpus analysis*, Vol. 14 of Hamburg Studies on Multilingualism, 25–46. Amsterdam: Benjamins.

Ishikawa, Shin'ichiro. 2019. The ICNALE spoken dialogue: A new dataset for the study of Asian learners' performance in L2 English interviews. *English Teaching* 74. 153–177.

Janssen, Maarten. 2016. TEITOK: Text-faithful annotated corpora. In N. Calzolari, K. Choukri, T. Declerck, S. Goggi, M. Grobelnik, B. Maegaard, J. Mariani, H. Mazo, A. Moreno & J. Odijk (eds.), *Proceedings of the tenth international conference on language resources and evaluation (LREC 2016)*, 4037–4043. Paris: European Language Resources Association (ELRA). https://aclanthology.org/L16-1637.pdf (accessed 27 January 2025).

Johannessen, Janne Bondi, Joel Priestley, Kristin Hagen, Tor Anders Åfarli & Øystein Alexander Vangsnes. 2009. The Nordic Dialect Corpus – An advanced research tool. In Kristiina Jokinen & Eckhard Bick (eds.), *Proceedings of the 17th nordic conference of computational linguistics NODALIDA 2009*, Vol. 4 of NEALT Proceedings Series, 73–80. https://aclanthology.org/W09-4612.pdf (accessed 27 January 2025).

Kilgarriff, Adam, Vit Baisa, Jan Bušta, Miloš Jakubíček, Vojtěch Kovář, Jan Michelfeit, Pavel Rychlý & Vít Suchomel. 2014. The Sketch Engine: Ten years on. *Lexicography* 1(1). 7–36. https://www.researchgate.net/publication/271848017_The_Sketch_Engine_Ten_Years_On (accessed 27 January 2025).

Kirk, John M. & Gisle Andersen (eds.). 2016. Compilation, transcription, markup and annotation of spoken corpora. *International Journal of Corpus Linguistics* 21(3). 396–418.

Knight, Dawn. 2010. The future of multimodal corpora. *Revista Brasileira de Linguística Aplicada* 11. 391–415. https://www.researchgate.net/publication/262499851_The_future_of_multimodal_corpora (accessed 27 January 2025).

Kosek, Michal, Anders Nøklestad, Joel Priestley, Kristin Hagen & Janne Bondi Johannessen. 2015. Visualisation in speech corpora: Maps and waves in the Glossa system. In Gintarė Grigonytė, Simon Clematide, Andrius Utka & Martin Volk (eds.), *Proceedings of the Workshop on Innovative Corpus Query and Visualisation Tools at NODALIDA 2015*, May 11–13, Vilnius, Lithuania, Vol. 25 of NEALT Proceedings Series, 23–31. May 11–13, 23–31. http://www.diva-portal.org/smash/get/diva2:812052/FULLTEXT01.pdf (accessed 27 January 2025).

Krause, Thomas & Amir Zeldes. 2016. ANNIS3: A new architecture for generic corpus query and visualisation. *Digital Scholarship in the Humanities* 31(1). 118–139. https://doi.org/10.1093/llc/fqu057 (accessed 27 January 2025).

Křen, Michael. 2015. Recent developments in the Czech national corpus. In Piotr Bański, Hanno Biber, Evelyn Breiteneder, Marc Kupietz & Harald Lüngen (eds.), *Proceedings of the 3rd workshop on challenges in the management of large corpora (CMLC-3)*, 1–4. Mannheim: Institut für Deutsche Sprache.

Kunze, Claudia & Lothar Lemnitzer. 2009. Lexical-semantic and conceptual relations in GermaNet. In *Proceedings of the Mannheim Colloquium on lexical semantic relations from theoretical and practical perspectives*, June 2008.

Lange, Herbert. 2022. Metadata formats for learner corpora: Case study and discussion. In *11th workshop on natural language processing for computer-assisted language learning (NLP4CALL 2022)*. https://doi.org/10.3384/ecp190011 (accessed 27 January 2025).

Leech, Geoffrey, Greg Myers & Jenny Thomas (eds.). 1995. *Spoken English on computer: Transcription, markup and application*. Harlow: Longman.

Love, Robbie, Claire Dembry, Andrew Hardie, Vaclav Brezina & Tony McEnery. 2017. The spoken BNC2014: Designing and building a spoken corpus of everyday conversations. *International Journal of Corpus Linguistics* 22(3). 319–344.

Love, Robbie (ed.). 2024. Innovations in the compilation and analysis of spoken corpora. [Special issue]. *Research in Corpus Linguistics* 12(2).

Machálek, Tomáš. 2017. KonText – A modern, customizable corpus query interface. In *Abstracts booklet for corpus linguistics international conference*, 681–683. University of Birmingham.

MacWhinney, Brian. 2007. The TalkBank project. In Joan C. Beal, Karen P. Corrigan & Herman L. Moisl (eds.), *Creating and digitizing language corpora: Synchronic databases*, Vol. 1, 163–180. Houndmills: Palgrave-Macmillan.

MacWhinney, Brian. 2017. TalkBank and CLARIN. In *Selected papers from the CLARIN Annual Conference 2016*, Vol. 136 of Linköping Electronic Conference Proceedings, 76–89. https://ep.liu.se/en/conference-issue.aspx?series=ecp&issue=136 (accessed 27 January 2025).

MacWhinney, Brian. 2024. *Tools for analyzing talk part 1: The CHAT transcription format*. https://doi.org/10.21415/3mhn-0z89 (accessed 27 January 2025).

MacWhinney, Brian & Johannes Wagner. 2010. Transcribing, searching and data sharing: The CLAN software and the TalkBank data repository. *Gesprächsforschung* 11. 154–173. http://www.gespraechsforschung-online.de/fileadmin/dateien/heft2010/px-macwhinney.pdf (accessed 27 January 2025).

Mauri, Caterina, Silvia Ballarè, Eugenio Goria, Massimo Cerruti & Francesco Suriano. 2019. KIParla corpus: A new resource for spoken Italian. In Raffaella Bernardi, Roberto Navigli & Giovanni Semeraro (eds.), *CLiC-it 2019 – Italian conference on computational linguistics. Proceedings of the sixth Italian conference on computational linguistics*.

Nøklestad, Anders, Kristin Hagen, Janne Bondi Johannessen, Michal Kosek & Joel Priestley. 2017. A modernised version of the Glossa corpus search system. In Jörg Tiedemann (ed.), *Proceedings of the 21st nordic conference on computational linguistics (NoDaLiDa)*, 251–254. https://www.duo.uio.no/bitstream/handle/10852/59550/NODALIDA-2017-G%25C3%25B8teborg-Glossa-trykt.pdf?sequence=2&isAllowed=y (accessed 27 January 2025).

Ochs, Elinor. 1979. Transcription as theory. In Elinor Ochs & Bambi Schieffelin (eds.), *Developmental pragmatics*. New York, San Francisco, London: Academic Press.

Parian-Scherb, Mahnaz, Peter Uhrig, Luca Rossetto, Stéphane Dupont & Heiko Schuldt. 2024. Gesture retrieval and its application to the study of multimodal communication. *International Journal on Digital Libraries* 25. 585–601. https://doi.org/10.1007/s00799-023-00367-0 (accessed 27 January 2025).

Pęzik, Piotr. 2015. Spokes – A search and exploration service for conversational corpus data. In *Selected papers from the CLARIN 2014 conference*, 99–109. Linköping University Electronic Press.

Rabus, Achim & A. Šymon. 2015. Na novŷch putjach isslidovanja rusyns'kŷch dialektu. Korpus rozhovornoho rusyns'koho jazŷka. In Kvetoslava Koporová (ed.), *Rusyn'skŷj literaturnŷj jazŷk na Slovakiji. 20 rokiv kodifikaciji* / The Rusyn literary language in Slovakia. 20th anniversary of its codification. IV. International Congress of the Rusyn Language. Prešov: Editor, 40–54.

Priestley, Joel, Anders Nøklestad, Kristin Hagen, Anu Laanemets & Dag Trygve Truslew Haug. 2024. Treebanks for the ordinary working grammarian. In *Proceedings of the Computational Humanities Research Conference (CHR) 2024*, 313–321. https://ceur-ws.org/Vol-3834/paper32.pdf (accessed 27 January 2025).

Ruhi, Şükriye, Michael Haugh, Thomas Schmidt & Kai Wörner (eds.). 2014. *Best Practices for spoken corpora in linguistic research*. Newcastle: Cambridge Scholars Publishing.

Rühlemann, Christoph & Alexander Ptak. 2023. Reaching beneath the tip of the iceberg: A guide to the Freiburg Multimodal Interaction Corpus. *Open Linguistics* 9(1). https://doi.org/10.1515/opli-2022-0245 (accessed 27 January 2025).

Sauer, Simon & Anke Lüdeling. 2016. Flexible Multi-Layer Spoken Dialogue Corpora. *International Journal of Corpus Linguistics* 21(3). 419–438. *Special Issue on Spoken Corpora*.

Schmidt, Thomas. 2005. Computergestützte Transkription – Modellierung und Visualisierung gesprochener Sprache mit texttechnologischen Mitteln. *Sprache, Sprechen und Computer*, Vol. 7. Frankfurt am Main/Berlin/Bern/Bruxelles/New York/Oxford/Wien: Lang.

Schmidt, Thomas. 2012. EXMARaLDA and the FOLK tools. Two toolsets for transcribing and annotating spoken language. In *Proceedings of the eighth conference on international language resources and evaluation (LREC-12)*, 236–240. Istanbul, Turkey: European Language Resources Association (ELRA).

Schmidt, Thomas. 2014. The Database for Spoken German – DGD2. In *Proceedings of the ninth international conference on language resources and evaluation (LREC'14)*, 1451–1457. European Language Resources Association (ELRA).

Schmidt, Thomas. 2016a. Construction and dissemination of a corpus of spoken interaction – Tools and workflows in the FOLK project. In Marc Kupietz & Alexander Geyken (eds.), *Corpus linguistic software tools*, Vol. 31 of Journal for Language Technology and Computational Linguistics (JLCL), 127–154. Berlin: GSCL. https://doi.org/10.21248/jlcl.31.2016.205 (accessed 27 January 2025).
Schmidt, Thomas. 2016b. Good practices in the compilation of FOLK, the research and teaching corpus of spoken German. In John M. Kirk & Gisle Andersen (eds.), *Compilation, transcription, markup and annotation of spoken corpora*, Vol. 21 of International Journal of Corpus Linguistics, 396–418. Amsterdam/Philadelphia: Benjamins.
Schmidt, Thomas. 2022. Werkzeuge für die Transkription gesprochener Sprache. In Michael Beißwenger, Lothar Lemnitzer & Carolin Müller-Spitzer (eds.), *Forschen in der Linguistik. Eine Methodeneinführung für das Germanistik-Studium*, 451–460. Paderborn: Brill/Fink.
Schmidt, Thomas. In print. Représenter et accéder à la parole dans les corpus oraux: diversification et adaptation des méthodes et technologies. In Layal Kanaan-Caillol, Céline Dugua, Lotfi Abouda & Annette Gerstenberg (eds.), *Représenter la parole*. Berlin/Boston: De Gruyter.
Schmidt, Thomas, Susan Duncan, Oliver Ehmer, Jeffrey Hoyt, Michael Kipp, Dan Loehr, Magnus Magnusson, Travis Rose & Han Sloetjes. 2009. An exchange format for multimodal annotations. In Michael Kipp, Jean-Claude Martin, Patrizia Paggio & Dirk Heylen (eds.), *Multimodal corpora: From models of natural interaction to systems and applications*, 207–221. Berlin/Heidelberg: Springer.
Schmidt, Thomas, Wilfried Schütte, Jenny Winterscheid, Mia Schürmann, Silke Reineke & Evi Schedl. 2023. cGAT. Konventionen für das computergestützte Transkribieren in Anlehnung an das Gesprächsanalytische Transkriptionssystem 2 (GAT2). https://doi.org/10.14618/chrz-zy56 (accessed 27 January 2025).
Schmidt, Thomas & Kai Wörner. 2014. EXMARaLDA. In Jacques Durand, Ulrike Gut & Gjert Kristoffersen (eds.), *The Oxford handbook of corpus phonology*, 402–419. Oxford: OUP.
Selting, Margret, Peter Auer, Dagmar Barth-Weingarten, Jörg R. Bergmann, Pia Bergmann, Karin Birkner, Elizabeth Couper-Kuhlen, Arnulf Deppermann, Peter Gilles, Susanne Günthner, Martin Hartung, Friederike Kern, Christine Mertzlufft, Christian Meyer, Miriam Morek, Frank Oberzaucher, Jörg Peters, Uta Quasthoff, Wilfried Schütte, Anja Stukenbrock & Susanne Uhmann. 2009. *Gesprächsanalytisches Transkriptionssystem 2 (GAT 2)*. http://www.gespraechsforschung-online.de/fileadmin/dateien/heft2009/px-gat2.pdf (accessed 27 January 2025).
Slavcheva, Adriana & Cordula Meißner. 2014. Building and maintaining the GeWiss corpus – Perspectives on the construction, sustainability and further enrichment of spoken corpora: A showcase. In Sukriye Ruhi, Michael Haugh, Thomas Schmidt & Kai Wörner (eds.), *Best practices for spoken language corpora in linguistic research*, 20–35. Newcastle: Cambridge Scholars Publishing.
Sloetjes, Han. 2014. ELAN: Multimedia annotation application. In Jacques Durand, Ulrike Gut & Gjert Kristoffersen (eds.), *The Oxford handbook of corpus phonology*, 305–320. Oxford: Oxford University Press.
Stern, Karen. 1997. The Longman Spoken American Corpus: Providing an in-depth analysis of everyday English. *Longman Language Review* 3. 14–17.
von Waldenfels, Ruprecht, Michael Daniel & Nina Dobrushina. 2014. Why standard orthography? Building the Ustya River Basic Corpus, an online corpus of a Russian dialect. In Komp'juternaja lingvistika i intellektual'nye technologii: Po materialam ežegodnoj Meždunarodnoj konferencii «Dialog» (Bekasovo, 4–8 ijunja 2014 g.) Vyp. 13 (20), Moskva. Izd-vo RGGU.
von Waldenfels, Ruprecht & Michał Woźniak. 2016. SpoCo – a simple and adaptable web interface for dialect corpora. *Journal for Language Technology and Computational Linguistics* 31. 155–170.

Werthmann, Antonina. 2025. From Spoken Language Data to TEI-based ISO Standard. In Piotr Bański, Ulrich Heid & Laura Herzberg (eds.), *Harmonising language data: Standards for linguistic resources*. Berlin/Boston: De Gruyter.

Westpfahl, Swantje, Thomas Schmidt, Jasmin Jonietz & Anton Borlinghaus. 2017. *STTS 2.0. Guidelines für die Annotation von POS-Tags für Transkripte gesprochener Sprache in Anlehnung an das Stuttgart Tübingen Tagset (STTS)*. https://nbn-resolving.org/urn:nbn:de:bsz:mh39-60634 (accessed 27 January 2025).

Wieling, Martijn, Jack Grieve, Gosse Bouma, Josef Fruehwald, John Coleman & Mark Liberman. 2016. Variation and change in the use of hesitation markers in Germanic languages. *Language Dynamics and Change* 6(2). 199–234.

Wilbur, Joshua. 2019. ELAN as a search engine for hierarchically structured, tagged corpora. In *Proceedings of the fifth international workshop on computational linguistics for Uralic languages*, 90–103. Tartu, Estonia: Association for Computational Linguistics. https://doi.org/10.18653/v1/W19-0308. (accessed 27 January 2025).

Verdonik, D., I. Kosem, A. Zwitter Vitez, S. Krek & M. Stabej. 2013. Compilation, transcription and usage of a reference speech corpus: the case of the Slovene Corpus GOS. *Language Resources and Evaluation* 47(4). 1031–1048.

Volodina, Anna. 2021. "Wieso" und nicht "Warum"! Von der Theorie zur Analyse kausaler Fragen in der Lehrer-Schüler-Interaktion. In Stephan Schicker & Sabine Schmölzer-Eibinger (eds.), *ar|gu|men|tie|ren. Eine zentrale Sprachhandlung im Fach- und Sprachunterricht*, 48–66. Weinheim/Basel: Beltz Juventa.

Xu, Jiajin. 2015. The CQPweb family. https://corpus.bfsu.edu.cn/info/1082/1844.htm (accessed 27 January 2025).

Erik Körner and Thomas Eckart

Accessing linguistic content in distributed research environments

Abstract: Many high-quality language resources are available all over the Internet which opens up new opportunities for federated search applications. This article is devoted to such functionality in the context of distributed research environments. The CLARIN Federated Content Search (FCS) is a decentralised search and retrieval framework that has established itself in the European context as a flexible and lightweight solution for making linguistic resources readily visible and easily searchable to researchers in a modern distributed research environment while leaving control of the data with its owners.

The current FCS Core 2.0 specification is the result of long-term development and has evolved as a stable, backwards-compatible, but also highly extensible standard. It describes how data communication takes place, which formats can be used to serialize data and how queries are to be formulated. The FCS stands on top of many established standards, such as SRU/CQL – specified by the Library of Congress and OASIS –, *XML* for data serialization, or annotation standards like the *Universal Dependencies Part-of-Speech Tagset*.

This core functionality has been used for years to provide annotated resources by a variety of institutions across Europe. New requirements are continuously determined in dialogue with users and are incorporated into the expansion of the platform specification and its software ecosystem. They address a number of current problems, such as the integration of search procedures in Single Sign-on authentication systems, the support of resource-specific content representation, or the increasing use of large knowledge bases in a "web of data".

Acknowledgement: This chapter is based on work within Text+, funded by the Deutsche Forschungsgemeinschaft (DFG, project number 460033370) as part of the German National Research Data Infrastructure (NFDI e. V.) and the Common Language Resources and Technology Infrastructure (CLARIN). The authors thank the funding bodies and acknowledge the contributions of all supporting institutions and individuals. The authors would like to thank Text+ and CLARIN for the funding and support. Furthermore, the authors would like to thank all members of the Text+ data domain *Lexical resources* and the *CLARIN FCS taskforce* for their continuous work.

Erik Körner, Saxon Academy of Sciences and Humanities in Leipzig, Karl-Tauchnitz-Straße 1, 04107 Leipzig, Germany; and CLARIN ERIC, Utrecht, The Netherlands, e-mail: koerner@saw-leipzig.de
Thomas Eckart, Saxon Academy of Sciences and Humanities in Leipzig, Karl-Tauchnitz-Straße 1, 04107 Leipzig, Germany, e-mail: eckart@saw-leipzig.de

https://doi.org/10.1515/9783112208212-015

Keywords: federated content search, research data retrieval, information retrieval, data models, query languages, search engine, data federation

1 Introduction

The extensive and, in many cases, publicly available inventory of digital language resources – including text corpora, dictionaries, or text editions – represents a great enrichment for scientific work in many disciplines and is often the prerequisite for exciting research questions. At the same time, accessing these resources in a variety of technical environments using a wide range of access methods and interfaces makes it difficult to obtain a broad overview of available data sets or to aggregate results from different sources. Federated search methods that query a large number of resource providers in parallel and provide their results centrally can support these tasks. Specifically usage scenarios or research interests that are not tied to a single, specific resource benefit from a broad view of available data.

A concrete, simple example is the search for references for a specific word or a specific linguistic expression in texts. Text corpora typically represent a limited object of observation – limited in time, space or otherwise. These can be, for example, texts from different countries speaking the same language or collections of texts written by different authors. For both a synchronic and a diachronic analysis of language, access to a wide variety of technical systems is required; any need for data aggregation must be dealt with by the respective scientist or research team. Federated access mechanisms can significantly reduce this workload, either through the results directly or simply through a brief overview of the number of results available in each resource, possibly followed by a deeper inspection of the resources identified as particularly relevant in their "home applications".

Similarly, these mechanisms can also be used for research questions on other resource types. This includes, among others, federated access to dictionaries. Here, parallel access also offers new options, ranging from analysing meaning change across different language periods – based on the respective historical dictionaries – to aggregating different types of information for the same lemma – such as supplementing morphosyntactic information from one dictionary with information on the frequency of use from another one.

1.1 Linguistic research data in a federated environment

The number of infrastructure projects dedicated to the utilization of existing and new research data in the field of linguistics and related disciplines has become quite extensive. The corresponding projects often face similar basic problems and address these with partly similar, partly different strategies that can cover the entire life cycle of research data. In such a broad and diverse thematic field, solutions that are geared towards data storage and access at a single location are often not feasible. Depending on the respective spatial and thematic scope, a large number of institutions with different degrees of autonomy must be taken into account with their different organizational and legal frameworks and working traditions. This often happens in a conflict with topics and requirements such as a high degree of usability, the development of "one face to the customer" while mitigating integration conflicts that arise from different levels of granularity or different scientific focus.

What holds an infrastructure together that consists of a large number of participating institutions, and how can a heterogeneous service and data landscape be structured in order to be able to provide competitive and sustainable services? A core problem to be considered in an infrastructure that is distributed both spatially and organizationally is, among other things, the degree of cooperation that can be expected and the type and extent to which jointly supported standards are used. The establishment of a federation – here meant in the sense of connecting otherwise autonomous institutions – is an obvious cooperation structure in the aforementioned environment and the quasi-standard from a certain minimum project size.

With regard to "views" on provided data sets, the large number of preceding work in the area of federated database systems, which has been dealing with similar problems since the 1980s, can serve as a model. Approaches to solutions are often discussed here along the lines of the three problem dimensions of autonomy, heterogeneity and distribution (Leser and Naumann 2007). Their significance for the area of research data infrastructures will only be briefly outlined here and illustrated by way of example:

- Large-scale research infrastructures are in most cases built and supported by a variety of institutions and individual researchers. As a consequence, available resources are stored in a physically *distributed* environment (such as different servers or other technical environments). Appropriate measures must be taken to overcome this spatial separation in uniform user interfaces like search engines that provide access to the overall inventory of resources considered.
- Participants in the infrastructure are – at least to some degree – *autonomous* in their decisions regarding the design of their data, the associated interfaces or implemented access restrictions. In research, these are typically derived from scientific, but in particular also from organizational or legal framework conditions and requirements.

- Data – even when established standards are used – is often highly *heterogeneous*, i. e. using a wide variety of formats or format dialects.[1] Additional integration efforts must be made to provide and access distributed data inventories in a common infrastructure.

This paper presents the Federated Content Search (FCS) as an example of how linguistic research data can be made available in a federated environment and discusses its design principles. These enable it to serve as a lightweight "view" of different types of resources without giving up specific features that are indispensable for highly specialised research questions but can hardly be harmonised in a distributed environment.

1.2 Infrastructure federation in the CLARIN project

The Federated Content Search was originally developed in the 2010s in the context of the European infrastructure project CLARIN (Hinrichs and Krauwer 2014, Fišer and Witt 2022). In order to better understand the basic motivation for the FCS and its potential importance for a distributed and user-friendly research environment, a few general structural principles of CLARIN are briefly outlined here.

CLARIN builds a digital infrastructure that offers data, tools and services for all kinds of research based on language resources. The infrastructure is supported by more than eighty "centres" all belonging to established research and infrastructure institutions spread across more than twenty – mostly European – countries. CLARIN centres provide their specific data stock, services, and expertise to the overall infrastructure. As a central means of building a common infrastructure from the multitude and heterogeneity of different participants, the project uses both established and self-developed standards, compliance with which is required of the centres as part of regular certification processes.

With regard to search and retrieval processes in the infrastructure, the CLARIN project distinguishes between the area of metadata, for searching in the combined resource inventory, and access to the textual content of these resources as part of a "content search". Both applications are backed by dedicated standards for data representation (like those of the Component Metadata Infrastructure (CMDI) ISO 2015) or communication protocols (like *OAI-PMH* Lagoze et al. 2015 and *SRU/searchRetrieve* OASIS 2013), and presented to the user via dedicated Web portals (like the Virtual Language Observatory VLO, van Uytvanck et al. 2012).

1 As an example, just refer to the different encoding variants of the Text Encoding Initiative (TEI) for similar text encoding requirements.

Both approaches are based on the assumption that a federated view of the distributed infrastructure can not reach the original level of detail in all cases. Accordingly, central applications always offer access to the specific resource in the context of its actual provider. These applications must therefore enable the user to recognize when the federated procedures and views do not provide a sufficient level of detail.

The Federated Content Search (Stehouwer et al. 2012) was developed in CLARIN for searching in the textual content of linguistic resources. As an example, Figure 1 shows the results for the single-term query "Elephant" in a CLARIN FCS search portal. More than 500 resources provided by 19 European institutions were requested in parallel during this search.

The remainder of this chapter describes the system in more detail with respect to key characteristics and its integration into a standards-focused research environment. This begins with an overview of key characteristics that were central to the conceptual design of the FCS and its implementation on the basis of established standards, followed by a presentation of its central standard components and an exemplary discussion of use cases with a focus on functionalities that have been newly developed in recent years (see also Trippel 2025).

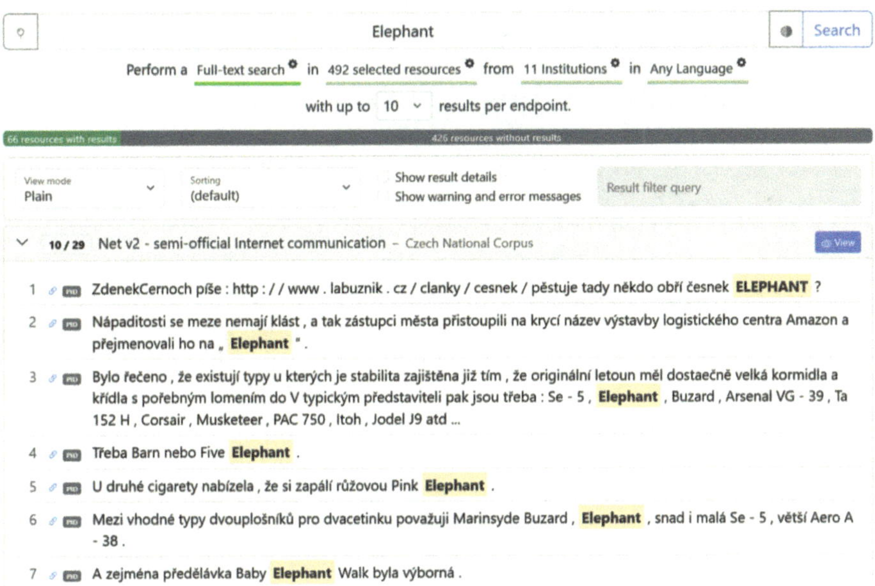

Figure 1: Search results for the query "Elephant" with results provided by 12 different European institutions in the CLARIN FCS.

2 Federated content search

2.1 Distributed retrieval of linguistic content

The general requirements of a distributed and diverse research landscape have led to various approaches to solving the problem of access to or retrieval of structured text data in decentralised “data stores” at an early stage. They are thus – among other things – in the tradition of bibliographic databases, which have been trying to solve similar problems for a long time and have developed strategies that are also useful for the area of “content search” addressed here.

A central idea, which is also the basis for the FCS, is the agreement on three core components: (i) a data model as a “mediator schema” that abstracts from local specificities, (ii) an access protocol through which messages are exchanged between clients and the data stores (called “*endpoints*” in the FCS), and (iii) a query language that enables selection and filtering by the requesting party. All three of these components are published in the form of standards that guarantee the interoperability of the distributed system. A general overview of this architecture is shown in Figure 2.

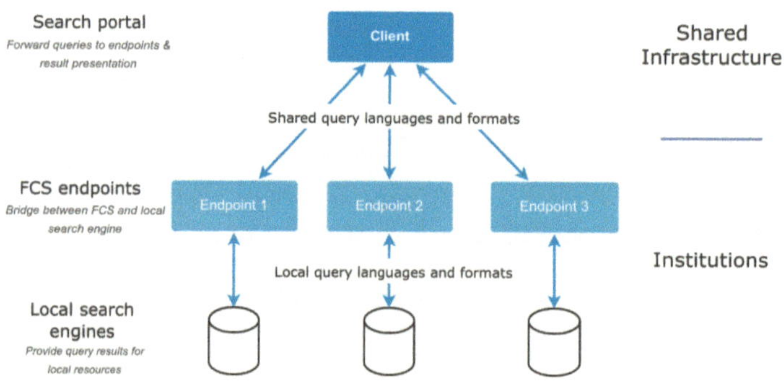

Figure 2: General architecture of the FCS.

The field of text editions in particular was very productive at an early stage and developed powerful applications. Some examples worth highlighting, especially in the field of text retrieval, include the Canonical Text Services CTS (Tiepmar and Heyer 2019), which developed a powerful protocol with a focus on TEI documents based on standardised citation rules (Smith 2010) for hierarchical, digital text structures, and its successor CITE. The latter also allows the serialization of a wide variety of resource types via a corresponding exchange format (CITE Exchange format, CEX) as plain text. The specification of Distributed Text Services DTS (Almas et al. 2023) follows a similar concept, also focusing on the retrieval process rather than on user-driven (full-text) searches. Several institutions provide resources using these systems, but there is not a particularly broad support across disciplines at the moment.

Parallel to these and comparable approaches, there were also early efforts to enable the encoding of and access to linguistic content using Linked Open Data (LOD) standards. One example of this is the NLP Interchange Format NIF (Hellmann et al. 2013), which clearly distinguishes itself from other LOD-based approaches that focus more on text metadata or individual text annotations. NIF consistently supports the encoding of linguistic resources using an RDF/OWL-based format – from plain text structures to linguistic annotations – with the aim of being able to carry out natural language processing methods directly on these structures. Accordingly, the relevant standards of the Semantic Web Community are used for publication, access protocol, and query language. To date, individual NIF-based services are still available, but there has been no widespread use. This can at least be seen as an indication that, despite the increasing popularity of related technologies such as knowledge graphs or the access to resources via authority data, the formats used to encode textual content will continue to be the established, often XML-based data formats. This makes publication of textual content based on them – despite standards such as *SPARQL Federated Query* (Prud'hommeaux and Buil-Aranda 2021) being available in principle – a reasonable choice in a federated search environment because of an expected higher acceptance rate and simpler integration procedures.

As a general and prominent example of the relevance of decentralised indexing and search solutions for textual content, reference should also be made to the *European Open Search Foundation* OSF,[2] even though its focus is on generic web search and not on annotated research data. One of the core motivations behind this project, however, is highly topical: the use of decentralised, federated infrastructure as opposed to monopolised ecosystems that have prevailed in the area of web search (Mager 2023, Khan 2025).

2.1.1 Aspect "content search"

The term "content search" is used here in contrast to providing access to data sets based on structured metadata, i. e. finding relevant resources based on their author, title, publisher and similar information. Providing descriptive metadata is an established basis for the provision and use of research data in accordance with the FAIR principles (Wilkinson et al. 2016). Corresponding protocols and access procedures

2 Open Search Foundation, https://opensearchfoundation.org

have been established for decades (see, for example, the *Protocol for Metadata Harvesting of the Open Archives Initiative*, OAI-PMH) and open up huge amounts of data to interested users via modern web interfaces. Searching in metadata records is a practical solution for filtering large amounts of resources with facets to identify a smaller subset for more in-depth examination. In most cases, direct search in the actual content of the filtered resources (like the textual content of a text corpus) is not part of the functionality provided by these portals.

Search engines for linguistic content that are dedicated to the use by scientists and which address both their needs and the specific features of the respective resource provide a special form of access to data. They especially stand out from generic Web search engines such as Google, Bing, Baidu, or Yandex in that they allow searching within scientifically curated linguistic resources while enabling powerful queries using linguistic search patterns rather than simple keyword or text phrase queries. There are a large number of these specialised search engines available, which offer a variety of search functionality (see, for example, corpus query engines like BlackLab (de Does et al. 2017), Open Corpus Workbench (Evert and Hardie 2011), KorAP (Diewald et al. 2016) or SketchEngine (Kilgarriff et al. 2014)). In some cases, they are specifically tailored to specific resources or resource types, and used to provide access to local resources without a dedicated focus of their application in a federated environment. The FCS is meant to be a rather slim compatibility layer on top of these applications.

The use of a federated content search in no way excludes the use of established metadata-based search environments. Rather, it complements existing access meth-

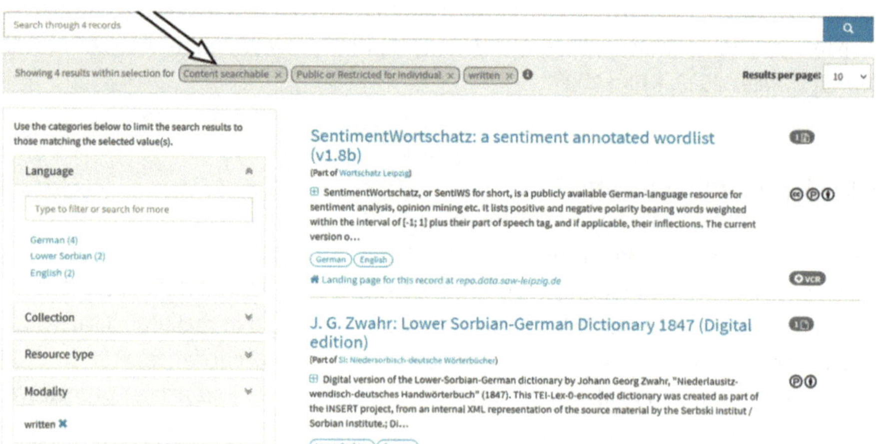

Figure 3: Combining metadata facets and content search in the CLARIN VLO.

ods with the additional option of transitioning from descriptive meta information to the actual content. Using metadata search as a filter on huge resource inventories followed by a subsequent content search is a powerful approach for researchers to find potentially useful data sets and assess their relevance. Figure 3 shows an example of how both forms of search can be combined in a user-friendly way. In this case, the metadata search engine VLO of the European CLARIN project offers the option of performing a distributed FCS-based search on the content of the resources already pre-filtered by the user (see also Trippel 2025).

2.1.2 Aspect "federation"

The "federation" aspect is a core feature and declared design goal of the FCS. Compared to conventional search engines, it offers many advantages for data providers in particular, which also encourages them to participate in the overall platform. One of the main advantages is that control over the data remains with its providers, who can determine means of access, update data without delay or withdraw resources in the event of problems and use their expertise to ensure an optimal search experience (e. g., optimised indexing and search evaluation based on the data, appropriate ranking of results). However, this comes with the drawback that the FCS infrastructure cannot guarantee the availability of the data when endpoints are unavailable and features such as global ranking of results and faceting based on metadata are not supported or only to a small extent (see Kamocki 2025).

2.2 FCS as a standard-driven application

Extensibility and backward compatibility are key design principles of the Federated Content Search. Whenever possible, established standards were used for all aspects of its specification, favouring those that are in the widest possible active use.

The central search protocol on which the FCS is based and which it extends is *Search/Retrieve via URL* (SRU), standardised by the Library of Congress and the standardisation organisation OASIS (OASIS 2013). SRU describes a rather generic search protocol on top of established Internet standards like RESTful APIs, Uniform Resource Identifiers (URIs) and several standards of the XML family of standards. It describes the communication protocol used including search requests to endpoints and self-configuration of clients via standardised endpoint descriptions.

SRU utilizes the query language *Contextual Query Language* CQL (Library of Congress 2023) (formerly Common Query Language) for formulating queries to information systems such as bibliographic catalogues. CQL is meant to be a user-friendly query language that still allows to express complex information needs. However, its orientation towards a Key-Value oriented data model was problematic for formulating queries on sequential textual content. As a consequence, *FCS-QL* is used in the FCS for formulating corpus queries since version 2.0. Although this query language is a new development, it is heavily oriented towards the existing query languages of established corpus engines (e. g., CQP within CWB, SketchEngine) and largely compatible with those.

In addition to these central components for communication and query formulation, the FCS uses established standards at various levels, including the recommendation of suitable vocabularies at the value level. This includes the use of the Universal Dependencies Part-of-Speech tag set[3] for POS annotations or the *Speech Assessment Methods Phonetic Alphabet* (SAMPA) for providing phonetic transcripts, which both are part of the core specification 2.0. In general, persistent references to vocabularies and vocabulary values are increasingly used in FCS data models.

2.3 Community standard FCS Core 2.0

The FCS Core 2.0 specification (van Uytvanck et al. 2017) published in 2017 is the current version on which the entire Federated Content Search architecture is built. This specification is expected to remain the final major version which can be supplemented by companion or extension specifications. As long as extensions maintain backward compatibility and are not over-adjusted to individual resources or use cases (i. e., they should apply to multiple endpoints and resources and there should be a minimum number of supporting institutions), they can complement the FCS[4] in various areas:

- the introduction of additional endpoint configurations, e. g. further metadata about provided resources or information about supported search features,
- new result formats (so called “Data Views”) to present additional information or alternative result structures,
- new query languages.

The specification explicitly provides “extension points” for modifications, whether in the XML schemas, when introducing new values, or adding specialised SRU parameters. The minimum requirement for each endpoint is only the support of a

3 Universal Dependencies, Universal POS tags, https://universaldependencies.org/u/pos/

4 Changes to the user interface of FCS clients are usually only the result of the implementation of specifications. The FCS specification only describes the protocol details, but does not provide any guidelines for the implementation and design of UIs.

so-called "basic search" and the signalling of errors or unsupported functionalities via standardised diagnostics.

The FCS was originally intended and designed for searching in text collections, with support for linguistic search patterns on annotated text. A recent extension of the FCS is support and integration of lexical resources as a new resource type. Due to their different structure in data representation, a new data model and a matching query language were introduced with the *LexFCS* specification (Körner et al. 2024) as a new CQL *Context Set*. The need for authentication using an Authentication and Authorization Infrastructure (AAI) is a motivation for the development of a FCS-AAI specification. Other enhancements, such as support of entity annotations in queries or the support for custom fonts, are being tested and have turned out to be promising.

As an open standard, it is always possible to make protocol-compatible changes in a custom FCS setup and still participate in the overall infrastructure. However, all former and current modifications and extensions of the FCS are mainly coordinated and developed in the context of large-scale research infrastructure projects. In particular, the European CLARIN project with its 24 national consortia is the organizational basis for requirements analysis, conception phases, implementation of central software libraries, and approval of specification updates as community standards. Work on FCS-related topics is carried out in separate working groups or task forces, such as the *CLARIN FCS taskforce*, by interested participants from different professional and scientific backgrounds.

3 Main components of the FCS

3.1 Communication protocol

The FCS Core 2.0 specification (van Uytvanck et al. 2017: Section 3) extends the SRU 2.0 standard and describes communication in a distributed client-server architecture (cf. Figure 2), where the "FCS Aggregator" is an example of a client, while the "FCS endpoints" are servers. Clients send requests via HTTP GET and endpoints respond with XML SRU responses that wrap records (results encoded in "Data Views") or errors (diagnostics).

The specification allows the following SRU operations for use in the FCS:

- *Explain*: Clients ask an endpoint for a description of features it supports, e. g., the list of available resources, annotation layers, supported Data Views and formats. Clients can use this for autoconfiguration, like the adaptation of user interfaces for improved user guidance and assistance.

- *SearchRetrieve*: Clients send the actual search request to an endpoint, containing the query, query type, and (optionally) resource selection and pagination parameters. The endpoint responds with the result set and/or diagnostics if problems occur.

The FCS specification extends the SRU protocol to especially include the following aspects:
- "Endpoint Description" to describe the capabilities of FCS endpoints, i. e. the resource list and supported features used in the response to an "Explain" request,
- supported query languages (e. g., FCS-QL) and their respective data models,
- "Data Views" to store results in data containers to correctly represent the returned information,
- custom SRU extension parameters for resource and result format selection,
- additional diagnostics for FCS-related protocol extensions.

3.2 Data models

Two major data models are in use: a format for describing text with (optional) annotation layers and a key-value oriented format introduced by the LexFCS specification for queries on lexical entries. In many cases, these two formats can only provide a "lossy" representation of the original data. Their design was motivated by a focus on simplicity and generic applicability, to allow most data formats for textual content to be transformed into them. This is also due to the fact that the FCS does not aim to replicate all the features of local search engines but rather to provide a generic and comparable basis that allows users to work on predictable text and annotation structures. Results provide references to the original landing pages of the resources at their home institutions which allows users, if needed, to work with a more detailed resource representation and dedicated query functionality for a more in-depth research there.

3.2.1 Sequential text with annotation layers

The primary data model for full-text and linguistic pattern search is based on sequences of characters. Besides a mandatory *Basic search* functionality that uses a simple data model focused on plain text and that provides results in the familiar *Keyword in Context* (KWIC) format, the *Advanced search*, introduced in FCS 2.0, uses a more complex data model with character spans based on character offsets.

This flexible approach allows the representation of simple plain text documents (including audio transcripts) and the specification of character sub-segments to encode text structure (tokens, sentences) or text annotation, e. g. for providing grammatical information, text normalisation and more. Search queries are therefore pattern-based filters on text segments and their differently typed annotation values. Figure 4 shows an example for such a layered structure with different annotations (see also Bański and Diewald 2025).

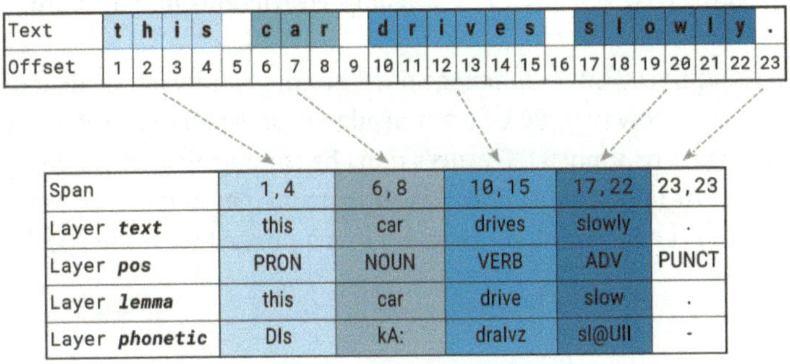

Figure 4: Exemplary illustration of the *Advanced search* data model.

3.2.2 Key-value data

The aforementioned data model is not suitable for resources with a complex key-value oriented data structure. This especially includes many lexical resources, like hierarchically structured word nets or dictionaries whose information can be mapped to a key-value structure. The LexFCS specification (Körner et al. 2024, Eckart et al. 2023) introduced a new data model which uses *entries* to represent lexical articles. Each entry contains values that are grouped by type into fields and may have additional attributes to encode language, references, and more.

3.3 Query languages

The FCS defines three query languages, of which two are already part of its core specification and one is part of the recent LexFCS extension:

– *CQL*: This query language is mandatory for all endpoints and is used in the *Basic search*. It is a dialect of the aforementioned Contextual Query Language CQL with a restricted feature set (such as supporting Boolean operators only).

- *FCS-QL*: This query language is used for the *Advanced search*. It is based on the aforementioned sequential data model and allows to build complex queries using multiple tokens with various annotation layers. Parentheses and Boolean operators are supported. Values can be specified using regular expressions.
- *LexCQL*: This query language is also a dialect of the Contextual Query Language CQL adapted for accessing lexical resources using the aforementioned key-value based data model. Various relation types and Boolean operators are supported. Using relation modifiers, field values can be evaluated under different criteria, e. g. taking case sensitivity or language restrictions into account.

Endpoints that want to support a query language must be able to fully parse all of its (structurally valid) queries. However, they do not need to support all features of the respective query language; unsupported features must be communicated via designated diagnostics. The CLARIN standard libraries support the parsing of queries to lower the entry threshold for new endpoints and the compliance with the specification.

4 Application- and domain-specific functionalities

The Federated Content Search is being used in a variety of application scenarios. This section gives a brief overview on supported functionalities with a focus on recent and future additions to the overall architecture. For more details, please refer to Körner et al. (2025) and the respective complementing specifications.

4.1 Text corpora and plain text resources

Searches through text collections, corpora, or plain texts are supported in both Basic and Advanced search modes by using the respective query languages (cf. Section 3.3) that operate on the default data model for full texts (cf. Section 3.2.1). An FCS-QL query to search through such resources is illustrated in Figure 5 where users of the FCS Aggregator web application are supported by a visual query builder.[5] Searches on plain text require a standard "text" layer that is also used for the most basic display of results. Additional annotation layers can be provided if supported by the resource. These annotation layers include:

5 Here creating a query for instances of three consecutive tokens: a word with the prefix "her" followed by a token with the lemma "Artznei", followed by a verb.

- *text*: Full text layer,
- *lemma*: Lemmatisation,
- *pos*: Part-of-Speech annotations using the Universal POS tags,
- *orth*: Orthographic transcription of (mostly) spoken resources,
- *norm*: Orthographic normalization of (mostly) spoken resources,
- *phonetic*: Phonetic transcription using SAMPA.

Each type of layer can be used multiple times in order to provide values in different vocabularies. That means, for example, that in addition to the default Universal POS tags, custom tagsets or other fine-grained grammatical features are allowed.

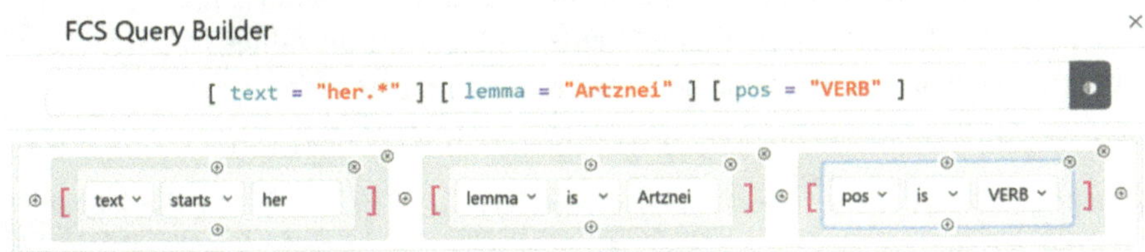

Figure 5: FCS-QL Visual Query Builder in the FCS Aggregator with a query that makes use of different annotation layers.

4.2 Lexical resources

The LexFCS extension (Körner et al. 2024) has been introduced as the data model and query language for corpora and plain texts was found to be unsatisfactory when working with highly structured lexical resources. In many of these, lexical entries that contain a potentially large number of information fields are in the centre. For this reason, the Lex data model (cf. Section 3.2.2) is focused on resources that can be encoded in a key-value data structure, i. e. the data model assumes lexical entries containing any number of typed fields with each having a (plain text) value.

In combination with additional features, this makes it a very flexible data model for different types of resources, including word graphs and dictionaries. A lexical entry is structured by fields that are typed using predefined categories, such as "lemma", "definition", "frequency", or "citation". The encoded value elements support a number of attributes that describe their content in more detail and can serve various purposes, like providing content language information or references to other parts of the entry which can be used for building information groups and hierarchical structures.

The LexFCS data model is – compared to established data models for lexical resources like TEI Lex-0 (Tasovac et al. 2018) or OntoLex-Lemon (Cimiano et al. 2016) – specifically designed to be a very simple format. This includes the lack of support for structures as they are possible in *feature structures*. However, recent work by participating institutions demonstrates the general feasibility of mapping a variety of lexical data formats into this data model. The LexCQL query language (cf. Section 3.3) that is also part of the new LexFCS specification is a dialect of the Contextual Query Language CQL and builds on indices provided by the data model's field types.

Figure 6 shows results for the query "Apfel"[6] provided by a bilingual Sorbian dictionary using the LexFCS. This new user interfaces offers – depending on the provided data – additional features such as the integration of audio files for pronunciation, hover effects to show related items, and tooltips on values with additional properties such as content language, references, and categories.

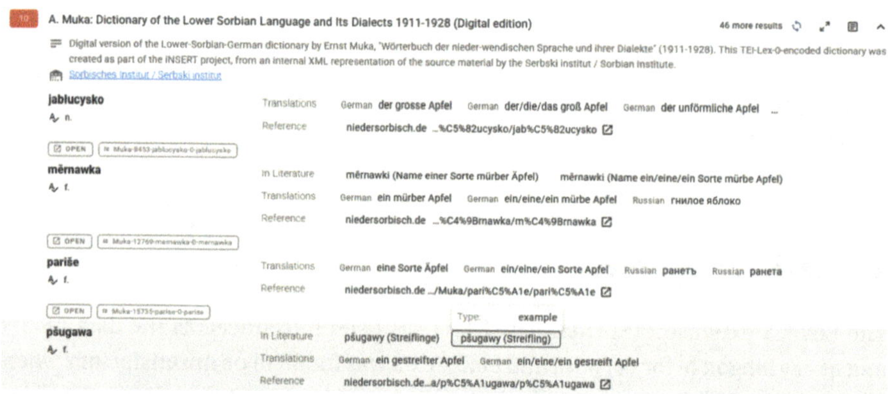

Figure 6: Visualisation of lexical resource results in an FCS frontend.

4.3 EntityFCS

The EntityFCS extension allows searches on entity- and sense-annotated full texts and lexical resources using global identifiers. The central idea is the annotation of "named entities" (such as people, places, organizations) with references to their entries in authority data (such as *Wikidata* or the Integrated Authority File

6 Query *citation* = *"Apfel"*, for lexical entries with the German word "Apfel" in their *citation* section.

GND) or the annotation of lexemes in dictionaries with their entries in lexical-semantic databases (such as *Princeton WordNet*). These annotations thus allow disambiguated queries for the corresponding entities.

Due to the different specific properties of Advanced and Lexical search, there are slightly different characteristics in the respective parts of the specification. They both entail modifications to the query language and to the support of entity representation in their data views. The Advanced search adds support for a new annotation layer "entity", while the Lexical search uses the "senseRef" field type which is already part of the LexFCS specification.

Aside from providing disambiguated query results, this enhancement of the FCS will also enable a new "Entity" search mode that allows for entity-oriented searches in full text and lexical resources and their aggregated presentation in the user interface. This would allow, for example, to identify dictionary entries for a given sense of the term "bank" while finding all occurrences in full texts that are annotated accordingly.

Figure 7 shows a query for all occurrences of the word "Leipzig" that are annotated with entity identifiers. These annotations can be viewed directly in the result presentation: all underlined words are annotated with GND references. By making use of an external API, additional information is dynamically displayed in an interactive tooltip (see also Khan 2025, Schwarz 2025).

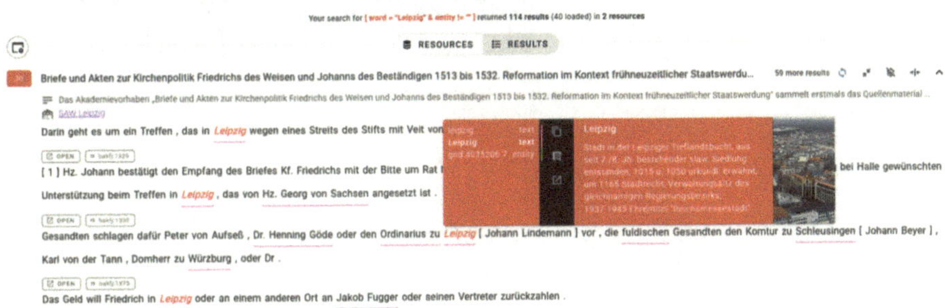

Figure 7: Integration of entity search and visualisation in an FCS frontend.

4.4 Adequate result presentation

Particularly for texts in historical languages or so-called "under-represented languages", the adequate representation of text can sometimes be a challenge. It cannot be assumed in every case that all characters used in the source material are supported by standard fonts or that characters and diacritics are even part of the

Unicode[7] standard or at least will be included in the near future. In the latter case, Unicode provides for the use of "private use areas", i. e. code points that are deliberately kept free for this use case and which in turn can only be meaningfully represented by using fonts adapted for this purpose.

The Federated Content Search is aimed not only at scientists who are often aware of the availability of such special fonts for their field, but also at non-specialist users and it aims to enable them to receive appropriate results both in central and decentralised FCS search applications. For this purpose, an extension currently under development provides optional information about required fonts in the endpoint description. Information on the name of the respective font, the license and, in particular, the URL at which it is available can be displayed directly in the user interface.

Direct integration and use of the referenced font in the FCS search portal, without direct user interaction, is also conceivable – analogous to the use of "web fonts" – but this can be problematic for data protection reasons. Figure 8 shows an early prototype of font-related hints in an FCS user interface. Here, results of the *Thesaurus Linguae Aegyptiae* with non-standard code points lead to major display problems. The web application provides a hint that the resource requires two specific fonts for adequate presentation and an external URL for more information.

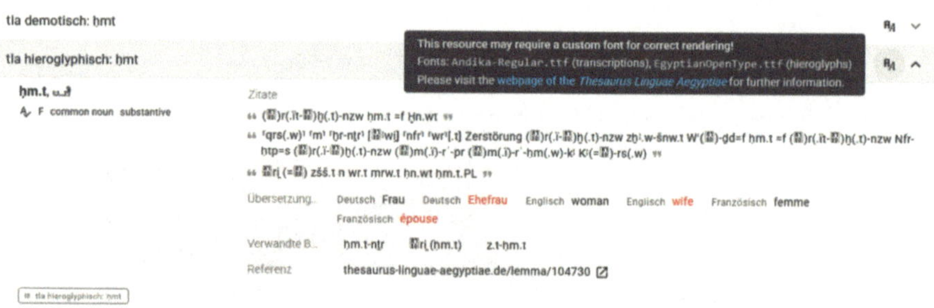

Figure 8: UI hint for required fonts in the FCS Aggregator (prototype).

As part of work in the Text+ project, further use cases were identified for resources which are intended for integration into the FCS. This includes a specific font for the representation of sign language data (Hanke 2004) and a font mostly used for the correct presentation of historical dictionaries. The popular *KompLett*[8] font

7 Unicode – The World Standard for Text and Emoji, https://unicode.org

8 KompLett, https://tcdh.uni-trier.de/en/projekt/komplett

includes – among others – letters with multiple accent marks[9] but also old currency and musical note symbols (see also Wartena 2025).

4.5 Restricted access to linguistic content

There are a number of reasons why linguistic resources cannot be made freely and publicly available. These include copyright, specific licensing agreements ("moving wall") or data protection restrictions. Even though there are various exceptions at national and European level, particularly for research, the publication of many resources is not possible or only possible to a limited extent.

At least for some of these problem cases, solutions exist in distributed infrastructures that can at least enforce restrictions on access by a limited group of people. These restricted user groups can be specific individuals, all members of a research project or a specific institution, or even the research community in general. Authentication and Authorization Infrastructures (AAIs) are established as basic services in modern research, so that scientists can use the identity provider of their respective home institution to access restricted services at other institutions as part of a convenient single sign-on solution.

A specification (Schonefeld et al. 2024) currently under development and first implementation prototypes based on it extend the existing FCS architecture with the corresponding support. This includes a number of sub-components, such as the option of logging in at the central search portals of the infrastructure, procedures for how endpoints communicate their respective requirements and the transfer of the corresponding security tokens as part of the communication protocol.

As usual, the decentralised endpoints (and thus their operating institutions or resource providers) make the decision about the approval of a request. For the rather common case of access to "academic use only" content, the knowledge that authentication has taken place with an identity provider of an established AAI (like eduGAIN) can already be sufficient; for more detailed restrictions, *SAML* (Security Assertion Markup Language) attributes such as *eduPersonPrincipalName* or *eduPersonTargetedID* are also available.

Surveys among operators of FCS endpoints made it clear that such control mechanisms can lead to the provision of additional resources. Furthermore, they highlighted a special case that will also be part of the future specification: the ability to signal the presence of possible results without being able to provide the actual data. Using separate references, users can be referred directly to the corresponding

9 Which can often only be inadequately represented by the use of combining different diacritics.

local access points via the FCS search interfaces, which might require separate authentication mechanisms. The inclusion of additional information on the restricted representation of resources for legal reasons – “derived text formats” (Schöch et al. 2020), such as sentence shuffling, limited text contexts, etc. – is currently under discussion.

A high level of acceptance for this additional access option is only conceivable on the basis of established infrastructure and standards. These range from the underlying AAI and familiar login interfaces (*Shibboleth*), the use of SAML attributes to Internet standards such as *JSON Web Tokens* for encoding the transmitted access tokens (see also Kamocki 2025).

5 Conclusion

Over the last twelve years, the Federated Content Search has developed into a mature and powerful platform for accessing linguistic research data in large-scale infrastructures. This development has been favoured by an increasingly extensive ecosystem of software, a steadily growing number of institutions that offer their resources within the framework of the FCS, as well as a key idea of the FCS: flexible mechanisms for its expandability based on and taking into account established data and communication standards.

The speed and dynamism with which the FCS has evolved in recent years can also be explained by its role as a central component in modern research infrastructure projects, which provide new impetus at both European (CLARIN) and national level (like Text+ in Germany) and formulate new expectations and requirements. A number of solutions that have emerged from the community as answers to real-world questions have been outlined in this paper. Direct communication channels and the offer of immediate support, for example in the context of problem-oriented and focused workshops and hackathons, were the basis for the iterative development of appropriate solution proposals. Not least due to the limited resources available, a balance is always struck between the effort required and the scope and degree of utilisation to be expected beyond the requesting institutions or users, as well as between the generic nature of possible solutions for their broad applicability and the specificity of these solutions, as a prerequisite for answering individual scientific questions.

The development of the FCS is by no means complete. The work considered here represents the state of a development of 2025 that is based on various earlier iterations. This approach is only possible by taking into account and adhering to established standards, backward compatibility and the continuous versioning of its own community standards. It is the strong intention to progress along this path, to further improve existing solutions and, if necessary, to develop new ones. Various enhancements are foreseeable and in some cases already in preparation, including the clearer description of resources and query results through structured metadata and the simplified use of FCS interfaces in external applications, which are to be seen both in the context of a stronger interlinking of highly integrated research environments and in the context of current developments that make high-quality data sets available via Retrieval Augmented Generation (RAG) using large generative language models.

Bibliography

Almas, Bridget, Hugh Cayless, Thibault Clérice, Vincent Jolivet, Pietro Maria Liuzzo, Jonathan Robie, Matteo Romanello & Ian W. Scott. 2023. Distributed text services (DTS): A community-built API to publish and consume text collections as linked data. *Journal of the Text Encoding Initiative* (Rolling Issue). 1–26.

Bański, Piotr & Nils Diewald. 2025. Dealing with multiple annotations. In Piotr Bański, Ulrich Heid & Laura Herzberg (eds.), *Harmonising language data: Standards for linguistic resources*. De Gruyter.

Cimiano, Phillip, John P. McCrae & Paul Buitelaar. 2016. *Lexicon model for ontologies*. W3C, 2016. https://www.w3.org/2016/05/ontolex/.

de Does, Jesse, Jan Niestadt & Katrien Depuydt. 2017. Creating research environments with blacklab. In *CLARIN in the Low Countries*, 245–257.

Diewald, Nils, Michael Hanl, Eliza Margaretha, Joachim Bingel, Marc Kupietz, Piotr Bański & Andreas Witt. 2016. Korap architecture – diving in the deep sea of corpus data. In Nicoletta Calzolari, Khalid Choukri, Thierry Declerck, Sara Goggi, Marko Grobelnik Bente Maegaard, Joseph Mariani, Helene Mazo, Asuncion Moreno, Jan Odijk & Stelios Piperidis (eds.), *Proceedings of the tenth international conference on language resources and evaluation (LREC 2016)*, Portorož, Slovenia, 3586–3591.

Eckart, Thomas, Axel Herold, Erik Körner & Frank Wiegand. 2023. A federated search and retrieval platform for lexical resources in Text+ and CLARIN. In *Electronic lexicography in the 21st century (eLex 2023): Invisible Lexicography. Proceedings of the eLex 2023 conference*, 280–292. Brno, Czech Republic: Lexical Computing CZ s. r. o.

Evert, Stefan & Andrew Hardie. 2011. Twenty-first century Corpus Workbench: Updating a query architecture for the new millennium. In *Proceedings of the Corpus Linguistics 2011 conference*, UK: University of Birmingham.

Fišer, Darja & Andreas Witt (eds.). 2022. *CLARIN – The infrastructure for language resources*. De Gruyter.

Hanke, Thomas. 2004. HamNoSys—Representing sign language data in language resources and language processing contexts. In *Workshop on the representation and processing of sign languages. 4th international conference on language resources and evaluation, LREC 2004*.

Hellmann, Sebastian, Jens Lehmann, Sören Auer & Martin Brümmer. 2013. Integrating NLP using linked data. In Harith Alani, Lalana Kagal, Achille Fokoue, Paul Groth, Chris Biemann, Josiane Xavier Parreira, Lora Aroyo, Natasha Noy, Chris Welty & Krzysztof Janowicz (eds.), *The semantic web – ISWC 2013*, 98–113. Berlin/Heidelberg: Springer Berlin Heidelberg.

Hinrichs, Erhard & Steven Krauwer. 2014. The CLARIN research infrastructure: Resources and tools for e-Humanities scholars. In *Proceedings of the ninth international conference on language resources and evaluation (LREC-2014)*, 1525–1531.
ISO. 2015. *ISO 24622-1:2015 Language resource management — Component Metadata Infrastructure (CMDI)*. https://www.iso.org/standard/37336.html.
Kamocki, Paweł. 2025. Taxonomy of legal and ethical metadata for language resources. In Piotr Bański, Ulrich Heid & Laura Herzberg (eds.), *Harmonising language data: Standards for linguistic resources*. De Gruyter.
Khan, Anas Fahad. 2025. Linguistic linked (open) data. In Piotr Bański, Ulrich Heid & Laura Herzberg (eds.), *Harmonising language data: Standards for linguistic resources*. De Gruyter.
Kilgarriff, Adam, Vít Baisa, Jan Bušta, Miloš Jakubíček, Vojtěch Kovář, Jan Michelfeit, Pavel Rychlý & Vít Suchomel. 2014. The Sketch Engine: Ten years on. *Lexicography* 1:7–36.
Körner, Erik, Thomas Eckart, Felix Helfer & Uwe Kretschmer. 2025. An enhanced federated content search infrastructure for the humanities and social sciences. In *Selected papers from the CLARIN annual conference 2024*. To be accepted.
Körner, Erik, Thomas Eckart, Uwe Kretschmer, Axel Herold, Frank Wiegand, Frank Michaelis, Matthias Bremm, Louis Cotgrove, Thorsten Trippel, Felix Rau, Anne Klee, Daniel Werning, Dominik Blöse & Claus Zinn. 2024. *Federated Content Search for Lexical Resources (LexFCS): Specification*. https://doi.org/10.5281/zenodo.7849753.
Lagoze, Carl, Herbert Van de Sompel, Michael Nelson & Simeon Warner. 2015. *The Open Archives Initiative Protocol for metadata harvesting*. Open Archives Initiative. https://www.openarchives.org/OAI/openarchivesprotocol.html.
Leser, Ulf & Felix Naumann. 2007. *Informationsintegration: Architekturen und Methoden zur Integration verteilter und heterogener Datenquellen*. Heidelberg: dpunkt-Verl.
Mager, Astrid. 2023. European Search? How to counter-imagine and counteract hegemonic search with European search engine projects. *Big Data & Society* 10(1).
OASIS. 2013. *searchRetrieve v1.0*. Organization for the Advancement of Structured Information Standards. http://docs.oasis-open.org/search-ws/searchRetrieve/v1.0/searchRetrieve-v1.0-part0-overview.html.
Library of Congress. 2023. *CQL: The Contextual Query Language*. The Library of Congress. https://www.loc.gov/standards/sru/cql/.
Prud'hommeaux, Eric & Carlos Buil-Aranda. 2021. SPARQL 1.1 Federated Query. W3C recommendation, W3C. https://www.w3.org/TR/sparql11-federated-query.
Schonefeld, Oliver, Leif-Jöran Olsson, Thomas Eckart, André Moreira & Erik Körner. 2024. *CLARIN Federated Content Search (CLARIN-FCS) – AAI 1.0*. https://clarin-eric.github.io/fcs-misc/fcs-aai-specs/fcs-aai.html.
Schwarz, Pia. 2025. Named entity recognition and entity linking. In Piotr Bański, Ulrich Heid & Laura Herzberg (eds.), *Harmonising language data: Standards for linguistic resources*. De Gruyter.
Schöch, Christof, Frédéric Döhl, Achim Rettinger, Evelyn Gius, Peer Trilcke, Peter Leinen, Fotis Jannidis, Maria Hinzmann & Jörg Röpke. 2020. Abgeleitete Textformate: Text und Data Mining mit urheberrechtlich geschützten Textbeständen. *Zeitschrift für digitale Geisteswissenschaften*.
Smith, Neel. 2010. *Citation in Classical Studies*, 151–172. Piscataway, NJ, USA: Gorgias Press.
Stehouwer, Herman, Matej Durco, Eric Auer & Daan Broeder. 2012. Federated search: Towards a common search infrastructure, In Nicoletta Calzolari, Khalid Choukri, Thierry Declerck, Mehmet Uğur Doğan, Bente Maegaard, Joseph Mariani, Asuncion Moreno, Jan Odijk & Stelios Piperidis (eds.), *Proceedings of the Eighth International Conference on Language Resources and Evaluation (LREC'12)*, 3255–3259. Istanbul, Turkey: European Language Resources Association (ELRA).

Tasovac, Toma, Laurent Romary, Piotr Banski, Jack Bowers, Jesse de Does, Katrien Depuydt, Tomaž Erjavec, Alexander Geyken, Axel Herold, Vera Hildenbrandt, Mohamed Khemakhem, Boris Lehečka, Snežana Petrović, Ana Salgado & Andreas Witt TEI. 2018. *Lex-0: A baseline encoding for lexicographic data*. DARIAH Working Group on Lexical Resources. https://dariah-eric.github.io/lexicalresources/pages/TEILex0/TEILex0.html.

Tiepmar, Jochen & Gerhard Heyer. 2019. *The canonical text services in classics and beyond*, 95–114. De Gruyter Saur.

Trippel, Thorsten. 2025. Metadata for research data. In Piotr Bański, Ulrich Heid & Laura Herzberg (eds.), *Harmonising language data: Standards for linguistic resources*. De Gruyter.

van Uytvanck, Dieter, Leif-Jöran Olsson, Oliver Schonefeld, Thomas Eckart, Erik Körner, Thomas Kisler, Peter M. Fischer & Eliza Margaretha Illig. 2017. *CLARIN Federated Content Search (CLARIN-FCS) – Core 2.0*. https://office.clarin.eu/v/CE-2017-1046-FCS-Specification-v20230426.pdf.

van Uytvanck, Dieter, Herman Stehouwer & Lari Lampen. 2012. Semantic metadata mapping in practice: The virtual language observatory. In Nicoletta Calzolari, Khalid Choukri, Thierry Declerck, Sara Goggi, Marko Grobelnik Bente Maegaard, Joseph Mariani, Helene Mazo, Asuncion Moreno, Jan Odijk & Stelios Piperidis (eds.), *Proceedings of the eight international conference on language resources and evaluation (LREC'12)*. Istanbul, Turkey: European Language Resources Association (ELRA).

Wartena, Christian. 2025. Character encoding and its importance for text resources. In Piotr Bański, Ulrich Heid & Laura Herzberg (eds.), *Harmonising language data: Standards for linguistic resources*. De Gruyter.

Wilkinson, Mark D., Michel Dumontier, Jan Aalbersberg, Gabrielle Appleton, Myles Axton, Arie Baak, Niklas Blomberg, Jan-Willem Boiten, Luiz Bonino da Silva Santos, Philip E. Bourne, Jildau Bouwman, Anthony J. Brookes, Tim Clark, Mercè Crosas, Ingrid Dillo, Olivier Dumon, Scott Edmunds, Chris T. Evelo, Richard Finkers, Alejandra Gonzalez-Beltran, Alasdair J. G. Gray, Paul Groth, Carole Goble, Jeffrey S. Grethe, Jaap Heringa, Peter A. C. 't Hoen, Rob Hooft, Tobias Kuhn, Ruben Kok, Joost Kok, Scott J. Lusher, Maryann E. Martone, Albert Mons, Abel L. Packer, Bengt Persson, Philippe Rocca-Serra, Marco Roos, Rene van Schaik, Susanna-Assunta Sansone, Erik Schultes, Thierry Sengstag, Ted Slater, George Strawn, Morris A. Swertz, Mark Thompson, Johan van der Lei, Erik van Mulligen, Jan Velterop, Andra Waagmeester, Peter Wittenburg, Katherine Wolstencroft, Jun Zhao & Barend Mons. 2016. The FAIR Guiding Principles for scientific data management and stewardship. *Scientific Data* 3.

Paweł Kamocki

Taxonomy of legal and ethical metadata for language resources

Abstract: Legal and ethical considerations are fundamental to the responsible creation, sharing, and reuse of language resources. This chapter presents a structured taxonomy of legal and ethical metadata designed to enhance compliance, transparency, and reusability in line with the FAIR principles. It emphasizes the importance of clearly documenting legal and ethical conditions through metadata to support proper attribution, usage compliance, and data protection. Aimed at researchers unfamiliar with legal frameworks, the chapter also offers a step-by-step guide to understanding lawful use of language data. Key topics include the role of the Data Steward, an overview of copyright and data protection laws, as well as ethical considerations. The proposed taxonomy serves as a practical tool to foster confidence and clarity in data reuse, while also highlighting ongoing challenges in this evolving area.

Keywords: metadata, copyright, personal data, ethics, licence

1 Introduction

Legal and ethical considerations play a crucial role in the creation, sharing, and reuse of language resources. Ensuring compliance with legal frameworks and ethical guidelines is not only a fundamental responsibility of researchers, but also an essential requirement for fostering trust and transparency in research. From the perspective of the FAIR principles, clear legal and ethical information is particularly important for enabling responsible and sustainable data reuse.

For re-users, understanding the legal and ethical conditions attached to a dataset is essential for ensuring proper attribution, respecting usage restrictions, and adhering to data protection and copyright requirements. To facilitate this, metadata provide an appropriate and structured means of documenting legal and

Acknowledgement: The author acknowledges the use of Large Language Models (LLMs) as writing aids in phrasing this chapter, based on the authors' notes, ideas, and concepts. The author retains full responsibility for the content.

Paweł Kamocki, Digitale Sprachwissenschaft, Leibniz-Institut für Deutsche Sprache, R5 6-13, 68161 Mannheim, Baden-Württemberg, Germany, e-mail: kamocki@ids-mannheim.de

https://doi.org/10.1515/9783112208212-016

ethical information. By integrating such details into metadata, language resources can be made more accessible and legally compliant, ultimately supporting their wider adoption and interoperability.

Just as there is only one way to eat an elephant – one bite at a time – there is only one way to approach the legal and ethical status of a language resource: step by step. This chapter is intended as a guide for researchers who may be unfamiliar with legal concepts but wish to understand what they can and cannot do with their language data. Moreover, it aims to help researchers document legal and ethical conditions clearly so that others – often equally uncertain about the law – can confidently re-use the data.

This chapter is structured as follows: Section 2 is devoted to the key information in legal metadata which is the identification of the Data Steward; Sections 3 and 4 provide some high-level overview of the most important legal frameworks affecting language resources, namely copyright (Section 3) and data protection (Section 4), and discuss how they can be addressed in the metadata; Section 5 elaborates on ethical metadata, Section 6 contains a representation of the proposed taxonomy for legal and ethical metadata, and Section 7 briefly mentions some future challenges.

2 Data stewardship

The first step in preparing the legal and ethical metadata for a language resource should be to define the data steward.[1] The data steward is a person (usually a legal person, i. e. an entity) who has oversight of the resource, i. e. who supervised its creation, had the possibility to intervene to correct errors in the process, and – perhaps most importantly – is accountable for it. According to the famous Spiderman adage: With great power comes great responsibility.

Often, the data steward is the university or research institution where the resource was first created. It is not necessarily the depositor, as a resource can be deposited by an individual researcher or even a reuser. It is also not the rightholder (see below), but it should normally be the controller of the personal data in the resource, although, at least theoretically, these two roles can be separated.

1 See Pisetta and Trippel (2025) for a detailed description of data stewards in repositories, their roles and functions.

3 Copyright metadata

Copyright is a legal framework that provides authors with exclusive rights in their *works*. In order to be protected by copyright (i. e., to qualify as a work), a creation must be original, i. e., according to the Court of Justice of the European Union (hereinafter: CJEU), it must be its author's own intellectual creation,[2] a threshold that most language data meet. Copyright-protected works can only be lawfully copied (reproduced) and shared (communicated to the public) with permission (i. e., a license) from the rightholder, or in cases covered by statutory exceptions (such as the relatively new exceptions for Text and Data Mining). Copyright is limited in time, and it generally expires 70 years after the death of the author.

The following subsections will discuss various aspects that can be reflected in copyright metadata of a language resource. Most importantly, the copyright status (in-copyright vs. public domain) of every resource should be identified in the metadata (3.1). Further, for those resources that are protected by copyright, the information about the author and the rightholder (3.2), and about the license (3.3) or the relevant statutory exception (3.4) should also be provided.

3.1 Copyright status of a language resource

Copyright status is one of the crucial elements of legal status that the re-user will have to assess before making use of the resource. The following information may be useful in the process.

Ultimately, only courts can make authoritative statements about the copyright status of a resource. Nevertheless, in some clear-cut scenarios researchers should be able to reliably assess that the resource is or is not protected by copyright.

If the author died more than 70 years ago, the work is in principle in the Public Domain and it should be labelled as such. However, some countries (like France) have rather elaborate rules on extensions of the term of protection, e. g. to compensate for time periods when there was no efficient copyright protection (such as both World Wars);[3] researchers dealing with historical texts (especially those from the late 19th and early 20th centuries), as well as librarians, should generally be aware of those rules. Nevertheless, as a rule of thumb, the copyright status of works of

2 CJEU, C-5/08, Infopaq.

3 Cf., e. g., https://www.kwf.org/contact/copyright/

authors who died before the beginning of the 20th century can be safely identified as “Public Domain”. It is a good practice to mark such resources with the Public Domain Mark (PDM),[4] a tool created by the Creative Commons foundation,[5] to increase their discoverability and avoid unnecessary effort multiplication.

If a resource contains large passages of freely written text (e. g., entire paragraphs or more), and the author is still alive or died less than 70 years before, the Copyright status of the resource can quite safely be identified as “In-Copyright”. This includes works of fiction (novels, short stories, poems) and non-fiction (newspaper articles), blog posts, student essays, song lyrics etc.

Still, a sizeable gray area exists, which includes very short texts or short snippets of text (Kamocki 2020), everyday speech, tweets (Kamocki et al. 2022), or content using only highly formulaic language (e. g., user manuals, product instructions) etc. Such content should not at all be labelled for Copyright Status, and the assessment should be left to the re-user. Obviously, when in doubt, it is safer to treat the resource as if it were in copyright.

If a resource contains content that is both “in-copyright” and “public domain”, it should always be labelled as “in-copyright”. However, for convenience of re-users, it may be advisable to make the “public domain” part easily separable from the rest (even as a separate resource).

To further complicate the situation, compilations of public domain material may be protected by copyright if their selection or arrangement is original (i. e., *a minima*, based on subjective criteria).[6] Therefore, an anthology of “100 most beautiful German love poems”, or a list of “10 best songs of 2002” may still be protected by copyright (belonging to the author of the compilation, typically the editor), regardless of whether the content is in copyright or not. However, if the compilation was made for research purposes, the selection process is normally based on objective criteria (such as representativeness and balance), and so the compilation should not meet the originality criterion and therefore it should not attract copyright. In case of doubt, compilations of public-domain materials should not be labelled for copyright status.

For resources with Copyright Status = Public Domain no further copyright metadata are needed or, as a matter of fact, useful.

4 https://creativecommons.org/public-domain/pdm/

5 https://creativecommons.org/

6 See Art. 10(2) of the TRIPS Agreement, Article 3 of the EU Database Directive (96/9/EC), and, e. g. § 4 of the German Copyright Act.

3.2 Information about the author and the rightholder

For in-copyright resources, whenever possible, the *Author* should be identified. Proper authorship attribution is a legal obligation under the so-called paternity right.[7]

It may happen, especially for older texts, that the author cannot be identified. European copyright rules address such cases. Briefly put, a work whose rightholders cannot be identified or contacted despite diligent search is called an "orphan work". Orphan works can, to a rather limited extent, be used by cultural and educational establishments.[8] They should also be registered in the Orphan Works Database held by the European Intellectual Property Office (https://euipo.europa.eu/orphanworks/). However, it should be kept in mind that the mere fact that it is difficult to identity the author is not enough to label a resource as "orphan", or to consider it an orphan work. Before the resource can be labelled as such, the procedure of diligent search as described in the law needs to be carried out, and relevant works should be registered in the Orphan Works Database. Only then the resource can safely be labelled as "orphan". Moreover, the Orphan work status should be a separate element of the metadata, since a work may be considered orphan also if the author or rightholder is identified, but simply cannot be contacted.

If the *author's death year* is known, it is useful to mention it in the metadata, in order to enable future re-users to keep track of the resource's copyright status – in principle, at the end of the 70th year after the author's death year (death year +70),[9] the work enters the public domain and so its Copyright Status can be automatically changed to Public Domain. For precisely this reason, it is useful to implement separability "per author" for resources that contain works from several authors.

The *Rightholder* is the person (natural or, perhaps more often, legal) who has exclusive rights in the resource. It may or may not be the same person as the Author. Under German copyright law (unlike in most other countries), copyright cannot be transferred[10] and it always remains with the author. However, even under German law the author can grant an exclusive license,[11] and by doing so assign the possibility to exercise exclusive rights in a work to the licensee. The rightholder is usually clearly identified in the copyright notice after the © sign; if a license to use the data

7 Art. 6bis of the Berne Convention, and, e. g., § 13 of the German Copyright Act.

8 EU Orphan Works Directive (2012/28/EU), and, e. g., §§ 61-61c of the German Copyright Act.

9 Art. 1(1) of the EU Copyright Term Directive (2006/116/EC), and, e. g., § 64 of the German Copyright Act.

10 § 29 of the German Copyright Act.

11 § 31 of the German Copyright Act.

was obtained, the Rightholder is the licensor (the person from whom the license was obtained). Often it is the publisher. It is useful to know the rightholder in cases where additional permission (exceeding the one granted in the license or in a copyright exception) is necessary.

3.3 License metadata

The *License, i. e. a permission granted by the rightholder*, is another crucial element of copyright-related metadata. First, a distinction should be made between "public" and "private" licenses.

A "public" license is a license in which the licensor (the rightholder) grants a permission to the general public, i. e. to everyone who has access to the work. The prototypical public license is the GPL (General Public License).[12] For example, Wikipedia articles are available under a public license (CC BY-SA 4.0).[13]

There are several standardised public licenses that are well-adapted for licensing of language datasets, such as Open Data Commons licenses (https://opendatacommons.org) or, most importantly, Creative Commons licenses (https://creativecommons.org/) (Kamocki and Ketzan 2014).

The Creative Commons licenses (like most public licenses) are based on the "some rights reserved" principle, which is a shift from the traditional copyright approach ("all rights reserved"). All CC licenses contain the BY ("attribution") requirement; furthermore, the rightholders may choose among other requirements: NC ("non-commercial" use only), ND ("no derivative" works allowed) and SA ("share-alike", i. e. all modified versions need to be shared under a compatible license). In total, 6 licenses are available: CC BY, CC BY-SA, CC BY-NC, CC BY-ND, CC BY-NC-ND and CC BY-NC-SA. Five versions of the CC licensing suite are available: 1.0 (released in 2002), 2.0 (in 2004), 2.5 (in 2005), 3.0 (in 2007) and the most recent 4.0 (released in 2013). Moreover, localised ('ported') versions of 3.0 and 4.0 CC licenses exist. A proper indication of such a license should therefore include the specific license (e. g., CC BY-SA), its version number (e. g., 3.0) and, if applicable, an indication of whether it is "ported" (e. g., DE for the German port, FR for the French one etc.) or "international" (Int; so, for example, the full indication should be CC BY-SA 3.0 Int or CC BY-SA 3.0 FR). Simply labelling the license as "CC" or "CC BY" is not enough to single out the text of the license, and consequently to identify all the conditions that apply to the resource.

12 https://www.gnu.org/licenses/gpl-3.0.en.html

13 Cf. https://en.wikipedia.org/wiki/Wikipedia:Copyrights (last visit: 13.02.2025).

The Creative Commons licensing suite is completed by two instruments that are not licenses: a CC0 copyright waiver ("no rights reserved")[14] and a Public Domain Mark (PDM)[15] used for labelling works in the Public Domain. Both only have one version (1.0), which should still be indicated, as a new version may be released at some point in the future.

Although technically CC0 is a waiver, and not a license, CC0 contains a "fallback license" (a license that applies only if and to the extent that the waiver has no effect), and as such it should still be listed in the License metadata field. It is so because under some national copyright systems there are doubts as to whether copyright can be waived – therefore, resources with CC0 cannot simply be treated as "public domain" and should instead be approached more like licensed resources, as the "fallback license" will often turn out to be applicable.

On the other hand, PDM is not a license, and it should only be applied to resources whose Copyright Status = Public Domain.

CLARIN PUB and ACA licenses[16] are also, arguably, public licenses, as they grant permissions not to specific persons, but to the general public (PUB) or at least to a group of persons defined in abstract terms (ACA, for researchers affiliated with an academic institution).

It is also possible, albeit rare in practice, to encounter a non-standardised public license, i. e. a license which grants rights to the general public, but which does not correspond to any standard license such as the CC licenses, Open Data Commons, Open Government License[17] etc. The text of such non-standard public licenses should be attached to the resource.

A "private" license is a license granted to a specific user (licensee); e. g. throughout the years, IDS Mannheim has obtained numerous private licenses from newspaper publishers. Resources under private licenses should be labelled as such. Whenever reasonably practicable, a private license should be attached to the resource, although the end-user should not be granted access to it, as it may contain confidential information.

Apart from the general type of license, some useful information should be extracted from a private license agreement:

– License expiry date: unlike public licenses that are generally granted for the entire duration of copyright (i. e., until the work enters the public domain), private licenses are usually limited in time (expressed in the number of years).

14 https://creativecommons.org/public-domain/cc0/

15 https://creativecommons.org/public-domain/pdm/

16 https://www.clarin.eu/content/licenses-and-clarin-categories (last visit: 14.02.2025).

17 https://www.nationalarchives.gov.uk/doc/open-government-licence/version/3/

Therefore, it is useful to indicate the date when the term of the license expires (usually specified in the license agreement). Some licenses may be automatically renewable, which means that, like a subscription, the license is automatically renewed (e. g. every year) until it is cancelled by one of the parties. In such cases, this should also be stated in the metadata (e. g. "expiry date: 2028, automatically renewable");

- Allowed uses: the uses can typically be described as reproduction (copying)[18] and/or adaptation (modification)[19] and/or communication to the public (sharing),[20] which correspond to the three basic rights granted by copyright law. Some licenses may only allow for copying, but not for sharing (reproduction only), or only for copying and sharing in unmodified form (reproduction + communication to the public), or for the "whole package".
- Restrictions on use: these must be read together with allowed uses. The logic is that the "allowed uses" are only allowed insofar as they are not restricted. Restrictions can take many forms (and so this metadata field should allow for a textbox option), but the most common ones include: attribution (requirement to attribute the work to the author), non-commercial use only, use only for scientific research purposes, use only within a specific project, use only on German (or other country's) territory, etc. In order to avoid confusion, the use of CC acronyms (BY, NC, ND) to describe restrictions on use in private licenses should be avoided.
- Fee: although many licenses are granted free of charge, some require a fee (calculated on an annual/monthly basis, as a flat rate or per end-user). This information is important in data management, as it is crucial to assess the perspectives for long-term storage of the resource.

When one resource contains material available under several different licenses, the resource as a whole should be treated in such a way as to respect all the applicable conditions. For example, if parts of the resource are available under a license that only allows reproduction (no adaptation and no communication to the public) and only for "non-commercial purposes", and other parts are licensed under a license that allows for reproduction, adaptation and communication to the public for scientific research purposes, then the whole resource should be treated as if the only

18 Article 2 of the EU Directive on Copyright in the Information Society (2001/29/EC), and, e. g., § 16 of the German Copyright Act.

19 E. g., § 23 of the German Copyright Act.

20 Article 3 of the EU Directive on Copyright in the Information Society (2001/29/EC), and, e. g., § 19a of the German Copyright Act.

allowed use was reproduction for non-commercial scientific research purposes. In order to avoid excessively restrictive outcomes, it is advisable to provide for a functional separation between the differently licensed parts.

3.4 Statutory exception metadata

It is also possible to build language resources without a license, but instead under a statutory exception, i. e. a specific provision of the law that allows for copyright-protected material to be used without permission from the rightholder in a strictly limited scenario.

Currently, the exception for text and data mining (TDM) for scientific research, introduced in Article 3 of the 2019 EU Directive on Copyright in the Digital Single Market (2019/790), and transposed in § 60d of the German Copyright Act, allows research organisations (as well as cultural heritage institutions) to make reproductions of lawfully accessible content in order to carry out TDM for scientific research purposes (Iacino et al. 2023). The copies (corpora) made for this purpose can be stored (with an appropriate level of security) and re-used for further research, and even (at least under the German national transposition) shared within a limited circle of persons for joint research.

Language resources built under this exception are "in-copyright", and although they have no "license", they were lawfully compiled, and can be lawfully stored and (at least to an extent) shared. For long-term storage, they should be labelled as built under an exception. Furthermore, the specific legal provision of applicable national law should be identified (e. g., § 60d UrhG). Since statutory exceptions, particularly those addressing new technologies, are quite likely to evolve over time, it is also useful to provide the complete wording of the exception in English and in the original language.

4 Data protection metadata

Another legal framework that should be addressed in the metadata is data protection.

Data protection law garnered significant attention from the general public when the EU General Data Protection Regulation (GDPR) became applicable in mid-2018, even though most of the data protection principles existed also before that date.

Language resources often contain personal data, which are defined very broadly as "any information related to an identified or identifiable natural person"[21] (i. e., a living individual). In particular, people's voice, image, and personal details (such as name, surname, address, age, gender, etc.) are personal data.[22]

Processing of personal data should follow the principles defined in Article 5 of the GDPR: (1) lawfulness, fairness and transparency, (2) purpose limitation, (3) data minimisation, (4) accuracy, (5) storage limitation, (6) integrity and confidentiality (also referred to as security) and (7) accountability. Some of these principles (e. g., security), are best addressed at the institutional level, rather than by individual researchers, but making certain basic data-protection-related information visible in the metadata facilitates the decision-making process and makes data workflows more transparent.

Firstly, resources containing Personal Data should be labelled as such.

One can argue here that every language resource contains (at least potentially) personal data, such as, at the very least, names of (living) authors. Although it is generally true, mere processing of the names of authors should not be enough to have an impact on the data workflows, mostly because names of authors are processed on the basis of a legal obligation[23] (copyright law, and more specifically the so-called paternity right, makes it a legal obligation for everyone to mention the name of the author whenever his or her work is used[24]). The Personal Data label should therefore be reserved to resources that contain non-negligeable amounts of personal data (such as speech and multimodal data, newspaper articles, non-anonymised student essays etc.).

Personal data can be anonymised, in which case they are no longer to be considered personal data.[25] However, anonymisation must be complete and irreversible; especially in the case of speech data anonymisation could significantly reduce the value of the data for scientific research. If a resource was anonymised, it can be labelled as containing no personal data, but information about the applied anonymi-

---

21 Article 4, (1) of the GDPR.

22 See e. g. Article 29 Data Protection Working Party, Opinion 4/2007 on the concept of personal data, June 2007 (WP 136), and (specifically regarding voice) European Data Protection Board, Guidelines 02/2021 on virtual voice assistants, version 2.0, adopted on 7 July 2021, available at: https://www.edpb.europa.eu/system/files/2021-07/edpb_guidelines_202102_on_vva_v2.0_adopted_en.pdf (last visit: 14.02.2025).

23 Art. 6.1(c) of the GDPR.

24 E. g., § 13 of the German Copyright Act.

25 Article 29 Data Protection Working Party, Opinion 05/2014 on Anonymisation Techniques (WP216), April 2014, available at: https://ec.europa.eu/justice/article-29/documentation/opinion-recommendation/files/2014/wp216_en.pdf (last visit: 14.02.2025).

sation technique should be added. If a pre-existing software solution was applied, it can also be named in the metadata. This information is useful for long-term storage, as over time, with progress of identification technologies, some anonymisation techniques may become obsolete and data that were anonymised at the moment of deposition may become personal data again, or require additional transformations in order to remain anonymised.

For resources that contain personal data, the Controller needs to be identified. A controller is, as per the GDPR's definition,[26] a person or entity who "determines the purposes and means of the processing of personal data", i. e. decides why, and (at least generally) how personal data are processed.[27] Usually, but not necessarily, it is the depositor's institution, and the same entity that was identified as the *data steward* (see Section 2 above).

If the Controller is not the same as the institution where the resource is deposited, the depositary is the data processor[28] acting on behalf of the Controller. Under the GDPR, the relation between the controller and the processor should be regulated in a contract known as the Data Processing Agreement (DPA).[29] The DPA should be appended to the metadata, as it regulates the conditions under which the resource should be stored, and – perhaps most importantly – stipulates whether the processor can appoint further sub-processors. However, the DPA should not be made publicly available.

For resources that contain personal data, it is useful to identify their categories, from the obvious ones such as: name, nickname, age, email, to more complex ones like native language (which may reveal ethnic origin), political opinions (e. g. in newspaper articles, or recorded discussions about politics), or health data (e. g. in disordered speech data). The information is useful to process access requests under the right of access,[30] and to comply with downstream reusers' self-assessment obligations, such as keeping a record of data processing activities[31] or the obligation to carry out a Data Protection Impact Assessment,[32] under the accountability

26 Art. 4, (7) of the GDPR.

27 European Data Protection Board, Guidelines 07/2020 on the concepts of controller and processor in the GDPR, available at: https://www.edpb.europa.eu/our-work-tools/our-documents/guidelines/guidelines-072020-concepts-controller-and-processor-gdpr_en (last visit: 14.02.2025).

28 Article 28 of the GDPR, cf. also European Data Protection Board, Guidelines 07/2020 (aforementioned).

29 Art. 28(3) of the GDPR.

30 Art. 15 of the GDPR.

31 Art. 30 of the GDPR.

32 Art. 35 of the GDPR.

principle. Furthermore, it allows to identify resources containing special categories of personal data (such as information revealing racial or ethnic origin, health, sex life, political opinions, religious beliefs), which are subject to stricter rules.[33]

Processing of personal data is lawful if and only if one of the legal bases listed in Article 6 of the GDPR applies to it. In the context of language research, the most commonly used legal bases seem to be consent[34] or legitimate interest.[35] There is no hierarchy between those legal bases, and the choice should reflect the circumstances in which the data were collected. For example, if the data are collected directly from the data subjects (e. g. via surveys or interviews), consent seems to be best adapted; if, however, the data are collected from publicly available sources such as TV, radio or social media, relying on legitimate interest is more realistic.

For data processed on the basis of (written) consent, it is useful to append a template with the consent form used.

For data processed on the basis of legitimate interest, it should be considered to append the documentation regarding the "balance of interests" tests. Such documentation is required by the GDPR.[36] However, it may be advisable not to make it downloadable to re-users.

Other legal bases (such as public interest[37] or performance of a contract[38]) may, albeit in rather exceptional cases, also be appropriate for processing personal data for research purposes.

Furthermore, the purpose (or purposes) for which the language resource was compiled should also be mentioned in the metadata. The purpose can be extracted from the consent form, where it should be clearly stated. If the resource was compiled on the basis of legitimate interest, the purpose should be stated in the documentation regarding the "balance of interests" test. As per the GDPR principle of purpose limitation, personal data can only be "collected for specified, explicit and legitimate purposes and not further processed in a manner that is incompatible with those purposes".[39] Although some leeway is allowed in the research con-

33 Art. 9 of the GDPR.

34 Art. 6.1(a) of the GDPR.

35 Art. 6.1(f) of the GDPR.

36 European Data Protection Board, Guidelines (1/2024) on processing of personal data based on Article 6(1)(f) GDPR, October 2024, available at: https://www.edpb.europa.eu/system/files/2024-10/edpb_guidelines_202401_legitimateinterest_en.pdf (last visit: 14.02.2025).

37 Art. 6.1(e) of the GDPR.

38 Art. 6.1(b) of the GDPR.

39 Art. 5.1(b) of the GDPR.

text,[40] merely stating that the data will be processed for "scientific research" would not meet the specificity requirement. In practice, the announced purpose may be phrased as, e. g. "research on the acquisition of German as a second or third language", "research on the use of the German language in news broadcasts", or even "research in the XYZ project" (with a link to a project's website). The data can further be reused for the same or a compatible purpose, it is therefore important to be able to assess the relation between the new purpose and the purpose for which the data was originally collected.[41]

Another element defined by the controller and communicated to the data subject (either in a consent form,[42] or in the information provided to the data subjects[43] or made publicly available[44]) are the recipients (or categories thereof) to which the data can be disclosed. These can be defined e. g. as "research teams in the field of Digital Humanities", or "partners in the XYZ project". Obviously, the data cannot be lawfully disclosed to those who do not fall within the defined categories.

According to the storage limitation principle,[45] personal data can only be stored for no longer than is necessary for the purposes for which they are processed. Although some leeway is allowed when the processing is carried out for research purposes,[46] personal data should not be stored indefinitely. A part of the controller's responsibility is to define the so-called "retention period", i. e. the period of time for which personal data will be stored before it's deleted or anonymised. In Germany, the DFG guidelines recommend research data to be stored "for at least 10 years",[47] but in some cases it may be advisable to delete (or anonymise) personal data before this deadline.[48]

---

40 Recital 33 of the GDPR.

41 Cf. Article 29 Data Protection Working Party, Opinion 03/2013 on purpose limitation, April 2013, available at: https://ec.europa.eu/justice/article-29/documentation/opinion-recommendation/files/2013/wp203_en.pdf (last visit: 14.02.2025).

42 Cf. European Data Protection Board, Guidelines 05/2020 on consent under Regulation 2016/679, May 2020, available at: https://www.edpb.europa.eu/sites/default/files/files/file1/edpb_guidelines_202005_consent_en.pdf (last visit: 14.02.2025).

43 Art. 13 of the GDPR.

44 Art 14.5(b) of the GDPR.

45 Art. 5.1(e) of the GDPR.

46 *Idem.*

47 DFG Guidelines on the Handling of Research Data, http://doi.org/10.2312/ALLIANZOA.019 (point 3).

48 See e. g. https://www.tilburguniversity.edu/about/conduct-and-integrity/privacy-and-security/research-data/data-minimization or § 27(3) of the German Federal Data Protection Act (BDSG).

It should also be kept in mind that when the data are reused in a new research project, their retention period can be extended. Furthermore, research data can be subject to long-term archiving under specific provisions of archiving law (e. g., in Germany, the *Bundesarchivgesetz*).

When the data are processed for research or archiving purposes with *appropriate safeguards*,[49] the processing benefits from numerous exceptions to or attenuations of the strict GDPR obligations.[50] It is therefore useful to specify in the metadata which safeguards have been implemented in the compilation of the resource. The choice of *appropriate* safeguards depends on the specific circumstances, but it may include, e. g., pseudonymisation, data encryption, functional separation (in short, measures to prevent reuse of data for an incompatible purpose), organisational measures (such as presence of an Ombudsperson for good scientific practice in the organisation), adoption of a Data Protection Concept Plan (*Datenschutzkonzept*), and potentially other measures and techniques.[51]

In particular, it is important to distinguish between anonymisation, which irreversibly transforms personal data into anonymised data, and pseudonymisation, which consists, in short, of replacing identifying information with "pseudonyms" (e. g., "person A") while keeping the actual identifiers separated from the data. In other words, the information that "person A" is in fact Max Mustermann from Münster is kept separately from the dataset, but can be retrieved under certain conditions. Unlike anonymised data, pseudonymised data are still to be considered personal data.[52]

Furthermore, if the controller carried out the Data Protection Impact Assessment (DPIA), either because it is mandatory[53] or as an additional safeguard, the DPIA can also be appended to the resource, as it may be useful for further re-use. For example, new measures to mitigate risks (e. g., by enhancing data security) may become available in the future, which may change the outcome of the DPIA, and enable the re-user to share the resource more broadly than originally planned.

---

49 Art. 89(1) of the GDPR.

50 Cf., Art. 89 of the GDPR, and, e,g., Art. 5.1(b) and (e), Art. 14.5(b), Art. 17.3(d) of the GDPR.

51 Cf. European Data Protection Supervisor, Study on the appropriate safeguards under Article 89(1) GDPR for the processing of personal data for scientific research (EDPS/2019/02-08), August 2021, available at: https://www.edpb.europa.eu/system/files/2022-01/legalstudy_on_the_appropriate_safeguards_89.1.pdf, last visit: 14.02.2025).

52 Cf. European Data Protection Board, Guidelines 01/2025 on pseudonymisation (version for public consultation), January 2025, available at: https://www.edpb.europa.eu/system/files/2025-01/edpb_guidelines_202501_pseudonymisation_en.pdf (last visit: 14.02. 2025).

53 Cf. Art. 35 of the GDPR.

5 Ethical metadata

In a related vein, ethical issues may also be represented in the metadata.

If the resource has undergone an assessment by an Ethics Committee, the assessment may be appended to the metadata. It should also be stated which Ethics Committee (at which institution) carried out the assessment.

Regardless of the potential committee assessment, the depositor may feel that the resource poses certain ethical challenges. The author of this chapter also co-authored a proposal for a taxonomy of ethical issues and an accompanying "checklist" (Kamocki and Witt 2024), which can be used as a basis for 'flagging' potential ethical issues in language resources by identifying the principle that was taken into consideration in the compilation process, or that should be taken into account by downstream re-users. The ethical principles identified in the above-mentioned paper are: 1) Privacy, 2) Property, 3) Equality, 4) Transparency, 5) Freedom, 6) Accountability, 7) Risk Anticipation and Mitigation and 8) Reliability and Limited Confidence.

6 Proposed taxonomy of legal and ethical metadata

The taxonomy of metadata proposed in this chapter to describe the legal and ethical status of a language resource can be represented as follows:

6.1 Data stewardship

The provision of legal and ethical metadata for a language resource may be very difficult and oftentimes almost impossible without specialised assistance. In order to avoid the chilling effect, only the information about the Data Stewardship (see above Section 2) should be mandatory. See Table 1.

Table 1: Data Stewardship metadata.

*DataSteward	Person or Organisation	A person (usually a legal person, i. e. an entity) who has oversight of the resource, i. e. who supervised its creation, had the possibility to intervene to correct errors in the process, and is accountable for it.

6.2 Copyright metadata

Copyright metadata can be divided into those concerning the Copyright Status (6.2.1), Authors and Rightholders (6.2.2), Licenses (6.2.3) and Exceptions (6.2.4). If a Copyright Status is "Public Domain", then no further copyright metadata are useful. If, however, copyright status is "In Copyright", Author and Rightholder Metadata should be provided. Further, if the resource was compiled on the basis of a license, License Metadata should be provided (which again will differ depending on whether the LicenseType is "public" or "private"). If, on the other hand, the resource was compiled on the basis of a statutory exception, Exception Metadata should be provided. Graphically, this can be represented in Figure 1.

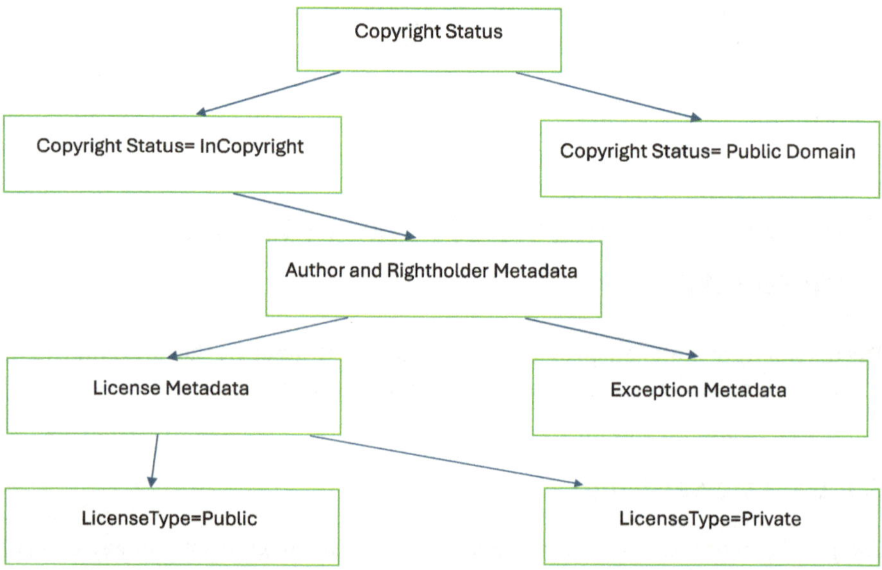

Figure 1: Copyright metadata structure.

6.2.1 Copyright status

The explanations regarding the Copyright Status of a language resource are provided in Section 3.1. See Table 2.

Table 2: Copyright Status metadata.

CopyrightStatus	"inCopyright" Or "Public Domain"	Describes whether the resource is in copyright or in the public domain. Public-domain resources need no further copyright metadata.

6.2.2 Author and rightholder metadata

The explanations regarding the Author and Rightholder Metadata are provided in Section 3.2. See Table 3.

Table 3: Author and Rightholder metadata.

Author	Person	
OrphanWork	"Yes" Or "No"	For works that can be found in the EUIPO's Orphan Works Database
AuthorDeathYear	Year	The year of the author's death is used to determine when the resource enters the public domain
Rightholder	Person Or Organisation	The person or entity who holds copyright in the resource.

6.2.3 License metadata

If the resource was built on the basis of a license, License Metadata need to be provided, as explained in Section 3.3. See Table 4.

Table 4: License Type metadata.

LicenseType	"Public" Or "Private"	A public license is a license granted to the whole public (everyone). A private license is granted to a specific licensee.

Public licenses should then be described according to the scheme in Table 5.

Table 5: Public License metadata.

PublicLicense	"CC BY 4.0 Int" "CC BY-SA 4.0 Int" ... "CC0" "CLARIN-PUB" ... Or Text	CC licenses (version 4.0 International) are a common choice. However, considering the high number of available options, a textbox should be included to enable the user to enter the full name.
PublicLicenseURL	URL	A URL pointing to the text of less-known public licenses
PublicLicenseText	Text (PDF, TXT)	Only useful if there is no PublicLicenseURL

Private licenses, on the other hand, should be described according to the scheme in Table 6.

Table 6: Private License metadata.

PrivateLicenseText	Text (PDF)	Should not be made publicly available
LicenseExpiryDate	Date Or Text Or "End of Copyright"	The date on which the license expires. A license can also be granted for the whole duration of rights, in which case it expires when the resource enters the public domain.
AllowedUses	"Reproduction" And/or "Communication to the public" And/or "Adaptation"	Reproduction (copying) and/or Communication to the public (sharing) and/or adaptation (modification). Restrictions on these uses are a separate metadata item. Multiple choice allowed.
RestrictionsOnUse	"Attribution" "Non-commercial" "Scientific research" "Project specific" + Text "Restricted Territory" + Text or Text	Conditions for AllowedUses to be made; Textbox should be available alongside common options. Multiple choice allowed.
Fee	Text	An amount to pay for re-use and how it is calculated

6.2.4 Exceptions metadata

The explanations regarding the Exceptions Metadata are provided in Section 3.4. See Table 7.

Table 7: Exceptions metadata.

Exception	LawArticleNumber	Article number from applicable national law (may include letters and other signs). § 60d UrhG is commonly used in Germany.
ExceptionDate	Date	Date at which the use covered by the exception took place
ExceptionText	Text	Preferably original language + English

6.3 Personal data metadata

As explained in Section 4, it should first be termined if the resource contains personal data (Personal Data = "Yes") or not (Personal Data = "No"), see Table 8. If there is no personal data in the resource, it should be stated whether and how it was anonymised, see Table 9. If, however, the resource contains personal data, information about the controller (Table 10), the categories of personal data (Table 11), the legal basis (Table 12), the purpose of processing (Table 13), the recipients (or categories thereof, Table 14), data retention (Table 15), the implemented safeguards (Table 16) and the potential Data Protection Impact Assessment (Table 17).

Table 8: Personal Data metadata.

PersonalData	"Yes" or "No"	Signifies whether personal data are present in the resource. If "PersonalData = no", no other personal data (apart from possibly the AnonymisationTechnique) metadata should be provided.

Table 9: Anonymisation Technique metadata.

AnonymisationTechnique	Text	The name (and description) of the anonymisation technique used, if applicable. To be filled only if PersonalData = "No".

Table 10: Controller and Processor metadata.

Controller	Person Or Entity	Usually the same as the DataSteward
DataProcessingAgreementText	Text (PDF)	If a data processor is used, the Data Processing Agreement should be included in the metadata.

Table 11: Personal Data Categories metadata.

PersonalDataCategories	“Name” Or “Pseudonym” Or “Age” Or “Address” Or “Email” Or “NativeLanguage” Or “Political opinions” Or “Health” Or Text	The types of personal data present in the resource. Common options should be included alongside a textbox. Multiple choice allowed.

Table 12: Legal Basis metadata.

ProcessingLegalBasis	“Consent” Or “Legitimate interest” Or “Public interest” Or “Performance of a contract” Or “Legal Obligation” Or “Vital Interest”	Legal bases for processing listed in Article 6 of the GDPR. Optionally: list only the first three + textbox.
If: ProcessingLegalBasis = “Consent”		
ConsentFormTemplate	Text Or URL	Template of the consent form used

Table 12 (continued)

If: ProcessingLegalBasis = "Legitimate Interest"		
BalanceOfInterestDocumentation	Text Or URL	Documentation of the balance of interest test required by the GDPR.

Table 13: Purpose of Processing metadata.

ProcessingPurpose	Text	The purpose of the processing as defined in the required documentation (consent form, information about the processing). Multiple choice allowed.

Table 14: Data Recipients metadata.

Recipient	Person Or Entity	Names of the persons or entities to which the data may be disclosed
or		
RecipientCategories	Text	Categories of the recipients

Table 15: Data Retention metadata.

DataRetentionPeriod	TimePeriod	The period of time for which the data will be stored (as defined by the controller)
DataRetentionEndDate	Date	The date at which the data retention period ends

Table 16: Data Protection Safeguards metadata.

DataProtectionSafeguards	"Pseudonymisation" Or "Encryption" Or "Organisational measures" Or "Functional separation" Or "Data protection concept plan" Or "Ethics committee assessment" Or "Data protection impact assessment" Or Text (PDF)	Appropriate safeguards required by the GDPR for processing of personal data for research purposes (Article 89(1) of the GDPR). Multiple choices allowed. PDFs accepted (e. g., for the Data protection concept plan).

Table 17: Data Protection Impact Assessment metadata.

DataProtectionImpactAssessment	Text (PDF)	Documentation of the Data Protection Impact Assessment, if applicable

The process is represented graphically in Figure 2.

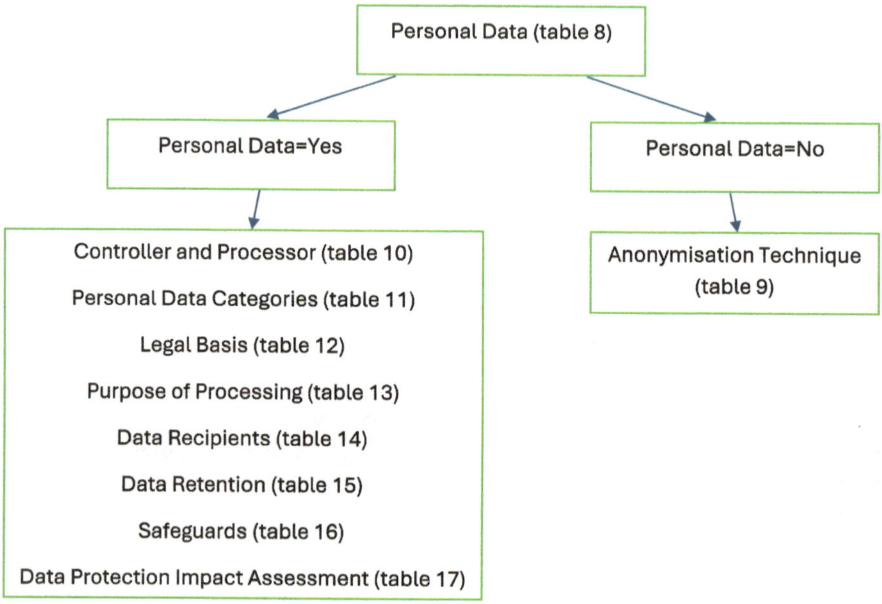

Figure 2: Personal Data Metadata structure.

6.4 Ethical metadata

The explanations regarding Ethical Metadata are provided in Section 5. See Table 18.

Table 18: Ethical metadata.

EthicsAssessment	Text (PDF)	
EthicsCommittee	Text	The Ethics Committee who delivered the Ethics Assessment

Table 18 (continued)

ObservedEthicalPrinciples	"Privacy" or "Property" or "Equality" or "Transparency" or "Freedom" or "Accountability" or "Risk Anticipation and Mitigation" or "Reliability and Limited Confidence" or Text	Ethical challenges addressed in the compilation and re-use of the resource. The typology proposed in Kamocki and Witt (2024) can be proposed as an option. Textbox should be included. Multiple choice allowed.

7 Future challenges

Although relatively future-proof, the legal and ethical metadata scheme is bound to evolve over time, as the applicable frameworks change, or new frameworks appear.

For example, Article 53.1(d) of the EU Artificial Intelligence Act (Regulation (EU) 2024/1689), which will enter into force in mid-2025 (several months after these words are written), stipulates that the providers of general-purpose AI models shall "draw up and make publicly available a sufficiently detailed summary of the content used for training of the general-purpose AI model, according to a template provided by the AI Office". This template, which has not yet been published, will certainly have an impact on how language resources should be described from the legal and ethical perspective.[54]

54 Cf. the proposal made in: Open Future, Sufficiently detailed? A proposal for implementing the AI Act's training data transparency requirement for GPAI, June 2024, available at: https://openfuture.eu/wp-content/uploads/2024/06/240618AIAtransparency_template_requirements-2.pdf, last visit: 14.02.2025.

8 Conclusion

Legal and ethical metadata are essential for ensuring the responsible and sustainable use of language resources. This chapter has outlined the key components of legal metadata, emphasizing the importance of identifying the Data Steward, and has provided an overview of the most relevant legal frameworks – copyright and data protection – and their implications for metadata. Additionally, ethical considerations have been discussed, highlighting their role in fostering transparency and trust. The proposed taxonomy of legal and ethical metadata offers a structured approach to documenting this critical information, supporting compliance with legal requirements and alignment with the FAIR principles. It would be useful to convert it into a standard or at least a best practice guideline. As the landscape of language resources continues to evolve, future challenges remain, particularly in adapting metadata standards to emerging legal and ethical developments (such as the adoption of the EU AI Act and the development of relevant best practices), and ensuring their widespread adoption across projects, institutions and communities.

Bibliography

Article 29 Data Protection Working Party. 2007. *Opinion 4/2007 on the concept of personal data (WP 136)*. June 2007.

Article 29 Data Protection Working Party. 2013. *Opinion 03/2013 on purpose limitation*. April 2013. https://ec.europa.eu/justice/article-29/documentation/opinion-recommendation/files/2013/wp203_en.pdf (accessed 14 February 2025).

Article 29 Data Protection Working Party. *Opinion 05/2014 on anonymisation techniques (WP216)*. April 2014. https://ec.europa.eu/justice/article-29/documentation/opinion-recommendation/files/2014/wp216_en.pdf (accessed 14 February 2025).

DFG. *Guidelines on the handling of research data*. http://doi.org/10.2312/ALLIANZOA.019.

European Data Protection Board. 2020a. *Guidelines 05/2020 on consent under Regulation 2016/679*. May 2020. https://www.edpb.europa.eu/sites/default/files/files/file1/edpb_guidelines_202005_consent_en.pdf (accessed 14 February 2025).

European Data Protection Board. 2020b. *Guidelines 07/2020 on the concepts of controller and processor in the GDPR*. https://www.edpb.europa.eu/our-work-tools/our-documents/guidelines/guidelines-072020-concepts-controller-and-processor-gdpr_en (accessed 14 February 2025).

European Data Protection Board. 2021. *Guidelines 02/2021 on virtual voice assistants*, version 2.0, adopted 7 July 2021. https://www.edpb.europa.eu/system/files/2021-07/edpb_guidelines_202102_on_vva_v2.0_adopted_en.pdf (accessed 14 February 2025).

European Data Protection Board. 2024. *Guidelines 1/2024 on processing of personal data based on Article 6(1)(f) GDPR*. October 2024. https://www.edpb.europa.eu/system/files/2024-10/edpb_guidelines_202401_legitimateinterest_en.pdf (accessed 14 February 2025).

European Data Protection Board. 2025. *Guidelines 01/2025 on pseudonymisation (version for public consultation)*. January 2025. https://www.edpb.europa.eu/system/files/2025-01/edpb_guidelines_202501_pseudonymisation_en.pdf (accessed 14 February 2025).

European Data Protection Supervisor. 2021. *Study on the appropriate safeguards under Article 89(1) GDPR for the processing of personal data for scientific research (EDPS/2019/02-08)*. August 2021. https://www.edpb.europa.eu/system/files/2022-01/legalstudy_on_the_appropriate_safeguards_89.1.pdf (accessed 14 February 2025).

European Union. 2016. *Regulation (EU) 2016/679 of the European Parliament and of the Council of 27 April 2016 on the protection of natural persons with regard to the processing of personal data and on the free movement of such data, and repealing Directive 95/46/EC (General Data Protection Regulation)*.

Federal Republic of Germany. 1965. *Urheberrechtsgesetz vom 9. September 1965 (BGBl. I S. 1273)* [German Copyright Act].

Iacino, Gianna, Paweł Kamocki & Peter Leinen. 2023. Assessment of the impact of the DSM-Directive on Text+. *Zenodo*. https://doi.org/10.5281/zenodo.12759960.

Kamocki, Paweł & Andreas Witt. 2024. Ethical issues in language resources and language technology – New challenges, new perspectives. In *LEGAL2024 @LREC-COLING-2024*, 19–23. https://aclanthology.org/2024.legal-1.4.pdf (accessed 14 February 2025).

Kamocki, Paweł & Erik Ketzan. 2014. Creative Commons and language resources: General issues and what's new in CC 4.0. *CLIC White Paper Series*, May 2014. https://ids-pub.bsz-bw.de/frontdoor/deliver/index/docId/3224/file/Kamocki_Ketzan_Creative_Commons_and_Language_Resources_2014.pdf (accessed 13 February 2025).

Kamocki, Paweł, Vanessa Hannesschläger, Esther Hoorn, Aleksei Kelli, Marc Kupietz, Krister Lindén & Andrius Puksas. 2022. Legal issues related to the use of Twitter data in language research. In Monica Monachini & Maria Eskevich (eds.), *Selected papers from the CLARIN Annual Conference 2021*, Vol. 189 of Linköping Electronic Conference Proceedings, 68–75. https://doi.org/10.3384/978917929444.

Kamocki, Paweł. 2020. When size matters: Legal perspective(s) on n-grams. In *Selected papers from the CLARIN annual conference 2020*. https://doi.org/10.3384/ecp18014.

Open Future. 2024. *Sufficiently detailed? A proposal for implementing the AI Act's training data transparency requirement for GPAI*. June 2024. https://openfuture.eu/wp-content/uploads/2024/06/240618AIAtransparency_template_requirements-2.pdf (accessed 14 February 2025).

Pisetta, Ines & Thorsten Trippel. 2025. Standards and practices for long-term digital archiving. In Piotr Bański, Ulrich Heid & Laura Herzberg (eds.), *Harmonising language data: Standards for linguistic resources*. Berlin & Boston: De Gruyter.

WIPO. 1886. *Berne Convention for the Protection of Literary and Artistic Works*. September 9, 1886.

Annette Preissner and Ulrich Heid

The life of an ISO standard

Abstract: This volume emphasizes the crucial role of standards and best practices for language data and language resource infrastructures in ensuring data sustainability, transparency and interoperability, especially within digital humanities. Many of the conventions and guidelines are international standards developed by various communities, organizations and consortia, and several of them have been developed by the International Organization for Standardization (ISO). This chapter focuses on ISO standardization.

ISO standardization work is organized into technical committees (TCs), which in turn can have thematically focused subcommittees (SCs). The ISO subcommittee in charge of "standardization of the modelling, specification, design, documentation and encoding of digital language resources to enable integration, interchange and replicability" is ISO/TC 37/SC 4 "Language resource management". This chapter provides a glimpse of the activities carried out in this ISO subcommittee, and it explains in detail the general consensus-based ISO process of standards development and how one can get involved in it.

Keywords: ISO, development of standards, development stages, maintenance of standards, national delegation principle, consensus, language resource management

1 Introduction

This volume emphasizes the crucial role of standards and best practices for language data and infrastructures in ensuring the sustainability, transparency, and interoperability of data, especially within language documentation and digital humanities.

Best practices and standards typically come into existence in at least two ways. The practice of a group of, e. g., researchers may be communicated to a broader scientific public and taken up by more and more colleagues. This practice may be seen by the community as a "best" practice and may thus become a "de facto standard".

Annette Preissner, DIN-Normenausschuss Terminologie (NAT), DIN Deutsches Institut für Normung e. V., Burggrafenstr. 6, 10787 Berlin, Germany, e-mail: annette.preissner@din.de
Ulrich Heid, Institut für Informationswissenschaft und Sprachtechnologie, Universität Hildesheim, Universitätsplatz 1, 31141 Hildesheim, Germany

https://doi.org/10.1515/9783112208212-017

On the other hand, professional associations, companies as well as researchers in universities contribute to well-organized consensus-building actions that lead to the publication of standards proposals. The institutions providing and organizing this structured path toward standards are mainly the national and international standards organizations, such as ISO, the International Organization for Standardization, but also professional associations and consortia of interested parties. There are various international standards-setting communities, organizations and consortia relevant to the field, for example the Internet Engineering Task Force[1] (IETF), the Organization for the Advancement of Structured Information Standards[2] (OASIS), and the World Wide Web Consortium[3] (W3C), just to mention some of them. They all have their own organizational structure, processes, responsibilities and functions, and for most of them, standardization activities focus on a certain industry or sector.

The three largest international standards organizations are the following, and there are tens of thousands of standards carrying their name: the International Electrotechnical Commission (IEC), the International Telecommunication Union (ITU), and the International Organization for Standardization (ISO), the latter in charge of all sectors except electrotechnology and telecommunication. ISO, IEC and ITU together constitute the World Standards Cooperation[4] (WSC) and promote the "voluntary consensus-based International Standards system". What is meant by "consensus" will be explained later in this chapter, and "voluntary" stands for the fact that ISO, IEC and ITU standards do not include contractual, legal or statutory requirements. Voluntary standards do not replace national laws, with which standards users are understood to comply and which take precedence.

ISO, IEC and ITU are based on the principle of "one member per country", and this is an aspect that distinguishes them from most of the other standards-setting communities, organizations and consortia.

Out of ISO, IEC and ITU, ISO is the international standards organization that is responsible for the field of language-related standardization. This chapter provides a glimpse of the activities carried out in the ISO subcommittee in charge of "standardization of the modelling, specification, design, documentation and encoding of digital language resources to enable integration, interchange and replicability", and it explains in detail the general ISO process of standards development and how one can get involved in it.

1 https://www.ietf.org/

2 https://www.oasis-open.org/

3 https://www.w3.org/

4 https://www.worldstandardscooperation.org/

2 ISO standards for language data and infrastructures

2.1 ISO members, committee structure and liaisons

2.1.1 ISO members

ISO is a network of national standards bodies (NSBs) that are considered as the leading (or, in the case of several national standards bodies for different industry sectors, as the coordinating) standards organizations in their country, for example DIN (Deutsches Institut für Normung, en: German Institute for Standardization) in Germany, IRAM (Instituto Argentino de Normalización y Certificación, en: Argentine Standardization and Certification Institute) in Argentina, JISC (Japanese Industrial Standards Committee) in Japan, SA (Standards Australia) in Australia, SABS (South African Bureau of Standards) in South Africa, SCC (Standards Council of Canada) in Canada. There is only one ISO member per country and there currently are more than 170 ISO members.[5]

About 130 of those ISO members are full members, and only full members can participate actively in standardization work.

2.1.2 ISO committee structure

At ISO, standardization work takes place in technical committees (TCs), with each TC representing one sector. In exceptional cases, when there is no TC for a certain sector, project committees (PCs) are established for the development of only one standard and are dissolved once this standard is completed, or they are transformed into a TC if further standardization is needed within its scope. Project committees cannot have subcommittees, but besides that, everything stated for technical committees in the following also holds for project committees.

There are currently more than 250 active technical committees at ISO, from ISO/TC 1 "Screw threads" to ISO/TC 349 "Cultural heritage conservation".[6] In general, the lower the number, the older the committee. Back in 1947, the year in which ISO was founded, there were 67 technical committees (ISO/TC 1 to ISO/TC 67).

Many technical committees are organized internally in such a way that there are different subcommittees (SCs) for different subsectors.

5 https://www.iso.org/about/members

6 https://www.iso.org/technical-committees.html

The general management of the technical committee structure is with the Technical Management Board (TMB). The TMB is responsible for the overall management of the technical work. It has a Chair and 15 member bodies and it decides on the establishment of technical committees. It also monitors the progress of the technical work and is responsible for the ISO/IEC Directives, which are the rules for the development of International Standards and other ISO deliverables.

Every ISO technical committee and subcommittee receives administrative support from an ISO member body, its *Secretariat* that is appointed by the TMB. The secretariat designates a *Committee Manager*, i. e. one person assuming responsibility for all administrative aspects of the committee. Committee Managers are expected to be impartial. This means they must not give privilege to, or favour the interests of, a particular ISO member body.

The Secretariat of a committee also nominates a Chair for that committee. The main function of the Chair is to support the committee in achieving consensus. Just like the Committee Manager, the Chair is required to be impartial. The Committee Manager and the Chair closely collaborate.

The actual work on documents in most cases does not take place in technical committees or subcommittees, but in separate working groups (WGs). There can be several working groups per technical committee or subcommittee, and a working group can work on just one project, i. e. a single standard, or on several projects, for example a standard series. Each working group is led by a Convenor who is appointed by the technical committee or subcommittee. The appointment needs to be approved by the Convenor's national body or nominating liaison organization (see Section 2.1.3).

Figure 1 gives an overview of the ISO committee structure.

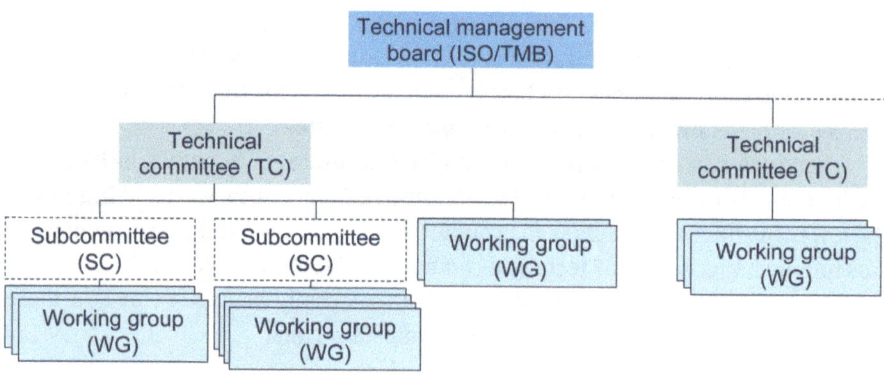

Figure 1: ISO committee structure.

Full members of ISO indicate for each technical committee and for each subcommittee whether they want to participate actively in its work (P-member), or whether they want to follow its work as an observer (O-member), or whether they are not interested in the sector at all. This of course has a lot to do with the sector concerned and whether it plays a role in the respective country. For example, SNV (Swiss Association for Standardization) is neither a P-member nor an O-member of ISO/TC 234 “Fisheries and aquaculture”, and no African country at all is a P-member or an O-member of ISO/TC 83/SC 4 “Snowsports equipment”.

The technical committee in charge of all linguistic issues is ISO/TC 37 “Language and terminology”.[7] ISO/TC 37/SC 4 “Language resource management” is one of currently five subcommittees within ISO/TC 37, and it is the one where ISO standards relevant for this volume have been and continue to be developed.

2.1.3 Liaisons

Not only P-members can take part in the development of ISO standards. ISO has established several mechanisms to ensure that all relevant stakeholders can participate. As one such mechanism, and probably as the most important one, liaisons can be established between different ISO committees, between ISO committees and committees of the International Electrotechnical Commission (IEC), and between ISO committees and not-for-profit organizations that are membership-based and open to members worldwide or over a broad region.

2.2 ISO/TC 37/SC 4 “Language resource management”

2.2.1 Standards and work programme of ISO/TC 37/SC 4

ISO/TC 37/SC 4 “Language resource management” is in charge of the “standardization of the modelling, specification, design, documentation and encoding of digital language resources to enable integration, interchange and replicability”. As for all other technical committees and subcommittees, there is an ISO website on ISO/TC 37/SC 4 with a lot of useful information.[8] Among other things, it contains links to the constantly updated list of publications[9] (standards and other deliverables) as well

7 https://www.iso.org/committee/48104.html

8 https://www.iso.org/committee/297592.html

9 https://www.iso.org/committee/297592/x/catalogue/p/1/u/0/w/0/d/0

as to the constantly updated work programme.[10] Earlier overviews of standardization activities in the field of language resource management are given by Herzog et al. (2015) and by Stührenberg (2012).

There are currently about 40 published standards and other documents that have been produced by ISO/TC 37/SC 4. In an attempt to organize them according to criteria related to their functions and objectives, as well as to the dimensions under which language resources are discussed in this volume, the present section suggests a (necessarily simplified) grouping of the relevant deliverables.

There are a few standards concerning infrastructures of language resources. They deal with persistent identifiers (ISO 24619 2011) for resources, with metadata (ISO 24622) and ways of defining metadata and of "packaging" them in a modular way; an upcoming part of this generic standardization infrastructure is a collection of specialized terms from the domain of language resources, as used in the existing standards: this collection will also allow ISO/TC 37/SC 4 to homogenize the terminology used both in new and in revised standards.

The origins of ISO/TC 37/SC 4 go back to the 1990s and 2000s, which was a period when computational linguistics was mostly based on symbolic and statistical processing. Consequently, the need was felt to have standard ways of representing data and of serializing attribute-value structures, as these were the basic representation formalism for most computational linguistic work. The two standards of the ISO 24610 series consequently dealt with feature structures and feature system declarations (as they were then used, for example, in typed representation formalisms).

On this basis, it became possible to describe details of feature-structure-based linguistic representation, from a phenomenon-oriented viewpoint: with respect to the representation of corpus data, the Linguistic Annotation Framework, LAF (ISO 24612 2012), serves this purpose and is thus a basis on top of which specific proposals can be made for the different "layers" of linguistic description (in the sense of traditional distinctions): the Morphosyntactic Annotation Framework, MAF (ISO 24611 2012), deals with the annotations typically produced by part-of-speech taggers and morphological analysers. The Syntactic Annotation Framework, SynAF (ISO 24615), provides ways of annotating structural data from syntax and includes a serialization proposal for data as they come in treebanks (indirectly modelled on the example of TIGER XML, cf. Brants et al. 2001). Finally, a broad array of aspects of semantics and pragmatics is the focus of the parts of the Semantic Annotation Framework series, SemAF (ISO 24617). All of these standards rely, at least, to some extent, on the LAF and feature structure infrastructure.

10 https://www.iso.org/committee/297592/x/catalogue/p/0/u/1/w/0/d/0

With a main focus on the Asian languages, Chinese, Japanese and Korean, a standard series on word segmentation (ISO 24614) was produced; it can, to some extent, also serve as a guideline for certain aspects of tokenization and for the analysis of morphologically complex words of other languages.

While the above mentioned feature-structure-based standards mainly target corpus data and their annotation, two further standards series focus on other types of language resources. The Lexical Markup Framework, LMF (ISO 24613), provides basic structures for encoding of entries in electronic dictionaries. For spoken language, there is (ISO 24624 2016), with guidelines for the transcription of spoken language and for the representation of transcribed material.

The standards described so far look at language resources from the angle of the data producer: which kinds of metadata and which kinds of linguistic annotations are recommended, and how they can be represented in order to be interoperable and reusable. In addition, a need was felt to also address the perspective of those who wish to consult language data, in particular by means of query systems. The two parts of the Corpus Query Lingua Franca series, CQLF (ISO 24623) concern basic principles of the interaction between corpus representation and query, and they come up, among other things, with a structured overview of the field of corpus query, highlighting which prerequisites are needed in order for certain types of phenomena to be queryable.

More recently, the aspect of workflows in the creation of corpus data has come into focus. A standard series on Corpus Annotation Project Management (ISO 24635) provides guidance in terms of organizational and managerial infrastructures for data creation.

Figure 2 diagrams the classification sketched above and distinguishes infrastructural, representational and descriptive, as well as organizational standards. As the area of linguistic description and annotation has been worked out in much detail, we indicate the different targeted types of language resources by means of colour-coding: the standard for word-segmentation, which targets surface strings and tokenization, is marked by a yellow background, standards concerning written text data are highlighted by a blue background, those for spoken language data in pink, and the standards series dealing with lexical data in green. Standards for the feature-structure-based representation and for query as well as workflows concern several types of language data.

The perspective common to standards classified and diagrammed above is their focus on language resources as artefacts. When, however, the focus is shifted to the *use* of language resources in various environments, other perspectives emerge, and standards that address them include, among others, the Multilingual Information Framework, MLIF (ISO 24616 2012), which provides a generic platform for modelling and managing multilingual information, among others from the perspective

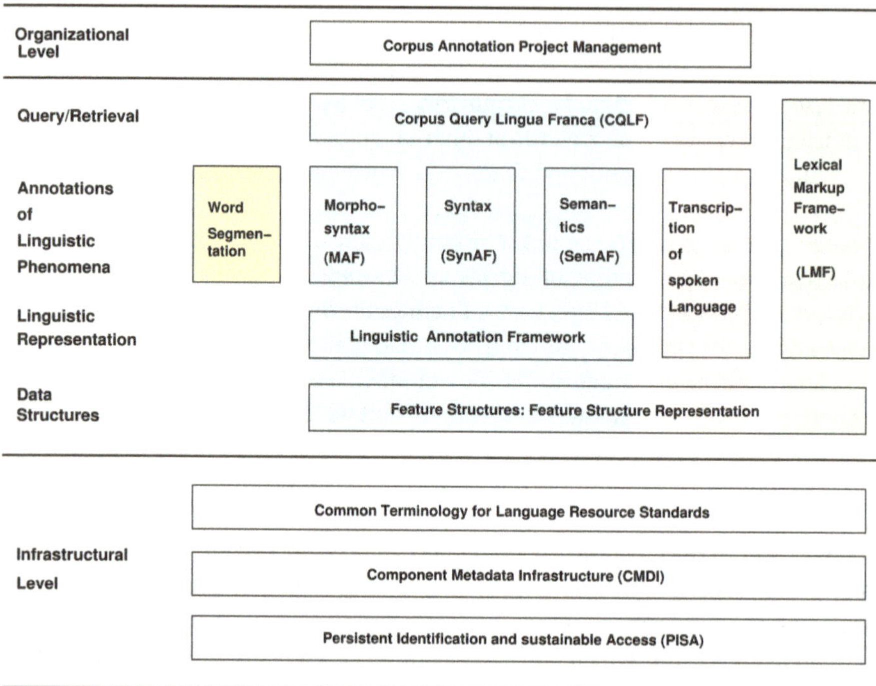

Figure 2: Thematical classification of ISO/TC 37/SC 4 standards.

of translation, localization and other applications in the language industries. Similarly, a few standards on Controlled Human Communication, CHC (ISO 24620) have been produced, which set out general guidelines for different types of controlled languages.

2.2.2 Members of ISO/TC 37/SC 4 and organizations in liaison

As stated in Section 2.1.2, full members of ISO indicate for each technical committee and for each subcommittee whether they want to participate actively in its work (P-member), or whether they want to follow its work as an observer (O-member), or whether they are not interested in the sector at all. There is an illustrative map on the ISO website on ISO/TC 37/SC 4[11] showing all its P-members and O-members. As an aside, one thing the map makes clear is that there is a much stronger interest of

11 https://www.iso.org/committee/297592.html?view=participation

the northern hemisphere in ISO/TC 37/SC 4 and its standardization activities than of the southern hemisphere. SABS (South Africa) currently is the only one out of more than 20 P-members that is from the southern hemisphere, and none of the current O-members at all is from the southern hemisphere. The discrepancy is less extreme in the other subcommittees of ISO/TC 37 "Language and terminology" and also in ISO/TC 37[12] itself.

The ISO website on ISO/TC 37/SC 4 also provides a list of the committees and organizations that are in liaison with ISO/TC 37/SC 4. The liaison mechanism also allows for liaisons between ISO technical committees or subcommittees and other standards-setting organizations. Examples for this are the liaisons between ISO/TC 37/SC 4 and the Text Encoding Initiative (TEI)[13] and between ISO/TC 37/SC 4 and CLARIN ERIC.[14]

3 ISO process of standards development

3.1 National delegation principle

As outlined in Section 2.1, ISO standards are developed in technical committees and subcommittees, with both P-members and liaisons as participants. The participation of P-members is realised by the *national delegation principle* as shown in Figure 3.

P-members of a technical committee or subcommittee typically have national committees in which representatives of all interested parties of the committee's sector come together at the national level. These national committees are called *mirror committees*. The interested parties vary from sector to sector, but typically include industry, research, politics and consumer protection, and others as appropriate.

The mirror committee of a P-member is responsible for determining the national position of that member via a consensus-based process. "Consensus" is the "general agreement, characterized by the absence of sustained opposition to substantial issues by any important part of the concerned interests and by a process that involves seeking to take into account the views of all parties concerned and to reconcile any conflicting arguments" (source: ISO/IEC Guide 59 2019: 3.2).

National mirror committees nominate delegates that have to express their national mirror committee's position in meetings of the ISO technical committee or

12 https://www.iso.org/committee/48104.html?view=participation

13 https://tei-c.org/

14 https://www.clarin.eu

subcommittee. Liaison representatives are also allowed to participate in committee meetings and to make comments, but they have no right to vote.

National mirror committees also appoint experts to work on the projects allocated to a working group. Working group experts typically work in the sector for which they are nominated and are selected for their expertise and experience. They act in personal capacity and therefore are not bound to the national position of the P-member that appointed them. However, they should understand this position and also keep the national mirror committee informed of work progress.

Decisions within working groups are reached through consensus, without formal votes. It is possible and not unusual at all that one person is both a national delegate in a technical committee or subcommittee and a working group expert in one, several or even all of the committee's working groups.

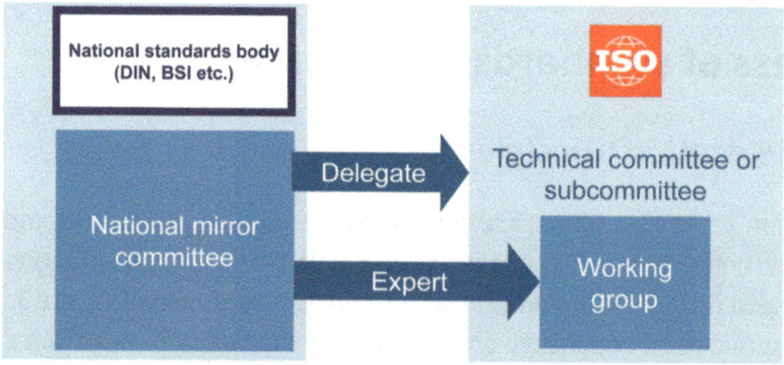

Figure 3: National delegation principle.

Liaison committees and liaison organizations can also send experts to a working group that work on its project(s) together with the experts appointed by P-members.

3.2 ISO and CEN cooperation

In addition to the national and international levels, there is also a regional level in standardization, e. g. concerning Europe. The national delegation principle is applied in European standardization work in the same way as on the international level.

At the European level, CEN (Comitée Européen de Normalisation, en: European Committee for Standardization), CENELEC (Comité Européen de Normalisation Electrotechnique, en: European Committee for Electrotechnical Standardization) and ETSI (European Telecommunications Standards Institute) are the three European standardization organizations that have been officially recognized by the European Union and by the European Free Trade Association (EFTA) as being responsible for developing and defining voluntary standards at the European level. All three European standardization organizations, just like ISO, IEC and ITU, are based on the principle of one member per country, CEN being the ISO counterpart, CENELEC the IEC counterpart, and ETSI the ITU counterpart.

However, there also are differences between CEN and ISO standardization. One major difference is that the adoption of international standards as national standards is voluntary, while the national adoption of European Standards is obligatory. Also, at CEN, there is weighted voting with weightings allocated to the CEN Members depending on their population.

In 1991, an agreement on technical cooperation, the *Vienna Agreement*,[15] was signed by CEN and ISO. Its primary aim was to avoid duplication of (potentially conflicting) standards between CEN and ISO. New standards projects are now jointly planned between CEN and ISO. It is possible to work on projects that are published as both European and international standards in the end. Whenever this path is chosen, work takes place at CEN or ISO level only, normally under ISO lead, so in the international committee. CEN lead is possible in exceptional cases.

There actually is no European committee corresponding to ISO/TC 37/SC 4, so there neither are purely European nor Vienna agreement projects in the field. This is why in the following the focus is again on ISO standardization.

3.3 Stages in the development of ISO standards

3.3.1 General

While there are also other ISO deliverables,[16] the focus is on standards in the following, also given that only two out of the almost 40 current ISO/TC 37/SC 4 deliverables are not standards, but technical specifications. Figure 4 illustrates the preparation of an ISO standard.

In Figure 4, stages in light blue are stages that are skipped in some cases, whereas stages in dark blue are mandatory at least for all first editions of ISO standards. The official procedures to be followed when developing and maintaining an ISO standard are given in the ISO/IEC Directives Part 1 and the Consolidated

15 Cf. ISO/CEN (2016), https://www.cencenelec.eu/about-cen/cen-and-iso-cooperation/

16 E. g. “Technical Specifications”, see https://www.iso.org/deliverables-all.html

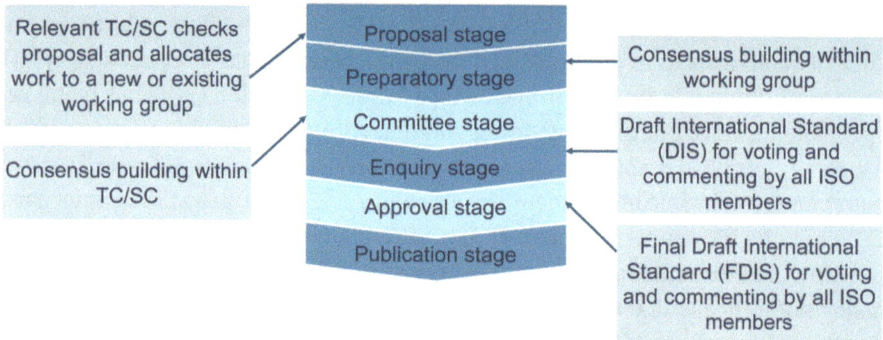

Figure 4: Preparation of an ISO standard.

ISO Supplement made available on the ISO website.[17] The ISO website also makes available a lot of additional information directly on the website or in downloadable brochures, for example "My ISO job – What delegates and experts need to know".[18]

It is important to note – especially because this is different in European standardization – that all ISO members are equally important when it comes to votes. This means that in committees where both MCCAA (Malta) and SAC (China) are P-members, they both have one vote.

3.3.2 Proposal stage

The first stage in the life of an ISO standard is to confirm that a new ISO standard in the subject area is really needed and will bring added value. This stage can only be skipped for revisions and amendments to ISO standards (see Section 3.4) that are already published and as long as their scope does not change, because for these, it is assumed that the added value was already checked and confirmed for the edition to be revised or amended. In all other cases, the proposal stage is mandatory.

The proposal stage consists of a new work item proposal (NWIP) being submitted to the technical committee or subcommittee for vote using a form called *Form 4*.[19]

Most often, a new project is proposed by a national standards body, by an organization in liaison, by the Secretariat of the technical committee or subcommittee

17 https://www.iso.org/directives-and-policies.html

18 Cf. ISO (2024), https://www.iso.org/publication/PUB100037.html

19 https://www.iso.org/sd/fetch/d0dndtMtgUSiz-WfmM12N1rh-a4Dcb8VpKtNUoHJ4fDeHTnxdJcJUHuZi4d80TPY

or by another committee. Form 4 contains detailed information on the proposal, such as, for example, title, scope, purpose and justification, the working group to which the project should be allocated or the suggestion to establish a new working group, names of the project leader(s), the intended deliverable (in the following, the focus is on standards, but the proposer could also suggest a technical specification) and the proposed development track including target dates for the most important milestones. The development track[20] determines the time granted to the development. There currently are three possible development tracks at ISO: 36 months, 24 months and 18 months. The proposal also comprises at least an outline description of the topic as an annex to Form 4.

The ISO tool used for voting is the electronic balloting portal. The ballot on new work item proposals (NP ballot) normally is a 12-week ballot.

The new project is accepted when two conditions are met: a 2/3 majority of the P-members of the technical committee or subcommittee approve the proposal and at least 4 or 5 of them (depending on the number of P-members in the committee) nominate experts to work on the project. If both is the case, the proposal formally becomes a standards project.

3.3.3 Preparatory stage

Usually, a new project is either allocated to an existing working group, or a new working group is set up by the technical committee or subcommittee to prepare a working draft (WD). As already stated, a working group comprises a Convenor, experts from P-members and from liaisons. Also, each project normally has a project leader.

During the preparatory stage of a project, experts keep working on a document. They start their work with the draft or outline that was attached to Form 4 in the NP ballot, and they only stop working on it when they agree on a document version that is good and publishable in their eyes. This process can involve several working drafts (WDs) being circulated in the working group for commenting. The project only goes to the next stage when consensus has been reached.

The draft is then forwarded to the working group's parent committee. The Convenor of the working group and/or the project leader can propose to skip the committee stage following a consultation with the experts of the working group to prove consensus. It is up to the parent committee to decide which stage to go to next (committee stage, see Section 3.3.4, or enquiry stage, see Section 3.3.5). The important

20 https://www.iso.org/stages-and-resources-for-standards-development.html

question is what can be expected to be gained by the committee stage (for example further understanding of an issue) compared to possible increases in costs and time (additional drafting and meetings). The final decision to skip the committee stage should be taken by the committee by consensus through a 4-week ballot or at a meeting.

3.3.4 Committee stage

The committee stage is optional, although, in most cases, it is kept. During the committee stage, the draft on which consensus was reached in the working group is shared with the members of the parent committee who are asked for their comments. The comments are then discussed within the working group, and accepted comments normally lead to changes to the draft. Just like working drafts (WDs) at working group level, successive committee drafts (CDs) can be circulated at committee level until consensus is reached in the committee.

Once this is the case, the project goes to the next stage.

3.3.5 Enquiry stage

Once consensus has been reached in the technical committee or subcommittee, the document is circulated as Draft International Standard (DIS) to all ISO members, not only to the members of the technical committee or subcommittee. So this is the point in the development process where SNV (Switzerland) can also vote and comment on fisheries and aquaculture standards, and where African ISO members also get the chance to vote and comment on standards on snowsports equipment. All ISO members get 12 weeks to vote and comment on the DIS.

Many ISO members make the DIS available for public review within their country. A list of standards that are currently at this stage can be found on the ISO website.[21]

The DIS is approved if two thirds of the P-members of the committee are in favour and not more than one quarter of the total number of votes cast are negative. Abstentions are excluded when the votes are counted, as well as negative votes not accompanied by a textual description of the technical reasons for the negative vote.

21 https://www.iso.org/advanced-search/x/title/status/U/docNumber/docPartNo/docType/0/langCode/ics/currentStage/true/searchAbstract/true/stage/40.20/stageDateStart/stageDateEnd/committee/sdg

Comments made to the DIS are again discussed in the working group, and accepted comments will most probably lead to changes to the draft. It makes a difference whether among these changes are technical changes or not. Technical changes are changes in content, so more than purely editorial changes. If the DIS is approved and no technical changes are introduced in the draft, the project goes directly to publication, skipping the approval stage. However, in case there are technical changes, the approval stage is mandatory.

Normally, the task of the working group is considered to be completed at the end of the enquiry stage. When there are no other projects in the working group, it should be disbanded by resolution of the parent committee. For any questions arising during the following stages, the project leader will be consulted.

3.3.6 Approval stage

This stage is skipped in all cases where the Draft International Standard (DIS) has been approved and no technical changes are introduced for publication.

However, in case technical changes are made as a consequence of comments made to the DIS, the approval stage becomes mandatory even if the DIS has been approved. It is needed to seek confirmation that the changed draft is still approved.

If this stage is used, the Final Draft International Standard (FDIS) is circulated to all ISO members for an 8-week vote, so to the same group that was also asked to vote and comment on the DIS during the enquiry stage. The focus now is on the vote and less on comments, because technical changes to the draft are no longer possible at this stage.

The standard is approved if two thirds of the P-members of the committee are in favour and not more than one quarter of the total number of votes cast are negative. Again, abstentions are excluded when the votes are counted, as well as negative votes not accompanied by any technical comments.

3.3.7 Publication stage

In case the approval stage was skipped because no technical changes have been introduced, this stage simply consists of the Committee Manager of the technical committee or subcommittee submitting the final document for publication.

If, however, the approval stage was not skipped, the Committee Manager together with the project leader may be asked to find responses to member body comments on the Final Draft International Standard (FDIS). At this stage, only editorial corrections can be made to the final text. Blatant errors can be corrected as well, but no other changes are permitted. Once responses have been found, the draft is updated in the sense of the responses.

Committee Managers and project leaders then get a two-week period for a last check of the document before the standard is published as an International Standard (IS). Please note that the capitalized spelling of "International Standard" is intended here. It is used in the ISO and IEC world for international standards developed by ISO, IEC and ITU, whereas "international standards" without capital letters is a more general term including standards developed by other international standards-setting communities and organizations.

3.4 Systematic review of ISO deliverables at least every five years

To ensure that ISO standards and other ISO deliverables remain up-to-date and globally relevant, they are reviewed at least every five years after publication. This process is called *systematic review*. During the systematic review, national standards bodies are asked to review the document and its use in their country and to decide – ideally in consultation with their stakeholders – whether it is still valid, should be updated, or withdrawn. After the systematic review, the ISO deliverable is either confirmed until the next systematic review is due, or revised, or withdrawn.

An example for a standard that is currently being revised as a consequence of a systematic review is (ISO 30042), the TermBase eXchange standard (TBX). Although the ISO/TC 37 subcommittee in charge of this standard and its revision is not ISO/TC 37/SC 4, but ISO/TC 37/SC 3[22] "Management of terminology resources", it should be mentioned here because it is special in two respects: first, the TBX standard has not been developed by researchers as it is the case for most standards in the field of language resources, but the proposal originated from an association of companies, the Localization Industry Standards Association (LISA, 1990–2011). Second, the original TBX standard was developed by LISA and only later adopted (and in part reworked and further refined) by ISO. As of 2025, the second edition of ISO 30042 (published in 2019) is under revision.

A committee may decide to initiate a revision at any time between systematic reviews, i. e. not only as the result of a systematic review. While revisions that impact the technical content of the standard have to follow the whole path as outlined in Figure 4, a shortened procedure called *minor revision* may be applied when there are only minor changes (e. g. updating and editorial changes) that do not impact the

22 https://www.iso.org/committee/48136.html

technical content of the standard. Once the decision for a minor revision has been made, the minor changes are implemented in the standard and the minor revision project then goes directly to the approval stage (see Section 3.3.6), and, if approved, the revised standard is published right after.

The decision for withdrawal is what actually puts an end to the life of a standard as outlined in this chapter.

4 Conclusion

There are many standards-setting communities, organizations and consortia working on language-related international standards. In this chapter, the focus was on the voluntary, consensus-based ISO standardization, involving one institutional member per country.

The voluntary aspect applies at all levels: from the active participation of the national standards bodies, over the decision, for each standards project, whether it is of relevance for a given country, its research and/or industrial community, down to the participation of individual experts in the working groups and/or (sub)committees.

The consensus-based work relies on technical quality (and on generalizability): no ISO member can block standards proposals without giving technical comments – which then have to be considered and, if relevant, accounted for in a next version of the document.

Readers wishing to participate actively in ISO standardization can either do so via their respective national standards body in case it is a P-member of the technical committee or subcommittee of interest, and the P-members of all technical committees and subcommittees are given on the ISO website, together with a possibility to reach out to them. Or they can try to participate via a liaison organization. Liaison organizations can also be found on the ISO website for all technical committees and subcommittees.

Bibliography

Brants, Sabine, Stefanie Dipper, Silvia Hansen, Wolfgang Lezius & George Smith. 2001. The TIGER Treebank. In *Proceedings of the first workshop on treebanks and linguistic theories (TLT2002)*. https://www.linguistics.ruhr-uni-bochum.de/~dipper/pub/tlt02_webVersion.pdf (accessed 26 February 2025).

Herzog, Gottfried, Ulrich Heid, Thorsten Trippel, Piotr Bański, Laurent Romary, Thomas Schmidt, Andreas Witt & Kerstin Eckart. 2015. Recent Initiatives towards New Standards for Language

Resources. In Bernhard Fisseni, Bernhard Schröder & Torsten Zesch (eds.), *Proceedings of the international conference of the German society for computational linguistics and language technology*, 154–156. https://ids-pub.bsz-bw.de/files/4358/Herzog_Heid_Trippel_Banski_Romary_Schmidt_Witt_Eckart_Recent_initiatives_2015.pdf (accessed 26 February 2025).

ISO. 2024. *My ISO job – What delegates and experts need to know* [Brochure]. https://www.iso.org/publication/PUB100037.html (accessed 26 February 2025).

ISO/CEN. 2016. *Guidelines for the implementation of the Agreement on technical cooperation between ISO and CEN (Vienna Agreement)* [Brochure]. https://boss.cen.eu/media/CEN/ref/va_guidelines_implementation.pdf (accessed 26 February 2025).

ISO 24610-1. 2006. *Language resource management – Feature structures – Part 1: Feature structure representation.*

ISO 24610-2. 2011. *Language resource management – Feature structures – Part 2: Feature system declaration.*

ISO 24611. 2012. *Language resource management – Morpho-syntactic annotation framework (MAF).*

ISO 24612. 2012. *Language resource management – Linguistic annotation framework (LAF).*

ISO 24613-1. 2024. *Language resource management – Lexical markup framework (LMF) – Part 1: Core model.*

ISO 24613-2. 2020. *Language resource management – Lexical markup framework (LMF) – Part 2: Machine-readable dictionary (MRD) model.*

ISO 24613-3. 2021. *Language resource management – Lexical markup framework (LMF) – Part 3: Etymological extension.*

ISO 24613-4. 2021. *Language resource management – Lexical markup framework (LMF) – Part 4: TEI serialization.*

ISO 24613-5. 2022. *Language resource management – Lexical markup framework (LMF) – Part 5: Lexical base exchange (LBX) serialization.*

ISO 24613-6. 2024. *Language resource management – Lexical markup framework (LMF) – Part 6: Syntax and semantics.*

ISO 24614-1. 2010. *Language resource management – Word segmentation of written texts – Part 1: Basic concepts and general principles.*

ISO 24614-2. 2011. *Language resource management – Word segmentation of written texts – Part 2: Word segmentation for Chinese, Japanese and Korean.*

ISO 24615-1. 2014. *Language resource management – Syntactic annotation framework* (*SynAF*) *– Part 1: Syntactic model.*

ISO 24615-2. 2018. *Language resource management – Syntactic annotation framework (SynAF) – Part 2: XML serialization (Tiger vocabulary).*

ISO 24616. 2012. *Language resource management – Multilingual information framework.*

ISO 24617-1. 2012. *Language resource management – Semantic annotation framework (SemAF) – Part 1: Time and events (SemAF-Time, ISO-TimeML).*

ISO 24617-2. 2020, *Language resource management – Semantic annotation framework* (*SemAF*) *– Part 2: Dialogue acts.*

ISO 24617-4. 2014. *Language resource management – Semantic annotation framework (SemAF) – Part 4: Semantic roles (SemAF-SR).*

ISO/TS 24617-5. 2014. *Language resource management – Semantic annotation framework (SemAF) – Part 5: Discourse structure (SemAF-DS).*

ISO 24617-6. 2016. *Language resource management – Semantic annotation framework (SemAF) – Part 6: Principles of semantic annotation (SemAF Principles).*

ISO 24617-7. 2020. *Language resource management – Semantic annotation framework (SemAF) – Part 7: Spatial information.*

ISO 24617-8. 2016. *Language resource management – Semantic annotation framework (SemAF) – Part 8: Semantic relations in discourse, core annotation schema (DR-core).*
ISO 24617-9. 2019. *Language resource management – Semantic annotation framework (SemAF) – Part 9: Reference annotation framework (RAF).*
ISO 24617-10. 2024. *Language resource management – Semantic annotation framework (SemAF) – Part 10: Visual information.*
ISO 24617-11. 2021. *Language resource management – Semantic annotation framework (SemAF) – Part 11: Measurable quantitative information (MQI).*
ISO 24617-12. 2025. *Language resource management – Semantic annotation framework (SemAF) – Part 12: Quantification.*
ISO 24617-14. 2023. *Language resource management – Semantic annotation framework (SemAF) – Part 14: Spatial semantics.*
ISO 24617-15.[23] *Language resource management – Semantic annotation framework (SemAF) – Part 15: Measurable quantitative information extraction (MQIE).*
ISO 24619. 2011. *Language resource management – Persistent identification and sustainable access (PISA).*
ISO/TS 24620-1. 2015. *Language resource management – Controlled natural language (CNL) – Part 1: Basic concepts and principles.*
ISO 24620-3. 2021. *Language resource management – Controlled human communication (CHC) – Part 3: Basic principles and methodology for controlled oral communication (COralCom).*
ISO 24620-4. 2023. *Language resource management – Controlled human communication (CHC) – Part 4: Basic principles and methodology for stylistic guidelines (BSG).*
ISO 24620-4.[24] *Language resource management – Controlled human communication (CHC) – Part 4: Basic principles and methodology for stylistic guidelines (BSG).*
ISO 24620-5. 2024. *Language resource management – Controlled human communication (CHC) – Part 5: Lexico-morpho-syntactic principles and methodology for personal data recognition and protection in text.*
ISO 24622-1. 2015. *Language resource management – Component Metadata Infrastructure (CMDI) – Part 1: The Component Metadata Model.*
ISO 24622-2. 2019. *Language resource management – Component Metadata Infrastructure (CMDI) – Part 2: Component metadata specification language.*
ISO 24623-1. 2018. *Language resource management – Corpus query lingua franca (CQLF) – Part 1: Metamodel.*
ISO 24623-2. 2021. *Language resource management – Corpus query lingua franca (CQLF) – Part 2: OntologyÏ.*
ISO 24624. 2016. *Language resource management – Transcription of spoken language.*
ISO 24635-1.[25] *Language resource management – Corpus Annotation Project Management – Part 1: Core model.*
ISO 24635-2.[26] *Language resource management – Corpus Annotation Project Management – Part 2: Training.*
ISO 30042. 2019. *Management of terminology resources – TermBase eXchange (TBX).*

23 Under preparation. Stage at the time of publication: ISO/DIS 24617-15:2024.

24 Under preparation. Stage at the time of publication: ISO/DIS 24620-4.

25 Under preparation. Stage at the time of publication.

26 Under preparation. Stage at the time of publication.

ISO 30042.[27] *Management of terminology resources – TermBase eXchange (TBX).*
ISO/IEC Directives Part 1. *Procedures for the technical work – Consolidated ISO Supplement – Procedures specific to ISO.* https://www.iso.org/sites/directives/current/consolidated/index.html (accessed 30 January 2025).
ISO/IEC Guide 59. 2019. *ISO and IEC recommended practices for standardization by national bodies.* https://www.iso.org/resources/publicly-available-resources.html?t=Ruvyk3OTE1FejG9wJie0LojrUDDf3weEqbMekT5NvH7ARf5jR7ng2dLlMyUmadiO&view=documents#section-isodocuments-top (accessed 30 January 2025).
Stührenberg, Maik. 2012. The TEI and current standards for structuring linguistic data. An overview. *Journal of the Text Encoding Initiative.* https://doi.org/10.4000/jtei.523 (accessed 26 February 2025).

27 Under preparation. Stage at the time of publication: ISO/WD 30042.

Index

In this index, **bold** page numbers indicate the location of the principal definition or extended discussion of a term. *Italic* page numbers refer to occurrences of the term in figures, tables, or other illustrative materials. Page numbers given in regular type denote additional references or relevant mentions throughout the volume.

https://doi.org/10.1515/9783112208212-018

Author index

https://doi.org/10.1515/9783112208212-019

FSC
www.fsc.org
MIX
Papier | Fördert gute Waldnutzung
FSC® C083411

Kolibri 360 GmbH
Ferdinand-Jühlke-Straße 7
99095 Erfurt, Deutschland
produktsicherheit@kolibri360.de